1. *China's Early Industrialization: Sheng Hsuan-huai (1844–1916) and Mandarin Enterprise.* By Albert Feuerwerker.
2. *Intellectual Trends in the Ch'ing Period.* By Liang Ch'i-ch'ao. Translated by Immanuel C. Y. Hsü.
3. *Reform in Sung China: Wang An-shih (1021–1086) and His New Policies.* By James T. C. Liu.
4. *Studies on the Population of China, 1368–1953.* By Ping-ti Ho.
5. *China's Entrance into the Family of Nations: The Diplomatic Phase, 1858–1880.* By Immanuel C. Y. Hsü.
6. *The May Fourth Movement: Intellectual Revolution in Modern China.* By Chow Tse-tsung.
7. *Ch'ing Administrative Terms: A Translation of the Terminology of the Six Boards with Explanatory Notes.* Translated and edited by E-tu Zen Sun.
8. *Anglo-American Steamship Rivalry in China, 1862–1874.* By Kwang-Ching Liu.
9. *Local Government in China under the Ch'ing.* By T'ung-tsu Ch'ü.
10. *Communist China, 1955–1959: Policy Documents with Analysis.* With a foreword by Robert R. Bowie and John K. Fairbank. (Prepared at Harvard University under the joint auspices of the Center for International Affairs and the East Asian Research Center.)
11. *China and Christianity: The Missionary Movement and the Growth of Chinese Antiforeignism, 1860–1870.* By Paul A. Cohen.
12. *China and the Helping Hand, 1937–1945.* By Arthur N. Young.
13. *Research Guide to the May Fourth Movement: Intellectual Revolution in Modern China, 1915–1924.* By Chow Tse-tsung.
14. *The United States and the Far Eastern Crises of 1933–1938: From the Manchurian Incident through the Initial Stage of the Undeclared Sino-Japanese War.* By Dorothy Borg.
15. *China and the West, 1858–1861: The Origins of the Tsungli Yamen.* By Masataka Banno.
16. *In Search of Wealth and Power: Yen Fu and the West.* By Benjamin Schwartz.
17. *The Origins of Entrepreneurship in Meiji Japan.* By Johannes Hirschmeier, S.V.D.
18. *Commissioner Lin and the Opium War.* By Hsin-pao Chang.
19. *Money and Monetary Policy in China, 1845–1895.* By Frank H. H. King.
20. *China's Wartime Finance and Inflation, 1937–1945.* By Arthur N. Young.

Harvard East Asian Series 9

Local Government in China under the Ch'ing

The East Asian Research Center at Harvard University administers research projects designed to further scholarly understanding of China, Japan, Korea, Vietnam, and adjacent areas.

LOCAL GOVERNMENT IN CHINA UNDER THE CH'ING

T'UNG-TSU CH'Ü

HARVARD UNIVERSITY PRESS
Cambridge, Massachusetts

Second Printing, 1970

Distributed in Great Britain by Oxford University Press, London

Preparation of this volume was aided by a grant from the Carnegie Corporation. The Corporation is not, however, the author, owner, publisher, or proprietor of this publication and is not to be understood as approving by virtue of its grant any of the statements made or views expressed therein.

Publication has been aided by a grant from the Ford Foundation

Library of Congress Catalog Card Number 62–11396

SBN 674–53675–4

Printed in the United States of America

ACKNOWLEDGMENTS

The author wishes to acknowledge his indebtedness to Professor John K. Fairbank and Professor L. S. Yang for going over the manuscript and giving helpful advice and criticism in the preparation of this work. Professors K. C. Hsiao, Harold D. Lasswell, James T. C. Liu, Benjamin I. Schwartz, and Mary C. Wright have read the manuscript; Professor Morris B. Lambie has read Chapters III to VI; Dr. T. T. Chow has read Chapter II; Professor S. H. Chou has read Chapter VIII; and Professor Judith N. Shklar has read Chapter X. For their comments and valuable suggestions the author is most grateful. He is indebted to Mrs. Elizabeth Matheson and Miss S. Ch'eng for their patience in the editing of the manuscript and for contributing toward its clarity and readability. Finally, the author wishes to thank Mrs. Bertha Ezell for typing the manuscript and preparing the Glossary.

CONTENTS

TABLES

CHART

INTRODUCTION

This book attempts to describe, analyze, and interpret the structure and functioning of local government at the chou and hsien levels in the Ch'ing dynasty. The chou and hsien were the units of local government that actually carried out administration and dealt directly with the people. An understanding of how they functioned can tell us much about how the populace was ruled in imperial China. Yet no systematic and comprehensive work on this subject has ever been published in Chinese, in Japanese, or in any Western language. The few available studies on Chinese government have dealt either with the central government or with provincial government, which merely exercised a supervisory function over the administration of local government.

It is my hope that the present book will contribute to an understanding of Chinese political institutions in the Ch'ing period and thus assist comparative studies of governments in the future. Historians and social scientists, who have displayed an increasing interest in the comparison of Chinese and Western governments, have inevitably been hampered by the lack of information on the Chinese side.

Although this book is not directly concerned with bureaucratic behavior, it is also hoped that it will provide data for the science of bureaucracy and administration. There is an increasing demand in the social sciences for research on bureaucracy, yet up to the present time most works in this field have been theoretical and speculative. There is a gap, as R. K. Merton has observed, between the theoretical study of bureaucracy and empirical data.[1] There can be no doubt that all behavioral analysis must be contextual—that is, we must consider any behavior as it is actually manifested in a concrete social and political situation. In this sense, the behavior pattern of Chinese bureaucrats in a particular political situation should also shed light on the science of administration and bureaucratic behavior in general.[2]

Certain basic concepts in this volume may be outlined as follows.

In dealing with the functions of local government, a distinction is made between those prescribed in administrative codes and government orders and those that were actually performed. With the latter as the chief focal point, the following questions are posed: What were the actual functions of the local government? How were they carried out and by whom? Who were the decision-makers?

The importance of the magistrate has long been recognized. But the significant role of his private secretaries has, by and large, been overlooked and deserves our special attention. As the chief advisers to the magistrates, they provide a vital key to an understanding of the local government operations.

Laws and statutes must always be a part of the data on political behavior, for they prescribe and in some ways condition the behavior of bureaucrats and the people under their jurisdiction. However, the study of a political system can never be completely adequate if it is based merely on laws and statutes. The laws are not always observed, and frequently there is a gap between the law in letter and the law in action. For this reason, I have sought to go beyond laws and administrative codes in order to construct a picture of the local government in action.

As the reader will see, this book is concerned not with the formally organized government alone. Government is conceived as a "participation in the governing process," and this concept inevitably encompasses both the "formal" and "informal" government, to use the terms of C. E. Merriam.[3] Needless to say, informal government exists in different forms in different social and political structures. In China, it was in the hands of the power group called the "gentry" or the local elite. As the gentry participated in local administration, influenced and sometimes even shaped local policy, a chapter is devoted to an examination of their role in order to see how the informal government functioned, how it was related to the formal government, and how the two complemented each other. A study of Chinese local government that left out the gentry would be as incomplete as a study of the Western political system that did not include parties and other pressure groups.

While it is undeniable that regional differences existed in China in administrative as well as in social practices, my belief is that those differences were of secondary importance, and that the dominant characteristic of Ch'ing government, brought about by centralization, was uniformity. Thus, I have chosen to survey the Chinese empire as a whole, with the exception of Manchuria and certain districts governed by local tribesmen (t'u-ssu), which had administrative systems peculiar to themselves. This approach is only partly necessitated by the fact that data are insufficient to permit the study of specific regions in detail; a more important consideration is that a broad approach to the little-explored subject of Chinese local administration seems to me to be more meaningful.

And finally, I have chosen to deal with the entire Ch'ing dynasty rather than with one period in the dynasty. Although changes occurred from time to time throughout the dynasty, as indicated in the revision or introduction of edicts and regulations, most of these changes were technical and procedural and therefore not of major importance. Furthermore, it is only by investigating a long time span that we can discover the common patterns and characteristics of the Ch'ing administration and whether it was marked by continuity or discontinuity.

The plan of the book is as follows: The opening description of the structure of local government gives the reader a background picture of the position of the chou and hsien in the provincial government, and the administrative relationships between the different levels. One chapter is devoted to each of the five groups of personnel in the chou and hsien government: the magistrate, clerks, runners, personal servants, and private secretaries. In order to give the reader an idea of who these yamen workers were, what they did, and how they did it, the discussions center around such factors as recruitment, social and legal status, duties, maintenance, promotion, supervision, and disciplinary control. Chapters VII through IX deal with the functions performed by the local government. The magistrate is taken as the focal point to which all the other elements are related. Through him we are able to see the local operations as an integrated process.

To the reader who may expect a section dealing with local finance, it will soon become apparent why there is none: the Chinese local government had no revenue of its own, and the magistrate was expected to defray both office and personal expenses from his own income. No distinction was made between public and private expenses. Thus it seemed more sensible to discuss local finance under the heading of the maintenance of the magistrate, where the system of "customary fees" (*lou-kuei*) is discussed.

The final chapter discusses the role of the gentry in local administration. By considering their status and position in the community and their relationships with the government officials as well as with the people, we may see how the formal and informal governments operated, interacted, and were integrated within the social and political order.

A few words should be said about the sources I have used. The basic data were provided by the laws, statutes, administrative codes, official compendia—such as the *Ta-Ch'ing hui-tien* (Collected statutes of the Ch'ing dynasty) and *Shih-li* (Cases)—and various encyclopedias. But even more valuable data were found in the handbooks or guidebooks written by magistrates, private secretaries, and personal servants. These materials, which served the practical purpose of guiding succeeding incumbents, contain advice based upon personal experience in office. Other valuable sources were official documents, records, correspondence, and memoirs (*pi-chi*) written by officials, private secretaries, and other persons versed in administration. These materials provide valuable information concerning the administrative operations and problems of local government, behavior of the groups attached to the bureaucracy, and interpersonal relations, including tensions and other psychological manifestations. Biographies, local gazetteers, essays, and miscellaneous works also yield pertinent information.

LOCAL GOVERNMENT IN CHINA UNDER THE CH'ING

————————— I —————————

CHOU AND HSIEN GOVERNMENT

In China in the Ch'ing dynasty local government was organized on the same principle at all levels. All administrative units, from the province down to the chou (department) and the hsien (district), which are the focus of our study, were designed and created by the central government, which financed their budgets, appointed their officials, and directed and supervised their activities. All local officials, including magistrates of the chou and hsien, were agents of the central goverment. There was no autonomy in the chou, the hsien, or in the towns and villages that constituted them. In fact, no formal government of any sort existed below the chou and hsien levels.

1. CHOU AND HSIEN, THE SMALLEST ADMINISTRATIVE UNITS

Chou and hsien, which were the smallest administrative units within a province, were grouped to form larger units: prefectures (*fu*), independent subprefectures (*chih-li t'ing*), or independent departments (*chih-li chou*); the last included only hsien.[1] The independent subprefectures and independent departments are not to be confused with the ordinary subprefectures and departments. The former were under the direct supervision of the provincial treasurer,[2] and had a status equivalent to that of the prefecture.[3] For this reason, they will be excluded from our study. What we refer to as chou and hsien are the ordinary departments and districts.

As Table 1 shows, the number of administrative units in local government varied in different periods. There were more than 100 ordinary chou and about 1200 to 1300 hsien in the empire. Table 2 shows the distribution of these and of larger administrative units in various provinces, according to the 1899 edition of *Ch'ing hui-tien* (Collected statutes of the Ch'ing dynasty).

The size of a chou or hsien, which was usually described in terms of length added to width at its widest point, varied from about one hundred to several hundred li.[4] It consisted of a district or department seat, which was a walled city,[5] surrounded by a few towns and several score or hundreds of villages,[6] the size of which varied.[7] The population in a chou or hsien varied from several tens of thousands to several hundred thousand households.[8]

There was a "head" in each rural area (*hsiang-chang*), town (*chen-chang*), and village (*ts'un-chang* or *chuang-t'ou*),[9] who was "elected" by the people themselves to take charge of local affairs, but this electing of a head had never developed into self-government. In fact the towns and villages had no legal status whatever. The government actually created artificial subadministrative units, whose size did not coincide with that of the towns and villages. First there were the tax and labor-service units (*li-chia*). As a rule, in a rural district every ten households were organized

Table 1. Number of administrative units

Period	Prefectures	Independent departments	Independent subprefectures	Depart-ments	Subprefectures	Districts
K'ang-hsi	177	—	—	267[a]	—	1261
Yung-cheng	167	65	—	149	—	1211
Ch'ien-lung	187	67[b]	—	154	—	1282
Chia-ch'ing	182	67	22[c]	147	74	1293
Kuang-hsü	185	72	45[c]	145	75	1303

[a] K'ang-hsi *Ch'ing hui-tien* does not specify whether these were independent departments or ordinary departments; however, it should be noted that 19 out of the total were departments not subordinate to the prefecture.

[b] Nineteen independent departments are mentioned under Szechwan in the Ch'ien-lung *Ch'ing hui-tien, chüan* 4. Obviously this is a copyist's error. The number should be 9 (see *ibid.*, 8:21, 22b–23; *Chin-shen ch'üan-shu* (1793), *ts'e* 4:1).

[c] Including the four subprefectures of the Metropolitan Prefecture, the *ssu-lu t'ing*, which were directly subordinate to the provincial treasurer. *Ch'ing hui-tien* (1899), 4:6.

Source: *Ch'ing hui-tien* (1690), *chüan* 18 and 19; *ibid.* (1732), *chüan* 24 and 25; *ibid.* (1764), *chüan* 4 and 8; *ibid.* (1818), *chüan* 4 and 10; *ibid.* (1899), *chüan* 6, 13–16.

Table 2. The distribution of administrative units in various provinces

Provinces	Prefectures	Independent departments	Independent subprefectures	Depart-ments	Subprefectures	Districts
Sheng-ching	2	—	1	5	2	14
Kirin	2	—	—	1	4	2
Heilungkiang	—	—	2	—	—	—
Chihli	10	6	4	17	4	123
Shantung	10	2	—	9	—	96
Shansi	9	10	—	6	7	85
Honan	9	4	—	6	1	96
Kiangsu	8	3	1	3	2	62
Anhui	8	5	—	4	—	51
Kiangsi	13	1	—	1	2	75
Fukien	9	2	—	—	6	58
Chekiang	11	—	1	1	2	75
Hupeh	10	1	—	7	—	60
Hunan	9	4	5	3	—	64
Shensi	7	5	—	5	7	73
Kansu	8	6	1	6	6	47
Sinkiang	2	4	11	—	—	11
Szechwan	12	8	4	11	8	112
Kwangtung	9	5	5	6	1	78
Kwangsi	11	2	2	15	2	49
Yünnan	14	3	5	26	10	39
Kweichow	12	1	3	13	11	33
Total	185	72	45	145	75	1303

Source: *Ch'ing hui-tien* (1899), *chüan* 13–16.

into a *chia* (tithe), and every 110 households into a *li* or *t'u* (rural zone); in a district seat the unit was called *fang* (ward), and in nearby places the unit was the *hsiang* (suburban ward).[10] The magistrate appointed the head of *chia* (*chia-chang* or *chia-shou*) and *li* (*li-chang*) as agents in charge of tax collection, population registration, and labor services.[11]

The government also organized the people into security units (*pao-chia*): 10 households comprised a *p'ai;* 100 households a *chia;* and 1000 households a *pao.* The magistrate appointed the heads (*p'ai-t'ou, chia-chang,* and *pao-chang*) as agents.[12]

The magistrate also assigned a *ti-pao* or *ti-fang,* known as local constable or land warden, to each ward or rural zone as a general agent.[13] The *ti-pao* served as the messenger to the magistrate, whose orders he passed on to the villagers or ward residents. It was also his duty to keep an eye on suspicious persons and to report cases of robbery, homicide, salt smuggling, fire, etc. He could report minor disputes, such as arguments over landed property or quarrels between relatives, but he was not authorized to settle them.[14]

It was the *ti-pao's* responsibility to see that the government was provided with things needed for a special purpose (as for an inquest) and that villagers required to render labor service were on hand.[15] However, it should be kept in mind that a *ti-pao* was merely a man rendering service to the yamen, and as such he had a very inferior social status.[16] He was often beaten by the magistrate for failing to report or carry out assignments promptly.[17] By no means should he be regarded as representing the villagers or as taking part in local government, as has been suggested by H. B. Morse, who assumed that *ti-pao* were nominated by the magistrate from among the village elders, with the consent of the villagers.[18] Apparently Morse confused the *ti-pao* with the "elders," *ch'i-lao,* who were selected by the magistrate from the venerable villagers and given the honor of wearing the official hat buttons.[19] The main activity of the elders was to attend the lectures in which the maxims of the Sacred Edict were expounded. The *Ch'ing-ch'ao wen-hsien t'ung-k'ao* (Encyclopedia of the historical records of the Ch'ing dynasty) points out clearly, however, that they were not concerned with the official business of the community;[20] they merely served as a symbol of veneration by virtue of their age.

In short, all these heads of the various units created by the government in the rural districts to perform specific administrative functions were but government agents, appointed by and subject to the control of the magistrates. None of them could be considered local leaders representing the villagers. Self-government was absent in towns and villages.[21]

2. Administrative Relations between Levels of Government

The administration of local government in China was highly centralized. Within a province, each governmental level was under a superior, and all levels were under the general supervision of the highest provincial authorities. A hsien magistrate (*chih-hsien*) was under the direct supervision of a prefect (*chih-fu*), or an independent department magistrate (*chih-li chou chih-chou*), or a subprefect in charge of an independent

CHART 1. PROVINCIAL GOVERNMENT

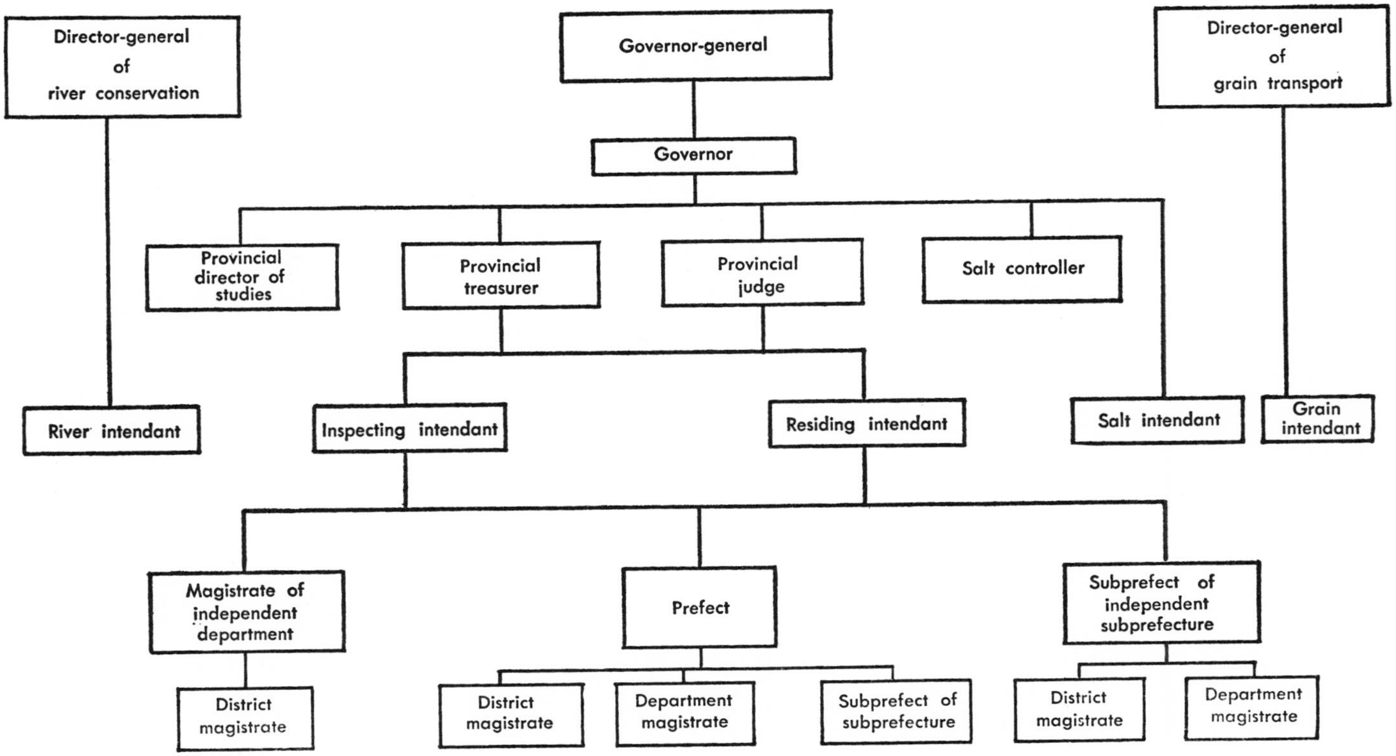

subprefecture (*chih-li t'ing t'ung-chih* or *chih-li t'ing t'ung-p'an*). An ordinary department magistrate (*chih-chou*) was supervised by a prefect, or a subprefect in charge of an independent subprefecture. Over a sub-prefect in charge of an ordinary subprefecture (*t'ung-chih* or *t'ung-p'an*) there was a prefect. The prefect, independent department magistrate, and subprefect of an independent subprefecture were under the circuit intendant (*tao*), who could be a resident intendant (*fen-shou tao*), an inspecting intendant (*fen-hsün tao*), or an intendant entrusted with one or more specific functions—for example, a river intendant (*ho-tao*),[22] grain intendant (*tu-liang tao* or *liang-chu tao*),[23] salt intendant (*yen-fa tao*), postal intendant (*i-ch'uan tao*), postal and salt intendant (*i-yen tao*), salt and tea intendant (*yen ch'a tao*).

Above the intendants there were the provincial treasurer or lieutenant governor (*ch'eng-hsüan pu-cheng shih*),[24] the provincial judge (*t'i-hsing an-ch'a shih*), and the salt controller (*yen-yün shih*).[25] The provincial judge supervised the administration of justice and the postal service in the province. The provincial treasurer, who supervised taxation and other financial affairs in the province, was authorized to examine and appraise the accomplishments of the various civil officials.[26]

There was a governor (*hsün-fu*) in each province, with the exception of Chihli,[27] Kansu, and Szechwan, where this position was held con-currently by a governor-general. The governor, the highest civil authority in a province, was subordinate to the governor-general (*tsung-tu*), who had one, two, or three provinces under his jurisdiction[28] and commanded both the civil and military officials. As a rule, the governor played the leading role in a province where there was no governor-general (Honan, Shantung, and Shansi), or in a province where the governor-general was not stationed. In a province where both the governor-general and governor were stationed, all administration was under the control of the former.[29]

Official orders issued by the governor-general and governor were passed to the lower levels, and the official at each level was responsible for seeing that the orders were carried out by his subordinates. It was the duty of the subordinate officials to submit periodic reports to their superiors on the implementation of orders from above. The inspecting intendant made inspection tours to check on the performance of local government, par-ticularly the handling of lawsuits.[30] The provincial treasurer often sent representatives to audit the funds and grain under the care of various local governments.[31]

Centralization also extended upward, from the local to the central government. The central government controlled the appointment and removal of the local officials, since all officials in a province, from the governor-general and governor down to the magistrates, were appointed by the Board of Civil Office. Although high provincial authorities could recommend promotion, demotion, or removal of their subordinate officials, the recommendation had to be made in accordance with the rules and procedure set up by the board, and it was the board that deliberated on each case and made the formal decision.

Most important of all, local officials, high or low, had to abide by the code of administrative regulations issued by the central government. When orders issued by the emperor and the boards reached the governor-general and governor, they passed them on to their subordinates. The governor-general and governor were obliged to memorialize to the throne and submit reports to the various boards, and imperial commissioners were sent to investigate local activities when the situation warranted.

The central government also had full control over the financial affairs of the local government. In fact, the provincial treasurer and other local authorities were agents of the central government in the collection of taxes. The budget and expenditures of the local government, including salaries and office expenses, were regulated by the Board of Revenue. The administration of justice was also supervised by the central government. While local officials at each level had a measure of judicial power, decisions made by the authorities at a lower level had to be reviewed and approved by a higher level.[32] All cases involving sentences more severe than penal servitude ($t'u$)[33] had to be reported by the highest provincial authority to the Board of Punishment and the sentences were subject to its approval.[34] If the board rejected a sentence, the case had to be retried, or the sentence altered by the governor-general or governor, or revised by the board.[35]

All death sentences had to be reported to the board, deliberated by central government officials in accordance with regular procedure, and referred for final decision to the emperor, the highest judicial authority in the empire.[36] If any case was appealed to a higher authority in the capital and the local officials were charged with injustice, the emperor might order the governor-general or governor of the province to try the case in person, or he might send an imperial commissioner to the province to reopen the case, or refer it to the Board of Punishment for retrial.[37]

3. Organization of Chou and Hsien Government

Under the chou magistrate (sub-fifth rank) and hsien magistrate (magistrate in the capital, sixth rank; ordinary magistrate, seventh rank), who were known as *cheng-yin kuan* (officials in charge of the seal) or *cheng-t'ang* (officials presiding in the main hall),[38] there were three groups of subordinate officials: assistant magistrates (*tso-erh*), chief officers (*shou-ling kuan*), and miscellaneous officials (*tsa-chih*). The officials subordinate to the chou magistrate were:

1) Assistant magistrates:

a) First-class assistant chou magistrate (*chou-t'ung*), sub-sixth rank, also known as *chou erh-shou* (deputy magistrate of a chou).

b) Second-class assistant chou magistrate (*chou-p'an*), sub-seventh rank, also known as *fen-chou* (subdepartment).[39]

2) Chief officer:

Jail warden (*li-mu*), sub-ninth rank, known also as *yu-t'ang* (official presiding in the right hall). As a *li-mu* was also in charge of police duties, his office was known as *pu-t'ing* or *tu-pu t'ing* (police bureau).[40]

3) Miscellaneous officials:

a) Subdistrict magistrate (*hsün-chien*), sub-ninth rank, known as *fen-ssu* (subdistrict), *shao-yin* (junior magistrate), or *hsün-tsai* (police commissioner)[41]—in charge of police duties within his subdistrict, or of river administration or salt administration.[42]

b) Postmaster (*i-ch'eng*), unclassed.

c) Tax collector (*shui-k'o-ssu ta-shih*), unclassed.

d) Granary supervisor (*ts'ang ta-shih*), unclassed.

e) Sluice keeper (*ch'a-kuan*), unclassed.

f) Fish tax collector (*ho-po-so kuan*).[43]

The officials under the hsien magistrate were:

1) Assistant magistrates:

a) Assistant hsien magistrate (*hsien-ch'eng*), eighth rank, known as *erh-yin* (deputy magistrate of a hsien), *fen-hsien* (maigstrate of a subdistrict), or *tso-t'ang* (official presiding in the left hall).

b) Registrar (*chu-pu*), ninth rank, known as *san-yin* (the second deputy magistrate).

2) Chief officer:

Jail warden (*tien-shih*), unclassed, known as *yu-t'ang, shao-wei,* or *lien-pu* (detect and arrest). His office too was known as *pu-t'ing*. He was also expected to assume the duties of an assistant hsien magistrate or a registrar if there were no such officials in a locality.[44]

3) Miscellaneous officials:

Same as those under a chou magistrate.[45]

All three groups were generally called *tso-tsa*,[46] and we shall refer to them as "subordinate officials."

4. THE INSIGNIFICANCE OF SUBORDINATE OFFICIALS

The duties of the chief officers and miscellaneous officials were indicated by their specific titles. But an assistant magistrate might have a general charge or a special one like land tax, police, river administration, or water works.[47] His title could be a plain one without a prefix, or it could indicate a special assignment—for instance, assistant magistrate in charge of river administration,[48] assistant magistrate in charge of water works,[49] assistant magistrate in charge of land tax.[50] Sometimes two or more responsibilities were indicated in a title, such as river administration and water works,[51] land tax and water works,[52] land tax and police,[53] or land tax, police, and water works.[54] Here it should be noted that an assistant magistrate or a registrar in charge of river administration (known as *hsün*) and a subprefect in charge of river administration (known as *t'ing*) were subordinate to the river intendant, who was under the supervision of a director-general of river conservation.[55] Such an assistant magistrate should not be confused with a regular assistant magistrate in charge of general administration.

Each subordinate official had his own office. The subdistrict magistrate was always stationed in a subdistrict (*fen-fang*) where he acted as police commissioner.[56] The postmasters and sluice keepers were stationed in a specified area where a post station or a sluice was located. A jail warden of a chou or a hsien always had his yamen near the prison.[57] The assistant magistrate in charge of river administration was always stationed on the bank of the river.[58] A regular assistant magistrate either had his yamen in the district seat where the magistrate's yamen was located,[59] or was stationed in a different locality to guard the peace in that area (*fen-fang*).[60]

In addition to these three groups of subordinate officials, there were two educational officers (*chiao-chih*) in each chou or hsien: the director of studies (*hsüeh-cheng* or *chiao-yü*) and the assistant director of studies (*hsün-tao*). They were under the provincial director of studies and were concerned with the supervision and direction of the students in the chou and hsien schools.[61] However, they were also entrusted with some administrative duties, such as opening the wrappings in which silver came from the taxpayers.[62] The magistrate also called upon the educational officers to help whenever a student was involved in administrative procedure. For example, an educational officer had to see that students who had failed to pay a tax made the payment. The law also required that he, together with the magistrate, hear cases in which the chastisement of a student was called for, since a magistrate was not allowed to administer punishment to a student.[63]

The three groups of subordinate officials occupied a very insignificant position in local administration. In the first place, with the exception of the "chief officer," that is, the jail warden, whose post existed in practically all chou and hsien,[64] there were very few subordinate officials. Among the miscellaneous officials in the empire, the 1899 *Ch'ing hui-tien* states that there were 925 subdistrict magistrates,[65] 65 postmasters, and 45 sluice keepers,[66] who were appointed only in places where water control was necessary. In some hsien there was more than one sluice keeper; for instance, there were five in Wen-shang, Shantung, and four in Ch'ing-ho, Kiangsu.[67] Tax collectors were found only in four hsien,[68] and fish tax collectors only in Nan-hai and P'an-yü, both in Kwangtung.[69]

The small number of *tso-erh*, the assistant magistrates, was most striking. According to the 1899 *Ch'ing hui-tien,* there were only 32 first-class assistant chou magistrates, 35 second-class assistant chou magistrates, 345 assistant hsien magistrates, and 55 registrars in the whole empire.[70] Table 3 shows their distribution among the various provinces.

It is interesting that there were no first-class and second-class assistant chou magistrates in Kiangsu, Shansi, and Kwangtung.[71] There were no first-class assistant chou magistrates in Chihli, and registrars were nonexistent in Chihli, Yünnan, and Singkiang. In fact, less than half of the chou (63) had assistant magistrates, and less than a third of the hsien (370) had assistant magistrates or registrars. In Table 3 the paucity of assistant hsien magistrates and registrars is particularly noticeable in the following provinces, where there were many hsien: Chihli, Szechwan, Shantung, Shansi, Shensi, Honan, Hunan, Yünnan, Kwangsi, and Kweichow (see Table 2 for the distribution of hsien). Obviously, many chou and hsien were not provided with an assistant magistrate.[72]

Many of the chou and hsien that had an assistant magistrate had only one type; that is, some chou had only a first-class assistant magistrate or a second-class assistant magistrate; some hsien had either an assistant

Table 3. The distribution of assistant magistrates in the various provinces

Province	Chou-t'ung	Chou-p'an	Hsien-ch'eng	Chu-pu
Chihli	—	5	10	—
Shantung	4	4	31	2
Shansi	—	—	6	1
Honan	1	3	17	1
Kiangsu	—	—	29	14
Anhui	3	1	15	4
Kiangsi	1	—	48	2
Fukien	—	—	23	1
Chekiang	—	1	45	11
Hupeh	2	5	18	4
Hunan	1	1	14	1
Shensi	2	1	18	3
Kansu	1	2	9	2
Sinkiang	—	—	1	—
Szechwan	2	2	18	3
Kwangtung	—	—	20	2
Kwangsi	11	5	9	2
Yünnan	1	3	3	—
Kweichow	2	2	9	1
Total	32	35	345	55

Source: *Ch'ing hui-tien* (1899), *chüan* 5.

magistrate or a registrar. Only a very few chou and hsien had both. According to the 1899 *Ch'ing hui-tien,* only three chou had both first-class and second-class assistant magistrates,[73] and only thirty-one hsien had both assistant magistrates and registrars.[74]

Although the *Ch'ing-ch'ao wen-hsien t'ung-k'ao* mentions that there were several assistant district magistrates and registrars in places where there was much official business,[75] such cases were rare. Moreover, some of these officials were in charge of river administration only. For instance, in Cho-chou there were four assistant magistrates, but three of them were in charge of river administration.[76] In both Pa-chou and T'ung-chou there was one first-class assistant magistrate and two second-class assistant magistrates, all of them in charge of river administration.[77] Hsiang-fu had two assistant district magistrates and two registrars; with the exception of one assistant magistrate, all of them were in charge of river administration.[78] There were three assistant district magistrates in Liang-hsiang, but two of them were in charge of river administration.[79] All three assistant district magistrates and two registrars in Wu-ch'ing were in charge of river administration.[80] Only three localities had more than one regular assistant magistrate: Ting-fan chou, Kweichow, with two second-class assistant magistrates; [81] Yüan-ho, Kiangsu, with two assistant district magistrates and one registrar; [82] and Fu-shun, Szechwan, with two assistant district magistrates.[83]

Besides being few in number, the subordinate officials played an insignificant role in local government. With the exception of those who were assigned to such special duties as river administration, postal service, police duty, and jail-keeping, most of them had trivial and sometimes ill-defined duties. An assistant magistrate or a miscellaneous official, for instance, might be sent to collect land tax in remote places where land tax receipts were given to taxpayers.[84] While a magistrate officiated in counting collected taxes, an assistant magistrate might be assigned to open the wrapping and count the silver handed in by taxpayers.[85] Assistant magistrates and miscellaneous officials were sometimes sent to supervise the collection of grain tribute[86] and the sale of government grain to the people at a low price (p'ing-ti).[87]

The law did not permit assistant magistrates or miscellaneous officials to accept a complaint; a magistrate who permitted them to do so or assigned them to hear a case was subject to punishment.[88] In practice, however, many magistrates allowed their assistant magistrates to accept complaints in order to give them some additional income,[89] although this practice was usually limited to trivial cases like quarrels, and an assistant magistrate was merely expected to settle the case by argument or by asking relatives and friends of the parties concerned to act as mediators.[90] In other words, an assistant magistrate was not permitted to deal with criminal cases or serious civil cases.[91] An assistant magistrate stationed in a different locality than the magistrate was authorized to arrest a person guilty of theft, gambling, or prostitution, but he was not permitted to try the offender; instead he had to deliver him to the magistrate for trial.[92] Sometimes, if a magistrate was too busy, he would assign the hearing of theft and robbery cases to a subordinate official. In such cases the deposition obtained was submitted to the magistrate for examination; the subordinate official was not permitted to search for stolen goods or to arrest an offender.[93] Other duties which might be assigned to a subordinate official were the examination of an injury received by someone involved in a lawsuit,[94] investigation of an area stricken by natural disasters,[95] and investigation into disputes over landed property or a graveyard.[96] An assistant magistrate or a jail warden could also be assigned to conduct an inquest or on-the-spot investigation of a robbery when the magistrate was absent.[97] However, many magistrates were reluctant to delegate investigations to a subordinate official on the grounds that he might accept a bribe or that his prestige was insufficient to command the respect of the people and their wilingness to accept his judgment.[98] Even a subordinate official with a specific assignment, such as *li-mu* or *tien-shih* (jail warden), might not actually discharge the duties indicated by his title. The jail wardens, although designated as officers in charge of police bureaus, actually had no voice in police affairs.[99]

This all points to the fact that the subordinate officials, particularly the assistant magistrates, who were referred to as *hsien-ts'ao* (idle officials) or *jung-kuan* (superfluous officials)[100] had very little function in the local government.[101] With the aim of relieving the burden of the magistrates, who alone were responsible for the collection of land tax, Lu Lung-ch'i (1630–1692), a statesmanly magistrate, suggested recruiting assistant magistrates and registrars from the successful candidates in the civil service examinations and assigning them as actual assistants in collecting land tax.[102] Lu I-t'ung (1805–1863), who saw that the subordinate officials had less authority than the clerks, suggested that a magistrate should hire two or three more subordinate officials and that they should be given more authority, so that a magistrate could actually secure their assistance and the clerks could be reduced in number and controlled.[103] The nonfunctioning of the subordinate officials inevitably led to a situation in which the magistrate became a one-man government, overburdened with all kinds of administration, and with little or no assistance from his official subordinates.

This point is most significant and deserves our special attention. It helps us better to understand the role of the magistrate, the way in which official business was carried out in his yamen, and the administrative problems with which he was faced. It also explains the role played by his private secretaries and personal servants, who were employed privately by him and were directly responsible to him. The insignificance of the subordinate officials made it necessary for the magistrate to rely upon the services of these two groups of aides.

THE MAGISTRATE

Chou and hsien magistrates (*chih-chou* and *chih-hsien*), although they were low in the hierarchy of local officials, played an extremely important part in local administration. As Lu I-t'ung pointed out, they were the administrative officials (*chih-shih chih kuan,* lit., "officials in charge of affairs"); their superiors—prefect, circuit intendant, provincial judge, provincial treasurer, governor, and governor-general—were the supervisory officials (*chih-kuan chih kuan,* lit., "officials in charge of officials").[1] In other words, the superior local officials merely gave orders to the magistrates and made reports to other superior local officials and to the boards of the central government. They supervised the work of the magistrates, for the most part, through documents. It was the magistrates who acted on routine administrative matters and the orders issued by their superiors. This was observed by Fang Ta-chih (d. 1886).

The provincial judge, provincial treasurer, circuit intendants, and prefects are able to talk about but unable to act on the desirable things that should be done and the undesirable things that should be removed. Even the governor and governor-general rely mainly on empty words. Only the department and district magistrates can be seen in real action.[2]

For this reason, magistrates were usually referred to as *ch'in-min chih kuan* (officials close to the people), or *ti-fang kuan* (local officials), and were addressed as *fu-mu kuan* (father and mother officials) by the people under their jurisdiction.

In short, it is no exaggeration to say that the local administration was in the hands of the magistrates. Without them it would have been at a standstill. Hsieh Chin-luan (*chü-jen* 1789), an instructor in a government district school, once remarked that there were only two groups of important officials in the empire; the grand secretaries in the capital and the magistrates outside the capital. And as Hsieh saw it, the magistrates were the more important because they had firsthand knowledge of the people's condition and of the administration's success or failure.[3]

1. The Role of the Magistrate

The magistrate's burden was not the same in all localities, of course. Departments and districts varied in size, population, area of cultivated land, amount of land tax and other taxes collected, means of communication, and so on. The magistrate of a hsien located in a communications center which was frequently visited by officials from other places had to devote a great deal of time and money to entertaining.[4] In the northern provinces labor service was levied on the people more frequently than in the south. Certain hsien in the lower Yangtze valley and along the canal had the additional responsibility of collecting and transporting tribute grain. Factors like these led to the descriptive classification of a local official's post: *ch'ung* (frequented, i.e., a center of communications), *fan* (troublesome, i.e., a great deal of official business), *p'i* (wearisome, i.e., many overdue taxes), *nan* (difficult, i.e., a violent populace, prone to crime).[5]

The relative importance of a post was indicated by the following terms: (1) most important (*tsui-yao ch'üeh*)—when all four conditions listed above were present; (2) important (*yao-ch'üeh*)—when three of the conditions were present; (3) medium (*chung-ch'üeh*)—two conditions; (4) easy (*chien-ch'üeh*)—only one condition. The first two were commonly referred to as busy posts (*fan-ch'üeh*); the last two as easy posts.[6] Wang Hui-tsu (1730–1807), a magistrate, said that it was much easier for an official to carry out his duties and be close to the people in an out-of-the-way place where business was light, and that one had little time to be close to the people in a communications center where official business was heavy.[7] A similar opinion was expressed by Fang Ta-chih, who maintained that it was difficult to hold a busy post, especially in a central location.[8]

There were certain duties, however, which were more or less common to all magistrates. As the chief executive of a chou or a hsien, a magistrate was expected to be familiar with all aspects of the local situation[9] and to assume the responsibility for everything within the territory under his jurisdiction. Above all, he was expected to maintain order in the area.

He was the judge, the tax collector, and the general administrator. He had charge of the postal service, salt administration, *pao-chia,* police, public works, granaries, social welfare, education, and religious and ceremonial functions. His over-all duty is summed up in the *Ch'ing shih kao* (Draft history of the Ch'ing dynasty):

> A magistrate takes charge of the government of a district. He settles legal cases, metes out punishment, encourages agriculture, extends charity to the poor, wipes out the wicked and the unlawful, promotes livelihood, and fosters education. All such matters as recommending scholars [to the court], reading and elucidating the law and imperial edicts [to the public], caring for the aged, and offering sacrifices to the gods, are his concern.[10]

A magistrate, although a civil official, also had to defend the city in an uprising or a foreign invasion. Failure to do so would incur dismissal and physical punishment.[11]

It is hardly necessary to mention that all these varied functions of a magistrate were not equal in importance. Next to the maintenance of order, the most important were the collection of taxes and the administration of justice.[12] His performance of these two was the basis for evaluating a magistrate's achievements, a process known as *k'ao-ch'eng.* If he failed in these duties he could be disciplined. Evaluation also took into consideration whether or not he met the official quota in the sale of salt. All the other duties, which did not affect the *k'ao-ch'eng,* the magistrates generally discharged with less devotion, if they did not actually neglect them.

The daily schedule of a yamen was usually announced and regulated by the sound produced by striking a bamboo tube (*pang*) and a small iron bar (*tien* or *yün-pan*). The yamen opened its doors before dawn[13] when the iron bar was struck seven times in the inner yamen (the magistrate's residence), and the bamboo tube was struck once in the outer yamen. The clerks, runners, and personal servants were expected to appear at that time. When the iron bar was struck five times and the bamboo tube twice, in the early morning,[14] documents were distributed to the clerks and the yamen personnel started their official business. The magistrate then presided over the "morning court," receiving and dispatching documents, receiving written and oral reports submitted by yamen personnel, questioning and examining persons under arrest or prisoners who were to be delivered to other yamen, and accepting any complaints. He then went to his office, the *ch'ien-ya fang* (lit., "the room for signing documents"), where he received and endorsed documents, including those relating to cases to be heard later that day.

As a rule the afternoon was reserved for hearing lawsuits.[15] About four o'clock[16] the iron bar was struck seven times and the bamboo tube once (the *wan-pang,* afternoon signal), which was a signal that the office was about to close. When the iron bar was struck five times and the bamboo tube twice, the documents were collected from the clerks and delivered to the *ch'ien-ya fang.* If there were too many cases to be heard during the "afternoon court," a hearing was held in the evening (called *wan-t'ang,* evening court). The administration of "deadline punishment" to those who had failed to pay overdue taxes sometimes took place in the evening also.

At about 7:00 P.M. the clerks, runners, and able-bodied adults who were assigned to night duty to guard the prison, treasury, and granary were checked in, and the main entrance of the yamen, as well as the door of the magistrate's residence, was locked.[17]

Certain days were officially designated each month for the people to submit their complaints (*fang-kao*), and the magistrate was expected to accept them when he presided over the morning court.[18] From the second month to the tenth month, the land tax collection period, several days were reserved each month for conducting deadline hearings in which runners who had failed to speed up the collection of the land tax or taxpayers who had failed to pay their taxes on time were questioned and flogged (*pi tse*).[19]

On the first and fifteenth days of every month[20] the magistrate was expected to visit the Confucian temple and the temple of the city god. These routines were supposed to be observed regularly throughout the year without interruption. The only legal holiday was the New Year, which began on the nineteenth, twentieth, or twenty-first day of the twelfth month.[21] During this period, called *feng-yin* (sealing the seal), the seal was not to be used or official business transacted. The seal was not used again until the nineteenth, twentieth, or twenty-first day of the first month of the new year, the period of *k'ai-yin* (opening the seal).[22] In addition to the New Year holiday, the farmers' busy season (*nung-mang*) was observed by suspending all civil cases. Of course, all the magistrates did not observe these routines with equal diligence. Some conscientious magistrates attended to all official business personally and read all official and legal documents daily, without delay. For instance, Wang Feng-sheng (1776–1834) reported that he usually read and revised documents in the morning, reviewed legal documents in the afternoon before the hearings, and, after returning from the court, read all the documents submitted to him on that day. When he had to leave the yamen to welcome or bid farewell to a commissioner or other superior passing through his locality, he always took the documents and read them while traveling by boat or carriage. The trials were then conducted in the evening after he had returned.[23] However, there were magistrates who did not read the documents but left them to the clerks and private secretaries.[24] T'ien Wen-ching (1662–1732), a governor-general, reported that magistrates could not avoid presiding over the court in the afternoon and evening, but that the practice of morning court was not observed by many magistrates who were too lazy to get up early in the morning. He said that only one or two magistrates out of ten held the morning court, and then only once or twice every ten days.[25]

2. Qualifications for Appointment

Magistrates came to their posts either by the "regular route" (cheng-t'u) or the "irregular route" (i-t'u). The first group included chin-shih, the Metropolitan Graduates;[26] chü-jen, the Provincial Graduates;[27] regular kung-sheng, the Senior Licentiates;[28] and yin-sheng, Honorary Licentiates.[29] The irregular route to a magisterial appointment was the purchase of an academic title—kung-sheng or chien-sheng (Student of the Imperial Academy)—followed by purchase of an official title.[30] A petty official, who would not normally be eligible for a magistracy, might be recommended (pao-chü) for the post by his superiors by virtue of meritorious service.[31]

In order to gain a general idea of the number of the above-mentioned groups appointed to the posts of chou and hsien magistrate, I have made use of the Chin-shen ch'üan-shu (Complete directory of officials). Two issues were selected as samples: those for 1745 (the tenth year of Ch'ien-lung) and 1850 (the thirtieth year of Tao-kuang). The first one represents the situation in the earlier Ch'ing, a period in which the government and bureaucracy are recognized to have been in good order. The second directory was selected as more representative of the later days of the dynasty, before the Taiping Rebellion and other uprisings. Readers are reminded that the situation was different from Hsien-feng on, because more candidates entered officialdom through purchase of title or recommendation based on military service.

Table 4 shows that, in both directories, the largest single category from which chou magistrates came was that of commoners who bought the title of Student of the Imperial Academy[32] (27.8 per cent in 1745 and

28.6 per cent in 1850); next came the *chin-shih* (22.9 and 25.9 per cent for the given years), and the *chü-jen* (13.9 and 13.3 per cent, respectively).

As a source of hsien magistrates, the *chin-shih* led with 44.6 per cent in 1745, and 34.7 per cent in 1850); next came the *chü-jen* (22.3 and 26.2 per cent respectively), and finally the commoner *chien-sheng* (12.7 and 13.4 per cent). It is interesting that more chou magistrates came from the commoner *chien-sheng* than from the *chin-shih* group, although the difference in the percentages acquired from the two groups is not very great.

If we put all regular degree holders into one group—including *chin-shih, chü-jen, pa-kung* (Senior Licentiates by selection), *yu-kung* (Senior Licentiates by recommendation), *fu-pang* or *fu-kung* (supplementary *chü-jen), en-kung* (Senior Licentiates by imperial favor), *sui-kung* (Senior Licentiates by seniority), *sheng-yüan, chiao-hsi,* and *t'eng-lu*[33]—and compare them with all those who purchased their academic titles—including *lin-kung* (stipendiaries who purchased the title of *kung-sheng), tseng-kung* ("additional" government school students who purchased the title of *kung-sheng), fu-kung* ("supplementary" government school students who purchased the title of *kung-sheng*), commoner *chien-sheng* who purchased the title of *kung-sheng,*[34] *lin-chien* (stipendiaries who purchased the title of *chien-sheng), tseng-chien* ("additional" government school students who purchased the title of *chien-sheng), fu-chien* ("supplementary" government school students who purchased the title of *chien-sheng*), and commoners who purchased the title of *chien-sheng*—we will find that the percentage of chou magistrates from the first group was only slightly higher than from the second group: 45.8 versus 37.5 in the 1745 list and 46.2 versus 44.0 in the 1850 list. Among the hsien magistrates, the number of the regular degree holders is overwhelmingly larger and the difference between the two groups is very significant in both years: 74.4 versus 16.5 per cent in the 1745 list and 69.5 versus 19.4 per cent in 1850.

The table also shows that there was a slight increase in those who entered officialdom by purchase between 1745 and 1850, and that the increase was greater among the chou magistrates. Among the chou magistrates, the officials by purchase increased from 37.5 to 44.0 per cent, whereas the regular degree holders increased only slightly, from 45.8 to 46.2 per cent. Among the hsien magistrates, the regular degree holders decreased from 74.4 per cent to 69.5, whereas the officials by purchase increased from 16.5 to 19.4 per cent. It may be noted that there was only a slight increase

Table 4. Background of chou and hsien magistrates[a]

	1745				1850			
	Chou magistrate		Hsien magistrate		Chou magistrate		Hsien magistrate	
Background	number of persons	per cent	number of persons	per cent	number of persons	per cent	number of persons	per cent
By examination:								
Chin-shih	33	22.9	573	44.6	37	25.9	444	34.7
Chü-jen	20	13.9	287	22.3	19	13.3	336	26.2
Pa-kung	8	5.5	60	4.6	1	0.7	50	3.9
Yu-kung	—	—	6	0.5	—	—	7	0.5
Fu-pang	1	0.7	21	1.6	1	0.7	19	1.5
En-kung	—	—	2	0.2	—	—	—	—
Sui-kung	—	—	—	—	—	—	1	0.1
Sheng-yüan	4	2.8	7	0.5	7	4.9	24	1.9
Chiao-hsi	—	—	1	0.1	—	—	—	—
T'eng-lu	—	—	—	—	1	0.7	9	0.7
Total	66	45.8	957	74.4	66	46.2	890	69.5
By purchase:								
Lin-kung								
Tseng-kung }	4	2.8	16	1.2	11	7.7	48	3.7
Fu-kung								
Kung-sheng	10	6.9	27	2.1	8	5.6	25	2.0
Lin-chien								
Tseng-chien }	—	—	6	0.5	3	2.1	4	0.3
Fu-chien								
Chien-sheng	40	27.8	163	12.7	41	28.6	171	13.4
Total	54	37.5	212	16.5	63	44.0	248	19.4
By other channels:								
Yin-sheng	1	0.7	3	0.2	4	2.8	10	0.8
Clerks[b]	—	—	1	0.1	—	—	14	1.1
Meritorious record[c]	7	4.9	38	3.0	4	2.8	42	3.3
Recommendation	4	2.8	27	2.1	2	1.4	22	1.7
Hereditary rank	1	0.7	—	—	1	0.7	—	—
Hsiao-lien fang-cheng[d]	—	—	—	—	—	—	1	0.1
Total	13	9.1	69	5.4	11	7.7	89	7.0
Unknown	11	7.6	48	3.7	3	2.1	53	4.1
Grand total	144	100.0	1286	100.0	143	100.0	1280	100.0

[a] Tribal magistrates excluded.

[b] Includes kung-shih, li-yüan, and chih-yüan.

[c] I-hsü (Evaluation of merit by the Board of Civil Office).

[d] This entry is given in the source as chao-shih (summoned to take examination) for the magistrate Feng Chen-tung. Chin-shen ch'üan-shu, 1850 fall ed., ts'e 4, p. 50.

in the *sheng-yüan* (students of prefectural, chou, and hsien schools) who purchased the title of *kung-sheng* (that is, *lin-kung, tseng-kung, and fu-kung*), and that the number of commoner *chien-sheng* remained more or less the same. The most noticeable change occurred within the groups of regular degree holders. The *chin-shih* decreased from 44.6 to 34.7 per cent and the *chü-jen* increased from 22.3 to 26.2 per cent. This was probably the result of attempts to give more magisterial appointments to the *chü-jen* (see note 27).

A *yin-sheng* (Honorary Licentiate) was the son or grandson of a high official who obtained his title by virtue of his father's or grandfather's bureaucratic status or by virtue of his father or grandfather having died in the service of the government. As Table 4 indicates, this was not an important group; the percentage of those who became magistrates was almost negligible. The table also makes it clear that the chances of a clerk's being promoted to magistrate were extremely slight.

As magisterial appointments were given to both Han Chinese and the Bannermen, particularly the Manchus, the question arises as to how many magistrates were Han Chinese and how many came from other groups. Table 5, based upon the same 1745 and 1850 directories, shows that most of the chou and hsien magistrates in these years were Han Chinese. The Bannermen, including Manchus, Mongols, and Chinese, constituted only 16.7 and 14.7 per cent of the chou magistrates in 1745 and 1850 respectively, and only 6.2 and 7.8 per cent of the hsien magistrates. Note that more Bannermen were appointed as chou magistrates than as hsien magistrates. The table also shows that among the Bannermen, the Manchus were in the lead, and that among the magistrates more were Chinese Bannermen than Mongol.

One regulation should be mentioned in connection with the appointment of a magistrate. Like all other local officials, he was permitted to hold office neither in his native province nor in a neighboring province within 500 li of his home town. There was also a law of "avoidance" (*hui-pi*) which prohibited clan members or maternal relatives from

---

According to the local gazette of Ch'u-chou, Feng was recommended under the category of *hsiao-lien fang-cheng* (filial, pure, and upright) and also passed the court examination—which qualified him for appointment to the post of magistrate. *Ch'u-chou chih*, 6B:33; 7D:37; on the system of *hsiao-lien fang-cheng* consult *Ch'ing shih kao*, 116:3b–4b.

Source: *Chin-shen ch'üan-shu* (1745, fall ed., and 1850, fall ed.).

Table 5. Racial origin of chou and hsien magistrates

	1745				1850			
	Chou magistrate		Hsien magistrate		Chou magistrate		Hsien magistrate	
Racial Origin	No.	Per cent	No.	Per cent	No.	Per cent	No.	Per cent
Manchu Bannermen	14	9.7	39	3.0	11	7.7	54	4.2
Mongol Bannermen	5	3.5	4	0.3	4	2.8	12	0.9
Chinese Bannermen	5	3.5	37	2.9	6	4.2	34	2.7
Han Chinese	120	83.3	1206	93.8	122	85.3	1180	92.2
Total	144	100.0	1286	100.0	143	100.0	1280	100.0

Source: *Chin-shen ch'üan-shu* (1745, fall ed., and 1850, fall ed.).

serving in the same province. Specifically, a magistrate could not hold office in the same province as his grandfather, grandson, father, son, father's brother, or brothers; nor could he serve in the same province as his paternal first cousin or any maternal relative who was included in the category "to be avoided." Moreover, he could not hold office in a province if any of the following officials was his clansmen or maternal relative: governor-general, governor, provincial treasurer, provincial judge, or an intendant who had the whole province under his jurisdiction.[35]

3. The Magistrate's Income and Local Finance

Under the Shun-chih and K'ang-hsi emperors a magistrate received only a nominal salary. From the Yung-cheng period on, in addition to this nominal salary he was given a substantial supplementary salary (*yang-lien yin,* lit., "money to nourish honesty").[36] For a chou magistrate the yearly nominal salary was only 80 taels, for a hsien magistrate in the capital 60 taels, and for an ordinary hsien magistrate 45 taels.[37]

The supplementary salary for a chou magistrate varied in different provinces, ranging from 500 to 2000 taels (see Table 6). In Yün-lung chou, Yünnan, a magistrate enjoyed the highest supplementary salary in the empire, 2000 taels. In other places 1400 was the maximum. The lowest salary (500–600 taels) was paid in Chihli, Shensi, Kansu, Szechwan, Kwangtung and Kweichow. In Kiangsi, Chekiang, Fukien, Hunan, and Shensi all chou magistrates in the same province received the same salary; in other provinces the salary was not uniform.

The supplementary salary of a hsien magistrate also varied among the provinces, ranging from 400 to 2259 taels (see Table 6). Excepting in

Table 6. Supplementary salary of magistrates in various provinces (Source: *Hu-pu tse-li, chüan 75*)

Chou magistrates

Taels	Chihli	Shantung	Shansi	Honan	Kiangsi	Chekiang	Hupeh	Kiangsu	Anhui	Fukien	Hunan	Shensi	Kansu	Szechwan	Kwangtung	Kwangsi	Yünnan	Kweichow
500–599	X																	X
600–699												X	X	X	X			X
700–799	X		X				X							X		X		X
800–899			X	X	X		X		X				X			X		
900–999	X						X	X	X		X			X	X		X	
1000–1099	X		X	X			X		X							X	X	
1100–1199													X					
1200–1299		X						X		X								
1300–1399																		
1400–1499		X		X		X										X		
1500–1599																X		
1600–1699																		
1700–1799																		
1800–1899																		
1900–1999																		
2000																	X	

Hsien magistrates

Taels	Chihli	Shantung	Shansi	Honan	Kiangsi	Chekiang	Hupeh	Kiangsu	Anhui	Fukien	Hunan	Shensi	Kansu	Szechwan	Kwangtung	Kwangsi	Yünnan	Kweichow
400–499	X						X				X							X
500–599						X	X				X		X	X				X
600–699	X		X			X	X		X	X	X	X	X	X				X
700–799	X		X		X	X	X				X				X	X	X	
800–899	X	X	X	X	X	X	X		X	X	X				X	X	X	
900–999	X				X		X	X			X				X	X	X	
1000–1099		X		X	X	X	X		X	X	X		X	X	X	X		X
1100–1199	X					X	X	X		X	X			X		X		
1200–1299						X		X			X				X	X	X	
1300–1399		X		X							X		X					
1400–1499								X								X		
1500–1599					X	X	X			X								
1600–1699															X	X		
1700–1799					X	X		X										
1800–1899						X		X										
1900–1999					X													
2000–2259		X		X	X													

Shensi, there were also marked differences between hsien in the same province. The magistrate's salaries were comparatively low in five provinces: Shansi, Anhui, Shensi, Szechwan, and Kweichow, where they ranged from 400 to 1000 taels. All other provinces went beyond the 1000 level. Twelve hundred taels was the highest pay in Chihli, Hunan, Kansu, and Yünnan. Nine provinces paid their magistrates more than 1400 taels: Shantung, Honan, Kiangsi, Chekiang, Hupeh, Kiangsu, Fukien, Kwangtung, and Kwangsi. But with the exception of Shantung and Honan, these higher salaries were limited to only a few hsien within the province.[38] We may conclude that high pay was rather exceptional and that the supplementary salaries of most magistrates ranged from 500 to 1200 taels. This roughly accords with the statement by Chou Kao (1754–1823) that the most a magistrate got was 1000 taels and the least 500 or 600 taels.[39]

Was such a salary sufficient to cover a magistrate's personal and official expenses? Besides supporting his family, the magistrate had to meet very heavy expenses entailed by his post. He had to pay for the services of his private secretaries and personal servants, and the salary of a private secretary, as we shall see, was very high. Indeed, Chou Kao once remarked that a magistrate's total salary was barely enough to pay for his private secretaries.[40]

Another heavy drain on the magistrate's income was the *t'an-chüan* (assigned contribution), a system under which magistrates and other local officials in a province were ordered by the provincial treasurer to contribute to the financing of government expenditure when the government funds were unavailable or inadequate.[41] Such a contribution was usually deducted by the provincial treasurer from the official's supplementary salary. As a rule, the assigned contribution that a magistrate was obliged to make was assessed according to the position of his income, in a scale of three grades. Only the lowest grade was exempted from the contribution.[42] One common "contribution" was a regular donation toward the defrayment of a number of administrative expenses, such as civil examination expenses, autumn assize expenses, or military supplies.[43] The magistrates also had to contribute regularly to the office expenses of superior yamen.[44]

Furthermore, all local officials might be ordered to contribute money to make up a deficit accumulated over a number of years (*li-nien k'uei-kung*). This often happened after an audit of treasuries and granaries (*p'an-ch'a*).

For instance, after all the treasuries and granaries in Chekiang had been audited in 1800, a deficit of 1,942,337 taels was disclosed, and the various chou and hsien magistrates were ordered to make a contribution within a period of sixteen years. Another audit was held in 1819, and the local officials were ordered to make up a deficiency of 954,085 taels within ten years. And again, in 1822, officials were ordered to contribute 1,701,003 taels within thirteen years.[45] It was reported that local officials in Shantung contributed 1,100,000 taels between 1803 and 1804 toward making up a deficit after an audit of treasuries and granaries.[46] These contributions certainly reduced the magistrate's income considerably.[47] One magistrate complained that one's nominal salary went to pay for forfeits[48] and one's supplementary salary went to assigned contributions.[49] In the opinion of some officials, these assigned contributions were largely responsible for the deficits that frequently occurred in the magistrates' government funds.[50]

The magistrate also bore the financial burden for entertaining his superior official or a high commissioner passing through his area. He had to provide a residence, furnishings, and food for them, and farewell gifts were customarily presented to a superior on his departure,[51] although this was not permitted by law.[52] Besides, money was usually demanded by the superior's petty officers, runners, and personal servants, who could number up to as many as a hundred.[53] It was also customary for the magistrate holding office in the provincial capital to repair the official residence and provide furnishings and fuel for a newly appointed governor-general, governor, or other superior. Such expenses were borne jointly by all the magistrates for their superiors.[54] Magistrates were also expected to present their superiors with customary fees and gifts when they arrived at a post, on birthdays, at the New Year, and on other festivals.[55]

A magistrate was obliged to pay various "customary fees" to the personnel in a superior yamen whenever he had dealings with them. He had to pay "door fees" (men-pao) to gate porters, "tea money" (ch'a-i) to runners and personal servants,[56] and other customary fees to the clerks on various occasions—at the audit of the treasury and granary, when submitting reports or delivering government funds to a superior yamen (chieh fei), or when transferring government funds and records at the time of leaving his post.[57]

Of course, the total of all these various expenses varied in different localities, but there is no doubt that it far exceeded the magistrate's total salary. According to Chou Kao, these expenses were several times greater than the total salary a magistrate received.[58] Hsieh Chen-ting (1753–1809), a censor, estimated that a magistrate's annual expenses (excluding salaries paid to private secretaries, food, daily expenses, and entertainment) varied from five or six thousand to more than ten thousand taels.[59] Salaries to private secretaries would add another one to three thousand taels, depending upon the number of secretaries employed.[60]

How could a magistrate meet these enormous expenses with his limited income? The answer lies in a practice called *lou-kuei* (customary fees; lit., "base custom"). By collecting fees on every imaginable occasion, members of the Chinese bureaucracy at every level were able to supplement their incomes. Although the practice was, as the term suggests, "irregular" and "low," it was nevertheless established and authorized and became widely accepted. It was thus within the toleration of the law.[61] It should not be confused with bribery or other forms of corruption, which were unlawful and prohibited. However, in some cases there was no sharp dividing line between the collection of a customary fee and corruption.

This practice in Chinese government deserves our special attention. It must be conceived as a system and examined together with the fiscal system, which was different from that of the West. In China, the basic fiscal principle was that each type of expenditure was met from a definite source, and that specific funds were earmarked for every item of government expenditure.[62] If no fund was provided for a certain expense, the official had to find some other means to finance it. For example, the magistrate had to collect taxes according to a quota and deliver the total amount to the treasurer; none of the cost of collection or delivery could be deducted from the tax fund. Only very small funds were provided for expenditures falling into the category of office expenses.[63] The wages of yamen personnel were insufficient to maintain them; in fact, in some cases they received no wages at all. All these deficiencies were met by the customary fees. In other words, it was the fees that made it possible for the magistrate to maintain himself and his staff, and pay the various office expenses.

Many officials held that customary fees could not be abolished because they provided the only means of paying the administrative expenses.[64] Wang Hui-tsu argued that customary fees obtained from the people were used for the public and not for enriching the officials.[65] H. B. Morse correctly pointed out that China's fee system was not unique; similar practices existed in Europe and America.[66] The system was probably more prevalent in China, where it remained the standard practice to the end of the dynasty. The government made no serious effort to abolish it, for it realized that unless office expenses were included in the government budget, as Cheng Kuan-ying (b. 1841) had once suggested they should be,[67] the fee system was indispensable. To increase the budget was to reduce the imperial revenue, unless the government instituted a corresponding rise in the tax rate, and this it was apparently unwilling to do.

Instead, the government merely attempted to regulate the fee system, without success. It was difficult to define just what constituted legitimate administrative expenses and how much was actually needed for them. Officials and yamen personnel soon began to abuse the practice of *lou-kuei* and created a serious administrative problem for the government. The variety of the fees increased, and so did the amounts. The whole matter was beyond the control of the government, especially the central government, which had no way of even knowing the different types of customary fees in use in various localities, let alone any way of checking their use.[68]

Consequently, control was left to the provincial authorities. Some of them, like Ch'en Hung-mou (1696–1771), a governor, did try to regulate the practice by listing fees that were permitted and abolishing the rest.[69] But since local governments at all levels depended on customary fees for administrative expenses, each yamen was obliged to demand such fees from the yamen at lower levels. Obviously, control of the system could hardly be effective if the higher officials could not restrain themselves and their own personnel from demanding customary fees from subordinate yamen.[70]

The magistrates were in a very difficult position, for they had to find the means both to pay customary fees to the superior yamen and to finance the administrative expenses of their own yamen. According to the established pattern, yamen personnel were allowed to share the benefits of customary fees with the magistrate. It must be kept in mind that the chou or hsien yamen, being the lowest rung in local government, had to collect its customary fees from the people directly or indirectly through the medium of local agents like the village head. Obviously, if the people were faced with excessive demands for fees, they became too impoverished to pay taxes. And it was the magistrate's duty to collect the full quota of taxes. The supervision and control of the yamen personnel, upon whom he had to depend to collect customary fees from the agents and the people, consequently became yet another serious problem for him. We will deal with this problem in the subsequent chapters on clerks, runners, and personal servants.

The government's tolerance of the fee system and the lack of institutional control over it meant that the whole matter of customary fees was left largely to the magistrates, who were expected to be reasonable and moderate. It does not follow, however, that a magistrate was free to demand customary fees at will. The extent of the fees was defined and regulated mainly by the custom of an area, which was known to all who lived there. The payers would consent to a fee that accorded in purpose and amount with the established rule; but they would refuse to pay if an official or any of the yamen personnel demanded higher fees or introduced new ones. Feng Kuei-fen (1809–1874) said that the people in Chü-jung, Kiangsu, always paid the land tax at a fixed conversion rate, although the market rate might change. If a magistrate increased the rate, a riot usually resulted.[71] Obviously, custom was the force that kept customary fees within certain limits, and a wise magistrate simply followed the established practice.[72]

Of the great variety of customary fees imposed in different areas, the following were widespread. One of the most common, which was collected from taxpayers before 1724, was the *huo-hao* (meltage fee),[73] an allowance to make up for the silver lost in the process of being melted (the small pieces of silver collected as tax had to be cast into ingots).[74] The allowance varied from ten to fifty per cent of the tax itself.[75] A magistrate who demanded only ten per cent of a tax as *huo-hao* was considered a good magistrate.[76] Another practice was the collection of copper coins in lieu of silver at a conversion rate higher than the market rate.[77] An extra allowance of grain was generally imposed on taxpayers paying grain tribute. And if cash was collected in lieu of grain, the price demanded was higher than the market price.[78]

The amount of income thus derived in the process of collecting land tax alone, as we shall see in Chapter VIII, was astonishing. It certainly contributed largely to the magistrate's ability to meet both his official and personal expenses. It covered the meltage loss of silver, wastage of grain in storage and transit, the cost of stationery, and tax collection and delivery expenses.[79] In addition, according to Ho Shih-ch'i (*chin-shih* 1822), a first-class assistant prefect (*t'ung-chih*), the magistrate could meet various of his yearly expenses out of the income derived from grain tribute collection.[80]

We must remember, however, that many items of customary allowance were not enjoyed by the magistrate alone, but were shared by other yamen personnel. For instance, the extra silver (*yü p'ing*)[81] obtained from the land tax payments was distributed in a certain local yamen in the following ratio: sixty per cent to the magistrate, ten per cent to the personal servants, and thirty per cent to the clerks.[82]

A few magistrates held that customary fees should never be received from clerks and runners, because it would then be impossible to control them.[83] But it seems that many magistrates collected many kinds of fees from the yamen personnel. They also collected fees from people who were not employed in the yamen but who had dealings with it. "Gift" money was often exacted from clerks, scribes (*tai-shu*), and runners by newly appointed magistrates.[84] Sometimes money was also expected from the clerk in charge of the silver chest or tribute grain, and from a runner who was appointed as chief of a group of runners.[85] There were even cases where the chief runners were told to hand in customary fees on the days they were on duty.[86]

The magistrates also collected fees from the rural people who were assigned as *li-chang* (head of a *li*), or as *ts'ui-t'ou* (a taxpayer assigned to speed the payment of land tax among five or ten families). Money was frequently offered to the magistrates or clerks by people who wanted to avoid such an assignment,[87] and by those rural residents who wanted to avoid being clerks in charge of the district treasury.[88] Furthermore, customary fees were obtained from shopkeepers (*hang-hu*) who provided the commodities and services for sacrifice and entertainment during the celebrations at the advent of spring.[89] Other fees collected by magistrates were charges for such things as door placards and records in connection with the administration of the *pao-chia* system, tax assessment notices (*yu-tan*), and the expenses involved in an investigation of a famine, census-taking, or land survey.[90]

We should also mention the practice of demanding commodities from the people without payment or at an "official price" (*kuan-chia*) which was lower than the market price. The goods used daily in the yamen— rice, meat, firewood, charcoal, cotton, silk, etc.—were either taken from the merchants without payment or bought at the "official price." [91] By law, an official who borrowed the people's property or purchased commodities below market price was guilty of bribery, and magistrates were frequently warned against these practices by their supervisors.[92] There was also a regulation to the effect that a local yamen was to buy only food in its own locality; cotton, silk, and other goods were either to be brought from home or bought in a neighboring district.[93] The practicability of this regulation was of course dubious.

The different attitudes of magistrates toward the widespread practice of buying at the official price are interesting because they reveal a conflict between what was considered right and what was considered practical. There were some magistrates, like Wang Chih (*chin-shih* 1721), who did not permit the use of an official price and always bought goods at the market price.[94] Wang Hui-tsu admitted that using the official price was not a good idea, and yet many things could not be done if the practice were abolished.[95] Another magistrate, Fang Ta-chih, held that although the practice was not altogether acceptable, it was better to keep it, since the people were used to it, than to demand customary fees. He suggested that a magistrate should check his income against outlay before making any changes. If the outlay could not be balanced by income, it was better to keep the old practice; but there should be a limit, and the magistrate's personal servants should not be permitted to demand goods from the people.[96] The fact that the system of official price was openly defended in their handbooks by such honest magistrates as Wang and Fang indicates that very few magistrates could do without it.

It is evident, then, that nearly all yamen expenses, which were not provided for in the government budget, were met by one or another form of customary fees at the expense of the local people. When a village head or yamen employee was required to pay a customary fee, he collected from the people, kept a part of the money for himself, and handed in the rest. Thus the local people had a dual burden—the regular tax or fees imposed by the government and an additional obligation imposed by the magistrate or other yamen personnel. In any given situation or event it was always the people involved who paid the various expenses entailed. Chao Shen-ch'iao (1644–1720) summed up the situation as follows:

All the public and private expenses [of the magistrate and other yamen personnel] are taken from the village people . . . The *lou-kuei* are too numerous to be counted. In short, there is not a single thing for which money is not privately extracted from the people; there is not a single fee which is not harshly demanded from the village units.[97]

Although the practice of *lou-kuei* was universal in the empire, the types and number of fees, as well as the amounts, varied in different localities.[98] That is why most magistrates were anxious to find out the kinds and amounts of customary fees available to them when they took office. There were also personal differences among the officials, not all of whom handled the matter in the same way. There were magistrates who took advantage of the system and enjoyed every kind of customary fee in existence. The complaint was sometimes made that when 100 coins were needed they would demand 1000 from the people.[99] At times they even created some new types of fees.[100] On the other hand, some honest and conscientious magistrates made a distinction between what could and could not be accepted. They also attempted to regulate the practice by approving some fees and abolishing or reducing others.[101] It was generally considered improper to accept customary fees from clerks and runners and in connection with the administration of justice, such as gift money for presiding over the court (*tso-t'ang li*) or fees paid by the two parties to sign a statement accepting the court's judgment (*ch'u-chieh ch'ien*).[102] There were magistrates who donated money out of their own pockets to cover an expense originally covered by a customary fee, so that the fee could be abolished.[103]

We may now ask whether the money from customary fees was sufficient to meet all the expenses of a magistrate. Since the amounts varied in different localities, the financial situations of magistrates also varied. A post in a locality where the amounts from customary fees were large was commonly considered a "good post" (*mei-ch'üeh*), and the holder of such a post need not worry about finances.[104] As a rule, nearly all posts had a moderate surplus.[105] It seems that surplus was even possible from a "bad post" (*ch'ou-ch'üeh*). Hsieh Chin-luan said that a magistrate would not suffer poverty even if he was not fond of money.[106] Probably only those who were extravagant in their personal expenses and social activities had the problem of a deficiency.[107] Hung Liang-chi (1746–1809) wrote that when he was a young man, magistrates could retire with a surplus that would keep their families well fed and well clad for several generations. In his later years, he added, the surplus was ten times greater than before.[108] Since a magistrate's salary remained the same, this statement implies that more customary fees were collected by magistrates as time went on.

4. Promotion, Demotion, and Removal from Office

Like all other officials in the empire, magistrates of accomplishment were rewarded by the recording of merits (*chi-lu*), advancement in grade (*chia-chi*), or promotion. A magistrate might be given one to three recordings, according to his merit. Advancement in grade, which was a higher reward, also varied from one to three grades. One advancement in grade was equivalent to four recordings of merit.

Promotion might be granted either upon completion of the current term (*feng-man chi-sheng*), or, in some cases, before completion of the current term (*pu-lun feng-man chi-sheng*).[109] In the first case a magistrate was required to have held office for a specified minimum period before he could be promoted. The term varied according to whether the chou or hsien was classed as an interior post (*fu-feng*) or a border post (*pien-feng*). The second category included both posts in a malarial area (*yen-chang ch'üeh*)[110] and posts in an area occupied by tribesmen (*Miao-chiang ch'üeh*).[111] A magistrate holding an interior post was not eligible for promotion until he had served for five years; the term was three years in a border post. However, a magistrate in a border post where the air and water were considered malignant (*shui-t'u o-tu*) could be promoted in less than three years. A magistrate in a coastal area (*yen-hai ch'üeh*)[112] or a river area (*yen-ho ch'üeh*)[113] was treated in the same way as a magistrate in a border post.[114]

All officials were subject to disciplinary measures when they neglected their duties, performed their duties incorrectly, abused their authority, engaged in corruption, or committed other crimes. The law distinguished between malfeasance in office (*kung-tsui*) and a personal crime (*ssu-tsui*), such as bribery or embezzlement. However, a personal crime committed unintentionally was also classified as a *kung-tsui,* whereas malfeasance in office connected with the performance of official duties, committed with intent, was classified as *ssu-tsui*.[115]

As a rule, malfeasance in office was punished less severely than a personal crime.[116] Also, an official could use his merit record and advancement in grade to cancel out a forfeit or demotion in the case of malfeasance, but this privilege was not granted in the case of a personal offense.[117] Since a personal crime implied moral degeneration, whereas malfeasance in office was almost inevitable owing to the profusion and complexity of the administrative regulations embodied in the Punitive Regulations of the Board of Civil Office (*Li-pu ch'u-fen tse-li*), some magistrates expressed the opinion that although one should never commit a personal crime, one might not be able to avoid malfeasance in office.[118]

When a magistrate violated any regulation or law and was impeached by his superior or a censor, the case was referred to the Board of Civil Office for deliberation in accordance with the articles provided in the Punitive Regulations or the Penal Code (*Ta-Ch'ing lü-li*).[119] The punishment might be a forfeit of nominal salary,[120] demotion,[121] or dismissal.

In a serious case an official could be permanently barred from appointment (*yung pu hsü-yung*).[122] When a magistrate was guilty of a crime for which the penalty, as defined in the Penal Code, was a beating, he could be punished instead by forfeiture of his nominal salary, demotion, or dismissal, because an official was entitled to be exempted from beating.[123] As dismissal was the maximum punishment provided in the Punitive Regulations which was applicable to an official whose crime called for a beating, the case of an official subject to more severe punishment was referred to the Board of Punishment and judged in accordance with the Penal Code.[124]

5. SERVICE RATINGS

Every three years there was a "great reckoning" (*ta-chi*) in all provinces, in which the achievements of all the local officials were assessed.[125] A report on each official was written by the immediate superior—prefect, independent department magistrate, or circuit intendant—and presented to the provincial treasurer and provincial judge, who added their evaluations (*k'ao-yü*) and handed the report on to the governor-general and governor. The last two reviewed the report, approved or modified the evaluations, and then submitted it to the Board of Civil Office.[126] In the course of this review, the magistrates were classified into three categories.

Those in the first category, whose achievements had been extraordinary, were recommended to the board as "outstanding and distinctive" (*cho-i*). An official thus recommended was qualified to have an audience with the emperor (*yin-chien*), and, as a rule, was given an advancement in grade by the board. A magistrate qualified for this distinction if he had imposed no extra tax and given no excessive punishments, if in his locality there was no robbery, no uncollected taxes, no deficit in the government funds or granary, and if the people's livelihood was secure and local conditions had been improved during his magistracy.[127]

By far the most important criterion was his ability to collect taxes. Thus a magistrate was not eligible for recommendation if he had been unable to collect the land tax according to the quota. A magistrate who had thus failed could be recommended only under the following conditions: (1) if he was honest and capable, if his post was a busy one characterized by at least three of the four descriptions (frequented, troublesome, wearisome, and difficult), and if he had served in the province for three years; (2) if he was not holding such a post but had served in the province for five years.[128] There was a regulation in Chekiang that a magistrate could not be recommended if he had been impeached or punished in connection with salt administration.[129]

There was a quota for recommendations in each province, varying according to the size of the province and the number of posts in it. The number of local officials, from chou and hsien magistrates up to circuit intendants, who could be recommended as "outstanding and distinctive" was as follows: five in Kweichow; six in Anhui, Fukien, Kwangsi, and Kansu; seven in Kiangsu, Hupeh, Hunan, Shensi, and Yünnan; eight in Kiangsi, Chekiang, and Kwangtung; and nine in Shantung, Shansi, and Honan. Szechwan had a quota of eleven. The highest quota was thirteen, in Chihli.[130] From this it is clear that the chance of a magistrate's inclusion in this category was very slight.

The second category included all those who were found to have been incompetent or corrupt. In the great reckoning system there were eight conditions or charges, known as *pa-fa* (eight proscriptions), that could lead to impeachment: avarice (*t'an*); cruelty (*k'u*); tardiness, weakness, or nonfeasance (*p'i-juan wu-wei*); impropriety (*pu-chin*); old age (*nien-lao*); infirmity (*yu-chi*); instability or hastiness (*fu-tsao*); incompetence (*ts'ai-li pu-chi*). From the Chia-ch'ing period on, any official charged with avarice or cruelty was subject to *immediate* impeachment; as a result these two proscriptions were removed from the list, leaving only six, known as *liu-fa*.[131]

An official guilty of avarice or cruelty was dismissed and permanently barred from appointment,[132] in addition to the punishment prescribed in the Penal Code. According to the code, an official who embezzled government funds in his charge was to be punished by beating or penal servitude, depending upon the amount he embezzled.[133] For bribery the punishment ranged from beating to strangling, according to the amount accepted and whether the action resulted in injustice.[134] The responsibility for impeaching an avaricious or cruel magistrate rested on all his superiors, from the prefect up to the governor-general or governor. They themselves were subject to punishment if they failed to report and impeach a magistrate guilty of these crimes.[135]

The penalties for the "six proscriptions" were: dismissal for impropriety and for tardiness, weakness, or nonfeasance; demotion of two grades for incompetence; demotion of three grades and transfer to another post for instability or hastiness. The aged and infirm were told to resign.[136]

Those magistrates who were listed neither for recommendation nor for impeachment were kept in their posts and were reported separately to the Board of Civil Office by the governor-general and governor. The majority fell into this third category. Their accomplishment was evaluated on the basis of four criteria: integrity (shou), ability (ts'ai), quality of administration (cheng), and age (nien). The report also indicated whether the government funds and grain under a magistrate's care were free from deficit.[137]

The great reckoning system, which was based mainly upon descriptive phrases in connection with the magistrate's performance, was devised to eliminate the unqualified officials, leaving only the competent and honest in their posts. The government hoped to encourage and reward the most efficient magistrates with advancement in grade and promotion. Since local administration actually rested in the hands of more than one thousand magistrates, from the central government's point of view it was a logical prerequisite to efficiency that good men be recruited for these posts and that they be kept under close scrutiny by the provincial authorities at various levels.

III

CLERKS

The clerks (*li* or *shu-li*), one of the four groups of aides in a magistrate's yamen, had a unique role in local administration. Their importance can be understood only through knowledge of the institutional framework within which they functioned.

All clerks were recruited within the province where they would serve; their situation thus contrasted with that of the magistrate who, as a stranger, was not familiar with the local situation and problems and might not even understand the native dialect. This explains why a magistrate could easily be deceived by the clerks.[1] Furthermore, the clerks had families, relatives, and friends who had lived in the same locality generation after generation. Their personal interest in matters concerning their relatives and friends inevitably led to favoritism and irregularities in taxation, labor service, and law suits. The magistrate, in contrast, had no personal relations with the local people except possibly with some members of the gentry.

Although a clerk's term of service was only five years, many of them actually remained in their posts after their terms expired, often by changing their names. If they were unable to hold the posts themselves, they tried to have the positions occupied by family members or relatives.[2] A magistrate, on the other hand, might be dismissed, transferred, or promoted. It was said that "there were shiftings and promotions among the officials but there was no change among the clerks."[3] Thus the local government was headed by a succession of more or less inexperienced magistrates under whom there were a number of experienced native clerks, who continued to hold their positions and perform the same duties.

This situation had two important consequences affecting the administration of local government. The inexperienced magistrate was forced to depend on the clerks to carry out official business. By the time he became more experienced, after a few years in office, it was time for him to leave. Another new man would then take over the post and he too would have to go through the same process of trial and error. As for the clerks, the longer they stayed in office the more versed they became in administrative affairs. At the same time, however, they became more experienced in manipulating situations and abusing their power. The magistrates, therefore, were in an unfortunate predicament. On the one hand, they had to rely upon the knowledge and experience of the clerks;[4] on the other, they had to deal with the problem of the clerks' corruption.

The magistrate's short term of office and the instability of his position made it extremely difficult for him to supervise and control the clerks efficiently. It took him years to become familiar with the administration, to understand the local situation, and to discover the clerks' abuses.[5] Even if an experienced and capable magistrate did detect and dismiss the corrupt clerks, he could exert no control after he left his post; they could return and serve again under a new magistrate.

The importance of the clerks was closely related to the existing administrative system and practice, under which the chou and hsien magistrates, who were the administrative officials, were supervised by their superiors.[6] This supervision was carried out mainly through the exchange of documents: orders were issued to magistrates via documents, and magistrates responded via documents.[7] Since it was the clerks who prepared and received the documents,[8] it is clear that they were in a strategic position.[9] Lu I-t'ung observed that the routine of preparing and presenting documents left the magistrate little time to perform more essential administrative functions and that this, though not good for the local administration, was advantageous to the clerks.[10]

Another factor that made it possible for the clerks to manipulate government affairs was the complexity of the government regulations and precedents. The officials, who could not know all of the regulations, were necessarily dependent upon the clerks' greater knowledge.[11] This was fully realized by Feng Kuei-fen, who remarked that the root of the clerk problem lay in the fact that the precedents were too numerous and consisted of extremely minute details, unrelated and sometimes contradictory. This gave the clerks an opportunity to manipulate regulations to their own advantage. He described li (clerks) and li (precedents) as two great misfortunes of the government and expressed regret that clerks were allowed to seek profit by taking advantage of the precedents.[12]

Finally, the clerks had access to the government files, which contained valuable information for the administration. In order to monopolize this information, they made every effort to make the files secret. The land tax record (*ch'ien-liang ts'e*) is a case in point. Only the names of the households (*hu-ming*) appeared in the official records, but the real names and the addresses of the taxpayers appeared in private copies made and kept by the clerks of revenue, who regarded them as their own valuable properties and were reluctant to show them to the magistrate and others.[13]

1. ORGANIZATION

Clerks served both in the magistrate's yamen and in the offices of his subordinate officials.[14] There was a quota for regular clerks to be employed in the various chou and hsien yamen, varying from a few to less than thirty.[15] The officials were also permitted to employ a number of copyists, called *t'ieh-hsieh,* to help the regular clerks to copy documents.[16] The number of these extra clerks to be employed in the various yamen was determined by the governor-general and governor, according to the actual needs of each office. The number had to be reported to the Board of Civil Office, and the local officials were not allowed to employ more than had been approved.[17]

However, this regulation was never strictly enforced. It was widely acknowledged that the enormous amount of paper work which was indispensable to the Chinese governmental routine necessitated many more clerks than the number officially allowed. An official once suggested that the number of clerks be drastically reduced and each regular clerk be allowed the help of only one extra clerk. This suggestion was considered impractical by two capable governors-general, T'ien Wen-ching and Li Wei (1687?–1738). The latter pointed out that each office (*fang*) needed more than ten clerks to take care of the routine.[18] A magistrate in Kwangtung reported that besides the ordinary documents and reports, the so-called *ping hsiang* (the informal and formal reports),[19] more than one hundred kinds of reports and guaranties (*ts'e-chieh*) had to be prepared every year and usually six or seven copies had to be made of each report to be submitted to the various supervising officials. Therefore more than one hundred copyists had to be employed for the work in a hsien where official duties were numerous; and even in a hsien in which official duties were relatively light, several dozen clerks were needed. In addition, it was sometimes necessary to have extra copyists to do odd jobs; these were paid according to the number of words they copied.[20]

However, not all the clerks whose names appeared on the government list actually served in the office. There were a number of nominal clerks (*kua-ming shu-li*). Yüan Shou-ting (1705–1782), a magistrate, wrote that the post of *tien-li* (clerk in charge of documents) was usually held by persons who were interested only in the honor attached to wearing official hats and belts (*kuan-tai*) but who did not actually engage in official business.[21] According to T'ien Wen-ching, these nominal clerks were members of the propertied class who were willing to pay a sum of money, ranging from two to four silver taels, for the nominal post as a protection for their properties and themselves,[22] or in order to avoid labor services.[23] The money paid by these men was used to buy stationery.[24]

The total number of clerks employed in a hsien yamen, including the regular clerks, the extra clerks, and the nominal clerks, seems to have varied with the size of the area. According to Hou Fang-yü (1618–1655), probably more than 1000 clerks were employed in a hsien.[25] Hung Liang-chi estimated that there were 1000 clerks in a large hsien, 700 to 800 in a medium-sized hsien, and at least 100 to 200 in a small hsien.[26] The estimate offered by Yu Po-ch'uan (*chin-shih* 1862) was even higher: 2000 or 3000 in a large hsien and 300 to 400 in a small one.[27]

Since the number of clerks employed in a hsien far exceeded the number actually needed for carrying out official business, various attempts were made to reduce their number. In 1826, upon the request of Na-yen-ch'eng, the governor-general of Chihli, an imperial edict was issued to reduce the number of clerks and runners in the various provinces. Eighty was proposed as the maximum quota for a chou or hsien yamen. As a result of this suggestion, more than 23,900 clerks and runners were dismissed in the province of Chihli alone.[28]

In accordance with the traditional division of official business in the Chinese government, the clerks of a chou or hsien yamen were organized into six *fang*: civil office, revenue, rites, military affairs, punishment, and works. Clerks were thus called "clerk of civil office" (*li-shu*), "clerk of revenue" (*hu-shu*), etc., each taking charge of affairs and documents relating to his particular office.

The office of civil office kept the personnel records on the assistant magistrate and other subordinate officials, the clerks, and the copyists serving in a chou or hsien government—recording their names, the date they entered the office, whether they had been recommended for merit or punished for faults.[29]

The office of revenue was responsible for the collection of taxes and all matters connected with the treasury and granary. It kept a record of the amount of the various taxes to be collected, the amount already collected, the amount transmitted to the provincial treasurer and to other offices, the amount of cash kept in the treasury, and the amount of grain stored in the granary. The office also kept a record of the names of tax agents (*li-chang*), the clerks assigned to collect the tax (*kuei-shu*), and a list of the taxpayers (*hua-hu*).[30] A clerk was usually assigned to take charge of the collection of land tax (*ch'ien-liang ching-ch'eng*). This post was given to those clerks of revenue who owned a considerable amount of property, and the term was limited to one year. However, it was not unusual for the post to be held by the same clerk for several years.[31]

Among the responsibilities of the office of rites were sacrificial ceremonies, temples, schools, examinations, and the conferring of honors (*ching-piao*).[32] The office of military affairs kept the records on the guards of city gates (*men-chün*), lictors, horsemen, commoner-guards, dispatch bearers (*p'u-ping*), and the records for the post stations.[33] The office of punishment kept the records on legal cases, prisoners, policemen, coroners, and jail-keepers, and had charge of the administration of *pao-chia*.[34] The office of works saw to repairs of government offices, granaries, prisons, post stations, bridges, ferries, and roads.[35]

In addition to these six offices, a chou or hsien might have other offices or clerks with special assignments: (1) The receipt and distribution office (*ch'eng fa fang*), which distributed documents to, and collected prepared drafts from, the six offices. It was this office that made direct contact with the magistrate's gate porter in connection with the handling of documents.[36] (2) Office of correspondence (*chien-fang*).[37] (3) Treasury office (*k'u-fang*), where money collected from land tax, official properties, and recovered stolen goods and weapons used in cases of homicide were stored. The clerk was required to keep a record of every item that was stored in or removed from the treasury.[38] (4) Granary office (*ts'ang-fang*).[39] (5) Office (or clerk) in charge of preparing records of land tax deadline hearings (*tsung-fang* or *tsung-shu*).[40] (6) Clerks responsible for making cadastres and land tax records for each *li* (*li-shu*, also known as *ts'e-shu* or *shan-shu*).[41] (7) Clerks in charge of the chests in which taxpayers' silver or cash was deposited (*kuei-shu*). It was their duty to give receipts to the taxpayers.[42] (8) Clerk in charge of the collection of tribute grain (*ts'ao-shu*).[43] (9) Office (or clerk) of deposition (*chao-fang* or *chao-shu*)— in charge of the writing of *chao-chuang,* that is, the questions asked by the magistrate and the depositions by the plaintiff, defendant, and witness.[44] (9) Clerk of postal service (*i-shu*), whose duty it was to keep a record of the number of couriers, grooms, boatmen, horses, and boats, and the expenses incurred for them.[45]

2. FUNCTIONS

The work of the various *fang* necessarily involved the preparation and processing of many documents, duties which fell mainly to the clerks. These duties may be summarized as follows.

1) Making a draft. Since there were many clerks and, as we shall see, the preparation of documents always brought some profit to them, the clerks usually took turns in preparing the drafts. The assignments were therefore distributed according to the names as they appeared on the muster roll (*mao-pu*).[46] The clerk whose turn it was to present a draft was expected to do so within a reasonable period of time. Sometimes definite deadlines were set for the preparation of drafts and of finished documents, depending upon the nature of the documents and the effort involved in preparing them. As a rule, the clerk preparing a draft was required to write his name at the end of it,[47] so that the document could be traced back to him if any questions arose. This draft was submitted for revision or approval to either the magistrate or his private secretary. The approved draft was returned to the original *fang* for copying. The finished copy was then sent in again for checking and sealing. After this the document was either sent out or posted, depending on the nature of the situation.[48]

As most of the clerks had had only very elementary training in reading and writing, they were not expected to prepare well-written documents. Hsieh Chin-luan remarked: "although the drafts are prepared by clerks, it is merely expected that the form is roughly there . . . Anyone who roughly understands the meaning of words and knows the format for the draft is capable of becoming a clerk." [49]

2) Preparing routine reports. It was the duty of the clerks to prepare the various routine reports that the magistrate regularly submitted to his superiors.[50] These included various kinds of annual reports and guaranty statements (*ts'e-chieh*).[51]

3) Writing a memorandum. Sometimes it was necessary to refer to old

documents before a trial could be conducted or an inquiry from a superior could be answered. It was then the duty of a clerk to look into the files relating to the case under investigation and submit a report. The usual practice was to write down the essential points on a piece of paper and attach it to the document itself, so that the magistrate could have a clear picture of the case.[52]

4) Issuing a warrant (*p'iao*). It was the duty of the clerks to prepare warrants authorizing the government runners to arrest culprits, or to summon witnesses or persons who had failed to pay tax. Since a distinction was made between an arrest and a summons, and since criminals under arrest could be chained, it was essential that the clerk specify clearly whether the warrant was for an arrest or merely a summons. Some magistrates had their clerks stamp a summons with the phrase: "No chains are to be used." If such a procedure was followed, the clerk was obliged to mark the warrant with such a stamp. Some magistrates also demanded that the clerk write on the draft of the warrant (*p'iao k̨ao*) the distance a runner had to go to reach his destination, so that the magistrate could determine a deadline for carrying out the mission.[53]

5) Preparing tax records. We have mentioned that the clerks prepared both the land tax records (*shih-ch'eng ts'e*) and the deadline-hearing records (*pi-pu*). It was their duty to check the payments made by tax-payers at each deadline and to write on the deadline-hearing record the amount owed by each to the government, so that the delinquent taxpayers, tax agents, or runners responsible for speeding the tax collection could be identified and summoned. This record was the basis for the deadline hearing.[54]

6) Filing the documents, an essential for any bureaucracy, was one of the most important functions of the clerks.[55] They were held responsible if any document was misplaced, lost, or removed from the files.[56]

This description of the functions of the clerks makes it clear that they played an indispensable part in the local administration, particularly in their control of the files. In discussing the power of the clerks Lu I-t'ung made the following remarks:

Why can the clerks not be abolished right away? Because the officials [of a chou or hsien government] do not attend to the administration personally; it is not in the hands of the officials . . . Clerks are consulted about bandits and thieves. Now the clerks are even consulted about the granary, prison, and postal service.[57]

On rare occasions the voice of the clerks was even more decisive than that of the magistrate. Thus Feng Kuei-fen remarked: "if a chou or hsien magistrate says 'yes,' and the clerk says 'no,' the result will be 'no.' "[58]

At the same time, clerks were held responsible for certain aspects of the administration. For example, when a chou or hsien failed to collect and deliver taxes to the superior officers, the provincial treasurer sent his runners to summon the clerk in charge of tax collection for investigation and punishment.[59]

3. RECRUITMENT, TERM OF SERVICE, AND PROMOTION

We have mentioned that members of the propertied class frequently held nominal posts, with the purpose of obtaining social prestige, or to protect their property or evade labor services. But most of the clerks who actually served in the office came from the propertyless class and economic reward was their primary motive. Yüan Shou-ting reported that those clerks who actually served in the office were poor, and since they enjoyed neither remuneration nor title, they conducted illegal activities and extorted money from the people in order to support themselves and their families.[60] In the case of those active clerks who had some property, their motives in seeking posts were probably very similar to those of the nominal clerks.

One of the official qualifications, as specified by law, was that all the clerks must come from good families (shen-chia ch'ing-pai), that is, from families not engaged in any of the "mean" occupations. A signed guarantee to this effect had to be obtained from the neighbors of the candidate before he applied for a post, and the local official had to present a stamped certificate to the Board of Civil Office. The official was subject to demotion of two grades if he failed to ascertain whether or not a clerk came from a good family.[61]

Since the main duty of a clerk was to handle documents, naturally the ability to read and write was one of the basic qualifications. For some of the duties an elementary knowledge of computation was also necessary. It was reported that some students who failed to make progress (that is, were unable to pass the lowest civil service examination) gave up their studies and entered upon the career of a clerk.[62]

It was up to the local official whether an examination was held for the candidates. An official might give the clerks an examination upon his arrival at a post. Huang Liu-hung's practice was to keep those who were able to write clear documents and whose handwriting was fairly good, and to dismiss those who did not meet these requirements. He noted that many of the clerks, when asked to prepare a document, were unable to continue after writing the introductory phrases.[63] Wang Chih had a similar experience in giving such examinations. He usually dismissed the aged and incompetent, but was lenient to those clerks who had served for a long time, who had some property, who were familiar with the official routine, or who were able to express themselves well orally.[64] Another common practice was to promote the *t'ieh-hsieh* to the post of regular clerk after they had been in office for a number of years.[65]

The clerk's term of appointment was five years.[66] A magistrate was held responsible if he retained a clerk whose term had expired or who had been dismissed. A magistrate was to be dismissed if he permitted a clerk to change his name or falsify his birthplace in order to serve again in an office. If an official failed to inquire into such a case through negligence, he was to be demoted two grades and transferred to another post.[67]

A clerk was entitled to enter officialdom after he had been in office for five full years. An examination for official appointment (*k'ao chih*) was given every autumn by the governor-general or governor. The examination consisted of writing one *kao-shih* (official notice) and one *shen-wen* (report to a superior).[68] The examination papers were sent to the Board of Civil Office. As a rule no more than fifty per cent of the candidates in a province were selected.[69] Those who passed the examination were graded and entitled to official appointment accordingly. The first grade corresponded to the post of the sub-ninth rank, and the second grade to the post below the regular rank.[70]

When a clerk obtained a rank and a certificate issued by the Board of Civil Office he gained a new status and was entitled to wear a button on his hat according to his rank.[71]

4. Financial Maintenance

Most of the sources state that the clerks in the various yamen received no remuneration,[72] and that they had to supply their own working equipment—writing brushes, ink, and papers.[73] However, it should be pointed out that wages, under the name of *fan-shih yin* (meal money), were given to them in the early years of the Ch'ing dynasty. *Ch'ing-ch'ao wen-hsien t'ung-k'ao* mentions that when the salary scale was first established both the clerks and the government runners in the various local governments were given wages in terms of silver and that their wages were later reduced from time to time.[74] According to the data in the *Fu-i ch'üan-shu* (The complete book of taxes and labor services) of Chihli, the annual payment for the various clerks serving in the chou and hsien governments was as follows:

Twelve office clerks	10.8 taels per person
Treasury clerk	12.0 taels
Granary clerk	12.0 taels

The same source reveals that a substantial cut was made in the ninth year of Shun-chih (1652): 4.8 taels for each of the office clerks, 6 taels for the treasury clerk and 6 taels for the granary clerk. Pay was altogether eliminated in the first year of K'ang-hsi (1662).[75]

The original wage for each of the twelve office clerks and the other two clerks serving in the magistrate's yamen of Hsiang-t'an, Hunan, as listed in the *Fu-i ch'üan-shu,* quoted in the local gazetteer, was the same as that in Chihli. This source also says that a cut similar to that in Chihli was made in 1652, and that the pay was altogether eliminated in 1662.[76] The local gazetteers of Hsien-ning, Shensi, and K'uai-chi, Chekiang, which list similar wages and a similar cut, also give 1662 as the date when the wage of the office clerks was totally eliminated.[77] As the cut and the elimination of the clerks' wages took place in the same year in these different provinces, it is reasonable to assume that the action was universal in the empire, and that the elimination of clerks' wages took place about the same time, that is, 1662 or early in the K'ang-hsi period. According to Lu Lung-ch'i (1630–1693), the magistrate of Ling-shou, Chihli, the wages for clerks and runners were eliminated after the "military expeditions" exhausted government funds. Lu also mentioned that after 1681 runners' wages were restored but that clerks' wages were not.[78] "Military expeditions" apparently refers to the liquidation of Ming forces in the south.

Since no remuneration was offered for their services, why were the clerks interested in holding their posts? In other words, what were their incentives? One, as we have mentioned, was the desire for protection. Another was the possibility of entering officialdom through service as a clerk. But for most of the clerks the most powerful attraction was the economic reward, and this explains why many people attempted to keep the posts after the expiration of their terms.

If the clerks received no wages, what were the sources of their income? One of the main sources was similar to the magistrate's *lou-kuei,* the "customary fees." In fact the whole pattern of customary fees among the clerks and other yamen personnel was a duplication, on a lower level, of what happened among magistrates.

The acceptance of customary fees by the clerks was justified on the ground that they received no remuneration for their services and no compensation for stationery expenses. How could they be expected to render services without eating?[79] Wang Feng-Sheng admitted frankly that clerks had to depend upon customary fees for a living.[80] Wang Hui-tsu once remarked that a magistrate should not go to the extreme of abolishing the customary fees which had been in practice for a long time and were necessary to the clerks as a means of livelihood, but that the clerks must not be allowed to practice corruption.[81] In the opinion of Liu Heng (1776–1841), it was difficult to get rid of those fees which paid for stationery and meals, but the clerks should not be allowed to take more than the customary amount.[82] Obviously the situation was beyond the control of a magistrate unless he was willing and able to pay the various expenses out of his own pocket. This was done by Liu Heng, who ruled that he would pay for paper, oil, and candles needed in conducting an inquest, and his clerks were not allowed to demand a single coin of the people on such occasions.[83]

Moreover, since the system of customary fees was an established practice at all government levels—in the capital as well as in the provinces—and was accepted as a necessary feature of the administrative system, the problem of irregularity could not be solved simply be controlling the government clerks at the lower levels. In point of fact, clerks in a higher yamen generally demanded fees from the clerks in a lower yamen, a practice mentioned in an edict of 1736.[84] A magistrate, Hsü Keng-pi (fl. 1874), once reported that unless the various documents and reports presented to a superior yamen were acompanied by fees they would be rejected on the ground that they contained copyists' errors or that they were not prepared in accordance with approved styles.[85] Not a single document could pass through the clerks of the superior yamen without a payment. Hence, the clerks of the superior yamen were feared and treated with respect by a magistrate, and the magistrate's own clerks would seek an income by any available means so that they could pay the customary fees whenever there were documents to be submitted.[86]

The problem now becomes very clear: How could the magistrate's clerks afford to pay the clerks of a superior yamen if they were not allowed to accept the customary fees accessible to them? There was no solution, unless the magistrate was able to talk to his superior and convince him that the customary fees paid to clerks of the superior yamen should be abolished. This was done by Wang Chih, a magistrate who reached an agreement with the provincial treasurer before he told his own clerks to abolish some of the fees.[87]

Realizing that the practice of customary fees was indispensable, but only within reasonable limits, some officials tried to work out a practical solution. For example, T'ien Wen-ching, the governor-general of Honan and Shantung, investigated all kinds of customary fees enjoyed by the clerks and runners of the two provinces, and then issued a catalog that listed the fees that were permissible and the amount of money that could be collected for each of them.[88] Thus the fees were openly authorized and codified, and by the highest local authority. Wang Chih held that since the customary fees varied among prefectures and hsien, it was better to leave this matter to the local officials. Whenever he arrived in a hsien, he always asked his clerks to list all the customary fees, telling them that he would take all of them into consideration and then decide which should be kept and which should be abolished.[89]

There were various kinds of customary fees. Some were enjoyed by the clerks exclusively (usually in the name of "money for pens and paper" (*chih-pi fei*), but most of them were shared by the clerks and the runners.

Various fees were collected from persons involved in a law suit. To begin with, there were fees for registration (*kua-hao fei*) and for handling a complaint (*ch'uan-ch'eng fei*).[90] Then the plaintiff had to pay a fee for getting a *p'i*, the official statement of the acceptance or rejection of a complaint (*mai-p'i fei*). As the usual procedure in opening a case called for such an official statement at the end of the complaint as an endorsement of the case, and it took many days to write a *p'i* after a complaint had been handed in, clerks and runners could take advantage of the situation and ask the plaintiff to pay some money to hasten the writing of the statement.[91] In addition there were fees to clerks for preparing the list of people involved in a case (*sung-kao chih-pi fei* or *k'ai-tan fei*)[92] and fees for the issuance of a warrant (*ch'u-p'iao fei*).[93] Fees collected from both plaintiff and defendant included fees for their arrival at the yamen for a trial (*tao-an fei* or *tai-an fei*),[94] and fees to clerks and runners for attending the court when the magistrate opened the trial (*p'u-t'ang fei* or *p'u-pan fei*).[95] Both parties had to pay fees for expenses incurred by a magistrate and his personnel in making on-the-spot investigations (as in a law suit involving a dispute over property boundaries [*t'a-k'an fei*]),[96] for the conclusion of a law suit (*chieh-an fei*),[97] and for the withdrawal of a law suit when an amicable agreement had been reached between the plaintiff and the defendant (*ho-hsi fei*).[98] Persons involved in homicide cases were required to provide food and traveling expenses for clerks and runners, stationery expenses, oil and candle fees, and many other kinds of fees in connection with an inquest (*ming-an chien-yen fei*).[99]

The clerk in charge of land tax collection usually demanded from taxpayers money for stationery and bookkeeping expenses.[100] There was a fee for issuing the "simplified tax notice" (*i-chih yu-tan*)—a statement giving the rate of tax imposed on various kinds and grades of land in a particular district[101]—and for issuing a land tax receipt (*ch'uan-p'iao* or *liang-p'iao*).[102] The fee for the latter varied from about three coins up to ten.[103] String money (*ch'uan-sheng ch'ien*) was also demanded from taxpayers who handed in coins.[104]

In the collection of tribute grain, various fees had to be paid to the clerks and runners: for carrying the grain into the granary (*chin ts'ang ch'ien* or *chin ao ch'ien*),[105] for a receipt,[106] for the granary clerk's stationery expenses, "tea and fruit" money (*ch'a-kuo ch'ien*), money for the grain measurer (*tou-chi*), for the granary watchman (*k'an ts'ang*), for the repair of the granary, and for the checking of grain measures (*chiao hu*).[107]

Customary fees also had to be paid for the collection of fish tax, wine tax, and other miscellaneous taxes. According to Wang Chih, a fee amounting to thirty to forty per cent of the tax was paid. He also stated that the list of taxpapers was prepared by the clerks of one *fang,* while collection was undertaken by the clerks of another *fang;* and each demanded a fee from the taxpayers.[108]

The same was true in the taxation of title deeds. When a house or a piece of landed property changed hands, a tax had to be paid to the government for having the title deed stamped with an official seal. A stamped certificate was affixed to the title deed to legalize the transaction; this was called the *ch'i-wei,* "the tail of the deed." [109] However, the clerks of one *fang* stamped the seal, and the clerks of another *fang* recorded the transaction (*kuo-ko* or *t'ui-shou*). Fees were thus charged separately for the same thing.[110]

A broker (*ya-hang* or *ya-hu*) had to get a license from the government, for which an examination was required each year, and for which the clerks collected a customary fee.[111]

The customary fees described above are but a few that are known to us. As the magistrate Hsü Keng-pi pointed out, fees were as numerous as the hairs on an ox.[112] Furthermore, although the practice of customary fees was universal in all provinces, the names of the various fees and the amount collected for each differed from place to place. Each locality followed its own pattern.[113]

5. FORMS OF CORRUPTION

Customary fees were only a part of the income of clerks, runners, and others who served in a local government. For additional income they engaged in various unlawful practices which were distinct from the authorized *lou-kuei* and may be called corruption.

We have mentioned that most of the customary fees were shared by clerks and runners—a fact suggesting that the two groups cooperated with one another in mutual interest. This cooperation extended to corrupt practices, including extortion.[114] Collaboration was most obvious where clerks and runners were assigned to work together, as in the case of the granary clerk and the grain measurer. Since runners had direct contact with the people, they often acted as liaison for the clerks. For instance, the runners who were sent ahead to make all practical arrangements in connection with an inquest usually negotiated for the clerk of punishment. On the other hand, since clerks were responsible for checking on the runners, reporting who failed to carry out their assignments within the prescribed deadline, it is obvious that the runners needed the cooperation of the clerks in order to avoid punishment. Above all, since the clerks were in a position to manipulate the documents, particularly warrants and land tax receipts, their collaboration was essential in most corrupt practices. Extensive corruption was possible only when there was close cooperation between the group that could manipulate the documents and the group that had the authority to summon and arrest people.

Many corrupt practices were connected with the administration of justice. The opening of a case could be purposely delayed if the defendant offered a clerk a bribe.[115] Or the clerk charged with writing a deposition, the *chao-shu,* could make some changes in the records.[116] Clerks frequently attempted to involve as many people as possible in a law suit so that money could be extorted from them. It was not uncommon for clerks to restore names on the summons list that had been crossed out by a magistrate or a secretary.[117] Huang Liu-hung once remarked that one of the common tricks of the clerks was to obtain a piece of blank paper on which a seal had been stamped. With this they could threaten the people and extort money from them, for when a seal was stamped on a piece of paper it could be used as a writ issued by the government.[118] An imperial edict of 1736 says: "before a legal case is tried and concluded the plaintiff and the defendant have spent a large sum of money, so that both of them are in great distress." [119]

Clerks sometimes tried to introduce certain changes into documents. Even when a draft was prepared by a private secretary, changes could still be made by a clerk when the draft was copied.[120] Wang Hui-tsu said that it was essential for all deeds and contracts submitted for examination to be handled personally by a magistrate; they should not be allowed to remain in the hands of a clerk, who could emend them by excising a piece of the original document and patching it with a piece of paper on which desired changes had been made.[121] It was also reported that sometimes original documents were removed from the file and fake documents put in their place.[122]

Most of the corrupt practices were connected with tax collection. The clerks in charge of the silver chest usually manipulated the scales in such a way that more than the fixed amount was collected.[123] According to regulations, silver was to be put in a sealed bag by the taxpayer himself when he delivered it to the silver chest clerk. However, there were frequent complaints that the silver was not actually put into the chest, and that often a package containing less silver was inserted by clerks as a substitute for the original one. Even if the silver had been placed in the chest, the package could still be taken out by paring down the revolving cylinder inside the slot through which it had been dropped.[124]

Land tax receipts came in books of one hundred, each one numbered consecutively and stamped with an official seal. One corrupt practice was for the clerks to duplicate the number of several receipts when these were sent in for stamping. If this was not discovered and the duplicate receipts got stamped, they were used to collect land tax which the clerks kept for themselves. This trick was not easily detected by the government since no number was missing on the stubs of the receipts.[125] Some clerks even collected tax with forged receipts.[126]

Another form of corruption was frequently resorted to by the clerks charged with the collection of land tax: they would enter into an agreement with taxpapers whereby, in return for a bribe, they would not hurry them in paying their land tax. Under this arrangement, every effort was made to help the taxpayers to delay payment, and their names were not included in the *pi-tan,* the list of overdue taxpayers subject to summons and punishment. The taxpayers were willing to pay a bribe in the hope that they could avoid paying the tax.[127]

Other corrupt practices were connected with the collection of tribute grain. During the time of collection, several clerks of the office of revenue were assigned to the various granaries. Theoretically their duty was merely to record the amount of grain paid by taxpayers and issue a receipt.[128] Actually they took charge of the collection and were thus in a position to be abusive. One way of extorting money from taxpayers was to delay the examination and receipt of grain. As it was extremely inconvenient for the taxpayer to wait and take care of his grain, he was willing to pay the clerks and runners so that he could hand in his grain and go home.[129]

The clerks sometimes forced the taxpayers to sift or winnow the grain, on the excuse that the grain brought in fell short of the accepted standard—it was either too small or not white enough.[130] This could be avoided, however, by offering money to the clerks. It was also usual for the granary clerks to cooperate with the grain measurers in an attempt to collect more grain from taxpayers.[131]

The government was fully aware of the consequences of the clerks' corruption. An imperial edict of 1736 stated that "before the regular land tax is collected by the government, the amount which has gone into the pockets of the wicked clerks amounts to twenty to thirty per cent of the tax collected from the people." [132] An investigation in 1736 disclosed that of the 3,000,000 taels of overdue land tax uncollected by the government in Shantung, 80,000 taels had been embezzled by clerks and runners.[133] In another instance, the clerks of Chü-jung hsien, Kiangsu, embezzled 3700 taels of tax money and 800 bushels of tribute grain.[134]

Many of the clerks had special connections with the owners of rice shops and the so-called *pao-hsieh,* the "lodging house owner–guarantors." Usually there were a number of rice shops near a granary. Taxpayers sometimes found it more convenient to buy grain from the shops than to transport it from ther homes. However, the taxpayers did not always transact this business voluntarily. By paying money to the granary clerk, the grain measurer, and the magistrate's personal servants who were

assigned to supervise the granary, the store owner secured their cooperation. Taxpayers who carried grain to the granary themselves were treated
in such a way that they were forced to buy grain from the rice shop
owners and ask them to pay the tax on their behalf. The shop owners were
able to gain great profit from this kind of arrangement.[135]

Sometimes it was a lodging house owner–guarantor who acted as a
middleman in tax payments. These were the people who provided lodging
to travelers coming to the hsien seat to pay tax.[136] They frequently talked
taxpayers into letting them make the payment on the ground that they
knew the clerks and runners. Since most of the men from the country
were afraid to see yamen clerks, and since this kind of arrangement could
expedite matters and enable them to shorten their stay in the city, they
were easily persuaded. The lodging house owner would embezzle the
money and give the taxpayer a false receipt, while the tax remained
unpaid. When the government sought out the people with overdue taxes,
the taxpayer, his "guarantor" having disappeared, could do nothing but
raise money for his overdue tax.[137] It was pointed out by Wang Yu-huai
(a private secretary in the eighteenth century) that clerks who had been in
office for a long time often designated their own fathers or brothers as
lodging house owner–guarantors, and that, conversely, the latter always
depended for business on their sons or brothers who were clerks. Frequently the runners were also relatives or friends of the clerks.[138]

It is most interesting to learn that the clerks received such large incomes
from lou-kuei and from illegal sources that a sum usually had to be paid
to a retiring clerk by his successor, as payment for the post. This was
mentioned in an imperial edict in 1800: "The clerks of the various yamen
at the various levels within and without the capital demand expenses for
all occasions. After a considerable length of time the practice has become
established and the amount derived from these sources has increased
gradually. When the term of a clerk expires, money is paid by his
successor for the post. This is called ch'üeh-ti."[139]

A law was then passed prohibiting the sale of clerical posts,[140] and any
official of the local government conniving at the violation of this law was
to be dismissed. For failure to inquire into such an offense, due to
negligence, the penalty was demotion by one grade and transfer to another
post. A governor-general or governor who had knowledge of, but failed
to impeach, a magistrate thus guilty, was to be demoted three grades and
transferred to another post.[141]

There was also evidence that in certain cases money was paid to a magistrate himself for the appointment of a clerk,[142] the fee varying from several tens to several hundred taels of silver.[143] Since the clerks in charge of the silver chest and the collection of tribute grain were in a position to extort money from taxpayers, the competition for these assignments was very keen, and bribes were often paid to a magistrate's personal servant or private secretary[144] in order to secure them. Sometimes a gift was offered to a magistrate for this purpose.[145]

6. Disciplinary Control

The law placed the responsibility for supervising the clerks on the shoulders of the magistrate and his superiors. It was ruled that the clerks of a prefecture, chou, or hsien government were under the supervision of the circuit intendant and the provincial judge.[146] It was their responsibility to investigate and punish a clerk for such offenses as controlling the local government, manipulating the letter of the law, using the name of an authority to swindle others, conducting negotiations and transmitting money for others in cases of bribery, handling law suits for others, embezzling tax receipts, shifting the burden of tax from one taxpayer to another, receiving bribes for releasing a robber, and falsely accusing and arresting innocent people. Should they fail to investigate a case, owing to negligence, these officials were to be fined the equivalent of a year's nominal salary. The prefect and the chou or hsien magistrate were to be dismissed if they had connived at the office.[147]

The clerk guilty of receiving a bribe was to be punished in accordance with the law.[148] The magistrate was to be dismissed, whether he had cooperated with the clerk in practicing bribery or had merely connived at it. The punishment was the same regardless of the size of the bribe. The magistrate's punishment for failure to inquire into the case, due to negligence, varied from a fine to demotion.[149]

However, the task of supervising clerks was not an easy one. It was generally agreed that clerks were extremely dishonest. As some officials pointed out, they merely came for profit and could not be moved by kindness.[150] Thus it was said that they should be looked upon and guarded against as "treacherous beings." [151] Nearly all the advice given on the subject emphasized that clerks and runners should be treated severely,[152] should not be received with anything but a stern face, and that no verbal exchange should take place between a magistrate and clerks except regarding official business.[153] The *Ch'in-pan chou-hsien shih-i* (Imperial directive on chou and hsien administration) advised that an official should not allow his outward behavior to betray his real attitude, and he should not accept clerks with smiles, which they might interpret as a sign of encouragement.[154]

The first concern of a magistrate was to prevent clerks from engaging in corruption.[155] Various measures were recommended; for instance, it was said that clerks should not be allowed to communicate with the magistrate's personal servants, lest they obtain information from them.[156] Most important of all, clerks should not be given any opportunity to manipulate power. Thus it was emphasized that they should be entrusted only with the job of copying documents; none should be drafted by them.[157] One able magistrate, Liu Heng, worked out rules to control his clerks.[158] There was also a legal stipulation that any official who left legal decisions in the hands of a clerk was to be dismissed for failure to carry out his duty.[159]

Wang Hui-tsu advised that rewards and punishments be meted out strictly.[160] It is worth noting, in passing, that although the status of a clerk was superior to that of a government runner,[161] nevertheless they were treated more or less in the same way where corporal punishment was concerned.[162]

Experts varied in their opinions on the matter of rewards to the clerks. A certain official suggested that a clerk who was diligent and dutiful should be rewarded either with money or with wine and food, rather than with an assignment which might be lucrative.[163] A different opinion was held by another official who argued that a magistrate could not afford to give money to everyone who served in a yamen and clerks and runners who had families to support were not merely interested in wine and food; therefore he suggested that it was necessary to assign an occasional legal case to the clerk so that he could get the "money for stationery expenses," but that he should not be allowed to go to the extreme of extorting money from people at will.[164]

As we have seen, it was extremely difficult for the magistrates to control the clerks, for most of the magistrates were not experienced in official business and therefore could be easily deceived by the clerks, who were experts in all kinds of tricks.[165] Besides, a magistrate did not have time to supervise all the routine business of his yamen.[166]

Even if a magistrate was experienced and energetic in supervising all kinds of activities, it was still impossible for him to handle the situation. This was clearly pointed out by Yüan Shou-ting: "If they [clerks] are dealt with leniently, they will seek personal profit by every means; if they are dealt with strictly they will submit a statement asking to resign. Since there are hundreds of things to be done daily, they can hardly be allowed to leave. This is the concealed problem of an official and it cannot be mentioned openly." [167]

The magistrate's helplessness in supervising his clerks merely reflected a larger problem—the inability of the government to control the clerks serving in the various higher yamen, provincial as well as central. The clerks' access to documents and their knowledge of administrative routine enabled them to manipulate government business. All in all, the government regulations for dealing with the clerks, though comprehensive and greatly detailed, remained ineffective.

IV

GOVERNMENT RUNNERS

Government runners, generally known as *ya-i,* served the local government as messengers, guards, policemen, or in other menial capacities. Like the clerks, they were natives of the province where they served. Also like the clerks, they held their positions as long as possible, often after their official terms had expired. These facts created the same type of problems that arose in connection with the clerks.

As we have seen, the exchange of documents between a magistrate and his superiors was an extremely important part of the local government routine. However, in carrying out orders issued by his superiors a magistrate was obliged to deal with the local people directly, for it was an essential function of any local yamen to make government orders known to the people. Since a hsien covered a large territory, within which a number of villages were widely scattered,[1] communicating efficiently with the head of each village, or the people, was a problem. The means of communication in those days being extremely limited, the only way to convey a magistrate's orders to the people in rural districts was to send out messengers. Thus the government runners were indispensable.

Moreover, the runners constituted an organized force upon which a magistrate could rely in enforcing law and order. Without these men under his command, he would probably not have been able to collect land tax and tribute grain. He would also have been unable to demand from the people such labor services as repair of the city wall, road construction, labor connected with water works, and the providing of carriages or other means of transportation for the government. The runners who served as policemen were also depended upon to serve summonses or make arrests and perform regular police duties.

A number of runners were also needed to take care of the granary and the jail, to administer chastisement, and attend to other matters essential to local administration. Thus a magistrate remarked that clerks and runners were an official's claws and teeth, and their services could not be dispensed with for a single day or in a single task.[2]

1. ORGANIZATION

The government runners were organized into four groups: *tsao-pan, k'uai-pan, min-chuang,* and *pu-pan.*[3] The first consisted of the *tsao-li,* the black-robed lictors. The second were the so-called *k'uai-shou* (swift hands), who were again divided into *ma-k'uai* (horsemen) and *pu-k'uai* (foot messengers).[4] The third group, *min-chuang* (commoner-guards), comprised the able-bodied commoners who were recruited to render service in a local government. The fourth group were the policemen, who were known as *pu-i* or *pu-k'uai.*[5] Each of the four groups was headed by a chief runner, *t'ou-i.*[6]

In addition to these groups, there were runners who served as doormen (*men-tzu*), jailers and prison guards (*chin-tsu, lao-i*), coroners (*wu-tso*),[7] treasury janitors (*k'u-tzu* [*ting*]), granary janitors (*ts'ang-fu*), grain measurers (*tou-chi*), sedan-chair bearers (*chiao-fu*), parasol and fan bearers (*san shan fu*), gong beaters (*ming-lo fu*),[8] pipers and drummers (*ch'ui ku shou*), lantern carriers (*teng-fu*), night watchmen (*keng-fu*), stove attendants (*huo-fu*), grooms (*ma-fu*), and dispatch bearers (*p'u-ping*).

The quotas for the various kinds of runners employed in a chou or hsien government were given in the *Fu-i ch'üan-shu* (The complete book of taxes and labor services) of the various provinces. Quotas for localities in Chihli, Honan, Kiangsi, Hunan, and Kiangsu are presented in Table 7.

The quota for policemen was not given in the *Fu-i ch'üan shu.*[9] The number in each hsien in Kiangsi was eight.[10] Usually policemen were stationed both in the hsien seat and rural district. For instance, in P'ing-hu, Chekiang, there were one police chief (*ya-pu tsung t'ou-i*), three captains (*pu-pan t'ou-i*), twelve *fang*[11] policemen, and a number of policemen in charge of the *i-fang,* where thieves were detained.[12] According to Ho Keng-sheng (*chin-shih* 1822), who was a magistrate in Shensi, there were a number of policemen in the surrounding rural districts. After Ho had dismissed several dozen policemen who were aged, incapable, or corrupt, there were still more then eighty left.[13]

However, as was pointed out by Wang Chih and Fang Ta-chih, the official quota for runners was too low, and more runners were actually needed to provide services.[14] As a matter of fact, the employment of extra runners was a common practice in all provinces. This was sanctioned in an edict of 1736 which said that if the official quota was insufficient to

Table 7. Quotas for runners in ten localities

Types of Runners	Ta-hsing[a]	Ch'ing-yüan[b]	Hsiang-fu[c]	An-yang[d]	Chien-ch'ang[e]	P'o-yang[f]	Heng-yang[g]	Ch'a-ling[h]	Chia-ting[i]	Pao-shan[j]
Doormen	2	2	2	2	2	2	2	2	2	2
Lictors	16	16	16	16	14	12	16	16	16	16
Coroners	—	4	—	—	1	3	—	—	—	—
Apprentice coroners	—	—	—	—	2	2	—	—	—	—
Horsemen	12	8	8	8	8	8	8	8	8	8
Jailers	8	8	8	8	7	8	8	8	8	8
Sedan-chair, parasol, and fan bearers	7	7	7	7	7	7	7	7	7	7
Lantern bearers	4	4	—	—	—	—	—	—	—	—
Treasury janitors	4	4	4	4	4	4	4	4	4	4
Grain measurers	4	4	4	4	4	4	4	4	4	4
Commoner-guards	50	50	50	50	15	29	50	50	30	35

[a] *Chi-fu fu-i ch'üan-shu*, Shun-t'ien fu, Ta-hsing hsien, 103–106b.
[b] *Ibid.*, Pao-ting fu, Ch'ing-yüan hsien, 111b–116.
[c] *Honan fu-i ch'üan-shu*, K'ai-feng fu, Hsiang-fu hsien, 70–72.
[d] *Ibid.*, Chang-te fu, An-yang hsien, 48–90.
[e] *Chiang-hsi fu-i ch'üan-shu*, Nan-k'ang fu, Chien-ch'ang hsien, 19a–b.
[f] *Ibid.*, Jao-chou fu, P'o-yang hsien, 25–26.
[g] *Hunan fu-i ch'üan-shu*, Heng-chou fu, Heng-yang hsien, 13–14.
[h] *Ibid.*, Ch'ang-sha fu, Ch'a-ling chou, 5–6.
[i] *T'ai-ts'ang chou fu-i ch'üan-shu*, Chia-ting hsien, 44–45b.
[j] *Ibid.*, Pao-shan hsien, 64–66.

meet the need, a local official was allowed to hire extra runners.[15] These extra runners were called *pai-i* or *pang-i*, that is, runners whose names were not listed in the government record.[16] According to Wang Chih, there were usually three or four *pai-i* under the command of one regular runner.[17] Hu Lin-i (1812–1861) reported that several thousand *pai-i* served in Shih-ch'ien prefecture, Kweichow.[18] When the regular runners were sent to the rural district, they were usually followed by several score of these *pai-i*, who participated in swindling and extorting money from the people.[19] There were also a number of *pai-pu,* extra policemen, and the complaint was made that they caused the people in the area of Chiang-nan to suffer, for they frequently arrested innocent people and seized their property under the pretext of catching thieves.[20]

There were also nominal runners (*kua-ming ya-i*), who were listed as government runners without actually serving.[21] Their motives were the same as those of the nominal clerks: as a nominal runner, a man could evade rendering labor service,[22] and could protect himself and his family property.[23] A governor reported that a sum of money, two to four taels of silver, was usually paid to the magistrate for such a nominal post in the province.[24] On the other hand, many poor people were willing to act as substitutes for the nominal runners because of the opportunity it afforded for making money.[25]

Thus the actual number of runners in a chou or hsien government, including both regular, extra, and nominal runners, far exceeded the number fixed by the official quota. In Hunan, for example, the runners serving in a hsien usually numbered several hundred.[26] According to the report of a censor, there were 1500 to 1600 runners in Jen-ho and Ch'ien-t'ang hsien, Chekiang, including both regular and extra runners.[27] A memorial presented by another censor in 1827 shows that the situation was similar in Shantung. The memorial mentions that in a large hsien the runners numbered more than 1000 and even in a small hsien there were several hundred.[28] There were even more runners in Szechwan. Liu Heng, the magistrate of Pa-hsien, reported that there were 7000 runners in his hsien. After he had been in office for a year, 6700 or 6800 of them resigned because they were unable to get sufficient income from their jobs to support themselves. Only about 100 remained in office there.[29]

Attempts were made to reduce the number of runners. There was a ruling that an official who connived at the maintenance of nominal runners was to be demoted three grades and transferred to another post; if nominal runners were kept without his knowledge, he was to be demoted one grade and retained in the same post.[30] Regulations were also issued to prohibit the employment of extra runners. A magistrate who kept extra runners in excess of the permitted number (*e-tseng pang-i*) was to be demoted one grade and kept in the same post.[31] A magistrate who gave a warrant to an extra runner or assigned to him some other official duty was to be demoted three grades and transferred to another post.[32] An official who failed to discover that a regular runner was accompanied by extra runners while performing his duty was to be fined six months' nominal salary. If extra runners shared the same post, while registering under a single false name, their supervisory official was to be demoted three grades and transferred to another post if he connived at the practice, or demoted two grades and transferred to another post if he neglected to inquire into the case.[33] A magistrate was required by law to submit a stamped statement to his superior guaranteeing that there were no instances of false registry in his yamen. He was also required to present to the Board of Civil Office at the end of each year a report listing the names of the regular runners, the date they entered the office, and the date their terms expired.[34]

It appears, however, that these regulations and penalties were rarely enforced. Liu Heng once suggested that a magistrate should only employ runners according to the quota and that even in a hsien located in a communications center, where official business was heavy, he should employ no more than "several tens" over the quota; all the superfluous runners should be dismissed. Liu admitted, however, that this was not an easy task, because even when runners had been officially dismissed they actually remained in office. This situation he described as "deceiving the one above but not deceiving those below." [35]

2. FUNCTIONS

There was a division of labor among the various runners. The lictors served as forerunners who cleared the way for the magistrate in public.[36] They always accompanied him when he made an inspection trip or conducted an inquest. In the latter case, as we mentioned earlier, a number of runners were sent to the place in advance to make practical arrangements. The lictors attended court when a trial was in progress. It was their duty to use torture to obtain confession from the suspects and to administer corporal punishment.[37]

The horsemen or foot messengers acted as night watchmen,[38] served summonses, made arrests,[39] attended court when a trial was in progress, and ran errands for the magistrate.[40] They were also sent to rural districts to speed the collection of land tax.[41]

The policemen were concerned mainly with catching robbers and thieves,[42] and sometimes they acted as night watchmen. They also escorted government funds (silver) in transit.[43] In the northern provinces policemen also served in connection with ordinary lawsuits; this was not permitted in the south.[44]

The commoner-guards, who were recruited for military training,[45] were assigned to guard the granary, treasury, and jail, and to escort government funds and criminals in transit. They served as a supplementary force to guard and defend the city.[46] In addition, they performed duties similar to those of the other runners. They helped to expedite land tax collection,[47] served summonses involved in civil cases,[48] and acted as bodyguards to the various local officials.[49]

The functions of certain other categories of runners are suggested by their titles—coroners, jailers, janitors, night watchmen. Only a few need explanation. A doorman, in addition to his routine duties, attended court when a trial was held. Holding the key to one of the gates[50] and a box containing the documents of the case, he stood in the hall to call the names of those who were to be questioned; he also had charge of the bamboo tallies.[51] The dispatch bearers were stationed at *p'u* (dispatch stations) to forward official documents.[52]

Now let us turn to the standard procedure by which the runners' services were distributed. It was universal practice for the runners to take turns, serving for five days at a time, under the command of a chief runner. This practice was called *tso-ch'ai*.[53] As every runner was anxious to get an assignment or a warrant when he was on duty, various means were used to facilitate a fair distribution of assignments. One common practice was to leave the matter to the chief runner, who allocated assignments to the runners under his command.[54] An able magistrate, however, neither allowed others to influence him in assigning jobs nor allowed runners to put their own names on a warrant. Instead, he distributed assignments according to the order of the muster roll so that each runner would get an assignment in turn.[55] Some magistrates preferred to assign jobs to runners according to their merits. One of them, Wang Feng-sheng, kept a record of merits (*chi-kung pu*) and assigned jobs to runners whose names appeared in this record before their turn came up according to the muster roll.[56]

3. Status, Recruitment, and Term of Service

It should be pointed out that although all four groups—the *tsao-pan*, *k'uai-pan*, *min-chuang*, and *pu-pan*—were considered government runners, they did not have the same social and legal status. The commoner-guards, as well as the treasury janitors, grain measurers, and dispatch bearers, had the status of ordinary commoners, but the lictors, horsemen, foot messengers, policemen, coroners, jailers, doormen,[57] archers, etc., were legally classified as "mean" people (*chien-min*), a status comparable to that of a prostitute, actor, or slave.[58] Like all other "mean" people, they were a negatively privileged group. They were not allowed to take civil service examinations and were prevented from entering officialdom. The law stipulated that any of them who took the civil service examination or purchased an official title was to be dismissed and given one hundred strokes. Their offspring were similarly deprived.[59] According to Ho Kengsheng, the policemen occupied the most inferior position of all the government runners.[60] This was probably because most of them were associated with thieves.[61]

Because of their mean occupation and their low legal status, the runners were looked down upon by the intelligentsia and the common people. It was mentioned in the *Ch'ing-ch'ao wen-hsien t'ung-k'ao* that the "*k'uai-shou* were not treated as equals by the intellectuals" and that the status of others who rendered miscellaneous services in a yamen was still lower.[62] This inferior social status was also reflected in the fact that certain families forbade their members to engage in such an occupation because it was a disgrace. Some families ruled that any member who chose to become a government runner was to be expelled from the clan.[63]

Since the social position of a government runner was in the lowest stratum, and since any man in that position had no prospect of ever rising from it, nor had his children, we may well ask why people were to be found who were willing to take such a job.

We have said that the nominal runners were people of the propertied class who secured their nominal posts in order to protect their properties. Among the active runners there were probably also people of the same class, who had the means to support their families and maintain a medium standard of living but secured jobs as runners for the same reason.[64] Also, exemption from labor services to be rendered in the yamen was available to *i-hu* (government-runner households). Hence people who did not qualify for exemption as members of the gentry (*kuan-hu*, official households, or *ju-hu*, scholar households) sought exemption through service as runners.[65]

Some runners who owned landed property took advantage of their position and their connection with the clerks and refused to pay land tax.[66] The jobs of jailer and archer were also occupied by people who had some property. There was a ruling that jailers and archers were to be recruited among people who paid less than three piculs and more than two piculs of land tax, and not from the well-to-do people who paid more.[67] However, most people were unwilling to serve as jailer and preferred to give money to the runners in order to avoid being recruited.[68] A similar situation prevailed in the recruitment of doormen.[69]

Most of the runners, however, were propertyless and poor, and they became runners in order to support themselves.[70] This was particularly true among the policemen, who owned no property and did not even have enough to eat and wear. They were described as persons in extreme poverty.[71] Some of them were former thieves who wanted to start a new life.[72]

Actually, the lot of the runners was not always as miserable as their legal and social status would indicate. Because they were in a position to abuse their power, they inspired awe among the people. The following may be cited as a case in point. A man whose surname was Chao served as a *k'uai-shou* in the prefecture government of Ch'ing-chou, Shantung. It was mentioned in a notice issued by Chou Liang-kung (1612–1672), the circuit intendant, that Chao was "arrogant and behaved as if he were a member of the gentry" (*hsiang-shen t'i-mien*). When he went to a banquet, he rode on a horse and was followed by a number of escorts. He formed alliances with others and had sworn brothers. He was addressed as *Chao-ssu t'ai-yeh* ("the fourth lord-master Chao"), and his wife as *Chao-ssu t'ai-t'ai* (Madame Chao).[73]

A runner's term of service was three years,[74] and a magistrate was held responsible if any runner continued to be employed after his term had expired or after he had been dismissed. In such a case, the magistrate received the same punishment as that for continuing to employ a similarly disqualified clerk.[75] The government thus required a newly employed runner to submit a statement that he had not been a runner before and was not re-entering the service under a different name. A guarantee to this effect, stamped with the official seal, was required of the magistrate.[76] However, this regulation was seldom strictly enforced. Many runners kept their posts by changing their names. Or, if they were unable to hold the posts personally, they attempted to transfer them to their family members or relatives. They were thus able to keep control over the posts year after year.[77]

4. FINANCIAL MAINTENANCE

The annual wage of the various government runners, including lictors, doormen, foot messengers, policemen, jailers, grain measurers, granary janitors, treasury janitors, sedan-chair bearers, parasol and fan bearers, pipers and drummers, night watchmen, and coroners, was about 6 taels of silver in most localities.[78] In Shensi and Kansu and some other provinces, wage scales were not uniform. The pay for the same types of service varied from hsien to hsien, and from 3 to 7 taels. In Kansu the pay for jailers varied from 3 to 11 taels.[79] In some other provinces the horsemen received more money, but out of this payment they had to buy horse fodder. For example, in Chihli and Anhui, they received 16.80 taels, and in Shantung 15.69. In Shensi and Kansu the pay varied from a little more than 11 to more than 16 taels.[80] It is interesting that although a coroner had to have some technical training—at least he had to be able to read and follow the Instructions for Coroners (Hsi-yüan lu)[81]—he received the same pay as other runners. The only exception occurred in Shantung, where the coroner was paid 11.21 taels. Other runners in Shantung, with the exception of horsemen, received only 5.6 taels.[82] The apprentice coroners of course received less pay than the regular coroners: only 2 or 3 taels.[83]

The scale was lower for many runners, including the bell and drum beaters, dispatch bearers, watchmen at a dispatch station, and archers. These were paid as little as 1 tael, and at no time more than 6 taels.[84] The commoner-guards received the same pay as the lictors, foot messengers, and policemen in most of the provinces—6 taels—although some localities paid them 7 to 8 taels, and in Chekiang their wage varied from 1 to 19 taels.[85]

We may conclude that the average annual pay of a government runner was 6 taels of silver. The highest pay, excepting for horsemen and commoner-guards, was less than 12 taels. In the lower wage group the pay ranged from 1 to 6 taels. It is obvious that such a low income could hardly support the wage earner. As Fu Wei-lin (chin-shih 1646) pointed out, a runner's wage was only 7 taels and 2 ch'ien, or no more than 12 taels. He got only 2 or 3 fen per day and this amount could only provide one meal for himself and his wife.[86] A similar remark was made by Fang Ta-chih, who said that the wage of a runner was only 2 *fen* per day, and on this he could hardly support himself, let alone his family.[87] There are reports which indicate that the runners used all their pay for office expenses, leaving nothing for themselves or their families.[88]

There was a historical reason for the runner's very low pay. In Ming times, service as a yamen runner was a kind of labor service (known as *chün-yao*, lit., "equal service") which the people were obliged to render. However, they were allowed to pay a sum in lieu of actual service, and this money the government used to hire men to render the service. This system was still practiced in Ch'ing times, and the pay thus came to be fixed at a very low rate.[89] Like the unpaid clerks, the runners were forced to depend upon customary fees, most of which were shared by the clerks and the runners. As a matter of fact, some fees, notably those collected from people involved in a lawsuit, were collected by a runner who then turned over to a clerk the share to which the latter was entitled.[90] When a homicide case was reported to the government, a number of runners were usually sent on in advance to erect a mat shed and make preparations for conducting an inquest. Upon their arrival, they demanded payments from any suspect for coolie services, horses, meals, and other inquest expenses. They also negotiated bribes for the clerk of punishment and the coroner.[91] When the magistrate arrived, he was accompanied by a large number of runners, personal servants, and other attendants.[92] As each of the attendants demanded a share in the customary fees, the money collected in connection with a homicide case sometimes amounted to several tens of thousands or several hundred thousand coins.[93] Although a government regulation required the magistrate to pay his attendants' expenses and prohibited his clerks and runners from demanding fees from the people,[94] only a few magistrates, like Liu Heng, abided by it.[95]

Some customary fees were enjoyed exclusively by runners. Those who were sent to the rural zones (*t'u* or *li*) to expedite land tax collection of course enjoyed such a source of income.[96] A provincial treasurer remarked that these runners were responsible for the government's failure to collect taxes because the more money they demanded from the taxpayers, the less tax was paid to the government.[97] Customary fees were also enjoyed by the runners who served in a granary.[98] As a rule, runners demanded from persons being arrested or summoned money for "shoes and socks" (*hsieh-ch'ien* or *hsieh-wa ch'ien*), wine and meal money, boat and carriage fare, and money for hiring a donkey.[99] The runners also collected fees from both plaintiff and defendant for bringing them to court for a trial. The plaintiff and the defendant were not allowed to see the magistrate or to go home until an agreed sum had been paid.[100] A convicted criminal also had to pay a fee (*chao chieh fei*)[101] for being taken to the superior yamen for retrial.[102]

Since the magistrates were aware that the runners' wages were inadequate for subsistence, they tolerated their collecting "boat fare" and "meal expenses." However, if a runner was accused by the people of extortion, he had to be dealt with according to the law.[103]

Since the policemen in the northern provinces were allowed to serve in connection with ordinary lawsuits, they were able to share the usual customary fees with the lictors and messengers. The policemen in the south, who had no such privileges, obtained monthly customary fees from prostitutes and those who slaughtered cattle illegally.[104] It was reported that the policemen in small, remote places, who were unable to obtain such customary fees, lived like beggars.[105]

The maintenance of policemen was a particular problem in local administration, for no funds were provided for expenses relating to the detection and arrest of robbers and thieves. The policemen had to pay for the services of an informer, for their own traveling expenses, and the expenses incurred in taking convicted criminals to the superior yamen after they had been tried by the magistrate.[106] It was generally acknowledged that the policemen were the most desperate among the government runners.[107] Realizing that a policeman could not be expected to perform his duty without financial help, some magistrates tried to solve the problem by donating money out of their own pockets. In some cases they gave supplementary monthly wages in cash or rice to the policemen, to make it possible for them to support their families.[108] Sometimes they gave them money to cover their expenses in obtaining information, traveling, and taking convicted criminals to a superior yamen.[109] According to Ho Keng-sheng's estimate, about 700 to 800 taels of silver were needed to cover these expenses and the rewards in a hsien where thefts were numerous and 500 to 600 taels were neded in a hsien where such cases were less numerous; 300 to 400 might be sufficient in some other localities. He pointed out that these were not impossible sums for the magistrate to pay, if he was moderately frugal in his own living expenses, employed fewer private servants and secretaries, and supported fewer of his relatives in the yamen.[110]

5. Forms of Corruption

Runners, like the clerks, engaged in various forms of corruption. The corrupt runner or clerk became almost a stereotype in the minds of Chinese.[111] This is understandable. In spite of the runners' negatively privileged status and their low wages, they still enjoyed being runners, mainly because it was lucrative. A magistrate once said: "Why are the clerks and runners willing to accept the inferiority and the humiliating corporal punishment [received from the magistrates], and enjoy them as though eating a delicious vegetable? Obviously they live on corruption."[112]

One of the common methods used by runners to extort money was to pay land tax owed by a taxpayer, without his knowledge, and then demand reimbursement plus interest. The land tax receipt said merely "money advanced by the runner," without specifying the name of the taxpayer. The runner was thus able to use this receipt to demand payment from any taxpayer.[113] The interest charged by the runners, according to an imperial edict of 1827, was as high as 100 per cent.[114] According to Wang Hui-tsu, this practice was resorted to by the runners who were sent to rural zones to expedite the collection of tax (*t'u-ch'ai* or *li-ch'ai*) and by local constables (*ti-pao*) who usually advanced money to pay land tax for orphans, widows, and families registered as middle households (*chung-hu*). For one *ch'ien* of silver advanced by the runner, the victim had to repay 230 to 250 coins; for one *sheng* of tribute rice the sum varied from 60 to 90 coins.[115]

Runners sent to rural areas to hasten land tax collection were in a good position to abuse their authority and extort money from the local people.[116] Sometimes a runner and a taxpayer reached an agreement to the effect that the former would assume the responsibility of handing in the latter's tax to the government. Such a proposition was frequently accepted by taxpayers in the hope that they could avoid going to the hsien seat in person. Actually, as Ch'en Hung-mou pointed out, the money for tax payment entrusted to runners under such an arrangement always went into the runners' pockets.[117]

A complaint submitted to the provincial treasurer by a group of students and commoners in Sung-chiang prefecture stated that the runners, including both the *tsao* group and the *k'uai,* could be divided into three categories according to their influence and their ability to extort money from people. The first group, nicknamed *ta-a-ko* (big brothers), included those runners who, in cooperation with the clerks of military affairs, public works, and land tax, collected money from residents of various rural zones in exchange for a guarantee that the residents would be exempted from the miscellaneous labor services. A sum of about 100 taels was collected from each zone for such protection. Usually three to four, or six to seven zones, and sometimes even more than ten zones were under the protection of a single runner. The second category was nicknamed *tsao-li ch'iang-shou* (lictors-snatchers) and included runners who collected money from the residents of the zone under the name of fees for delivering messages (*ch'ai-ch'ien*), or for receiving a flogging at a deadline hearing (for having failed to expedite the payment of overdue taxes).[118] These runners also demanded rice and wheat after each harvest, under the pretext that they would look after all the affairs of the rural zone. The third group, which had the nickname of *ting-t'u lao-hu ch'uan* (butting tiger boat), included those irregular runners who were sent to collect land tax and tribute grain. Upon arrival in the rural zone, they demanded "soil money" (*ti-ch'ien*), wine and meal money, and boat fare. In addition, the people were asked to pay them a sum of money for bearing a message (60 to 70 taels in a small zone, and 100 to 200 in a large zone).[119]

Various tricks were used by a grain measurer to collect extra tribute grain from a taxpayer, such as kicking the measure so that it could contain more grain, or heaping grain in the measure in such a way that it was filled more than level.[120]

Runners always attempted to extort money from the people they arrested or summoned. They often threatened their victims with the use of chains (even when chains had not been authorized) which would not be removed unless "chain-release money" (*chieh-so ch'ien*) was offered.[121] When runners failed to obtain money from the people under arrest, they resorted to tricks: they would destroy the warrant, tear up their own clothes, and report to the magistrate that the party had resisted arrest. This would anger an inexperienced magistrate and cause him to punish the alleged offender.[122]

Runners were even more abusive when they were sent to serve a summons with a bamboo tally (*t'ang-ch'ien*).[123] Wang Hui-tsu reports that when he was a commoner living in the country, he saw many families go bankrupt because of the runners. He says that a runner bearing a bamboo tally was as fierce as a tiger or wolf, and that the summoned frequently lost all their property before going to court.[124]

People involved in homicide cases also suffered great financial losses. Besides the enormous amount in customary fees demanded by clerks and runners, the latter also attempted to extort money by various other means. According to reports, the family property of the murderer or the suspect was not only thus exhausted, but all the wealthy families residing within twenty or thirty li were also targets of extortion. If these families failed to produce money, they could be falsely accused and involved in the case.[125]

One of the unlawful devices frequently employed by runners was to detain a suspect in the *pan-fang*.[126] The prisoner was usually kept in a dirty place, exposed to the sun in summer and the cold in winter, until he agreed to pay money to the runner. Wang Hui-tsu reported that many detained people died of disease before their release was ordered. He therefore advised that a suspect should not be detained unless it was absolutely necessary, and that if he was detained, a magistrate should inspect the place of detention personally.[127] Sometimes a runner even set up a private prison in his home where a person summoned by him was unlawfully detained without the magistrate's knowledge. The prisoner was not allowed to see the magistrate until he had paid the runner.[128]

Since the job of serving summonses and of expediting tax payment in rural districts offered opportunity for extortion, these assignments were much sought after by the runners, who sometimes "bought" them—for example, by bribing the clerks in charge of land tax to appoint them as *li-ch'ai* or *t'u-ch'ai*. The bribes reportedly varied according to the size and the productivity of a rural zone.[129] The runners also offered money to the magistrate's personal servants in order to obtain a warrant. Sometimes they even tried to ask the magistrate to grant them an assignment as a favor.[130]

Before a policeman would do anything about investigating a theft or robbery, he would first collect from the victim money for traveling, for wine and meals, for the services of any informer, and a "reward." If the owner of the stolen goods was influential, he would get half of the recovered goods back; if not, he would get nothing but lies and excuses.[131] In fact, it was common knowledge that nearly all the policemen were associated with the thieves and robbers, as well as with those who harbored them or shared the stolen goods.[132] The policemen depended upon thieves as a means of support and the thieves depended upon the policemen for protection.[133] It was reported that thieves gave customary fees to the policemen every month, and when there was a large theft the stolen goods were shared with them.[134] Thus the policemen were seldom anxious to catch thieves, and as a consequence, very few cases of theft were solved.[135] Wang Hui-tsu held that the only way to catch a thief or robber was to punish the policemen when they failed to bring in the offender within a specified period.[136]

Frequently a former thief or robber, or even an innocent person, was arrested and forced to confess to a larceny. Sometimes the "stolen" goods were even produced as evidence for the false accusations.[137] There were also cases in which an arrested thief was instructed by a policeman to trump up a charge against an innocent person, either accusing him of receiving or buying stolen goods or of being an accomplice in larceny. This was a device to involve more people in the case, thus increasing the opportunities for extorting money. Even if these people were released later, they would not get their money back.[138] Thus it was suggested that a thief should never be put in the custody of a policeman.[139]

Policemen were known to go to people's houses and, under the pretext of searching for stolen goods, demand money or seize the owner's possessions.[140] When real stolen goods were recovered, only a small quantity was reported and handed in to the magistrate; most of the valuable things were distributed among the policemen themselves.[141]

Other forms of corruption were practiced by other types of runners. A coroner could be bribed into making a false report on the cause of death.[142] Many prisoners were maltreated by jailers and prison guards who had failed to extract money from them.[143] A lictor might temper the administration of flogging as he had been bribed to do.[144] We may conclude, with T'ien Wen-ching, that there was not a single type of runner who did not engage in some kind of corruption.[145]

6. DISCIPLINARY CONTROL

As in the case of the clerks, the responsibility for supervising the runners rested with the magistrate. He was subject to dismissal if he connived at a runner's remaining in office for a long time, controlling the local government, acting as negotiator or transmitter of funds in a bribery, shifting the tax burden from one taxpayer to another, manipulating law suits, falsely accusing innocent people, or receiving bribes for release of a robber.[146] A runner guilty of embezzling tax funds was required to pay the money back to the government. For failing to prevent such a practice, the magistrate was subject to dismissal.[147] For receiving a bribe a runner was punished in accordance with the law,[148] and his magistrate was subject to dismissal, whether he had merely connived at the bribery or had actually shared the money, and regardless of the amount of the bribe. The punishment for failure to investigate a case of bribery, due to negligence, ranged from a fine to demotion.[149] A magistrate was also held responsible if a runner beat a person under arrest in order to obtain money from him.[150] The law required the magistrate to examine any arrested person to see whether he had been beaten and tortured. If he failed to conduct such an examination and injustice was later discovered, he was to be demoted three grades and transferred to another post.[151] Moreover, the law stipulated that a magistrate who purposely tolerated a runner who made trouble was to be dismissed.[152]

A magistrate was accountable if he failed to discover that his extra runners, the *pai-i*,[153] accompanied the regular runners on trips for purposes of extortion; for this he could be fined six months' nominal salary. If he employed extra runners who engaged in corruption, he was to be punished according to the amount received in bribes by the extra runners.[154]

A magistrate failing to investigate a case where a policeman associated with thieves and shared stolen goods with them was to be demoted two grades and transferred to another post.[155] If a policeman falsely accused an innocent person of being a thief or a robber and unlawfully tortured him, the magistrate was to be demoted three grades if the victim survived, and dismissed if death was caused.[156] The magistrate's superiors were also punishable if they failed to inquire into the case.[157]

A magistrate was subject to dismissal if he knew that a prisoner had died because of ill treatment by a jailer but failed to investigate the case, or if he connived at such abuse even though it did not lead to the death of a prisoner. If he failed to inquire into such a case, due to negligence, he was to be demoted two grades if the prisoner died, and one grade if death did not result.[158]

How did a magistrate actually supervise and control his runners? The runners, like the clerks, were generally regarded as dishonest, treacherous, and concerned only with lucre.[159] Liu Heng once remarked that all runners were scoundrels who could not be moved by reason, sentiment, virtue, or kindness, and that they feared only the law.[160] The standard advice on how to treat clerks was also extended to the runners: they should be treated severely and received with a stern face (and only in the presence of others),[161] and they should not be allowed to communicate with the magistrate's personal servants.[162] Most important of all, runners should not be given opportunities to abuse their authority. For example, they were not usually allowed to use chains in ordinary civil cases.[163] One magistrate printed a number of regulations on making arrests and serving summonses, having to do with such matters as the number of runners to be sent on a mission and whether chains were to be used; these he attached to the warrant, so that the person concerned would know the regulations. He was permitted to beat a gong and make a complaint before the magistrate if the runners abused him.[164]

Runners were required to bring a criminal or a witness to court within a specified time. The deadline was often written down on the warrant, and any runner who failed to bring a required person to court by the given deadline was subject to investigation and corporal punishment.[165] When a criminal or a witness was brought in, the runner was required to report it immediately to the magistrate and not detain him privately.[166] Since a warrant, if not canceled, could be used again by runners as a tool of extortion, it was emphasized that the warrant must be returned when the mission had been carried out and the case had been closed.[167]

Usually several runners were sent to make an arrest or serve a summons. It was reported that as many as seven or eight runners were sent on civil cases in Hupeh.[168] Realizing that more runners meant more demands for money, some magistrates tried to save the people's money by sending only one or two runners on each mission.[169] For the same reason they also tried to minimize the number of runners who accompanied them on trips to conduct inquests.[170]

Special regulations were formulated by some magistrates to control the policemen. They were not permitted to make an arrest or search for stolen goods without a warrant, nor were they permitted to arrest a person whose name was not listed on the warrant.[171] Usually a deadline was set for solving a case of robbery or theft, and policemen were subject to inquiry and corporal punishment if they failed to carry out their assignment within the time limit.[172] In fact, beating became standard punishment for any runner who failed to carry out an order promptly, or who engaged in corruption.[173]

It was recognized that rewards were necessary to encourage the runners to carry out their duties. Usually money or wine and food were given to a runner who was diligent and dutiful.[174] Some magistrates also gave money to policemen as a reward for catching a thief or robber.[175] Opinion differed among the magistrates as to whether warrants should be granted to runners and policemen as rewards. Some magistrates felt that a runner should not be rewarded with a warrant lest he use it as a means of extortion.[176] Although the law stipulated that a magistrate who rewarded runners with warrants was subject to dismissal,[177] the practice was not unusual[178] and was even recommended by some officials. Fang Ta-chih's contention was that the runners, like the clerks, needed money as well as wine and food, and the magistrate could not be expected to give money to everyone in the yamen. He therefore believed it necessary to reward the runners with warrants so that they could thus collect "money for straw sandals," though they should be prohibited from resorting to extortion.[179]

Although the runners rendered only menial service and occupied a lower position in the yamen than the clerks, it was equally difficult to supervise and control them. It was impossible for the magistrate to keep an eye on his hundreds of runners, whose duties involved direct contact with the people, and who were in a position to abuse their power in dealing with the people, although their social and legal status was much inferior to that of the commoners.

PERSONAL SERVANTS

Ch'ang-sui (lit., "permanent attendants"), the personal servants of a magistrate, occupied an important and unique position in local administration. Although a great many clerks and runners served in a yamen, some official tasks still remained unassigned. These were left to the magistrate's personal servants, who, though not employed by the government, became thus involved in local administration.[1] Only a few of them did menial and domestic work for the magistrate; most of them discharged one or another kind of official duty.

It was not the fact that a magistrate's personal servants worked in an official capacity that made them as important and indispensable as they actually were, for there was no reason why their duties could not have been assigned to regular government employees. The explanation must be sought in the institutional framework within which a magistrate functioned.

As we know, a magistrate, who was a stranger and unfamiliar with the local situation, could not trust the native clerks and runners upon whom he had to depend to carry out routine official duties. Moreover, he realized that it was almost impossible for him to supervise and control them. This situation could lead to one, or even both, of the following consequences: the local people could become the victims of corruption on the part of the clerks and runners; or the magistrate himself could suffer the consequences of his failure to supervise them (for the government regulations were such that any negligence toward the irregular practices of a clerk or runner could ruin the official's career). The situation obviously placed a magistrate under great strain. He had to depend upon someone to check and supervise the clerks and runners. Here he found his personal servants more reliable and less dangerous on the following grounds.

In the first place, since the servants were not usually natives[2] of the locality in which their employer officiated, they had no personal interest in the local community and no personal connections with the local people. Second, since they were hired and paid by the magistrate himself, they had a personal contact with him, and perhaps even a sense of loyalty toward him. Furthermore, the end of the magistrate's career also meant the end of the servant's job. And third, the magistrate knew his servants fairly well, since some of them had been his family servants previously and others had been recommended by his relatives and friends. Wang Hui-tsu, for example, hired one of his old servants as a gate porter, realizing that this post required a trustworthy person. When the man was accused of irregularity, Wang did not believe it, because he thought the servant was simple and very timid about official business. He did not know the truth until the servant's guilt was disclosed a year later.[3]

A magistrate usually regarded his servants as persons whom he could trust and depend upon. Hsieh Chin-luan, director of studies in a hsien school, held that it was advisable for an official to retain family servants upon whom he could depend. He believed that one dependable person could usually be found among five or six servants.[4] The employment of servants to check on clerks and runners obviously eased the strain on the magistrate. The most confidential job, handling the official seal, was also entrusted to servants.[5] A Manchu magistrate sent his trusted servants with the policemen to catch robbers because he thought there were no reliable runners.[6] Some magistrates even discussed official affairs with their personal servants.[7] In short, the servants served not only as a magistrate's eyes and ears,[8] but in a way they were also his *fu-hsin* (lit., "stomach and heart"), confidential aides.[9]

Personal servants gained further in importance because many magistrates found their administrative duties tedious and preferred to leave them to their servants.[10] And the magistrate also depended upon the servants to remind him of the things he had to do himself.

Obviously, personal servants were indispensable to a magistrate who was interested in practicing corruption. As Fang Ta-chih said, no magistrate could negotiate for bribes personally; he had to use his servants as go-betweens.[11] It was also easier for others to approach the magistrate's servants than to deal with him directly.

1. Types of Personal Servants

The number of personal servants in a yamen was determined by its size and duties. Chou and hsien government more or less universally included personal servants in the following capacities: one or two gate porters (*ssu-hun* or *men-shang*), one document-endorsement attendant (*ch'ien-ya,* also known as *kao-an*), one or two granary supervisors (*ssu-ts'ang*), one kitchen superintendent (*kuan-ch'u*), and the magistrate's personal attendant (*ken-pan*).[12] Additional servant personnel included a court attendant (*chih-t'ang*), correspondence attendant (*shu-ch'i*), seal attendant (*yung-yin*), servant in charge of land tax and grain tribute (*ch'ien-liang* or *ch'ien-ts'ao*), jail supervisor (*kuan-chien*), post station supervisor (*kuan-hao*), and servant in charge of miscellaneous taxes (*shui-wu*).[13] Ho Shih-ch'i, a magistrate, reported that in many provinces more than ten personal servants were needed for each magistrate, and that more than twenty were hired in a locality where the volume of official business was greater. In the Chiang-nan area, where the collection of tribute grain was an important function of the local government, twenty to thirty servants were employed.[14]

A more complicated picture was given by Hsieh Chin-luan, who reported that the category of gate porter was subdivided into several further categories: servant in charge of lawsuits (*an-chien*), servant in charge of complaints (*ch'eng-tz'u*), servant in charge of land tax (*ch'ien-liang*), servant in charge of miscellaneous taxes (*tsa-shui*), servant charged with the practical arrangements in entertaining superior officials (*ch'ai-wu*), and visiting-card attendant (*chih-t'ieh ch'uan-hua*). Thus, seven, eight, ten, or even more persons could be employed in the category of gate porter alone.

The category of *ch'ien-ya*, document-endorsement attendant, was divided into similar subcategories, with the addition of two more: servant in charge of registration (*hao-chien*), and the warrant writer (*shu-p'iao*).[15] Sometimes a personal servant was stationed away from the yamen, in the provincial capital or prefecture, to serve as liaison; he was known as *tso-sheng chia-jen* (servant stationed in a provincial capital) or *tso-fu chia-jen* (servant stationed in the prefecture).[16]

A quota for personal servants employed by local officials was not set until 1702[17]—twenty for a chou or hsien magistrate, and ten for an assistant magistrate. For Manchu officials the number was doubled. An official whose personal servants exceeded the quota was to be demoted one grade,[18] but the situation here was different from that connected with the quota for clerks and runners, since personal servants were hired and paid by the magistrate himself. Normally an official would not employ more servants than were necessary. From the above data, it seems likely that the number of servants serving in a chou or hsien government varied from five to about thirty.

2. FUNCTIONS

Since some of the yamen duties, such as the handling of documents, were assigned to more than one type of personnel and thus overlapped, it seems best to study the activities of the personal servants through an examination of the government functions in which they participated. This process will not only give a complete picture of the routine administration, but will also show the interrelation of the various types of servants and the interaction between them and the other people employed in a yamen— the clerks, runners, and private secretaries.

Functions Relating to the Control of Personnel

1) Watching the people who entered and left the yamen. This was the duty of a gate porter. No personal servants, cooks, and coolies in the yamen were permitted to leave the main entrance except when sent out on a mission. It was the gate porter's responsibility to ask why they were leaving and to keep a record of it. Even the magistrate's relatives who were staying with him and his private secretaries, on the infrequent occasions when they left the yamen, were questioned and their departure reported.[19] The gate porter checked and reported all visitors to the magistrate before they were allowed to enter.[20] If the visitor was a commissioner sent by a superior official, or another official stationed in the same city, or a member of the local gentry, it was the duty of the visiting-card attendant to take his card to the magistrate and accompany him to the visiting room.[21]

2) Acting as an intermediary between the magistrate and clerks and runners. This important function was also assigned to a gate porter, who passed the magistrate's orders to the clerks and runners.[22] When it was necessary to read a document, to make an inquiry about a case, or to expedite some official business, a note was usually issued by the magistrate to a servant in charge of documents, who then gave it to the gate porter to give to a clerk or runner. As a rule, a servant in charge of documents

was not allowed to make direct contact with clerks and runners.[23] By the same token, a report made by a clerk or runner had to pass through the gate porter's hands before it could reach the magistrate. When a warrant was issued to a runner by the magistrate, it was transmitted through the gate porter.[24]

Functions Relating to the Flow of Documents

1) Receiving incoming documents. All incoming documents sent from a superior yamen or another yamen of the same level went first to the gate porter, who opened and delivered them to the document-endorsement attendant. Sometimes it was the latter who opened them.[25] In either case, the document-endorsement attendant then presented them to the magistrate to be marked with the date.[26]

2) Supervising and centralizing the procedure in handling documents. This most important function was assigned to the gate porter, servant in charge of registration, document-endorsement attendant, and seal attendant. After documents had been presented to the magistrate or his private secretary[27] for the official rescript (p'i), they were sent to the servant in charge of registration.[28] Then they were delivered by the document-endorsement attendant to the gate porter, and thence to the "receipt and distribution office" (ch'eng-fa fang). Here they were distributed to the clerks of the various offices who were to prepare drafts according to the instructions given in the rescript.

The drafts, when prepared, were collected by the receipt and distribution office in the afternoon and turned over to the gate porter. He then delivered them to the document-endorsement attendant, who presented them to the private secretaries for revision and then submitted them to the office of the magistrate for his endorsement. The documents were then sent back to the gate porter, through whom they were relayed to the clerks to prepare the final copies.[29]

After the final copies had been prepared, they were delivered to the gate porter, who passed them on to the document-endorsement attendant, who in turn passed them on to the seal attendant for the official seal.[30] The documents were then delivered to the document-endorsement attendant, who saw that the documents were properly finished by writing the appropriate official code and adding the flourishes in red ink in accordance with the established pattern, a procedure known as piao-p'an.[31]

Finally, the documents were registered again and delivered to the gate porter. If they were outgoing documents, he checked and sealed them. He had to make sure that there were no copyist's errors and that the number of enclosed documents was correct.[32]

Thus, in the preparation of documents the clerks were supervised by the servants. First, the gate porter was expected to see that clerks did not delay in preparing the documents.[33] When a document was urgent, it was the duty of the document-endorsement attendant to instruct a clerk to prepare it without delay.[34] Second, all documents were checked carefully by the personal servants in charge of documents to prevent tampering by the clerk and to ensure an authentic file. Special care was taken in handling important documents like depositions, statements of decision, documents enclosing title deeds or promissory notes.[35] When a document was to be stamped, it was the seal attendant's duty to see that no changes had been made by a clerk.[36] When a warrant was issued, an official seal was usually stamped over the character *hsing* (approved) and over the name of the assigned runner, so that it would be impossible for a clerk to add the name of another runner on the warrant.[37]

Functions Relating to the Magistrate's Court

1) Superintending the preparation of trials. When a complaint was received by a gate porter, he passed it on to a private secretary. The secretary wrote the official rescript, which was later submitted to the magistrate for his approval and stamp. It was then copied by another secretary, and a clerk was called in to write a complaint placard (*chuang-pang*).[38] This was marked with a red brush[39] and delivered to the gate porter to be registered and posted on the bulletin board.[40] It was the gate porter's duty to check in the early morning the number of lawsuits to be heard on that day, to call the clerks and runners, and to see that the witnesses and other persons required to attend the court were brought in so that the trial could proceed. The same routine was followed in the late afternoon if there were more cases to be heard.[41] When the gate porter had made sure that all the necessary persons were present, he attached a report of the arrival of plaintiff, defendants, and witnesses (*tao-tan*) to the legal document of the case and handed it to the court attendant. The court attendant submitted these papers to the magistrate and ascertained from him the time the court was to open and which case was to be heard

first. The clerks and runners were then instructed to attend the court, and the runners were told to bring in the persons in their charge. Finally, the magistrate was requested to preside over the trial.[42]

When someone beat the drum at the entrance of the yamen, indicating that he wanted an audience with the magistrate, it was the gate porter's task to find out what it was about, and whether there was a complaint.[43] If it was serious, the magistrate was requested to hear the case and to issue a warrant for the arrest of the offender.[44]

When a homicide was reported, it was the duty of the gate porter to examine the report and present it to the magistrate and to notify the clerk of punishment, the coroner, and other runners to attend the court. When the date for the inquest had been set, the gate porter made all necessary arrangements: he sent runners in advance to erect a mat tent, prepared horses and coolies, notified the clerk of punishment and coroner to accompany the magistrate, and handed the depositions and inquest forms to the court attendant who would accompany the magistrate.[45]

2) Attending the trial. The court attendant took care of the routine related to a trial. He placed the legal documents in front of the magistrate,[46] and he stood in court throughout the trial, listening carefully to the testimony and seeing that no changes were made by a clerk in the deposition. When an injury had to be examined, the court attendant called in the coroner and watched the examination closely in order to prevent a false report. The court attendant could, if necessary, ask the injured about the conditions under which the injury had been inflicted and the kind of weapon used by his assailant. He then told the clerk of deposition to write down the statement and the clerk of punishment to copy the list of injuries. When torture was used, the court attendant was expected to watch closely and make sure that it was properly administered. When a witness was released, the attendant reminded the magistrate to check him off the list of witnesses, and when a person was ordered to be imprisoned he told the clerk of punishment to prepare a card and request the magistrate to endorse it. If any property was returned to an owner, the court attendant had to get a receipt which was dated by the magistrate and was kept in the file.[47]

At the end of a trial, it was the court attendant's duty to ask the plaintiff and defendant to sign a statement accepting the judgment.[48] The deposition, which had been copied by a clerk, was checked by the court attendant for accuracy and then presented to the magistrate for endorsement. After the deposition and *tsun-i* or *kan-chieh* (statement of willingness to accept the decision) had been read and marked with the character *yüeh* (read) by the magistrate, they were checked by the court attendant in the presence of the clerks, put into a folder, and delivered to the document-endorsement attendant.[49] Finally, the documents were delivered to the gate porter, through whom they were returned to the clerks and put back in the files.[50]

The court attendant also attended inquests. He was expected to watch the coroner's examination and to fill out the inquest form, on which the magistrate made necessary marks with a red brush.[51]

3) Dispatching of other judicial details. The court attendant was concerned with the routine involved during a trial, while the gate porter and document-endorsement attendant attended to the preliminaries and aftermath of the trial. Their concern was not only the distribution of documents, but also the routine procedures related to the administration of justice. Both the gate porter and the document-endorsement attendant kept a record of the names of the plaintiff, the defendant, and the clerks and runners in charge of the case, as well as other kinds of records pertaining to lawsuits.[52] It was their duty to remind the magistrate to issue a warrant and to instruct the office of punishment to prepare a list of deadlines for the runners to close cases of robbery or homicide.[53] A document-endorsement attendant could request the magistrate to assign the case to a different runner, or to appoint additional runners, if necessary.[54] Personal servants were customarily sent by magistrates in Kiangsi to escort the delivery of criminals in major crimes to superior yamen for retrial.[55]

Functions Relating to the Jail

It was the duty of a gate porter or the jail supervisor, if there was one,[56] to supervise the detention of prisoners. Both of them were authorized to ask the office of punishment to submit a daily list of those imprisoned or merely detained in the *pan-fang* (a place where material witnesses or people guilty of minor offenses were detained temporarily). It was their duty to deliver a new prisoner to the jail, to check the fetters worn by prisoners while the clerk of punishment called the roll, to see that the jailers kept the jail clean, and to take care of sick or dying prisoners.[57] A handbook prepared by an anonymous personal servant, the *Ko-hang shih-chien* (Activities within the various specialties), mentions that a jail supervisor should check the prisoners' rice ration daily, in order to prevent a jailer from reducing it. Another handbook, the *Kung-men yao-lüeh*

(Essentials in a public office), states that jailers usually maltreated those prisoners from whom they could not extort money, and that it was the duty of a jail supervisor to investigate any such maltreatment.[58]

When escorted criminals were passing through a hsien, the jail supervisor there checked their number, ordered the clerk of punishment to check their fingerprints, examined their fetters, put them in prison, and delivered them to the escort runners at the time of their departure, giving back the delivery certificate[59] to the latter.[60]

Functions Relating to Taxation[61]

1) Seeing that all the essential information about taxation was duly prepared by the clerks. When a newly appointed magistrate arrived at his post, the servant in charge of land tax and grain tribute was authorized to ask the clerk of revenue to submit a Complete Book of Taxes and Labor Services; to ask the office of revenue, the clerk in charge of silver chests, and the clerk of the treasury to make a report on the quota of land tax and various other taxes to be collected, the amount already collected and delivered, the amount kept in the treasury, and the amount not yet collected; and to ask the granary clerk to make a report on the amount of rice stored in the granaries. If there was a deficit in tax funds, the servant was expected to get a written statement from the various clerks in charge of silver chests guaranteeing that the deficit was caused not by their embezzlement but by the taxpayers' failure to pay taxes. A guarantee was also obtained from the granary clerk and the grain measurer stating that the amount of grain stored in the granary was the same as that listed in the record and that they would be responsible for any deficit and for damage caused by damp and mildew.[62]

The servant in charge of land tax and grain tribute was advised in the handbook *Men-wu che-yao* (Essentials in gate administration) to examine all tax records in order to have a full knowledge of all taxes collected, delivered, or uncollected.[63] However, as we shall see, this was the responsibility mainly of the private secretary in charge of taxation. Apparently the servant was merely expected to obtain information from the various clerks and to have a rough idea of these matters. It seems to have been the secretary's duty to examine and check carefully the records in his office, whereas the servant's duty was to make direct contact with clerks in order to secure these records and reports for the secretary, who was not allowed to make direct contact with clerks.

The importance of the servant in charge of land tax and grain tribute cannot be overlooked. According to *Kung-men yao-lüeh,* only two copies of tax quota records were prepared by the office of revenue, one of which was submitted to the magistrate and the other was kept by the servant for reference.[64]

2) Speeding tax collection. Prior to a deadline it was the duty of the servant in charge of land tax and grain tribute to ask the clerks of revenue and land tax to submit a list of delinquent taxpayers, or of *t'u-ch'ai* (runners sent to a rural zone to hasten the collection of taxes) who were subject to inquiry and punishment for failing to carry out their mission. He then asked the magistrate to preside over the court and punish the guilty runners.[65]

3) Supervising clerks and runners. Through the above processes, the servant in charge of land tax and grain tribute was expected to see that the clerks made no attempt at deceit in connection with the issuing of land tax receipts.[66] He was also charged with seeing that the tax collected by the clerks in charge of silver chests and by the runners sent to the rural districts was handed in daily.[67]

4) Delivering tax funds. The servant in charge of land tax and grain tribute was frequently asked to escort, along with runners and soldiers, the delivery of silver.[68] It was his duty to count the money received from the treasury and to see that it was packed into barrels or hollowed logs. While the money was in transit he was to make sure that the barrels or logs were secure. Upon arrival at the destination, he supervised the unpacking of the barrels or logs before delivery.[69]

5) Supervising the collection and delivery of grain tribute. The servant in charge of land tax and grain tribute was entrusted with the task of supervising clerks and runners handling tribute grain. This was made clear in the *Ch'in-pan chou-hsien shih-i,* which mentions that since the task of measuring and collecting grain could not be performed by the magistrate himself it had to be assigned to clerks and runners, and personal servants had to be employed to supervise them in order to prevent corruption.[70] The servant was authorized to examine the quality of the tribute grain and could reject grain of poor quality.[71] The transportation of tribute grain was the job of the Bannermen (*Ch'i-ting*), who were likely to be overbearing and difficult to deal with, and the ability to deal with them became a basic qualification for appointment as a servant in charge of grain tribute.[72] A government regulation permitted the servants to

help the magistrate to check the sailing of the transport junks by putting down the date of their arrival and departure on the form which was to be submitted by the magistrate to the yamen concerned.[73]

Functions Relating to the Granary

The servant appointed as granary supervisor was stationed in the granary, as a rule.[74] It was his duty to see that storerooms were kept locked and that the doors were firmly sealed with strips of paper bearing the official seal. He could open the doors when an investigation was necessary, and he helped to examine the rice stored in the granary when a newly appointed magistrate assumed office. He was also authorized to supervise the grain measurers. The *Ch'ang-sui lun* (On personal servants) advised servants in charge of granaries not to reprimand or punish a grain measurer because if offended he would deliberately cause a shortage in the granary; instead the measurer should be won by kindness.[75]

Functions Relating to Post Stations

Servants were stationed in post stations[76] as supervisors to oversee the routine of dispatching official messages, to supervise the grooms who cared for the horses, and to receive guests and messengers. When a message arrived at a station the supervisor examined its condition and noted the date and hour of its arrival on a piece of paper which was then attached to it. He then ordered the grooms to prepare a horse and deliver the message to the next station, bringing back a return receipt (*hui-chao*). He received officials who were on a mission and entitled to the service of the station, and prepared horses and attendants for each in accordance with the specifications on his certificate (*k'an-ho*).[77]

Miscellaneous Functions

There were in a yamen a number of servants who handled special funds for wages to runners, for rations to prisoners, and for sacrifices;[78] took charge of correspondence;[79] acted as night watchmen;[80] supervised the kitchen;[81] or waited upon the magistrate.[82]

There was a *pan-ch'ai* or a *ch'ai-tsung* who oversaw the reception and entertainment of superior officials arriving in or passing through the district on a mission. He might also arrange for housing, furniture, decorations, and coolies for them. Usually the *ch'ai-tsung* had a number of *liu-ch'ai* (errand boys) serving under him.[83]

A servant was frequently stationed in the provincial capital or in a prefecture to serve as liaison. His principal duty was to maintain close contact with the personal servants of his magistrate's superior official.[84] The inside information thus obtained frequently put the magistrate in a more favorable position in dealing with his superiors. Sometimes when a magistrate had a document to submit to his superior, a favorable arrangement would be made beforehand through the personal servants of both officials.[85] There was a law prohibiting magistrates from stationing servants in the provincial capital or prefecture,[86] but few observed it.[87]

This examination of the functions of the personal servants shows that, with the exception of the visiting-card attendant, the personal attendant, and the kitchen superintendent, all the personal servants were concerned with official business in one way or another. "They were not government employees, yet all things under their care were government affairs." [88] Especially important among them were the gate porter, the document-endorsement attendant, the seal attendant, the court attendant, the servants in charge of taxation, the granary supervisor, the post station supervisor, and the jail supervisor.[89]

An analysis of the various functions described above reveals that personal servants served three purposes. First, they assisted in the office routine in order to lighten the magistrate's excessive burden. As long as the assistant magistrate and other subordinate officials remained inactive (see Chapter I), the magistrate, the only executive in a yamen and hence over-burdened with all kinds of administrative duties, had to have a group of aides to help him to look after the routine. It is obvious that the less energetic and experienced the magistrate was, the more responsibility rested with his personal servants. A handbook prepared by a personal servant mentions that a document-endorsement attendant should see that all legal papers were kept in the file but that if the magistrate was capable and alert, this need not worry a servant.[90]

Second, the personal servants coordinated the activities of the various departments of the yamen: between clerks and runners, private secretaries and clerks, and between all these and the magistrate. The coordinating role of the servants was indispensable because secretaries, clerks, and runners, each serving as isolated units, were not allowed to contact one another directly. As Wang Chih summed it up, personal servants were the agents through whom clerks and runners received their orders and through whom the division of labor among the clerks and runners was coordinated.[91] Although a magistrate was free to see any employee under him, he was in fact unable to see all of them, especially the numerous clerks and runners. Thus personal servants were relied upon as intermediaries between the official and his personnel. Even when the official was in close contact with his private secretaries, personal servants were still useful in transmitting documents and messages.[92]

An attempt was once made by a capable magistrate, Liu Heng, to eliminate the services of a gate porter in handling documents and giving orders to clerks and runners.[93] His servants were employed merely to wait upon him, as personal attendants and in other menial capacities.[94] However, Liu's method was considered exceptional and unconventional and few officials were willing to introduce similar innovations. Liu, in his capacity as prefect, left the magistrates to decide whether or not to adopt his practice and did not try to force it upon them.[95]

Finally, the personal servants were employed to supervise the government employees. This was explicitly expressed in the writings of both magistrates and personal servants.[96] It seems that the servants were well aware of the supervisory nature of their position and considered themselves confidants of the officials, while they looked down upon the clerks as "wicked clerks" (chien-hsü).[97]

3. STATUS AND RECRUITMENT

The personal servants in a yamen had an inferior legal status. They were included in the category of "mean" people[98] and received the same treatment as slaves, domestic servants, and government runners. They were not allowed to take the civil service examination or enter officialdom,[99] and their descendants could not do so until three generations after their discharge.[100] Their social status was also inferior; for example, they could not be seated in the presence of the magistrate or his private secretary.[101]

Some magistrates' servants had been old family servants;[102] others had been recommended by relatives, friends, colleagues, or superior officials.[103] Some had served as personal servants in a yamen before and hence were familiar with the official routine. All of them had to be able to read and write.

All servants did not have the same economic status. Although the majority of them were poor, some had considerable wealth and property.

It was reported that some people offered large sums of money to those who recommended them for the job of a magistrate's personal servant.[104] There were cases where money was advanced by a personal servant to a newly appointed magistrate who lacked funds for traveling and other expenses.[105] A contemporary writer reported a practice that was common in the capital in the late Ch'ing: Loans were made available at silversmiths' shops to those who wanted to purchase an official title; when the shop owner granted such a loan he frequently recommended a personal servant to the debtor, who was obliged to hire the person recommended.[106] The motive of a person who was willing to lend money to a magistrate and become his personal servant was obvious—to gain profit by engaging in corruption. The loan was in the nature of an investment.[107]

Since the servants were hired on a personal basis, they could be employed and dismissed at the discretion of the magistrate. He could keep a servant as long as he wished. Only one official regulation had to be observed: when a servant was employed, his name, birth place, and social origin as well as the official duty assigned to him had to be reported to the superior yamen within three months of his employment. When a servant was dismissed, a report also had to be submitted.[108]

4. Financial Maintenance

As a rule, a servant received wages (*kung-shih*) according to his ability and the nature of his assignment.[109] However, this pay was usually nominal. What a personal servant counted upon was *lou-kuei,* customary fees of various kinds. Thus Wang Hui-tsu observed that if a servant was employed but not given a specific assignment, he could enjoy no income except regular meals.[110]

Many of the customary fees were shared by the servants with clerks and runners. The following fees are mentioned in *Ko-hang shih-chien:* fees for presenting a complaint,[111] for summoning defendants and witnesses to court, for withdrawing a lawsuit, for signing a statement by the plaintiff and defendant accepting the judgment of the magistrate, for securing a personal bond, for land tax receipts, for taxes on title deeds, salt, fish, wine, and pawnshops, for broker's licenses, and for boat licenses.[112] Fees were paid to the court attendant and document-endorsement attendant in a trial.[113] In a certain district in Kiangsu, besides the inquest fees paid to the clerks and runners, 3000 coins had to be paid to the magistrate's personal attendant, and 2200 to the court attendant.[114]

There were also customary fees that were enjoyed exclusively by personal servants. Among the best known of these was the so-called *men-pao,* a gift given to the gate porter by one who wanted to see the magistrate or deliver something to him. Such a gift had to be given even by clerks and runners serving in the same yamen.[115] Customary fees were paid to personal servants by the treasury clerk or clerk in charge of land tax and grain tribute, the silversmith who was assigned to melt the silver handed in by taxpayers, a scribe who wrote complaints for others, the local constables, the superintendent of a charity granary, a student of a hsien school who was given a stipend (*pu-lin*), a student who was promoted to a Senior Licentiate, and a person who purchased an official title.[116] The servants usually deducted a certain amount of money from the runners' wages,[117] from sacrificial funds,[118] and from funds for construction and repairs.[119] In addition, there were such fees as the "gift for arriving at a post" (*tao-jen li*), the "festival gift," and the "New Year gift,"[120] which people seeking favors would give to a magistrate's personal servants.

Although it was generally recognized that customary fees were necessary to the maintenance of personal servants in a yamen,[121] many officials found it necessary to regulate them. The types and amounts of the customary fees varied in different localities;[122] some magistrates, after studying those of their locality, would approve some and eliminate others,[123] thus authorizing and codifying the fees. Usually a portion of the fees was reserved for the office expenses of the gate porter and the document-endorsement attendant, and the remainder was distributed among the personal servants seasonally or during each of the three major festivals.[124] The share of each servant varied according to his diligence and seniority, and this was usually determined by the magistrate himself in order to avoid disputes.[125] When the customary fees obtainable in a locality were insufficient to support the personal servants employed in a yamen, funds were sometimes donated by the magistrate himself in order to keep them.[126]

5. Forms of Corruption

Nearly all types of personal servants engaged in one or another form of corruption. The gate porter was in an excellent position to manipulate situations and abuse his authority as all documents and reports had to pass through his hands.[127] He often procrastinated in distributing a document or delivering a warrant to a runner if money had not been offered him.[128] Once an official notice ordering the people to wipe out locusts was prepared by a magistrate upon the request of a *pao-chia* head. The magistrate found out later that, because he failed to give money to the gate porter, the notice was never given to the *pao-chia* head.[129] On the other hand, the complaint was often made that a report submitted by a clerk or a runner did not reach the magistrate because of the deliberate intervention of a gate porter.[130] When defendants and witnesses in a lawsuit were brought in by the runners, the gate porter would not report it to the official unless a satisfactory amount of money was offered to him, frequently using the excuse that not all of the witnesses were present.[131] The following case was reported by Liu Heng:

> A magistrate was ordered to arrest a criminal by his superior. A reward of 1000 silver dollars was offered and a deadline was set for the arrest. The wanted criminal was brought in by the runner within the deadline. The gate porter, however, instructed the runner to detain the criminal in a private house, told the magistrate that the criminal had fled, and suggested raising the reward to 3000 dollars. The magistrate agreed to pay 2000 dollars, but got no result. When the official wanted to punish the runner, the gate porter hid him and asked for postponement of his punishment. Finally a 3000-dollar reward was offered by the magistrate and the criminal was delivered to him.[132]

It is obvious, then, that the gate porter was the person who blocked communication between the official and the clerks, runners, and people.[133]

It is most interesting that while servants were considered confidants of the magistrate and were entrusted with the duty of supervising the clerks and runners,[134] many of them were accused of cooperating closely in corruption with the other two groups. Wang Chih pointed out that servants depended upon clerks and runners to negotiate business and obtain money from them; in return, they tolerated and connived at the others' corruption.[135] In other words, servants relied upon clerks and runners as their agents, and the latter relied upon the former as their protectors.[136] The servants frequently helped the clerks and runners to conceal their faults before the magistrate, and when necessary they asked an official to postpone disciplinary action against clerks and runners.[137] The clerks and runners, in turn, sought from the servants information that could be of value to them.[138] There was a case where a clerk made a monthly payment of 30,000 coins to a gate porter who agreed to show him all the documents, official rescripts, and drafts before they were distributed to the various *fang*.[139] Land tax receipts were sometimes sold to clerks by servants.[140] Sometimes the two groups cooperated in stealing depositions and substituting sections of them.[141]

A frequent complaint was that servants supervising granaries not only connived at the corruption of the clerks and grain measurers, but also cooperated with them so that each of them would get a share from the collection of tribute grain.[142] Feng Kuei-fen estimated that the average income derived from customary fees and corruption by a servant and a clerk in charge of grain tribute in a hsien in Kiangsu amounted to 10,000 taels each.[143] Cooperation was also found between the jail supervisor and the jailers and prison guards.[144]

Thus many personal servants whom a magistrate regarded as his confidential aides actually turned out to be the collaborators of his clerks and runners. A case may be cited as an example:

A newly appointed magistrate was deceived by his gate porter, who worked out a scheme with one of the clerks, telling the official that the local government had failed to collect the tax quota for years. The magistrate did not know what to do and asked for advice. "Why not ask a clerk to contract for the collection of taxes?" When the official agreed and an invitation was extended to the clerk, the latter pretended that he could not do it. After a few days the gate porter again urged him, and the request was accepted this time. The embezzlement was disclosed years later and the official was indicted.[145]

The most common tactic used by a personal servant was to ingratiate himself with the magistrate, use artful means to deceive him, and feign loyalty in order to win his confidence.[146] There was also a more direct and aggressive approach. As Fang Ta-chih pointed out, not all official business could be carried out strictly in accordance with government regulations, and a corrupt gate porter could take advantage of this situation and intimidate the official, so that the latter would tolerate his unlawful activities.[147] Also, it was hard for a magistrate to dismiss a servant to whom he owed money and was therefore obligated.[148] If a magistrate was corrupt himself, and especially if he had received money from a servant for an assignment,[149] it was even easier for a personal servant to intimidate him.[150] In such a case the servant certainly had a free hand in practicing corruption; indeed the two might even cooperate to their common interest. Probably this was the reason for the law that when a magistrate was indicted for accepting a bribe his personal servants were also to be detained and tried.[151]

6. DISCIPLINARY CONTROL

Personal servants who received a bribe or extorted money from others were subject to the same punishment as clerks and runners guilty of these crimes.[152] The punishment was two degrees more severe if they fled when their masters were impeached for corruption.[153]

With the servants, as with the clerks and runners, the law placed the responsibility of supervision on the magistrate. Thus an official who connived at extortion by a servant was to be dismissed; if he failed to inquire into the case, due to negligence, he was to be fined or demoted according to the extent of the servant's crime.[154] A magistrate was also subject to demotion when he failed, due to negligence, to inquire into a case where one of his personal servants abused his authority and assaulted another person.[155]

As we have said, many of the officials trusted their personal servants and relied upon them to supervise the clerks and runners. However, many officials realized that few of the servants were dependable, and that they had to be supervised constantly.[156] Since the government employees and the personal servants cooperated in corruption, it became clear that the system of using servants to supervise government employees was unworkable. Instead of easing the burden of the magistrate, it only created further difficulties for him, for it was even more difficult to supervise the servants than to supervise the clerks and runners,[157] and it was obvious that unless such servants as the gate porters could be controlled there could be no hope of controlling the clerks and runners.[158] Wang Hui-tsu claimed that, in his experience, there were some clerks who were law-abiding, but all the personal servants had no principles and were concerned only with profit. Thus if an official relied upon them, his administration would be ruined.[159] Liu Heng, a capable magistrate and later a prefect, advised his subordinates not to use gate porters, admitting frankly that he was unable to control them.[160] It was even more difficult to supervise a servant in charge of a granary or post station because they were stationed outside the yamen.[161] One commonly offered solution to the problem of controlling the servants was that authority should not be given to them and they should not be allowed to make decisions on official business.[162]

Since gate porters were in a position to postpone the delivery of documents and reports for their own purposes, some magistrates tried to prevent this kind of offense by demanding that documents be delivered daily without delay.[163] Wang Feng-sheng ruled that clerks and runners must put the date on any report when they submitted it and that the gate porter must deliver it at once to the magistrate who would again date it before sending it on to his private secretary. His clerks and runners were also permitted to submit reports directly to the magistrate when he was in court. Wang also ruled that all documents approved for posting and warrants issued to runners must be dated by the magistrate so that delay on the part of a gate porter could be checked.[164]

In a direct effort to prevent collaboration among the servants, the clerks, and the runners, which was the source of most corruption, one magistrate, in a *Shu-kuei* (yamen regulations for personal servants), ruled that the servants were forbidden to make friends with clerks and runners or to drink and gamble with them.[165] He further warned his servants against cooperating with clerks and runners in any attempt to engage in corrupt practices.[166] However, these were merely rules on paper; in practice things were quite different.

──────── VI ────────

PRIVATE SECRETARIES

Private secretaries, *mu-yu* or *mu-pin* (lit., "friends or guests serving in a tent")[1] or *shih-yeh* (a colloquial expression; lit., "teacher-master"), were administrative experts employed by local officials. They were not members of the regular bureaucracy and were not paid by the government. Their emergence as a group was the outcome of functional necessity, and is understandable only in terms of the institutional framework of the Chinese educational and bureaucratic system.

1. The Need for Administrative Experts

Ever since the introduction of the civil service examination system, the basic qualification for taking the examinations had been a knowledge of the classics and the ability to write essays and poems. Hence, scholars concentrated their efforts on these subjects. But once they passed the examinations, they were given official appointments and were expected to handle administrative affairs. This did not mean that they possessed the kind of knowledge essential for fulfilling their official duties; on the contrary, they were not at all prepared for them. This discrepancy between training in literature and a career in administration had long been recognized by Chinese statesmen like Wang An-shih (1021–1086) and others. In the words of Wang:

What a student should learn is practical matters concerning the world and the nation. Now all these are put aside, and students are taught instead to learn literary essays in which they are later examined. They are asked to spend all their energy and time in these [literary pursuits], and yet when they are appointed officials, they are asked to put aside [what they have learned], and are obliged to deal with matters concerning the world and the nation. . . Now their energies are diverted and their time is occupied with learning impractical things day and night; and when they are entrusted with [government] affairs, suddenly we demand that their services be used for the world and the nation. It is no wonder that few of them have the ability to accomplish anything.[2]

The discrepancy became even wider during the Ming and Ch'ing because of the primary importance given to the *pa-ku* (eight-legged essay). In the T'ang and Sung, students had at least been required to study the law and to write judgments. In the Ming and Ch'ing periods students no longer studied the law;[3] they were concerned almost exclusively with the prevailing style of essays and poems.

Max Weber, wondering how the officials who had no specialized training were able to assume administrative duties, suggested that while they proved their "charisma"[4] through the canonical correctness of their literary forms, "the actual administrative work could rest on the shoulders of subordinate officials."[5] Weber overlooked the fact that practically all officials, high or low, central or local, received the same training and took the same kind of examinations. Thus the subordinate officials faced exactly the same practical problems. Furthermore, the roles of subordinate officials might vary on different levels, and there were also historical variations in different periods. Their role cannot be generalized. We cannot here go into a detailed discussion, but a few remarks may be made in connection with local government.

Higher provincial officials, who were concerned mainly with documents and the supervision of their subordinates, could of course leave the actual administration to the magistrates. But on the hsien level, the magistrate had to assume direct responsibility for all administrative duties in his area. Here the gap between training and actual practice was at its widest,[6] for no other official was entrusted with responsibility for so many technical administrative details. Obviously the problem of preparation for an official career was more serious in the case of a magistrate than in that of any other official. He could learn his job only through trial and error, a very time-consuming process. Yet the magistrates received little help from their subordinates. This was particularly so during the Ch'ing, when the subordinate officials, as we saw in Chapter I, did very little administrative work, and everything fell upon the shoulders of the magistrate. A further point is that no talented man was willing to accept the post of a subordinate official because of its inferior status and because the chance of promotion was slight.[7] Hence there was little possibility of recruiting magistrates from those who had started their careers as subordinate officials. This meant that nearly all newly appointed magistrates were inexperienced.

The immediate problem precipitated by this situation was how to keep the administrative machinery in operation until such time as the magistrate had gained some experience. Obviously there had to be some means of reducing the technical inadequacy; otherwise the local administration would cease to function. We may assume that there were two alternative solutions to this problem: either the magistrate had to be given specialized training before he took up his post, a measure that would have required a fundamental change in the educational and examination systems, or an expert had to act as his substitute. The second was precisely the solution adopted during the Ch'ing period.[8]

There consequently emerged a large group of administrative experts—private secretaries—who personified the bridge between the scholar and the official. They were learned men who had undergone specialized training in administrative matters, not for the purpose of becoming officials (at least not immediately) but for the purpose of serving as professional advisers to officials. They possessed the technical knowledge and skill to run a government. In this they stood in sharp contrast to candidates for officialdom whose objective was an official career, although they were not prepared for actual administration.

It seems clear that the services of these administrative experts were absolutely necessary to a nonexpert official. One or two quotations will suffice to prove this point.

All one has to do in order to pass an examination is to master the art of *pa-ku*. Once one is appointed an official, all matters of taxation and administration of justice are left to private secretaries.[9]

An official who is appointed for the first time should be careful [in employing a private secretary]. As he has not studied law and accounting before, how can he understand matters concerning law and taxation in a moment when they are imminent? He has to depend upon someone to help him to deal with the numerous perplexing matters.[10]

Therefore when an official obtained an appointment, one of his first important tasks was to find competent and reliable secretaries to act as his advisers and aides.[11] There was a case where a newly appointed magistrate was told by his superior that his district was difficult to rule, that his predecessor would have been sentenced to death for a wrong judgment had he not had a very able man as his private secretary, and that hence the new magistrate should ask the same man to be his secretary.[12]

The services of private secretaries were needed even by experienced and capable magistrates for the reason that a magistrate's duties were so numerous that few, no matter how energetic they might be, could manage to discharge all of them.[13] The case of Liu Heng is an example. He himself had been a private secretary for many years[14] and was well known for his knowledge of law and his remarkable success in abolishing the employment of gate porters; yet he still needed the assistance of private secretaries. According to Liu's preface to his *Yung-li yung-yen* (Ordinary words of an ordinary official) and the preface written by Wu Shou-ch'un, one of his private secretaries, Liu himself wrote all the documents presented to superior officials, official notices, and statements of decision. Even so, he could not dispense with the services of a secretary.[15] The only magistrate known to have been without a private secretary was Wang Hui-tsu, and even he had had a secretary at one time. Wang's case was exceptional, however: he had been a private secretary himself for many years, and he was an unusually energetic person.[16]

It should be pointed out that private secretaries were employed not only in the chou and hsien governments, which dealt directly with the practical details of administration, but also in higher-level local governments, which supervised the administration of chou and hsien governments.[17] Since these administrative experts were relied upon by local officials of all levels, it was logical that actual local administration fell in their hands. Their importance was fully realized by Han Chen (early nineteenth century), who observed that local government might be divided into two categories: the "visible" and the "invisible."

> The ssu [provincial treasurer or provincial judge] and *tao,* who supervise prefects and magistrates, and the governor-general and governor, who supervise the *ssu* and *tao,* may be called the visible government outside the capital. . . [the invisible government outside the capital is run by] private secretaries who are in charge of the duties of the magistrates, prefects, *ssu, tao,* governors, and governor-general, and carry out the administration of the seventeen provinces on their behalf.[18]

Han's statement may have been an exaggeration. Nevertheless, it reveals the invisible function played by these administrative experts, often overlooked and underestimated.

2. Types of *Mu-yu* and Their Functions

Private secretaries serving in a chou or hsien yamen may be divided into the following categories: *hsing-ming*, secretary of law; *ch'ien-ku*, secretary of taxation (lit., "money and grain"); *cheng-pi*, secretary in charge of the enforcement of tax collection; *kua-hao*, secretary of registration; *shu-ch'i* or *shu-ping*, secretary of correspondence; [19] *chu-mo* or *hung-hei pi*, secretary of red and black brushes; [20] *chang-fang*, bookkeeper.[21] According to Hsieh Chin-luan, there was, in addition to the secretary of taxation, a *ch'ien-liang tsung*, secretary in charge of land tax.[22] Besides the secretary of law, Hsieh also mentions the *an-tsung*, secretary in charge of lawsuits.[23]

Only the first five or six of these categories seem to have been universal in all chou and hsien governments; the rest were optional, depending upon the size and demands of a locality. Hsieh Chin-luan pointed out that it was impossible for a yamen where the magistrate's burden was moderate to have all types of secretaries; therefore each of his secretaries had to assume more than one class of duties.[24] However, the same type of work might be assigned to more than one secretary. In one yamen in which Wang Hui-tsu served as secretary, there were two secretaries of law. At one time Wang himself was the assistant to a secretary. At another time, he and another secretary had the same duties, with each of them responsible for a specified geographic area.[25] According to Wang, who listed only the first five types of secretaries, more than ten private secretaries were needed in a locality where the administrative load was heavy, whereas in a less busy locality only two or three persons were employed to take care of the five posts.[26] As no quota was set by the government for the employment of private secretaries, this matter was left entirely to the local official. Since the salary was rather high, and since it was paid by the official, it is obvious that no magistrate would employ more secretaries than were necessary. The tendency seems to have been to keep the number at a minimum.

Private secretaries always lived in the yamen,[27] occupying quarters isolated from the other yamen personnel. They were free to consult with each other, but they could have complete privacy if they preferred. They did not have a common office; each attended to his business in his own room.[28]

The functions assigned to private secretaries may be summarized under the following categories.

Functions Relating to Legal Cases

This was one of the most important functions performed by private secretaries. Legal cases might be the charge of the secretary of law or the secretary of taxation. As a rule civil cases involving a dispute over property, loans, and business transactions, regardless of whether fighting was involved, were assigned to a secretary of taxation. Cases involving fighting, fraud, marriage, disputes over graveyards or the designation of an heir, and other cases in which family members were involved, regardless of whether a loan or property was involved, were assigned to a secretary of law. Cases of homicide and larceny came under the jurisdiction of the latter exclusively.[29] Thus when a complaint was received by the magistrate it was handed over to one of the secretaries, the choice depending upon the nature of the case. It was then the duty of the secretary concerned to read the complaint and write an official rescript at the end of the duplicate of the complaint. After the official rescript had been approved and endorsed by the magistrate, it was copied by the secretary in charge of the black brush on the original copy of the complaint. Finally it was copied by a clerk and posted on a bulletin board.[30] In order to insure that the content was kept confidential before its release, the rescript written by a secretary was frequently sealed and submitted to the magistrate through a personal servant.[31]

The importance of an official rescript lay in the fact that it determined the endorsement or rejection of a complaint, that is, whether a hearing would be granted, or whether a dispute over landed property would be investigated.[32] Wang Yu-huai pointed out that a lot of cases could be settled by a rescript without a trial, if a private secretary was able to find out at the beginning whether the complaint was justified.[33] It was emphasized by an expert that a good rescript that could convince a plaintiff and prevent a pettifogger from exaggerating the case could be written only by a secretary who had a thorough knowledge of law, was able to use his reasoning power, was experienced in discerning fact from fraud, and able to express his points clearly in a statement. The reason for rejecting a complaint had to be clear and convincing; otherwise the plaintiff would try to appeal to a superior yamen.[34]

Sometimes a rescript was more than an endorsement; it was tantamount to a decision. Wang Yu-huai suggested that in some cases the situation was so clear that they could be judged without a hearing. Sometimes it was necessary merely to examine a title deed or a genealogical chart.[35]

There was one case where a widow wished to designate an heir for her deceased son, but the clansmen of her husband argued that the son was not qualified to have an heir because he had not been married. The magistrate ruled that the matter should be discussed and decided by the clansmen. However, after eighteen years no agreement had yet been reached. Finally, Wang Hui-tsu, then a private secretary, wrote a rescript in which he decided that an heir should be designated according to the widow's will.[36] In another case involving a dispute over the designation of an heir, a man wanted to designate himself as the heir of some deceased relatives who had no son but only a married daughter. Wang decided in his rescript that a part of the property involved was to be given to the daughter, the rest of it to be reserved as a sacrificial fund for the deceased couple, and that no heir need be designated.[37]

The dates of hearings were also arranged by a private secretary. He was expected to consider such factors as the urgency of the case, the distance which the persons involved had to travel, and the estimated time needed to hear the case.[38] Before the trial, he went over the legal documents and prepared a brief summary of the case so that the magistrate would know what it was about and how to proceed.[39] A private secretary also decided who had to be summoned to attend court.[40]

It was the magistrate who presided over the court and announced the judgment. However, he would usually seek advice from his private secretaries both before and after a trial.[41] As a secretary never attended court,[42] the written deposition became his primary source of information. Besides this, the magistrate usually gave him a detailed description of the hearing. Details of an inquest or investigation were also reported to him.[43] Advice was then given by the secretary, and doubts raised by him often led to a second hearing.[44]

The fact that a private secretary did not participate in trials certainly was an obstacle to the efficient handling of legal cases, for, as Chang T'ing-hsiang, a private secretary in the nineteenth century, pointed out, it prevented him from direct observation and investigation.[45] He was not in a position to know all the details.[46] Besides, the deposition was not always reliable, for changes might purposely be introduced into the record by a clerk.[47] This impasse could not be overcome unless a secretary was willing to follow the unconventional practice of Wang Hui-tsu, who used to stand behind the courtroom to listen to the hearings in serious cases, that is, in cases involving at least a sentence of penal servitude. Whenever he felt that a deposition was doubtful, he requested the magistrate to have a second hearing, and urged him to be patient and avoid the use of torture. Sometimes a case was heard as many as eight or nine times.[48] The following case illustrates how decisive a secretary's role could be:

A man named Sheng Ta, suspected of robbery, was caught along with seven other persons. They all confessed, and an allegedly stolen quilt was recovered and claimed by the owner. Wang Hui-tsu, however, considered the case doubtful on the ground that the confessions made by the eight persons were exactly the same. A second hearing was held the next day and the magistrate examined the group one by one. This time the confessions were not at all alike, and several of the previously indicted persons even denied that they had committed the crime. Wang then mixed the allegedly stolen quilt together with other quilts, and asked the owner to identify it. The latter failed to do so. The suspects were again questioned and they all denied that they had engaged in robbery. Finally it was discovered that Sheng Ta, a runaway soldier, who thought he would die anyway, had made a false confession. The group was found not guilty and released.[49]

Private secretaries frequently made important decisions.[50] This is understandable since all judgments had to be based upon law or precedents, with which most of the officials were not familiar. If the magistrates did not follow the advice of these legal experts, they might find themselves unable to keep their posts because of a wrong decision.[51]

The more serious cases, those involving sentences of penal servitude, banishment, or death, had to be reported to the superior officials and approved by them,[52] and the preparation of a detailed report became the responsibility of a private secretary. In common practice, when a confession had been signed by a criminal all the papers relating to the case were handed to a private secretary.[53] He then prepared a report containing: the original report of the plaintiff or constable;[54] a record of inquiry made by the magistrate, and depositions made by the witnesses, suspects, or offenders;[55] a proposed statement of decision, in the form of a *k'an-yü* (lit., "statement of consideration"). The statement of decision was called *k'an-yü* because a magistrate was supposedly not in a position to pass a judgment and therefore merely suggested what he saw fit in accordance with the law and submitted it for approval.[56]

Usually the report submitted to a superior was a detailed report (*hsiang-wen*). Sometimes a brief report (*ping*) was also included. The *ping* might be submitted prior to a *hsiang-wen*, along with a *hsiang-wen*, as a substitute for a *hsiang-wen*, or after a *hsiang-wen* had been rejected. A *ping* was used either because the case was a serious one or because there were doubtful points that required a detailed explanation.[57] In preparing a report, whatever its form, a private secretary had to be able to outline the case clearly, including all the essential information gained from the inquest or investigation.[58] He had to see that there was no inconsistency between the actual incident, the deposition, and the judgment. Above all, the judgment had to be convincing and in accordance with law so that it would not be questioned and rejected by the superior official.[59]

When a proposed decision was rejected[60] by a superior official, it was the duty of a private secretary to reply to all the points raised by the superior so that the case could be closed. In this connection, it should be pointed out that it was actually the private secretaries of the superior officials who criticized and rejected or accepted reports.[61] This was only natural since local official, high or low, depended upon these legal experts to fulfill their legal duties.

Functions Relating to Taxation

When a magistrate assumed a post, it was the secretary of taxation who helped him to take over the accounts and government funds from his predecessor. It was his duty to check thoroughly The Complete Book of Taxes and Labor Services and other tax records,[62] stubs of land tax receipts, government fund delivery certificates (*p'i-hui*), cash receipts (*ling-chuang*), and records of the transfer of government funds to the new magistrate[63] in order to find out the amount of various taxes to be collected in a particular locality, the actual amount already collected, the amount unpaid by taxpayers, the amount already delivered to the superior yamen, and the amount kept in the treasury. He also had to ascertain the amount embezzled by the former official or other personnel serving in the yamen.[64] Obviously this kind of checking and auditing was fundamental during a transfer, which involved not only government funds but also the liability of a magistrate. The magistrate was liable for any embezzlement or unauthorized expenditure that he might overlook during the process of taking over government funds.[65]

Before tax collection began, the secretary of taxation went over The Complete Book of Taxes and Labor Services and other government records in order to figure out the total amount of various taxes required to be collected in the chou or hsien.[66] A record of land tax (*shih-cheng ts'e*) was then prepared by the clerks of revenue, under the supervision and examination of the secretary,[67] for each family, *chia* (unit of ten households), and *li* or *t'u* (unit of 110 households).[68] Usually two copies were prepared and submitted to the secretary. One copy was kept by the latter, and the other was given back to the clerks during the collection period, so that the amount collected from taxpayers could be listed under their names. These figures were later inserted in the secretary's copy.[69]

The most important task assigned to a secretary of taxation was to check the amounts paid and owed by taxpayers. Those who failed to pay within a specified time were called to appear for a "deadline hearing and flogging" (*pi tse*), a practice which was generally held to be necessary in tax collection.[70] Since this checking was tedious work, a secretary in charge of enforcement of tax collection was sometimes employed to assist the secretary of taxation.[71]

We have mentioned that the deadline-hearing record, which provided the basis for checking tax payments and conducting deadline hearings and floggings, was prepared by the clerks. But it was the private secretaries who went over these deadline-hearing records, the deadline-hearing certificates (*pi-chao*), and/or the canceling certificates (*hsiao-chao*) and other records[72] in order to extract the names of taxpayers who had failed to pay taxes within the deadline and to cancel the record of overdue taxes after they had been paid—a procedure known as *nei-chai nei-hsiao* (lit., "to pick out and to cancel in the inner [office]").[73] The names extracted were then identified with a stamp reading "first selection," "second selection," or "third selection."[74] A private secretary was empowered to issue bamboo tallies to summon and flog the *t'u-ch'ai* or *li-ch'ai* (the runners sent to rural zones to expedite tax payments),[75] and the delinquent taxpayers.[76] The usual practice was to punish the runners first; the taxpayers were summoned after the runners had been flogged, if their taxes were still unpaid.[77]

Many officials and secretaries maintained that the kind of authority exercised by the secretaries of taxation in the procedure described above should be invested only in a private secretary.[78] A clerk with this authority would be prone to procrastination, embezzlement, and all kinds of corruption. A clerk might try to exempt a taxpayer from appearing at the hearings by falsely reporting that he had paid the tax, crossing out or covering his name on the deadline-hearing record, or not calling his name during a hearing.[79] The clerks also would have a tendency to pick out the small taxpayers instead of the large taxpayers.[80]

Even as it was, some private secretaries experienced difficulty in compiling the lists because the clerks did not submit the record of land tax to them until the beginning or the middle of the tax collection period, with the result that the secretary was unable to check and compute the record.[81] Nonetheless, effective supervision of clerks still depended on the efficiency of secretaries.[82] Ch'en Hung-mou reported that since there were not always enough secretaries to supervise tax collection, and since some of them were either inexperienced or found the work too tedious, they sometimes merely went over the records roughly and ordered clerks to prepare the list of taxpayers to be called for hearings. This gave the clerks an opportunity to omit some names or change the amount owed by a taxpayer. This situation was aggravated by the fact that some short-sighted magistrates, in an effort to keep salaries at a minimum, employed inexperienced secretaries who were not capable of checking the corruption of the clerks.[83]

Private secretaries also supervised the issuing of land tax receipts. They counted the receipts contained in each book before they were stamped and given to each of the silver-chest clerks, so that the latter would be prevented from obtaining duplicate receipts.[84] When a book of one hundred receipts had been used up, the stubs were returned to the secretary before a new book could be issued.[85] The clerk in charge of the silver chest was required to report daily the amount collected from taxpayers. Further, the cash on hand and the receipt stubs were presented every evening to the secretary who examined them to see that the two corresponded. He also kept a daily record of the total amount deposited in the various silver chests.[86]

A secretary of taxation also examined and kept a record of all other kinds of taxes collected by the government,[87] in addition to the land tax.

Finally, the expenditure and the delivery of government funds came under his supervision. He was expected to check The Complete Book of Taxes and Labor Services to find out the items and amounts of authorized disbursement and have necessary funds delivered to the various superior yamen. He also assigned priorities to the various funds to be thus delivered. He went over all cash receipts and certificates of delivery[88] and kept a record of all funds expended or delivered.[89]

Functions Relating to Accounts

The duty of the *chang-fang,* the bookkeeper, who also served as the cashier, differed from that of a secretary of taxation, who was concerned with auditing but not with the actual money received and expended.[90] The *chang-fang* was concerned with miscellaneous incomes and disbursements,[91] such as gifts for the various superior officials on their birthdays, at each new year, and on other occasions; fees paid to gate porters of a superior yamen; and various expenses for entertaining visiting officials.[92] Since a *chang-fang* handled funds, this post was usually entrusted to a magistrate's confidant.[93] Sometimes it was occupied by a relative of the magistrate,[94] a practice that was considered inadvisable by some officials.[95]

Functions Relating to Registration

The secretary of registration registered all incoming and outgoing documents, official notices, and warrants. In this way he could see at a glance what action was required in connection with each of the documents, and whether action was being taken on time according to priority, without delay on the part of clerks and runners. For this reason, the *Ch'in-pan chou-hsien shih-i* emphasized that registration, which was frequently considered unimportant by many officials, was actually an important task.[96] In the experience of Wang Hui-tsu, the process of registration served as a stimulus also to the secretaries of law and taxation who frequently did not attend to their duties promptly.[97]

Preparation of Documents

Documents were prepared both by secretaries of law and secretaries of taxation, depending upon their nature. As a rule, a draft was prepared by a clerk and revised by a secretary.[98] Since the clerks were limited in their ability to prepare drafts, and documents prepared by them alone might not be acceptable to a superior, an efficient secretary sometimes first outlined the essential points for the clerk.[99] In complicated cases requiring experienced judgment and greater skill, the secretary often drafted the document himself.[100]

The secretary of red and black brushes[101] was entrusted with the duty of copying in black the rescripts and other drafts written by a secretary of law or taxation.[102] He used red brushes to write the key words appearing on official notices, warrants, and other documents, and to add red signs and flourishes on documents (*piao-p'an*).[103]

Functions Relating to Correspondence

The secretary of correspondence drafted letters and presented them to the magistrate for approval. The approved draft was then copied either by a secretary or by a correspondence attendant.[104]

Functions Relating to Examination Papers

It was a magistrate's duty to give preliminary examinations[105] to those who wanted to take the formal civil service examination given by the Provincial Director of Studies, and those of his secretaries who had sufficient literary training were expected to help him to read the examination papers.[106]

In summary, the private secretaries constituted a "brain trust" who helped the magistrate to operate the government machinery. They gave technical advice on legal, financial, and other administrative matters.[107] They also assumed responsibility for certain aspects of high-level administrative routine. In point of fact, the two most important aspects of local administration—justice and taxation—were in the hands of the private secretaries, and these were the very aspects in connection with which a magistrate's accomplishment (k'ao-ch'eng) was judged by his superiors.[108]

Of course the contribution and the influence of a secretary depended upon the experience and efficiency of his magistrate. It may be assumed that the less experienced an official was, the more he relied upon his secretaries. Thus, an official who was entering officialdom for the first time or who had purchased his post frequently left all administrative matters to his private secretaries.[109] An experienced and efficient magistrate, on the other hand, tended to play a more active part in administration. Wang Hui-tsu, a magistrate with thirty-four years of experience as a private secretary, maintained that an official should not rely entirely upon his private secretaries, but should attend to his duties himself. He argued that a magistrate who was unfamilar with administrative matters would be unable to judge whether a secretary was competent; furthermore, there were occasions when an official had to take action immediately without the advice of a secretary.[110] Huang Liu-hung advised officials to attend to all matters, big or small, when they had time to do so.[111] There were capable officials who preferred to write the rescripts themselves whenever possible.[112]

Although it was generally believed that an official should consult his private secretaries on all official matters[113] and not be obstinate about accepting a secretary's advice if it was reasonable,[114] many capable magistrates insisted that an official should make the final decisions, so that he could retain his authority and prevent abuses.[115] Many magistrates also advised that an official should judge all cases on the evidence and not be unduly influenced by the rescripts prepared by his private secretary. When there was disagreement between the official and his secretary, the former should use his own judgment.[116] However, there were secretaries who insisted that their rescripts could not be changed or that cases had to be judged according to their suggestions, and who would resign rather than give in.[117]

In addition to serving as administrative experts, the private secretaries performed another important function: they supervised the clerks, runners, and personal servants. Chang T'ing-hsiang recommended that a private secretary should see whether the gate porters, clerks, or runners were engaged in corruption or were attempting to deceive the officials. He believed that although a secretary stayed in the inner office he should be able to detect what was happening by checking the documents.[118] The matter of supervision of clerks was emphasized by Wang Hui-tsu in the following statement:

There are clerks serving in the six offices in a yamen. Legal matters are in the charge of the clerk of law, and taxation is in the charge of the clerk of taxation. There is no lack of experienced personnel. Yet the reason [an official] relies upon his private secretaries is that the duties of a private secretary consist of assisting the official and supervising the clerks. A proverb says, "an incorrupt official cannot escape a wicked clerk." While an official has clerks under his command, all the clerks use their energy in looking for an opportunity when the official is not on the alert. As an official attends to numerous matters of business, it is impossible for him to supervise each of them. Every private secretary, on the other hand, has his special duty and is able to check the corruption of clerks.[119]

One of the methods Wang employed to prevent clerks from making changes in a title deed or a contract submitted for investigation was to stamp the back of the document where the key words appeared.[120] He also would not allow a clerk to send any extra runner on a mission when one runner had already been assigned.[121] He also advised that a private secretary should see that a suspect or witness was not unwillingly detained by runners.[122]

This sort of supervision, which ran counter to the personal interests of the clerks, runners, and servants in a yamen, frequently led to conflict between them and the secretaries. As an example: one private secretary succeeded in preventing certain clerks from falsely accusing people of gambling in an attempt to extort money from them. The clerks then conspired with a gate porter who went to the magistrate and falsely charged the secretary with receiving a bribe from the gamblers.[123]

3. Status and Recruitment

Private secretaries were recruited mainly from among the intelligentsia. Some were former clerks who were versed in administrative affairs.[124] Some were former officials who had experienced a decisive failure in their official careers.[125] A number of them were students who had failed to pass the civil service examinations.[126] But most of the private secretaries were holders of the first degree. Since holders of such a degree were not yet qualified for official appointment, they had to have some means of support while preparing to take a higher examination. They became teachers or private secretaries or engaged in other occupations; and some teachers gave up teaching to become secretaries[127] because secretaries had a better income.[128] Many secretaries regarded their posts as temporary ones which they would leave as soon as they succeeded in passing a higher examination. Thus they took leave at regular intervals to participate in the civil service examinations. If they did not pass they either returned to their original post or took a similar post in a different yamen.[129]

A holder of the second degree, *chü-jen,* was qualified for official appointment. However, some secretaries who had their *chü-jen* degrees remained private secretaries either because there was no official post available or because they preferred not to start their official career until they had passed the highest examination. Wang Hui-tsu remained a private secretary for seven years after he became a *chü-jen,* and while he was a secretary he took the metropolitan examination four times.[130] It was unlikely that a holder of the third degree, *chin-shih,* would be willing to be a private secretary in a local government (except for personal reasons), for he was in a very favorable position to enter officialdom and could be appointed as a magistrate.[131] Of course, many private secretaries turned out to be secretaries for life because they were unable to pass a higher examination.

Private secretaries enjoyed a superior social status, partly because of the prestige of the position itself, and partly because of their scholarly status. The scholar had a status superior to that of a nonscholar commoner, for his training, which qualified him for the civil service examinations, was most esteemed by society. A degree holder commanded still more respect because he was a potential candidate for membership in the bureaucracy, and he was given a number of legal privileges.[132] As a private secretary might be a holder of a lower or higher degree, it may be assumed that his status varied, depending upon his degree.

Private secretaries were not government officials; nevertheless, they were considered the equals of the officials.[133] The term *mu-yu* or *mu-pin* itself suggests that a secretary was the "friend" or "guest" of the host, the official.[134] When a secretary was given a letter of appointment, it was written on a full-sized red card on which he was addressed as *lao-fu-tze* ("old master"; a conventional title of respect for a teacher), and his *tzu* (style) instead of his name was mentioned. The magistrate referred to himself as *chiao-ti,* "younger brother under instruction." The secretary addressed the magistrate as *tung-weng* (Mr. Host) or *lao-tung* (old host).[135] He referred to himself formally, in writing, as *wan-sheng* (born-late),[136] and informally as *hsiung-ti* (younger brother).[137]

Private secretaries were treated with respect and politeness by magistrates.[138] They were served with good food,[139] and the magistrate visited them and entertained them with wine and feasting on New Year and other festivals.[140] At a banquet, when there were no outside guests, they were given the seats of honor. The secretary of law, whose status was superior to that of other secretaries, usually occupied the first seat except when there was a private tutor. The secretary of taxation sat next to the secretary of law.[141] Lack of courtesy on the part of a magistrate was considered intolerable by private secretaries and constituted grounds for resignation.[142] The secretaries' self-respect was generally reflected in the concept of *pu-ho tse-ch'ü* (leaving when not in accord [with the magistrate]). They might resign when no compromise was possible between their viewpoints and those of the official, or when the official showed lack of trust in them.[143] Wang Hui-tsu once resigned beacuse his advice was not accepted by an official; he returned only when the magistrate sent a relative to apologize for him and asked Wang to come back.[144] Thus we see that of all the aides in a yamen the private secretaries were the only group who enjoyed a superior status and were treated as equals by the officials. The clerks, the runners, and the personal servants, in contrast, were looked down upon and treated as inferiors by the officials.

We have stressed the point that a private secretary was an expert in administration. This meant that in order to qualify as a secretary, a man with a general education in classics and literature had to undergo specialized training, usually under the private tutorship of a professional secretary.[145] The most important part of the training was in law or in taxation. To become a legal expert, a knowledge of law and the handling of legal cases was fundamental.[146] Another basic requirement was the ability to write official documents clearly and properly.[147] Finally, in addition to professional competence, the necessity for personal integrity was stressed.[148]

Since secretaries of law and taxation were concerned with the most important function of local administration, an expectant official frequently looked for such competent persons when he was still waiting for his appointment or immediately after he had received an appointment but prior to his taking office.[149] Recommendations for private secretaries often came to an official from a relative, a friend, or a colleague.[150] There was a law that prohibited a superior official from recommending a secretary to his subordinate.[151] However, a subordinate official usually found it difficult to refuse such a recommendation.[152] Wang Hui-tsu advised that in a case like this it was better to accept the secretary, treat him nicely, but not trust him with any important duty.[153] The private secretaries of a superior official also had a tendency to recommend their students and friends to a newly appointed magistrate.[154] Some magistrates preferred to accept such recommendations in the hope that a connection thus established with the superior yamen might prevent the rejection of documents submitted to it.[155] Sometimes a magistrate simply retained one of his predecessor's secretaries.[156] Secretaries of lesser importance, like the secretary of registration or the secretary of correspondence, were frequently recommended to the magistrate by his secretary of law or of taxation.[157]

Usually an informal interview was held between the magistrate and a secretarial candidate. Huang Liu-hung tested his candidates by asking them to draft a letter or an official order.[158] When a candidate proved competent, a formal letter of appointment, which mentioned the stipulated salary, was then given to him.[159]

Since the reason for having a private secretary was to get expert technical assistance, the primary criterion in hiring him was his record of achievement, and the magistrate's fundamental concern was with the secretary's competence in performing his duties. Contrary to expectation, nepotism did not enter into the picture significantly. Although it was common practice for the family members and relatives of a magistrate to accompany him to his yamen and to receive special favors, there was a strong tendency on the part of magistrates not to employ relatives as private secretaries because they were not experts. Wang Hui-tsu pointed out that supervising the granary and treasury were the only jobs that could be assigned to a relative, and that all administrative affairs should be handled only by private secretaries.[160] There were cases where relatives of officials were assigned to posts requiring little in the way of technical qualification, such as the post of bookkeeper[161] or secretary of correspondence.[162] However, even this was not encouraged because, as Wang Hui-tsu pointed out, relatives thus employed might take advantage of their connection with the magistrate and engage in corruption, and an official usually found it difficult to punish them. A private secretary who had no kinship with an official, on the other hand, could be dismissed or even punished without personal complications.[163] Thus Wang suggested that the magistrate's best solution was to support his relatives financially but not to entrust them with official duties.[164] This obviously was a compromise which took into consideration personal relations—or in sociological terms, "particularism" [165]—without permitting them to interfere with the application of the achievement criterion. Apparently the magistrates realized that they could not afford to risk their own careers by employing incompetent secretaries as their advisers.

Since the private secretary was hired and paid by the official, the government did not interfere in the matter of the appointment. The law only required the official to report to the Board of Civil Office the names and career statements of his secretaries.[166] A regulation promulgated in 1723 prohibited an official from employing as his private secretary a native of the province in which he held office. A similar regulation, announced in an edict of 1772, also decreed that a private secretary could not serve in a neighboring province within 500 li of his native town.[167] There was also a regulation prohibiting the employment of a secretary whose family lived in the same province or locality.[168] However, none of the regulations concerning the employment of a native secretary seems to have been strictly enforced. Wang Hui-tsu, a native of Shao-hsing prefecture, a place well known for producing private secretaries,[169] reported that when he was about to resign in 1773, in response to the regulation of 1772, the governor of Chekiang ordered that a prefect or magistrate could ask to keep native secretaries temporarily if their services were needed. Wang was kept in Hai-ning yamen for more than a year, until the magistrate was dismissed.[170]

An imperial edict of 1776 stated that the emperor had thought it reasonable to prohibit the employment of native residents or natives of a neighboring place as secretaries, and had accordingly ordered the provincial authorities to submit yearly reports on their secretaries. However, the edict revealed, no such reports had ever been made. The emperor concluded that his request for annual reports was ineffectual and ordered it discontinued.[171] Although the edict did not mention the abolition of the 1772 regulation, it was in effect an announcement that the old regulation could be discarded. It is interesting to note that from 1775 to 1785, thirteen years after the promulgation of the regulation, Wang continued to serve as a private secretary in Chekiang, his native province.[172] A censor in the nineteenth century reported that about half of the secretaries serving in Kwangtung were natives of the province.[173]

4. TERM OF SERVICE

A private secretary's appointment was based upon a personal contract which normally contained no clause on tenure.[174] The magistrate had complete freedom to annul the contract any time he was dissatisfied with the secretary's work.[175] The secretary was obliged to resign if he failed to render satisfactory service or if he committed an error that affected the career of the official.[176] He was also free to resign if the terms of employment were not acceptable to him.[177] On the other hand, a secretary might be kept in office for as long as the official found his work satisfactory. There were cases where a secretary served under the same official for more than ten years.[178] It was not unusual for an official to keep the same secretary as long as he himself remained in the same post. He might even take his secretary with him when he was transferred to a new post.[179]

It was ruled in 1723 that a private secretary employed by a governor-general or a governor could be recommended by his employer for official appointment. Under a 1736 regulation, a secretary serving in a yamen of lower officials, from provincial judge or provincial treasurer down to magistrate, was also qualified for such recommendation after he had served continuously for six years. However, this privilege was limited to a secretary of law or taxation.[180] A secretary thus recommended by a local official to the governor-general or governor was given an examination by the latter. The examination papers were then presented to and reviewed by the Board of Civil Office. Those who passed the examination were given an official title, or if they already possessed a title, were given priority of appointment to office. Those who were too old for appointment were given the honor of wearing an official hat button of an appropriate rank.[181]

The local official who made the recommendation was held responsible and was subject to demotion if the secretary proved poor in writing, or incompetent in law, or if he was found guilty of corruption and dismissed after he had been appointed to office.[182]

However, the chances of a private secretary's entering upon an official career through this sort of recommendation were very slight. Wu Ying-fen, the Vice-Minister of War, pointed out in 1736 that although one or two secretaries had been recommended by a governor-general or governor in accordance with the edict issued by the Yung-cheng emperor, the practice was not in wide use and was gradually disappearing.[183] Thus most private secretaries remained secretaries for life, unless they could pass the civil service examinations or purchase official titles.

5. FINANCIAL MAINTENANCE

A private secretary was paid by the magistrate, who also provided his board. Remuneration varied according to the secretary's ability, his responsibilities, and the income of the magistrate. The annual salary of a secretary of correspondence and registration in the 1750's ranged from about 40 or 50 taels to about 100.[184] The salary of a secretary of law or taxation was two to five times more, and a secretary of law was the best paid of all, because his knowledge was more technical and necessitated more training. Thus in the 1750's a secretary of law could have a yearly salary of 260 taels, while a secretary of taxation could have 220.[185] Their pay was increased considerably in the last years of the dynasty. Wang reported that it gradually increased after the 1760's, and during the 1780's was as high as 800 taels.[186] In the nineteenth century there was again a tremendous increase. Chang P'eng-chan, a censor, reported in 1800 that the salary of a secretary in P'an-yü and Nan-hai hsien, Kwangtung, varied from 1500 to 1900 taels.[187] According to Yang Hsiang-chi (1825–1878), a secretary of law or taxation got a salary as high as 2000 taels, almost equivalent to the salary of a magistrate.[188] Some magistrates advised officials not to be stingy when hiring a private secretary, so that they might secure the services of a competent person.[189]

A comparison of the incomes of secretaries and those of runners and servants, who received merely nominal wages, makes it obvious that the secretaries were the only group of aides in the yamen who received a salary sufficient to maintain themselves and their families. They were also the only group that did not have a share in the customary fees that were a main source of income for other yamen employees.[190] According to Wang Hui-tsu, even a secretary of correspondence and registration could have an income sufficient to maintain a family of eight.[191] A secretary of law or taxation was usually able to put aside some savings. Ch'en Pi-ning pointed out that the financial position of a secretary was more favorable than that of a magistrate, because an official was obliged to contribute money to the common fund (for administrative expenses) of his prefecture or province and to make up any deficiency in government funds under his care.[192] Thus many officials suffered losses, while many secretaries could accumulate savings.[193] Wang Hui-tsu's case is an example. After serving as a private secretary for thirty-four years (as a secretary of law for twenty-six years), he was able to save enough money to buy seventy *mou* of land. He admitted that he could not afford to buy any more land after four years as a magistrate (although he did buy a house in the hsien seat, which presumably cost less than seventy *mou* of land).[194] But Wang was an honest man who, before taking a post as secretary, swore before his mother that he would not accept any money that it was improper for him to receive.[195] Obviously a secretary who was less honest could have had more income. A certain secretary in a governor's yamen was accused by a censor of amassing more than 100,000 taels of silver.[196]

6. Supervision

Private secretaries were frequently accused of forming cliques with secretaries of other yamen in the same province in order to consolidate their position and enhance their prestige and influence. (Secretaries who came from other provinces and had no connection with them met with hostility and found it difficult to keep their posts.)[197] A censor reported a case in Kwangtung where the governor's secretary had relatives and disciples serving as secretaries in other prefectures and hsien.[198] Many secretaries also had personal ties with the secretaries of a superior yamen.[199] We have mentioned that some of the secretaries in a magistrate's yamen had been recommended by their teachers or friends who were secretaries in a superior yamen. These people frequently allied with one another for personal gain.[200] Secretaries in a lower-level yamen frequently took advantage of this kind of connection in dealing with the magistrate. A censor reported that a secretary with connections in a higher yamen was very overbearing and if his magistrate failed to meet his demands he would seek to create dissension between the magistrate and the superior official, or cooperate with the latter's secretary so that any legal case presented by the magistrate would be rejected.[201]

Although most private secretaries were respected as men of integrity, some of them did not live up to this expectation[202] and were accused of accepting bribes[203] and engaging in corruption.[204] There were corrupt secretaries who cooperated with gate porters or other yamen personnel.[205] There were also secretaries who cooperated with magistrates in an effort to render false accounts during the time of transferring government funds and accounts to a new magistrate.[206]

In order to isolate private secretaries the emperors from time to time issued edicts ordering the local officials to prevent their secretaries from too freely leaving the yamen to associate and make connections with outsiders.[207] Some capable officials also tried to prevent their secretaries from communicating with other personnal in the yamen. In order to forestall cooperation in malpractice, the gate porter, the clerks, and the magistrate's subordinate officials were prohibited from seeing the secretaries.[208] A cautious secretary would avoid suspicion by giving the magistrate the names of people who came to visit him and those whom he visited.[209] Chang T'ing-hsiang mentioned that in order to avoid possible suspicion he never communicated with any member of the local gentry.[210]

As a private secretary was under the direct supervision of the magistrate, the latter was held responsible by law if his secretary communicated with people outside the yamen to engage in swindling.[211] At the same time, the law put the responsibility of supervising the magistrate's private secretaries on the provincial treasurer and provincial judge. If these two officials failed to investigate any abuse or malpractice on the part of a magistrate's secretary for which the magistrate was subsequently indicted by the governor or governor-general, they were subject to demotion varying from one to three grades. A governor or governor-general who failed to indict the magistrate in such a case was in turn subject to demotion of one grade.[212]

It may also be noted that although private secretaries played an extremely important role in local administration, they were not held accountable for wrong decisions or maladministration. In the first place, they were not formally employed by the government. Furthermore, they served mainly in the capacity of advisers, and it was for the magistrate to make final decisions. Therefore he alone was responsible for the administration.

One situation in which a private secretary shared liability with his magistrate was when the magistrate was punished for engaging in a corrupt action that had been instigated by the secretary.[213] The secretary was also punishable for inspiring the magistrate to engage in improper activities for which he incurred punishment. The penalty for the secretary was either the same as, or one degree more severe than, that of the magistrate, depending upon the severity of the magistrate's punishment.[214]

Under the circumstances prevailing in the Ch'ing, the training and employing of a group of administrative experts in a yamen did serve a practical purpose—it made it possible for the inexperienced magistrates to run the government more or less effectively, under certain limitation. Obviously despite the fact that the private secretaries discharged their duties in accordance with objective rules, their attitudes and behavior were conditioned to a considerable extent by personal factors. Owing to the emphasis on the personal relationship between the magistrates and their private secretaries which characterized the *mu-yu* system, the secretaries were often more concerned with their employers' *k'ao-ch'eng* and careers than with the administration. As a result their first consideration was adherence to government regulations and precedents so that the magistrates could avoid punishment.[215]

The Ch'ing government, which apparently was aware of the personal tie, insisted upon treating the private secretaries as personal aides of the magistrates, not as government employees. Thus the secretaries were not subject to disciplinary actions applicable to other yamen personnel nor were they rewarded with promotion in office.[216] As the government did not carry out its plan to recommend private secretaries for official appointment and thus left them with no channels for promotion, it failed to recruit officials from the experienced administrative experts. The experts and the officials remained two distinct groups throughout the dynasty, with no possibility of interchange.

ADMINISTRATION OF JUSTICE

In the previous chapters we have discussed the position and role of the magistrate and his four groups of aides in local government. We shall now proceed to deal with the various aspects of local administration, beginning with the administration of justice, which was one of the most important functions of the chou and hsien government.

The chou and hsien yamen were the lowest tribunals in the empire. People could appeal to a higher yamen only if a magistrate had refused to receive their complaints and if his decision in the case was felt to be unjust. To appeal to the higher yamen without first going to the chou or hsien authorities was against the law, and a violation of this law was punishable with fifty strokes.[1]

The magistrate heard all cases in his area, civil as well as criminal. But he was more than a judge. He not only conducted hearings and made decisions; he also conducted investigations and inquests, and detected criminals. In terms of modern concepts his duties combined those of judge, prosecutor, police chief, and coroner. They comprised everything relating to the administration of justice in its broadest sense, and failure to carry out any of these duties incurred disciplinary actions and punishments, as defined in the many laws and regulations. In this chapter we shall mention only the most important of these laws and regulations in order to outline what a magistrate was expected to do in connection with the administration of justice. We shall also see how justice was actually administered by a magistrate, with the help of his legal adviser.

1. Judicial Power of the Magistrate

As the judge of the lowest tribunal, a magistrate was only authorized to pronounce sentences in civil and minor criminal cases where punishment was no more severe than beating or imposing the cangue; such cases were usually referred to as *tzu-li tz'u-sung* (lawsuits under a magistrate's own jurisdiction).[2] His judgments did not have to be approved by a superior, but he had to report monthly to his superior the number of complaints he had accepted, the number of cases that had been closed and how they were closed, and the number of cases that had not yet been closed.[3] In this way the superior official was kept informed on the magistrate's handling of lawsuits. The court records were then checked personally by the inspecting intendant whenever he arrived at a chou or hsien on an inspection tour, to see whether cases had been closed without delay, and whether all cases had been listed in the record.[4] If he found any evidence of injustice, he was authorized to review the documents relating to the particular case and reverse or alter the sentence as he saw fit.[5] A party involved in a civil case could appeal to a higher yamen, which had the authority to review the case and to conduct a retrial.[6]

Serious cases which called for penal servitude had to be reported to the magistrate's superior officials and his recommended sentences were subject to their approval. After he had tried such a case, the magistrate was required to deliver the criminals to the prefect, or to the subprefect of an independent subprefecture, or to an independent chou magistrate for retrial—a procedure known as *shen-ch'uan* (lit., "to retry and pass on"). When a case had been retried and approved by the higher official, it was in turn referred to a still higher authority. Finally, all cases involving a sentence of penal servitude were reported collectively every season to the Board of Punishment by the governor and governor-general.[7] Cases involving a sentence of exile, banishment, or penal servitude when it was a penalty for homicide were retried by the provincial judge,[8] and each case was reported individually to the board by the governor and governor-general.[9]

All cases involving death sentences had to be retried by the governor-general and governor. Where the sentence was immediate execution, they tried the case together with the provincial judge and the intendants, and then reported the case to the board. If the sentence was detention for execution, the case was retried by all these provincial authorities during the time of the "autumn assize" (*ch'iu-shen*) and reported to the board before the specified deadline.[10]

Thus a magistrate was under the supervision of the various provincial authorities in the administration of justice, particularly in cases involving penalties more severe than beating. Each of the superior officials empowered to review and retry cases served as judge of a higher court. The superior official could order the magistrate, or a different official assigned by him, to rehear the case if the judgment was found doubtful or if the confessed criminal retracted his original testimony during a retrial. When an appeal was made to the superior officials the case had to be retried, either by themselves or by a commissioner.[11]

The final approval of a sentence more serious than beating came from the Board of Punishment, which reviewed all the cases reported by the highest provincial authority. A sentence which had been approved by the provincial authorities but rejected by the board still had to be retried by an official assigned by the governor-general, and the necessary adjustment had to be made in accordance with the instructions of the board.[12]

2. CIVIL CASES

Six or nine[13] days of each month were reserved for the acceptance of civil complaints, except during the "busy season for farmers," that is, from the first day of the fourth month to the thirtieth day of the seventh month. (During this period cases involving disputes over family matters, marriage, landed property, and various minor matters were not heard.[14]) The magistrate was required to preside in court in person on the specified days to receive complaints from the people. His first step was to determine by means of interrogation whether a complaint should be rejected or accepted.[15] An official rescript (*p'i*) was then written at the end of the statement of complaint either endorsing it or giving the reasons for its rejection.

The practice in writing official rescripts varied from person to person. Some capable and efficient magistrates were known to have written the rescript themselves, either upon receipt of the complaint and in the presence of the plaintiff, or after discussing the cases with their private secretaries.[16] Some magistrates, although they themselves did not write the rescripts, preferred to discuss the cases with their secretaries and assert their own opinion.[17] Most magistrates, however, were not familiar with the law and were incompetent to prepare rescripts, and they asked their secretaries to do so.[18] Fang Ta-chih advised only experienced magistrates to try to write a rescript in the court, for one that was written by an inexperienced official might be unconvincing and even absurd.[19]

The law required that a civil case under the jurisdiction of a magistrate be closed within twenty days.[20] However, there were frequent complaints that many magistrates paid little attention to deadlines because there was no penalty for procrastination.[21]

3. CRIMINAL CASES

Criminal cases, including homicide, robbery, theft, adultery, and kidnapping, could be reported to a magistrate at any time, not only on the days reserved for civil complaints.[22] One magistrate allowed the people to beat the gong in his yamen to signal their request for a hearing.[23]

Homicide

As determination of the nature of a fatal injury was crucial in judging any case in which a death was involved, conducting inquests became one of a magistrate's important duties. The law required that a magistrate personally conduct an inquest at the spot where the victim had been killed or where the body had been found. A magistrate who failed to conduct an inquest promptly was subject to demotion of one grade and transfer to another post.[24] He was to be sentenced to sixty strokes if the delay caused any change in the condition of the corpse.[25] If the magistrate was absent on an official mission when the crime was reported, the magistrate of a neighboring district was to conduct the inquest for him.[26] An assistant magistrate could be assigned this task only if the neighboring magistrate was at a great distance or if he too was absent on an official mission.[27]

Nearly all the magistrates' handbooks recommended that an inquest be conducted as soon as possible in order to avoid further complications and possible changes in the corpse, especially in warm weather.[28] However, the customary procedure was first to send yamen runners to set up a mat shed and make the preparations necessary for the inquest.[29] The magistrate, sitting in a sedan chair and accompanied by a number of runners and clerks and a coroner, arrived later. Although the magistrate's entourage on such a mission was legally limited to one coroner, one clerk, and two runners,[30] it frequently swelled to sixty or seventy or even to a hundred escorts.[31] Two magistrates, Liu Heng and Fang Ta-chih, were notable exceptions in that they actually observed the regulation.[32]

The problem of the lack of legal training among the local officials was particularly serious when it came to handling homicide cases. The conducting of an inquest required a highly specialized technique and a body of practical knowledge which were entirely unfamiliar to scholars trained in literature and the classics. In view of this, an inexperienced magistrate was not expected to identify an injury correctly.[33]

Of course there were professional coroners under the magistrate's command; but it must be kept in mind that they were not medical experts but merely yamen runners assigned to examine injuries.[34] As the reader may recall from Chapter IV, these runners had a very low status and received hardly any pay. They were unlikely to be either intelligent or skilled, and they frequently took bribes.[35] The magistrates, therefore, could not rely on them and had to supervise their work closely. Recognizing this fact, the government ruled that a magistrate who allowed a coroner to make a report that was incomplete, incorrect, or false was to be punished by forfeiture of one year's nominal salary, or demotion of one to two grades.[36] In such cases, both the magistrate and the coroner were also subject to corporal punishment.[37] Therefore most magistrates found it necessary to check all the findings reported by the coroner before filling out the inquest form.[38]

As to practical details in conducting an inquest, some experienced officials warned magistrates not to avoid the unpleasant odor of a corpse, but to examine it with their own hands. They should also match the alleged weapon with the injury in order to make sure that the coroner's report was correct.[39] However, it was reported that many magistrates tried to avoid touching the body, sat at a great distance, and left the examination entirely to the coroner. They merely wrote down on the form what had been announced by the latter,[40] and then asked the coroner to sign a statement to the effect that there was no omission or false statement.[41]

In order to equip himself to supervise coroners, a magistrate could study Hsi-yüan lu (Instructions to coroners), which gave the methods for determining the cause of death.[42] Since this was the only authoritative guidebook,[43] a magistrate was on safe ground as long as he followed it closely.

After he had conducted an inquest the magistrate was required to submit a detailed report to his superior at once. Delay in making such a report was punishable.[44] If a family member of the deceased objected to the outcome of the inquest and appealed to a superior yamen, the magistrate might be ordered to conduct a second inquest. However, it was not permissible to conduct three inquests in the same case.[45] In certain cases where the cause of death could not be ascertained by examining the corpse, the bones were steamed and examined in accordance with a procedure given in *Hsi-yüan lu*.[46]

After an inquest had been held it was the duty of the magistrate to detect and apprehend the person responsible for the homicide within the prescribed time limit. Failure to apprehend the criminal by the imposed deadline led to impeachment and punishment as follows.

First deadline (six months)—suspension without pay
Second deadline (one year)—forfeiture of one year's nominal salary
Third deadline (one year)—forfeiture of two years' nominal salary
Fourth deadline (one year)—demotion of one grade and retention in the same post

There were only three deadlines for the apprehension of a criminal involved in a homicide which was considered more serious (such as the killing of a senior relative by a junior, or a husband by his wife or concubine, or of a master by his slave, or the killing of three or four persons in a single case). Failure to meet these deadlines subjected a magistrate to the following punishments.

First deadline (six months)—suspension without pay
Second deadline (one year)—demotion of one grade and retention in the same post
Third deadline (one year)—demotion of one grade and transfer to another post

When a magistrate had left his post, the apprehension of the killer then became the responsibility of his successor, who was given another year to carry out the assignment. If he failed he forfeited one year's nominal salary.[47]

The law required that a person convicted of homicide by a magistrate be delivered to the superior yamen, where he was tried again. The total time limit for the closing of an ordinary homicide case by the magistrate and his superior officials was six months. But the magistrate was required to finish his trial within three months of apprehending the criminal, after which the case was referred to the superior yamen. Cases with a total time limit of four months (involving a sentence of immediate execution) were to be tried and referred to the superior yamen by the magistrate within two months. Cases with a total limit of two months (the more serious cases mentioned above) had to be tried and referred to the superior yamen within one month.[48] If a magistrate failed to complete a trial by the specified time he was subject to impeachment. After a six-month or a four-month deadline, the officials were automatically given an extension of four months for closing the case, and the magistrate was required to complete his trial within two months. For a case with an original time limit of two months, an extension of another month was given, and the magistrate was obliged to complete his trial within twenty days. Failure to complete the trial at the end of the extended deadline was punishable by a second impeachment and dismissal.[49]

Robbery and Theft

The apprehension of thieves and robbers was the duty of a magistrate. If the stolen goods in a case of theft had a value of more than 100 taels, he was required to close the case within six months. If he failed to meet the first deadline, the magistrate was subject to forfeiture of six months' or one year's nominal salary, depending upon the value of the goods stolen. If the case was still not solved after a one-year extension, the penalty was forfeiture of one or two years' nominal salary.[50]

When a robbery was reported to the magistrate, it was his duty to make an immediate on-the-spot investigation together with the military officials stationed in the chou or hsien. Failure to make an investigation in person was punishable by dismissal.[51] Delay also carried a penalty.[52] An assistant magistrate could make an investigation on behalf of the magistrate only when the latter was absent on an official mission, but the law insisted that a second investigation be made by the magistrate of a neighboring district.[53] The magistrate was required to submit a report to his superior without delay after the investigation.[54]

A four-month time limit was set for the detection and apprehension of robbers. A magistrate who was able to apprehend all robbers wanted in a case within this period was rewarded with two recordings of merit.[55] A new magistrate who, within a year of taking office, apprehended robbers whom his predecessor had failed to apprehend could win an advancement in grade or a recording of merit.[56] A magistrate who caught a robber wanted for grand larceny was rewarded by a recommendation from the governor-general and governor to the Board of Civil Office for an audience with the throne.[57]

On the other hand, a magistrate was subject to impeachment for neglecting to take precautions (*su-fang*) if he failed to apprehend the robbers by the end of four months (first deadline). A distinction was made between a robbery that occurred within the city walls and one that took place in a village or on a public road. In the first place, the magistrate was subject to suspension of one year's nominal salary at the first deadline, and was to be demoted one grade and transferred to another post if he still failed to apprehend the robbers at the end of another year (second deadline). In the second case, there were four deadlines. The punishment for failing to meet the first deadline was the same as in the first instance, but three more deadlines (one year for each deadline) were granted. Although the magistrate was subject to demotion of one grade after the second deadline, he was to be kept in his post for two more years. He suffered actual demotion and transfer to another post only after the fourth deadline. In other words, he was given three years and four months to solve the case.[58] In a case where one household was robbed repeatedly or several households were robbed on the same day, whether within the city walls, in a village, or on a public road, the magistrate was to be impeached, demoted two grades and transferred to another post immediately if he failed to apprehend robbers at the end of four months.[59]

However, governors-general and governors who were lenient often transferred a magistrate to a different post before the last deadline was reached in an effort to save him from actual demotion; thus the deadline laws were not always strictly enforced.[60] A new regulation was formulated in 1814 to prevent high provincial authorities from transferring a magistrate to another post prior to the last deadline.[61]

In contrast, however, there were governors-general and governors who not only gave strict observance to the regulations concerning impeachment, but at times even took action more severe than the regulations demanded. They requested the emperor either to order the board to consider punishing a magistrate in advance of the deadline, or to permit them to take away his hat button (as a token of disgrace), or even to remove him from office prior to the deadline while at the same time ordering him to assist his successor to apprehend the robbers by the deadline. They might also request that the magistrate be punished more severely than the regulations required.[62]

Besides the deadline for the apprehension of robbers, there was also a deadline for closing a case of robbery. The time limit set for the magistrate and his superiors was four months after the apprehension of the robbers,[63] and the magistrate was required to complete the trial and deliver the criminal to his superiors for retrial within two months. If he failed to do so, he was subject to impeachment. An extension of another four months was then granted and the magistrate had to complete the trial within the first two of them. Dismissal was the punishment if he failed to meet the second deadline.[64]

The record of a magistrate's accomplishments in solving thefts and robberies was reviewed at the end of each year. For every five cases in which less than half of the total number of thieves and robbers had finally been apprehended, one demerit was recorded for the magistrate. For every five cases in which more than half had been apprehended, one merit was recorded. If a magistrate had apprehended more than ten robbers within one year, he could win an audience with the throne.[65]

Under the pressure of these various regulations, the detection and apprehension of thieves and robbers became one of the magistrate's principal concerns, for his official career was determined, to a large extent, by his success in this direction.

As mentioned earlier, nearly all of the government runners who acted as policemen were in illegal contact with thieves and robbers;[66] consequently the only hope of solving a theft or robbery lay in forcing the policemen to carry out their orders promptly. It therefore became standard practice throughout the empire to set deadlines for policemen to catch thieves and robbers, and to flog those who failed to meet the deadline.[67] The law permitted the magistrate to take a policeman's family members into custody if thieves or robbers were not apprehended by the deadline.[68] Some magistrates, however, chose to encourage the policemen by giving them traveling expenses for delivering criminals to the superior yamen and rewards. They also provided funds for the services of an informer.[69]

4. TRIAL AND JUDGMENT

Very few magistrates were able to go over the legal documents relating to a case before presiding over its trial in court, as Wang Feng-sheng did.[70] Hence, most of them relied upon the summary of the case prepared by their private secretaries for information needed in conducting the hearing.[71] The magistrates also sought advice, both before and after the trial, from their secretaries, who were not allowed in court while a trial was in session.[72]

In the court, the magistrate was accompanied by a court attendant, a clerk of deposition, a doorman in charge of bamboo tallies,[73] and a number of runners to guard the prisoners and to administer torture. All persons involved in a case were required to kneel on the ground: the plaintiff and the defendant on either side and the witnesses in the middle.[74] Local people were often allowed to stand as spectators to the trial.[75]

A magistrate, during interrogation, was allowed to use torture to obtain a confession from the suspect, except when the person interrogated was over seventy, under fifteen, or an invalid.[76] The forms of torture permitted by law were flogging,[77] slapping,[78] squeezing the fingers[79] or ankles,[80] and other forms described below. All instruments of torture had to accord with standard sizes and forms and they had to be examined and branded by the superior yamen.[81] Officials were prohibited from making unlawful instruments of torture.[82] Among the lawful instruments of torture was the ankle-squeezer, which could never be applied to a woman. It could be used only in cases of homicide and robbery, and officials were required to report to the governor-general and governor whether they had used it in a particular case.[83] It was legitimate to have a person kneel upon an iron chain or to press a stick against the back of his knees only in cases of robbery or homicide where the suspect refused to confess.[84]

The attitudes of magistrates toward the use of torture ranged from viewing it as a valid recourse for securing confessions to the view that an official should avoid using it because an innocent person might thus be forced to confess to a crime he did not commit.[85]

When a suspect made a confession the statement of deposition was read to him before he was asked to sign or make his mark on it.[86] No official was permitted to delete or alter any part of the statement.[87] As omissions or changes might purposely be introduced by a clerk of deposition, it was the responsibility of the magistrate, often with the help of his court attendant, to go over the statement and correct any errors.[88]

All sentences had to accord with an existing law or statute. They could not be based upon a determination announced by a special imperial edict in connection with a particular case but not decreed as a law. The penalty for violation of this regulation was the same as for inflicting punishment that was either inadequate or excessive for the crime, whether with intent or by error. Nor could a sentence be based upon the determination of a prior case which had not been declared a precedent. Only the governor-general and governor were authorized to cite a prior case and request the approval of the Board of Punishment.

In determining a sentence, a magistrate could refer to only one particular law or statute applicable to that case; he was not allowed to refer to more than one. For violation of this ruling he was punishable in accordance with the law governing the infliction with intent of punishment excessive for the crime. Moreover, a magistrate was required to quote the complete legal article he was referring to in forming a judgment; the penalty for omission was thirty strokes.[89]

As a rule, the statement of decision was shown and read to the plaintiff and the defendant in court before they were asked to write a statement accepting the judgment.[90] The law required that when a person was convicted of an offense punishable by penal servitude, banishment, or death, he and his family members living within a distance of 300 li should be informed of the sentence, and a written statement pleading guilty or protesting the sentence should be secured from the person convicted.[91]

Some magistrates wrote down the statement of decision (*p'an-yü* or *shen-yü*) in the presence of the plaintiff and defendant in the court.[92] Obviously a magistrate could write a statement of decision while presiding in court only if he understood the law and was experienced in preparing such a document. Thus Fang Ta-chih was of the opinion that it was better for a magistrate to write the statement after the trial so that he could have time to think about it,[93] or consult his private secretaries.[94]

It should be pointed out that decisions were announced by the magistrate immediately after the hearing only in civil and minor criminal cases which came under the jurisdiction of the magistrate. The procedure involved in more serious cases, in which the decision had to be approved by the superior officials, was different. The reader may recall that the preparation of the *k'an-yü* (statement of consideration), which required much deliberation and careful wording, was the duty of a private secretary.[95] The magistrate's duty was done as soon as he had conducted the trial and secured a confession. All the documents relating to the case were then handed over to the private secretary, so that he could prepare the report. A magistrate might discuss the case with his secretary, but, as a rule, he did not prepare the report himself.

It is evident that there was a division of labor between the magistrate and his private secretary, each playing his part in the administration of justice in accordance with legal and customary procedures. As a rule, the magistrate presided in court, made arrests, interrogated suspects, pronounced sentences, administered punishments, and conducted inquests and other investigations. The secretaries reviewed legal documents, wrote the official rescripts, prepared summaries for the magistrate, wrote reports to the superior yamen, and gave legal advice to the magistrate.

It is obvious that a knowledge of law was essential to a magistrate in the administration of justice; without it he would be unable to make legal decisions.[96] But the complexity of the law and the pressure of his work made it impossible for him to make a thorough study of the law. The experience of Liu Heng, a conscientious and efficient magistrate, proves this. Liu's grandfather had taught him law when he was waiting at home for an official appointment. Yet he admitted that he was not familiar with the legal code when he was a magistrate in Kwangtung, where he remained for seven years. He studied law intensively for a period of eight months while relieved from official duties during the period of mourning for one of his parents. During that time he also served as a private secretary to his uncle, who was a prefect. When he was reappointed as magistrate he was able to write official rescripts and to judge cases.[97] Certainly few magistrates had such opportunity and determination to study law in a systematic manner. Mu-han pointed out in his handbook that since officials did not study law before they entered officialdom they could not have much legal knowledge when they became officials. Moreover, he said, it was difficult for an official to gain the legal knowledge while holding a post, for he was so burdened with numerous duties that he might read law books one day and be forced to forget all about them three days after.[98] It was the magistrate's private secretary who had to make a thorough study of the legal code, which consisted of more than 1000 articles,[99] and of numerous recorded cases, so that he would be able to advise his employer. The magistrate himself was expected merely to have a general and elementary knowledge of law,[100] and he concerned himself only with the laws relating to judicial procedure and trials, and with that part of the law which he dealt with most frequently.[101]

But even this modicum of legal knowledge took a considerable time to acquire. According to Mu-han, it took about half a year to gain a working knowledge of ming-li (general law).[102] Many magistrates were unwilling to make such an investment of time and energy. As a result, they had to rely almost exclusively upon their private secretaries for the administration of justice.[103]

5. Punishment for Wrong Judgment

The liability for a wrong judgment, however, lay not with the private secretaries, who gave advice and might even play a decisive role in making decisions, but with the magistrate. This is understandable, because the legal advisers were not government employees and were responsible only to the magistrates. It was the latter who, as formal authorities, announced decisions, and therefore they were held responsible.

A magistrate was subject to impeachment if he failed to get the actual facts of a case.[104] He was also subject to disciplinary action if he made a wrong judgment. Here a distinction was made in the law between *shih-ch'u* (pronouncing through error a sentence inadequate to the crime) and *shih-ju* (pronouncing through error a sentence excessive for the crime). In the latter case, the magistrate's penalty was forfeiture of one year's nominal salary, demotion, or dismissal, depending on the seriousness of the case. The magistrate was subject to dismissal if the sentence had already been executed.[105] In the case of *shih-ch'u,* the magistrate's penalty varied from forfeiture of six months' nominal salary to demotion.[106] In all cases, whether the punishment was inadequate or excessive, the superior officials of the magistrate, who were responsible for retrial, and the provincial judge, governor, and governor-general were also subject to disciplinary action as stipulated in the regulations.[107] The magistrate could be exempted from punishment or his punishment reduced if the sentence recommended by the magistrate in the case in question was rejected by the superior officials and subsequently corrected by the magistrate.[108] The same rule was applicable when the Board of Punishment rejected the sentence approved by the governor-general and governor and ordered them to retry the case.[109]

As with all other officials, a magistrate guilty of a wrong judgment might incur corporal punishment as defined in the Penal Code.[110] If he wilfully pronounced an unjust sentence which was carried out, he was to be penalized in the same way as the condemned person. In other words, if he recommended sentencing an innocent person to, say, penal servitude, he himself would also be given penal servitude. Or, if he acquitted a person who should have been banished, then he himself would be subject to banishment.

If the sentence was not wholly unjust but was either aggravated or mitigated with intent, his punishment was to be determined by the difference between the sentence which should have been applied to the case and that which was actually pronounced and executed.[111] If an unjust sentence of death was recommended with intent and the person was executed after approval, the magistrate's punishment was death.[112]

If, however, an unjust sentence had been recommended or pronounced not with intent, but through error, the punishment was reduced. In such a case, the law put the principal responsibility on the clerk in charge, the reason, as stated in the commentary attached to the relevant legal article, being that a clerk of law should know the law and therefore call attention to an error whenever it occurred.[113] The penalty for the clerk who failed to point out an error was reduced by three degrees if the injustice consisted of aggravation; and by five degrees, if it consisted of mitigation. For the same offense, the chief officer (that is, the jail warden),[114] received a punishment reduced one more degree; the assistant magistrate,[115] reduced two more degrees; and the magistrate, three more degrees. Thus when an unjust sentence proved unintentional, the clerk would be the principal person penalized, while the magistrate, whose punishment was three degrees less than that of the clerk, might suffer no punishment at all.[116]

The penalty for wrong judgment incurred by an official was reduced by one degree in all the above cases if an unjust sentence had only been recommended or pronounced but not yet executed, or if a prisoner who had been unjustly acquitted and dismissed was later apprehended or if he had died a natural death.[117]

From the above, we can see that the penalty for a wrong decision was extremely severe. It was not limited to disciplinary action, but included such punishments as penal servitude, banishment, and the death penalty, depending upon the case. This sort of liability explains the absolute necessity for the magistrates who were unfamiliar with the law and precedents to have the services of competent legal advisers. It was not merely a matter of efficiency. Without proper advice, the magistrates were not only unable to keep their posts; they might suffer corporal punishment or even lose their lives for a wrong decision.

TAXATION

The magistrates were the collectors of land tax, grain tribute, and all other taxes, with the exception of customs duties and likin. The collection of customs was the responsibility of the commissioners of customs[1] or the taotai of the maritime customs established in the treaty ports. The likin (a local tax on commodities in transit), which was introduced in 1853 to meet exigencies created during the Taiping Rebellion, was under the likin bureaus headed by commissioners appointed by the governor-general and governor. The commissioners were recruited from the active and expectant officials awaiting appointment, and from gentry members.[2] An imperial edict of 1862 ordered the commissioners to be abolished and replaced by the local officials—magistrates, prefects, or intendants—but objections were raised by a few provincial authorities and they were permitted to retain the old system.[3] The collection of likin became the duty of magistrates only in places where such duty was transferred to them.[4]

The land-and-labor-service tax and other taxes were collected by magistrates in accordance with the items and quotas given in the Complete Book of Taxes and Labor Services (*Fu-i ch'üan-shu*), prepared by the office of the provincial treasurer for each hsien, chou, subprefecture, prefecture, intendancy, and province.[5] The *Fu-i ch'üan-shu* gave the number of male adults (*ting*),[6] the local land holdings, and the rates and quotas for land-and-labor-service tax, grain tribute, and other taxes. It also listed the amounts of cash to be delivered to the superior yamen (such funds were known as *ch'i-yün*), and the amounts to be kept by the magistrate's yamen for expenses (*ts'un-liu*).[7] In addition, it gave information on special regional products to be sent to the capital as tribute, such as wood oil, colors for paint, and medicinal herbs.

Since the quotas for land-and-labor-service tax and other taxes might change in a locality from time to time—because of land reclamation, abandonment of eroded land, or simply by order of the government[8]—the Complete Book of Taxes and Labor Services was theoretically revised every ten years.[9] But in fact it sometimes was not revised for several decades,[10] and therefore the collection of taxes could not be based entirely upon this book.[11] It was necessary to consult the provincial account book (*k'uai-chi ts'e*),[12] the provincial annual expenditure report (*tsou-hsiao ts'e*),[13] and other official documents[14] in order to compute the amount of various taxes to be collected in a particular year.[15] This first and basic step in tax collection was the responsibility of the secretary of taxation.[16]

1. LAND-AND-LABOR-SERVICE TAX

The land-and-labor-service tax, generally referred to as "principal tax" (*cheng-hsiang ch'ien-liang*),[17] constituted the principal source of support for the emperor's court, the government, and the army. In the early part of the Ch'ing dynasty, taxes were imposed separately on land and on persons liable to labor service. The land tax, which was paid in money, was levied according to the fertility of the soil; its rate consequently varied in different provinces and also in different chou and hsien within the same province.[18] The labor-service tax (*ting yin,* male adult tax), was in theory imposed on male adults aged sixteen to sixty, in lieu of labor service.[19] Hence it was also known as *yao yin* or *yao-li yin* (labor service money). Its rate varied in different provinces and also within the same province.[20] In Chihli, Honan, Shansi, Shensi, Kansu, and some localities in Shantung, the rates were classified into three grades (upper, middle, and lower) and nine divisions (upper-upper, middle-upper, lower-upper, upper-middle, middle-middle, lower-middle, upper-lower, middle-lower, lower-lower) according to the taxpayer's economic status; but no such classification was made in the south and in certain parts of Shantung.[21] In order to keep the labor-service tax revenue abreast of any population increase, a registration was undertaken at regular intervals. In 1713, however, the registration for 1711 was fixed as a permanent basis for collecting the labor-service tax. That part of the population which had come into being after 1711 was called *sheng-shih tzu-sheng jin-ting* (lit., "increased population of the flourishing age"). Population in excess of the quotas of 1711 was not counted for tax purposes; the quotas remained as before. Thereafter the term *ting* came to mean a tax unit.[22] Another important change took place in many provinces between 1716 and 1729, when labor-service tax ceased to be collected as an independent item; instead it was combined with the land tax, and the two together were now called *ti-ting yin* (land-and-labor-service tax). As a result, the people who owned no landed property were exempted from paying labor-service tax.[23]

It should be noted that, together with the land-and-labor-service tax, a definite amount was collected under the name of "meltage fee" (*huo-hao*, i.e., silver lost in the process of melting). Before 1724 this item had been collected as a kind of customary fee and kept by the magistrate to meet various official and personal expenses. In 1724, with the emperor's permission, the collection of this fee was legitimatized and the money thus collected became a part of the tax funds known as *hao-hsien* (surplus). It was not submitted to the Board of Revenue, however; instead it was delivered to the provincial treasurer and was reserved exclusively for the supplementary salaries (*yang-lien yin*) of officials in the province and for certain types of office expenses in the various yamen.[24]

Tax Schedules

In all the provinces except Kwangtung, Yünnan and Kweichow,[25] the collection of land-and-labor-service tax began in the second month, and in theory half of the tax was to have been collected by the end of the fourth month.[26] Tax collection was suspended between the fifth and seventh months, the farmers' busy season. It was resumed in the eighth month[27] and continued till the end of the eleventh month.[28]

As the collection of land-and-labor-service tax was one of a magistrate's most important duties, his collection record was used by his superiors as a basis for evaluating his accomplishment (*k'ao-ch'eng*). A magistrate who failed to collect the proper quota of land-and-labor-service tax within a given time was subject to punishment, which was determined by the percentage of tax uncollected. If the uncollected portion was less than ten per cent, he was not entitled to promotion and was subject to forfeiture of one year's nominal salary. The punishment was demotion of one to four grades if the portion uncollected was ten, twenty, thirty, or forty per cent respectively. If he failed to collect more than fifty per cent, he was subject to dismissal. A magistrate responsible for a tax deficiency of less than fifty per cent was given an extension of one year to make it up. If he failed to do so by the end of the extension, he was then demoted or dismissed, depending upon the percentage uncollected at the time of his first impeachment.[29] The superior officials—independent chou magistrates, prefects, grain intendants, provincial treasurers, governors, and governors-general—were also subject to punishment (varying from forfeiture of salary or demotion, to dismissal) if their subordinate officials failed to collect the proper quota of land-and-labor-service tax.[30]

Such a regulation, demanding 100-per-cent collection, would seem to be a very strict one,[31] and apparently few magistrates could attain this goal. If this regulation had been strictly enforced, probably no magistrate could have avoided impeachment. A provincial treasurer of Kiangsu reported that in Wu-hsien and fourteen other hsien, not a single magistrate had been promoted from the reign of Shun-chih to his own time (early K'ang-hsi). He added that within the prefectures of Su-chou, Sung-chiang, Ch'ang-chou, and Chen-chiang there had never been a full collection in any year and thus there was not a single official who had not been impeached.[32] A governor of Kiangsu reported that numerous officials had been dismissed because of failure to collect the land-and-labor-service tax, and no magistrate in Su-chou, Sung-chiang, and other prefectures could hold his post for more than one or two years.[33] Apparently total tax collection was particularly difficult in Kiangsu, especially in Su-chou and Sung-chiang prefectures, where the land tax rate was the highest in the empire.[34] Possibly the magistrates in the other provinces had less difficulty in collecting land tax.

Those magistrates who succeeded in collecting the full quota of land-and-labor-service tax before the time for submitting the annual expenditure report (*tsou-hsiao*) were rewarded with recordings of merit, advancement in grade, or promotion, depending upon the total amount of taxes collected in a district.[35]

With the magistrates under this sort of positive and negative pressure, it is not hard to believe that many of them would resort to devious means in order to keep their posts. Government funds were often misappropriated to make up the uncollected tax.[36] There were also cases where wealthy magistrates advanced money for the tax owed by taxpayers.[37] Many magistrates resorted to harsh measures like flogging, in an attempt to force people to pay their taxes.[38]

Collection of Land-and-Labor-Service Tax

Preparation of land tax records. Before starting the collection, each yamen prepared "land tax records" (*shih-cheng ts'e*), which were based upon the Complete Book of Taxes and Labor Services and other records, for each *li* or *t'u* (a rural zone comprised 110 families) and each *chia* (a unit of ten households), in order to ascertain the rate of land tax imposed on each type of land, the rate of labor-service tax, and the quota of land-and-labor-service tax.[39]

Then a "simplified tax notice" (*i-chih yu-tan*) was issued to the taxpayers[40] giving the rate of tax imposed on various kinds and grades of land in a particular district.[41] The cost of printing this notice was paid by the taxpayers when they received it. In fact, they were usually charged a fee several times the actual cost. This abuse eventually led to suspension of the notice in 1688 in all provinces except Kiangsu. Thereafter the magistrates were ordered to make the taxes known to the people by engraving the items of taxation and their rates on a stone tablet placed in front of the yamen.[42]

Deadlines for tax payment. The standard practice in collecting land tax was to set a number of deadlines and divide the tax owed by a taxpayer into a number of payments corresponding with these deadlines. As a rule, payment was to be made by ten principal deadlines, ten per cent of the tax being due each month.[43] After the deadlines and the portions due had been established, the clerks were ordered to prepare a "deadline-payment form" (*hsien-tan*) and a "deadline-hearing record" (*pi-pu*) for each *li, chia,* and individual taxpayer. The form and the record listed the amount of tax due at each deadline. At the time of tax collection, the amount handed in by a taxpayer and the amount he still owed were entered into the forms and records by the clerks of land tax. Thus the payment and balance due could be examined at a glance, and the taxpayers who failed to hand in their taxes could easily be singled out for investigation.[44]

Receiving tax payments. Clerks in charge of silver chests were assigned to receive payments, but the taxpayers were allowed to weigh the silver themselves,[45] using the official scale (*k'u-p'ing*) approved by the Board of Revenue and the highest provincial authorities.[46] The silver was then placed in a paper bag, bought from the clerks,[47] and sealed by the taxpayers themselves. After the clerk had written on the bag the name of the taxpayer, the amount paid, the date, and his own name, and had entered the payment in the tax journal (*liu-shui shou-pu*), the bag was inserted into the silver chest in the presence of the taxpayer,[48] who was then given a receipt.[49]

The lack of uniformity in the fineness of silver[50] presented a special technical problem in tax collection. In order to ensure that the silver handed in by taxpayers was up to the standard, an authorized silversmith (*kuan yin-chiang*) was required to melt it and put a seal on it.[51] This practice, which was convenient to the magistrates, gave the authorized silversmith a chance to demand money from the taxpayers. Besides charging a fee for the melting and for his seal, the silversmith often purposely underestimated the fineness of the taxpayer's silver in order to get more from him.[52] For this reason, some magistrates dispensed with the authorized silversmith. Huang Liu-hung, for instance, allowed the taxpayers to ask any silversmith to melt their silver. Under his system it was not necessary to have the seal of a silversmith to certify the quality of the silver if it was up to the standard; all the taxpayers had to do was to put the name of the silversmith on the paper bag when the silver was handed in.[53]

As a rule, taxpayers were allowed to hand in copper coins in lieu of silver at a conversion rate which was established by the highest provincial authority in accordance with the current market rate, and which the magistrates were not permitted to exceed.[54] However, the prevailing custom among the magistrates was to insist upon payment in copper coins in lieu of silver,[55] and at a rate higher than the market rate. The magistrate's rate, as reported in some specific cases, was as high as 142 per cent to 175 per cent of the market rate.[56]

Although this practice was contradictory to the letter of the law, in the words of Hsieh Chin-luan it was not actually considered to be a "violation of the law," and therefore was not prohibited. Hsieh defended the practice on the ground that there was no other means to provide stationery and other expenses connected with the delivery of tax funds to a superior yamen.[57] Moreover, obtaining a surplus by using a higher conversion rate made it easier for a magistrate to meet the strict requirement of collecting 100 per cent of his tax quota, for he could use a part of the surplus thus obtained to make up the deficiency.

Tax agents. One hundred and ten households constituted a tax unit (*li*) and the head of this unit (*li-chang*) was recruited from among the ten households having the largest number of male adults. These ten households rotated in supplying a *li-chang* each year, who was responsible for urging the households within the *li* to pay their land-and-labor-service tax. The remaining 100 households were divided into 10 *chia,* each headed by a *chia-shou.* This rotating system, which was copied after the Ming pattern, was known as *li-chia*,[58] and the man currently serving as *li-chang* was called *p'ai-nien* (lit., "to serve for the year by turn") or *hsien-nien* ("to serve in the current year").[59] He was to see that all the taxpayers in the whole *li* handed in their land-and-labor-service tax on time. He was given the deadline-payment forms so that he was in a position to know the amount of tax due at each deadline from the taxpayers in the *li* or *chia*. To show that he had paid his tax, the taxpayer would give to the *hsien-nien* a part of his receipt, the "deadline-hearing certificate" (*pi-chao*).[60] The *hsien-nien* would then enter the payment on the deadline-payment form. Before a deadline hearing it was the duty of the *hsien-nien* to present to the magistrate's yamen the deadline-payment form and all the deadline-hearing certificates handed in by the taxpayers. If all the taxpayers in his *li* had paid their taxes on schedule, the *hsien-nien* was given a "deadline-flogging exemption certificate" and allowed to go home to do his farming (*kuei-nung mien-pi p'iao*). But if any taxpayers had failed to pay, which was likely to be the case, the *hsien-nien* was required to appear at the deadline hearing and was subject to flogging.[61]

The *hsien-nien* was obviously placed in a hopeless position, because there were always poor people unable to pay taxes on time, and there were also powerful persons, such as members of the gentry, whom he had no way of forcing to make payment. Yet he alone was responsible for all the taxpayers in a *li* and suffered flogging because of them.[62] Moreover, the runners sent to the rural districts to expedite tax payment all took advantage of the situation and demanded customary fees from the *hsien-nien*. He was obliged to pay the runners an annual fee, escort fees for taking him to the magistrate's court, fees for postponing deadline hearings, and fees for hiring someone else to receive a flogging in his place. On top of all this he had to meet travel and board expenses while attending the deadline hearings.[63] Numerous *hsien-nien* were reputed to have gone bankrupt because of this tremendous burden.[64] Because of its obvious unfairness, the system was abolished in the K'ang-hsi period,[65] and other measures were adopted.

One of these new measures was to designate a *chia-chang* to be the agent to hasten tax payment in ten households. He was given a form (*ch'ang-tan* or long folded sheet) which listed the names of the ten households, the amount of landed property owned by them, the land-and-labor-service tax to be paid by them, and the amount to be paid by each deadline.[66] With this information he was supposed to be able to see that the households paid taxes to the yamen on time. He could request the magistrate to summon taxpayers who refused to cooperate. But, as in the case of the *hsien-nien,* he alone was responsible for attending the deadline hearing and was subject to flogging if the taxes were not paid on time.[67] The main difference between a *hsien-nien* and a *chia-chang* was that one was responsible for the whole *li* and the other for a *chia* only. The *chia-chang's* task was somewhat easier because his unit was much smaller and the households within it were more accessible. Thus the *chia-chang* system was commended by Huang Liu-hung either as a substitute for the *hsien-nien* system, or to provide a supplementary agent to share the burden of the *hsien-nien.*[68]

In addition to these local tax agents, government runners (*t'u-ch'ai* or *li-ch'ai*) were stationed in each *t'u* or *li* to enforce payment of land-and-labor-service tax. Their main function was to keep an eye on the *hsien-nien* or *chia-chang* in order to ensure that they would be present at the deadline hearings. The runners were authorized to bring these agents to the magistrate's court if they failed to appear voluntarily.[69] These runners, who demanded various customary fees from the tax agents, became a considerable burden to the rural population.

Another system was to organize taxpayers into units of five to ten households, with a member of the household owing the most tax acting as the tax agent (*ts'ui-t'ou*). A form, known as *kun-tan* (rolling form), which listed the amount of land-and-labor-service tax to be paid by each of the households at each of the deadlines as well as the amount outstanding, was designed in 1700 to facilitate the enforcement of payment. This form was given by the *chia-chang* to the *ts'ui-t'ou.* The latter could request the magistrate to punish the taxpayers who failed to cooperate. But, again, it was the tax agent who attended the deadline hearings and was flogged if the payments, including his own, were not made. After he had paid his tax, the chore of being *ts'ui-t'ou* would fall to one of the remaining households, in the order of the amount of tax owed. Thus the rolling form went from hand to hand until the last deadline.[70]

This system was considered the best by many officials and private secretaries because it did not necessitate stationing runners in the rural districts, where they collected customary fees.[71] However, if the *ts'ui-t'ou* failed to attend a deadline hearing, runners were sent to summon him.[72]

It should be noted that even though it was not always necessary, some magistrates still stationed runners in the rural districts to enforce tax payment.[73]

Of course, the rolling form system was feasible only when the record of taxpayers was made household by household according to actual residence, and all the landholdings of a taxpayer, though they might be located in different villages, were listed under a single name; when all of the five or ten households were in the same village, it was possible for one household to urge the other households to pay their taxes.[74] This system was found impracticable in the province of Chihli, where Chinese and Bannermen lived together,[75] nor was it practiced in Kwangsi and Szechwan.[76]

Deadline hearings. The primary means used to enforce tax payment by the prescribed deadlines, regardless of the type of agent assigned to encourage collection, was to conduct a deadline hearing, at which the delinquent taxpayers or the tax agents were flogged. This was standard practice all over the empire, and the hearings were conducted by the magistrate himself.

Prior to the hearings it was necessary to determine the status of each taxpayer with regard to payment. As land-and-labor-service tax was payable in a number of installments the record had to be checked and computed at each of the deadlines. This tedious task was assigned to clerks and private secretaries. The clerks prepared the deadline-hearing record (*pi-pu*), which listed the amount due by each deadline, the amount paid, and the balance owed.[77] This record was then checked by a private secretary against the deadline-payment forms, the tax journal, the stubs of receipts, the deadline-hearing certificates (*pi-chao*) and/or the canceling certificates (*hsiao-chao*).[78] Paid taxes were then canceled, and delinquent taxpayers were listed to be called in for flogging.[79] As a rule, the ones owing the largest amount were listed first.[80]

The list of delinquent taxpayers was then handed over to the magistrate for use at the deadline hearings. As we have already mentioned, the persons flogged were not always the taxpayers themselves. They might be the tax agents (*hsien-nien* or *chia-chang*),[81] or the runners stationed in the rural districts to hasten tax payment.[82] Most of the magistrates preferred to flog the agents or runners because this was much simpler than summoning individual taxpayers, who were widely scattered.[83] As a rule taxpayers were summoned and flogged when they ignored the warnings of the "hastener" and the deadlines.[84] However, some officials held that it was better to flog the taxpayers than the runners on the ground that not all the uncollected taxes were actually owed by the taxpayers, but were often embezzled by the runners. It was thought that if the taxpayers were summoned to the hearing, the runners would not dare to embezzle tax payments freely.[85] A further argument was that if the runners were flogged instead of the taxpayers, the runners would then have an excuse for demanding compensation from the taxpayers.[86]

Many sources indicate that a large number of magistrates resorted to flogging as the only means to enforce tax payment,[87] in spite of the fact that the principle of benevolence toward the people was very much emphasized by officials in connection with tax collection.[88] Even reputedly kind magistrates frankly admitted that it was not easy to put this principle into practice.[89] An exceptional case was that of Fang Ta-chih who personally went on a tour to the rural districts to encourage people to pay their taxes; he was able to avoid flogging entirely for five years while he was magistrate in Kuang-chi.[90]

Some magistrates used means other than flogging to enforce tax payment. For instance, Wang Hui-tsu refused to accept a complaint unless the plaintiff had paid his taxes.[91] There were also magistrates who relied upon encouragement, rewarding the commoner-taxpayers with decorations and wine, and sending drummers and pipers to accompany them out of the yamen, or granting tablets to the gentry-taxpayers.[92]

Delivery of Tax Funds

After the land-and-labor-service tax had been collected, the silver chests were taken to the magistrate's court, where the silver was unwrapped, counted, and entered in the record in the presence of the magistrate, often with the help of his subordinate officials or the director of studies.[93] The prefect or independent chou magistrate was required by law to supervise the unwrapping and counting of the tax funds.[94]

The magistrate was allowed to keep a specific amount out of the tax funds for such expenses as the chou or hsien government salaries and wages, expenses for post stations, stipends for government school students, and relief rations for the poor. The amount kept for these purposes (*ts'un-liu*) was specified in the Complete Book of Taxes and Labor Services.[95] The rest of the land-and-labor-service tax fund, together with the fund collected for "miscellaneous taxes," was to be delivered to the provincial treasurer without delay.[96]

Runners, often under the supervision of a magistrate's personal servant,[97] were assigned to deliver the funds. The magistrates of the localities through which the funds passed were obliged to send soldiers and commoner-guards (*min-chuang*) to escort the runners within the territory under their jurisdiction. Both the magistrate who sent the funds and the magistrates of the places en route were responsible for the safety of the funds. They were required to replace the funds if any loss occurred in transit.[98]

2. GRAIN TRIBUTE

Grain tribute, a tax in kind, was collected in Shantung, Honan, Hunan, Hupeh, Kiangsi, Kiangsu, Anhui, and Chekiang, mainly in the form of husked rice.[99] Prior to the period of sea transport,[100] it was shipped through the Grand Canal to the granaries in Peking (direct tribute, *cheng-tui*) or to T'ung-chou (indirect tribute, *kai-tui*).[101] The amount of grain collected per *mou,* like the land tax, varied both among the different provinces and among the localities within a province.[102]

Not all grain tribute was collected in kind; a portion was collected in silver in lieu of grain and was called *yung-che* (commuted permanently to cash).[103] There were places where taxpayers handed in cash to the magistrates, who bought the grain.[104]

Grain tribute was subject to a number of surcharges. A definite allowance for wastage (*hao-mi*) was collected for every picul of grain, in order to cover any loss in transit or in storage.[105] In addition, taxpayers were required to pay various surtaxes to cover the cost of transport and of repairs to the granary, and other expenses.[106]

In actual practice, the regular tax and the official surcharges were only a part of the taxpayers' burden, for extra surcharges were imposed by the magistrates. Even more irregularities were practiced in connection with grain tribute than in the collection of the land-and-labor-service tax, because more expenses were incurred in collecting and transporting grain than in handling money. As Feng Kuei-feng pointed out, it was impossible for a magistrate to deliver the exact amount of grain that had been collected, and the collection of a surplus was necessary to cover the expenses involved.[107] The collection of this surplus eventually took the form of an extra surcharge levied upon the taxpayers and designated as "cost of grain tribute collection" (*ts'ao-fei*). This kind of irregularity, since it was inherent in the method of tax administration, was generally considered inevitable and justifiable by the officials.[108]

The government's problem was where to draw the line between what was necessary and what was superfluous. The situation was further complicated by the fact that the actual cost of collection varied in different localities and therefore the extra surcharges varied accordingly.[109] For these reasons it was difficult for the government, central and provincial, to check any excessive collection of extra surcharges, with the result that the whole matter of extra surcharges remained almost entirely in the hands of the local officials. Whenever they found it impossible to meet the expenses, they increased the extra surcharge. As more and more persons depended for an income upon the collection and transport of grain tribute, the cost of collection increased, and with rising costs, the extra surcharge also increased. Moreover, many magistrates and their aides seized the opportunity to collect more than was needed to cover costs, in an attempt to enrich themselves. This situation was summed up by Wang Ch'ing-yün (1798–1862): "[The government] puts no limit on its levies or on its expenditures. All this begins with the collection of extra surcharges by the chou and hsien magistrates."[110] In certain cases there were even agreements between the clerks in charge of grain tribute and their magistrates, whereby the clerks would guarantee collection of the full quota of grain plus a surplus, a certain percentage of which would be turned over to the magistrate.[111]

There were two common methods of gathering a surplus in collecting the grain tribute. One was to collect extra grain from taxpayers—for example, by heaping the grain in the measure, although this was prohibited by law.[112] In the early years of Ch'ien-lung, it was the practice to heap grain one to three fingers above the level of the bushel.[113] Gradually there developed a custom of collecting grain on a "discount basis": a picul of grain (10 *tou*) was counted as only 7, 8, or 9 *tou;* that is, an excess of 10 to 30 per cent was extracted from the taxpayer.[114] Later when the "discount" increased to 40–50 per cent some court officials in Peking suggested setting the limit on discounts at 20 per cent.[115] According to Feng Kuei-fen's estimate, taking into consideration the extra surcharges exacted by the magistrate and his aides (clerks, runners, and personal servants), the taxpayer paid 2.5 or 2.6 piculs for every picul of grain tribute. In other words, the actual payment was about 250 per cent of the legal tax.[116]

Another way of obtaining a surplus in collecting grain tribute was to collect cash in lieu of grain. It was unlawful to demand cash from taxpayers, but cash could be accepted when a taxpayer preferred to pay cash, and the conversion rate was to accord with the market rate.[117] However, an edict of 1756 stated: "The magistrates frequently demand cash in lieu of grain to obtain more grain. This cannot be prohibited in spite of the existence of the law." [118] One assumes that the grain collected by chou or hsien magistrates over and above the quota set by the government might not be as easily disposed of as cash.[119] Thus when the quota of grain tribute had been reached, the officials would demand cash from the remaining taxpayers.[120]

Evidence indicates that there was more irregularity in the collection of cash than in the collection of grain.[121] According to an edict of 1829, taxpayers in Lin-chang, Honan, had to pay 9000 coins for one picul of wheat, 8000 for one picul of rice, and 7000 for one picul of beans, whereas the market rate for rice and wheat was less than 2000 coins.[122] Later the rate was increased to 16,000 to 20,000 coins in many areas for one picul of grain, and an attempt was made by Hu Lin-i (1812–1861) and other provincial authorities to set the limit at about 4000 to 6000 coins in Hupeh, Kiangsu, and Shantung.[123] The conversion rate in Kiangsu, as reported by Feng Kuei-fen, was as high as 300 per cent to 400 per cent of the market rate—three to four piculs for one picul of tax imposed. It is obvious that the burden of the taxpayers was the heaviest when the grain tribute was converted into cash.[124]

The collection of grain tribute, which began in the tenth month, customarily ended at the close of the eleventh month so that the grain would be ready for transportation in the twelfth month.[125] For failing to collect grain tribute on schedule in accordance with the quota a magistrate was punished in the same way as for failing to collect land-and-labor-service tax.[126]

Payment of grain tribute, like payment of land-and-labor-service tax, was enforced by flogging. Taxpayers had to deliver their grain to the government granary within the collection period. Before the granary was closed, the grain tribute record and the stubs of receipts were checked by the secretary of taxation, and delinquent taxpayers or the runners responsible for their payment were called in for a hearing and flogging.[127]

Grain tribute was transported and delivered to the granaries by the taxpayers. This posed a problem for those who lived far away from the district seat where the granary was located. Rural granaries, which were convenient for the rural residents, were built only when funds for their erection could be raised among the local residents, most of whom, it was said, were willing to share this expense in order to save themselves both time and traveling expense.[128] Without rural granaries, rural taxpayers had either to transport grain from home or to buy grain from rice shops at the district seat.[129]

At each of the granaries, a clerk was assigned to receive grain, issue receipts, and to record all transactions.[130] To be acceptable, the tribute grain had to be dry and of average size.[131] If any grain fell short of the standard, it was sifted or winnowed.[132]

The measure used in the granaries was made to specifications issued by the Board of Works and approved by the grain intendant.[133] The law permitted taxpayers to level the top of the grain in the measure by scraping it with a wooden stick. It was unlawful to pile the grain into a heap in an attempt to collect more grain.[134] However, these matters were entirely out of the control of the taxpayers. There is ample evidence that this law, like many other laws, was not observed. We have mentioned that collecting more grain than was due was a prevailing practice all over the empire. The actual measuring was done by the grain measurer, who by and large followed the customary practice of the locality, often with the consent of the magistrate.[135]

In theory, a magistrate was expected personally to supervise the collection of grain at the granary in his district; if he was absent on an official mission he was required to assign subordinate officials to act in his place.[136] But, since thousands of bushels of grain were involved in each collection,[137] and there might be more than one granary in a district,[138] it was impossible for a magistrate to be present at all times. A common practice was to station a reliable personal servant in the granary to supervise the clerks, grain measurers, and other personnel.[139] But the servant often cooperated with the clerks and runners, engaging in such forms of corruption as collecting extra grain or extorting money from the taxpayers.[140] A few magistrates employed a granary secretary (ao-yu) to supervise the collection.[141]

In the early days of the dynasty, grain tribute was delivered directly by the taxpayers to the transport officers and boatmen in charge of tribute junks, who demanded various fees for their services. After 1652 the magistrate was responsible for delivering the collected grain to the transport officers and boatmen, thus avoiding direct negotiation between them and the taxpayers.[142]

As the tribute junks were scheduled to sail for T'ung-chou annually at the end of the twelfth month, it was the magistrate's duty to deliver the grain at the specified time without delay.[143] He was subject to punishment if the grain had not yet been collected when the junks arrived or if the delivery was made after the twelfth month.[144] As soon as the grain was delivered to the transport officers and boatmen, the magistrate's responsibility was ended.[145] However, it was not easy to deal with these men. They often refused to accept the grain under the pretext that it fell short of the standard. When this happened, the grain would pile up in the granary. As a rule, a receipt (*t'ung-kuan*) had to be obtained from the transport officers when grain had been handed over.[146] But they often refused to issue the receipt unless a fee was paid to them. The magistrates, who had to meet a deadline in the delivery of grain tribute, were forced to accept their terms and pay the fees.[147] Some magistrates left the negotiations with the transport officers and boatmen to their clerks and personal servants, who knew how to deal with them.[148]

There were exceptionally capable magistrates who took upon themselves the task of personally supervising the collection and delivery of grain tribute. They saw to it that the grain collected from the taxpayers was up to par so that the transport officers and boatmen could not object to its quality. When the junks arrived, they were there to make the delivery, and to assign to the boatmen the storerooms from which the grain was to be taken. Finally, when delivery had been made, they ordered the junks to sail without delay.[149]

The magistrates of the districts along the Grand Canal had the additional responsibility of getting the junks to move along without blocking the river traffic.[150] It was also their duty to see that the grain tribute was not stolen or sold,[151] and to keep an eye on the boatmen so that they would not make trouble with the local people, smuggle salt, or sell private goods.[152]

3. Miscellaneous Taxes

The magistrates were also obliged to collect "miscellaneous taxes": [153] title deed taxes on land and on houses,[154] brokerage tax,[155] pawnshop tax, [156] tax on the sale of cattle, pigs, and other livestock, and on the sale of cotton, tobacco, wine, and other commodities,[157] shop tax (*men-t'an shui*),[158] tax on commodities collected at the time of unloading either at a transit point or at a destination (*lo-ti shui*),[159] fish tax,[160] and a number of other taxes.[161] Of these, only the brokerage tax, the pawnshop tax, and the tax on title deeds were universal in all provinces.[162] The specific taxes to be collected in each locality were given in the Complete Book of Taxes and Labor Services, which might or might not specify a quota.[163] In the latter case, the magistrate was required to deliver to the provincial treasurer the entire sum collected from the taxpayers.[164] Failure to collect and delay in delivery were punishable.[165]

The collection of miscellaneous taxes seems to have presented no great problem to the magistrates because the proceeds were relatively small,[166] and because it was easier to collect taxes from a limited number of brokers and store owners than from the scattered rural populace. The magistrate's task was particularly simple when no quota was set for a tax. Apparently the magistrates were given more freedom in handling these taxes than in administering the land-and-labor-service tax and grain tribute. For example, they could, as Huang Liu-hung suggested, be more generous to the poor people engaged in small businesses and exempt them from tax payment as they saw fit.[167] However, this freedom also afforded them opportunities to engage in embezzlement.[168]

4. Salt Gabelle

As a rule, the magistrates were not concerned with the collection of salt gabelle, which was the duty of the salt officials.[169] However, there were places where the magistrates also were responsible for the salt administration (chien-kuan yen-wu). For instance, the tax on salt manufacture (tsao-k'o) in a number of localities in Shantung and Chekiang was collected and delivered to the salt controller by the magistrates.[170] The certificate tax (yin-k'o, that is, the fee paid for a certificate to sell salt) was collected by magistrates in Yang-ch'ü and in twenty-nine other chou and hsien in Shansi, where certificates to sell native salt (t'u yen-yin) were issued.[171] The salt gabelle was also collected by magistrates in places where no salt certificates were issued.[172]

A penalty was imposed on a magistrate charged with salt administration if he failed to collect the proper quota of salt gabelle. As in the case of the land-and-labor-service tax, the dergee of punishment was determined by the percentage of uncollected tax. Penalties, in order of severity, were suspension of promotion, reduction in nominal salary, and demotion in grade (if the uncollected portion of the tax ranged from less than ten per cent to sixty per cent), and dismissal (if the uncollected portion was eighty per cent or more). After a failure of this kind, a magistrate was given a one-year extension to collect the tax. If he failed again, he was punished with demotion from one to five grades or dismissal, depending upon the percentage of uncollected tax.[173]

With some exceptions, the issuance of certificates for the transport and sale of salt was not in the hands of the magistrates. In the Huai River area, where the salt ticket system (*p'iao-fa*), introduced in 1832, was in use, the right to sell salt was not monopolized by the licensed merchants but extended to any merchant who bought a ticket.[174] There the magistrates were authorized to issue tickets to merchants for buying salt in the field.[175] The law also authorized the magistrates of Kiangsu, Anhui, and Chekiang to issue permits to poor people over sixty or under fifteen, the disabled, and women having no relatives to support them, so that they could buy a small quantity of salt from the manufacturer.[176]

All magistrates, whether in charge of salt administration or not, were required to see that the salt merchants sold all the salt they bought, that is, the amounts indicated on the certificates issued by the government. Their success or failure in the discharge of this responsibility was taken into account in their record of accomplishment (*k'ao-ch'eng*). A magistrate who failed to carry out this duty was punished according to the percentage of salt quota unsold in an area: ten per cent or less, suspension of promotion; twenty to thirty per cent, reduction in nominal salary; forty per cent, demotion of one grade; fifty to seventy per cent, demotion of two to four grades and transfer to another post; eighty per cent or above, dismissal.[177]

Conversely, a magistrate of a district where the annual quota of salt was sold was rewarded in the same way as when the full quota of land-and-labor-service tax was collected. The same reward was also given to magistrates who were successful in collecting the salt tax.[178]

Every magistrate was supposed to urge the people to buy salt. But about all he could do was to issue a notice encouraging people to buy salt from the salt merchants.[179] It was unlawful to apportion salt to the people and force them to buy it, and such action was punishable by dismissal.[180] The problem was that smuggled salt was always cheaper than licensed salt and consequently the people preferred to buy it.[181] As a result the licensed salt could not be sold in full quota, and it became a major concern of the government to stop the illegal manufacture and sale of salt.

The magistrates were held responsible for any unauthorized manufacture, smuggling, or illegal sale of salt. They were subject to punishment for failing to detect illegal manufacture or sale,[182] and also for failing to apprehend smugglers who either imported or exported salt.[183] By the same token, magistrates who did arrest smugglers were rewarded with a "recording of merit" or advancement in grade.[184]

Finally, it may be noted that some magistrates were directly concerned with the transport and sale of salt in places where such business was under government management (*kuan-pan*). These magistrates had the responsibility of buying salt certificates from the government with official funds, and then transporting and selling salt within their districts.[185]

5. Tea Tax

Tea certificates (*ch'a-yin*), required for the sale and transport of tea, were issued principally by the Board of Revenue and in certain localities by the magistrates.[186] In most instances the tea certificates carried by merchants were examined at the inner customs stations. In certain areas, however, this examination was the duty of the magistrates.[187] The tea tax (*ch'a-shui*)[188] was collected from tea merchants either at the customs stations or by the magistrates as one kind of miscellaneous tax.[189]

The magistrates were supposed to prevent the sale of "private" tea, that is, tea sold without benefit of a certificate. If they neglected to do so, they were punished in the same way as for failing to prevent salt smuggling.[190]

OTHER ASPECTS OF ADMINISTRATION

The last chapters have been devoted to the two most important functions of local government, the administration of justice and taxation. In this chapter we shall discuss briefly the remaining aspects of local administration: population registration, security, courier sevice, public works, public welfare, and educational, cultural, religious, ceremonial, and other functions. This list indicates that the local government's functions were comprehensive; they incorporated not only those activities which could be performed only by the government, but also the supervision of those activities which were, or could have been, handled by private agencies. Underlying this situation was the Chinese philosophy of government, which decreed that every organized activity that concerned the general welfare of the populace was the concern of the government. Therefore all community activities were either governmentalized or under direct government supervision.

1. POPULATION REGISTRATION

In theory, the Yellow Registers (*Huang-ts'e*) were the records of "land holdings, households, and mouths"[1] in a locality. But since the Ch'ing government was interested in registering the population mainly for the purpose of imposing labor-service tax on male adults (as a substitute for labor service), the Yellow Registers listed only the male adults (*ting*) between the ages of sixteen and sixty, who were liable to the labor-service tax. Female adults were also registered in Kiangsi, Fukien, and Kwangtung, where they were subject to the salt gabelle. The names of the *ting* were listed by *chia-chang* and *li-chang* on the records for each *chia* and *li*. The magistrate, on the basis of all the records submitted to him by the various *li-chang,* compiled a register for the whole hsien and submitted it to his direct superior, who in turn submitted it to the provincial treasurer. The latter then compiled the register for the whole province and submitted it to the Board of Revenue. The Yellow Register was compiled in this way every ten years, until it was discontinued in 1668.[2]

The compilation of Yellow Registers constituted but a part of the magistrate's routine. His real responsibility was the registration and assessment (*pien-shen*) of *ting* and their landed property at regular intervals (in the early years of the dynasty, every three years; from 1656 until 1772, every five years). Such a registration-assessment was indispensable during the period when the labor-service tax was imposed on male adults as an independent item.[3] It was a means of ensuring that the labor-service tax collected kept pace with any increase in the adult male population. All males aged sixteen and above were registered and the names of the aged (sixty years and over), the deceased, and those who had moved away were eliminated from the record.[4] The assessment was more complicated in Chihli, Honan, Shansi, Shensi, Kansu, and in some localities in Shantung, where the labor-service tax was divided into three grades and nine divisions, corresponding to ownership of landed property.[5] In these areas, change in an individual's economic status called for a corresponding adjustment in his tax rate at the time of the assessment. Hence it was necessary to reassess landed property when its ownership was transferred, so that landowners would be reclassified according to any increase or decrease in their holdings.[6] The assessment of *ting* was less complicated in the south and in some parts of Shantung, where labor-service tax was not divided into grades.

We have mentioned that after 1713, the 1711 registration of *ting* was used as a permanently fixed basis for collecting the labor-service tax. However, since any male who had reached the age of sixty had to be replaced on the records by another adult of his family, or by one of his relatives, or by someone within the same *chia* or *li,* an assessment continued to be made every five years in order to maintain the 1711 quota.[7] When the labor-service tax was merged with the land tax in most provinces, between 1716 and 1729, this quinquennial assessment became less significant, and in 1740 the provincial authorities were ordered to report annually to the emperor the number of households and mouths and the amount of grain stored in a province. This annual report was based on *pao-chia* records, not on an actual assessment like the quinquennial assessment.[8] The quinquennial assessment, which continued concurrently with the annual reports instituted in 1740, was finally abolished in 1772. The edict abolishing it stated that its purpose had been to prevent adults from evading labor service, but since the labor-service tax was now collected on the fixed basis of 1711 and, moreover, had been merged with the land tax, the quinquennial assessment no longer served any practical purpose, and should, therefore, be abolished forever.[9]

2. SECURITY

It was a magistrate's duty to organize the households in his district into units of *p'ai* (10 households), *chia* (100 households), and *pao* (1000 households) and to appoint heads for each unit (*p'ai-t'ou, chia-chang,* and *pao-cheng* or *pao-chang*).[10] The magistrate issued annually to each household a door placard listing the name, age, and occupation of the family head and the names of other persons in the household, including relatives and servants.[11] Whenever a member moved in or out, the family had to report it to the *chia-chang,* who was obliged to put it on the *pao-chia* record and to revise the door placard.[12] As a rule, two copies of this record were prepared for each *chia,* one of which was kept by the *chia-chang* and the other by the magistrate. The two copies were used in rotation at regular intervals: when copy A was revised by the *chia-chang* in accordance with the actual changes in population within his *chia* and presented to the magistrate, copy B was given back to the *chia-chang* for similar revision, and so on. In this way the *pao-chia* records were to be kept up to date.[13]

The *pao-chia* organization was used in both the district seat and the villages. All residents were included in it, including the unemployed, ex-convicts, prostitutes, and other delinquents.[14] The fundamental function of *pao-chia* was to set up a police network to detect lawbreakers, particularly robbers and bandits.[15] Under some officials it also incorporated such functions as encouraging good conduct and thus improving local custom.[16] The main idea behind the *pao-chia* system was that one's activities could hardly escape the eyes and ears of one's neighbors, and if the neighbors were organized and a register of their households kept, it would be difficult for strangers and lawbreakers to hide among the law-abiding residents.[17]

Consequently, the principal task of the heads of *pao-chia* was to watch the local residents and report any unlawful activities in the various families (gambling, religious heterodoxy, selling of unlicensed salt, illegal coining of money, harboring of fugitives or other criminals), and to keep an eye on suspicious strangers. They were to record the name of everyone who came and left.[18] They were also required to submit a signed statement to the magistrate twice a month reporting whether there had been any unlawful activities.[19] They were held responsible for failure to report any case involving robbery or the harboring of a robber.[20]

In addition, the *pao-chia* also performed the function of local patrol. The *chia-chang* could assign villagers to keep watch at the street gates day and night. When an alarm warned of the approach of robbers and bandits, the *chia-chang* led the villagers in pursuing the invaders and guarding the village.[21] It should be noted that the *t'uan-lien* (local militia), whose purpose was to train local adults as a supplement to the regular government force in defending an area against outside invaders, was not identical to the *pao-chia*. The two might supplement one another,[22] but in most cases the *t'uan-lien* was not included in the *pao-chia*.[23] As the next chapter will show, the local militia was organized under the leadership of the gentry, not under the heads of *pao-chia*, who were generally commoners.

Now let us consider the over-all situation into which the *pao-chia* fitted. In China in the period under discussion, the majority of the populace under the jurisdiction of a magistrate lived in widely scattered villages. The magistrate, whose yamen was located in the district seat, normally had no direct contact with the villagers. Not many towns had subdistrict magistrates stationed in them to detect and arrest lawbreakers.[24] Thus the villages and many of the towns were left outside the surveillance of the government. The *pao-chia* was an apparatus that enabled the government to extend its control beyond the lowest administrative unit and thereby fill this gap.[25]

Most writers on this subject have tended to overemphasize the effectiveness and formidability of the *pao-chia* system of surveillance and the harsh punishment meted out to its heads when, for instance, they failed to report crimes. These writers seem to assume that the rural population was thoroughly controlled by the government. The question of how successful the *pao-chia* actually was has not been given sufficient attention.[26] In point of fact, it was on the whole ineffective.[27] The system was first introduced under the Ch'ing in 1644. Local officials neglected to follow it, and an edict was issued sixty-four years later by the K'ang-hsi emperor to enforce adherence to it. But we find the following statement by the Yung-cheng emperor in an edict of 1726: "Since the enforcement of *pao-chia* in the forty-seventh year of K'ang-hsi [1708], there has frequently existed only the name, not the reality. The local officials are afraid of the difficulties, considering [the system] a formality, not actually observing it, and not strictly carrying out the surveillance." Following this edict, rules of reward and punishment were promulgated to encourage enforcement.[28] Yet the government still found it necessary to reiterate its policy from time to time as the officials continued to regard the administration of *pao-chia* as a formality.[29]

To be sure, there were isolated cases where the magistrates took the matter seriously. Liu Heng and Wang Feng-sheng,[30] for example, were known for their accomplishments in *pao-chia* administration. But they were more the exception than the rule. The policy of such magistrates, which was not carried on by their successors, soon became obsolete. By and large, the magistrates seem to have been halfhearted in executing and supervising the *pao-chia* administration. As the statements of Huang Liu-hung, T'ien Wen-ching, Wang Hui-tsu, and other officials indicate, *pao-chia* was not actually enforced in their times—the K'ang-hsi, Yung-cheng, and Ch'ien-lung periods, respectively.[31] According to Wang Feng-sheng, a magistrate in the Chia-ch'ing period, the *pao-chia* had remained a formality for the past several hundred years.[32] In the nineteenth century, Feng Kuei-fen declared that despite the many decrees issued by the emperors and provincial officials to enforce the *pao-chia,* it was seldom carried out and on the few occasions when it was, it produced no effect.[33]

It is obvious that the magistrates could not, and were not expected to, visit all the villages and register the households in person.[34] This was customarily done by the *pao-chia* personnel or *ti-pao,* who apparently took no great pains in performing their duty.[35] The magistrates knew that the household records prepared by them were unreliable,[36] but at best they could do no more than check the records occasionally by selecting at random a few households to be investigated when they next went into the villages.[37]

As we have mentioned, each household in a district was issued a door placard by the magistrate, listing all the members of the household.[38] But frequently these placards were found only on the doors in a district seat.[39] No effort was made to revise the records and door placards; they remained the same, although changes took place from time to time within the households.[40] A certain magistrate pointed out that these records were useless unless they were kept up to date, though constant revision was extremely difficult.[41] It was reported by one prefect that the rotating records actually were not exchanged between the magistrates and the heads of the *pao-chia* as specified by regulation. He also mentioned that the heads did not actually carry out their assignments.[42]

Some of these shortcomings were undoubtedly attributable, in whole or in part, to lack of funds. No funds were provided by the government for defraying the expenses involved in registering the households, making records, and issuing door placards. The necessary funds could be obtained in only two ways: by securing donations from the magistrates,[43] or by putting the financial burden on the local residents. For example, the residents were frequently called on to pay the cost of stationery and of door placards.[44] Here again, the clerks and runners took advantage of the situation and demanded various fees from the people.[45] The *pao-chang* also were subjected to extortion when they went to the yamen to exchange records or to submit their signed semimonthly statements.[46] Liu Heng once observed that while the *pao-chia* failed to keep the people under surveillance, it disturbed them by causing them to pay fees.[47]

Finally, something should be said about the place of the gentry in the *pao-chia* administration. The law provided that members of the gentry be included in the organization together with the commoner households, but that they be exempted from night watch duty, and not recruited to serve as heads of *pao-chia*.[48] However, the gentry were reluctant to have their names registered in the *pao-chia* records, and they were often allowed by the magistrate to be registered separately and exempted from displaying a door placard. It was commonly considered improper to register their names together with those of commoners in the same record or to ask the gentry to display a placard on their door and to have them supervised by the *p'ai-chang*.[49] In point of fact, the heads of *pao-chia,* having no access to the gentry households, were not in a position to supervise them anyhow, so that, whether the gentry households were included in the *pao-chia* organization or not, they were outside the surveillance of government agents.

In general the gentry did not participate in the administration of *pao-chia*.[50] Fang Ta-chih once expressed the opinion that although he needed the help of the gentry in administering the *pao-chia,* the honest gentry were unwilling to participate, because they wanted to avoid suspicion and enmity, as well as work. The poor members of the gentry, on the other hand, were busy making a living and had no free time to participate in *pao-chia* activities, while the dishonest gentry were not reliable and therefore could not be trusted.[51]

3. COURIER SERVICE

The post stations (*i-chan*), which provided horses (carriages in Chihli) and meals for the imperial commissioners, tribute-bearers, high provincial officials en route to their posts or to the capital, and couriers carrying official dispatches and memorials, were set up on thoroughfares. The number of post stations in a chou or hsien varied from one to three, depending upon need; there were sixty to seventy horses at each station. In a lonely place, only a few horses were prepared for the dispatching of official documents.[52] There were also *p'u,* where dispatch bearers (*p'u-ping*) were stationed to convey official documents to various yamen within the province, mainly between the magistrate's yamen and that of his superior, or between different magistrates.[53] Boats were also provided in places near a river.[54]

In most cases the post stations were under the magistrate's jurisdiction; but in some places they were under a post station master (*i-ch'eng*). Even in the latter case, the over-all supervision was the magistrate's and he had charge of the funds.[55] Thus it was his duty to see that the horses were well fed, well cared for, and reasonably used,[56] that horses and rations were given according to the specifications in the certificate allowing the bearer to use the post service (*k'an-ho* or *huo-p'ai*),[57] and that there was no delay in the delivery of dispatches.[58]

It was extremely difficult for a magistrate personally to supervise the post stations, especially when they were located in towns outside the district seat; [59] hence a relative or personal servant was often assigned to a post station to supervise the clerk and the grooms (*ma-p'ai*).[60]

However, this did not exempt the magistrate from many of the burdens connected with the post service, particularly the burden of welcoming a commissioner or high official. It was not only necessary to supply horses and escorts, but also to provide residence and food, and to present gifts to the official and his attendants. Failure to satisfy the attendants often led to humiliation and trouble.[61] Of course much of the routine was taken care of by the magistrate's servants, but their inferior status made it impossible for them to handle the entire situation. Hence the magistrates, particularly those located in centers of communication, were forced to keep a strenuous schedule.[62]

Although the unauthorized use of post horses was prohibited,[63] many traveling officials demanded more horses than were specified in their certificates. The magistrates seldom dared to offend them by refusing to comply with their demands; still less did they have the courage to report such occurrences to the Board of War.[64] Some of the higher officials using the post service even demanded all sorts of supplies, and their attendants also demanded fees from the magistrate.[65]

The clerks of the post station also practiced abuses, and the postal service thus became a great burden to the local people. Sometimes they were asked to feed the horses at the station,[66] or to pay the expenses of the post station.[67] Or they had to supply horsefeed without charge, or sell it cheaply.[68] Sometimes a horse broker would be forced to replace a thin horse with a fat one. At other times a tax agent (*hsien-nien*)[69] would be asked to contribute money to buy a horse to replace a dead one.[70] According to regulations, in places where no carriages were provided by the post station, they could be rented from the local people.[71] In actuality, many local households supplied carriages and donkeys without charge, or gave money instead.[72] Sometimes horses and donkeys were commandeered from the people when there were not enough horses at the station to meet the need, although such action was unlawful and any magistrate guilty of it was subject to demotion.[73] In short, it was the local people who suffered through the administration of the post stations.[74]

4. Public Works

Water conservation and water works of the principal rivers, like the Yellow River and Yung-ting River, were under the officials in charge of river administration, and were financed by government funds.[75] But river tributaries, reservoirs, and dams which affected merely the irrigation of local farms were left to the local officials and people. In theory, it was the magistrate's responsibility to see that the rivers were properly dredged and the dams kept in good condition so that the local people could have the benefit of irrigation.[76] As no funds were provided by the government for these works,[77] the magistrate had to finance them by other means. The customary way was either to recruit local residents to do the labor[78] or to secure contributions from them in proportion to the extent of their landed property.[79] Sometimes a special fund was raised by means of donations when work on a large scale was called for. For instance, the repairs on a collapsed dike of Ch'ien-t'ang River in Chekiang were financed through a fund amounting to 140,000 taels contributed by the people of three hsien and some salt merchants.[80]

It was the duty of the magistrate to see that the main roads and important bridges were in good condition. He was subject to punishment if they were in such a poor state as to impede communication.[81] The city walls and government buildings (yamen, treasury, granary, jail, and government temples) also had to be maintained, and if any of them collapsed the magistrate was held responsible.[82] He was allowed to recruit local people to repair the city wall if the expense of construction was less than 1000 taels.[83]

As a rule, any large-scale repair or construction project had to be approved by a superior authority;[84] otherwise it had to be financed by the magistrate. There were two common ways of meeting such expenses: by a donation from a magistrate[85] or by inducing the gentry and the wealthy people to contribute. A third but less common way was to impose a fine on parties involved in minor violations of the law.[86] In one instance, the expense of repairs to a city wall (3400 taels of silver) was shared by the people of a district.[87] Yamen buildings were often repaired by borrowing money from the government, with the understanding that the loan would be paid back by deducting it from the magistrate's supplementary salary.[88] Many magistrates also contributed to the repair of the local shrine to honor the loyal, righteous, chaste, and filial.[89] An edict of 1727 indicated that it was proper for a magistrate to donate money to repair shrines, for he could afford to make such a small contribution. If the official was allowed to use public funds, the edict continued, it might lead to embezzlement by officials and clerks.[90] Since a magistrate was held responsible if any construction done under his supervision collapsed within a specified period,[91] and since he would have to pay customary fees to clerks in the superior yamen if he requested funds, few magistrates requested government funds for repair work unless it was absolutely necessary and urgent. For this reason, an official once advised that a magistrate undertake no works that could be avoided, lest he get himself into trouble by initiating them.[92]

5. Public Welfare

Granaries

There was an "ever-normal granary" (*ch'ang-p'ing ts'ang*) in each chou or hsien, under the charge of the magistrate. These granaries were so called because part of the grain[93] stored in them could be sold to local residents at a price lower than the market price in the spring when the market price was high; in the autumn the granaries could replenish their supplies with the funds obtained from the spring sale.[94] In time of famine the poor farmers could borrow grain from these granaries and pay it back after the harvest without interest. Such loans had to be reported to the magistrate's superior officials and approved by them.[95]

Before any grain was sold from the granary the magistrate had to report to his superior the price and the quantity to be sold.[96] The proceeds from the sales were turned over to the provincial treasurer, and in some cases to an intendant.[97] The grain had to be replaced through purchase within six months; delay would incur penalties for the magistrate ranging from forfeiture of nominal salary to dismissal.[98] Prior to the purchase, the governor-general and governor were informed of the quantity to be purchased as well as the source of supply. Then the funds obtained from the spring sale would be returned to the magistrate to be used for the purchase. The newly bought grain was examined by the prefect or the independent chou magistrate, who then submitted a signed statement to the provincial treasurer reporting the purchase.[99]

The magistrate was to see that the grain under his care was kept in good condition. He was held responsible if it was spoiled through dampness. The granary was inspected every year by the prefect or an intendant. A magistrate leaving his post had to leave a fixed quantity of grain to his successor. He was further responsible for making up any deficiency within a year.[100]

Although the system of the ever-normal granary was devised to benefit the poor, it actually did not work out to their advantage. In the first place, since the granary was located at the district seat, it was out of reach for the villagers living at a distance. According to regulations, temporary stations were to be established in rural districts where the magistrate's subordinate officials were to be sent to direct the sale of grain.[101] But apparently this was rarely done, for there were frequent complaints that only those who lived in or close to the cities were benefited.[102] Taking advantage of the lower price of the government grain, the households of government students, runners, and grain brokers, with the cooperation of the granary clerk, often bought large quantities by using false names,[103] although this was forbidden by law.[104] The granary clerks and runners often demanded money from the people who purchased grain from the granary, or asked them to return more grain than they had borrowed.[105]

To get rid of their old stock, some magistrates forced the people to buy grain, even when they did not need it.[106] A further burden on the people was that the magistrate often bought grain at a price lower than market price from the people under his jurisdiction, who were then obliged to transport it from the villages to the granary.[107] For this reason, a regulation was promulgated to the effect that grain must be bought from a neighboring hsien; a magistrate was to buy grain on his own locality only if no water transport existed between his locality and neighboring districts.[108]

There are indications that there was frequently a shortage of grain in many of the granaries. One reason for this was that the superior yamen was so slow in arranging for the transfer of funds to the magistrate that by the time the funds arrived the market price of grain might have gone up. This situation was aggravated by a tendency on the part of the superior officials to cut the purchase price reported by the magistrate, regardless of the actual market price. Consequently many magistrates found it impossible to buy grain at the rate set by their superiors and simply deposited the funds in the treasury without making the purchase.[109] Embezzlement of grain also contributed to the deficiency of government grain.[110]

In addition to the ever-normal granary, many chou or hsien had "community granaries" (she-ts'ang) and/or "public granaries" (i-ts'ang),[111] from which local residents could borrow grain, with or without interest, depending upon the local harvest condition.[112] These granaries were established in the villages and towns by the local residents, through voluntary donations. To encourage such donations the government rewarded the donors with decorations, tablets, or official hat buttons.[113] This type of granary was managed by a director nominated by the local residents and approved by the magistrate.[114] The only provinces where the community granaries were under the management of a magistrate were Shensi and Kwangsi, where the granaries were established with government funds.[115]

The community and public granaries were under the over-all supervision of the magistrates. The name of the director nominated by the local residents was registered in the yamen. After years of satisfactory service, the director might be rewarded with a decoration, tablet, or official hat button. If his service had not been satisfactory, or if he had committed embezzlement, he could be dismissed and punished, and the magistrate could order him to pay back the funds.

In principle, the magistrate was not allowed to interfere in the financial affairs of the community granary, but the director was required to submit to him an annual report as to the amount of grain received, lent, and stored. He had to report also when the granary was repaired.[116] Magistrates were generally advised to examine the management of the community granary carefully, since its success depended largely upon their supervision.[117]

However, community and public granaries were not established universally, and even where they did exist there was frequently a shortage of grain. A private secretary once stated that since the magistrates could not investigate these granaries in person, they merely sent runners to secure a bonded statement from the directors; thus the supervision was but a formality.[118] An edict of 1727 mentioned that the governor-general of Hunan and Hupeh, Yang Tsung-jen, was well known for his efforts in promoting the community granary, and yet an investigation disclosed that the grain kept in the granaries in his provinces was much less than he had previously reported. This discovery caused the emperor to question the practicality of the much advocated system.[119] Wang Hui-tsu reported that although the community granary of Ning-yüan in Hunan had a quota of 2000 piculs, its operations were restricted to cash accounts being transferred from one director to another.[120] In another instance, a magistrate of P'ing-hu in Chekiang discovered that out of the 10,000 piculs of grain in the community granary, 9000 had been embezzled by the director, who had never lent grain to the people in a period of thirty years.[121] In general, the directors were indifferent and the management poor; in many areas the community granaries operated ineffectively or even ceased to operate.[122]

Famine Relief

As natural calamities were a constant threat to the people all over the empire, it was an unavoidable task of the local government to deal with them. Whenever there was a flood or drought, it was the magistrate's duty to make a preliminary investigation and report his findings to his superior at once.[123] Delay was punishable by forfeiture of nominal salary, demotion, or dismissal, depending upon the extent of delay. A magistrate who failed to report a calamity at all was subject to dismissal.[124] The preliminary investigation was followed by a second investigation by commissioners assigned by the magistrate's superior officials, in which the magistrate also assisted. Within forty days of the second investigation, the magistrate was to submit a report on the seriousness of the calamity. As this report was the basis for decisions relating to famine relief and the reduction of the land-and-labor-service tax, it was up to the magistrate to see that it was accurate.[125] The percentage of tax reduction varied according to the degree of crop damage.[126] As a rule, the collection of tax (minus the reduction agreed upon) was postponed for one to three years after the calamity.[127]

The computation of tax reduction was a complicated task, for it had to be done for each household with reference to the damage on each piece of land. Thus it was necessary for the magistrate to prepare for each household a tax record listing the damage, reduction, and amount to be collected.[128] He was required also to announce the rate of reduction as approved by the emperor and to notify each taxpayer as to the amount deducted and owed.[129]

The administration of famine relief was equally complicated. To begin with, it was necessary for the magistrate or commissioner to interview the calamity-stricken people in their homes, determine how much relief, if any, should be given,[130] classify them into such categories as "extremely poor" or "less poor," and make a report to the superior officials.[131] In the case of a flood, the magistrate examined the damaged houses and the bodies of drowned people and livestock, in order to allocate money for house repairs and for burial of the dead.[132]

In the experience of one magistrate, Fang Ta-chih, the business of calamity investigation was beset with evils. If it was assigned to the clerks and the heads of *pao-chia,* they would engage in various forms of corruption; [133] if it was entrusted to the gentry, they would be prone to favoritism; and yet it was extremely difficult for the magistrate himself to visit and examine all the households in person.[134] Wang Feng-sheng suggested that the best way was to have a record of the people stricken by calamity prepared by the village heads, examined by the gentry, and then sent to the commissioners for further investigation.[135]

Cards listing the number of persons eligible for relief were given to the households, entitling them to receive money or rice from the government.[136] These were distributed in person by the magistrates and the commissioners, both at the stations set up in the district seat and in the rural areas.[137]

As government relief was often inadequate to meet the needs of the poor people, it was necessary to raise funds for additional relief—for example, in the form of rice-gruel kitchens.[138] Such funds were secured mainly through contributions from the gentry and other well-to-do people, especially shop owners.[139] For instance, during a flood in Chekiang, government relief was administered for four months, and relief for an additional three months was made possible through contributions by the gentry and the owners of pawnshops, saltshops, and other large shops.[140] To initiate fund-raising campaigns, the magistrates often found it necessary to make a contribution themselves.[141] Frequently a relief board was established and members of the gentry were appointed by magistrates as directors to manage and distribute the relief funds.[142]

In a case of calamity caused by locusts, the magistrates were required to make a report to the superior officials without delay and to supervise the peasants in exterminating the insects. Under the law, it was the duty of the magistrates to destroy the pupal locusts. A magistrate failing to do so and thus permitting the pest to mature and destroy the crops was subject to dismissal.[143]

Poorhouses and Foundling Homes

In every district there was a poorhouse, variously known as *p'u-chi t'ang, yang-chi yüan,* or *liu-yang chü,* where the aged, disabled, and poor were housed and given rations, clothing, and medical care. It was the magistrate's duty to take care of persons in these categories in accordance with the local quota, which varied in different localities.[144] As the poorhouse usually had limited funds and a small quota,[145] only a small number of poor people could be admitted. For this reason, conscientious magistrates found it necessary to raise funds to meet the need, often through contributions from the magistrates themselves and from the gentry and well-to-do commoners.[146] Most of the foundling homes were in the provincial capitals;[147] with a few exceptions[148] no official funds were provided for such institutions in the chou and hsien. Thus, as in the case of the poorhouses, it was left to the magistrates and/or the gentry to raise money to establish foundling homes.[149] The funds and the foundling home might be managed by the government, often under the direct care of the clerks and runners,[150] or by the gentry.[151]

6. EDUCATION AND PROMOTION OF CULTURE

According to the government regulations, there should be community schools (*she-hsüeh*) and charity schools (*i-hsüeh*) in the cities and rural districts of each chou and hsien to provide education for children and adults who could not otherwise afford it. The magistrates were required to report to the provincial director of studies the names of the teachers and the pupils attending the schools.[152] But, with the exception of such a place as Shun-t'ien prefecture, no funds were provided for this purpose.[153] Therefore the establishment and maintenance of these schools were left to the magistrates. Schools were often established by conscientious magistrates through contributions from themselves and from local gentry.[154]

The students of the chou and hsien schools (*sheng-yüan*) were under the supervision of the director of studies and an assistant director of studies; but some magistrates also took an active interest in the students' academic activities, asking them to lecture on the classics, examining them at regular intervals,[155] or admitting brilliant students to the academies (*shu-yüan*) for advanced study.[156]

The magistrates played a part in the examination system by administering the preliminary "district" examination (*hsien-shih*) required of the *t'ung-sheng* (lit., "junior students").[157] Only after a candidate had passed this examination and another one given by the prefect (*fu-shih*, prefectural examination) could he take the examination given by the provincial director of studies (*yüan-shih*). In general, the task of reading the examination papers was left to the magistrate's private secretaries; only a few magistrates read the papers or gave the students an oral examination.[158] But the responsibility for conducting a fair examination always rested on the magistrate. Thus he was punishable with demotion or dismissal for permitting anyone to take the examination who was not eligible,[159] for passing any who should not have been passed, or for allowing his private secretaries or clerks to accept a bribe from candidates in connection with the examination.[160]

In addition to formal education, the government also concerned itself with indoctrinating the masses. This was not only essential according to the Confucian doctrine of moral influence; it was also, as the rulers well knew, of vital importance to the social order and security of the dynasty. For this purpose Sacred Edicts[161] were created and expounded to the people at public lectures twice a month, a practice known as *hsiang-yüeh*. The magistrates were required to marshal the gentry and the people to these lectures. In the rural areas, members of the gentry and, more frequently, students in government schools were selected as speakers (*yüeh-cheng* and *yüeh-fu*) to expound the Sacred Edicts to the local residents.[162]

The magistrates were required to make an inspection tour of the villages from time to time to supervise these lectures,[163] which were held in such public places as temples. The Confucian concept of moral influence was further applied by the government's instructing the magistrates to investigate the custom of their locality, seek to improve it, and encourage the people to be filial, chaste, honest, industrious, frugal, and law-abiding. The officials were also enjoined to wipe out bad customs like idleness, gambling, infanticide, heterodoxy. The magistrates were instructed to visit the villages frequently in order to learn the good and bad customs and try to rectify the bad ones. They were also advised to adopt the lecture system and to discuss with the gentry the customs and problems of their locality.[164]

In particular the magistrates were concerned with two of the moral precepts advocated by the government: honoring the aged and honoring the virtuous. The first was demonstrated through the ceremony of a local banquet (*hsiang-yin*) which was held in the first and tenth months of every year at the district school, where the magistrate was host to the aged and worthy people of the locality.[165] Women of chastity, married or unmarried, and filial sons were also honored. They were reported to the government by the magistrates and educational officials, so that their names could be preserved on a stone tablet or an arch and they could be worshipped after their death in the shrine to chaste and filial women (*Chieh-hsiao tz'u*) or the shrine to filial and brotherly men (*Hsiao-ti tz'u*).[166] Needless to say such acts were meant to encourage deeds of virtue.

In spite of the ceremonial importance attached to virtuous deeds, cultural and moral activities remained theoretical, having little significance in practice. Not many people seemed to take them seriously. There were conscientious magistrates who really made an effort to enforce the lecture system and took part in the lectures themselves.[167] But as evidenced in an edict of 1813, few magistrates actually adopted the system.[168] In the district seats, lectures may have been given as a formality, but in the villages even this was not done.[169] Since the magistrates seldom visited the rural districts, except when on official tours, they were not in a position to enforce and supervise the lecture system there. At best, they could only round up the villagers to attend a lecture while they were on a visit to the villages.[170] Thus the system did not operate successfully in the villages, where the Sacred Edicts had no way of reaching the illiterate rural population at large, whom the emperors were seeking to indoctrinate.[171]

Nor was the ceremony of the local banquet observed by many magistrates.[172] Wang Hui-tsu reported that when he announced his intention to observe the ceremony, no one could tell him the details of how it should be done, and the ceremony, when held, attracted a large crowd of spectators as a rare event.[173] The government finally decided in 1843 to eliminate the appropriation for this purpose.[174]

7. CEREMONIAL OBSERVANCES

From the earliest days of Chinese history, offering sacrifices to Heaven and other supernatural forces had always been a sacred task of the government. From the emperor down to his agents at the lowest level, every official took part in sacrificial activities as prescribed in the Book of Sacrifices kept by the government. As soon as an emperor or official took office, these observances became a part of his routine. In this chapter we shall deal only with the religious duties performed by the magistrates.

Upon his arrival at a new post, it was customary for the magistrate to hold a fast, and if possible, to stop overnight in the temple of the city god.[175] Whether he slept in the temple or not, he offered a sacrifice at the temple the next morning, and read a sacrificial address to the city god. The address usually contained an oath that he would not engage in corruption or injustice, invoking punishment from the god if the oath were violated.[176] The oath thus gained the magistrate a measure of supernatural sanction.

Only after this sacrifice had been held would the magistrate proceed to his yamen. And before he took over the post, he was expected to offer sacrifices to the spirit of the middle gate of the yamen (*i-men*) and the local earth god (*T'u-ti*).[177] Within three days of arriving at his post, the magistrate was also expected to pay a visit to the Confucian temple, the temple of the city god, and temples of other gods included in the list of regular sacrifices (*ch'ang-ssu*).[178]

Thereafter it was the magistrate's duty to burn incense on the first and fifteenth days of each month at the temples of Confucius, the city god, the god of war (Kuan-ti), and the god of literature (Wen-ch'ang). Spring and autumn sacrifices were offered in the second and eighth months to Confucius, and to the gods of earth and grain (She-chi), of wind, cloud, thunder, rain, mountains, streams, and city (Ch'eng-huang). Sacrifice was also offered to the god of agriculture (Hsien-nung) in the third month.[179] In addition, sacrifices were offered in spring and autumn at the shrines to famous local officials (*Ming-huan tz'u*), to virtuous local gentry (*Hsiang-hsien tz'u*), to loyal and righteous men (*Chung-i tz'u*), to filial and brotherly men (*Hsiao-ti tz'u*), and to chaste and filial women (*Chieh-hsiao tz'u*).[180] There was also a sacrifice to those ghosts who had no one to offer sacrifices to them (*li*).[181]

A magistrate who failed to visit the temples or offer sacrifices on schedule, or who held a banquet during a fast was subject to impeachment. Failure to provide adequate sacrificial articles was also punishable.[182]

In addition, it was the magistrate's obligation to pray whenever there was a calamity. Thus a prayer meeting was often held before the city god, the gods of earth and grain, the gods of wind, cloud, thunder and rain, and the god of agriculture in time of drought, flood, or locusts.[183] Some magistrates also offered sacrifice to the god of locusts,[184] although this duty was not included in the Book of Sacrifices.

Some magistrates took praying very seriously. They demonstrated their sincerity by wearing dark clothing and walking to the altar where the sacrifice was offered,[185] and they often instructed the people to stop the slaughter of animals before a prayer meeting took place.[186]

The religious activity of local officials was not determined altogether by government regulations and requirements. It was also influenced by the expectations of the people. In time of drought, for example, people demanded that the magistrate pray for them.[187] They not only expected him to offer prayers to gods approved by the government, but also to worship any god whom they worshipped and whom they conceived of as presiding over the calamity. To them the magistrate was the chief priest of the locality. It was not unusual for the local people to take the image of some god to the yamen and demand that the magistrate offer sacrifice to it. When this happened, the official was really in a dilemma. He was not supposed to worship any spirit not listed in the government Book of Sacrifices,[188] but his refusal to cooperate with the local people would displease them and give them the impression that he was not concerned with their suffering; such an impression might lead to further, serious consequences. Wang Hui-tsu reported that the local people once took more than twenty images to his yamen, demanding that he pray to them for rain. He refused, on the ground that these gods were not orthodox. He maintained that his refusal could have led to disturbance had he not already won the confidence of the people.[189]

Among the local deities the city god occupied a particularly important position. In the minds of the traditional Chinese, there was a similarity between this deity and the magistrate: both were concerned with the people's welfare and with justice in the territory under their jurisdiction. One was appointed by the emperor; the other was appointed by the supreme god.[190] There were even instances in which a magistrate, after his death, was worshipped as the city god.[191] The magistrate was responsible for things within the range of human power, while the gods were responsible for what was beyond human power.[192] The city god was called upon to maintain a harmonious natural order, protect the people against epidemics, bestow good harvests, protect the innocent, punish the guilty, and supervise government administration and the personal conduct of officials.

In the belief that a man's crime could escape the eyes of human beings but not of the gods, the city god in particular was frequently called upon to help the magistrate to administer justice more satisfactorily.[193] There was a case where a magistrate prayed before the city god, asking for instruction through the medium of a dream to help him to identify a murderer.[194] Of course, not all officials actually believed in the supernatural, but they made use of the people's belief in it. As the people feared supernatural sanction more than law, one could take advantage of their credulity to induce suspects to confess. For this purpose, trials were sometimes held in the temples of the city god.[195]

The ceremonies performed by the magistrates included celebrations of the advent of spring, the local banquet honoring the aged and the virtuous, and drum-beating to save the sun or moon during an eclipse.[196] To welcome the advent of spring, a clay ox, whose color corresponded to the color of the year,[197] was carried to the yamen from the east suburb, together with the image of Mang-shen (the driver of the clay ox). On the first day of spring (*li-ch'un*) the ox was whipped by the magistrate and his subordinates.[198] This ceremony, which symbolized the beginning of the influence of spring, the season to start agriculture, was observed everywhere in the empire.

8. MISCELLANEOUS

The magistrates were charged with many further duties, such as encouraging the people to engage in farming and in the cultivation of mulberry trees,[199] encouraging them to dredge rivers and build dams,[200] and reporting to their superior officials on the local conditions with regard to rain and snow.[201] The magistrate was also the fire warden of his district,[202] and was punished when any official building or private dwelling was destroyed by fire.[203] It was also his duty to defend the city against attack.[204] The magistrates were required to enforce the prohibition of unlawful coinage,[205] unlawful mining,[206] unlawful slaughtering of cows,[207] heterodox beliefs,[208] gambling,[209] and violations of the sumptuary law.[210] Negligence in the detection of such unlawful activities was punishable by law in most cases.

In sum, the magistrate was given over-all authority to deal with all matters in his locality, except those under the charge of special officials: educational officials, military officials, and officials in charge of river administration, salt, and customs. New duties might be assigned to magistrates as dictated by necessity. For instance, after the introduction of opium into China, the magistrates were made responsible for prohibiting opium smoking and the planting of opium seeds.[211]

Needless to say, not all of the magistrate's functions were performed with equal seriousness. Some of them were mere formalities. It is quite apparent that those tasks whose performance did not affect the magistrate's career and whose accomplishment could not be measured were more or less neglected. Thus the majority of the officials did only lip service in exerting moral influence, and those who made genuine efforts were ridiculed by their colleagues as "dogmatic and doltish."[212] The encouragement of farming and irrigation was regarded in the same light. An imperial edict complained that it was difficult to find officials who would concern themselves with such things as farming and irrigation, which in ancient times had been encouraged by good officials.[213] The absence of activities in connection with moral influence and encouragement of farming was well documented by the officials themselves.[214]

X

THE GENTRY AND
LOCAL ADMINISTRATION

1. THE GENTRY AS AN INFORMAL POWER

As we have seen, the chou and hsien governments considered all matters concerning the common good of the community—welfare, custom, morality, education, agriculture, and so on—to be within the scope of their activities. Many of these matters, regarded by the Chinese as within the province of governmental "administration," would in other societies have been the responsibility of civic associations. Certainly the government was not in a position to carry out all these functions with equal effectiveness. It was the local gentry that performed some of the functions which the local government was unable or not well qualified to perform. As we shall see, there was a traditional division of function between the local governmental authority and the gentry. The latter, in fact, were indispensable to the realization of certain of the government's aims.

The gentry were the local elite[1] who shared with the government the control of local affairs. They represented an informal power, in contrast to the formal power invested in the local government.[2] While the two groups depended upon one another, each exercised its power in a different way. The interplay of these two forms of power shaped the power relationship into patterns of coordination, cooperation, and conflict.

An important feature of the Chinese gentry was that it was the only group that could legitimately represent the local community in discussing local affairs with the officials and in participating in the governing process. This privilege was not extended to any other social group or association. The merchants' guild[3] was not powerful enough to have a voice in matters concerning the common good of the community, still less in the governing process. In fact, with the exception of a few wealthy members, such as those engaged in the salt business,[4] the merchant class was not treated with courtesy by the government officials and had no access to them. The merchants' strongest means of protest against the authorities was to close their shops. This situation persisted until the latter part of the nineteenth century, when the merchants were allowed to join the gentry in discussions of local affairs (hence the gentry and merchants came to be mentioned together as *shen shang*).[5] But they were still under the domination of the gentry and failed to form an independent power group.[6] Thus, for a long time the gentry's leadership and power went unchallenged, except during a rebellion or other crisis when the *status quo* could not be maintained.

In the sense that the gentry and the officials belonged to the same group, as either members or potential members of the bureaucracy, their power was derived from the political order. Thus, despite the distinction between formal and informal power, it was actually the same power group that controlled society. The same group of men were officials in their public capacity and gentry in their private capacity. The result was that the politically based power was the power that dominated and only those who possessed it, actually or potentially, were admitted into the elite and allowed to participate in the act of governing.

2. Definition of "Gentry"

The term "gentry," borrowed from English history, has been the cause of much confusion and debate when applied to the Chinese scene. To this confusion has been added the fact that the composition of the gentry in China was not the same in all periods.

The early Chinese term, *chin-shen,* which can be traced back to before the Ch'in and Han, was simply a synonym for officials.[7] The term *shen-shih* or *shen-chin* was used in Ming and Ch'ing times, indicating the emergence of a new status group—degree holders (*shih* or *chin*). The Ch'ing inherited both its examination system and the structure of its gentry from the Ming dynasty.

In view of the evolution in the composition of the group, it is misleading to discuss the Chinese gentry without specifying the period. We are concerned here only with the gentry under the Ch'ing. Since the term has no equivalent in English, it would be better either to use the Chinese term or to designate this class in China as the "local elite," meaning a power group which controlled local affairs by means of informal power. While "local elite" might seem rather too general, it does not have the misleading associations that "gentry" has. But, wishing to avoid further confusion through the injection of a new term, I shall keep the commonly accepted term "gentry," emphasizing the rather unique features of the Chinese gentry.[8]

The privileged status of the Chinese gentry was not determined on a purely economic basis. Membership in the gentry did not derive from wealth or the ownership of landed property, as some scholars have assumed.[9] No doubt there was a close connection between wealth and gentry membership and the significance of the former should not be overlooked. The possession of property made possible the leisure necessary for acquiring the education that enabled a person to take the civil service examinations. The characteristic style of life of the gentry was also impossible without some degree of wealth.[10] However, there is a distinction between the conditions facilitating entrance into a privileged class and the actual attainment of privileged status. Wealth or landed property per se was not the qualification for gentry status. The commoner-landlords did not belong to the gentry group, no matter how much land they owned. Probably the connection between wealth and status became closest at times when it was possible to buy from the government an official rank or academic title (student status in the Imperial Academy)—a common practice in the Ch'ing, particularly in the nineteenth century when exigencies forced the government to seek additional revenue.[11] This was the only condition under which wealth could be translated directly into status, bypassing the examinations. But landlords and merchants who did not purchase an official rank or academic title remained commoners.[12]

On the other hand, anyone holding a degree or receiving an official appointment immediately became a member of the gentry, regardless of land ownership. There were poor *sheng-yüan,* holders of the lowest degree, who owned no landed property,[13] and lived on their stipends or incomes from teaching or other occupations. The poorest ones even received relief from the government during a famine.[14] Thus both propertied and propertyless persons belonged to the same status group.[15] While it is true that most gentry members did possess property, particularly landed property, the fact is often overlooked that many of them, as portrayed in the satirical novel, *Ju-lin wai-shih* (The Scholars), acquired landed property after they had acquired gentry membership. In their case land ownership was the effect rather than the cause of status. All these factors would argue that, although landed property was closely linked with gentry status, it is ambiguous and misleading to define landlords as gentry.

It is also important to keep in mind that a distinction existed between the literati and the gentry, although there was of course a certain degree of overlap. Education was usually a prerequisite to becoming a gentry member, but education alone did not automatically qualify one. It was necessary to pass the civil or military examinations in order to attain this status. For example, a junior student (*t'ung-sheng*) who had passed the preliminary examination given by a magistrate or a prefect (*hsien-shih* or *fu-shih*) was not admitted to the gentry until he had passed the examination given by the provincial director of studies (*yüan-shih*),[16] thus acquiring the First Degree and the status of a student in the government schools. There were learned scholars who never became gentry because they had failed to pass this examination or refused to take it. These men were known as *pu-i* (lit., "wearers of cotton-cloth garments"; that is, commoners).[17] On the other hand, nonliterati might acquire gentry status by purchasing an academic title or official rank.

What, then, were the qualifications for gentry membership? The answer is to be found in the political order; that is to say, membership was based upon the attainment of bureaucratic status or of the qualifications for such status. The gentry class in the Ch'ing period, as it was defined legally, officially, and popularly, was composed of two groups: (1) officials: active, retired, or dismissed, including those who purchased their official titles or ranks;[18] (2) holders of degrees or academic titles, including civil and military *chin-shih* (holders of the Third Degree, or those who had passed the metropolitan examination); civil and military *chü-jen* (holders of the Second Degree, or those who had passed the provincial examination); *kung-sheng* (Senior Licentiates, including those who purchased their titles);[19] *chien-sheng* (Students of the Imperial Academy, including those who purchased their titles);[20] and civil and military *sheng-yüan* (students of government schools, who were holders of the First Degree, popularly known as *hsiu-ts'ai*).[21]

These two groups constituted the gentry, known as *shen-shih* or *shen-chin*.[22] But within the gentry, as is indicated in the *Hsien-kang ts'e* (Essentials to government; records prepared by magistrates for their superiors) and other official records in which the names of local gentry were listed, a distinction was made between *shen*[23] and *shih* (or *chin*).[24] *Shen* referred only to the officials (group 1), whereas *shih* referred to the holders of degrees or of academic titles who had not yet entered official-dom (group 2).[25] In other words, a distinction was made between officials and nonofficials, between what may be called, respectively, the "official-gentry" and the "scholar-gentry." [26]

The "scholar-gentry" belonged neither to the ruling class, nor to the ruled; they were an intermediate group.[27] They did not participate in the formal government, but they enjoyed a large measure of the prestige, privileges, and power of the ruling class—a fact which characterized them as the elite and separated them from the masses. As potential candidates for membership in the bureaucracy, they may also be called the potential ruling class.

In view of these factors, I am strongly convinced that the distinction between the official-gentry and the scholar-gentry has considerable socio-logical significance in the analysis of the Ch'ing power structure. As we shall see, the official-gentry had a superior status, had more privileges, and were more influential than the scholar-gentry. The first group formed the locus of power, whereas the second was rather on the periphery. The way in which the groups exercised their influence or power was also different.

Both the official-gentry and the scholar-gentry were referred to as *chü-hsiang shih-ta-fu* (scholar-officials living in their home town) because of the close connection between the gentry and their native communities. The degree-holders generally lived in their native places, except when they took employment (for example, as private secretaries) in other areas. The officials, under the "law of avoidance," which prohibited their holding a post in their native province,[28] had a dual status—that of an official in one locality, and that of gentry member in their native province. We might call such an official an "absentee gentry member" because he could assume his role only in an indirect way. He assumed it directly when he was at home on leave, say to observe the mourning period for a parent, or when he had retired or been dismissed. Then he became a *hsiang-huan* or *hsiang-shen* (lit., "official living in his home town").

It was within this territorial sphere that the gentry acted their role and maintained the various forms of interpersonal relations with the local officials. Because their ties with their native places were permanent ones that engendered a sentimental attachment, the gentry seem to have felt that it was their responsibility to guard and promote the welfare of these communities. This sentiment was lacking among the magistrates and other local officials, who were nonnatives.

3. Prestige and Privileges of the Gentry

The gentry had a status superior to that of the rest of society. They had a class consciousness and a sense of belonging to one group. They identified each other as members and shared similar attitudes, interests, and values (specifically, Confucian values). They felt that they were distinct from the rest of the populace. This fact apparently underlay their common sentiments and collective action. An insult to one member, from an outsider, for example, was considered an insult to the whole group. A magistrate once said: "Please one *shih*, and the whole group *of shih* will be pleased; humiliate one *shih*, and the whole group of *shih* will be resentful." [29]

On the whole, the gentry were treated by local officials with courtesy and respect, the extent of which was graded according to the individual's status within the gentry stratum. Only the official-gentry and holders of higher degrees (*chin-shih* and *chü-jen*) were equals of the magistrates; and some among these, having higher official ranks, were considered superior to the magistrates. The holders of the lowest degrees (*sheng-yüan*) were regarded as inferior to the magistrates. The members of this subgroup, having no bureaucratic status, were regarded as merely "heads of the commoners." [30] This status scale was clearly evident in the conventional way in which the gentry referred to themselves before the magistrate[31] and the way in which they were received by him.[32] While the official-gentry or holders of higher degrees had free access to the magistrate, the *sheng-yüan* did not.[33] Under the law, the *sheng-yüan* and those who purchased the titles of *kung-sheng* and *chien-sheng* were under the supervision and control of both the local and educational officials,[34] who were required to report to the provincial director of studies on the conduct of the students.[35] As we shall see later, the students could be and were chastised or dismissed in accordance with a prescribed procedure. In short, while the gentry as a whole enjoyed a status superior to that of the commoners, the status of the *sheng-yüan* and of the *chien-sheng* was inferior to that of the official-gentry and the holders of higher degrees. As Feng Kuei-fen pointed out, it was difficult for a magistrate to inflict hardships on the official-gentry, but easy to inflict them on the *sheng-yüan* and *chien-sheng*. They could be deprived of their titles upon the magistrate's request, or humiliated or ruined by him in some other way.[36]

The gentry enjoyed certain social, economic, and legal privileges. The law allowed them the privilege of a particular style of life. They were entitled to wear a certain kind of hat button, and an official robe and belt.[37] The holder of a higher degree or academic title, from *chin-shih* down to *kung-sheng*, could display on his door a horizontal tablet inscribed with his title, and erect a flagpole in front of his residence to show his superior status.[38] All the gentry had the privilege of observing special ceremonies at weddings, funerals, and sacrifices.[39]

The official-gentry were not placed under the judicial power of their local authority and were not subject to the regular judicial procedures. An official could not legally be tried or given a sentence without the emperor's permission.[40] The same applied to retired or dismissed officials, unless their discharge had been dishonorable.[41]

The scholar-gentry were accorded treatment different from that of the commoners in court. *Sheng-yüan* and purchasers of the title of *kung-sheng* or *chien-sheng* could not be beaten by a magistrate without permission from the educational officials.[42] When corporal punishment was decreed, it was administered by the latter in the presence of the magistrate, in a hall in the government school which was named, literally, "Understand Relations Hall" (*Ming-lun-t'ang*). A magistrate who disregarded this regulation was subject to punishment.[43] When a serious offense was involved, the suspected offender had first to be deprived of his academic title or degree on the recommendation of the magistrate before a trial could be held.[44]

Official-gentry and scholar-gentry were also exempted from punishment short of penal servitude. The law permitted them to cancel a beating by pecuniary redemption. But by mandate, when an offense called for punishment by 100 strokes, an official was to be impeached and a *chin-shih*, *chü-jen*, *kung-sheng*, *chien-sheng* or *sheng-yüan* was to be deprived of his degree or academic title.[45]

When a member of the official-gentry or scholar-gentry was involved with a commoner in a dispute over marriage or landed property, or in any other civil lawsuit, he was permitted by law to send a family member or servant to act as his representative at the trial.[46] A commoner who injured an official, whether active or retired, was punished more severely than if the injured man had been his equal.[47]

All these privileges meant that the gentry received legal protection such as was not enjoyed by the commoners. From earlier chapters the reader will recall that the common people, including wealthy landlords, were subjected to all kinds of persecution and annoyance by officials and their subordinates.[48] Only when wealth was combined with political power could the people secure protection for themselves and their families.[49] This helps to explain the eagerness to become degree holders or officials.[50]

4. Gentry Channels of Influence

The gentry's influence in their community was exerted in two spheres. One was the sphere of the commoners, from whom they commanded respect and obedience. As social leaders of the community, they settled disputes,[51] conducted fund-raising campaigns, commanded local defense, and provided other kinds of leadership. The people also expected the gentry to protect them against injustice, to give them relief in time of calamity, and to take an active part in promoting local welfare.[52]

The other sphere of influence was that of the local officials. In this connection, a distinction has to be made between authority and influence. Only an official had the authority to make decisions and to issue orders through the government apparatus. A gentry member, lacking such authority in his native area, could only exert his influence upon the officials in their decision-making—that is, induce the officials to initiate, modify, or withdraw a decision or action. Influence is here defined as operative whenever it induces a change in decisions.[53]

Needless to say, not all the gentry were equally influential. There were prominent members who had influence in a whole province; others had influence only in a prefecture, a hsien, or a village. The degree of influence was determined largely by the local situation. For example, in Kiangsu or Chekiang, where there was a large number of degree-holders, a *chü-jen* was not likely to have a great deal of influence. On the other hand, even the holder of a low degree could be influential in a place where degree-holders were rare; for instance, a *sheng-yüan* might occupy a leading position in a small place, such as a village.[54]

Among the prominent gentry in a community, there were usually a few at the top who were the most influential of all. Their word carried more weight than that of any other gentry members and they often assumed leadership among the group.[55] In general, the official-gentry were more influential than the scholar-gentry, and the holder of a higher official post or of a higher degree was more influential than the holder of a lower post or of a lower degree. The reason is obvious. Official-gentry as well as holders of higher degrees had closer connections with the power hierarchy. They invariably had ties with high officials both in the central and provincial governments. They were able to bypass the magistrate and go directly to the provincial or central officials to influence decisions at a higher level.[56] The official-gentry with superior status might even appeal to the monarch directly.[57] Thus, although the gentry represented the informal power in a local community, they were linked to the formal power at all levels, and it was this link that gave them power to influence the local officials. They were by no means an isolated local power.

An important point here is that the gentry's connection with formal power must be examined within the institutional framework, for the connection was based not merely on random and unorganized personal relations, such as between friends or fellow officials; it was based primarily upon specific relationships connected with the examination system. These relationships existed among three groups of people associated with the examinations: (1) teachers (*tso-shih* and *fang-shih*)—the examiners who passed a candidate in his examinations; (2) students (*men-sheng*)—those who passed the examination, thereby becoming known as the students of the examiner; and (3) fellow degree-holders (*t'ung-nien*)—those who passed the same examination in the same year.

The behavior patterns of the scholar-officials were to a large extent conditioned by these relationships. Once a relationship of this sort was established, it lasted a lifetime. The scholar-officials were under obligation to be loyal to their teachers, students, and fellow degree-holders, and also to the children of all of them, and to help each other in trouble—an obligation observed by all scholar-officials.[58] This was the kind of particularism that Ku Yen-wu noted as the cause of cliques among the scholar-officials.[59] Such institutionalized and organized personal relationships, then, were the channel through which the gentry exerted their influence.

With this in mind it is not hard to see why retired or dismissed officials could still be influential. While they no longer had the formal power, they were not cut off from the power hierarchy and they usually retained some affiliation with it. On the other hand, officials lacking such affiliation, such as those who entered officialdom through the purchase of a title, were much less likely to be influential. In this connection, it was not so much lack of esteem for purchased titles as lack of proper connections that placed the group at a disadvantage.

As the *sheng-yüan* were outside the power hierarchy, they were the least influential among the gentry. Any power or strength they had derived mainly from group solidarity and collective action—as, for example, in joint petitions, or mass refusals to participate in an examination.[60] At times, acting as a group, they even defied and insulted the local magistrate, who often found it difficult to control or punish them.[61] But as individuals, the *sheng-yüan* had little influence with a magistrate.

Nevertheless, the strength and influence of the *sheng-yüan* should by no means be underestimated. The following statement from an essay by Ku Yen-wu describes some of their activities. Ku's essay dealt with the *sheng-yüan* of the Ming dynasty, yet to a considerable extent his description is applicable to the Ch'ing.

It is the *sheng-yüan* who visit the yamen and interfere with the administration of the government; it is the *sheng-yüan* who rely upon their influence to be arbitrary in the villages; it is the *sheng-yüan* who associate with the clerks— some of them are even clerks themselves; it is the *sheng-yüan* who get together and riot when the government officials do not comply with their wishes . . . it is impossible for the officials to punish them, or to liquidate them. When they are treated with even slight harshness, they will say: "This is to kill the scholars. This is to bury the scholars." [62]

5. Gentry Families

Strictly speaking, only a man possessing the qualifications described above (section 2) had the status of gentry. But his prestige and privileges were shared by his family members, not merely on a *de facto* basis, but within the provision of the law. Most important, the status of an official might legitimately be transferred to his family members through the system of bestowal (*feng-tseng*)—a system under which an honorary official title was bestowed on an official's father and/or grandfather. An honorary title, such as *fu-jen* or *ju-jen,* was also bestowed on his wife, mother, and/or grandmother.[63] Upon acquisition of such an honorary title, an official's family member attained the legal status of an official, and was entitled to all such privileges as wearing the official hat button and garment, observing the etiquette and ceremonies prescribed for officials, and legal protection.

Technically, the law treated holders of honorary titles (known as *feng-*

tseng kuan, bestowed officials) in the same way as regular officials.[64] They could be arrested, tried, and punished only in accordance with the law governing the arrest, trial, and punishment of officials. In fact, such legal privileges were also extended to certain family members not possessing an honorary title. There was a law to the effect that the grandparents, parents, wife, sons, and grandsons of high officials in the category of *pa-i* (lit., "the eight deliberations")[65] could not be arrested or sentenced without approval from the emperor. The parents and wife of an official of the fourth or fifth rank, as well as his son or grandson who was entitled to the privilege of *yin* (that is, holders of the title *yin-sheng*), could be arrested and tried by the court, but the sentence had to be approved by the emperor.[66]

An official's father who acquired an honorary title was not himself considered a member of the gentry.[67] While fathers of officials did not participate in such formal gentry activities as meetings, they were not necessarily without influence in the community. They were usually regarded as elders and treated with respect by the local populace and local officials. The form of address used by degree-holders for the father of a fellow degree-holder was *nien-po* (lit., "uncle [who is the father of a] *t'ung-nien*"), a title which implied a sense of kinship and respect. It was not inconceivable for the father of a gentry member to exert a measure of influence on the local magistrate through his son, since sons were expected to be obedient to their fathers. Thus relatives of a gentry member often found it easier to approach him indirectly through his father.

Other relatives of any gentry member—brothers, uncles, nephews, sons, and grandsons—because of their connections with this one gentry member were also often very influential in their community.[68] The higher the gentry member's position, the greater the influence of his relatives. This influence was frequently exerted with greater freedom when the gentry member was away than when he was present to exercise some control.[69] Numerous complaints were made about relatives who used a gentry member's power to oppress the local people, engage in unlawful activities, and interfere with the local administration. Against such practices the local magistrate was helpless.

To deal with this situation, a law was passed to the effect that any relative of an official, other than his father, wife, or son, who relied upon the official's influence to oppress the local people and to insult government authority was to be penalized one degree more severely than commoners guilty of similar offenses.[70] There was also a law holding officials in the capital responsible for the actions of their sons and younger brothers in their home town. The officials themselves were subject to dismissal if their family members used their influence to intimidate the local authority.[71]

In the instructions he left for his children, Wang Hui-tsu warned that the gentry should instruct their family members to abide by the law and not incite them to intimidate or resist the magistrates.[72] For their part, the magistrates were advised in the *Ch'in-pan chou-hsien shih-i* to inform the gentry that punishment would be meted out to their family members if they violated the law.[73]

Women in traditional Chinese society were excluded from membership in the gentry and did not participate in any community activity. However, the wives of gentry members could associate with the wives of magistrates or other local officials, and thus could approach the local officials through their wives.[74]

Even the servants in a gentry family were known to use their master's influence when engaging in unlawful activities.[75] To counter this situation, a law was passed similar to that governing gentry relatives: a slave or servant of an official who relied upon his master's influence to oppress the people or to defy the government authority was to be punished one degree more severely than someone without gentry connections.[76]

All these facts indicate that although the family members of the gentry lacked the formal status of gentry, their activities could not be entirely disassociated from the gentry members themselves. For this reason, they must be included in any survey of the power group; otherwise we see only part of the picture. The point is that the fathers and other close relatives of gentry members were not only more influential than the commoners, but they could actually be as influential as the gentry themselves. Family members of important official-gentry might even be more influential than the low-ranking official-gentry and the scholar-gentry.

As a background factor, we should, of course, keep in mind that the family was the basic unit in Chinese society, and the attitudes and behavior of the gentry were strongly dominated and conditioned by family solidarity. There was a permanent tie between the kinship unit and the local community within which the member's livelihood and the perpetuation of lineage were deeply rooted. Any disturbance in the community naturally threatened the interest of the family. It therefore became the prime responsibility of all family members to protect the collectivity. Similarly it was the obligation of all to help and defend any individual member when he was in trouble, especially when an injustice was done to him by an outsider. An insult to an individual was considered a humiliation to his entire family.

In this environment, one's ability to protect one's self and one's family depended primarily on one's position in the bureaucratic hierarchy.[77] It followed that each family or clan looked upon the gentry member within it as its protector. He in turn accepted this responsibility. Thus, inability to protect the family from encroachment and injustice meant a lack of influence, and group humiliation was equated with personal humiliation.

6. The Gentry's Role in Local Administration

As the magistrate was never a native of the province where he held office, he was likely to have little or no knowledge of the local situation and find it necessary to seek advice from the gentry.[78] In the present context, it is important to note that while regional differences existed in the vast territory of the empire, the administrative code was extremely rigid and contained few provisions for dealing with these differences. The gentry, being more familiar with the local situation, were presumably in a position to offer advice that took the local situation into account.

Information concerning local residents, particularly such undesirable ones as local bullies and pettifoggers, was also sought from the gentry. In this sense, they were considered the "eyes and ears" of the magistrate.[79] It was argued that if the magistrates did not seek information and advice from the gentry, they would have to seek it from another group of natives —the government clerks and runners—who in the minds of most officials were people of less integrity and reliability.[80]

As the official-gentry did have some administrative experience, the magistrates often consulted them on administrative matters like public works or local defense, or when a situation was too complicated for the magistrate to make a decision alone. In this sense the gentry participated in policy decisions. For instance, in 1666 Li Fu-hsing, the magistrate of Lou-hsien, Kiangsu, intended to introduce for taxation purposes a new measure whereby landholdings in the whole district would be grouped into a number of equal units. This required making new records of landholdings and involved many complicated technical problems. The magistrate called a conference with the gentry and got their support for the measure. The book recording this reform attributes success in implementing this new measure mainly to one member of the gentry, a *chü-jen,* on whose advice the magistrate had acted.[81]

In another instance, when the magistrate of Hai-ning, Chekiang, requested that an agent (*li-ts'ui*) be appointed to hasten the collection of land tax in a rural area, the governor, who questioned the suggestion, ordered him to have a conference with the gentry. With the gentry's support the request was finally approved.[82] These examples show that the advice of the local gentry was not only frequently sought by the magistrates voluntarily but at times was required by his superior officials. Sometimes high local officials themselves consulted the gentry on certain administrative matters.[83]

Between the magistrate and the people the gentry assumed an intermediary role, which was facilitated by the traditional respect they commanded from the local populace. Many officials found that it was much easier to pass an order to the people through the gentry than through the formal government channels.[84] At the same time, since they were the only natives who had access to the magistrate, the gentry could make the people's reactions known to the government. Through this channel the magistrate learned, for example, about complaints connected with his administration or his aides.[85]

It is generally assumed that the gentry shared common interests with the local people.[86] Let us see to what degree this was true. In traditional China what the sociologists call community sentiment—that is, a sense of belonging to the same community[87]—was dominant and served to give cohesion to both the gentry and the peasants. Under normal conditions both groups desired a stabilized and orderly society. But such a society was even more important to the gentry because their security and privileges depended upon it. Any great disaster among the peasants would lead to disturbance of the community and thereby threaten the position of the gentry.

On the other hand, as a privileged class the gentry were primarily concerned with the interests of their families and relatives,[88] interests at times necessarily divergent from those of the masses. In times of local crisis community sentiment could emerge forcefully, but in general class interest was more decisive in determining the behavior of the gentry. We conclude that it was only when their own interests were not jeopardized that the gentry took the general interest of the community into consideration and mediated between the magistrate and the local people.

Whether the gentry acted individually or collectively, as a pressure group, on behalf of the community, they were the only group that could voice a protest or exert some pressure on the magistrate or higher officials through recognized channels. One gentry member once addressed a letter to a magistrate stating that the land-and-labor-service tax collected from the people was frequently embezzled by government employees and that taxpayers should be treated more leniently.[89] On one occasion the gentry members of Shan-yin and K'uai-chi, Chekiang, complaining about the excessive charges demanded by the clerks for registering the transfer of landed property, held a meeting and decided that only 800 coins should be charged for such a transfer. They forwarded their resolution to the prefect, asking him to authorize this sum as the permanent official charge. The request was granted.[90] When a suggestion or complaint from the gentry was ignored by a local official, they could, as we have suggested above, directly approach his superiors and exert a greater pressure upon him.[91]

In addition to giving advice, the gentry participated in the following aspects of local administration.

Public Works and Public Welfare

The gentry contributed to the building and repairing of dikes, dams, city walls, roads, and bridges, and the establishment of poorhouses, foundling homes, and widows' homes.[92] The magistrate had to depend upon them for help, because, as we said in the preceding chapter, government funds for public works and public welfare were limited.[93] A common procedure was for the government to set up a commission and appoint gentry members as directors to collect and take charge of funds contributed by the local officials, gentry, and commoners. Further, the gentry were often requested by the magistrate to direct or supervise a construction project or manage a charitable organization.[94] Many officials maintained that under the supervision of the gentry the construction work and public services were performed more efficiently and at less expense than in the hands of clerks.[95]

In time of famine or flood, the gentry not only contributed funds for relief[96] but also directed relief commissions[97] in interviewing famine-stricken people and actually distributing food or money.[98] Many community granaries were under the management of the gentry.[99]

The gentry also participated in the attempted construction of provincial railways when China began to modernize her means of communication in the latter part of the nineteenth century. While the merchants were also financially involved in this venture, it was the gentry who took the lead in negotiating with the government officials for the right to build local railways. For this reason, the directors of the railway companies were eventually selected from the gentry members,[100] although in terms of actual accomplishment this meant very little.

Educational Activities

Contributions for repairs to the local Confucian temple, the examination hall, and school buildings came mainly from the gentry, who considered themselves guardians of the Confucian teachings.[101] They also contributed to the establishment of academies (*shu-yüan*),[102] and some of them became chancellors or lecturers in these institutions.[103] They were also expected to assist the magistrates in enforcing the semimonthly lecture system in the rural districts, where the magistrates could not be present themselves.[104] However, this function was apparently rather nominal. The reader may recall that even in the district seat the lecture system was a formality.

Pao-chia *Administration*

As we have already noted, the gentry as a rule were not actually included in the *pao-chia* organization and the commoners who were heads of *pao-chia* were not in a position to supervise them.[105] However, attempts were made by some magistrates to enlist the help of the gentry in such matters as checking the households against the records made by local constables.[106] There was one case where gentry members were appointed as heads of *pao-chia* in the rural district to supervise the heads of minor units (*chia* and *p'ai*) and to visit the magistrate at regular intervals to exchange the rotating *pao-chia* records.[107] Possibly this was not only an attempt to make the *pao-chia* administration more efficient, but also a device to include the gentry in the network of surveillance.

Local Militia

Although the gentry, by and large, did not take an active part in the *pao-chia* administration, they always played a leading role in organizing the local militia[108] in order to protect their native towns, where their homes and properties were located. As a privileged class, they were eager to maintain the *status quo,* opposing any force that might overthrow the established social order. Naturally the task of local defense, which demanded strong leadership and financial support, fell to the gentry, who commanded the respect and obedience of the local residents and had access to the governmental authorities.

The Ch'ing government, since it was too weak to maintain peace, tolerated,[109] and even depended upon, gentry organization and command of the local militia. A comparable situation had been the organization of local defense by the Ming gentry against the Manchu invaders.[110] This was repeated in the Ch'ing, particularly in the nineteenth century during the Taiping Rebellion. While the regular force was collapsing, the government encouraged the gentry to organize the local militia. Some of the eminent official-gentry on leave in their native provinces, like P'ang Chung-lu (1822–1876) of Ch'ang-shu, Hou T'ung (*chin-shih* 1820) of Wu-hsi, and Tseng Kuo-fan of Hsiang-hsiang, were ordered by the emperor to organize and command the local militia in their native provinces.[111] Some active officials holding high posts in the central or provincial government—for example, Lü Hsien-chi (1803–1853) and Li Hung-chang—were sent back to their native provinces to take charge of local defense.[112] During the Sino-French War, Governor-general Chang Chih-tung also requested the gentry to organize the local militia in Kwangtung to help the government troops resist the invasion.[113]

Often a number of defense corps were organized in the various towns and villages, under the command of a local gentry member.[114] These corps were financed by the gentry themselves, or by voluntary or assigned contributions from the local residents, or by proceeds from a special tax, the likin.[115] Public bureaus were established to collect funds.[116]

In theory the local militia was an auxiliary of regular troops. Most cities were jointly defended by government troops and the local militia,[117] under the over-all command of the magistrate or other local officials.[118] But since the official-gentry often had a status superior to that of the lower-level local officials (in some instances they were the equals of the governor or governor-general), the gentry could sometimes command the local officials. For example, in the defense of Ch'ang-shu and Chao-wen, it was P'ang Chung-lu who directed the defense, with the two magistrates under his command.[119]

The gentry activities described in this section were prescribed by law or custom and were generally accepted. The magistrate was expected to accept the role played by the gentry and allow them to participate in community activities. If a magistrate failed to do what the gentry expected him to do or if he denied their established status and role he was faced with opposition. On the other hand, the gentry were expected by the magistrate and by the people to perform their functions in accordance with the established tradition. The failure of any gentry member to meet these expectations usually brought dissatisfaction and complaint from the officials and the local people and even censure from other members of the gentry.

7. Exploitation and Unlawful Activities

So far we have been concerned with the positive contributions of the gentry to their society. Now we must turn to the other side of the coin, to the gentry's exploitation of their privileged position.

In the early Ch'ing, as in the Ming, the practice of land tax evasion among the gentry was widespread. Although the law gave the gentry only limited exemption (two to thirty piculs per person), they sometimes ignored this limit and evaded land tax altogether. This practice continued despite an edict in 1657 which canceled all previous exemptions.[120] A few years after this edict the Ch'ing government ordered investigations in certain areas in Kiangsu and Chekiang where a large number of gentry members appeared to be tax delinquents. It was disclosed in 1661 that in the prefects of Su-chou, Sung-chiang, Ch'ang-chou, and Chen-chiang, and in Li-yang hsien, 13,517 gentry members owed tax and their names were reported to the court by the governor.[121] The investigations, together with a generally more rigorous policy toward the gentry members, seem to have been a part of the Manchus' efforts to consolidate their political power over South China during the early days of their rule.[122] Nevertheless, they give an indication of the extent to which the gentry evaded the land tax in those days.

To cope with the situation, special laws and measures were introduced by the Ch'ing government whereby delinquent taxpayers among the gentry were singled out and their names reported by the magistrate to the provincial authorities.[123] The tax delinquents were penalized by dismissal from office, loss of degree or academic title, beating, or the cangue, depending upon the amount of overdue tax. Their titles could be restored only after they had completed payment.[124]

Such measures, together with a regulation requiring the magistrates to hand in the full amount of tax owed,[125] made it more difficult for the gentry to evade tax payment than had been the case in the Ming dynasty, since magistrates would be risking their own careers if they tolerated tax evasion by the gentry. This does not mean, however, that there were no cases of the gentry refusing to pay land tax and grain tribute, although such cases were comparatively rare during the Ch'ing.[126]

A more serious problem faced by the government in tax collection was the inequality between payments by the gentry and by commoners. In the tax record the gentry households were designated as "official-gentry households" (*shen-hu*), "official households" (*kuan-hu*), "scholar households" (*ju-hu*), or "large households" (*ta-hu*); the commoner households were designated as "people's households" (*min-hu*), or "small households" (*hsiao-hu*).[127] The commoners, who were required to pay the extra surcharges,[128] paid more in tax than the gentry. The latter were reluctant to pay the extra surcharges on the grounds that they were not a part of the legal tax, and that the magistrates and the yamen personnel collected more extra surcharges than were justified to meet the collection cost. Hence it was impossible for the magistrate to collect from them the same amount in extra surcharges as was imposed on the commoner households. In general the gentry paid their land tax and grain tribute at a rate slightly higher than the legal rate. Some of them were even able to refuse to pay the extra surcharges.[129] Actually, the taxation rate was not the same among all gentry taxpayers. The extent to which they could avoid the payment of extra surcharges depended upon their status and influence; the more influential the gentry member, the lower the rate of the extra surcharge, and hence the closer his tax payment came to the legal rate.[130]

As the local officials could not argue with the gentry on the legality of collecting extra surcharges or setting a higher conversion rate, they had to accept the lower rate paid by the gentry households in accordance with established usage, and meet the cost of collection and other yamen expenses covered by extra surcharges by shifting the burden onto the commoners, who were unable to protest and protect themselves under the law. Thus the commoner-taxpayers bore the greatest share of the cost of collection and of other yamen expenses. In fact the part of the tax left unpaid by some gentry-landowners was also covered by the extra amounts collected from the commoner-landowners. Therefore the tax burden of the gentry was decreased, while the burden of the commoners was proportionately increased.[131] Throughout the dynasty the tax rates for the gentry households remained different from those of the commoner households—the rate increased as the status and influence of the taxpayer decreased. Governor-general Tso Tsung-t'ang reported to the emperor in 1864 that the gentry in Shan-yin, K'uai-chi, and Hsiao-shan, Chekiang, paid only 1.06 to 1.4 taels for 1 tael of land-and-labor-service tax, whereas the commoners, who were obliged to pay coins in lieu of silver, paid from 2800 up to 4000 copper coins for 1 tael of tax.[132] Similar inequality existed in the payment of grain tribute. According to an estimate by Feng Kuei-fen, the gentry paid only 1.2 or 1.3 piculs for 1 picul of tax (at most they paid 2 piculs). Among the commoners, the payment varied from about 2 piculs to 3 or 4 for 1 picul of tax.[133] The governor of Kiangsu, Ting Jih-ch'ang, also reported that the commoner-taxpayers in the Chiang-pei area had to pay 6000 to 7000 coins, or even as much as 15,000 to 16,000, for 1 picul of grain tribute, whereas the gentry paid only 2000 to 3000 coins.[134]

It is obvious that such economic privileges were obtained through political status, and were therefore not extended to commoner-landlords (a fact that again illustrates the impossibility of identifying landlords as gentry, although many of the latter were landlords). The government vainly attempted from time to time to abolish the distinction between the gentry households and commoner households for purposes of tax payment.[135] The gentry refused to give up their special privileges and banded together to defend their common interests.[136]

Another way in which the gentry abused their privileged position was to act as transmitters of tax payments for the commoners (*pao-lan ch'ien-liang*), although a law prohibited such activity and the magistrates were required to investigate any violation of this law.[137] The commoners sometimes sought this arrangement in order to avoid direct dealing with yamen personnel and their numerous techniques of extortion. The gentry stood to profit by collecting tax funds at the commoner-taxpayer's rate (a rate that included the customary extra surcharges) and paying to the government at the lower rate for gentry households, pocketing the difference.[138] Often when the gentry delivered the tax payment to a clerk, the silver contained in the sealed bags was either deficient in amount or inferior in quality.[139] And for grain tribute they often delivered grain of poor quality as payment.[140] An edict declared in 1696 that the large households in Hunan deliberately prevented the small households from paying their taxes directly to the government.[141] In fact, *pao-lan* was so prevalent in the empire that it became a great concern to the government, which was unable to put an end to the practice.[142]

Many gentry members, particularly the *sheng-yüan* and *chien-sheng,* also took advantage of the magistrates' collection of extra surcharges on grain tribute by demanding a share of the profit. In each of the several hsien in Kiangsu as many as 300 or 400 gentry members thus obtained grain tribute fees (*ts'ao-kuei*) from the magistrate. The source of these fees was obviously the commoner-taxpayers; the larger the share of customary fees for the gentry, the more the extra surcharges levied upon the people.[143]

The gentry were exempted from the labor-service tax, the revenue from which was used to hire men to render services to the government. In the earlier days of the Ch'ing dynasty this exemption was extended to the gentry's family members, who might number from two to thirty persons, depending upon the status of the particular gentry member.[144] In 1657 the exemption became limited to the gentry member himself.[145] The gentry were also exempted from "miscellaneous labor service" (*tsa-fan ch'ai-yao,* or simply, *ch'ai-yao*) not covered by the labor-service tax, for example, labor service in connection with public works, government transportation, and the *pao-chia* administration.[146] As a result, the burden of such labor service, which sometimes was rendered in money,[147] was borne by the commoners.[148] It was for this reason that Ku Yen-wu maintained that the official-gentry, scholar-gentry, and clerks and runners, who were all exempted from labor service, were the groups that caused the people to suffer. He suggested that only "the abolition of the *sheng-yüan*" could alleviate the suffering of the people.[149]

Although the law limited labor-service exemption to the gentry members themselves, in practice it was frequently extended to their relatives as well.[150] In many instances, the gentry made arrangements with commoner-landowners, permitting them to register their landed property under the names of the gentry. By this arrangement the commoners could avoid rendering miscellaneous labor service while the gentry profited, in the method described above, by keeping part of the commoners' tax money.[151] Thus a member of the official-gentry in the northern provinces, according to a magistrate's report, often had several tens of such persons under his protection (these were known as *kung-ting*), and a member of the scholar-gentry could also have several. Once a commoner became thus attached to a gentry member, the government agent in the villages did not dare to assign miscellaneous labor service to him.[152] Consequently all the burden of miscellaneous labor service was borne by the commoner-villagers who had no way to appeal,[153] and as more households or land came under the "protection" of the gentry members, fewer households or landowners were left to share the burden.[154]

In general, in the words of one magistrate, "when a project planned by the hsien government is disadvantageous to the gentry, they advance arguments to prevent it from being carried out."[155] Conversely, something useful, like newly reclaimed land or irrigation facilities, would be monopolized by some of the gentry for their own use.[156]

The influence that the gentry was frequently able to exert over the local magistrate was also applied in judicial affairs. True, there were gentry members who helped the innocent for the sake of justice. But more frequently their actions were motivated by nepotism or by financial gain.[157] Some gentry members, according to an imperial edict, presumed upon their position and frequently interfered with the administration of justice.[158] While *chien-sheng* and *sheng-yüan* could not see the magistrate freely, they often had connections with clerks and runners. Thus they were able to become pettifoggers, prompting litigation, handling lawsuits on behalf of others, and making arrangements for their "clients" with the yamen personnel.[159]

That such corruption was prevalent among the *sheng-yüan* is suggested by the fact that one of the eight imperial instructions engraved on a stone tablet (*wo-pei*) placed in all government schools warned the students to keep away from the yamen, not to get involved in lawsuits, and not to appear in court as witnessses. Further, they were instructed to send a deputy instead of going to court personally, even when they were directly involved.[160] Laws were also promulgated to impose punishment on *sheng-yüan* who appeared in court as witnesses, wrote complaints for others, or engaged in pettifoggery.[161]

Gentry members were often accused of being overbearing and tyrannical in their community and of being a menace to local residents, who dared not offend them. An imperial edict of 1747 reads:

Previously the official-gentry in the various places relied upon their influence and were arbitrary and tyrannical in their native places, bullied their neighbors, and constituted a great source of harm to the local area. After an effort was made in the Yung-cheng period to rectify this situation and to strictly prohibit [their unlawful activities], the official-gentry and the scholar-gentry began to obey the law and dared not be involved in affairs not concerning them. Yet recently the old habit has revived. They do not heed the laws but act arbitrarily.[162]

Some gentry members engaged in unlawful activities in an even more flagrant manner—falsely accusing innocent people,[163] seizing the landed property or graveyards of others,[164] beating their own tenants, assaulting others,[165] and swindling.[166] An edict stated that a number of *sheng-yüan* collected fees from boats navigating on rivers, and taxes from people trading at country fairs.[167] The gentry commanding the local militia were even more abusive, for they could make arrests freely.[168] They were accused of disturbing the local communities,[169] and of killing arbitrarily.[170]

Realizing the potential threat posed by the gentry to the peace and security of the local community, the Ch'ing government passed special laws to deal with it. These laws ruled that officials on leave at home who interfered with local government business or engaged in unlawful activities were to be dismissed. Retired and dismissed officials and degree-holders who interfered with government affairs, controlled government officials, or brought harm to the people or to the administration, were to receive eighty strokes. Another law authorized the local officials to impeach any member of the official-gentry or scholar-gentry who was found to be interfering with yamen affairs or oppressing the local people. At the same time the government placed the responsibilty for supervising and investigating the gentry on local officials, that for the *sheng-yüan* on the educational officials in particular. The local authorities were to be punished if they connived in or failed to report any gentry wrongdoing to their superiors.[171]

Despite these laws, the imperial government failed to prevent the gentry from exploiting their privileged position and engaging in unlawful activities. The law leaving the responsibility of supervising them to the local officials remained ineffective. In general these officials were not in a position to control the gentry, especially those of superior status and great influence. Moreover, normally the local officials had a tendency to maintain friendly relations with the gentry, avoiding any offense to them. Nor could the honest and upright gentry members be expected to go out of their way to use their influence to check the activities of the gentry of bad repute, except by expressing their disapproval and dissociating themselves from the group. Under these circumstances, it is no exaggeration to say that the presence in any community of the oppressive gentry, customarily referred to as *lieh-shen* (the bad gentry), constituted a menace to the populace who were at their mercy.[172]

8. Cooperation and Conflict between Magistrate and Gentry

Cooperation and conflict between local officials and the gentry were manifested in various ways and in varying degree. In general, conflict of interests occurred between the magistrate and individual members of the gentry rather than the local gentry as a whole. Only occasionally did a conflict involve all or the majority of the group—either because the interest of the whole group was involved or because the group sentiment was so strong that all the gentry members felt obliged to participate.[173]

The magistrate and the gentry, of course, had interests in common. The magistrate needed the gentry's cooperation and support, without which his administration could not be carried out smoothly. Even his career and reputation depended to a large extent, if not entirely, upon the gentry. As one magistrate, Ho Keng-sheng, put it: "As the gentry are leaders of a locality, the good or bad reputation of the official often hinges on their opinion."[174] Sometimes the gentry even helped the magistrates to make up deficits in government funds by claiming to the government that the local people were willing to contribute money. Actually, as an edict by the Yung-cheng emperor in 1724 indicated, these so-called "voluntary contributions" were a means to force the local residents to share the financial burden.[175] For these reasons, the magistrates treated the gentry with special favor and maintained friendly relations with them.[176]

On their part, the gentry depended upon the magistrate to maintain both their influence in the local community and such special privileges as paying tax at a favorable rate and sharing customary fees collected by the magistrate. A profit-seeking gentry member and a corrupt magistrate often cooperated closely for mutual benefit.[177] The gentry could also cooperate with the magistrate's relatives, private secretaries, personal servants, and yamen clerks.[178] Through these connections the gentry could ask favors of the magistrate either for themselves or on behalf of others.

However, this pattern of cooperation or collusion between the gentry and the magistrate was reversed whenever there was a clash of interests between the two—for example, when the magistrate insisted on enforcing laws that the gentry customarily violated, or when he prevented them from seeking personal gain. There were magistrates who adopted a policy of showing no weakness toward the gentry:

Those who dare to overstep the bounds by making trouble, to slander the officials by submitting complaints, or to contemn them orally in public, must be disciplined, and their errors must be emphatically rectified. They should never be given a chance to get their wish lest they become overbearing in the future.[179]

Conflicts also arose when the gentry had military power in their hands. Some of them not only treated officials with contempt, but often went beyond the traditional bounds of informal power and intruded into the area of formal power. In other words, they ceased to observe the customary way of exercising their influence, and were inclined to strive for superiority, usurp the power of the local authorities, and take the law into their own hands, even making arrests and meting out punishments. Tseng Kuo-fen, who himself had been a gentry member in charge of local militia and an expert in gentry-official power relations, described the situation in his warning to the gentry in 1860:

> First [the gentry] request from magistrates an appointment as commissioners of the local militia bureau to obtain honor. Then the power goes down [from the officials to them], and they have nothing to fear. The yamen is dependent upon them for its food and other needs. They bestow rewards and inflict punishment at will, and contemn the officials. Now I want to warn the gentry that they should respect and stand in awe of the officials and observe this rule as a first principle.[180]

Under the circumstances, it was inevitable that the gentry came into direct conflict with the local authorities, magistrates as well as higher officials. Several instances were reported by Hsüeh Fu-ch'eng (1838–1894), who was aware of the problems involved in authorizing the gentry to organize the local militia.[181] Obviously there were tensions between the local officials and the gentry. To a magistrate, the maintenance of harmonious relations with and proper control of the gentry was a very difficult problem. He was always under the threat of fault-finding, intimidation, slander,[182] and accusations[183] on the part of the gentry.

The gentry were likewise subject to stresses and strains because of their uncertainty as to the attitudes of the magistrate, who might not tolerate their exploitation of privileges and their unlawful activities. Open conflict with the magistrate could ruin them, particularly in the case of the scholar-gentry, whose status was less secure than that of the official-gentry.

While there were sometimes clashes of interest between individual gentry members and individual local officials, they seem never to have been serious enough to cause a change in the power structure and the established social and political order. Such conflicts should be interpreted as conflicts within the same power group or social class, not between two different groups or social classes. Since both the gentry and the officials belonged to the same privileged class, they depended upon each other for the *status quo,* with the result that they remained entrenched in their perpetuation of their common interests; this permitted them to maintain position of privilege and power for a long period in China's history.

CONCLUSION

At the beginning of this book I made the point that local government in China under the Ch'ing was highly centralized. The Chinese system, with the government of the various subdivisions of a province, down to the chou and hsien, under the control of the central government and administered by officials appointed by it, was parallel to the French system, where the prefect is directly responsible to the central government. But China had no local autonomy corresponding to that of the French communes. There was no government or council in the towns or villages, either in name or in fact. In this sense, the Chinese local government was even more centralized than the French.

The magistrate, who was under the supervision of officials at higher levels, was not empowered to make major decisions. Excepting in certain routine matters like the handling of minor civil cases, which were under his jurisdiction, the magistrate had to report to his superior and secure approval on most details of administration. This situation led Ku Yen-wu to conclude that "the magistrates possessed the least power among all officials." [1]

Local government under the Ch'ing was ruled by an administrative code that was very comprehensive and apparently aimed at uniformity, rationality, precision, conformity, and centralization. But, paradoxically, these regulations also created technical difficulties and were inefficient. First, they were too rigid to allow the magistrate to exercise personal judgment or initiative.[2] Second, the code made little allowance for regional differences, thus preventing the magistrate from adjusting administration to any special conditions in a locality.

It has been said that conformity is the universal value observed by all bureaucrats and often becomes an end in itself.[3] Bureaucrats everywhere are disciplined to conform to the rules by a system of reward and punishment, which produces in the officials an attitude of timidity and an over-concern with conformity per se. In China this was carried to the extreme, for the administrative regulations were extraordinarily numerous and infractions always incurred punishment. Moreover, as we recall, for violating certain regulations, Chinese officials could not only be demoted or dismissed from office but could also be subjected to corporal punishment. This means that Chinese officials were liable to more severe punishment than are their counterparts in countries where a distinction is made between punishment for an administrative fault and for a criminal offense. In this situation it is to be expected that the main concern of most officials was to avoid punishment.[4] This became even more accentuated because magistrates relied on their private secretaries in the conduct of local administration. The secretaries, being personally employed by the magistrate, felt obliged to avoid anything that would jeopardize the careers of their employers. Their guiding principle was apparently that strict adherence to regulations was the safest policy.

Yet at the same time we find that many laws and regulations were not actually in operation and had become more or less a formality. This occurred in almost every aspect of administration—for example, in relation to the term of service for the clerks and runners, and in the matter of customary fees. However, this did not mean that the officials and their aides could act entirely according to their own will. If the formal regulations governing some procedure were not operative, they had to follow the established custom. Any change from the established custom was likely to be resisted by the people. Thus the entire yamen staff developed a code of behavior acceptable both to themselves and to the local populace.

Local finance was also highly centralized, at least in theory. Officials of the local government, from the province down to the chou or hsien, acted only as agents of the central government in collecting and delivering taxes in accordance with the quotas set by the central government. They were not allowed to levy any taxes except likin, the local transit tax introduced in 1853. The local government thus had no revenue of its own, and even its operating budget was determined by the central government. No portion of the centrally administered taxes was allocated for local expenditure, with the exception of some limited items like the nominal salaries for officials, wages for runners, and sacrificial expenses. Nor was the local government allowed to add a centime to any national tax for local purposes. Consequently the local government was not provided with funds to meet the expenditures of local administration, including the collection and delivery of taxes to the central government.

This situation gave rise to the "customary fees" from which local government at various levels derived its revenue. Thus, while local finance was intended to be highly centralized, in practice it was decentralized. The fee system had no fixed rates, so the local officials had almost complete freedom in collecting and spending the fees. No distinction was made between yamen expenses and the personal expenses of the magistrate. The higher provincial officials had no control over the fees; they merely took their share of them.

From the data presented in the preceding chapters we may conclude that throughout the Ch'ing dynasty there was an over-all continuity in local administration, despite periodic revision of administrative regulations and formulation of new ones, all documented in great detail in the *Ch'ing hu-tien shih-li* (Collected statutes and cases of the Ch'ing dynasty). Most of these changes were technical and procedural and not very significant, particularly at the chou and hsien level. The organization of the yamen, its personnel, and their functions, and the pattern of supervision and of local finance all remained basically the same.

As we have seen, the functions of the local government were very comprehensive, the most important among them being tax collection and the administration of justice. In the sense that all these functions were under the magistrate's charge, he was a "one-man government," while his subordinate officials played a markedly insignificant role. Between the magistrate and his four groups of aides—clerks, runners, personal servants, and private secretaries—there was no intermediate authority; all were directly responsible to the magistrate.

The clerks, personal servants, and private secretaries all played an important part in local administration.[5] But the role of the secretaries, who were the real administrative experts, was most significant. They were the nerve center of the yamen. The popular notion that Chinese bureaucracy was run by "amateurs" should be somewhat offset by the "expertness" of the magistrate's private secretaries, whose professional qualifications and experience were well recognized.

The magistrate stood in two distinct relationships to his aides. The clerks and runners, being natives and employed by the government, maintained a formal and impersonal relationship with the magistrate. The secretaries and personal servants were usually not natives; they were employed by the magistrate himself and were not considered government employees. Thus they maintained an informal and personal relationship with the magistrate.

As bureaucracy is characterized by a rational structure based on formal and impersonal relationships,[6] the presence of informal and personal relationships in a government is often considered a hindrance to efficiency.[7] However, the case of China seems to suggest that these elements have to be re-examined against a particular bureaucratic structure. The employment by the magistrate of aides with whom he maintained an informal and personal relationship may be viewed as a device to check and supervise the formal and impersonal group, whose efficiency depended upon such supervision. It should be kept in mind that, despite the informal and personal arrangement between the magistrate and his private secretaries, their employment was based primarily upon technical qualifications—competence and achievement. And in the discharge of their duties, they were mainly guided by administrative rules. Although they were not entirely free from consideration for their employer's professional security, their actions still had to be based on objective and calculable rules. Hence the "irrational" elements in local administration were reduced to a minimum.

Recent studies on industrial workers and military personnel have indicated the importance of the informal primary group in raising output and morale. Such findings show that "the human, the interpersonal, the informal factors," which have been generally ignored by students of the traditional science of public administration and bureaucracy, including Max Weber, "are of crucial administrative consequence." [8] The private secretaries and personal servants of the magistrates seem to provide another example of how the informal and personal factors may operate within a formal structure to reduce administrative strain and gain greater efficiency. From this vantage point, supported by recent findings in the science of human relations in the West, one might well question the validity of the common notion that personal and informal relations are *always* incompatible with bureaucratic efficiency.[9] The point is that efficiency cannot be examined superficially, merely in terms of personal versus impersonal and formal versus informal relations. We must also take into account other factors—criteria of eligibility, method of selection, terms of employment, and the like. Our data indicate that such factors had a profound influence on the behavior of all groups in the yamen.

Specifically, the superior status, pecuniary reward, and other attractions of a private secretaryship provided incentives for capable persons to embark on that career. Conversely, the lack of such attractions in the jobs of the clerks, runners, and personal servants made them unappealing to persons who could find better employment. Usually the opportunity for extralegal income was the chief motive in taking jobs that were otherwise so unrewarding.

Earlier chapters have shown that the private secretaries, as a rule, were devoted to their jobs and were more honest and reliable than the notorious personal servants. The fact that both groups had a personal and informal relationship with their employer and yet manifested different behavior patterns suggests that the difference must be examined further against other factors, such as the ones mentioned above.

In sociological terms, the deviant behavior (from the point of view of morality and law) of the clerks, runners, and servants was largely a consequence of the dissociation of cultural values and social position.[10] In other words, when one has no legitimate means to secure the desired values—pecuniary reward, career opportunity—owing to one's unprivileged position, one tends to seek these values by illegitimate means. To be sure, such dissociation occurs among all other unprivileged groups in society. But the crucial point here is that the personnel attached to a yamen not only had access to the illegitimate means but in fact also had immunity from prosecution, despite the formal regulations. "Accessibility with immunity" is an invitation to deviant behavior. Moreover, if the majority of the members of an occupation are engaged in deviant behavior, it is likely that they will exert pressure on the remaining members by demanding conformity. Nonconformity on the part of some members may cause group sanction in varying degrees. Thus what the government and the public consider deviant behavior or corruption may be regarded as conformity to the occupationally defined norms of behavior.

The inefficiency of the Chinese local government was largely due to poor organization and lack of coordination. One manifestation was the duplication of duties among the secretaries, clerks, and personal servants. The government policy of isolating personnel—that is, allowing them no opportunity for contact with one another—as a means of control made effective supervision difficult. Another source of inefficiency was the policy of not permitting private secretaries to participate in direct observation or investigation, a policy which resulted in judgments based on documents and other indirect sources of information.

With regard to the gentry, we have identified them as the local elite whose right to represent the local community was recognized by both the government and the public. They served as intermediary between the local officials and the people, gave advice to the former, and frequently took an active part in certain aspects of local administration. As participation of the local community in the administration of local affairs has often been considered a condition of local self-government, it is logical to ask whether the gentry's participation meant local self-government.[11]

The answer to this question is no. In the first place, participation was limited to the gentry as a minority group. Second, the gentry were neither elected by the local people as their representatives nor appointed by the government as such. They were accepted as spokesmen for the community by dint of their privileged status. But their participation in government and their right to speak on behalf of the community were not formally defined, as in the case of an elected council in the West. There were no rules as to which gentry members should be consulted or invited to take part in administrative affairs. This was left largely to the local officials. Although the gentry might, and frequently did, intervene, there was no legal procedure whereby they might challenge or reject decisions made by the officials. In fact, the gentry's intervention took place mainly on a personal basis, and its effectiveness depended largely on the influence commanded by a particular member.

While the gentry could represent their own interests to the local government, there was no agent to represent other groups in the community. At most, the gentry were likely to be concerned with the welfare of the people only in the interest of general stability in the community. However, the gentry had no legal or political responsibility to protect the people. Any obligation they had was primarily moral and was carried out largely on a voluntary and informal basis. Furthermore, as a privileged group, the gentry's interests were at times in conflict with those of the rest of the community. This fact is again incompatible with self-government, which requires that the interests of the community as a whole be represented.[12]

The gentry enjoyed status and privileges similar to those of the officials. Although the officials were linked with formal power and the gentry with informal power, the power of both groups derived from the political order. Only persons having such a politically determined status had access to the local officials and could have a voice in local policy. Thus the gentry was the only pressure group. They and the local officials together determined the local policy and administration and shared the control of society. As power means participation in the governing process or "participation in the making of decisions,"[13] we may conclude that local power in China under the Ch'ing was distributed only among the officials (formal government) and the gentry (informal government).

The action and interaction of all the groups we have studied in detail indicate that there were strains and tensions among them: between the magistrate and his superior officials, between the magistrate and the clerks, runners, and personal servants, between the officials and the local gentry, between the people and the officials and their subordinates, and between the people and the gentry. As strains and tensions are often stimuli to change, we naturally ask why they induced no noticeable change in the Chinese situation. A decisive factor, I suggest, is that all these groups, with the single exception of the common people, secured maximal returns under the existing system. Therefore, in spite of the tensions and conflicts among them, they were not interested in altering the *status quo,* and we find stability and continuity in the social and political order. This stability was threatened only when the dissatisfaction of the people was intense enough to culminate in open revolt. But so long as their dissatisfaction was not translated into effective action, the *status quo* was maintained.

NOTES

INTRODUCTION

1. R. K. Merton, *Social Theory and Social Structure* (Glencoe, Ill., 1949), p. 118.

2. This notion implies that historical research on bureaucracy is not only of significance to the historians, but, to quote C. J. Friedrich, is "the only basis for empirical data on the social phenomena abstractly described as bureaucracy. Whatever aspects or criteria a working concept should stress is a question which should be settled, not by an intuitional typology, but by relevant historical documents" ("Some Observations on Weber's Analysis of Bureaucracy" in R. K. Merton, *et al.*, eds., *Reader in Bureaucracy*, Glencoe, Ill., 1952, p. 29).

3. C. E. Merriam, *Systematic Politics* (Chicago, 1945), p. 118.

CHAPTER I. CHOU AND HSIEN GOVERNMENT

1. A prefecture was divided into a number of smaller units: ordinary subprefectures (*shu-t'ing* or *san-t'ing*), ordinary chou (*shu-chou* or *san-chou*), and hsien. An independent department had a few hsien under its jurisdiction. Some of the independent subprefectures also contained ordinary chou and hsien. (According to *Ch'ing hui-tien,* 4:3, all independent departments had a number of hsien under their jurisdiction, whereas only two of the independent subprefectures incorporated ordinary chou and hsien: Feng-huang t'ing in Fengt'ien, and Shu-yung t'ing in Szechwan.)

2. *Ch'ing hui-tien,* 4:3.

3. *Ch'ing-ch'ao wen-hsien t'ung-k'ao* (hereafter *Ch'ing t'ung-k'ao*), 85:5610.

4. *Ch'ing shih-lu,* Kao-tsung, 47:6b; *Ching-shih wen hsü-pien,* 21:2. According to Lu Lung-ch'i (1630–1692), the chou and hsien in the north were smaller than in the south (*Ling-shou hsien-chih,* 10:25b).

5. However, there were instances where two hsien shared one walled city. This happened when one hsien was divided into two. When Ch'ang-chou and eleven other hsien and one chou in Kiangsu were divided into two in 1724, each of the newly established hsien were ordered to share the same walled city with the old chou or hsien: e.g., Ch'ang-chou and Yüan-ho; Ch'ang-shu and Chao-wen (*Ch'ing shih-lu,* Shih-tsung, 24:4–6). It was also customary for a

hsien yamen located in a prefectural city to share the same city with the prefectural yamen.

6. For example, there were 79 villages in Shen-tse, Chihli (*Shen-tse hsien-chih*, 1:32); 156 in Luan-ch'eng, Chihli (*Luan-ch'eng hsien-chih*, 2:25b); 407 in Nei-huang, Honan (*Nei-huang hsien-chih*, 2:19b); 894 in Tung-p'ing chou, Shantung (*Tung-p'ing chou chih*, 2:7); 411 in Shou-yang, Shansi (*Shou-yang hsien-chih*, 1:13b); 400 in Hsien-yang, Shensi (*Hsien-yang hsien-chih*, 1:5b); 41 in Wu-ling, Hunan (*Wu-ling hsien-chih*, 7:2b); approximately 1000 in Nan-feng, Kiangsi (*Nan-feng hsien-chih*, 2:16); 1560 in Li-yang, Kiangsu (*Li-yang hsien-chih*, 2:6b ff); 73 in P'ing-hu, Chekiang (*P'ing-hu hsien-chih*, 1:85a–b); 510 in Ch'ang-t'ing, Fukien (*Ch'ang-t'ing hsien-chih*, 2:2b ff); 511 in Hsin-hui, Kwangtung (*Hsin-hui hsien-chih*, 2:57 ff); 242 in Huai-chi, Kwangsi (*Huai-chi hsien-chih*, 1:10–11); 79 in Ch'eng-kung, Yünnan (*Ch'eng-kung hsien-chih*, 1:25–26b); and 26 in P'eng-shui, Szechwan (*P'eng-shui hsien-chih*, 1:30).

7. The average village contained several score to about 100 families, but a small village had only a few families, and a large village had several hundred (*Fu-hui ch'üan-shu*, 21:6–7). For instance, in Hsien-yang the number of families in a village varied from 4 or 5 to more than 200; in the largest village there were 270 (*Hsien-yang hsien-chih*, 1:5b–19). For additional information on the size and other physical aspects of a village see Hsiao Kung-chuan, *Rural China; Imperial Control in the Nineteenth Century* (Seattle, 1960), pp. 14 ff.

8. *Hsiao-ts'ang shan-fang wen-chi*, 15:6; *Kung-ch'ih-chai wen-ch'ao*, 4:1b; *Mu-ling shu*, 1:18; *Pao-chia shu*, 33:3a–b.

9. *Fu-hui ch'üan-shu*, 2:14b; 21:6a–b.

10. *Ta-Ch'ing lü-li hui-chi pien-lan* (hereafter *Ch'ing lü-li*), 8:47b–48. "*Li*" was called *t'u* in Chiang-nan and Chekiang (*Chia-ting hsien-chih*, 1:28; *Sung-chün chün-i ch'eng-shu, ts'e* 9:340; *Shan-yin hsien-chih*, 6:1b; *Jih-chih lu chi-shih*, 22:15b). A chou or hsien comprised several hundred *li* or *t'u*. In the province of Chiang-nan, according to a provincial treasurer of that area, there were 300 or 400 *t'u* in a small hsien, and 600 or 700 in a large hsien (*Chiang-nan t'ung-chih*, 68:4b). For instance, there were 183 *t'u* in Lou-hsien, Kiangsu (*Lou-hsien chih*, 3:2–4); 23 *fang* and 186 *t'u* in Shan-yin, Chekiang (*Shan-yin hsien-chih*, 6:1b–3b).

11. *Ch'ing lü-li*, 8:47–48, mentions that *li-chang* expedited land tax collection and took charge of other matters concerning the government (*kou-she kung-shih*). Among these matters were population registration and labor service. *Ch'ing lü-li*, 8:3–4; *Ch'ing hui-tien* (1764), 9:4b; *Ch'ing hui-tien shih-li* (1818), 133:1a–b; *Ch'ing t'ung-k'ao*, 19:5024; 21:5045; *Shih-ch'ü yü-chi*, 3:10b. For discussions of similar practice during the Ming, see: *Ming-lü chi-chieh fu li*, 4:2a–b, 20; *Ming shih*, 78:4a–b, 7b–8b; Liang Fang-chung, *The Single-Whip Method of Taxation in China*, tr. Wang Yü-ch'uan (Harvard University, East Asian Research Center, 1956), pp. 5–6.

12. See below, Chap. IX, sec. 2.

13. *Ch'ing t'ung-k'ao*, 21:5043, 5045; *Sung-chün chün-i ch'eng-shu, ts'e*

2:60a–b; *Fu-weng chi, hsing-ming,* 1:13; *Chiao-pin-lu k'ang-i,* A:13. The distribution of *ti-pao* given in the local gazetteer of Yung-ch'ing, Chihli, compiled by Chang Hsüeh-ch'eng (1738–1801), is as follows: 2 *ti-pao* in the district seat; 1 for each of the 4 suburbs; 1 for each village or for 2 or 3 villages: 66 in the eastern rural district of 78 villages; 61 in the southern rural district of 74 villages; 60 in the western rural district of 63 villages; and 61 in the northern rural district of 63 villages (*Yung-ch'ing hsien-chih,* 13:2–5; *Chang-shih i-shu wai-pien,* 9:132–137).

14. *Ch'ing t'ung-k'ao,* 21:5043, 5045; *Ch'ing lü-li,* 23:68b–69; *Li-pu tse-li,* 42:41a–b; *Liu-pu ch'u-fen tse-li,* 47:19; *Fu-weng chi, hsing-ming,* 1:13; *P'ing-hu-hsien pao-chia shih-i,* pp. 9b–10, 28b; *Pan-an yao-lüeh,* p. 31a–b; *Ching-shih wen-pien,* 33:3. The law permitted the local constables and *hsiang-yüeh* (heads of *hsiang*) to report a dispute to the magistrate, who would then make a decision, but the magistrate could not authorize them to settle it. The magistrate was not permitted to ask them to investigate a robbery, homicide, or other serious case (*Ch'ing lü-li,* 30:33b–40; *Li-pu tse-li,* 42:41a–b; *Liu-pu ch'u-fen tse-li,* 47:19). *Ching-shih wen-pien,* 23:13a–b and 74:11b, identifies the *hsiang-yüeh* as the head of a *hsiang* (*hsiang-chang*). Here the term *hsiang-yüeh* as a person should not be confused with *hsiang-yüeh* as the lecture system; the people conducting lectures in the *hsiang-yüeh,* known as *yüeh-cheng* and *yüeh-fu,* were the scholars (Chap. IX, sec. 6). According to *Tzu-t'ung hsien-chih,* 1:14 and 17, in each rural district there was a *hsiang-yüeh* who shared with the *pao-chang* and *li-chang* responsibility for reporting suspects to the magistrate. It was reported that people in Szechwan, Kweichow and Yünnan, particularly in remote places, often appealed to the *hsiang-yüeh* when there was a dispute (*Mu-ling shu,* 8:44–45).

15. *Ch'ing t'ung-k'ao,* 21:5045.

16. Thus a *ti-pao* was described by Feng Kuei-fen as a man "with a status below the commoners," who rendered "humble service" (*Chiao-pin-lu k'ang-i,* A:13). See similar remarks by Wang Feng-sheng in *P'ing-hu-hsien pao-chia shih-i,* p. 10.

17. *Ch'ing t'ung-k'ao,* 21:5045; *Fu-weng chi, hsing-ming,* 1:13b.

18. H. B. Morse, *The Trade and Administration of the Chinese Empire* (Shanghai and Hong Kong, 1908), pp. 48, 73–74.

19. Commoner-elders who were eighty or over were granted official hat buttons of the eighth rank (*Ch'ing lü-li,* 8:47a–b; *Ch'ing t'ung-k'ao,* 76:5556–57). For a study of *ch'i-lao* see Negishi Tadashi, *Chūgoku shakai ni okeru shidō so—kirō shinshi no kenkyū* (Tokyo, 1947), pp. 25–31, 69–72; Chang Chung-li, *The Chinese Gentry; Studies on Their Role in Nineteenth-Century Chinese Society* (Seattle, 1955), pp. 15–17; Hsiao, *Rural China,* pp. 553–555.

20. *Ch'ing t'ung-k'ao,* 21:5044; *Ch'ing hui-tien,* 30:13; *Li-pu tse-li,* 49:4b–5.

21. In his *Rural China* (p. 267), K. C. Hsiao correctly observes that *ti-pao* and other rural headmen were "in reality subadministrative government agents, serving largely the purpose of rural control." Hsiao believes that the government attempted to exercise rural control in all its aspects—police control,

ideological control and the like. He concludes (p. 263): "where the government abstained from interfering with its affairs the village enjoyed a measure of autonomy. It enjoyed autonomy, however, not because the government intended to give it something like self-government, but because the authorities were unable completely to control or supervise its activities. Such 'autonomy,' in other words, was a result of incomplete centralization; the government never hesitated to interfere with village life whenever it deemed it necessary or desirable."

22. The river intendant was under the supervision of the director-general of river conservation. The post of director-general in charge of the Yellow River and the Grand Canal (*tsung-ho*) was established in 1644, and that of deputy director-general (*fu tsung-ho*) was established in 1724. Later the title of *tsung-ho* was changed to *tsung-tu Chiang-nan ho-tao* (director-general of the river administration in Chiang-nan), and *fu tsung-ho* was changed in 1729 to *tsung-tu Honan Shantung ho-tao* (director-general of the river administration in Honan and Shantung).

In the following year the post of director-general in charge of rivers and water works (*ho-tao shui-li tsung-tu*) was established in Chihli. This post was abolished in 1749 and its duties were assigned to the governor-general of Chihli. The directorate-general of river administration in Chiang-nan was abolished in 1858, and its duties taken over by the director-general of grain transport (*ts'ao-yün tsung-tu*). Finally, the directorate-general of river administration in Honan and Shantung was abolished in 1902 and the work assigned to the governors of Shantung and Honan respectively. See *Ch'ing hui-tien* 6:16a–b; *Ch'ing-ch'ao hsü wen-hsien t'ung-k'ao* (hereafter *Ch'ing hsü t'ung-k'ao*), 132:8616–17; *Ch'ing shih kao*, 123:6; H. S. Brunnert and V. V. Hagelstrom, *Present Day Political Organization of China* (Shanghai, 1912), pp. 399–400.

23. Grain intendants were found in every province (two in Kiangsu) with the exception of Shansi, Kansu, Szechwan, and Kwangsi, where their duties were performed by the provincial treasurer. Grain intendants were under the supervision of the director-general of grain transport, who had eight provinces under his jurisdiction: Shantung, Honan, Kiangsu, Anhui, Kiangsi, Chekiang, Hupeh, and Hunan. Grain administration not under the jurisdiction of the tribute grain commsisioner was under the supervision of the governor-general and governor (*Ch'ing hui-tien,* 6:14a–b; *Ch'ing shih kao,* 123:12).

24. There was one provincial treasurer for each province, with the exception of Kiangsu, where there were two after 1760: one stationed in Chiang-ning (Nanking), and the other in Soochow (*Ch'ing shih kao,* 123:9a–b).

25. There were salt controllers in Chihli (Ch'ang-lu), Shantung, Kiangsu (Liang-Huai), Chekiang (Liang-Che), Kwangtung, and Shansi (Ho-tung; the post was abolished in Shansi in 1792). In all other areas salt administration was under the salt intendants (*yen-fa tao*) (*Ch'ing hui-tien,* 6:15; *Ch'ing shih kao,* 123:10b–12; Brunnert and Hagelstrom, pp. 414–415, 422–423).

26. *Ch'ing shih kao,* 123:8b, 9b, mentions that the provincial treasurer

guided the prefect and the chou and hsien magistrates, examined their abilities and graded them accordingly, and reported to the governor and governor-general. The provincial judge also examined the accomplishments of the officials during the time of "great reckoning."

27. At first there were three governors in Chihli, but they were abolished one after another during the Shun-chih period (*Ch'ing shih kao*, 123:3b–4).

28. With the exception of the governors-general of Chihli and of Szechwan, all governors-general had more than one province under their jurisdiction: Kiangsu, Anhui, and Kiangsi (*Liang-Chiang tsung-tu*); Shensi and Kansu; Fukien and Chekiang; Hupeh and Hunan; Kwangtung and Kwangsi; Yünnan and Kweichow. The governor-general's title, number of posts, and the provinces under his jurisdiction changed from time to time. For instance, once there had been a governor-general for Chihli, Shantung, and Honan. For a short period, there had been a governor-general in each of the following provinces: Chiang-nan, Kiangsi, Fukien, Chekiang, Kwangtung, and Kwangsi. For details see *Ch'ing shih kao*, 123:3b–5b.

29. For an illuminating discussion of the power of the governor-general over the governor see Kuo Sung-tao's (1818–1891) memorial in *Ch'ing hsü t'ung-k'ao*, 132:8915–16.

30. *P'ei-yüan-t'ang ou-ts'un kao*, 40:20–23; *Ch'ing shih kao*, 155:2.

31. For instance, see *Che-sheng ts'ang-k'u ch'ing-ch'a chieh-yao*.

32. Thus a case involving a sentence more severe than penal servitude (see below, n. 33) had to be retried by the superior yamen; cases originally tried by a hsien magistrate, ordinary chou magistrate, or a subprefect of an ordinary subprefecture were retried by the prefect, independent department magistrate, or a subprefect of an independent subprefecture; cases tried by a prefect, an independent department magistrate, or a subprefect of an independent subprefecture were retried by an intendant (and in some localities by the provincial judge). All cases involving banishment, or penal servitude related to a case of homicide, were retried by the provincial judge. Cases involving a death sentence were retried by the governor-general and governor, together with the provincial judge, provincial treasurer, and the intendants. In all cases, it was the responsibility of the governor-general and governor to report the case to the Board of Punishment. For details, see *Ch'ing lü-li*, 37:44b ff, 60 ff; *Ch'ing hui-tien*, 55:2b–3b; *Ch'ing shih kao*, 155:1, 2, 5, 6a–b. See also below, Chap. VIII, sec. 1.

33. We do not follow the usage of Staunton and Boulais who render *t'u* as "temporary banishment" or "exil temporaire" because the penalty was not banishment in the ordinary sense. Actually it was a sort of penal servitude, whose term could be for 1, 1½, 2, 2½, or 3 years. In the Ming, criminals given such punishment were assigned to making salt or smelting iron. In the Ch'ing, they were sent to a post station within the same province, or to serve as water carriers, kitchen stove attendants, or to perform other coolie services in a local yamen in a district where there was no post station (*Ch'ing lü-li*, 5:105a–b, 114b–115; *Ting-li hui-pien*, 34:3–4; *Ch'ing shih kao*, 154:1). Yünnan was the only place where criminals guilty of serious offenses who were given the *t'u*

punishment were sent to make salt or smelt lead; but this practice was abolished in 1787 (*Ta-Ch'ing lü-li an-yü*, 1:154b–155, 158b–159; *Ting-li hui-pien*, 34:3–4). For this reason, we translate *t'u* as "penal servitude." The term "banishment" is reserved only for real banishment (*liu*, which Staunton and Boulais render as "permanent banishment" and "exil perpetuel").

34. Thus, within the Board of Punishment, there were a number of divisions (*ch'ing-li ssu*), each responsible for the judicial affairs of one province. Each division reviewed the legal documents presented by its province, drafted suggestions as to the acceptability of the original decision, and presented them to the minister or vice-minister of the board for approval (*Ch'ing hui-tien*, 57:1a–b; *Ch'ing shih kao*, 155:1b).

35. *Ch'ing lü-li*, 37:31–33; *Ch'ing hui-tien*, 53:1b–3; *Ch'ing shih kao*, 155:2b–3b.

36. Cases involving a sentence of "immediate execution" (*li-chüeh*) had to be reviewed by the board, together with the Censorate (Tu-ch'a Yüan) and the Court of Judicature and Revision (Ta-li Ssu), and approved by the emperor. Cases involving "detention for strangling" (*chiao chien-hou*), and "detention for beheading" (*chan chien-hou*) were considered during the "autumn assize" (*ch'iu-shen*). These cases had to be reported by the governor-general and governor, reviewed by the Board of Punishment and the two other judicial bodies just mentioned, and deliberated jointly by the nine ministers and other officials. Finally they were presented to the emperor for approval (*Ch'ing lü-li*, 37:31–33; *Ch'ing hui-tien*, 53:1b–3; 57:13–15; *Ch'ing shih kao*, 155:2–3).

37. *Ch'ing lü-li*, 37:26–28b; *Liu-pu ch'u-fen tse-li*, 47:31 ff; *Ch'ing hui-tien*, 54:11b; *Ch'ing shih kao*, 155:5. A case in point occurred in 1824. A man accused of rape was judged by the magistrate to be guilty of adultery with consent, a verdict that caused the victim to take her own life. Her family appealed to the authorities in the capital. The emperor ordered the governor of Shansi, Ch'iu Shu-t'ang, to retry the case in person. The latter memorialized supporting the original judgment. He was charged by a censor with not having conducted the trial in person, and the case was referred to the Board of Punishment by order of the emperor. Eventually the magistrate was found guilty of receiving a bribe and causing injustice, and was sent to Ili to perform hard labor. The prefect and two chou magistrates were banished and the provincial judge was dismissed. The governor was demoted to a provincial judge (*Ch'ing lü-li*, 37:25b–26b).

38. *Huan-hsiang yao-tse*, 3:45.

39. *Ch'ing hui-tien*, 5:1; *Huan-hsiang yao-tse*, 3:45b.

40. *Ch'ing hui-tien*, 4:3b; *Liu-pu ch'u-fen tse-li*, 49:2a–b; *Ch'ing shih kao*, 123:14b; *Huan-hsiang yao-tse*, 3:45b; Brunnert and Hagelstrom, p. 435.

41. *Huan-hsiang yao-tse*, 3:45b; 7:13; Brunnert and Hagelstrom, p. 435.

42. *Ch'ing hui-tien*, 6:15, 16; *Ch'ing shih kao*, 123:15b.

43. *Ch'ing hui-tien*, 6:18b–19; *Ch'ing shih kao*, 123:15b–16. Brunnert and Hagelstrom's rendering (p. 429), "river police inspector," is not followed here because this officer's duty was mainly the collection of fish tax.

44. *Ch'ing shih kao*, 123:14b; *Huan-hsiang yao-tse*, 3:45b; 7:13.

45. *Ch'ing hui-tien*, 6:18b–19; *Ch'ing shih kao*, 123:15b–16.

46. *Ch'ing hui-tien*, 3:14b.

47. *Ch'ing t'ung-k'ao*, 85:5b; *Ch'ing shih-kao*, 123:14b.

48. E.g., there were *kuan-ho chou-t'ung* (first-class assistant chou magistrates in charge of river administration) in T'ung-chou, Te-chou, and Tung-p'ing chou (*Ta-Ch'ing chin-shen ch'üan-shu*, 1899, *ts'e* 2:22b, 77, 78b); *kuan-ho chou-p'an* (second-class assistant chou magistrates in charge of river administration) in T'ung-chou, Cho-chou, Pa-chou, and Tung-p'ing chou (*ibid., ts'e* 2:22b, 24, 78b); *kuan-ho hsien-ch'eng* (assistant hsien magistrates in charge of river administration) in Liang-hsiang, Yung-ch'ing, Wu-ch'ing, Hsiang-fu, and Chung-mou (*ibid., ts'e* 2:21b, 22a–b, 111, 113); and *kuan-ho chu-pu* (registrars in charge of river administration) in Wu-ch'ing and Wu-hsien (*ibid., ts'e* 2:23, 48b).

49. E.g., there was a *shui-li chou-p'an* (second-class assistant chou magistrate in charge of water works) in Pin-chou (*Chin-shen ch'üan-shu*, 1899, *ts'e* 2:80); *shui-li hsien-ch'eng* (assistant hsien magistrate in charge of water works) in Ching-yang and Hua-yang (*ibid., ts'e* 3:3b; *ts'e* 4:2b).

50. E.g., there were *kuan-liang chu-pu* (registrars in charge of land tax) in Ch'ang-chou, Yüan-ho, Hsiu-shui, Chia-shan, and P'ing-hu (*Chin-shen ch'üan-shu*, 1899, *ts'e* 2:48b, 49; *ts'e* 3:48a–b).

51. E.g., there was a *kuan-ho shui-li chou-p'an* (second-class assistant chou magistrate in charge of river administration and water works) in Cheng-chou (*Chin-shen ch'üan-shu*, 1899, *ts'e* 2:112b).

52. E.g., there were *liang-wu shui-li chou-p'an* (second-class assistant chou magistrates in charge of land tax and water works) in Cho-chou and Yü-chou (*Chin-shen ch'üan-shu*, 1899, *ts'e* 2:24, 113); *liang-wu shui-li hsien-ch'eng* (assistant district magistrates in charge of land tax and water works) in Lu-i and Kao-an (*ibid., ts'e* 2:115b; *ts'e* 3:69b); and a *liang-wu shui-li chu-pu* (registrar in charge of land tax and water works) in Wu-chiang (*ibid., ts'e* 2:48b).

53. E.g., there was a *liang pu chou-t'ung* (first-class chou magistrate in charge of land tax and police) in Hsi-lung chou; and a *liang pu chou-p'an* (second-class chou magistrate in charge of land tax and police) in Kao-t'ang chou (*Chin-shen ch'üan-shu*, 1899, *ts'e* 2:79b; *ts'e* 4:46).

54. E.g., there was a *liang pu shui-li hsien-ch'eng* (assistant hsien magistrate in charge of land tax, police, and water works) in Chiang-ning (*Chin-shen ch'üan-shu*, 1899, *ts'e* 2:46b).

55. *Ch'ing hui-tien*, 6:16a–b.

56. *Ibid.*, 4:3b.

57. For example, see *Tz'u-chou chih*, 1:4; 5:3; *Lou-hsien chih*, 2:6b, 8.

58. For instance, the *chou-t'ung* and *chou-p'an* in charge of river administration in Pa-chou were stationed at Yung-ting River. The *hsien-ch'eng* and *chu-pu* in charge of river administration in Wu-ch'ing hsien were also stationed on the bank of Yung-ting River. In Hsiang-fu hsien, the *hsien-ch'eng* and *chu-pu* in

charge of river administration were stationed at the Yellow River (*Chin-shen ch'üan-shu,* 1899, *ts'e* 2:23, 24a–b, 111; *Ch'ing hui-tien,* 6:17a–b).

59. *Ch'ing hui-tien,* 4:3b.

60. *Ibid.* For instance, the second class assistant chou magistrate of Pa-chou was stationed at Lung-kuan chen (*Chin-shen ch'üan-shu,* 1899, *ts'e* 4:7b). For Ting-fan, one of the second-class assistant chou magistrates was stationed at Ta-t'ang and another at Ch'ang-chai (*ibid., ts'e* 4:69b). The assistant hsien magistrate of Wan-p'ing was stationed at Men-tou kou (*ibid., ts'e* 2:21). In Fu-shun, one assistant hsien magistrate was stationed at Tzu-liu ching and another at Teng-ching kuan (*ibid., ts'e* 4:10). The assistant hsien magistrate of Wu-hsien was stationed at Mu-tu chen (*ibid., ts'e* 2:48b). The assistant hsien magistrate of Hsiang-shan was stationed at Macao (*ibid., ts'e* 4:25). In Kuei-an, the registrar was stationed at Ling-hu (*ibid., ts'e* 3:49).

61. *Ch'ing hui-tien,* 6:1; *Ch'ing shih kao,* 123:15a–b.

62. This was the duty of an assistant magistrate; however, it was assigned to an educational officer in a hsien where there was no assistant magistrate (*Hu-pu tse-li,* 9:10a–b).

63. *Li-pu tse-li,* 28:19a–b; *Liu-pu ch'u-fu tse-li,* 30:26.

64. According to the 1764 *Ch'ing hui-tien,* 4:12a–b, 13a–b, there were 164 *li-mu* (in 221 independent and ordinary chou), and 1282 *tien shih* (in 1282 hsien); according to the 1818 *Ch'ing hui-tien,* 4:28a–b, there were 219 *li-mu* (in 214 independent and ordinary chou), and 1294 *tien-shih* (in 1293 hsien). The 1899 *Ch'ing-hui-tien,* 5:13, gives the number of *li-mu* as 221 (in 217 independent and ordinary chou), and that of *tien-shih* as 1296 (in 1303 hsien).

65. This number includes only the regular subdistrict magistrates in charge of police duties. In addition, there were 11 subdistrict magistrates in charge of river administration, and 5 subdistrict magistrates in charge of salt administration (*Ch'ing hui-tien,* 5:5, 6:15, 16a–b, 18).

66. *Ch'ing hui-tien,* 6:19.

67. *Ibid.,* 6:20b–21.

68. Liu-ho, I-cheng in Kiangsu, and Ch'ien-t'ang and Jen-ho in Chekiang (*Ch'ing hui-tien,* 6:19b).

69. *Ch'ing hui-tien,* 6:21.

70. *Ibid.,* 5:1. These figures do not include the chou or hsien assistant magistrates and registrars in charge of river administration. The officials in charge of river administration included 5 first-class assistant chou magistrates, 13 second-class assistant chou magistrates, 317 assistant hsien magistrates, and 42 registrars (*Ch'ing hui-tien,* 6:16a–b).

The small number of registrars probably was the consequence of a decision in 1646 to eliminate such posts in the various hsien (*Ch'ing hui-tien shih-li,* 1818, 27:1). For detailed information as to the establishment and abolition of the posts of assistant hsien magistrates, registrars and other subordinate officials in the various localities from time to time, see *Ch'ing hui-tien shih-li* (1818), *chüan* 27 and 28 and *ibid.* (1899), *chüan* 30 and 31.

71. There was no chou in Fukien and Sinkiang.

72. *Ch'ing t'ung-k'ao*, 85:5617.

73. Mien-yang chou, Hupeh; Hsi-lung chou, Kwangsi; and Chen-hsiung chou, Yünnan (*Ch'ing hui-tien*, 5:2b–3).

74. Nine in Chekiang (Ch'ien-t'ang, Jen-ho, Chia-hsing, Hsiu-shui, Chia-shan, P'ing-hu, Wu-ch'eng, Kuei-an, and Ch'ang-hsing; 8 in Kiangsu (Wu-hsien, Ch'ang-chou, Yüan-ho, Wu-chiang, Pao-shan, Lou-hsien, Shanghai, and Ch'ing-p'u); 2 in Shantung (Li-ch'eng and T'ai-an); 2 in Hupeh (Chiang-ling and Chien-li); 2 in Kiangsi (Nan-ch'ang and Hsin-chien); and 1 in each of the following provinces: Anhui (Hsüan-ch'eng), Hunan (Pa-ling), Shensi (Ch'ang-an), Kansu (P'ing-lo), Szechwan (P'ing-wu), Fukien (Min-hsien), Kwang-tung (Nan-hai), and Kweichow (Chen-yüan).—*Ch'ing hui-tien*, 5:3–5.

75. *Ch'ing t'ung-k'ao*, 85:5617.

76. There was one *chou-t'ung* in charge of river administration, two *chou-p'an* in charge of river administration, and one *chou-p'an* in charge of land tax and water works (*Ch'ing hui-tien*, 5:3, 6:17).

77. *Ch'ing hui-tien*, 6:17.

78. *Ibid.*, 5:3b; 6:17.

79. *Ibid.*, 5:3b; 6:17a–b.

80. *Ibid.*, 6:17a–b. Thus Li Wei (1687?–1738), the governor-general of Chihli, mentioned that although there were many assistant magistrates in his province, most of them took charge of river administration and were not concerned with local administration (*Chu-p'i yü-chih*, Li Wei's memorials, 6:11b).

81. *Ch'ing hui-tien*, 5:3.

82. *Ibid.*, 5:3b, lists only one assistant hsien magistrate in Yüan-ho; however, two are listed in *Chin-shen ch'üan-shu* (1899), ts'e 2:49.

83. *Ch'ing hui-tien*, 5:4b.

84. *P'ei-yüan-t'ang ou-ts'un kao*, 46:37; *Mu-ling shu*, 11:27b.

85. *Hu-pu tse-li*, 9:10a–b.

86. *Ibid.*, 19:1–2b; *Mu-ling shu*, 11:43a–b.

87. *Hsüeh-chih t'i-hsing lu*, B:13.

88. *Ch'ing hui-tien*, 55:2b; *Ch'ing shih-lu*, Hsüan-tsung, 323:28a–b. An assistant magistrate or a miscellaneous official who accepted a complaint and conducted a hearing was to be demoted one grade and transferred to another post, and the magistrate who failed to inquire into the case due to negligence was to be fined one year's nominal salary. If the acceptance of a complaint caused the death of the accused person (e.g., by suicide), the subordinate official was to be dismissed and the magistrate demoted two grades and kept in the same post. A magistrate who ordered his subordinate official to hear a case was to be demoted two grades and transferred to another post, and the subordinate official was to be demoted two grades and kept in the same post. If the action caused the death of a person, the magistrate was to be dismissed and the subordinate official demoted three grades and transferred to another post (*Li-pu tse-li*, 42:39b–40b; *Liu-pu ch'u-fen tse-li*, 47:23–25; *Hsüeh-chih shuo-chui*, 2b–3; *Hsüeh-chih t'i-hsing lu*, A:10).

89. A sum of money was usually collected from a plaintiff for the acceptance of a complaint (*Fu-hui ch'üan-shu*, 31:9; *Chung-ya-t'ang wen-chi*, 8:28; *Hsüeh-chih t'i-hsing lu*, A:9b; *Mu-ling shu*, 18:3b–4).

90. *Fu-hui ch'üan–shu*, 31:9.

91. *Yü Ch'ing-tuan kung cheng-shu*, 5:99b–100; *Chang Wen-hsiang kung ch'üan-chi, kung-tu*, 95:15b; *Ching-shih wen hsü-pien*, 22:20.

92. *Liu-pu ch'u-fen tse-li*, 47:23b.

93. *Hsüeh-chih hsü-shuo*, p. 10b; *Hsüeh-chih t'i-hsing lu*, A:20b.

94. An assistant magistrate or a jail warden was allowed to examine an injured person when the magistrate was too busy or too far away (*Liu-pu ch'u-fen tse-li*, 43:4; *Hsüeh-chih t'i-hsing lu*, A:5).

95. *Huang-cheng pei-lan*, A:5.

96. *Hsüeh-chih t'i-hsing lu*, B:2.

97. For details, see below, Chap. VII, sec. 3.

98. *Hsüeh-chih t'i-hsing lu*, B:2; *Hsüeh-chih i-shuo*, B:7b–8.

99. As a provincial judge pointed out in 1759, the jail wardens (*li-mu* or *tien-shih*), although known as police officers (*pu-kuan*), did not command the policemen, who were under the command of the magistrates. The jail wardens were not informed of cases of theft; only occasionally did the magistrates ask their assistance in cases of grand larceny. The judge therefore suggested to the Board of Punishment that the jail wardens should be given the responsibility of commanding and supervising the policemen. The board, however, considered that the jail warden had too humble a position to control the policemen, and furthermore that he might abuse his authority if empowered to give assignments to the policemen. The board therefore ruled that police duty should remain under the control of the magistrates, but that the jail warden should be allowed to assist the magistrates in supervising the policemen. Like the magistrates, they too would be subject to punishment if the policemen were guilty of bribery or of unlawfully beating the prisoners (*Ting-li hui-pien*, 3:1–3).

100. *Hsiao-ts'ang shan-fang wen-chi*, 15:28; *Chung-ya-t'ang wen-chi*, 8:28.

101. Li Wei, who realized how insignificant the role of the magistrate's subordinate officials was, said in a memorial: "As they are unable to share the responsibility [of the magistrates] and are concerned merely with self interest, they are prohibited from receiving complaints and attending to government affairs. They are ordered to take charge only of the duties assigned to them" (*Chu-p'i yü-chih*, Li Wei's memorials, 4:25).

Describing the assistant magistrate in his native district as superfluous official "without duty," Chiang Shih-ch'üan (1725–1785) summed up the situation in the following words: "In name he is assistant magistrate, yet he is subject to punishment if he accepts complaint at will; in name he is in charge of the land tax bureau (*liang-t'ing*), yet he has no part in the collection of grain tribute" (*Chung-ya-t'ang wen-chi*, 8:28). Lu I-t'ung concluded that an assistant magistrate could have no voice in matters of law or taxation, in cases of grand larceny, or in serious civil lawsuits (*Ching-shih wen hsü-pien*, 22:2a–b). Wang

K'an (b. 1795) also stated that all authority was in the hands of the magistrates and that the assistant magistrates, registrars, subdistrict magistrates, and jail wardens had nothing to do (*Fang yen*, 47b–48).

102. In order to secure good and competent persons for these jobs, Lu also suggested that the assistant magistrates and registrars should be rewarded with promotions (*Ling-shou hsien-chih*, 10:25b).

103. *T'ung-fu lei-kao*, 1:15a–b.

CHAPTER II. THE MAGISTRATE

1. *T'ung-fu lei-kao*, 1:11b; see also similar remarks by Cheng Kuan-ying (b. 1841) in *Sheng-shih wei-yen*, 1:18.

2. *P'ing-p'ing yen*, 1:10.

3. *Mu-ling shu*, 1:51b.

4. *Hsiao-ts'ang shan-fang wen-chi*, 15:27a–b; *Hsüeh-chih t'i-hsing lu*, A:2b–3.

5. *Ch'ing t'ung-k'ao*, 55:5367; *P'ing-p'ing yen*, 1:25b; cf. Brunnert and Hagelstrom, pp. 426–427.

6. *P'ing-p'ing yen*, 1:25b; *Chin-shen ch'üan-shu, passim*; cf. Brunnert and Hagelstrom, pp. 426–427.

7. *Hsüeh-chih i-shuo*, A:10a–b.

8. *P'ing-p'ing yen*, 1:25b.

9. The title *chih-chou* or *chih-hsien* itself suggests that a magistrate should "know" (*chih*) all the conditions of a locality. See *Ch'in-pan chou-hsien shih-i*, p. 41.

10. *Ch'ing shih kao*, 123:14b.

11. *Ch'ing lü-li*, 19:266 ff; *Liu-pu ch'u-fen tse-li*, 37:25–26; Gui Boulais, *Manuel du code chinois, Variétés Sinologiques* (Shanghai, 1924), pp. 421–422.

12. The *Ch'in-pan chou-hsien shih-i*, p. 42b, mentions that "the duties which concern a chou or hsien magistrate are but the administration of justice and taxation." Huang Liu-hung says in his handbook, *Fu-hui ch'üan-shu, fan-li*, p. 3b: "Taxation and the administration of justice are important duties of an official, and the administration of justice is more important than taxation." However, in *ibid.*, 6:1, he says that "among the duties of an official probably taxation is the most important." This contradiction seems to indicate that the relative importance of the two functions depends upon one's approach to the problem: whether one thinks in terms of justice or in terms of government revenue.

13. The custom was to begin the day before dawn. According to the schedule of Ho Keng-sheng's yamen, the day began at 3:45 A.M. in summer and autumn, and 4:45 in the spring and winter (*Hsüeh-chih i-te pien*, 62).

14. Taking Ho's schedule as an example (see n. 13), this would be 5:15 A.M. in summer and autumn and 6:45 in spring and winter; cf. *Kung-men yao-lüeh*, quoted in *Chung-ho*, 2.10:73 (Oct. 1941).

15. *Hsüeh-chih t'i-hsing lu*, A:3. Wang Hui-tsu, *Ping-ta meng-hen lu*, 13:41b, stated that he usually presided over court from *ssu* (9–11 A.M.) to *yu*

(5–7 P.M.) and that sometimes the hearings were not concluded until *hsü* (7–9 P.M.) or *hai* (9–11 P.M.).

16. According to Ho's schedule (see n. 13), this would be 3:45 P.M. in summer and autumn, and 4:45 P.M. in spring and winter (*Hsüeh-chih i-te pien*, 62; cf. *Kung-men yao-lüeh*, quoted in *Chung-ho*, 2.10:73).

17. *Fu-hui ch'üan-shu*, 2:8 ff; *Hsüeh-chih i-te pien*, p. 62a–b; *Hsüeh-chih t'i-hsing lu*, A:3; *Mu-ling shu*, 2:3b–4, 17; *Huan-hsiang yao-tse*, 2:11 ff; *Ko-hang shih-chien, Kung-men yao-lüeh*, and *Ch'ang-sui lun*, quoted in *Chung-ho*, 2.10:73–74.

18. For details see below, Chap. VII, sec. 2.

19. For instance, Huang Liu-hung reserved ten days each month in which to conduct deadline hearings: from the first day to the fifth, and from the twenty-first to the twenty-fifth (*Fu-hui ch'üan-shu*, 7:4a–b). Wang Hui-tsu arranged his routine for every ten days as follows: seven days for hearing lawsuits, two for deadline hearings, and one day for preparing documents to be submitted to his superiors (*Ping-t'a meng-hen lu*, B:9b).

20. *Fu-hui ch'üan-shu*, 24:9.

21. *Ch'ing-pai lei-ch'ao, Shih-ling lei*, p. 44. The exact day was to be announced by the Board of Astronomy, Ch'in T'ien Chien.

22. *Ch'ing-pai lei-ch'ao, Shih-ling lei*, p. 34.

23. *Hsüeh-chih t'i-hsing lu*, A:3.

24. Ch'en Hung-mou, a governor who served in many provinces, mentioned that many officials attempted to avoid reading documents, arguing that drafts could be made by the clerks and revised by the private secretaries. They claimed that it was impossible for an official, who had so many duties, to read every document personally (*P'ei-yüan-t'ang ou-ts'un kao*, 13:31 ff).

25. *Ch'in-pan chou-hsien shih-i*, p. 24a–b.

26. A *chin-shih* might be given a post in the Hanlin Academy or in the central government, or appointed as a magistrate. (Under a regulation of 1646, a *chin-shih* could be appointed a chou magistrate, a *t'ui-kuan* [judicial official under a prefect], or a hsien magistrate. The post of *t'ui-kuan* was abolished in 1667 and the post of chou magistrate was ordered not to be given to *chin-shih* in 1659; then both the *erh chia* and *san chia*, i.e., those whose names appeared on the second and third lists of the metropolitan graduates, were given the post of hsien magistrate.) Those who had been *shu chi shih* (a *chin-shih* admitted to the Department of Study [*Shu-ch'ang Kuan*] of the Hanlin Academy) for three years were required to take the dismissal examination (*k'ao san kuan*). Those who did best were retained in the Hanlin Academy. The rest were released and appointed as *chu-shih* (second-class secretaries of boards), *nei-ko chung-shu* (secretaries of the Grand Secretariat), hisen magistrates, or instructors in the chou or hsien schools (*Ch'ing hui-tien*, 7:9b; *Ch'ing hui-tien shih-li, chüan* 60 and 72; *Ch'ing shih kao*, 115:12). Hanlin who left the academy and were appointed magistrates were popularly known as "Tiger Class" (*lao-hu pan*) because they had high priority in getting posts.

In the early days of the dynasty, only five appointments as magistrate were given to *chin-shih* in even months (*shuang yüeh*). It was reported that one had to wait more than ten years for a post. In 1724, upon the request of Shen Chin-ssu, vice-minister of the Board of Civil Office, four appointments were also given to *chin-shih* in odd months. As a result, a *chin-shih* had to wait only two or three years for a post (*Ch'ing shih kao*, 117:12a–b; *Ch'ing t'ung-k'ao*, 50:321–322).

27. Under the earlier practice of the dynasty, known as *chien-hsüan* (selection), a *chü-jen* who had taken but failed to pass the metropolitan examination and whose age and energy still permitted him to be a magistrate could be registered at the Board of Civil Office as candidate for a magistracy. A *chü-jen* from a remote province could register immediately atfer he had taken the metropolitan examination, but in nearby provinces only a *chü-jen* who had taken the examination five times (after 1698 it was changed to three) was qualified for such registration. The governor-general and governor were authorized to determine whether the applicant's age and energy were suitable for the appointment and to issue a paper to him so that he could go to the board for registration. An elderly *chü-jen* could be registered as a candidate for appointment as an educational official (*Ch'ing hui-tien*, 7:9b; *Ch'ing hui-tien shih-li*, *chüan* 43 and 73).

As there were only a limited number of vacancies for magistrates, it was extremely difficult for a *chü-jen* to get an appointment; it was reported that they often had to wait for more than thirty years. The system of *ta-t'iao* (great selection) was introduced in 1752 to hasten appointment. In the *ta-t'iao*, which took place every six months, a number of *chü-jen* from remote provinces who had taken the metropolitan examination once and failed and *chü-jen* from nearby provinces who had failed three times were selected by imperial commissioners. As a rule, those *chü-jen* who had participated in the four most recent examinations (after 1800, in the last three examinations) were excluded from the "great selection." At first, there was a quota for each province. Later the selection was made on a percentage basis. The selection was based principally upon appearance and age. Those who were selected as "first grade" were appointed as magistrates on probation. The elderly *chü-jen* were classified as "second grade" and were appointed directors or assistant directors of studies in the hsien schools (*Ch'ing hui-tien*, 7:13; *Ch'ing hui-tien shih-li*, *chüan* 73; *Ch'ing t'ung-k'ao*, 50:3321–2; *Ch'ing shih kao*, 117:12b; *Huang-ch'ao cheng-tien lei-tsuan*, 200:8).

28. Both the *pa-kung* (Senior Licentiates by selection) and the *yu-kung* (Senior Licentiates by recommendation) who had passed the court examination (*ch'ao-k'ao*) could be appointed as hsien magistrates, local officials below the rank of the latter, or to educational posts (*Hsüeh-cheng ch'üan-shu*, 50:10a–b, 14b–16b, 23; *Ch'ing hui-tien shih-li*, *chüan* 60; *Ch'ing shih kao*, 113:5–6).

29. A *yin-sheng* who was given a post outside the capital could be appointed to one of the following posts: (1) first-rank *yin-sheng*, *fu t'ung-chih* (first-class

assistant prefect); (2) sub–first-rank *yin-sheng*, chou magistrate; (3) second-rank *yin-sheng*, *t'ung-p'an* (second-class assistant prefect); (4) third-rank *yin-sheng*, hsien magistrate.

A *nan-yin-sheng*, a title bestowed on a man by virtue of his father's or grandfather's death in the service of the government, could also be appointed a chou magistrate, if the deceased official had been of the third rank or above, and a hsien magistrate, if the deceased official had been below the fourth rank (*Ch'ing hui-tien shih-li, chüan* 74).

30. *Ch'ing hui-tien shih-li, chüan* 71.

31. A recommendation might be made on the basis of military achievement, meritorious service in connection with river construction, or solicitation of contributions for relief funds (*Ch'ing shih-kao*, 117:14b). Liu Ju-chi, a censor, reported that recommendation on the basis of meritorious service in connection with river construction was frequently used by the high provincial officials as a means to compensate their subordinate officials for their service. Thus a subordinate official of a hsien could be promoted to chou or hsien magistrate. According to another censor, Chang Ju-hsin, as many as 500 to 600 persons were recommended on a single occasion as a reward for participation in river construction in Shantung (*Ch'ing shih kao*, 117:14a–b).

32. The *chien-sheng*, students of the Imperial Academy, included (1) *en-chien* (students by imperial favor); (2) *yu-chien* (students by recommendation); (3) *yin-chien* (*yin-sheng*, the Honorary Licentiates admitted to the Academy); (4) *li-chien* (students by purchase, including both the government school students who purchased the title of *chien-sheng* [*lin-chien, tseng-chien*, and *fu-chien*] and the commoners who purchased the title of *chien-sheng*). (*Ch'ing hui-tien*, 76:5; *Ch'ing shih kao*, 113:1b ff; see below, Chap. X, n. 20 for an explanation of these titles. But in the *Chin-shen ch'üan-shu* only the commoner–*chien-sheng* were listed as *chien-sheng*; all other types of *chien-sheng* were listed under their specifications.)

33. *Chiao-hsi* (instructors who taught members of the imperial members of the Eight Banners, or the family members of those who served in the *Nei-wu Fu*) were recruited exclusively from among *chin-shih, chü-jen*, or the five regular *kung-sheng*. *T'eng-lu* (copyists who served in the *Yü-tieh Kuan* [Office of the Imperial Genealogical Records], *Shih-lu Kuan* [Commission of Historiography], and *Kuo-shih Kuan* [State Historiographer's Office], were recruited from *chü-jen, kung-sheng, chien-sheng*, and *sheng-yüan*; therefore they are here classified as regular degree-holders).

34. Normally both the regular *kung-sheng* (i.e., *en-kung, pa-kung, fu-kung, sui-kung*, and *yu-kung*) and the *li-kung* (i.e., those who purchased the title of *kung-sheng*, including both the government school students [*lin-kung, tseng-kung*, and *fu-kung*] and the commoner–*chien-sheng* [*chün-hsiu chien-sheng*]) were all addressed as *kung-sheng*. (*Ch'ing hui-tien*, 32:12b–15b; 33:2b; 76:4b–5; *Ch'ing shih kao*, 113:1b, 6; *Hsüeh-cheng ch'üan-shu*, 51:28 ff. See below, Chap. X, n. 19, for an explanation of the various types of *kung-sheng*. But in the *Chin-shen ch'üan-shu* only the commoner–*kung-sheng* were listed as *kung-*

sheng; all other types of *kung-sheng* were listed under their specifications.)

35. *Li-pu tse-li,* 1:4–5b; *Liu-pu ch'u-fen tse-li,* 3:30b–35b.

36. The supplementary salary was given to local officials because the government realized that their regular salaries were insufficient to support them and to meet administrative expenses. The funds for the supplementary salaries came from a different source than the nominal salaries—from a surplus (*huo-hao,* meltage fee, or *hao-hsien,* lit., "surplus from wastage allowance") collected together with the regular land tax by the local government, at a rate set up by the central government (see below, n. 73) and delivered to the provincial treasurer. This surplus provided for the supplementary salaries and also for certain administrative expenses for the various officials. This system was first introduced in 1724 in Shansi by its governor, No-min. It was adopted by other provinces with the approval of the Yung-cheng emperor in 1728. From that time on the system was institutionalized, and supplementary salaries became a regular part of official salaries in the empire (*Ch'ing t'ung-k'ao,* 90:5648–49; *Ch'in-pan chou-hsien shih-i,* p. 45a–b; *Shih-ch'ü yü-chi,* 3:47–48b; see also Iwami Hiroshi, "Yosei jidai ni okeru kōhi no ikkōsatsu," *Tōyōshi kenkyū,* 16.4:65–99, March 1957). As surplus was collected both officially by the government and unofficially by the magistrates, we find it necessary to make a distinction between the "official" surplus or surcharges, and the "customary" surplus or extra surcharges.

37. *Hu-pu tse-li,* 73:22a–b.

38. In Shantung 40 hsien paid their magistrates a salary of 1400 taels, and in Honan 38 magistrates received a similar salary. In all other provinces high pay was rare: 2 hsien in Kwangtung (Nan-hai and P'an-yü) and 2 in Kwangsi (Hsüan-hua and Ma-p'ing) paid 1500 taels; 4 hsien in Chekiang (Chia-hsing, Hsiu-shui, Wu-ch'eng, and Kuei-an), 1 in Hupeh (Chiang-hsia), and 2 in Fukien (Min-hsien and Hou-kuan) paid 1600 taels; 1 hsien in Kiangsi (Hsin-chien) and 1 in Kwangsi (Ts'ang-wu) paid 1700 taels, and 2 hsien in Chekiang (Jen-ho and Ch'ien-t'ang) and 6 in Kiangsu (Chiang-ning, Shang-yüan, Ch'ang-chou, Yüan-ho, Wu-hsien, and Ch'ing-ho) paid 1800 taels. The 4 hsien that paid the highest salaries in the empire (2000 taels or above) were: Li-ch'eng in Shantung, Hsiang-fu in Honan, Nan-ch'ang in Kiangsi, and Lin-kuei in Kwangsi. Of these the pay in Lin-kuei was the highest: 2259 taels.

39. *Mu-ling shu,* 23:19. Hsieh Chen-ting also mentions that the salary of a magistrate was only a little over 1000 taels (*ibid.,* 23:39b).

40. *Ibid.,* 23:19.

41. *Ching-shih wen hsü-pien,* 16:2b; *Chang Wen-hsiang chi, tsou-i,* 27:30b.

42. *Ch'ing shih-lu,* Hsüan-tsung, 120:28a–b; *Nai-an tsou-i ts'un-kao,* 1:27; *Ching-shih wen hsü-pien,* 16:3a–b. In a list prepared by the provincial treasurer in 1803 for the assigning of contributions in Chekiang, the 77 chou and hsien were classified into three grades according to the magistrates' supplementary salary and the tax revenue of the localities: 20 chou and hsien as "big posts" (*ta-ch'üeh*); 28 as "medium posts" (*chung-ch'üeh*); and 16 hsien as "small

posts" (*hsiao-ch'üeh*). For every hundred taels of contribution, the share of each member of the first group was 2.273 taels; of the second group, 1.515 taels; of the third group, 0.757 taels. Only 13 hsien whose magistrates had a poor income were exempted from the "assigned contribution" (*Chih Che che'ng-kuei*, 3:47–48b). According to the estimate of Chang Chih-tung (1837–1907), the burden of a magistrate in connection with the assigned contribution in Shansi and Kwangtung varied from several hundred to about 2000 taels each year (*Chang Wen-hsiang chi, tsou-i*, 5:1b–2; 27:30b).

43. Chang Chih-tung enumerated 17 items of regular assigned contribution in Shansi, and 15 in Kwangtung (*Chang Wen-hsiang chi, tsou-i*, 5:1b–2; 27:30b–31). He mentioned that the contributions might be assigned by the provincial treasurer or provincial judge (*ssu t'an*), intendants (*tao-t'an*), or prefects (*fu-t'an*) (*ibid., kung-tu*, 95:15b; cf. below, n. 44).

44. An account book of the Fu-ning hsien yamen, Kiangsu (*Fu-i k'uan-mu pu*) reveals that the magistrate contributed the following sums to his superior officials for their general office expenses: 60 taels to the provincial judge; 240 taels to the intendant; 720 taels to the prefect. He also contributed to certain specific administrative funds, such as funds for *fu-shih* and *yüan-shih* (examinations given by the prefect and the provincial director of studies), for autumn assize, repair of the examination hall, etc. In addition, the magistrate helped to support the personnel employed by his superior. For instance, he paid the prefect's private secretaries for their services in connection with cases that were assigned to their yamen for trial (*fa-shen*). Various fees under the general name of *hsin-kung yin* (wages) or *chih-kung yin* (stationery and labor expenses) were paid to clerks of the various superior yamen for their services in connection with official business. Among these were: a fee for checking the records on collected land tax submitted to the provincial treasurer by the magistrate, a fee for making reports on the price of grain, a fee for *pao-chia* reports, and a fee for services connected with criminal cases, making monthly and annual reports, etc. According to the same source, the total sum of the various kinds of "contributions" amounted to more than 2800 taels. In another hsien in the same province, Ju-kao, the total of assigned contributions (excluding the magistrates' contribution to the funds of his own yamen), was more than 2700 taels, of which 500 taels went to the independent department yamen, T'ung-chou (*Ju-kao chiao-tai ts'e*).

Whenever a magistrate failed to hand in a contribution it was noted in the *Chiao-tai ts'e* (government fund transfer record) and he was requested by his successor to make it up (See *Hai-chou chiao-tai po-ts'e; Shan-yang chiao-tai po-ts'e; Ch'ing-ho chiao-tai po-ts'e; Yang-i chiao-tai po-ts'e; Fu-ning chiao-tai ts'e*).

45. *Che-sheng ts'ang-k'u ch'ing-ch'a chieh-yao*, pp. 16–18.

46. *Nai-an tsou-i ts'un-kao*, 1:24; *Ching-shih wen hsü-pien*, 16:3.

47. *Cheng wen lu*, 2:5. For a discussion of assigned contributions and other factors in connection with the deficit of magistrates' government funds during

the Chia-ching and Tao-kuang eras, see Suzuki Chūsei, "Shin matsu no zaisei to kanryō no seikaku," *Kindai chūkoku kenkyū*, 2:246–248 (1958).

48. *P'ing-p'ing yen*, 1:41b.

49. *Pu-ch'ien-chai man-ts'un*, 5:127; an edict of 1820 also mentions that since assigned contributions were deducted from their supplementary salary, the magistrates received no salary at all (*Ch'ing shih-lu*, Hsüan-tsung, 4:18b).

50. *Ch'ing shih-lu*, Hsüan-tsung, 120:28; *Nai-an tsou-i ts'un-kao*, 1:23b; *Ching-shih wen hsü-pien*, 16:2b; *Mu-ling shu*, 23:19. Thus it was generally realized that it was necessary to reduce assigned contributions in order to prevent a deficit in the magistrates' government funds and to prevent embezzlement, which was a common means of meeting the deficit (*Ch'ing shih-lu*, Mu-tsung, 40:18b–19b; *Chang Wen-hsiang chi, tsou-i*, 5:1b–2; *ibid., kung-tu*, 95:15a–b).

51. *Ch'ing shih-lu*, Jen-tsung, 170:19b; *ibid.*, Mu-tsung, 40:18b–19b; *Liu-pu ch'u-fen tse-li*, 15:8; 35:10; *Fu-hui ch'üan-shu*, 28:2b–4; *Chang Wen-hsiang chi, kung-tu*, 95:17.

52. *Ch'ing lü-li*, 31:11b–12; *Li-pu tse-li*, 13:8b; *Liu-pu ch'u-fen tse-li*, 15:14, 15.

53. *Liu-pu ch'u-fen tse-li*, 15:8; *Fu-hui ch'üan-shu*, 28:2b–4.

54. *Liu-pu ch'u-fen tse-li*, 15:8. It was recorded in an account book (*Fu-i k'uan-mu pu*) that 66.43 taels were contributed by the magistrate of Fu-ning for the winter furnishings used in the prefect's yamen and 52.54 taels were given for mat awning in the summer.

55. *Liu-pu ch'u-fen tse-li*, 15:9b; *Hu-pu tse-li*, 100:21–22; *Mu-ling shu*, 23:8, 19; *Ching-shih wen hsü-pien*, 16:15; *Chang Wen-hsiang chi, tsou-i*, 4:31b; 27:30; *ibid., kung-tu*, 95:17; *Shang-hai yen-chiu tzu-liao*, 535–536. It may be noted that there was a law prohibiting a magistrate from giving a birthday gift to his superior (*Liu-pu ch'u-fen tse-li*, 13:15).

56. *Mu-ling shu*, 23:8a–b; *Ching-shih wen hsü-pien*, 16:15.

57. *Chu-p'i yü-chih*, T'ien Wen-ching's memorials, 5:55a–b; *Ch'ing shih-lu*, Mu-tsung, 40:18b–19b; *Liu-pu ch'u-fen tse-li*, 15:9b; *Mu-ling shu*, 23:19, 39b.

58. *Mu-ling shu*, 23:19.

59. Hsieh mentioned the following items among the expenses: assigned contributions, subsidies for office expenses in a superior yamen, delivery expenses, record fees, and a fee for examination hall repairs (*Mu-ling shu*, 23:39b). According to Chang Chih-tung, the governor-general of Kwangtung and Kwangsi, the expenditure of a magistrate in Kwangtung, including the assigned contributions, customary fees paid to the superior yamen, and expenses incurred in entertaining high officials and commissioners and providing supplies to troops, varied from 300 to 5000 taels, depending upon the magistrate's income (*Chang Wen-hsiang chi, kung-tu*, 95:16).

60. This estimate is based on information given between 1750–1780, the same period during which Hsieh made his estimates. The salary was much higher in the nineteenth century (see Chap. XI, sec. 5).

61. This situation was summed up by the Tao-kuang emperor in an edict: "These *lou-kuei* have been handed down for a long time. In name, they are prohibited; in fact, every person takes them and they are found in all places" (*Ch'ing shih-lu*, Hsüan-tsung, 5:2b). In another edict he said: "Outwardly, the higher provincial officials prohibit their subordinates from taking the fees; secretly they tolerate them" (*ibid.*, Hsüan-tsung, 4:19).

62. Morse, *Trade and Administration*, pp. 80, 82.

63. Administrative expenses were not provided for by the government until 1724–1728, when it ordered the magistrates to deliver all money obtained from *huo-hao* to the provincial treasurers, to provide for the "supplementary salaries of the various officials and the local administrative expenses" of the province. (*Ch'ing hui-tien shih-li*, 1818, 143:14b; see also n. 73 below. Prior to 1724–1728 the magistrates could collect and keep the *huo-hao*.) But it should be pointed out that the fund secured from *huo-hao* covered only a small part of the administrative expenses of the chou and hsien yamen. This can be seen from the detailed information given by Chu Yün-chin (*chü-jen* 1789), who consulted the official documents of Honan and listed all the expenses that were met by the *huo-hao* in that province. The total income of *huo-hao* in Honan was 421,117 taels each year, of which 64.39 per cent (211,150 taels) was reserved for supplementary salaries, and the rest for the various expenses of the province. Included among these expenses were: (1) the meal money (*fan-yin*) paid to the clerks of the various boards, amounting to 10,842 taels; (2) stationery expenses of the governor's yamen, 1500 taels; (3) wages for clerks serving in the governor's and provincial treasurer's yamen, 4892 taels; (4) office expenses of the various chou and hsien, amounting to 23,480 taels, which were distributed as follows.

4 independent departments	1200 taels
43 large chou and hsien	10,320 taels
49 middle hsien	9800 taels
12 small chou and hsien	2160 taels

This indicates that in Honan only the yamen of the governor and provincial treasurer were provided with sufficient funds for office expenses, whereas the portion allotted to the yamen of the chou, hsien, and independent departments was more or less negligible. While the total amount appropriated for their office expenses constitutes only 5.57 per cent of the *huo-hao*, each yamen obtained only 180 to 300 taels on the average (for further details see *Yü-sheng shih-hsiao lu*, A:10b ff). According to *Yung-ch'ing hsien-chih*, 10:53, which lists the amount of *hao-hsien* derived from the land tax, in Yung-ch'ing, Chihli, the appropriation for the magistrate's yamen expenses was even less: 100 taels.

64. *Hsüeh-chih hsü-shuo*, pp. 2b–3; *P'ing-p'ing yen*, 1:39–40; *Mu-ling shu*, 11:52a–b; *Ching-shih wen hsü-pien*, 21:14. That *lou-kuei* was indispensable to local administration was also acknowledged by the Tao-kuang emperor who said in an edict of 1820 that even an honest official could not cook without rice. He had to depend upon *lou-kuei* to meet the deficiency (*Ch'ing shih-lu*, Hsüan-tsung, 4:18b).

65. *Hsüeh-chih hsü-shuo*, pp. 2b–3.

66. Morse, *Trade and Administration*, pp. 80–82.

67. *Sheng-shih wei-yen*, 2:9b–10.

68. The Tao-kuang emperor, immediately after he had ascended the throne in 1820, made an attempt to control the *lou-kuei*. Believing that it would be better to devise regulations to fix the amount of *lou-kuei* than to leave these matters to the local officials, he ordered the governors-general and governors to investigate the practice in each province in order to determine which fees should be kept and which should be abolished (*Ch'ing shih-lu*, Hsüan-tsung, 4:18b–20; 5:1b–3; 7:37–38). However, many officials opposed the edict on the ground that it was improper to legitimatize the *lou-kuei* openly in the government regulations. The emperor, admitting that he was not yet familiar with the administration and the situation and thus had made a wrong decision upon the suggestion of an official, Ying-ho (1771–1839), issued another edict canceling his previous order (*Ch'ing shih-lu*, Hsüan-tsung, 10:25–26b).

69. *P'ei-yüan-t'ang ou-ts'un kao*, 24:36–37.

70. *Mu-ling shu*, 23:8a–b.

71. *Hsien-chih-t'ang kao*, 5:32.

72. *Mu-ling shu*, 3:12b.

73. *Huo-hao*, also known as *hao-hsien* (surplus) had been in practice since the Ming dynasty (*Ch'ing t'ung-k'ao*, 3:4872). It was made unlawful in the early Ch'ing. A 1644 edict made it clear that the practice would be dealt with as bribery. However, the collection of this fee was in practice all over the empire and few higher officials were willing to impeach the magistrates because they themselves also depended upon the income from this source. The attitude of noninterference was even held by the K'ang-hsi emperor, who told one of his governors that it was tolerable if a magistrate imposed a 10 per cent *huo-hao* on the regular tax. The governor replied that it was kind of the emperor, but that magistrates should not be told openly that such a practice was permitted (*Shih-ch'ü yü-chi*, 3:46b–47).

Between 1724 and 1728, *huo-hao* was legitimatized and its revenue was used to provide supplementary salaries for the local officials and a part of the administrative expenses of the local government. It was delivered together with the regular tax to the provincial treasurer (see above, n. 36). The Yung-cheng emperor mentioned in an edict that although he wished that a magistrate would not take fees from the people, it was practically impossible to insist on such a policy because the supplementary salaries and administrative expenses in a province were derived from this source. At first, he refused to set an official quota for the collection of *huo-hao*, as some officials suggested, on the ground that the amount should be adjusted to the actual financial situation of the locality, and he hoped that this item might be abolished in the future (*Ch'ing shih-lu*, Shih-tsung, 22:3–6; *Ch'ing t'ung-k'ao*, 3:4871–72). But later the amount of *huo-hao* was fixed, varying in different localities and in different provinces (*Sun Wen-ting kung tsou-su*, 8:44–50; *Ch'ing hui-tien*, 1818, 11:23–25b; *Ch'ing hui-tien shih-li*, 1818, 139:9 ff; *Shih-ch'ü yü-chi*, 3:48; *Ch'ing shih kao*, 128:5b). On *huo-hao* see Abe Takeo, "Kōsen teikai no kenkyū," *Tōyōshi kenkyū*, 16.4:108–251 (March 1958); Iwami Hiroshi, "Yōsei jidai ni okeru kōhi no ikkōsatsu," *Tōyoshi kenkyū*, 15.4:87–97 (March 1957). For details on administrative expenses in connection with *hao-hsien*, see above, note 63.

74. *Mu-ling shu*, 3:12b.

75. Ch'ien Ch'en-ch'un (1686–1774) reported in a memorial that the rate in the K'ang-hsi period varied from 1 to 2 *ch'ien* for 1 *liang* of tax, but that in a small hsien where the tax quota was only 100 or 200 *liang*, the rate might be several times the tax (*Ching-shih wen-pien*, 27:5).

T'ien Wen-ching mentioned that the rate in Honan and Shantung varied from more than 1 *ch'ien* to 2 *ch'ien* (*Chu-p'i yü chih*, T'ien Wen-ching's memorials, 1:80b; 6:84).

Wang Ch'ing-yün (1798–1862) gave 1 *ch'ien* as the average rate for the empire, but noted that 2 to 3 *ch'ien* were collected in Hunan, and 4 to 5 *ch'ien* in Shensi (*Shih-ch'ü yü-chi*, 3:46b–47). This accords with an edict of 1723 which mentions that the rate in some localities was as high as 4 or 5 *ch'ien* for 1 *liang* of tax (*Ch'ing shih-lu*, Shih-tsung, 3:14).

76. *Shih-ch'ü yü-chi*, 3:46b; *Mu-ling shu*, 23:8b.

77. See below, Chap. VIII, sec. 1.

78. See below, Chap. VIII, sec. 2.

79. *Mu-ling shu*, 3:12b.

80. *Ibid.*, 11:48b.

81. Tax was often paid in small pieces of silver, which sometimes weighed slightly more than the amount required. When the magistrate delivered the tax to the government treasury, however, the fund was weighed in large packages. Thus there was a difference in the totals. This difference was called *yü-p'ing* (surplus due to a difference in scales). It was not obtained by manipulating the scale purposely (see *Ch'ing lü-li*, 11:44, note on top margin; *Chu-p'i yü-chih*, T'ien Wen-ching's memorials, 1:20; *ibid.*, Shih Lin's memorials, A:37a–b). According to T'ien, such a surplus might be as little as 2 or 3 taels, or up to 6 or 7 taels, per thousand taels (*Chu-p'i yü-chih*, T'ien's memorials, 1:20).

82. *Mu-ling shu*, 11:52b.

83. *Hsüeh-chih hsü-shuo*, pp. 2b–3; *P'ing-p'ing yen*, 2:26b.

84. *P'ing-p'ing yen*, 2:26b.

85. *Mu-ling shu*, 8:19b–20, 37b.

86. *Hsüeh-chih t'i-hsing lu*, A:8b.

87. *Mu-ling shu*, 8:37b–38; *Fu-hui ch'üan-shu*, 3:22b.

88. *Fu-hui ch'üan-shu*, 3:22b.

89. *Ibid.*, 3:22b; 24:16b–17. On the celebrations at the advent of spring see below, Chap. IX, sec. 7.

90. *Mu-ling shu*, 8:24b.

91. *Ch'in-pan chou-hsien shih-i*, pp. 30b–31; *Mu-ling shu*, 8:20b, 23b, 24; *Chang Wen-hsiang chi, kung-tu*, 86:32b, 35b.

92. *Ch'ing lü-li*, 31:31a–b; *Li-pu tse-li*, 21:7b–8; *Liu-pu ch'u-fen tse-li*, 22:24; *Hu-pu tse-li*, 100:34; *Ch'in-pan chou-hsien shih-i*, p. 31a–b; *Mu-ling shu*, 28:20b, 23b–24; *Tzu-chih hsin-shu*, 13:26 ff.

93. *Ch'ing lü-li*, 31:37–38.

94. *Mu-ling shu*, 11:40.

95. *Hsüeh-chih hsü-shuo*, p. 4b.

96. *P'ing-p'ing yen*, 1:38b–39b.

97. *Chao Kung-i sheng-kao*, 6:8.

98. *Ch'ing shih-lu*, Hsüan-tsung, 4:19a–b; 5:2; *Hsüeh-chih hsü-shuo*, 2b–3; *P'ing-p'ing yen*, 1:39.

99. *Mu-ling shu*, 8:24b.

100. As an example: since there were no funds in P'ing-yüan with which to pay supplementary salaries, the officials ordered the taxpayers to pay 1600 taels of silver in addition to tribute grain. This practice continued until a new magistrate, Wang Chih, took over (*Mu-ling shu*, 11:40a–b).

101. *Hsüeh-chih hsü-shuo*, pp. 2b–3; *P'ing-p'ing yen*, 1:39–40. For an instance of abolishing and reducing the amounts of *lou-kuei*, see *Mu-ling shu*, 11:41.

102. *Hsüeh-chih hsü-shuo*, p. 3; *P'ing-p'ing yen*, 1:39b–40.

103. *Yung-li yung-yen*, pp. 12b–13; *Mu-ling shu*, 11:41.

104. *Hsüeh-chih hsü-shuo*, p. 3b; *P'ing-p'ing yen*, p. 43b.

105. *P'ing-p'ing yen*, 1:41b.

106. *Mu-ling shu*, 3:10b–11b.

107. *P'ing-p'ing yen*, 1:41b.

108. *Chüan-shih-ko wen, chia-chi*, 1:20b.

109. *Ch'ing hui-tien*, 11:2b–3.

110. E.g., Ya-chou, Kan-en, Ch'ang-hua, and Ling-shui in Kwangtung; Pai-se, T'ai-p'ing, Ning-ming, and Ming-chiang in Kwangsi (*Ch'ing shih kao*, 117:12).

111. E.g., Chen-hsiung, En-lo, En-an, Yung-shan, and Ning-erh in Yünnan; Yung-feng and Li-po in Kweichow (*Ch'ing shih kao*, 117:12).

112. E.g., T'ai-ts'ang and Shanghai in Kiangsu; Jen-ho and Hai-ning in Chekiang; Chu-ch'eng and Chiao-chou in Shantung; Tung-kuan and Hsiang-shan in Kwangtung; Min-hou in Fukien (*Ch'ing shih kao*, 117:12).

113. E.g., Liang-hsiang and T'ung-chou in Chihli; Hsiang-fu and Cheng-chou in Honan; Te-chou and Tung-p'ing chou in Shantung; Shan-yang and P'ei-chou in Kiangsu (*Ch'ing shih kao*, 117:12).

114. *Ch'ing hui-tien shih-li, chüan* 59; *Ch'ing shih kao*, 117:12.

115. *Ch'ing hui-tien*, 11:4b–5.

116. See below, n. 123.

117. *Ch'ing hui-tien*, 11:4b–5; *Li-pu tse-li*, 2:10b–12; *Liu-pu ch'u-fen tse-li*, 1:6–7.

118. *Hsüeh-chih i-shuo*, B:20b–21.

119. *Ch'ing hui-tien*, 11:4a–b; *Liu-pu ch'u-fen tse-li*, 1:3b.

120. The nominal salary forfeits could consist of salary for 1 month, 2 months, 3 months, 6 months, 9 months, 1 year, or 2 years (*Ch'ing hui-tien*, 11:1).

121. The different degrees of demotion were: (1) Retention in the original post, with demotion of 1, 2, or 3 grades. (2) Transfer to a different post, with demotion of 1, 2, 3, 4, or 5 grades (*Ch'ing hui-tien*, 11:1a–b).

122. *Ibid.*, 11:1b–2.

123. *Ibid.*, 11:4b–5. The penalties corresponding to corporal punishment were as follow:

(1) Punishment for malfeasance in office:

10 strokes with a light bamboo stick (*ch'ih*)—forfeit of 1 month's nominal salary

20 strokes—2 months' nominal salary

30 strokes—3 months' nominal salary

40 strokes—6 months' nominal salary

50 strokes—9 months' nominal salary

60 strokes with a heavy bamboo stick (*chang*)—forfeit of 1 year's nominal salary

70 strokes—demotion of 1 grade and retention in the same post

80 strokes—demotion of 2 grades and retention in the same post

90 strokes—demotion of 3 grades and retention in the same post

100 strokes—loss of title and retention in the same post.

(2) Punishment for a personal crime:

10 strokes—forfeit of 2 months' nominal salary

20 strokes—3 months' nominal salary

30 strokes—6 months' nominal salary

40 strokes—9 months' nominal salary

50 strokes—1 year's nominal salary

60 strokes—demotion of 1 grade and transfer to another post

70 strokes—demotion of 2 grades and transfer to another post

80 strokes—demotion of 3 grades and transfer to another post

90 strokes—demotion of 4 grades and transfer to another post

100 strokes—dismissal

(See *Li-pu tse-li*, 2:1a–b; *Liu-pu ch'u-fen tse-li*, 1:3–4b; *Ch'ing-lü-li*, 4:48, 60.)

124. *Ch'ing hui-tien*, 11:2.

125. Regularly held in the *yin*, *ssu*, *sheng*, and *hai* years (*Ch'ing hui-tien*, 11:8a–b).

126. *Ibid.*, 11:10b. According to Huang Liu-hung, although it was the governor-general or governor who signed the memorial, the actual evaluation statements were made by the prefect or intendant of the circuit and presented to the provincial treasurer and provincial judge, who then jointly made the recommendation (*Fu-hui ch'üan-shu*, 24:3).

127. *Li-pu tse-li*, 4:7b; *Liu-pu ch'u-fen tse-li*, 6:7; *Ch'ing hui-tien*, 11:10b. Huang Liu-hung mentioned that such actions as the public reading and interpretation of certain imperial edicts, the establishment of a free school, or the

repair of a Confucian temple were frequently referred to as "outstanding and distinctive" accomplishments. The following statements were included in most recommendations: "pure, incorrupt, and loves the people," "has educated and exerted moral influence upon the people," "has abolished the 'melting fee,'" "has not executed cruel punishment and has not engaged in corruption" (*Fu-hui ch'üan-shu*, 24:2a–b).

128. *Liu-pu ch'u-fen tse-li*, 6:7b–8b.

129. *Li-pu tse-li*, 4:18.

130. *Liu-pu ch'u-fen tse-li*, 6:3–4b.

131. The "eight proscriptions" appear in the K'ang-hsi *hui-tien* (10:15a–b), Yung-cheng *hui-tien* (15:21b), and Ch'ien-lung *hui-tien* (6:1b). Only the "six proscriptions" appear in the Chia-ch'ing *hui-tien* (8:14) and the Kuang-hsü *hui-tien* (11:4b, 10b, 11). See also *Liu-pu ch'u-fen tse-li*, 61:1a–b; *Fu-hui ch'üan-shu*, 24:2b; *Shih-ch'ü yü-chi*, 2:23; *P'ing-p'ing yen*, 1:27b–28.

132. *Liu-pu ch'u-fen tse-li*, 6:16.

133. For embezzlement of
less than 1 tael—80 strokes
  1 tael to 2 taels, 5 *ch'ien*—90 strokes
  5 taels—100 strokes
  7 taels, 5 *ch'ien*—60 strokes and 1 year of penal servitude
  10 taels—70 strokes and 1½ years of penal servitude
  12 taels, 5 *ch'ien*—80 strokes and 2 years of penal servitude
  15 taels—90 strokes and 2½ years of penal servitude
  17 taels, 5 *ch'ien*—100 strokes and 3 years of penal servitude
  20 taels—100 strokes and banishment to a distance of 2000 li
  25 taels—100 strokes and banishment to a distance of 2500 li
  30 taels—100 strokes and banishment to a distance of 3000 li
  40 taels—beheading
It should be noted that banishment and beheading were not actually carried out in cases of embezzlement. Instead, 4 or 5 years of penal servitude were substituted for banishment and beheading, respectively (*Ch'ing lü-li*, 23:48–49).

134. For accepting a bribe and causing injustice in the administration of law (*wang-fu tsang*):
less than 1 tael—70 strokes
  1–5 taels—80 strokes
  10 taels—90 strokes
  15 taels—100 strokes
  20 taels—60 strokes and 1 year of penal servitude
  25 taels—70 strokes and 1½ years of penal servitude
  30 taels—80 strokes and 2 years of penal servitude
  35 taels—90 strokes and 2½ years of penal servitude
  40 taels—100 strokes and 3 years of penal servitude
  45 taels—100 strokes and banishment to a distance of 2000 li
  50 taels—100 strokes and banishment to a distance of 2500 li
  55 taels—100 strokes and banishment to a distance of 3000 li

80 taels—"detention for strangling"
For accepting a bribe without causing injustice in the administration of law
(*pu wang-fa tsang*):
less than 1 tael—60 strokes

1–10 taels—70 strokes
   20 taels—80 strokes
   30 taels—90 strokes
   40 taels—100 strokes
   50 taels—60 strokes and 1 year of penal servitude
   60 taels—70 strokes and 1½ years of penal servitude
   70 taels—80 strokes and 2 years of penal servitude
   80 taels—90 strokes and 2½ years of penal servitude
   90 taels—100 strokes and 3 years of penal servitude
  100 taels—100 strokes and banishment to a distance of 2000 li
  110 taels—100 strokes and banishment to a distance of 2500 li
  120 taels—100 strokes and banishment to a distance of 3000 li
over 120 taels—"detention for strangling"
(*Ch'ing lü-li*, 31:2–5b; cf. G. T. Staunton, *The Tsing Leu Lee; Being Fundamental Laws, and a Selection from the Supplementary Statutes, of the Penal Code of China*, London, 1810, pp. 379–382; Boulais, pp. 654–656. *Pu wang-fa tsang* and *wang-fa tsang* were misunderstood by Staunton as meaning "for a lawful purpose and for an unlawful purpose" respectively. No bribery could be lawful.)

135. If the governor or governor-general impeached a magistrate, the officials from the provincial treasurer down were subject to demotion or forfeiture of salary for having failed to make the impeachment. The law made a distinction between superior officials stationed in the same city as the magistrate and those who were not. In the first case, the independent department magistrate or the prefect was to be demoted two grades and transferred to another post, and the circuit intendant, the provincial judge, and the provincial treasurer were to be demoted one grade and retained in the same post. In the second case, the independent department magistrate or the prefect was to be demoted one grade and retained in the same post, and the circuit intendant, the provincial judge, and the provincial treasurer were to be punished by forfeiture of one year's nominal salary (*Liu-pu ch'u-fen tse-li*, 4:42; cf. *Li-pu tse-li*, 3:15a–b). When the circuit intendant, the prefect and the independent department magistrate had been told by the governor-general, governor, provincial judge, or provincial treasurer to investigate the case of a corrupt magistrate, or when a magistrate had been accused by the local people, and yet the circuit intendant, the prefect, and the independent department magistrate still failed to report the case, they were to be demoted three grades and transferred to another post (*Liu-pu ch'u-fen tse-li*, 4:42b; cf. *Li-pu tse-li*, 3:15b–16).

If a corrupt magistrate was impeached by a censor, the governor and the governor-general who had failed to make the impeachment due to negligence were subject to demotion of one grade or forfeiture of one year's nominal salary.

If a governor or a governor-general connived in a corrupt practice, he was to be demoted three grades and transferred to another post (*Liu-pu ch'u-fen tse-li*, 4:42b).

136. *Ch'ing hui-tien*, 11:14b; *Liu-pu ch'u-fen tse-li*, 6:16.

137. *Ch'ing hui-tien*, 11:10b; *Li-pu tse-li*, 4:15a–b; *Liu-pu ch'u-fen tse-li*, 6:1b; *Fu-hui ch'üan-shu*, 24:3a–b; *P'ing-p'ing yen*, 1:28. For the form used in the report see *Fu-hui ch'üan-shu*, 24:4a–b.

CHAPTER III. CLERKS

1. *Ch'ing shih-lu*, Hsüan-tsung, 191:15; *Ching-shih wen hsü-pien*, 21:13b.

2. *Chuang-hui-t'ang wen-chi, i-kao*, p. 12b; *T'ing-lin wen-chi*, 1:12; *Sheng-shih wei-yen*, 2:8. Thus Ku Yen-wu (1613–1682) compared the magistrates to guests who passed through a place only once, whereas the clerks were the hosts there (*Ku chung sui-pi*, p. 53).

3. *Ching-shih wen-pien*, 24:7.

4. Huang Liu-hung points out that the *hsü-chih* (lit., must know) prepared by the clerks included all the information relating to the local situation which was essential to the local government (*Fu-hui ch'üan-shu*, 2:11 ff).

5. *Ku chung sui-pi*, p. 53.

6. See above, Chap. I, sec. 2.

7. *Ching-shih wen-pien*, 24:1b.

8. *T'ung-fu lei-kao*, 1:11b.

9. *Ching-shih wen-pien*, 24:6b.

10. *T'ung-fu lei-kao*, 1:11b–12. Lu suggested that one way to deal with the problem was to reduce the number of supervising officials, so that the magistrate would be able to concentrate on administrative affairs and deal with the clerks (*ibid.*, 1:13, 15).

11. *Ibid.*, 1:11.

12. He therefore suggested that all the records of precedents should be burned and that a collection of simplified descriptions of precedents be made. These should be so worked out that an official, even if not versed in official business, would be able to understand and apply them. Feng had in mind particularly the clerks of the central government, who were in a position of considerable power, since they could reject the documents submitted by officials to the various boards of the central government. However, his remarks on the power of the clerks were also applicable to the less powerful clerks in the local government. Within the local government, the clerks in chou and hsien yamen were again less powerful than those in yamen at a higher level, since the latter were in a position to reject documents presented by the chou and hsien officials. See *Chiao-pin-lu k'ang-i*, A:17–18b; cf. the remarks of K'ou Yung-hsiu, *Ching-shih wen-pien*, 24:6b.

13. *P'ing-p'ing yen*, 4:60b; *Mu-hsüeh chü-yao*, p. 20.

14. *Ch'ing hui tien*, 12:13b, mentions that all the clerks who served in the government of *ssu* (provincial treasurer or provincial judge), *tao*, *fu*, *t'ing*, chou, and hsien were called *tien-li* (see also *Ch'ing hui-tien shih-li*, *chüan*

148–151). There were one or two *tien-li* in each office (*fang*). They were the quota clerks whose names were listed in the record of the Board of Civil Office (*Yung-ch'ing hsien-chih*, 9:3b–4; *Chang shih i-shu wai-pien*, 9:4b–5).

The clerks in the treasury office and the granary office and those who served in the yamen of the magistrate's subordinate officials were called *tsuan-tien* (*Ch'ing hui-tien*, 12:13b; *Ch'ing lü-li*, 5:97a–b; *Yung-ch'ing hsien-chih*, 9:3b; *Chang-shih i-shu wai-pien*, 9:4b).

15. The quota for regular clerks was first introduced in 1668. Both the K'ang-hsi and Yung-cheng *Hui-tien* mention that the quota for clerks serving in the chou yamen ranged from 6 to 12, in the hsien yamen from 2 to 12 (*Ch'ing hui-tien* [1690], 15:1, 17, 18a–b; *ibid.* [1732], 21:16, 17a–b). According to the 1899 *Ch'ing hui-tien shih-li*, most hsien had 10 to 14 clerks; a few had more than 16; and 1 hsien, Chung-wei of Kansu, had a quota of 25 (for details see *chüan* 148–151).

16. *Ch'ing hui-tien*, 12:13b; *Ch'ing hui-tien shih-li*, 21:4; *Ch'ing t'ung-k'ao*, 21:5045; *Fu-hui ch'üan-shu*, 4:23b. According to T'ien Wen-ching, *t'ieh-hsieh* were the beginners who were just learning to copy documents (*Chu-p'i yü-chih*, T'ien Wen-ching's memorials, 6:114).

17. Excess clerks were to be dismissed and the officials who violated this regulation were to be demoted one grade (*Ch'ing hui-tien shih-li, chüan* 146; *Liu-pu ch'u-fen tse-li*, 16:1b, 2b, 7).

18. *Chu-p'i yü-chih*, T'ien Wen-ching's memorials, 6:114b–115; *ibid.*, Li Wei's memorials, 4:23.

19. Both *ping* and *hsiang* were types of documents submitted by a magistrate to his superior. *Hsiang* refers to *hsiang-wen. Ping* refers to *ping-t'ieh;* it was less formal and was preferred when a complicated case called for a detailed explanation which the official hesitated to discuss freely in a *hsiang-wen.* For their use and style see *Fu-hui ch'üan-shu*, 5:1 ff.

20. *Pu-ch'ien-chai man-ts'un*, 5:123.

21. *T'u-min lu*, 2:26.

22. *Chu-p'i yü-chih*, T'ien Wen-ching's memorials, 6:115b–116; *ibid.*, Li Wei's memorials, 4:22b; *Mu-ling shu*, 8:23.

23. *Mu-ling shu*, 8:23, 10:6; *Ching-shih wen-pien*, 33:10b; *Liu-pu ch'u-fen tse-li*, 16:14.

24. *Chu-p'i yü-chih*, T'ien Wen-ching's memorials, 6:114b.

25. *Chuang-hui-t'ang wen-chi, i-kao*, 13b–14.

26. *Chüan-shih-ko wen, chia-chi*, 1:22.

27. *Ching-shih wen hsü-pien*, 22:16b.

28. *Ch'ing hsü t'ung-k'ao*, 27:7791.

29. *Fu-hui ch'üan-shu*, 2:12; *Yung-ch'ing hsien-chih*, 9:3b ff; *Chang-shih i-shu wai-pien*, 9:4 ff.

30. *Fu-hui ch'üan-shu*, 2:12b; *Yung-ch'ing hsien-chih*, 10:3 ff; *Chang-shih i-shu wai-pien*, 9:10b ff; *Hsüeh-chih i-te pien*, pp. 25 ff.

31. *P'ei-yüan-t'ang ou-ts'un kao*, 46:42. A clerk often had to serve more than

ten years before he became a *ching-ch'eng*, a clerk with a special assignment (*Ch'ing hsü t'ung-k'ao*, 89:8483).

32. *Fu-hui ch'üan-shu*, 2:12b–13; *Yung-ch'ing hsien-chih*, 11:2b ff; *Chang-shih i-shu wai-pien*, 9:108 ff.

33. It may be noted that of the records of the government runners only those of *tsao-li*, *k'uai-shou*, and *min-chuang* (see Chap. IV, sec. 1) were kept in this office; the records of policemen and coroners were kept in the Office of Punishment (*Fu-hui ch'üan-shu*, 2:13–14; *Yung-ch'ing hsien-chih*, 12:1b ff; *Chang-shih i-shu wai-pien*, 9:119b ff).

34. *Fu-hui ch'üan-shu*, 2:14a–b; *Yung-ch'ing hsien-chih*, 13:1b ff; *Chang-shih i-shu wai-pien*, 9:122 ff.

35. *Fu-hui ch'üan-shu*, 2:14b–15; *Yung-ch'ing hsien-chih*, 14:1b ff; *Chang-shih i-shu wai-pien*, 9:132 ff.

36. *Fu-hui ch'üan-shu*, 11:9; *Huan-hsiang yao-tse*, 2:12; *Ch'ien-ku pi-tu*; *Kung-men yao-lüeh*, quoted in *Chung-ho*, 2.10:73 (Oct. 1941).

37. *Fu-hui ch'üan-shu*, 4:12b–13b.

38. *Fu-hui ch'üan-shu*, 3:9b; *Yung-ch'ing hsien-chih*, 10:77b; *Chang-shih i-shu wai-pien*, 9:104b; *Huan-hsiang yao-tse*, 2:4b; *Ch'ien-ku pi-tu*. It should be pointed out here that the post of *k'u-shu* or *k'u-li* (treasury clerk) was not always occupied by a clerk. Since it was difficult to find an honest man among the clerks, and since embezzlement was a recurrent problem, a magistrate usually found it more convenient to ask the *t'u* or *li* to recommend for the post a person living in the rural district. However, many were unwilling to accept the post because the *k'u-shu* was frequently asked by the magistrate to provide silk, furniture, and other things without payment. Thus the local residents often paid a bribe (called *mai-mien*, buying the exemption) in order not to be recruited. The recommendation itself became an opportunity for the *t'u* or *li* to extort money from the wealthy people living in the rural district. Attempts were usually made to recommend the wealthy people one by one, so that each of them would pay a sum for exemption. According to Huang Liu-hung this was the greatest irregularity in the southeast. He advised that *k'u-shu* be selected from the clerks of the various *fang*, if possible, and that the local resident be asked to take the post only when no qualified man could be found among the clerks. He also advised magistrates not to demand anything from the *k'u-shu* (*Fu-hui ch'üan-shu*, 3:22b; 6:3a–b).

39. *Fu-hui ch'üan-shu*, 3:10; *Yung-ch'ing hsien-chih*, 10:72b ff; *Chang-shih i-shu wai-pien*, 9:97b ff; *Ch'ien-ku pi-tu*.

40. *Fu-hui ch'üan-shu*, 6:2b; 7:3b–6b; *Ch'ien-ku shih-ch'eng*, pp. 20b, 23.

41. *Chiang-nan t'ung-chih*, 7:11b; *T'ao Yün-t'ing hsien-sheng tsou-su*, 10:42. The name of *shan-shu* was given because in certain places in Kiangsu and Chekiang a number of *li* were grouped into a *shan*, two of which constituted a *ch'ü*, a subdivision of a *hsiang* (*Chia-ting hsien-chih*, 1:28b). K'o Sung's memorial quoted in the *Chiang-nan t'ung-chih* mentions that *li-shu* were employed in Kiangsu and Chekiang. However, their employment was not

limited to the south. For instance, *Ning-yüan hsien-chih*, 2:8, mentions that there were fourteen such clerks in Ning-yüan, Kansu, where there were fourteen *li*.

42. *Mu-ling shu*, 8:27; *Ch'ien-ku pei-yao*, 1:7b–8; *Ch'ien-ku pi-tu*. According to Wang Yu-huai, this post was not always occupied by the clerks of revenue. Since several silver chests were needed, several clerks had to be assigned to take charge of them during the time of tax collection. The clerks were selected from the various *fang* (*Ch'ien-ku pei-yao*, 1:7b).

43. *Hsing-ch'ien pi-lan*, 6:14.

44. *Fu-hui ch'üan-shu*, 2:9b–10; *Yung-li yung-yen*, 13; *Ch'ien-ku pi-tu*; *Hsüeh-chih ou-ts'un*, 4:18b–19; *Hsüeh-chih t'i-hsing lu*, A:6b–7.

45. *Fu-hui ch'üan-shu*, 2:13–14.

46. *Hsüeh-chih t'i-hsing lu*, A:7b.

47. *Hsüeh-chih ou-ts'un*, 4:17a–b; *P'ing-p'ing yen*, 2:27b; *Mu-ling shu*, 4:30b.

48. See *Fu-hui ch'üan-shu*, 4:11b; *Ching-shih wen-pien*, 22:19b, 20; *Mu-ling shu*, 4:30b–31; *Hsüeh-chih ou-ts'un*, 4:19a–b; *Hsüeh-chih t'i-hsing lu*, A:6b. According to the last source, the practice adopted by the various yamen was as follows: each *fang* had a wooden stamp with the name of the *fang* written horizontally across the top and the following five items written vertically below: *Fa-fang* (send the document to the *fang*); *Sung-kao* (present the draft); *P'an-fa* (approve the draft); *Sung-ch'ien* (send in the document for stamping); *Fa-hsing* (issue the document). The clerks were expected to affix this stamp to documents and fill in the date under each of the five items.

49. *Mu-ling shu*, 4:31.

50. *Hsüeh-chih ou-ts'un*, 4:17b.

51. *Ching-shih wen hsü-pien*, 21:14b.

52. *Hsüeh-chih ou-ts'un*, 4:17.

53. *Ibid.*, 4:18a–b; *Yung-li yung-yen*, 11b.

54. For details see below, Chap. VIII, sec. 1.

55. *Ch'ing hui-tien shih-li*, chüan 146.

56. *Hsüeh-chih ou-ts'un*, 4:18.

57. *T'ung-fu lei-kao*, 1:15.

58. *Chiao-pin-lu k'ang-i*, A:15.

59. *Tzu-chih hsin-shu*, 12:24. A provincial judge could also send his runners to summon a clerk when the magistrate failed to close a case of homicide or robbery (*P'ei-yüan-t'ang ou-ts'un kao*, 10:34b).

60. *T'u-min lu*, 2:26.

61. *Liu-pu ch'u-fen tse-li*, 16:1.

62. *Tzu-chih hsin-shu*, 12:29b. *Hsüeh-cheng ch'üan-shu*, 26:2, mentions that a *sheng-yüan* (holder of a first-degree or government school student) who achieved the lowest (sixth) grade in the *sui* examination given by the provincial director of studies was to be made a clerk, but this was optional with the *sheng-yüan*. According to Chang Hsüeh-ch'eng, none of the students had ever become clerks in this way (*Yung-ch'ing hsien-chih*, 9:4; *Chang-shih i-shu wai-pien*, 9:5). In fact, the law prohibited the *sheng-yüan* and *chien-sheng*

(students of the imperial academy) from being clerks (*Li-pu tse-li*, 57:5b; 59:4b). A candidate for the post of clerk was customarily required to submit to the magistrate a signed guarantee stating that he had not committed any crime and that he was not a *sheng-yüan* or *chien-sheng* (*Yung-ch'ing hsien-chih*, 9:4; *Chang-shih i-shu wai-pien*, 9:5).

63. *Fu-hui ch'üan-shu*, 3:20b–21.

64. *Mu-ling shu*, 4:32a–b.

65. *Ch'ing hui-tien shih-li*, chüan 146; *Ching-shih wen-pien*, 24:4b.

66. *Li-pu tse-li*, 14:3b; *Liu-pu ch'u-fen tse-li*, 16:5b–6, 7a–b. A clerk who continued to serve after his term had expired was to be dismissed and receive 100 strokes (*Ch'ing lü li*, 6:117b–118). Thus the law required a newly employed clerk to submit a statement saying that he had not served before and was not re-entering the service under a different name. The magistrate was also required to prepare a guarantee stamped with the official seal (*Li-pu tse-li*, 14:3b; *Ch'ing lü-li*, 6:117b–118).

67. *Li-pu tse-li*, 14:5b; *Liu-pu ch'u-fen tse-li*, 16:13.

68. *Fu-hui ch'üan-shu*, 4:14b–15; *Huan-hsiang yao-tse*, 1:16a–b.

69. *Ch'ing hui-tien*, 12:13b–14; *Ch'ing t'ung-k'ao*, 21:5044–45.

70. This was a regulation of 1790. Under the earlier regulations of 1655 and 1664, a clerk could be given a rank ranging from the eighth rank to the miscellaneous post (*tsa-chih*) below the regular rank. See *Ch'ing hui-tien* (1690), 15:20b–21; *ibid.* (1732), 21:23b; *ibid.* (1899), 12:13b–14; *Ch'ing hui-tien tse-li*, 10:16, 17a–b; *Ch'ing hui-tien shih-li* (1818), 58:8b, 10, 11b–12; *Li-pu ch'üan-hsüan tse-li*, 4:88b–89b.

71. *Ch'ing hui-tien shih-li*, chüan 97 and 146.

72. *Ching-shih wen-pien*, 24:4b; *Tso-chih yao-yen*, 5; *Hsüeh-chih t'i-hsing lu*, A:7b; *P'ing-p'ing yen*, 2:29; *Mu-ling shu*, 4:33b; *Chi-fu t'ung-chih*, 87:75.

73. *Ching-shih wen-pien*, 21:14b.

74. *Ch'ing t'ung-k'ao*, 21:5045. In theory, service as a clerk was considered a labor service rendered to the yamen by the people (*Ch'ing t'ung-k'ao*, 21:5044–45); but the people actually paid a sum of money in lieu of service, and this money was used by the government to hire clerks (see below, Chap. IV, sec. 4). However, no attempt was made by the government to restore the clerks' wage after its elimination (*San-yü-t'ang wai-chi*, 1:16b).

75. *Chi-fu t'iao pien fu-i ch'üan-shu*, Shun-t'ien fu, Ta-hsing hsien, pp. 101b–102b; Shun-t'ien fu, Pa-chou, pp. 44b, 48b; Shun-t'ien fu, Liang-hsiang hsien, pp. 74, 77b–78; Pao-ting fu, Ch'ing-yüan hsien, pp. 111a–b, 115a–b; Pao-ting fu, Ting-hsing hsien, pp. 56a–b, 60a–b; Shen-chou, pp. 31b, 35b; Ting-chou, pp. 74a–b, 78; *Pa-chou fu-i ts'e*, pp. 44a–b, 47–48.

76. *Hsiang-t'an hsien-chih*, 10:6b–7b.

77. *Hsien-ning hsien-chih*, 3:7, 8, gives 1662 as the date when the clerks' pay was totally eliminated, but the date of the cut is not given. *K'uai-chi hsien-chih*, 11:13b, 14b, which gives 1652 as the date for the cut, mentions that the pay for the twelve office clerks was eliminated in 1662, and that the pay for the treasury clerk and the granary clerk was eliminated in 1663.

78. *San-yü-t'ang wai-chi*, 1:16b. *Wu-chiang hsien-chih*, 18:14b, which reports that the clerks' pay was completely eliminated in the K'ang-hsi period, without specifying the date, also mentions that their wages were eliminated to provide pay and rations for the troops.

79. *Ching-shih wen-pien*, 28:3; *Mu-ling shu*, 4:33b; *Pu-ch'ien-chai man-ts'un*, 5:123a–b.

80. *Hsüeh-chih t'i-hsing lu*, A:7b.

81. *Tso-chih yao-yen*, p. 5.

82. *Yung-li yung-yen*, p. 12b.

83. *Ibid.* Magistrates in Kiangsu were ordered by Governor Ting Jih-ch'ang to donate money to meet various expenses encountered in conducting an inquest (*Fu Wu kung-tu*, 34:3).

84. The edict mentioned that fees had to be paid to the clerks of the superior yamen by the clerks of the chou or hsien government when land tax or tribute grain was delivered to the superior yamen. Fees also had to be paid when a document was received at the superior yamen. The clerk who received the document was asked to prepare a draft rescript and then hand it in for approval; he was, therefore, in a position of possible manipulation with regard to the approval or disapproval of the document, and with regard to the time involved in handling it (*Ch'ing shih lu*, Kao-tsung, 21:5a–b; *Ch'ing hui-tien shih-li* [1818], 77:9).

85. *Pu-ch'ieh-chai man-ts'un*, 5:123a–b.

86. *Ching-shih wen pien*, 24:7.

87. *Mu-ling shu*, 4:33b–34.

88. *Ibid.*, 4:34.

89. *Ibid.*, 4:33.

90. *P'ing-p'ing yen*, 2:36b; *Cheng wen lu*, 2:21b–22.

91. *Ching-shih wen hsü-pien*, 21:3. As a rule, the plaintiff had also to pay fees to clerks and to the court attendant (Chap. V, sec. 1) for stamping the complaint (*ch'o ch'ien*) (*Liang-shan hsien-chih*, 3:18a–b).

92. *P'ing-p'ing yen*, 2:36b; *Liang-shan hsien-chih*, 3:17a–b; *Ching-yen hsien-chih*, 4:25.

93. A regulation concerning fees for clerks and runners ("Shu-i t'iao-kuei") issued in 1877 by a magistrate in Liang-shan, Szechwan, indicates that both plaintiff and defendant were obliged to pay fees for the issuance of a warrant (*Liang-shan hsien-chih*, 3:16a–b).

94. *P'ing-p'ing yen*, 2:36b; *Ching-shih wen hsü-pien*, 21:3.

95. *Tseng Wen-cheng kung ch'üan-chi, tsa-chu*, 2:63b–64; *P'ing-p'ing yen*, 2:36b–37; *Fu Wu kung-tu*, 35:9b; 36:5a–b, 7b; *Cheng wen lu*, 2:21b–22; *Mu-ling shu*, 8:38b–39; *Ching-shih wen hsü-pien*, 21:3; *Liang-shan hsien-chih*, 1:16b–17; *Ching-yen hsien-chih*, 4:25b.

96. *P'ing-p'ing yen*, 2:36b–37; *Liang-shan hsien-chih*, 3:19a–b.

97. *Shu liao wen-ta*, 13b; *P'ing-p'ing yen*, 2:36b–37; *Ching-shih wen hsü-pien*, 21:2b.

98. *Tseng Wen-cheng chi, tsa-chu*, 2:64; *P'ing-p'ing yen*, 2:37; *Ching-shih*

wen hsü-pien, 22:7b; *Liang-shan hsien-chih*, 3:16; *Ching-yen hsien-chih*, 4:25b.

99. *Yung-li yung-yen*, 12b; *Shu liao wen-ta*, 13b; *P'ing-p'ing yen*, 2:37; *Ching-shih wen hsü-pien*, 22:8b; *Mu-hsüeh chü-yao*, 14; see below, Chap. IV, sec. 4.

100. *Mu-ling-shu*, 8:37b.

101. *Ibid.*, 11:35a–b; *Hsien-chih-t'ang kao*, 5:37.

102. *Mu-ling shu*, 8:37b; *Ching-shih wen hsü-pien*, 22:8.

103. See *P'ei-yüan-t'ang ou-ts'un kao*, 21:18b, 19b; 25:44a–b; *Ping-t'a meng-hen lu*, 35a–b, 38; *Mu-ling shu*, 12:19.

104. *Ch'ien-ku pei-yao*, 1:7b; *Hsüeh-chih ou-ts'un*, 3:12.

105. *Mu-ling shu*, 11:42.

106. *P'ei-yüan-t'ang ou-ts'un kao*, 22:2a–b.

107. *Fu-hui ch'üan-shu*, 8:2; *P'ei-yüan-t'ang ou-ts'un kao*, 25:43b.

108. *Mu-ling shu*, 4:34; 11:41.

109. *Liu-pu ch'eng-yü chu-chieh*, p. 64.

110. *Mu-ling shu*, 4:34; 11:41.

111. *Shu liao wen-ta*, 13b; *P'ing-p'ing yen*, 1:39b–40.

112. *Mu-ling shu*, 11:45.

113. *Ibid.*, 11:41.

114. *Hsüeh-chih ou-ts'un*, 4:16.

115. *Hsüeh-chih t'i-hsing lu*, A:6b.

116. *Ibid.*, A:15b; *Hsiao-ts'ang shan-fang wen-chi*, 18:7; *Ch'ien-ku pi-tu*.

117. *Hsüeh-chih t'i hsing lu*, A:6b; *Hsiao-ts'ung shan-fang wen-chi*, 18:7.

118. *Fu-hui ch'üan-shu*, 4:11. For other tricks practiced with seals obtained on a blank paper see *Huan-hsiang yao-tse*, 2:12b–13.

119. *Ch'ing shih-lu*, Kao-tsung, 21:4; *Ch'ing hui-tien shih-li, chüan* 146.

120. *Ching-shih wen-pien*, 22:20.

121. *Hsüeh-chih i-shuo*, A:17.

122. *Ch'in-pan chou-hsien shih-i*, p. 26; *P'ei-yüan-t'ang ou-ts'un-kao*, 46:31b.

123. *P'ei-yüan-t'ang ou-ts'un-kao*, 21:18a–b.

124. *Hsing-ch'ien pi-lan*, 5:8, 21; *Mu-ling shu*, 8:37b; *Ch'in-pan chou-hsien shih-i*, p. 12b. It should be pointed out here that although the regulation permitted the taxpayers to put the silver in a sealed bag themselves (see below, p. 134), most of the magistrates, fearing that the silver contained in the bag might be less than the amount indicated, authorized the clerks to examine the silver before it was put into the chest (*Ch'ing shih-lu*, Kao-tsung, 50:6). This procedure naturally gave the clerks an opportunity to tamper with the silver.

125. *Hsing-ch'ien pi-lan*, 5:7a–b; *Ch'in-pan chou-hsien shih-i*, p. 44b. Another trick commonly used by clerks was to make a false report on the number of land tax receipt books distributed to them so that they could keep the extra books for the purpose of collecting land tax privately (*Ch'ang sui lun*, quoted in *Chung-ho*, 2.9:54).

126. *Ch'ing hui-tien shih-li, chüan* 172; *P'ei-yüan-t'ang ou-ts'un kao*, 46:35b.

127. *P'ei-yüan-t'ang ou-ts'un kao*, 46:8, 35b; *Ch'ien-ku shih-ch'eng*, p. 20. For such an arrangement, according to the petition submitted to the prefect

in 1671 by the government school students and the commoners of Sung-chiang, taxpayers had to bribe the runners with ten per cent of the tax and the clerks with another ten per cent (*Sung-chün chün-i ch'eng-shu, ts'e* 8:300b).

128. *Hsing-ch'ien pi-lan*, 6:14a–b.

129. *P'ei-yüan-t'ang ou-ts'un kao*, 14:22a–b; 21:14; 45:37b–38.

130. *Ibid.*, 21:14; *Ch'in-pan chou-hsien shih-i*, p. 47a–b; *Mu-ling shu*, 11:46.

131. See below, Chap. IV, sec. 5.

132. *Ch'ing shih-lu*, Kao-tsung, 21:4; *Ch'ing hui-tien shih-li* (1818), 77:8b.

133. *Ch'ing shih-lu*, Kao-tsung, 17:1b.

134. *Ch'ing hsü t'ung-k'ao*, 1:7501.

135. *Mu-ling shu*, 11:42b.

136. *Fu-hui ch'üan-shu*, 6:18.

137. *Mu-ling shu*, 11:46; *Hsing-ch'ien pi-lan*, 5:23b–24; *Chiang-nan t'ung-chih*, 76:11b. Wang Yu-huai remarked that clerks were responsible for the fact that the government could never know the exact situation with regard to tax collection and that lodging house owner–guarantors were responsible for the fact that the govermnent was unable to collect tax from the people (*Hsing-ch'ien pi-lan*, 5:23b).

138. *Hsing-ch'ien pi-lan*, 5:23b.

139. *Ch'ing hui-tien shih-li* (1818), 77:19. According to Cheng Kuan-ying, the price for such a post varied from one hundred to several thousand taels (*Sheng-shih wei-yen*, 2:8).

140. A clerk who sold his post was subject to the same punishment as that prescribed by law for acceptance of a bribe causing injustice in the administration of law (*wang-fa shou-ts'ai*), the penalty for which ranged from beating to detention for strangling depending upon the size of the bribe (the death sentence was applicable when the bribe was 500 taels or more). The person who bought the post was to be punished for offering a bribe to obtain a favor (*i-ts'ai hsing-ch'iu*), the punishment being 100 strokes and 1 year of penal servitude when the money involved amounted to 500 taels or more (*Ch'ing lü-li*, 31:10a–b; cf. 4a–b).

141. *Liu-pu ch'u-fen tse-li*, 16:9.

142. *Mu-ling shu*, 8:20.

143. *Ching-shih wen-pien*, 24:3b. In some localities (e.g., Tung-kuan and Shun-te in Kwangtung) the fee paid for such an assignment was several hundred to 2000 taels (*Mu-ling shu*, 4:34).

144. *Mu-ling shu*, 8:37b; 11:31b.

145. *Ibid.*, 8:19b, 37b, 45b; *Ch'in-pan chou-hsien shih-i*, p. 26b.

146. *Li-pu tse-li*, 14:3a–b; *Liu-pu ch'u-fen tse-li*, 16:5a–b.

147. The official was demoted one grade and kept in the same post if the punishment for the guilty clerk was beating and penal servitude; he was demoted one grade and transferred to another post if the clerk's punishment was exile; he was demoted two grades and transferred to another post if the clerk's punishment was beheading or strangulation (*Li-pu tse-li*, 14:3b; *Liu-pu ch'u-fen tse-li*, 16:5a–b).

148. The law concerning the acceptance of bribes distinguished between two groups of *kuan-li* (officials and clerks): (1) those having emoluments (*yu-lu jen*), i.e., those whose monthly salary was more than one picul of rice; (2) those having no emoluments (*wu-lu-jen*), i.e., those who received no salary or whose monthly salary was less than one picul of rice. The punishment for the latter group was one degree less severe than for the former. The punishment for clerks who belonged to the second category (see notes to the relevant article in *Ch'ing lü-li,* 31:7), was as follows:

(1) For accepting a bribe causing injustice in the administration of law (*wang-fa tsang*):

Bribe (in taels)	Punishment
below 1	60 strokes
1–5	70 strokes
10	80 strokes
15	90 strokes
20	100 strokes
25	60 strokes, plus 1 year of penal servitude
30	70 strokes, plus 1½ years of penal servitude
35	80 strokes, plus 2 years of penal servitude
40	90 strokes, plus 2½ years of penal servitude
45	100 strokes, plus 3 years of penal servitude
50	100 strokes, plus banishment to 2000 li
55	100 strokes, plus banishment to 2500 li
80	100 strokes, plus banishment to 3000 li
120	detention for strangling

(2) For accepting a bribe not leading to injustice in the administration of law (*pu wang-fa tsang*):

Bribe (in taels)	Punishment
below 1	50 strokes
1–10	60 strokes
20	70 strokes
30	80 strokes
40	90 strokes
50	100 strokes
60	60 strokes, plus 1 year of penal servitude
70	70 strokes, plus 1½ years of penal servitude
80	80 strokes, plus 2 years of penal servitude
90	90 strokes, plus 2½ years of penal servitude
100	100 strokes, plus 3 years of penal servitude
110	100 strokes, plus banishment to 2000 li
120	100 strokes, plus banishment to 2500 li
above 120	100 strokes, plus banishment to 3000 li

In all cases the guilty clerk was to be dismissed and could not be employed again (*Ch'ing lü-li*, 31:2–6; cf. Staunton, pp. 379–382; Boulais, pp. 654–656).

If a clerk threatened and extorted money from poor people, the punishment was more severe:

below 1 tael	100 strokes
1–5 taels	100 strokes, plus wearing the cangue for 1 month
6–10 taels	100 strokes, plus 3 years of penal servitude
above 10 taels	exile to a nearby frontier
120 taels	detention for strangling
extortion causing the suicide of the victim	immediate strangling
beating victim to death	immediate beheading

(*Ch'ing lü-li*, 31:7b–8b. Only *tu-i*, the rapacious runners, are referred to in this statute. However, according to the interpretation of the Board of Punishment, quoted in *ibid.*, this law was applicable to clerks as well. See also *Ting-li hui-pien*, 5:126–128b.)

149. If the punishment for the guilty clerk was beating or penal servitude, the official responsible was to pay a fine equivalent to six months' nominal salary; if the clerk's punishment was exile, the fine was one year's salary; and if the clerk's punishment was beheading or strangling, the official was to be demoted one grade and kept in the same post (*Liu-pu ch'u-fen tse-li*, 16:11).

150. *Chuang-hui-t'ang wen-chi, i-kao*, p. 12b; *Hsüeh-chih i-te pien*, p. 31.

151. *Mu-ling shu*, 1:45b. However, this does not mean that there were no good men among the clerks (*Hsüeh-chih hsü-shuo*, 13a). A conscientious clerk in Lou-hsien was given credit for helping a magistrate to make new land tax records in order to equalize the burden of labor services among the people. His devotion greatly displeased other clerks and runners serving in the same yamen. For details, see *Sung-chün chün-i ch'eng-shu, ts'e* 3:116a–b; *ts'e* 8:288 ff, 301–307. But such cases were rare. The average clerk is described as dishonest and corrupt in most sources, including the popular literature. For example, a novel by Li Po-yüan (1867–1906) entitled *Huo-ti yü* (Living Hell) chiefly described the corruption of clerks and runners. In his prologue (*hsieh-tzu*, p. 1) Li stated that while he could not say that there was no honest official, he was sure that there was not a good clerk and runner. They could not be expected to serve on empty stomachs. From whom could they extort money except the people?

152. *Hsüeh-chih i-shuo*, B:10b; *Hsüeh-chih i-te pien*, p. 31.

153. *T'u-min lu*, 2:22b.

154. *Ch'in-pan chou-hsien shih-i*, p. 26b.

155. *Ibid.*

156. *Mu-ling shu*, 23:32.

157. *Ibid.*, 23:32; *Ching-shih wen-pien*, 22:20.

158. *Yung-li yung-yen*, pp. 11b–13.

159. *Li-pu tse-li*, 11:2b–3. A clerk who tampered with documents was punishable by law. A statute provided that a clerk who manipulated documents was to be punished one grade more severely than an offender who was not a

government employee, and that if he accepted money he was to be punished according to the amount received. Another statute provided that if a clerk was permitted by an official to make a draft and was guilty of manipulating documents, he was to be punished according to the law governing acceptance of a bribe causing injustice in the administration of law, and that if no bribe was accepted, the offender was to be punished with eighty strokes (*Ch'ing lü-li*, 31:11).

160. *Hsüeh-chih i-shuo*, B:10b.

161. Thus Liu Heng remarked that although clerks were people rendering services in a yamen, they had some prestige and were different from government runners. For this reason, he was frequently lenient to those clerks who committed faults unintentionally. His hope was that this might arouse their sense of shame and their conscience (*Yung-li yung-yen*, 11).

162. *Fu-hui ch'üan-shu*, 2:10–11; *Hsüeh-chih i-te pien*, p. 41.

163. *Mu-ling shu*, 4:24b.

164. *P'ing-p'ing yen*, 2:28b–29.

165. *Ching-shih wen-pien*, 23:2b.

166. *Tso-chih yao-yen*, p. 5.

167. *T'u-min lu*, 2:26. The governor-general of Chihli reported in 1728 that all the clerks and runners serving in a certain hsien left the yamen because the magistrate punished them too severely (*Chu-p'i yü-chih*, I Chao-hsiung's memorials, 116b).

CHAPTER IV. GOVERNMENT RUNNERS

1. See above, Chap. I, sec. 1.

2. *Hsüeh-chih i-te pien*, p. 31.

3. The government runners were customarily classified into three groups (*san pan*): tsao-pan, k'uai-pan, and min-chuang (*Fu-hui ch'üan-shu*, 3:6; *Ching-shih wen hsü-pien*, 21:10b). However, as is clearly pointed out in the "Chi-pu chang-ch'eng" (Police Regulations) formulated by the provincial judge of Chekiang, the government runners serving in a chou or hsien yamen had always been classified into four *pan:* the above three groups plus the policemen (*Chih Che ch'eng-kuei*, 8:66).

4. *Ch'ing t'ung-k'ao*, 21:5045. According to the *Fu-i ch'üan-shu* there were both *ma-k'uai* and *pu-k'uai* in a prefectural yamen, but only the former in a chou or hsien yamen (see *Chi-fu fu-i ch'üan-shu, passim; Honan fu-i ch'üan-shu, passim; Chiang-hsi fu-i ching-chih ch'üan-shu, passim; Hunan fu-i ch'üan-shu, passim; T'ai-ts'ang chou fu-i ch'üan-shu, passim*). However, in a document addressed to the Board of Rites, the provincial director of studies for Chihli mention that *pu-k'uai* were also employed in the chou or hsien yamen in the various provinces, in addition to the *ma-k'uai* (*Hsüeh-cheng ch'üan-shu*, 43:10b). The seeming discrepancy between these two sources may be explained by a statement found in *Hsiang-yin hsien t'u-chi*, 21:23b, which reads: "*min-chuang* are also called *pu-k'uai.*"

5. *Ch'ing t'ung-k'ao*, 21:5045; 23:5053; 24:5060.

6. *Fu-hui ch'üan-shu*, 3:7; *Mu-ling shu*, 4:29; *Hsüeh-chih i-te pien*, 40.

7. The quota for coroners was set in 1728 as follows: three in a large chou or hsien; two in a medium chou or hsien; one in a small chou or hsien. In addition, there were two apprentice coroners. However, an edict of 1740 pointed out that the employment of coroners was not a standard practice; some localities still did not have a coroner and usually attempted to borrow one from the neighboring hsien when an inquest was necessary. The edict warned that each hsien had to have coroners according to the quota and that a magistrate who failed to observe this order was to be demoted two grades (*Ch'ing t'ung-k'ao*, 23:5055; *Ch'ing lü-li*, 37:86–87b).

8. The gong beaters and the parasol and fan bearers, generally referred to as *chih-shih fu*, proceeded in front of the magistrate's sedan chair when he was on a tour (*Liu-pu ch'eng-yü chu-chieh*, p. 71).

9. A memorial mentioned that policemen were generally employed to catch thieves in chou and hsien governments, but that they were not listed in the *Ching-chih ch'üan-shu* (*Fu-i ch'üan-shu* was also called *Fu-i ching-chih chüan-shu*), and hence no funds were provided for them (see *Ch'ing t'ung-k'ao*, 23:5053; 24:5060). Thus when the magistrate of Ching-chou employed eight new policemen in his yamen, a certain amount of money was transferred from the other two groups of runners, *k'uai* and *min-chuang*, to supply wages for them (*Ching-chou chih*, B:11b).

10. *P'ei-yüan-t'ang ou-ts'un-kao*, 10:14a–b; *Hsi-chiang cheng yao*, 2:19b. Eight policemen are also listed in *Yung-ch'ing hsien-chih* of Chihli (13:8b) and *P'u-tai hsien-chih* of Shantung (2:20b). According to *Chih Che ch'eng-kuei*, 8:65b, there were six policemen in a large hsien in Chekiang, and only two or four in a small hsien. Yüan Mei (1716–1798) reported that as many as thirty policemen were employed in Chiang-ning (Nanking) (*Hsiao-ts'ang shan-fang wen-chi*, 15:28).

11. *Fang* (ward) was a subdivision of a city. As is indicated in the *Hsi-chiang cheng yao*, 36:6, each policeman was assigned one or more *fang* as his zone. Although this practice was prohibited by the government, *fang* policemen were still found in many chou and hsien in Kiangsi.

12. *Hsüeh-chih i-te pien*, p. 40. On *i-fang* see *Hsüeh-chih t'i-hsing lu*, B:4b.

13. *Hsüeh-chih i-te pien*, p. 53.

14. *Mu-ling shu*, 4:35; *P'ing-p'ing yen*, 2:29.

15. *Ch'ing shih-lu*, Kao-tsung, 21:4b; *Ch'ing hui-tien shih-li*, chüan 146.

16. *Ch'ing shih-lu*, Kao-tsung, 21:4; *Ch'ing hui-tien shih-li*, chüan 146; *Ch'ing t'ung-k'ao*, 21:5045; *Fu-hui ch'üan-shu*, 3:1; *Chu-pi yü-chih*, T'ien Wen-ching's memorials, 6:114.

17. *Mu-ling shu*, 4:35.

18. *Ching-shih wen hsü-pien*, 21:6.

19. *Liu-pu ch'u-fen tse-li*, 16:16a–b.

20. *Shih-hsüeh ta-sheng*, 8:78a–b.

21. T'ien Wen-ching points out that nominal runners were found among

the doormen, grooms, jailers, grain measurers, city-gate guards, and other types of runners (*Ching-shih wen-pien*, 24:4; *Mu-ling shu*, 3:23).

22. *Li-pu tse-li*, 14:10; *Liu-pu ch'u-fen tse-li*, 16:14; *Mu-ling shu*, 10:6.

23. *Chu-p'i yü-chih*, T'ien Wen-ching's memorials, 6:114a–b.

24. *Mu-ling shu*, 8:22.

25. *Ibid.*, 10:6.

26. *P'ei-yüan-t'ang ou-ts'un kao*, 48:45.

27. *Ch'ing shih-lu*, Jen-tsung, 171:3b–4b. This memorial was presented in 1806.

28. *Ch'ing hui-tien shih-li, chüan* 98.

29. *Shu liao wen-ta*, p. 10.

30. *Liu-pu ch'u-fen tse-li*, 16:14.

31. *Ibid.*, 16:17.

32. *Ibid.*, 16:15.

33. *Ibid.*, 16:17.

34. *Li-pu tse-li*, 14:6a–b.

35. *Yung-li yung-yen*, p. 4b.

36. *Tzu-chih hsin-shu*, 2:6.

37. *Ibid.; Mu-ling shu*, 20:46b.

38. *Fu-hui ch'üan-shu*, 5:15.

39. Both the horsemen and the foot messengers had the duty of arresting criminals (*kou-she jen-fan*) (*Tzu-chih hsin-shu*, 2:6), but as a rule the arrest of robbers and thieves was the special responsibility of the policemen. It was made clear in the *Ch'ing-ch'ao wen-hsien t'ung-k'ao*, 21:5045; 24:5060, that the *k'uai-shou* ran errands and waited upon the officials and that those with the duty of arresting robbers and thieves were called *pu-i, chien-k'uai*, or *ying-pu*. A report submitted to the provincial director of studies by Ting-chou, Chihli, also mentions that the foot messengers were not concerned with catching thieves. Instead they were expected to act as escorts in the delivery of criminals or government funds, to expedite the payment of land tax, and to render service in connection with law suits (*Hsüeh-cheng ch'üan-shu*, 43:10b). However, according to Chang Wo-kuan, the magistrate of K'uai-chi (1727–1730) in Chekiang province, and Shen Pao-chen (1820–1879), governor-general of Kiangsu, Kiangsi and Anhui, the horsemen were concerned with police duty, detecting and catching the thieves. Chang also formulated rules for rewarding them for their accomplishments and punishing them for their failure to catch thieves (*Fu-weng chi, hsing-ming*, 1:13a–b; *Shen Wen-su kung cheng-shu*, 7:41b). While these statements appear to be contradictory, they seem to indicate that the policemen were always concerned with the catching of thieves, but that horsemen might also be given the same assignment in some localities.

40. *Mu-ling shu*, 8:39.

41. The term *ts'ui-liang k'uai-shou* (*k'uai-shou* expediting land tax collection), appears in the *Fu-hui ch'üan-shu*, 5:15. *Hsüeh-cheng ch'üan-shu*, 43:10b, also mentions that the foot messengers were obliged to expedite land tax

payment. Runners who were sent to the rural zones for such a purpose were called *t'u-ch'ai* or *li-ch'ai* because one runner was assigned to each *t'u* or *li* (*Fu-hui ch'üan-shu*, 6:15a–b, 18b; *Hsüeh-chih i-shuo*, B:7; *Hsing-ch'ien pi-lan*, 5:6). According to Ch'en Hung-mou, there were three kinds of "land tax hasteners" (*ts'ui-ch'ai*) in Kiangsu province: (1) *shun-ch'ai*, the runners who served as "hasteners" year after year, but did not actually go to the rural zone; (2) *t'u-ch'ai*, who were picked from the runners by means of an annual drawing of lots; (3) *pan-ch'ai*, the runners who bribed the regular runners so that they could accompany them on a trip to a *t'u* to collect "customary fees" (*P'ei-yüan-t'ang ou-ts'un kao*, 46:42a–b).

42. *Ch'ing t'ung-k'ao*, 21:5045; *Fu-hui ch'üan-shu*, 17:7b; *Fu-weng-chi, hsing-ming*, 1:14–15; *P'ei-yüan-t'ang ou-ts'un kao*, 10:15b; *Hsüeh-chih i-te pien*, p. 39; *Mu-ling shu*, 20:41b; *Chih Che ch'eng-kuei*, 8:66.

43. *Mu-ling shu*, 20:41b.

44. *Ibid.*, 20:55b; *Chih Che ch'eng-kuei*, 8:66.

45. *Hu-pu tse-li*, 3:17a–b; *Liu-pu ch'u-fen tse-li*, 16:22a–b; *Ch'ing t'ung-k'ao*, 23:5053; *Mu-ling shu*, 20:47; 21:30. However, the military training was merely a formality in the Ch'ing (*Mu-ling shu*, 21:30; *Ching-shih wen hsü-pien*, 21:10b. See also Saeki Tomi, "Min Shin jidai no minsō ni tsuite," *Tōyōshi kenkyū*, 16.4:62, March 1957).

46. *Liu-pu ch'u-fen tse-li*, 16:22–23; *Hu-pu tse-li*, 3:17; *Ch'ing t'ung-k'ao*, 21:5045; 24:5060; *Chu-p'i yü-chih*, T'ien Wen-ching's memorials, 8:68b; *Mu-ling-shu*, 21:30; *Ching-shih wen hsü-pien*, 21:10b.

47. *Mu-ling shu*, 11:20a–b, says that a bribe was usually paid to the clerk of revenue by a *min-chuang* in order to secure such an assignment.

48. As a rule, *min-chuang* were concerned with summonses to defendants and witnesses involved in civil cases (*Mu-ling shu*, 21:30; *Ching-shih wen hsü-pien*, 21:10b; *Tzu-chih hsin-shu*, 2:6). However, they also gave assistance in arresting thieves and robbers (*Hu-pu tse-li*, 3:17; *Chu-p'i yü-chih*, T'ien Wen-ching's memorials, 8:68b).

49. *Ch'ing t'ung-k'ao*, 23:5053; *Chu-p'i yü-chih*, T'ien Wen-ching's memorials, 8:67.

50. I.e., the *i-men*, the gate in a yamen between the entrance gate and the principal hall. As a rule, the *i-men* was locked when the magistrate was presiding in the hall.

51. *Fu-hui ch'üan-shu*, 2:8b, 9b; *Mu-ling shu*, 2:4b. Bamboo tallies (*ch'ien*) were used as tokens of summonses or warrants for arrest (see below, n. 123), or of orders to carry out chastisement (see Chap. VII, n. 73).

52. *Hsüeh-cheng ch'üan-shu*, 43:18b; *P'ei-yüan-t'ang ou-ts'un-kao*, 48:47.

53. *Hsüeh-chih t'i-hsing lu*, A:8–9; *Chih Che ch'eng-kuei*, 8:34.

54. *Mu-ling shu*, 4:35b.

55. *Fu-hui ch'üan-shu*, 11:11; *Yung-li yung-yen*, p. 15a–b; *Hsüeh-chih t'i-hsing lu*, A:7b.

56. *Hsüeh-chih t'i-hsing lu*, A:7b.

57. The doormen serving in the yamen of the director of studies, *ju-hsüeh*

men-tou, however, had a status superior to that of ordinary doormen. They were treated as commoners (*Hsüeh-cheng ch'üan-shu,* 43:19a–b).

58. *Ch'ing hui-tien,* 17:4b. For the categories of "mean" people and their legal statuses in the Ch'ing dynasty, see Ch'ü T'ung-tsu, *Law and Society in Traditional China,* Le Monde d'outre-mer—passé et présent (Paris and The Hague, 1961), pp. 129–132.

59. *Ch'ing lü-li,* 8:16; *Hsüeh-cheng ch'üan-shu,* 43:1, 5–6b, 8–11, 12b–13b, 26b–27; *Li-pu tse-li,* 60:6a–b.

60. *Hsüeh-chih i-te pien,* p. 36b; *Chih Che ch'eng-kuei,* 8:66.

61. See below, Chap. IV, sec. 5.

62. *Ch'ing t'ung-k'ao,* 2:5045.

63. Hui-chen Wang Liu, *The Traditional Chinese Clan Rules* (New York, 1959), pp. 164–165, 256.

64. *Tzu-chih hsin-shu,* 12:27.

65. Four categories appeared in the *Sung-chün chün-i ch'eng-shu:* (1) *Kuan-hu* or *hsiang-shen* (or *shen*), official households; (2) *Ju-hu* or *chin,* scholar households, or to be more exact, the households of the students of prefecture, chou, or hsien schools, i.e., the holders of the first degree; (3) *i-hu,* the government-runner households; (4) *min-hu,* commoner households. The first three categories were customarily exempted from labor services (*ts'e* 1:40, 41b, 42b, 44a–b; *ts'e* 2, 49; *ts'e* 5:174–175).

66. *Sung chün chün-i ch'eng-shu, ts'e* 5:174–175.

67. *Ch'ing t'ung-k'ao,* 21:5045.

68. In order to be free from such recruitment and extortion, the people of Lou-hsien finally donated a piece of land, the rent from which was used to hire the jailers (*Sung-chün chün-i ch'eng-shu, ts'e* 2:73b–74b).

69. *Ibid., ts'e* 2:75a–b.

70. *Tzu-chih hsin-shu,* 12:27.

71. *P'ing-p'ing yen,* 4:20; *Hsüeh-chih i-te pien,* pp. 36b, 55a–b.

72. *Hsüeh chih i-te pien,* p. 55b.

73. Later, when his arrest was ordered by Chou Liang-kung, he fled. His wife was arrested and died in prison. His brothers and a son were also imprisoned (*Tzu-chih hsin-shu,* 12:29b).

74. A runner who re-entered service after the expiration of his term was to be dismissed and punished with 100 strokes. The punishment was 100 strokes and 3 years of penal servitude if the runner who re-entered service, either in the original yamen or in a different yamen, had been guilty of embezzlement and bribery (*Ch'ing lü-li,* 6:117b–118).

75. *Li-pu tse-li,* 14:5b; *Liu-pu ch'u-fen tse-li,* 16:13; see above, Chap. III, sec. 3.

76. *Li-pu tse-li,* 14:3b; *Ch'ing lü-li,* 6:118.

77. *Ching-shih wen-pien,* 24:5b.

78. In Chihli, Shansi, Honan, Kiangsu, Anhui, Chekiang, Hupeh, Hunan, Szechwan, Kwangtung, Kwangsi, Yünnan, and Kweichow, the pay was 6 taels. In Fukien, it was 6.2 taels; in Kiangsi, 5.9; and in Shantung, 5.6. However,

wages were irregular among pipers and drummers, night watchmen, sedan-chair bearers, and parasol and fan bearers in Kiangsu, Chekiang, Anhui, Honan, and Hupeh. Jailers got a higher pay in Shantung (11.21 taels). The pay of the policemen was higher in Anhui (8.0 taels) (*Hu-pu tse-li, chüan* 78). According to Yüan Mei, the pay of a policeman in Chiang-ning in Kiangsu was only about 2 taels (*Hsiao-ts'ang shan-fang wen-chi*, 15:28a–b).

79. *Hu-pu tse-li*, 78:30 ff.

80. *Ibid.*, 78:10b, 13a–b, 19, 30b–31, 38b–39. In all other provinces the pay was about 6 taels.

81. It was mentioned in a memorial that a coroner had to go through a training period before he could master the necessary technique. Apprentice coroners, who were candidates for regular coronerships, were expected to learn by practice. There was a regulation that each of them was to be given a copy of *Hsi-yüan lu* to study under a clerk of punishment, and they were to be examined yearly by the prefect or independent department magistrate (*Ch'ing hui-tien*, 55:7b–8; *Ch'ing lü-li*, 37:86b–87; *Ch'ing t'ung-k'ao*, 23:5055). Although the job was important, its status was inferior and the remuneration slight, so that an intelligent person obviously could not be expected to take such a job (*Hsi-yüan lu chieh*, p. 1; *Mu-ling shu*, 19:3b–4).

82. *Hu-pu tse-li*, 78:14.

83. The position of apprentice coroner existed in such provinces as Chihli, Kiangsi, Kansu, and Szechwan (*Hu-pu tse-li*, 78:11, 21a–b, 41, 46b).

84. However, a few exceptions may be mentioned. The pay of a dispatch bearer in Kiangsu was 7.2 taels; in Anhui it ranged from 3 to 8 taels; in Kwangsi from 2 to a little more than 2. The watchmen of the *p'u* in Honan had an income of from 6 to 11 taels. The pay of the archers ranged from a little more than 1 to more than 8 in Kiangsu. In other provinces, the pay for the three categories was 6 taels (*Hu-pu tse-li, chüan* 78).

85. In Shantung, Shansi, Honan, Kiangsu, Anhui, Kiangsi, and Hupeh, the pay was 7 to 8 taels (*Hu-pu tse-li, chüan* 78).

86. *Ching-shih wen-pien*, 24:9.

87. *P'ing-p'ing yen*, 2:29. Wang Feng-sheng also said that the wage of a runner was insufficient to support himself and his family (*Hsüeh-chih t'i-hsing lu*, A:7b).

88. *Mu-ling shu*, 2:56. It may be noted that runners who were assigned to deliver a criminal or a document to another yamen had not only to pay their own travel expenses, but also to pay customary fees to the clerks and runners of the superior yamen who accepted the delivery (*Pu-ch'ien-chai man-ts'un*, 5:123b; see also below, Chap. IV, sec. 4, on the financial burden of policemen).

89. *Ming shih*, 78:1, 7b–8; *Ch'ing hui-tien* (1764), 9:4b; *ibid.* (1818), 11:15b; *ibid.* (1899), 18:1b–2; *Ch'ing t'ung-k'ao*, 21:5044–45; *Ching-shih wen-pien*, 33:4b; see also Liang Fang-chung, *The Single-Whip Method of Taxation in China*, pp. 4–6. Thus Lu Lung-ch'i pointed out that all the runners' wages listed in the Complete Book of Taxes and Labor Services were the *ku-i ch'ien* (money to hire service) paid by the people (*San-yü-t'ang wen-chi*, 3:19a–b).

90. *P'ei-yüan-t'ang ou-ts'un kao*, 13:18a–b.

91. *Ch'in-pan chou-hsien shih-i*, 20a–b; *Yung-li yung-yen*, p. 36; *Mu-hsüeh chü-yao*, p. 14; *Ching-shih wen hsü-pien*, 22:8b.

92. It was a government rule that a magistrate could only bring with him one clerk, one coroner, and two runners (*Ch'ing lü-li*, 37:81b), but only a few magistrates (e.g., Liu Heng and Fang Ta-chih) observed this regulation (*Yung-li yung-yen*, 32, 37; *P'ing-p'ing yen*, 3:58a–b). T'an Ch'eng-tsu reports that the attendants who accompanied a magistrate usually numbered more than 100 (*Ching-shih wen hsü-pien*, 22:8b). According to Fang Ta-chih, a magistrate of Kuang-chi, the total number of runners and servants who accompanied a magistrate, including the cook, stove attendants, sedan-chair bearers, and coolies, was more than 90 (*P'ing-p'ing yen*, 3:58a–b).

93. *Yung-li yung-yen*, p. 29; *Ching-shih wen hsü-pien*, 22:8b. Ting Jih-ch'ang, governor of Kiangsu, reported that fees paid to the clerks and runners in connection with an inquest amounted to more than 10,000 coins in a certain district (*Fu Wu kung-tu*, 35:9b; 36:5b).

94. See *Ch'ing lü-li*, 37:81b–82.

95. *Yung-li yung-yen*, pp. 12b, 32b–33, 37a–b; *Huan-yu chi-lüeh*, A:9.

96. *Mu-ling shu*, 11:13; *Tzu-chih hsin-shu*, 1:1b.

97. *Mu-ling shu*, 11:20a–b.

98. According to the report of Ch'eng Yung-yen, the magistrate of Chang-an, the following customary fees were collected from tribute grain payers: by the grain winnower, 10 coins per picul of grain; by the grain measurer, 1 to 3 *sheng* for pouring the grain into the storeroom; by the grain carrier, 5 coins per *hu*, or 1 per *tou* of grain. See *P'ei-yüan-t'ang ou-ts'un kao*, 27:21.

99. *Fu-hui ch'üan-shu*, 20:29b; *Ching-shih wen hsü-pien*, 22:7b. Ch'en Hung-mou reported that sometimes several, or even 10, taels of silver were demanded from a plaintiff or a defendant under the name of travel expenses (*P'ei-yüan-t'ang ou-ts'un kao*, 13:18a–b).

100. *Ching-shih wen hsü-pien*, 22:7b. A regulation concerning fees for clerks and runners ("Shu-i t'iao-kuei") in Liang-shan, Szechwan, indicates that fees were collected from plaintiff and defendant by the runners each time they were brought in for a trial. In addition, there were fees for runners to attend the court (*p'u-t'ang fei* or *p'u-pan fei*). See *Liang-shan hsien-chih*, 3:16–17.

101. *Chao-chieh* means to deliver to a superior yamen for retrial a prisoner who had made a confession (*Liu-pu ch'eng-yü chu-chieh*, p. 99). The runners who served as escorts in charge of a prisoner were called *chieh-ch'ai*.

102. *Yung-li yung-yen*, p. 36.

103. *Hsüeh-chih t'i-hsing lu*, A:7b.

104. *Hsiao-ts'ang shan-fang wen-chi*, 15:28b.

105. *Ibid*.

106. *P'ei-yüan-t'ang ou-ts'un kao*, 10:14a–b; *Chih Che ch'eng-kuei*, 6:21b; 8:65b–66; *Hsüeh-chih t'i-hsing lu*, A:21a–b; *Hsüeh-chih i-te pien*, p. 36b; *Ming-hsing kuan-chien lu*, p. 31a–b; *Tseng Wen-cheng chi, tsa-chu*, 2:65b, *P'ing-p'ing yen*, 4:20.

107. *Hsüeh-chih i-te pien*, p. 36b.

108. For details see *Hsüeh-chih i-te pien*, p. 40; *P'ing-p'ing yen*, 4:20; *Hsüeh-chih t'i-hsing lu*, A:21a–b; *Mu-ling shu*, 20:46b.

109. Money for travel expenses and other expenses involved in delivering criminals was usually given in accordance with the distance a policeman had to travel (see *Ch'in-pan chou-hsien shih-i*, p. 17; *Hsüeh-chih t'i-hsing lu*, A:21a–b; *P'ing-p'ing yen*, 4:20; *Hsüeh-chih i-te pien*, pp. 40, 55b; *Ming-hsing kuan-chien lu*, p. 31b; *Mu-ling shu*, 20:55b). Since expenses were inevitable in taking convicted criminals to the superior yamen and yet no funds were available, the magistrates were sometimes told by their superior to donate money to provide fees for the policemen (*Chih Che ch'eng-kuei*, 8:66a–67b).

110. *Hsüeh-chih i-te pien*, p. 56a–b.

111. See Chap. III, n. 151.

112. *Pu-ch'ien-chai man-ts'un*, 5:123.

113. *Pei-yüan-t'ang ou-ts'un kao*, 46:40b–41.

114. *Liu-pu ch'u-fen tse-li*, 25:51a–b.

115. *Meng-hen lu yü*, pp. 34b–35.

116. *Fu-hui ch'üan-shu*, 6:19.

117. *P'ei-yüan-t'ang ou-ts'un kao*, 46:36b–37.

118. The runners who were sent to rural zones to expedite tax payment were often flogged during the deadline hearings by the magistrates, instead of the delinquent taxpayers (see Chap. VIII, sec. 1). This practice led the runners to demand fees for receiving the flogging, the so-called *chang-ch'ien* or *pi-fei*. Actually the runners often hired substitutes to take their punishment (*P'ei-yüan-t'ang ou-ts'un kao*, 46:39b–40).

119. *Sung-chün chün-i ch'eng-shu*, t'se 5:171a–b.

120. *Ch'ing shih-lu*, Kao-tsung, 46:5b–6; *Ch'in-pan chou-hsin shih-i*, p. 47b; *Fu-hui ch'üan-shu*, 8:2b; *P'ei-yüan-t'ang ou-ts'un kao*, 21:14; 25:43b. See *Ch'ing lü-li*, 11:42b, for an explanation of these tricks.

121. *T'u-min lu*, 2:23b; *Shu liao wen-ta*, p. 6.

122. *Tso-chih yao-yen*, p. 11b; *Hsüeh-chih hsü-shuo*, p. 14; *Hsüeh-chih t'i-hsing lu*, A:7.

123. *T'ang-ch'ien* was a bamboo tally issued during a trial to summon a person to appear in court immediately.

124. *Hsüeh-chih shuo-chui*, p. 3.

125. *Yung-li yung-yen*, p. 36b; *Ching-shih wen hsü-pien*, 22:8b.

126. *Shu liao wen-ta*, p. 6b. *Pan-fang* was a place where material witnesses and people guilty of minor offenses were detained while awaiting investigation. Legally only suspects in major crimes could be put in prison; all other criminals and people involved in a case were to be released after they secured a bond from a person guaranteeing their appearance in court. A magistrate was punishable if his clerks and runners unlawfully set up a *pan fang* for detaining criminals and others involved in a case. The punishment varied from forfeiture of nominal salary to dismissal. The superior officials were also punishable if they neglected to investigate such a violation (*Ch'ing hui-tien shih-li* [1818],

110:9b; 111:22b–23; *ibid.* [1899], *chüan* 134, 135; *Liu-pu ch'u-fen tse-li*, 49:7b–8).

127. *Hsüeh-chih shuo-chui*, pp. 1b–2.

128. *Hsüeh-chih ou-ts'un*, 4:22; *Ch'ing shih-lu*, Jen-tsung, 146:9 ff; 365:16–17; *Tso-li yao-yen*, "kuan-chien," p. 26b.

129. *Fu-hui ch'üan-shu*, 6:18b; *Mu-ling shu*, 11:20a–b.

130. *Ch'in-pan chou-hsien shih-i*, pp. 26b–27, 32b.

131. *P'ing-p'ing yen*, 4:18; *Tzu-chih hsin-shu*, 14:35a–b.

132. *Fu-hui ch'üan-shu*, 17:3b, 7b, 9b; *Chu-p'i yü-chih*, Li Wei's memorials, 4:21b; *Ch'in-pan chou-hsien shih-i*, p. 17; *P'ei-yüan-t'ang ou-ts'un kao*, 10:14a–b, 16b; *Yung-li yung-yen*, p. 67; *Hsüeh-chih t'i-hsing lu*, B:5a–b; *Hsüeh-chih i-te pien*, p. 36b; *Tseng Wen-cheng chi, tsa-chu*, 2:65b; *P'ing-p'ing yen*, 4:17b. As is shown in Kao P'an-lung's *Tse-ch'eng chou-hsien t'iao-yüeh* (Instructions to the chou and hsien magistrates), the close association between thieves and policemen was already a common practice in the Ming (*Ts'ung-cheng i-kuei*, B:8b).

133. *P'ing-p'ing yen*, 4:17b; *Hsüeh-chih i-te pien*, p. 39; *P'ei-yüan-t'ang ou-ts'un kao*, 44:23a–b; 35:30, 32.

134. *Tzu-chih hsin-shu*, 14:35a–b; *P'ei-yüan t'ang ou-ts'un kao*, 35:30.

135. *Hsüeh-chih i-te pien*, p. 39.

136. *Hsüeh-chih i-shuo*, B:5a–b.

137. *Ch'in-pan chou-hsien shih-i*, p. 26b; *Fu-hui ch'üan-shu*, 17:19; *P'ing-p'ing yen*, 4:18–19; *Mu-ling shu*, 20:34 ff; *Hsing-ch'ien pi-lan*, 3:13b.

138. *Tso-chih yao-yen*, p. 8b; *Hsüeh-chih hsü-shuo*, 9a–b; *Yung-li yung-yen*, 7–8b; *P'ing-p'ing yen*, 4:19; *Hsüeh-chih i-te pien*, p. 36b; *Hsing-ch'ien pi-lan*, 3:13b–14; *Mu-hsüeh chü-yao*, p. 10.

139. *Hsing-mu yao-lüeh*, p. 22; *Hsing-ch'ien pi-lan*, 3:17b.

140. *P'ing-p'ing yen*, 4:19b.

141. *Mu-hsüeh chü-yao*, pp. 10, 11b; *Hsing-ch'ien pi-lan*, 3:12b.

142. *Ch'in-pan chou-hsien shih-i*, p. 26b; *Shih-hsiang pi-lu*, pp. 9b–10.

143. *Ch'in-pan chou-hsien shih-i*, 35a–b; *P'ei-yüan-t'ang ou-ts'un kao*, 11:19b; *Mu-ling shu*, 18:40b; *Kung-men yao-lüeh*, quoted in *Chung-ho*, 2.10:98.

144. *Fu-hui ch'üan-shu*, 11:29–30.

145. *Ch'in-pan chou-hsien shih-i*, p. 26b.

146. *Li-pu tse-li*, 38:27a–b; *Liu-pu ch'u-fen tse-li*, 16:18, 19.

147. *Li-pu tse-li*, 25:16.

148. A runner who accepted a bribe from a person involved in a legal case or who threatened and extorted money from the common people was subject to the same punishment as clerks (*Ch'ing lü-li*, 31:2a–b; 7b–8b; see above, Chap. III, n. 148). A runner who unlawfully detailed, beat, or in some other way abused a person under summons because he had failed to submit to extortion was to be put in a cangue for two months and exiled to the areas of Yünnan, Kweichow, Kwangtung, or Kwangsi. A runner who unlawfully detained a victim without otherwise maltreating him was to be punished with 100 strokes and three years of penal servitude (*Ch'ing lü-li*, 31:14). A runner

convicted of bribery was tattooed with two characters: *tu-fan*, "rapacious criminal." This tattoo was either on his arm or face, depending upon the seriousness of the crime (*Ch'ing lü-li*, 25:117a–b).

149. If the punishment of the guilty runner was beating or penal servitude, the responsible official was to be fined six months' nominal salary; if the runner's punishment was banishment the official was fined a year's nominal salary; if the runner's punishment was beheading or strangulation, the official was to be demoted one grade and kept in the same post (*Liu-pu ch'u-fen tse-li*, 16:11; cf. *Li-pu tse-li*, 14:7b).

150. When unlawful beating led to death, the magistrate who connived at the crime was subject to dismissal; if the beating was not fatal, the magistrate was subject to demotion of three grades and transfer to another post. If the magistrate failed to inquire into the case due to negligence, he was to be demoted two grades if a death had been brought about and one grade if no death had occurred. A magistrate was also subject to demotion of two grades if any of the prisoners' family members committed suicide as a result of threats and extortion on the part of the runners (*Li-pu tse-li*, 38:27a–b; *Liu-pu ch'u-fen tse-li*, 16:18, 19).

151. *Liu-pu ch'u-fen tse-li*, 16:18b.

152. *Ibid.*, 16:18.

153. A regular runner who took a *pai-i* with him was subject to dismissal and 100 strokes. A *pai-i* who was guilty of bribery was subject to the same punishment as a regular runner (*Ch'ing lü-li*, 31:8b–9b).

154. In the earlier regulations, the official was to be demoted one grade and transferred to another post if the bribe was less than one tael; he was to be demoted two grades if the bribe was more than one tael; he was to be dismissed if the bribe was over 100 taels (*Li-pu tse-li*, 14:8). More severe regulations were formulated later: the official was to be demoted three grades and transferred to another post for employing an extra runner, and if the latter engaged in corrupt practices, the official was to be dismissed (*Liu-pu ch'u-fen tse-li*, 16:15).

155. *Li-pu tse-li*, 38:29a–b.

156. For falsely accusing an innocent person of being a thief and torturing him, the magistrate and the official in charge of the police (jail warden) were to be demoted one grade and transferred to another post. For falsely accusing an innocent person of being a robber and torturing him, the magistrate and the jail warden were to be demoted three grades and transferred to another post. If the accused person died of torture, whether he was falsely accused of being a thief or a robber, the magistrate and the jail warden were to be dismissed (*Liu-pu ch'u-fen tse-li*, 42:23a–b; cf. *Li-pu tse-li*, 28:27b–28).

157. If an innocent person was falsely accused of being a thief and tortured, the prefect, subprefect, or the magistrate of an independent department was to be demoted 1 grade; the circuit intendant was to be fined one year's nominal salary; the provincial judge, six months' salary; and the governor and the governor-general, three months' salary. If an innocent person was falsely

accused of being a robber and tortured, the prefect, subprefect, or the magistrate of an independent department was to be demoted one grade and transferred to another post, the circuit intendant demoted one grade and kept in the same post; the provincial judge fined one year's nominal salary, and the governor and the governor-general, six months' salary. If a policeman caused the death of an innocent person, whether he was falsely accused of being a thief or a robber, the prefect, subprefect, or the magistrate of an independent department was to be demoted two grades and transferred to another post. The circuit intendant was to be demoted one grade and transferred to another post; the provincial judge demoted one grade and kept in the same post; and the governor and the governor-general were to pay a fine of one year's nominal salary (*Liu-pu ch'u-fen tse-li*, 42:23a–b; cf. *Li-pu tse-li*, 38:27b–28).

158. *Liu-pu ch'u-fen tse-li*, 49:7, 8.

159. *Ch'in-pan chou-hsien shih-i*, p. 26; *Hsüeh-chih i-te pien*, p. 31.

160. *Yung-li yung-yen*, p. 20.

161. *Hsüeh-chih i-shuo*, B:10b; *Hsüeh-chih i-te pien*, p. 31; *T'u-min lu*, 2:22b; *Yung-li yung-yen*, pp. 14a–b, 20a–b.

162. *Mu-ling shu*, 23:32.

163. *Hsüeh-chih ou-ts'un*, 4:21b–22; *Yung-li yung-yen*, pp. 8b, 17b, 18b, 22a–b. In order to prevent runners from using chains privately, Yüan Shou-ting kept all the chains, giving them to runners only when the situation called for their use (*T'u-min lu*, 12:23b).

164. *Yung-li yung-yen*, pp. 18–19.

165. *Fu-hui ch'üan-shu*, 2:9b; *Huan-yu chi-lüeh*, A:21; *Hsüeh-chih ou-ts'un*, 4:21a–b; *Yung-li yung-yen*, pp. 15b–16, 18b–19, 45–46. It was emphasized that a runner who delayed in making an arrest was to be punished with beating (*P'ing-p'ing yen*, 4:34b). The following regulation was set up by Liu Heng: if the delay was 1 day beyond the deadline, the runner had his name listed on the record of demerits; 2 days beyond the deadline, he reecived 10 strokes; 3 days beyond the deadline, 20 strokes; 4 days beyond the deadline, put in cangue and dismissed (*Yung-li yung-yen*, p. 18b).

166. *Yung-li yung-yen*, pp. 18b–19; *Hsüeh-chih ou-ts'un*, 4:22; *Mu-ling shu*, 18:23b.

167. *Hsüeh-chih ou-ts'un*, 4:21b; *Li-pu tse-li*, 41:29.

168. *P'ing-p'ing yen*, 2:37b–38.

169. Both Liu Heng and Lu Wei-ch'i ruled that only one runner was to be assigned to carry a warrant (*Yung-li yung-yen*, 15a–b, 18; *Hsüeh-chih ou-ts'un*, p. 21b). Fang Ta-chih limited the number to two (*P'ing-p'ing yen*, 2:37b–38). A more unconventional procedure was also adopted by Liu Heng, who attempted to abolish the system of sending runners to summon a defendant or witness in a civil case. Instead, a subpoena was given to the plaintiff, who was required to hand it to the head of the *hsiang*. The latter would then notify the defendant to attend court on a specified date. Both the plaintiff and the defendant then made an appointment with the witnesses so that they could all attend court together. The subpoena stated clearly that this arrangement was

made in the hope that the abuses of the runners could be eliminated (*Yung-li yung-yen*, pp. 10a–b, 15).

170. See above, note 92.

171. *Yung-li yung-yen*, pp. 7–8b.

172. *Fu-weng-chi, hsing-ming*, 1:13b; *P'ing-p'ing yen*, 4:20a–b; *Hsüeh-chih i-te pien*, pp. 37, 40b–41b.

173. *Fu-hui ch'üan-shu*, 2:8b–10b, 11b; *P'ing-p'ing yen*, 4:34b.

174. *Mu-ling shu*, 4:24b.

175. *Ch'in-pan chou-hsien shih-i*, pp. 17b–18; *Fu-weng chi, hsing-ming*, 1:13b; *Chih Che ch'eng-kuei*, 6:21b–22; 8:66b; *Hsüeh-chih i-te pien*, pp. 37, 41a–b, 55b–56; *Ming-hsing kuan-chien lu*, pp. 29a–b; 31b; *Mu-ling shu*, 20:55b.

176. *Mu-ling shu*, 4:24b.

177. *Liu-pu ch'u-fen tse-li*, 16:15.

178. *Mu-ling shu*, 4:24b.

179. *P'ing-p'ing yen*, 2:28b–29.

CHAPTER V. PERSONAL SERVANTS

1. Presumably it was the assignment to the magistrates' personal servants of official business normally carried out by clerks in most governments that led a foreign observer like Byron Brenan, the British consul-general in Shanghai, to identify them as clerks. He described the clerks, *shu-li*, as "permanent clerks" (*The Office of District Magistrate in China*, Shanghai, 1899, p. 5).

2. Some of the personal servants recommended to a magistrate by his superiors might be natives of the locality where he was posted (*P'ei-yüan-t'ang ou-ts'un kao*, 34:28b–29). However, most of the servants came with the magistrate, either from the latter's home town or from the capital. Thus, the employment of native servants was rather exceptional.

3. *Hsüeh-chih i-shuo*, A:4b–5.

4. *Mu-ling shu*, 4:13b–14. Obviously not all personal servants were dependable, nor did they all have the confidence of their employers. Witness the statement of Wang Hui-tsu that servants were not permanently attached to a master, and as the names and native places claimed by them were usually not genuine, it was difficult to find one or two loyal, sincere, and dependable servants out of 100 (*Hsüeh-chih i-shuo*, A:3b–4). Thus instead of having servants who could relieve them of worry about the clerks and runners, the magistrates were subjected to the further strain of not being able to trust their servants. This problem will be discussed more fully in the section on supervision. However, it seems that in most cases officials found their personal servants more dependable than clerks and runners.

5. Weng Tsu-lieh (*chin-shih* 1836), a magistrate, mentioned that the jobs of gate porter and document-endorsement attendant must be assigned to several honest and confidential servants (*Huan-yu sui-pi*, 3:58). P'an Shao-ts'an said that when the documents were sent in for endorsement every day, it was always the servant closest to a magistrate who used the seal (*Mu-ling shu*, 2:8b).

6. *Ming-hsing kuan-chien lu*, pp. 25b–26.

7. *P'ing-p'ing yen,* 2:20b. Ho Keng-sheng, a capable magistrate, told his personal servants in his *Shu-kuei* (yamen regulations for personal servants) that they were not allowed to make decisions and should only act on instructions from him. But if a decision of his was not appropriate, they could present their opinions so that the matter could be discussed in order to avoid mistakes (*Hsüeh-chih i-te pien,* 60a–b).

8. Fang Ta-chih once pointed out that since a magistrate was not familiar with the local situation he usually relied upon his servants as eyes and ears (*P'ing-p'ing yen,* 22a–b).

9. *Yung-li yung-yen,* p. 42b; *P'ing-p'ing yen,* 2:15.

10. *Shu liao wen-ta,* p. 2; *P'ing-p'ing yen,* 2:20b, 21b–22.

11. *P'ing-p'ing yen,* 2:22.

12. For instance, Wang Hui-tsu, a magistrate of Ning-yüan in Hunan, employed only five personal servants: a gate porter, a document-endorsement attendant, a granary supervisor, a kitchen superintendent, and a personal attendant (*Hsüeh-chih i-shuo,* A:4b). Wang Chih, a magistrate in Chihli, employed two gate porters (one assistant gate porter), two granary supervisors, one document-endorsement attendant, one kitchen superintendent, and one servant to run errands. A post station supervisor was employed in a hsien where there was postal service (*Mu-ling shu,* 4:14b). Hsieh Chin-luan held that only five or six servants should be employed by a capable magistrate (*Mu-ling shu,* 4:13b).

13. *Mu-ling shu,* 4:12b–13b.

14. *Ibid.,* 4:12a–b.

15. *Ibid.,* 4:13b. Two types of servants in charge of documents are also mentioned in the *P'ing-p'ing yen,* 2:22b–23; one connected with the gate porter, known as *kao-an men-ting,* and the other connected with the document-endorsement attendant, known as *kao-an ch'ien-ya.*

16. *Ch'ing shih-lu,* Shih-tsung, 4:19b; *ibid.,* Kao-tsung, 94:2a–b; *Mu-ling shu,* 4:14b; 23:41.

17. The problem of controlling the personal servants of local officials was discussed in 1685, but the Board of Rites considered it inconvenient to fix a quota (*Ting-li ch'üan-pien,* 15:55).

18. The general term, *chia-jen,* which could mean either family members or domestic servants (*Ch'ing lü-li,* 31:41) was used in this statute. However, it was made clear that the quota applied to persons other than an official's wife, children, or brothers. Women were included in this quota (*Ting-li ch'üan-pien,* 15:55a–b; *Hu-pu tse-li,* 4:2).

19. *Hsüeh-chih i-te pien,* pp. 30, 61a–b; *Hsüeh-chih i-shuo,* A:4b; *Ch'ang-sui lun,* quoted in *Chung-ho,* 2.10:72 (Oct. 1941).

20. *Hsüeh-chih i-te pien,* 61b; *Ch'ang-sui lun,* quoted in *Chung-ho,* 2.10:72.

21. *Ko-hang shih-chien* and *Kung-men yao-lüeh,* quoted in *Chung-ho,* 2.10:79.

22. *Hsüeh-chih i-shuo,* A:4b; *Hsüeh-chih i-te pien,* pp. 62b–63; *P'ing-p'ing yen,* 2:19; *Yung-li yung-yen,* pp. 23a–b, 26.

23. *Hsüeh-chih i-te pien*, p. 62b.

24. *P'ing-p'ing yen*, 2:19b; *Hsüeh-chih t'i-hsing lu*, pp. 4b–5. According to Fang Ta-chih, actually a gate porter merely ordered the attending junior servant to tell the guard at the entrance to the magistrate's residence to summon a clerk or runner to receive a document or a warrant (*P'ing-p'ing yen*, 2:19b).

25. See *Ko-hang shih-chien*, quoted in *Chung-ho*, 2.10:85. Some capable magistrates prevented their servants from opening documents and correspondence (*P'ing-p'ing yen*, 1:58; *Hsüeh-chih i-te pien*, p. 61). However, this was largely a matter of personal preference. According to *Kung-men yao-lüeh*, a document might be opened either by a gate porter, by a document-endorsement attendant, or by the magistrate himself. Only a sealed envelope could not be opened by a servant (*Chung-ho*, 2.10:87; cf. *Ko-hang shih-chien*, quoted in *Chung-ho*, 2.10:75). As a matter of fact, a gate porter was authorized to open a sealed document and to check whether the number of accompanying documents corresponded with the number specified on the envelope. If there was a discrepancy, the messenger was questioned. All documents arriving after the closing of the yamen's main gate were received and opened by the gate porter (*Kung-men yao-lüeh*, quoted in *Chung-ho*, 2.10:72, 85). Both handbooks cited above emphasized that it was necessary for a gate porter or a document-endorsement attendant to open documents in order to ensure that a document involving an urgent matter would be attended to instantly (*Kung-men yao-lüeh* and *Ko-hang shih-chien*, quoted in *Chung-ho*, 2.10:72, 85).

26. *Ko-hang shih-chien* and *Kung-men yao-lüeh*, quoted in *Chung-ho*, 2.10:75, 86.

27. According to *Kung-men yao-lüeh*, a document might be sent first to the magistrate and then to the private secretary, or vice versa. Also there were cases where documents were prepared without being read first by a magistrate or a secretary (quoted in *Chung-ho*, 2.10:86–87).

28. A servant in charge of registration was assigned to keep a record of all legal cases (names of plaintiffs, defendants, witnesses, clerks and runners in charge, and a brief summary of the case), incoming and outgoing documents, placards, warrants, and other kinds of records. As a rule, each document was registered three times: before and after it was delivered to a private secretary, for the official rescript, and again after a copy had been marked with a red brush (*piao-p'an;* see below, n. 31). See *Ko-hang shih-chien* and *Kung-men yao-lüeh*, quoted in *Chung-ho*, 2.9:58 (Sept. 1941); 2.10:86, 88; 2.11:95 (Nov. 1941). The second source mentions that, although the documents were registered by a private secretary before they were registered by the servant in charge of registration, the secretary's registration was merely a matter of form, and the servants' registration was more important (*Chung-ho*, 2.11:95). The importance of registration in a yamen was stressed in the *Ch'in-pan chou-hsien shih-i*, p. 28b; as follows: "It is the key to all kinds of administration. It enables one to know at a glance the affairs which have to be transacted, replied to, investigated, or hastened. Thus matters can be attended to within the specified

time and deception on the part of clerks and runners can be prevented." For detailed information on the procedure of registration and the various kinds of registration records, see *Ko-hang shih-chien, Kung-men yao-lüeh, Ch'ang-sui lun*, quoted in *Chung-ho*, 2.11:92–96; *P'ien-t'u lun ko ssu shih*.

29. *Ko-hang shih-chien, Kung-men yao-lüeh*, and *Ch'ang-sui lun*, quoted in *Chung-ho*, 2.9:58; 2.10:73, 88; *P'ing-p'ing yen*, 2:19b.

30. *Ko-hang shih-chien* and *Kung-men yao-lüeh*, quoted in *Chung-ho*, 2.9:58, 86, 88, 92. As a rule all official documents, records, guarantees, land tax receipts, salt certificates, and warrants, had to be stamped with an official seal. This job was usually assigned to a seal-attendant. Before a seal was stamped on a document, it was his duty to see whether the document had been endorsed by the magistrate and whether the personal seal of a private secretary had been affixed. See *Ko-hang shih-chien*, quoted in *Chung-ho*, 2.10:92. For details on the use of seals see *P'ien-t'u lun ko ssu shih; Ko-hang shih-chien, Kung-men yao-lüeh*, and *Men-wu che-yao*, quoted in *Chung-ho*, 2.10:92–95.

31. *Ko-hang shih-chien* and *Kung-men yao-lüeh*, quoted in *Chung-ho*, 2.9:58; 2.10:86, 88. As a rule, a certain standard code symbol was written with a red brush on documents issued to an inferior yamen, or on official notices, warrants, certificates, and papers connected with the delivery of a prisoner or funds. The key character or characters appearing on the document were also marked with a red sign. This practice was called *piao-p'an*. For instance, the code *tsun* (obey) appeared on most of the official notices; *ching* (reverence), *ch'eng* or *ch'ien* (sincerity) on a sacrificial notice; *shen* (caution) or *hu* (guard) on papers connected with the delivery of funds; *su* (haste) on a warrant; an inverted *huo* (capture) on a warrant authorizing the capture of a robber; *chao* (certificate) on a certificate; and *fei* (fly) on a paper authorizing the immediate delivery of a document. Some of the key characters that were required to be marked with a red sign were: *wei* (for the sake of), *cha* (document issued to an inferior), *kao-shih* (official notice), *shih* (order), *yü* (instruction), *hsien* (time limit), *shih-t'ieh* (to be posted). The standard signs used on official notices were: a red dot on *wei;* a red circle around *lin-tsun* (obey with awe) or *wu-wei* (do not disobey); a red stroke along *yu-yang* (the above order is to be obeyed). The date was written with a red brush; a red circle was drawn at the end of a notice; and the character *hsing* (enforce) was written with a red brush in the "running style" (for details see *Huan-hsiang yao-tse*, 1:20–24; *Ko-hang shih-chien*, quoted in *Chung-ho*, 2.11:89–92).

Kung-men yao-lüeh states that *piao-p'an* was usually done by a relative of the magistrate, or a private secretary, or a seal attendant. It also mentions that a servant assigned to such a job was to do the work on behalf of the official; therefore he should not use the red brush without instructions from the official (quoted in *Chung-ho*, 2.10:95; 2.11:92).

32. *Ko-hang shih-chien* and *Kung-men yao-lüeh*, quoted in *Chung-ho*, 2.10:75, 88.

33. *Kung-men yao-lüeh*, quoted in *Chung-ho*, 2.10:73.

34. *Ko-hang shih-chien*, quoted in *Chung-ho*, 2.10:87.

35. *Kung-men yao-lüeh*, *Men-wu che-yao*, and *Ko-hang shih-chien*, quoted in *Chung-ho*, 2.10:73–74.

36. *Ko-hang shih-chien*, quoted in *Chung-ho*, 2.10:92.

37. *Ibid.*, 2.10:88.

38. *Chuang-pang* was a placard on which the complaints accepted by the magistrate were listed. Rejected complaints, together with the reasons for their rejection, were listed on a separate placard (*Fu-hui ch'üan-shu*, 11:7, 8a–b).

39. The character *tsun* (obey) was written in red on a placard concerning the hearing of a case (*Ko-hang shih-chien*, quoted in *Chung-ho*, 2.11:89). For other practices in connection with *piao-p'an* (see above n. 31).

40. *Kung-men yao-lüeh*, and *Ch'ang-sui lun*, quoted in *Chung-ho*, 2.10:85–86; *Hsüeh-chih i-te pien*, p. 63; *Fu-hui ch'üan-shu*, 11:7.

41. *Hsüeh-chih i-te pien*, p. 62b.

42. *Ko-hang shih-chien*, quoted in *Chung-ho*, 2.10:75, 81, 85.

43. If there was no written complaint, the plaintiff would be told to prepare a statement (*Ko-hang shih-chien*, quoted in *Chung-ho*, 2.10:76).

44. *Ko-hang shih-chien*, quoted in *Chung-ho*, 2.10:73.

45. *Ibid.*

46. *P'ing-p'ing yen*, 2:23b–24.

47. *Ko-hang shih-chien*, quoted in *Chung-ho*, 2.10:81.

48. The statement signed by a plaintiff was called *tsun-i;* and a similar statement signed by a defendant was called *kan-chieh* (*Ko-hang shih-chien*, quoted in *Chung-ho*, 2.10:81).

49. *P'ing-p'ing yen*, 2:24; *Ko-hang shih-chien*, quoted in *Chung-ho*, 2.10:81–82; *P'ien-t'u lun ko ssu shih*. Ho Keng-sheng, in his yamen regulations for personal servants, told his personal servants in charge of documents to check the depositions and other documents in the presence of clerks in order to avoid theft or substitution of the papers by clerks (*Hsüeh-chih i-te pien*, p. 63b).

50. *Ko-hang shih-chien*, quoted in *Chung-ho*, 2.10:75.

51. *Ko-hang shih-chien*, quoted in *Chung-ho*, 2.10:81–82.

52. *Ko-hang shih-chien* and *Cheng-yü tsa-chi*, quoted in *Chung-ho*, 2.10:74, 78, 84, 89.

53. The runners assigned to make an arrest were summoned for investigation and punishment if they failed to accomplish their mission by the deadline (*Kung-men yao-lüeh* and *Ko-hang shih-chien*, quoted in *Chung-ho*, 2.10:74, 84).

54. *Ko-hang shih-chien*, quoted in *Chung-ho*, 2.10:89.

55. It was ruled in Kiangsi in 1788 that when confessed criminals guilty of serious offenses were delivered to a superior yamen for retrial, the magistrates should send a personal servant to oversee the delivery along with two escort runners. Also, the legal document relating to the case should be entrusted to the servant whose duty it was to submit it upon arrival at the destination, in order to prevent the runners from opening the document privately. According to Kiangsi's provincial judge's report to the governor, the practice of having a

servant escort the criminals (a practice which had been authorized years ago), had been observed by chou and hsien magistrates for years (*Hsi-chiang cheng yao*, 27:2–3).

56. *Hsüeh-chih i-te pien*, 32b, mentions that a gate porter supervised the jail and those detained. The gate porter still played a part in these matters even when another servant was assigned as a jail supervisor. Thus *Ko-hang shih-chien* mentions that when a jail was inspected in the evening, "the friend who took care of the jail" (*kuan-chien p'eng-yu*, i.e., the jail supervisor) watched outside while the gate porter went in with the clerk of punishment to call the roll, examine the fetters, and check the jailers and guards who were on duty (quoted in *Chung-ho*, 2.11:97–98). However, the division of labor between the two is not very clear, for it is not specified in *Ko-hang shih-chien*, *Kung-men yao-lüeh*, and *Ch'ang-sui lun* whether a particular function was that of a gate porter or of a jail supervisor (quoted in *Chung-ho*, 2.10:74, 87–88; 2.11:97–98).

57. *Ko-hang shih-chien*, *Kung-men yao-lüeh*, and *Ch'ang-sui lun*, quoted in *Chung-ho*, 2.10:87–88; 2.11:96–99; *P'ien-t'u lun ko ssu shih*. Cf. *Hsüeh-chih t'i-hsing lu*, B:3.

58. Quoted in *Chung-ho*, 2.11:98; see also *P'ing-p'ing yen*, 4:38.

59. A certificate was always issued for the delivery of a prisoner. It was called *hui-chao* (return certificate). When the prisoner had been delivered, the receiving yamen acknowledged the delivery by stamping the certificate with an official seal. The certificate was then given back to the escort runner who submitted it to the original yamen.

60. *Ko-hang shih-chien*, and *Kung-men yao-lüeh*, quoted in *Chung-ho*, 2.10:74; 2.11:97–98.

61. There was usually a servant in charge of land tax and grain tribute (*ch'ien-liang men-ting* or *ch'ien-ts'ao men-ting*). Sometimes there was also a *tsa-shui men-ting* or *shui-ch'i men-ting*, who was concerned only with miscellaneous taxes and the tax on title deeds (*P'ing-p'ing yen*, 2:23a–b; *Mu-ling shu*, 4:13b).

62. *Ch'ang-sui lun*, *Kung-men yao-lüeh*, *Men-wu che-yao*, and *Ko-hang shih-chien*, quoted in *Chung-ho*, 2.9:52–56; see also *Fu-hui ch'üan-shu*, 3:10.

63. Quoted in *Chung-ho*, 2.9:53.

64. *Ibid.*

65. *Ko-hang shih-chien* and *Kung-men yao-lüeh*, quoted in *Chung-ho*, 2.9:59. According to the second source, the servant in charge of land tax and grain tribute was authorized to go over the list and put under the name of the *t'u-ch'ai* one or more red circles, the number varying according to the amount of overdue taxes whose payment they had failed to expedite. Each red circle called for five to ten strokes. However, it should be noted that the actual examination of tax records and determining of which runners were to be punished was the responsibility mainly of a private secretary. See below, Chap. VI, sec. 2.

66. *Ch'ang-sui lun*, quoted in *Chung-ho*, 2.9:54. See above, Chap. III, sec. 5.

67. *Ko-hang shih-chien,* quoted in *Chung-ho,* 2.9:59.

68. *Fu-hui ch'üan-shu,* 7:20; *Tzu-chih hsin shu,* 1:18a–b; *Ch'ien-ku pei-yao,* 1:16.

69. *Ch'ang-sui lun,* quoted in *Chung-ho,* 2.9:60.

70. *Ts'ao-yün ch'üan-shu,* 9:5, ruled that magistrates' relatives or personal servants should be stationed in the granaries to supervise the clerks to collect tribute grain.

71. *Ko-hang shih-chien,* quoted in *Chung-ho,* 2.9:63.

72. *Mu-ling shu,* 4:12b.

73. *Ch'ing hui-tien shih-li, chüan* 205.

74. *Hsüeh-chih i-te pien,* p. 63b.

75. *Ch'ang-sui lun,* quoted in *Chung-ho,* 2.12:102–103 (Dec. 1941).

76. *Hsüeh-chih i-te pien,* 63b.

77. *Mu-ling shu,* 4:12b; *Kung-men yao-lüeh,* quoted in *Chung-ho,* 2.12:101–102; *P'ien-t'u lun ko ssu shih.* A *k'an-ho* was a certificate issued by the Board of War to facilitate the use of the post service. The number of horses and attendants permitted to be used by an official was written down on the certificate (*Ch'ing hui-tien,* 51:6).

78. *Ko-hang shih-chien,* quoted in *Chung-ho,* 2.9:62.

79. Correspondence submitted to a superior official, known as red and white *ping-t'ieh.* (The official title and a brief summary statement were written on the red copy; the details on the white copy. See *Huan-hsiang yao-tse,* 3:36 ff.) It was the duty of the correspondence attendant to deliver the correspondence drafted by a private secretary to the magistrate for approval, and to see to it that the approved draft was copied by a secretary if he himself was unable to do it (*P'ien-t'u lun ko ssu shih*). According to *Kung-men yao-lüeh,* in the early days correspondence was copied by a private secretary of correspondence, but later usage shifted this job to a correspondence attendant (quoted in *Chung-ho,* 2.9:66).

80. It was the duty of the gate porter before locking up the yamen each night to check the runners on night duty and the *min-chuang* guarding the jail, granary, and treasury (*Kung-men yao-lüeh,* quoted in *Chung-ho,* 2.10:73). Several personal servants were also assigned to patrol the yamen every night and to keep check on the watchmen (*Fu-hui ch'üan-shu,* 22:10b–11).

81. This was a duty assigned to a kitchen superintendent (*Hsüeh-chih i-shuo,* A:5; *P'ing-p'ing yen,* 2:24; *Mu-ling shu,* 4:13b, 14b; *Men-wu che-yao,* quoted in *Chung-ho,* 2.12:104). According to Fang Ta-chih, this job might be assigned to a servant or a relative of the magistrate (*P'ing-p'ing yen,* 2:24).

82. *Hsüeh-chih i-shuo,* A:4b; *Hsüeh-chih i-te pien,* p. 64b; *P'ing-p'ing yen,* p. 59; *Ko-hang shih-chien,* quoted in *Chung-ho,* 2.10:80; *P'ien-t'u lun ko ssu shih.*

83. *Ko-hang shih-chien,* quoted in *Chung-ho,* 2.11:99–101; 2.12:100.

84. In discussing the situation prevailing in Kwangtung, an edict of 1739 mentions that a servant stationed in the provincial capital made friends not

only with the personal servants of the superior officials, but with their private secretaries and clerks as well (*Ch'ing shih-lu*, Kao-tsung, 94:2a–b).

85. *Ch'ing shih-lu*, Shih-tsung, 4:19b; *ibid.*, Kao-tsung, 94:2a–b; *Mu-ling shu*, 23:41.

86. A magistrate who stationed a servant in the provincial capital was to be demoted one grade and kept in the same post, and his superior official who tolerated such a practice was to be fined six months' nominal salary (*Ch'ing hui-tien shih-li* [1818], 76:21; *Li-pu tse-li*, 41:28b–29).

87. The *Chih Che ch'eng-kuei*, 2:29a–b, mentions that personal servants were stationed in the provincial capital to seek information for the magistrates of the various chou and hsien in Chekiang, although this was prohibited by law. Wang Chih, who did not station a personal servant in the provincial capital, seems to have been rather exceptional among the magistrates (*Mu-ling shu*, 4:14b).

88. *Mu-ling shu*, 4:14b.

89. Thus Wang Hui-tsu remarked that the posts of gate porter, document-endorsement attendant, granary supervisor, and post station supervisor were important. The gate porter and document-endorsement attendant in particular, he said, could affect the magistrate's reputation and career (*Hsüeh-chih i-shuo*, A:4b–5), a view shared by Wang Feng-sheng and Ho Keng-sheng, who held that the gate porter and document-endorsement attendant were the keys to a district yamen and therefore both had to be competent persons (*Hsüeh-chih t'i-hsing lu*, A:5b; *Hsüeh-chih i-te pien*, p. 32b). According to the experience of Ho Shih-ch'i, the servant in charge of land tax and tribute grain was most important among the personal servants. And among those whose duties were related to the using of the seals (*k'an-yin*) the most important was the one in charge of the endorsement of documents; next was the court attendant; then the servant in charge of correspondence; and last, the seal attendant. The jail supervisor and post station supervisor were also very important (*Mu-ling shu*, 4:12b).

90. *Ko-hang shih-chien*, quoted in *Chung-ho*, 2.10:90.

91. *Mu-ling shu*, 4:14b.

92. Thus Wang K'an held that it was necessary for a magistrate to have confidential personal servants to transmit documents (*Fang yen*, p. 56; see also *Kung-men yao-lüeh* and *Ko-hang shih-chien*, quoted in *Chung-ho*, 2.9:66–67; 2.10:86, 88–89).

93. Liu Heng used the following method to avoid the use of gate porters: two tables were placed side by side in the hall. On each table, space was reserved for each of the six *fang*, and the name of each *fang* was painted on the space assigned to it. A clerk handing in a document put it in the assigned space on the first table and signaled by striking the little bell or bamboo tube on the table. The documents which were to be distributed to clerks in the various *fang* were placed in the reserved space on the second table by the document-endorsement attendant, and the runner guarding the entrance to the

magistrate's residence was notified to call the clerk to collect the documents. A wooden box divided into sections, one reserved for each of the rural zones (*li*), was used by the runners for depositing their reports and cancel warrants. All warrants were issued and given to runners by the magistrate in person in the court (*Yung-li yung-yen*, pp. 27–28).

94. *Yung-li yung-yen*, p. 26a–b.

95. *Ibid.*, preface, pp. 1b–2, 26a–b. It may be noted that the popular opinion among the officials was that a magistrate who had newly entered officialdom must have a good gate porter (*Chiang-chou pi-t'an*, 15b).

96. *Ch'ang-sui lun*, *Men-wu che-yao*, *Ko-hang shih-chien*, and *Kung-men yao-lüeh*, quoted in *Chung-ho*, 2.9:54; 2.10:74, 81, 88, 92; 2.11:98; 2.12:101, 103.

97. *Ch'ang-sui lun*, quoted in *Chung-ho*, 2.9:54.

98. *Ch'ing hui-tien*, 17:4b.

99. Violation meant punishment and dismissal. Two cases were reported in the Ch'ien-lung period where two men having the status of personal servants (one of them was the son of a personal servant) bought official titles. Since the law at that time provided no punishment, the cases were judged in accordance with a similar case and the men were sentenced to three years of penal servitude (*Ch'ing lü-li*, 8:11b–12; *Hsüeh-cheng ch'üan-shu*, 43:5a–b). A statute was introduced in 1786, whereby prostitutes, entertainers, and government runners and their sons who took an examination or bought an academic title were punishable with 100 strokes (*Ch'ing lü-li*, 8:16b; see *Tu-li ts'un-i*, 9:20, for the date of this statute). This statute was applicable to personal servants also. In one instance a holder of the first degree and a commoner who had purchased official titles were dismissed and punished with 100 strokes when it was discovered that their deceased father had been the personal servant of a grand secretary (*Hsüeh-cheng ch'üan-shu*, 43:24b–25).

100. *Hsüeh-cheng ch'üan-shu*, 43:24b.

101. Ch'ih Chuang, "Ch'ing-tai chih mu-pin yü men-ting," *Ta-lu*, 5.2:16 (July 1952).

102. *Hsüeh-chih i-shuo*, A:4b; *Mu-ling shu*, 4:14.

103. *Hsüeh-chih i-shuo*, A:4; *P'ei-yüan-t'ang ou-ts'un kao*, 10:16a–b; 31:36; 34:28b–29.

104. *Hsüeh-chih i-shuo*, A:4; *Mu-ling shu*, 4:8; *Ting-li hui-pien*, 5:139.

105. *Hsüeh-chih i-shuo*, A:5b; *Fu Wu kung-tu*, 24:4b; *Huan-yu sui-pi*, 3:59; *Ch'ung-ming man-lu*, 1:31b.

106. Ts'ai Shen-chih, "Ch'ing-tai chou-hsien ku-shih," *Chung-ho*, 2.12:106 (Dec. 1941).

107. *Hsüeh-chih i-shuo*, A:5b; *Ch'ung-ming man-lu*, 1:31b.

108. *Li-pu tse-li*, 5:17; *Liu-pu ch'u-fen tse-li*, 7:39b–40.

109. *Fu-hui ch'üan-shu*, 1:14b–15. Ch'ih Chuang, however, mentions that no wages were given to servants; they were merely provided with meals ("Ch'ing-tai mu-pin," p. 16).

110. *Hsüeh-chih i-shuo*, A:4; see also *Huan-yu sui-pi*, 3:58b.

111. There were fees for registering and handling a complaint (*kua-hao fei*

and *ch'uan-ch'eng fei*). As a rule, an extra fee was demanded for presenting a complaint outside the regular period for accepting complaints, *kao-ch'i* (*Fu Wu kung-tu*, 36:6a–b; on *kao-ch'i*, see below, Chap. VII, sec. 2). A complaint might be accepted or rejected during the regular period, but when one was presented outside the regular period and the *ch'uan-ch'eng fei* had been paid, the case was always accepted (*Chih Che ch'eng-kuei*, 8:55; *P'ing-p'ing yen*, 2:40b). Hence many people were willing to pay the extra fee. According to Fang Ta-chih, this fee was either enjoyed exclusively by the servants, or half the amount was used to subsidize the magistrate's meal (*P'ing-p'ing yen*, 2:40b). But Ting Jih-ch'ang reported that such a fee was shared by servants, clerks, and runners (*Fu Wu kung-tu*, 3:1).

112. Quoted in *Chung-ho*, 2.10:75, 91. According to the same source, the customary fees in connection with lawsuits were collected from the runners when they handed in the report of the arrival of persons summoned to court (*Chung-ho*, 2.10:75).

113. *Fu Wu kung-tu*, 36:8b.

114. *Ibid.*, 35:9b.

115. *T'u-min lu*, 1:16b; *Kung-men yao-lüeh*, quoted in *Chung-ho*, 2.10:80. Yüan Shou-ting, who considered this practice unreasonable, prohibited his gate porter from demanding such fees from the clerks and runners (*T'u-min lu*, 1:16b).

116. *Ko-hang shih-chien*, quoted in *Chung-ho*, 2.9:56; 2.10:91; *P'ei-yüan-t'ang ou-ts'un kao*, 46:42.

117. The rate of discount varied in different provinces (*Ko-hang shih-chien*, quoted in *Chung-ho*, 2.9:62).

118. The various sacrifices, excepting the sacrifice offered to Confucius, were in the charge of the Office of Rites. Sacrificial money was given to this office for each ceremony (*Ko-hang shih-chien*, quoted in *Chung-ho*, 2.9:61–62). According to the same source, 100 to 200 coins were usually deducted by the gate porter from each string of coins given to the Office of Rites for such a purpose (*Chung-ho*, 2.9:62).

119. *Ko-hang shih-chien*, quoted in *Chung-ho*, 2.10:91.

120. *Ibid.*, 2.10:91. It is not clear from whom these gifts were collected. Probably all government employees had to contribute.

121. *Hsüeh-chih t'i-hsing lu*, A:6.

122. *Ko-hang shih-chien*, quoted in *Chung-ho*, 2.9:62.

123. *Hsüeh-chih t'i-hsing lu*, A:6; *P'ing-p'ing yen*, 2:25; *Mu-ling shu*, 4:14b.

124. *Hsüeh-chih t'i-hsing lu*, A:6.

125. *Ibid.*, *P'ing-p'ing yen*, 2:25; *Hsüeh-chih i-te pien*, p. 65; *Mu-ling shu*, 4:14b.

126. *P'ing-p'ing yen*, 2:25; *Hsüeh-chih t'i-hsing lu*, A:6; *Mu-ling shu*, 4:13.

127. *P'ing-p'ing yen*, 2:16.

128. *Hsüeh-chih i-shuo*, A:4b–5; *P'ing-p'ing yen*, 2:16a–b; *Hsüeh chih t'i-hsing lu*, A:4b–5.

129. *P'ing-p'ing yen*, 2:16b.

130. *Hsüeh-chih i-shuo*, A:4b–5.

131. *P'ing-p'ing yen*, 2:16; *Shu liao wen-ta*, p. 11b; *Mu-ling shu*, 8:28b.

132. *Yung-li yung-yen*, pp. 23b–24.

133. *P'ing-p'ing yen*, 1:38.

134. *Fu-hui ch'üan-shu*, 6:18b; *P'ing-p'ing yen*, 2:22b; *P'ei-yüan-t'ang ou-ts'un kao*, 13:18; *Ch'in-pan chou-hsien shih-i*, pp. 26b–27, 32.

135. *Mu-ling shu*, 4:15; *Fu Wu kung-tu*, 36:8.

136. *Yung-li yung-yen*, p. 42b.

137. *Yung-li yung-yen*, pp. 17a–b, 21b; *P'ing-p'ing yen*, 2:15b; *Mu-ling shu*, 4:15.

138. *Yung-li yung-yen*, p. 23b; *P'ing-p'ing yen*, 2:15b.

139. *P'ing-p'ing yen*, 2:15b–16.

140. *Hsüeh-chih i-te pien*, p. 60b.

141. *Ibid.*

142. *Ch'in-pan chou-hsien shih-i*, p. 47; *Chao Kung-i sheng-kao*, 6:11a–b; *P'ei-yüan-t'ang ou-ts'un kao*, 21:14b; 25:45; 45:37.

143. *Hsien-chih-t'ang kao*, 5:37b. Because, in Kiangsu, a servant in charge of grain tribute, known as *ts'ao-tsung* (tribute grain chief), was able to make a fortune (as much as 20,000 to 30,000 taels), Feng reported that some were willing to pay the magistrate several thousand taels for such an assignment (*ibid.*, 10:4a–b).

144. *P'ei-yüan-t'ung ou-ts'un kao*, 11:19b; *P'ing-p'ing yen*, 4:38; *Ch'i-pu-fu-chai ch'üan-chi, cheng-shu*, 4:19b.

145. *Yung-li yung-yen*, p. 24.

146. *P'ing-p'ing yen*, 2:17b.

147. *Ibid.*, 2:18b.

148. *Hsüeh-chih i-shuo*, A:5b; *Ch'ung-ming man-lu*, 1:31b. For a fictitious case in point see *Kuan-ch'ang hsien-hsing chi*, chaps. 5 and 6.

149. See above, n. 143.

150. *P'ing-p'ing yen*, 2:18b.

151. *Li-pu tse-li*, 5:17; *Liu-pu ch'u-fen tse-li*, 7:39b–40.

152. Personal servants guilty of extortion were also punishable by the tattooing of two characters, *tsang-fan* (bribery criminal), either on their arms or faces, depending upon whether it was the first or second offense. An official was not permitted to employ a tattooed servant (*Ch'ing lü-li*, 31:37a–b; *Ting-li hui-pien*, 5:139–142b). Another law decreed that a personal servant who was guilty of receiving money, gifts, or loans from the people under his master's jurisdiction, of demanding service without payment, or of engaging in unfair trading with the people incurred punishment less severe by two degrees than his master would have incurred under similar conditions (*Ch'ing lü-li*, 31:41; Staunton, p. 388).

153. *Ch'ing lü-li*, 31:37a–b; *Ting-li hui-pien*, 5:141–142b. A personal servant was also punishable if his magistrate was indicted for improper activities in which the servant had inspired him to engage. The servant's punishment ranged from beating to three years of penal servitude if the magistrate's penalty

was demotion, dismissal, or penal servitude. The servant's punishment was the same as the magistrate's if the latter incurred a penalty more severe than four years of penal servitude (*Ch'ing lü-li*, 32:45b–46b).

154. *Liu-pu ch'u-fen tse-li*, 15:36. The magistrate's punishment was the same as for failure to detect the acceptance of a bribe by a runner. Thus if the punishment of a guilty servant was beating or penal servitude, the magistrate was to be fined six months' nominal salary; if the servant's punishment was banishment or exile, the magistrate was to be fined one year's salary; and if the servant was sentenced to death, the official was to be demoted one grade and kept in the same post (*Ch'ing hui-tien shih-li* [1818], 77:16a–b; *Li-pu tse-li*, 16:11).

155. The official was to be demoted one grade and transferred to another post. If the servant had caused the death of a person, the official was to be demoted two grades. If a servant engaged in fighting with someone and caused his death, the official was to be fined one year's nominal salary (*Ch'ing hui-tien shih-li* [1818], 77:16a–b; *Liu-pu ch'u-fen tse-li*, 15:36).

156. *Mu-hsüeh chü-yao*, p. 43b.

157. *Mu-ling shu*, 4:7b.

158. Liu said that it was impossible to control runners if one trusted one's gate porter (*Yung-li yung-yen*, 17a–b, 47a–b).

159. *Hsüeh-chih hsü-shuo*, p. 13.

160. *Yung-li yung-yen*, p. 26.

161. *Hsüeh-chih i-te pien*, pp. 63b–64.

162. *Yung-li yung-yen*, pp. 25b–26; *Hsüeh-chih t'i-hsing lu*, A:5b; *Hsüeh-chih i-te pien*, p. 60.

163. *Hsüeh-chih i-te pien*, p. 63b.

164. *Hsüeh-chih t'i-hsing lu*, A:4b–5.

165. *Hsüeh-chih i-te pien*, pp. 64 ff; cf. *Yung-li yung-yen*, pp. 25b–26.

166. *Hsüeh-chih i-te pien*, pp. 60b–63b.

CHAPTER VI. PRIVATE SECRETARIES

1. This term is derived from military usage in the Han and subsequent dynasties. A scholar who served as a secretary (*chi-shih*) or staff member of a general often had his office in a tent (*mu-fu*), hence he was called a *mu-liao*, *mu-yu* or *mu-pin* (colleague, friend, or guest in a tent). See *Ch'eng wei lu*, 22:9b–12.

2. *Lin-ch'uan hsien-sheng wen-chi*, 39:7b.

3. In the T'ang and Sung one of the various types of civil service examination was one on law (*ming-fa*) for scholars who were versed in this subject (*Hsin T'ang shu*, 44:1, 2b; *Sung shih*, 155:1b–2, 9b–10; 157:9b–11b). Candidates who had passed a civil examination were also required to take a test in which they wrote statements of decision (*p'an*), before they were given an appointment (*T'ung-tien*, 15:84; *Hsin T'ang shu*, 45:1a–b; *Sung shih*, 58:3b–4, 7b). Although the candidates who took the *chü-jen* examination were still required to write *p'an* in the Ming and early Ch'ing, it had become a mere formality.

Ku Yen-wu pointed out that all the candidates had to do was to remember a few articles of law (*Ming shih,* 70:1b; *Ch'ing shih kao,* 115:1b–3b; *Jih chih lu chi-shih,* 16:21b). The test on the writing of *p'an* was finally abolished in 1757 (*Ch'ing shih kao,* 115:3b).

4. "Charisma" refers to the inborn qualities, physical and spiritual, of a leader, which were believed to be supernatural. For a detailed discussion, see *From Max Weber: Essays in Sociology,* tr. H. H. Gerth and C. W. Mills (New York, 1946), pp. 245 ff.

5. Max Weber, *The Religion of China, Confucianism and Taoism,* tr. H. H. Gerth (Glencoe, Ill., 1951), p. 132. Cf. Weber's remark on the nature of Chinese education and examinations, pp. 120–121.

6. See the postscript by Tu Kuei-ch'ih (1824–1901; an expert in law who served as a private secretary to Fang Ta-chih) to *P'ing-p'ing yen,* p. 3b. Wang Lan-kuang (a magistrate in the Tao-kuang period) emphatically pointed out that newly appointed magistrates were incompetent in the administration of justice because of their lack of training (preface to *Ming-hsing kuan-chien lu,* p. 3). They were also incompetent in the area of taxation (*Ch'in-pan chou-hsien shih-i,* p. 28; *Ching-shih wen hsü-pien,* 21:13b).

7. This was again a situation different from that of the Han, T'ang, and Sung, when scholars were found among the subordinate officials and many magistrates and higher-level officials came from this group (*Chüan-shih-ko wen, chia-chi,* 1:21).

8. Literati had been employed in earlier dynasties as advisers and secretaries to generals and high officials (see above, n. 1). But the employment of private secretaries in local government began in the Ming. It was mentioned in the biography of K'uang Chung (1383–1443), a prefect in Soochow, that no private secretary was invited to work in his inner office, and that he himself made all decisions in such matters as official documents and lawsuits (*K'uang t'ai-shou chih Su chi,* 3:3). This implies that it was rather exceptional for a local official not to have a private secretary in the Ming. Another Ming source mentions that a certain magistrate frequently consulted his private secretary on matters on which he could not make a decision (*Ku chin t'an kai,* 1:14). According to Li Kung (1659–1733), all officials serving in the central and local government in the Ming employed *mu-pin.* Li held that officials in the Later Han, T'ang, and Sung could appoint competent scholars as their subordinate officials, but that this was no longer possible in the Ming, when one could enter officialdom only by taking the civil examinations and obtain a post only through appointment by the Board of Civil Office. The officials, unable to handle their duties alone, were forced to employ private secretaries (*Yüeh shih hsi shih,* 3:3). From a different angle, Tsung Chi-ch'en (1792–1867) explained the need for private secretaries in the light of the degeneration of the subordinate officials. Successful examination candidates were highly respected, but the subordinate officials were looked down upon in the Ming dynasty; hence literati were unwilling to assume these humiliating posts. Consequently, talented men were scarcely to be found among the subordinate officials and learned scholars were

invited to serve in the capacity of advisers. This practice, Tsung claimed, continued up to his time without change (*Kung-ch'ih-chai wen-ch'ao*, 2:58).

9. *Ching-shih wen hsü-pien*, 23:1. A similar statement was made by a magistrate, Hsü Ken-pi: "Now the magistrates come from three channels: by examination, by military merits, and by purchase. Before they enter officialdom they have not studied administrative matters. . . Since they are unfamiliar with taxation, military affairs, and law, they do not know how to implement them or to make decisions. Therefore they regard the private secretaries as their guides" (*Pu-ch'ien-chai man-ts'un*, 5:120a–b).

10. *Ch'in-pan chou-hsien shih-i*, p. 28.

11. *Ibid.; Fu-hui ch'üan-shu*, 1:12b–13b.

12. *Ping-t'a meng-hen lu*, A:30b.

13. *Hsüeh-chih i-shuo*, A:2; *Huang-Ch'ing tsou-i*, 33:25a–b; *Huan-yu sui-pi*, 3:57.

14. *Yung-li yung-yen*, p. 36.

15. *Ibid.*, Wu's preface, p. 2; *Yung-li yü-t'an*, Liu's preface, p. 1.

16. *Ping-t'a meng-hen lu*, 3:5b, 8b–9, 40b.

17. *Ch'in-pan chou-hsien shih-i*, p. 28.

18. Actually Han had two types of "visible" and "invisible" government in mind: one pair in the central government, the other pair in local government. Visible government in the capital consisted of the officials of the various boards; invisible government consisted of the clerks (*Ching-shih wen-pien*, 23:1).

19. These categories appear in *Tso-chih yao-yen*, p. 15; *Hsüeh-chih i-shuo*, A:2b; *Ch'in-pan chou-hsien shih-i*, p. 28b; *Mu-ling shu*, 4:6, 13b.

20. *Mu-ling shu*, 4:6, 13b.

21. *Ibid.*, 4:6.

22. *Ibid.*, 4:13b.

23. *Ibid.*

24. *Ibid.*

25. *Ping-t'a meng-hen lu*, A:10b, 15b, 18b.

26. *Tso-chih yao-yen*, p. 15; *Hsüeh-chih i-shuo*, A:2b–3.

27. For instance, see *Lou-hsien chih*, 1:6.

28. Ch'ih Chuang, p. 15.

29. *Pan-an yao-lüeh*, pp. 28b–29.

30. *Hsüeh-chih i-te pien*, p. 29; *P'ing-p'ing yen*, 2:42b–43; *Ming-hsing kuan-chien lu*, pp. 32b–33; *Mu-ling shu*, 18:11b–12; 23:32a; *Pan-an yao-lüeh*, pp. 27b–28b; *Kung-men yao-lüeh* and *Ko-hang shih-chien*, quoted in *Chung-ho*, 2.10:86, 88.

31. *Hsüeh-chih t'i-hsing lu*, A:5; *Kung-men yao-lüeh*, quoted in *Chung-ho*, 2.10:86.

32. *Nai-an kung-tu ts'un-kao*, 2:36b; *Hsü tso-chih yao-yen*, pp. 2b–3.

33. *Pan-an yao-lüeh*, pp. 27–28b; *Hsü tso-chih yao-yen*, pp. 1b, 2b.

34. *Pan-an yao-lüeh*, pp. 27–28b; *Mu-hsüeh chü-yao*, pp. 1, 5b.

35. *Hsing-ch'ien pi-lan*, 7:2b.

36. *Ping-t'a meng-hen lu*, A:16.

37. *Ibid.*, A:25a–b.

38. *Tso-chih yao-yen*, p. 6a–b; *Mu-hsüeh chü-yao*, p. 5a–b. Wang Hui-tsu suggests that since a magistrate had to attend to numerous matters, it was necessary that a private secretary encourage him to conduct hearings without delay (*Tso-chih yao-yen*, 13b–14). He also advised that a secretary, in making arrangements for a hearing, should take into consideration the ability and efficiency of the official so that the latter would be able to manage (*ibid.*, p. 6).

39. *Ching-shih wen-pien*, 21:15b.

40. Wang Hui-tsu advised that a secretary should be cautious about serving summonses and that he should summon only those whose presence was absolutely necessary to a hearing (*Tso-chih yao-yen*, pp. 6, 10b–11; *Hsü tso-chih yao-yen*, pp. 1, 2a–b, 3b).

41. *Shu liao wen-ta*, p. 4.

42. S. W. Williams was wrong in maintaining that private secretaries were in waiting during a trial. One of the illustrations in his book shows a secretary standing behind the magistrate, who presided in the court (S. W. Williams, *The Middle Kingdom*, 2 vols., New York, 1883, 1:504).

43. *Ming-hsing kuan-chien lu*, p. 20; "Chui-yen shih-tse," pp. 4–5.

44. *Ming-hsing kuan-chien lu*, p. 20.

45. "Chui-yen shih-tse," p. 4b–5.

46. *Ming-hsing kuan-chien lu*, p. 20; *Ping-t'a meng-hen lu*, p. 11b.

47. Wang Hui-tsu questioned the reliability of any judgment based solely upon a deposition (*Hsü tso-chih yao-yen*, p. 4).

48. *Hsü tso-chih yao-yen*, pp. 4–5b; see also *Chia-yen sui-chi*, 1; "Tso-chih yao-yen che-yao," p. 12a–b.

49. *Ping-t'a meng-hen lu*, A:21b–22b.

50. For example, see cases of Wang Hui-tsu, *ibid.*, A:18b, 22b–23, 42 ff, 43b ff.

51. *Sheng-shih wei-yen pu-pien*, 4:21b; *Mu-ling shu*, 17:3; *Ching-shih wen hsü-pien*, 21:13b.

52. See below, Chap. VII, sec. 1.

53. *Ming-hsing kuan-chien lu*, p. 19b.

54. *Pan-an yao-lüeh*, p. 31 ff.

55. This record, known as *kung-chuang*, was an expanded version of the depositions (*ts'ao-kung*) written down by a clerk during the trial. The depositions of various persons involved in a homicide case were arranged in the following order: constable, family members of the victim, neighbors acting as witnesses, offenders deserving light punishment, and offenders deserving severe punishment (*Hsing-mu yao-lüeh*, p. 2; *Pan-an yao-lüeh*, p. 3b). For the technique of writing a deposition, see *Pan-an yao-lüeh*, pp. 36–40; *Hsing-ch'ien pi-lan*, pp. 1–5, 7–11b; *Hsing-mu yao-lüeh*, pp. 1–2b.

There was a regulation prohibiting any yamen employee from changing or eliminating any part of the deposition (see Chap. VII, sec. 4; *Mu-hsüeh chü-yao*, pp. 1b–2); but this was rarely strictly observed (*Ming-hsing kuan-chien lu*, p. 19b; *Hsing-ch'ien pi-lan*, 1:12). Mu-han (nineteenth century), a

Manchu magistrate, instructed his private secretaries, since depositions were read in court and signed by the persons who made them, not to change a single word (*ibid.*).

56. *Fu-hui ch'üan-shu*, 12:10b–11b. For the style of the *k'an-yü*, see *ibid.*, 12:12–23b; *Fu-weng chi, hsing-ming*, 2:1 ff; 4:8–13b; 5:15–19.

57. *Pan-an yao-lüeh*, p. 43.

58. This procedure was called *hsü-k'an* (to describe an investigation). Practice varied in different provinces. In some places both a chart and a description were required; in other places, only the description (*Pan-an yao-lüeh*, pp. 32b ff; *Hsing-mu yao-lüeh*, p. 4).

59. *Fu-hui ch'üan-shu*, 12:9b–10; *Hsing-ch'ien pi-lan*, 1:9b, 12 ff; *Hsing-mu yao-lüeh*, p. 1 ff; *Pan-an yao-lüeh*, p. 31 ff.

60. A decision might be rejected by a superior on any one of the following grounds: inconsistency between the plaintiff's charges and the defendant's final deposition, among the various depositions made by different persons, or between a confession and a statement of judgment; discrepancies found in a report; incompatibility between the fatal injury and the weapon used in a homicide case; an incomplete inquest; disagreement between descriptions of injuries and the Instructions for Coroners (*Hsi-yüan lu*); lack of agreement between a judgment and the law or precedent; retraction of a confession by a suspect during retrial (*Pan-an yao-lüeh*, p. 44b). It is interesting to note that, as pointed out by a magistrate and a private secretary, not a single serious case that was reported to a superior yamen could avoid rejection (*Fu-hui ch'üan-shu*, 12:11; *Mu-hsüeh chü-yao*, p. 2).

61. *Pan-an yao-lüeh*, p. 44. The same source mentions that a secretary in the chou or hsien government should be able to handle all necessary aspects of a case, leaving no doubtful points in his report, whereas a secretary in a *yüan* (governor), *ssu*, or *fu* government should be able to evaluate all the essentials in a case and, if necessary, to refute the given decision on the crucial points (*ibid.*, p. 45b).

62. See below, Chap. VIII.

63. The record of the transfer of government funds (*chiao-p'an ts'e*) was a record of accounts and funds prepared by an outgoing magistrate for his successor. It included the following four parts, the so-called *ssu-chu ts'e* (four-column record): (1) *chiu-kuan*, the amount taken over by the outgoing magistrate from the previous administration; (2) *hsin-shou*, the amount of revenue collected during the term of the outgoing official; (3) *k'ai-ch'u*, the amount already expended and the amount delivered to the superior yamen; (4) *shih-tsai*, the balance of grain and money stored in the granary and treasury. See *Ch'in-pan chou-hsien shih-i*, pp. 2b–3b; *Hsien-ch'ien pi-lan*, 5:1b–3; *Fu-hui ch'üan-shu*, 3:15.

64. *Hsing-ch'ien pi-lan*, 5:1b–3, 11; *Ch'ien-ku pei-yao*, 1:17–18b; *Mu-hsüeh chü-yao*, pp. 24, 25; *Ch'in-pan chou-hsien shih-i*, pp. 2b–4; *Fu-hui ch'üan-shu*, 3:14 ff.

65. The rule was that if an unauthorized expenditure or embezzlement by

a former magistrate was disclosed and reported by a new magistrate, the money was to be replaced by the former. But if it was not disclosed or reported by a new magistrate, both the former and the new official were subject to punishment, and the latter was obliged to replace the money (*Li-pu tse-li*, 6:10b–12; *Liu-pu ch'u-fen tse-li*, 8:9b; *Ch'ien-ku pei-yao*, 1:6a–b, 18a–b).

66. *Ch'ien-ku pei-yao*, 1:1b; *Ch'ien-ku shih-ch'eng*, pp. 4–5.

67. *Ch'ien-ku shih-ch'eng*, pp. 20a–b, 23a.

68. As a rule, the kinds of land owned by a family and the amount of tax to be paid were listed in the household record (*hu-ts'e*). This served as a basis in the preparation of records for each *chia*, *t'u*, and finally, for the chou or hsien as a whole. However, in a large area with many households, the practice was to drop the household and *chia* records, and use only the *t'u* record and the hsien record. See *Fu-hui ch'üan-shu*, 6:9b–11; *Ch'ien-ku pei-yao*, 1:10a–b; *Hsing-ch'ien pi-lan*, 5:3b, 19a–b.

69. *Hsing-ch'ien pi-lan*, 5:19a–b; *P'ei-yüan-t'ang ou-ts'un kao*, 46:38, 40.

70. See below, Chap. VIII, sec. 1.

71. *Tso-chih yao-yen*, p. 15; *Mu-ling shu*, 4:6, 13b.

72. *Fu-hui ch'üan-shu*, 7:2b–3; *Ch'ien-ku pei-yao*, 1:7; *Hsing-ch'ien pi-lan*, 5:22a–b; *Mu-ling shu*, 11:16. The *pi-chao* and/or *hsiao-chao*, both of which were parts of the land tax receipt (see Chap. VIII, note 49), were inserted in the deadline-hearing record by clerks and presented to the secretary for checking. If only a three-part receipt was in use, the *pi-chao* was given back to the clerk together with the deadline-hearing record, after a corner of the certificate had been cut off by the secretary. The certificate was destroyed by the secretary after the clerk had entered payment in the land tax record. If a four-part receipt was in use, the *hsiao-chao* was destroyed immediately after it had been examined by the secretary (*Ch'ien-ku pei-yao*, 1:7a–b; *Hsing-ch'ien pi-lan*, 5:25a–b).

73. *Ch'ien-ku shih-ch'eng*, pp. 20a–b, 22; *Hsing-ch'ien pi-lan*, 5:19b.

74. *Hsing-ch'ien pi-lan*, 5:25b–26.

75. According to Wang Yu-huai, there were three types of bamboo tallies, varying according to the seriousness of the case: the "wind tally" (*feng-ch'ien*), "fire tally" (*huo-ch'ien*), and "thunder tally" (*lei-ch'ien*). All of them were kept in the office of the secretary (*Hsing-ch'ien pi-lan*, 5:6a–b).

76. If the taxpayers whose names had been selected and who had been warned by the runners still failed to hand in their taxes by the next spring, a stamp reading "arrest with a tally (warrant)" would be used above their names on the land tax record. There were three kinds of tallies, varying according to the emergency of the case: *pi-wan ch'ien* (overdue tax must be paid), *jen-yin pi-tao ch'ien* (both taxpayer and tax must be present), and *pu-su ch'ien* (not allowed to remain overnight). See *Hsing-ch'ien pi-lan*, 5:25b–26.

77. *Hsing-ch'ien pi-lan*, 5:23.

78. *P'ei-yüan-t'ang ou-ts'un kao*, 46:37b; *Hsüeh-chih i-shuo*, B:7b; *Hsing-ch'ien pi-lan*, 5:19b, 22b; *Mu-hsüeh chü-yao*, pp. 22b–23; *Ch'ien-ku shih-ch'eng*, pp. 20a–b, 22; *Mu-ling shu*, 11:51a–b.

79. *Hsing-ch'ien pi-lan*, 5:4b, 22b; *Mu-hsüeh chü-yao*, p. 23; *P'ei-yüan-t'ang ou-ts'un kao*, 46:37b–38; *Fu-hui ch'üan-shu*, 7:3; *Mu-ling shu*, 11:51a–b.

80. *Hsüeh-chih i-shuo*, B:7b.

81. Thus both Hsieh Ming-huang and Wang Yu-huai, private secretaries in the Ch'ien-lung period, suggested that the land tax record should be submitted before the collection period so that it could be checked and the tax computed (*Ch'ien-ku shih-ch'eng*, pp. 20b, 23; *Hsing-ch'ien pi-lan*, 5:19a–b).

82. *Fu-hui ch'üan-shu*, 7:2–3b; *Mu-hsüeh chü-yao*, p. 23.

83. *P'ei-yüan-t'ang ou-ts'un kao*, 46:37b–38.

84. *Hsing-ch'ien pi-lan*, 5:7a–b, 20a–b; see above, Chap. III, sec. 5.

85. *Ch'ien-ku pei-yao*, 1:7b–8; *Hsing-ch'ien pi-lan*, 5:7a–b, 20a–b.

86. *Hsing-ch'ien pi-lan*, 5:7b–8, 20a–b; *Ch'ien-ku pei-yao*, 1:8a–b; *Fu-hui ch'üan-shu*, 6:6b, 9.

87. *Hsing-ch'ien pi-lan*, 5:26.

88. The certificates of delivery (*p'i-hui*), which, as a rule, were issued by the provincial treasury in advance, were kept by a secretary of taxation. When funds or grain were to be delivered, a certificate specifying the tax and amount would be issued upon the request of the clerks. Another type of certificate, which was used to deliver a fund other than land tax, was issued by the chou or hsien government itself (*Fu-hui ch'üan-shu*, 7:18–19). In either case, the certificate was stamped by the receiving yamen and given back to the messengers who escorted the delivery to acknowledge receipt of the funds.

89. *Hsing-ch'ien pi-lan*, 5:10a–b, 12b–15; *Hsüeh-chih t'i-hsing lu*, B:21b.

90. *Hsü tso-chih yao-yen*, p. 7b; *Mu-ling shu*, 3:5a–b.

91. *Mu-ling shu*, 3:5b. Yamen accounts as a rule were grouped under four categories: (1) Regular income (*cheng-ju*): tax funds derived from land tax and miscellaneous taxes. (2) Regular disbursement (*cheng-ch'u*): funds delivered and expended, including the official's salary, secretaries' salaries, and wages paid to other yamen personnel. (3) Miscellaneous income (*tsa-ju*): income derived from various kinds of customary fees. (4) Miscellaneous disbursements (*tsa-ch'u*): contributions, gifts, food, and other daily expenses paid by the magistrate (*Hsüeh-chih shuo-chui*, p. 4b).

92. As gifts and fees had to accord strictly with usage, a record which listed all the items and amounts paid to various officials on all occasions became a valuable guidebook. It is reported that a fee had to be paid by the *chang-fang* to the *chang-fang* of the former magistrate for securing such a record (*Kuan-ch'ang hsien-hsing chi*, chap. 41).

93. *Mu-ling shu*, 4:6.

94. See *Kuan-ch'ang hsien-hsing chi*, chaps. 5, 40, 41.

95. *Mu-ling shu*, 3:5b.

96. Pp. 28b–29. *Mu-hsüeh chü-yao* also mentions that a large portion of administrative action would be delayed if an official considered registration unimportant and did not assign it to a competent person. It also suggests that a good salary should be given to such a secretary (p. 1).

97. *Hsüeh-chih i-shuo*, A:3.

98. See above, Chap. III, sec. 2.

99. *Mu-ling shu*, 4:5a–b.

100. See *Ping-t'a meng-hen lu*, A:10b–11, 11b–12, 13a–b, 18b–19, 25b–27.

On an extremely complicated case, Wang Hui-tsu once spent 4 days and evenings in preparing a statement of decision and the draft was revised more than 10 times (*ibid.*, p. 24b).

101. *Mu-ling shu*, 4:6, 13b.

102. See above, Chap. VI, sec. 2.

103. For details on the practice of *piao-p'an*, see above, Chap. V, n. 31.

104. See above, Chap. V, n. 79.

105. See below, Chap. IX, sec. 6.

106. *Ping-t'a meng-hen lu*, B:38.

107. *Tso-chih yao-yen*, pp. 9b, 12b, 17; *Hsü tso-chih yao-yen*, pp. 12b–13, *Ping-t'a meng-hen lu*, A:9b; *Fu-hui ch'üan-shu*, 1:13; *Hsüeh-chih t'i-hsing lu*, A:4; *P'ing-p'ing yen*, 2:20b; *Ming-hsing kuan-chien lu*, p. 20. Chang T'ing-hsiang stated that, with the exception of a magistrate's personal affairs, there was not a single thing with which a private secretary was not concerned ("Chui-yen shih-tse," p. 3).

108. *Tso-chih yao-yen*, p. 15; *Hsüeh-chih t'i-hsing lu*, A:3b.

109. *Ching-shih wen hsü-pien*, 23:1; *Mu-ling shu*, 4:2; 17:3.

110. *Hsüeh-chih i-shuo*, A:3b; cf. *Mu-ling shu*, 4:5b; *Huan-yu sui-pi*, 3:58.

111. *Fu-hui ch'üan-shu*, 1:12b–13.

112. *Yung-li yung-yen*, pp. 44–45b; *Ming-hsing kuan-chien lu*, pp. 32b–33.

113. *Fu-hui ch'üan-shu*, 1:12b–13; *Hsüeh-chih shuo-chui*, 9b.

114. *Ming-hsing kuan-chien lu*, p. 20.

115. *Fu-hui ch'üan-shu*, 1:12b–13.

116. *Hsüeh-chih i-te pien*, p. 29; *Mu-hsüeh chü-yao*, p. 3b.

117. *Ping-t'a meng-hen lu*, A:16b, 22b, 28b.

118. "Chui-yen shih-tse," p. 3a–b.

119. *Tso-chih yao-yen*, p. 5.

120. *Hsüeh-chih i-shuo*, A:17.

121. *Hsü tso-chih yao-yen*, p. 3b.

122. *Ibid.*, p. 3a–b; "Chui-yen shih-tse," p. 3.

123. *Ping-t'a meng-hen lu*, A:46a–b.

124. *Chu-p'i yü-chih*, Hsien-te's memorials, p. 104b; *Mu-hsüeh chü-yao*, p. 6. The case of Wang Tsung-lu (1703–1753) may be cited. After he had failed many times to pass the preliminary civil service examination (*t'ung-shih*), he went to the capital and became a clerk of the Board of Punishment, where he studied law for six years. He then served as a secretary of law under various magistrates in Fukien for nearly thirty years (*Chang-shih i-shu*, 17:45b).

125. *Mu-hsüeh chü-yao*, p. 6. An imperial edict of 1747 ruled that a dismissed prefect or magistrate should not seek a post as private secretary in the province where he had held office (*Ch'ing shih-lu*, Kao-tsung, 285:17a–b). After Wang Hui-tsu had been dismissed, he was invited by several high provincial officials and his earlier employers to be their private secretary, but he refused their offers (*Meng-hen lu-yü*, p. 1–2).

126. E.g., Wang Tsung-lu (see above, n. 124) and Wang Hsien-i (d. 1855) (*Chia-yen sui-chi*, 1: "Yüeh-li ou-t'an," p. 1b).

127. E.g., Wang Hui-tsu had been a teacher before he became a private secretary (*Ping-t'a meng-hen lu*, A:6b–7b).

128. *Mu-hsüeh chü-yao*, pp. 6, 7b. Wang Hui-tsu reported that a teacher's income could only reach more than ten silver taels a year, whereas the salary of a private secretary might be more than ten times that of a teacher (*Tso-chih yao-yen*, pp. 3b, 4b; see below, Chap. VI, sec. 5, for concrete figures).

129. E.g., Wang Hui-tsu took the provincial examination six times during his period of service as a private secretary, not succeeding until the sixth time. With the exception of the second time, he returned to the same yamen after each attempt (*Ping-t'a meng-hen lu*, A:11b, 14b–15, 17, 23b). He took four metropolitan examinations, failing three times. Each time he first resigned his secretaryship in order to take the examination, and then took a post in a different yamen after he had returned from the capital (*ibid.*, pp. 23, 34b–35, 35b, 36b). His reason for resigning before a metropolitan examination was probably that it was difficult to be on leave for the length of time required for a trip to Peking.

130. See n. 129. The careers of Tso Tsung-t'ang (1812–1885) and Chang Ch'ien (1853–1926) may also be cited. Tso, who was a *chü-jen* but failed to pass the metropolitan examination, became a private secretary to Chang Liang-chi and Lo Ping-chang, both governors of Hunan (*Tso Wen-hsiang-kung nien-p'u*, 1:29b–35). Chang Ch'ien first served as a secretary to the provincial commander-in-chief when he was a holder of the first degree. After he had passed the provincial examination, he became secretary to a prefect (*Chang Chi-tze chiu-lu, ts'e* 1, *chien-p'u*).

131. Wang Hui-tsu was rather exceptional. His mother died shortly after he had passed the metropolitan examination in 1775. Thus he was prevented from entering officialdom, and continued to be a private secretary. He remained in this occupation for a number of years after the termination of his mourning period, probably out of personal loyalty to the magistrate. He did not become an official until 1786 (*Tso-chih yao-yen*, pp. 19–20b; *Ping-t'a meng-hen lu*, A:36b ff).

132. For a discussion of the status of scholars in general and the connection between status and bureaucratic qualification, see Ch'ü T'ung-tsu, "Class Structure and Its Ideology," in J. K. Fairbank, ed., *Chinese Thought and Institutions* (Chicago, 1957), pp. 246–247, 250. For the legal privileges given to degree-holders, see below, Chap. X, sec. 3; Chang Chung-li, *Chinese Gentry*, pp. 32 ff.

133. *Meng-hen lu-yü*, pp. 1b, 53b. Here it should be made clear that this statement applied only to a magistrate. The status of a higher official was decidedly superior to that of his secretaries. Wang Hui-tsu explained that the reason he accepted a secretarial appointment in a chou or hsien government was that there a magistrate and a private secretary were of equal status. He refused to be the secretary of a *ssu* or *fu* (governor), because there would be great distance between their status and his, and he would not tolerate the attitude of a high official (*Meng-hen lu-yü*, p. 53b). The distance is also

reflected in the way a superior official was addressed by his private secretary. A high official (a prefect or higher) was usually addressed by his informal official title (e.g., *chih-chün* for a governor-general, *fang-po* for a provincial treasurer, etc.), and a secretary referred to himself by his personal name (Ch'ih Chuang, p. 15).

134. *Mu-ling shu*, 4:1b, 6b; *Tso-chih yao-yen*, p. 1b; *Hsü tso-chih yao-yen*, p. 7b; *Ch'in-pan chou-hsien shih-i*, p. 28. A private secretary was even considered as being between a guest and a teacher (*pin-shih*) (*Hsüeh-chih i-shuo*, A:2b; *Tso-chih yao-yen*, p. 1b; "Chui-yen shih-tse," p. 1). The colloquial term *shih-yeh* (teacher-master) also carried honor and esteem.

135. *Chia-yen sui-chi*, 1: "Yüeh-li ou-t'an," p. 16b; Ch'ih Chuang, p. 15.

136. *Mu-ling shu*, 4:1b.

137. Ch'ih Chuang, p. 15.

138. *Hsüeh-chih t'i-hsing lu*, A:4; *Mu-ling shu*, 4:6a–b; 23:34b.

139. *Mu-ling shu*, 23:34b–35; *Hsü tso-chih yao-yen*, pp. 7b–8.

140. *Hsüeh-chih t'i-hsing lu*, A:4; *Mu-ling shu*, 4:6b.

141. *Mu-ling shu*, 4:1b–2; Ch'ih Chuang, p. 15.

142. *Hsü tso-chih yao-yen*, p. 7; *Hsüeh-chih i-shuo*, A:2b.

143. *Hsüeh-chih i-shuo*, A:2b, B:21; *Tso-chih yao-yen*, pp. 1b–2; *Chia-yen sui-chi*, 1: "Shen Han lun," p. 2; "Chui-yen shih-tse," p. 3b.

144. *Ping-t'a meng-hen lu*, A:12b–13. In another instance, Feng Kuei-fen, who was a private secretary to a magistrate, resigned because he disagreed with the magistrate, who insisted upon punishing a degree-holder for failure to pay his land tax (*Hsien-chih-t'ang kao, chüan-shou*, epitaph, p. 1b).

145. Wang Hui-tsu reported that some of his relatives and friends studied the secretarial art under him (*Hsü tso-chih yao-yen*, p. 16b). He himself learned law from a secretary of law while he was a secretary of correspondence. He was given an opportunity to practice the handling of documents, and after six years of apprenticeship he became a secretary of law (*Ping-t'a meng-hen lu*, A:9b; *Tso-chih yao-yen*, preface, p. 1a–b). As another example, Wang Hsien-i studied law under a secretary to the provincial judge for two years and then became a secretary (*Chia-yen sui-chi*, 1: "Yüeh-li ou-t'an," p. 1b; 4:73b, 75b).

146. *Tso-chih yao-yen*, pp. 9a–b, 16b. Wang Hui-tsu advised his son, who intended to learn secretarial technique, to study law and the statutes, read the Peking Gazette (*Ching-pao* or *Ti-ch'ao*), and practice writing *p'i* and making decisions on legal cases. According to his own experience, one could become competent after a year of concentrated study (*Meng-hen lu-yü*, p. 25; on the nature of the Peking Gazette see J. K. Fairbank and S. Y. Teng, "On the Types and Uses of Ch'ing Documents," *Harvard Journal of Asiastic Studies*, 5.1:61–62, 1940). Wang Hsien-i also recommended the reading of the Peking Gazette, for it included the revised statutes (*Chia-yen sui-chi*, 1: "Yüeh-li ou-t'an," p. 17). As the ability to make decisions was a necessary qualification, those who studied secretarial techniques in Chihli province frequently started by learning how to process a legal case ("Chui-yen shih-tse," pp. 1b–2). Others began with practice in writing statements, arguing and rejecting unacceptable

decisions prepared by others (*po-an*) (*Chia-yen sui-chi*, 1: "Yüeh-li ou-t'an," p. 18b).

147. *Mu-hsüeh chü-yao*, p. 6b; "Chui-yen shih-tse," p. 1b.

148. *Fu-hui ch'üan-shu*, 1:13; *Shuang-chieh-t'ang yung-hsün*, 5:12; *Meng-hen lu-yü*, p. 25; "Chui-yen shih-tse," p. 1b.

149. *P'ing-p'ing yen*, p. 20; *Fu-hui ch'üan-shu*, 1:12b–13b; *Hsüeh-chih i-shuo*, A:2.

150. *Fu-hui ch'üan-shu*, 1:13; *Hsüeh-chih i-shuo*, A:2a–b.

151. The superior official who forced his subordinate official to accept a private secretary whom he had recommended was subject to dismissal. The subordinate official who failed to report such a recommendation by a superior official was also subject to dismissal (*Ch'ing lü-li*, 31:36; *Liu-pu ch'u-fen tse-li*, 15:32b–33; *Ch'ing hui-tien shih-li, chüan* 97).

152. *P'ei-yüan-t'ang ou-ts'un kao*, 16:16a–b; 31:36 ff; 34:28 ff; *Yü-ping-ko tsou-i*, 51:5.

153. *Hsüeh-chih i-shuo*, A:2. Since the magistrates often found it difficult to refuse a recommendation from their superiors, and yet were unwilling to assign actual duties to secretaries thus recommended, they began to assign them to sinecures (*kan-hsiu*, salary without service), a practice which was regarded as "interfering neither with human feeling nor with the administration" (*Huan-yu sui-pi*, 3:57b; *Ching-shih wen-pien*, 20:10). According to Wu Wen-jung (1792–1854), the governor of Chekiang, a nominal post as secretary of correspondence, of registration, or of the enforcement of tax collection, in many of the yamen in the province, was often given to a man recommended by a superior official. Such a secretary, who did not actually come to the office, received a *kan-hsiu* varying from several tens to several hundreds of taels a year (*Wu Wen-chieh kung i-chu*, 19:4).

154. *Ch'ing shih-lu*, Hsüan-tsung, 232:24b–25. For a concrete example see the letter written by Hsü Keng-pi, a magistrate, who refused to accept the recommendation made by a private secretary serving in the yamen of the governor-general. The letter indicates that pressure was brought to bear by the secretary in an attempt to recommend his student (*Pu-ch'ien-chai man-ts'un*, 6:6–7). It was reported that sometimes an annual fee was paid to secretaries for making recommendations (*Ch'ing hui-tien shih-li, chüan* 97).

155. *Ch'ing shih-lu*, Kao-tsung, 285:17a–b; *Ching-shih wen hsü-pien*, 23:2b.

156. This practice, however, was prohibited by law in 1800 (*Ch'ing hui-tien shih-li, chüan* 97; Liu Chien-shao's comment on the top margin, in *Mu-ling shu*, 4:40b–41).

157. *Tso-chih yao-yen*, p. 16.

158. *Fu-hui ch'üan-shu*, 1:13b.

159. *Ibid.*; see also Ch'ih Chuang, p. 15; Doolittle, I, 325.

160. *Hsüeh-chih i-shuo*, B:13. Another magistrate, Weng Tsu-lieh, indicated that only about half of the minor secretarial posts (i.e., posts other than those of secretary of law and secretary of taxation) could be given to the magistrate's relatives (*Huan-yu sui-pi*, 3:58).

161. See above, Chap. VI, sec. 1.

162. Wang Hui-tsu began his professional career as a secretary of correspondence to his father-in-law for two years (*Ping-t'a meng-hen lu*, A:8–9). Wang was very skilled in *p'ien-t'i* writing (double-harnessed prose), a fashionable style used for correspondence (*ibid.*, A:9b–10).

163. *Ibid.*, B:11a–b; for a similar viewpoint expressed by Ho Shih-ch'i, see *Mu-ling shu*, 3:5a–b.

164. *Hsüeh-chih i-shuo*, B:12.

165. For the meaning of "particularism" and Talcott Parsons' discussion of China's "particularistic achievement pattern" see T. Parsons, *Social System* (Glencoe, Ill., 1951), pp. 62–63, 195–198.

166. *Li-pu tse-li*, 3:12b.

167. *Ch'ing hui-tien shih-li* (1818), 58:5b; 76:18a–b; *ibid.* (1819), *chüan* 75 and 97.

168. *Ch'ing hui-tien shih-li* (1818), 58:6b–7; 76:13; *ibid.* (1899), *chüan* 87. The reason was that if a private secretary's family was in the same locality where he held office he would be free to communicate with outsiders, and it would be difficult for the magistrate to enforce the policy of "isolation" (*Ch'ing hui-tien shih-li*, 1818, 76:13, 14, 15a–b; *ibid.*, 1899, *chüan* 97). Customarily a private secretary was required to live alone within the yamen and therefore left his family in his native town. Only in exceptional cases did they live together with their family members (see the cases of Wang Hsien-i and his son, Wang Chung-lin, also a secretary—*Chia-yen sui-chi*, 1: "Yüeh-li ou-t'an," p. 30b; 4:5b). Some secretaries married or kept a concubine in the locality where they held office, a situation which caused concern on the part of government officials and the emperor (*Ch'ing hui-tien shih-li*, 1818, 76:14, 15a–b). In the experience of Wang Hsien-i, there were both advantages and disadvantages to living with family members, and going home too often could lead to suspicion. Hence he held that a secretary should not bring his family with him unless he was on good terms with the magistrate and unless he had money enough to permit his family to move freely (*Chia-yen sui-chi*, 1: "Yüeh-li ou-t'an," p. 19). The fact that Wang did not take into consideration the law prohibiting a secretary from living with his family implies that the law was something of a formality. It seems that in general the practical reasons mentioned by Wang were the main factors that guided a private secretary's decision in this matter.

169. Hence the colloquial term, *Shao-hsing shih-yeh*. Li Wei, governor-general of Chekiang, once remarked that many natives of Shao-hsing were roughly familiar with the law and statutes (*Chu-p'i yü-chih*, Li Wei's memorials, 2:47a–b). A more specific statement was made by Chang Hsüeh-ch'eng, a native of K'uai-chi (Shao-hsing prefecture), who observed that since the men of his native town were intelligent and the land did not produce enough to support the population, many of them were engaged in the study of official documents and law, and became private secretaries (*Chang-shih i-shu*, 17:45). A statement by Hsieh Chao-chih (*chin-shih* 1592), a Ming scholar, quoted in Ku Yen-wu's *Jih-chih lu chi-shih*, 8:18b–19, reads: "All the clerks

as the thirteen sections of the Board of Revenue are natives of Shao-hsing." Both Ch'üan Tseng-hu and Miyazaki Ichisada suggest that this may explain the prevalence of private secretaries from Shao-hsing (Ch'üan Tseng-hu, "Ch'ing-tai mu-liao chih-tu lun," *Ssu-hsiang yü shih-tai*, 32:39, March 1944; Miyazaki Ichisada, "Shindai no shori to bakuyu," *Tōyōshi kenkyū*, 16.4:9, March 1958). However, it should be pointed out that Hsieh's original statement in his *Wu tsa-tsu*, 15:5b, reads, "are natives of Wu and Yüeh [Kiangsu and Chekiang]," not "are natives of Shao-hsing." Much confusion has been caused by the erroneous quotation.

The popular notion about Shao-hsing private secretaries seems to be an exaggeration. Except for a few individual cases, we have little knowledge of the actual geographical distribution of private secretaries. See Ch'üan Tseng-hu, 32:38–42, on a discussion of biological and environmental factors in connection with Shao-hsing private secretaries. Byron Brenan's statement, "[the secretaries] are nearly always from the Chekiang province, and usually from Shao-shingfu... In this way the office of secretary in all the yamens almost become a monopoly of the Chekiang province" (*The Office of District Magistrate in China*, p. 5), is an exaggeration based upon the popular notion.

170. *Ping-t'a meng-hen lu*, A:35b.

171. *Ch'ing hui-tien shih-li* (1818), 58:7–8; 76:18b–19; *ibid.* (1899), *chüan* 75 and 97.

172. He served in the following five localities in Chekiang: Tz'u-hsi, Hai-ning, P'ing-hu, Wu-ch'eng and Kuei-an (*Tso-chih yao-yen*, p. 20a–b; *Ping-t'a meng-hen lu*, A:38b, 39, 40b, 41b, 45b, 47).

173. *Yü-ping-ko tsou-i*, 5:5.

174. A regulation was promulgated in 1772 limiting the term of service of a private secretary to five years, and ordering the magistrates and other local officials to report the dismissal of secretaries whose terms had expired to the governor-general and governor, who were obliged to report annually to the Board of Civil Office. However, an edict of 1776 mentions that the board did not receive report of a single case in which a private secretary who had served for more than five years was dismissed. The edict ordered that the practice of making an annual report be discontinued (*Ch'ing hui-tien shih-li*, 1818, 58:6b–8; 76:18b–19; *ibid.*, 1899, *chüan* 75 and 97).

175. *Mu-ling shu*, 4:6b; 23:35.

176. *Ping-t'a meng-hen lu*, A:78b, 43a–b.

177. See above, Chap. VI, sec. 3.

178. Liu's marginal comment, *Mu-ling shu*, 4:3.

179. *Tso-chih yao-yen*, pp. 19–20b.

180. The regulation also specified that an official's son or relative who had assisted in the administration could not be recommended (*Ch'ing shih-lu*, Kao-tsung, 33:3; *Ch'ing hui-tien tse-li*, 10:5b, 11:21b; *Ch'ing hui-tien shih-li*, 1818, 58:6, 76:12; *ibid.*, 1899, *chüan* 75; *Li-pu tse-li*, 3:13b).

181. According to *Ch'ing shih-lu*, Shih-tsung, 5:6–7; *ibid.*, Kao-tsung, 33:3–4b; *Ch'ing hui-tien tse-li*, 10:15–16; *Ch'ing hui-tien shih-li* (1818), 58:5b–6b,

76:12–13; and *ibid.* (1899), *chüan* 75, the regulation concerning the recommendation of private secretaries serving under a governor-general or governor was introduced in 1723, whereas the one concerning the secretaries of the lower officials was formulated in 1736. But *Ch'ing hui-tien shih-li* (1818), 63:10b–11b; and *ibid.* (1899), *chüan* 81, give 1723 as the date of both regulations.

182. *Ch'ing shih-lu,* Kao-tsung, 33:4a–b; *Ch'ing hui-tien tse-li,* 11:21a–b; *Ch'ing hui-tien shih-li* (1818), 63:11a–b, 76:12b–13; *ibid.* (1899), *chüan* 81 and 97; *Li-pu tse-li,* 3:13a–b.

183. Thus Wu suggested that capable private secretaries should be rewarded with official recommendation in order to encourage them (*Huang-Ch'ing tsou-i,* 33:26b–28). According to Wang Ka'n (nineteenth century), Shen Chin-men was the only private secretary in the previous 200 years who had become an official through recommendation. Shen became a subdistrict magistrate. As this was very rare, his friends presented him with a seal engraved as follows: "The first official honor in the flourishing dynasty" (*Chiang-chou pi-t'an,* p. 4).

184. *Tso-chih yao-yen,* p. 15b. The case of Wang Hui-tsu, who provided this information, is an example. He was paid only 3 taels a month when he served as a secretary of correspondence in 1752 in the yamen of his father-in-law. Two years later he received a yearly salary of 74 taels, serving as a secretary of correspondence in a prefecture yamen, and he got an increase of 8 taels a year later (*Ping-t'a meng-hen lu,* A:8, 9a–b).

185. *Ping-t'a meng-hen lu,* A:24b, 47b. A secretary named Tung was given a nickname "Tung Three Hundred," because he would not accept an appointment for less than 300 taels (*ibid.,* A:47b).

186. *Ping-t'a meng-hen lu,* A:47b. The pay was even higher in certain other localities. For instance, Wang was offered a yearly salary of 1600 taels by the prefecture of Taiwan in 1766 (*ibid.,* A:28).

187. *Ching-shih wen-pien,* 20:10. According to Teng Ch'eng-hsiu, the salary of secretaries serving in Kwangtung was the highest in the empire (*Yü-ping-ko tsou-i,* 5:5).

188. *Ching-shih wen hsü-pien,* 23:2.

189. *Fu-hu ch'üan-shu,* 1:13b; *Hsüeh-chih t'i-hsing lu,* A:3.

190. *Tso-chih yao-yen,* p. 15b; *Huan-yu sui-pi,* 3:57b.

191. *Tso-chih yao-yen,* p. 16.

192. For details see above, Chap. II, sec. 3.

193. *Ching-shih wen hsü-pien,* 23:1.

194. *Ping-t'a meng-hen lu,* B:50b–51; *Meng-hen lu-yü,* p. 21.

195. *Tso-chih yao-yen,* preface, p. 1a–b; *Meng-hen lu-yü,* p. 25.

196. *Meng-hen lu yü,* p. 25.

197. Thus private secretaries in the same clique cooperated so that official documents prepared by one of its members in one yamen could be approved by another member serving in a superior yamen. They found fault with and rejected the documents prepared by secretaries outside the clique (*Ch'ing shih-lu,* Hsüan-tsung, 118:7b–8; *Huang-Ch'ing tsou-i,* 33:26a–b; *Ching-shih wen-pien,* 20:10).

198. *Yü-ping-ko tsou-i*, 4:13a–b. Similar cases were also disclosed in Kiangsi and Kweichow where relatives served as private secretaries in the various yamen in the same province. They were ordered to be dismissed and sent back to their home towns by the emperor, who recognized that relatives serving in the same province could cooperate with each other for personal advantage (*Ch'ing shih-lu*, Hsüan-tsung, 120:31a–b; 232:24b–25b).

199. *Ch'ing shih-lu*, Hsüan-tsung, 232:24b–25b, 26a–b; *Ch'ing hui-tien shih-li, chüan* 97.

200. *Ch'ing hui-tien shih-li* (1818), 76:13b; *ibid.* (1899), *chüan* 97; *Ching-shih wen hsü-pien*, 23:2b.

201. *Ching-shih wen-pien*, 20:10.

202. Wang Hui-tsu mentions that in his early years it was possible to find four or five honest men out of ten (*Hsüeh-chih hsü-shuo*, p. 13). However, lamenting the degeneration in the integrity of secretaries, in his later days, he says that only two or three out of ten were honest men (*Hsüeh-chih i-shuo*, A:2b). Wang Chih thought that only one or two per cent of them were men of integrity and ability (*Mu-ling shu*, 4:2).

203. Wang Hui-tsu reported that once a man attempted to offer a bribe to him and also gave him advice on ways of accepting bribes. Wang rejected the bribe, but another secretary accepted it. This corruption was disclosed later and the guilty persons fled (*Hsü tso-chih yao-yen*, p. 13a–b; *Ping-t'a meng-hen lu*, A:17). In another instance, a notorious secretary was charged with demanding gift money from others through the medium of a gentry member (*Fu Wu kung-tu*, 15:8).

204. *Huang-Ch'ing tsou-i*, 33:25b–26.

205. *Mu-ling shu*, 4:2.

206. *Hsüeh-chih t'i-hsing lu*, 3:22b.

207. *Chi'ng hui-tien shih-li* (1818), 76:13, 14b–15; *ibid.* (1899), *chüan* 97. Some officials thus authorized gate porters to ask secretaries leaving the yamen about their destination (*Hsüeh-chih i-te pien*, p. 30).

208. *Mu-ling shu*, 2:44b; 4:2; *Ching-shih wen-pien*, 2:12b.

209. *Hsü tso-chih yao-yen*, p. 6.

210. "Chui-yen shih-tse," p. 3.

211. The official was subject to dismissal if he connived at such a practice, and subject to demotion if he failed to investigate the case due to negligence (*Liu-pu ch'u-fen tse-li*, 15:32b; *Ch'ing hui-tien shih-li, chüan* 97).

212. *Liu-pu ch'u-fen tse-li*, 15:32a–b; *Ch'ing hui-tien shih-li, chüan* 97.

213. *Ch'ing hui-tien shih-li* (1818), 76:19; *ibid.* (1899), *chüan* 97. This statute was formulated in 1790 when it was disclosed that a secretary had advised his magistrate to report a feud as ordinary fighting. Both the magistrate and the secretary were exiled to Sinkiang (*Ting-li hui-pien*, 37:7 ff; 39:58b).

214. According to a statute formulated in 1792, if the magistrate incurred demotion, dismissal, or penal servitude, the punishment for the secretary varied from beating to three years of penal servitude. The punishment was the same as that of the magistrate if the latter's punishment was more severe than four

years of penal servitude. It may be pointed out that this statute was also applicable to personal servants, clerks, and runners (*Ch'ing lü-li*, 32:45b–46; *Ting-li hui-pien*, 39:57–60b).

215. Realizing this, some magistrates who considered administration of primary importance held that an official should have the courage to assume personal responsibility in making a decision (*P'ing-p'ing yen*, 2:12b; *Pu-ch'ien-chai man-ts'un*, 5:120b; *Mu-ling shu*, 1:43a–b).

216. See Wu Ying-fen's memorial, *Huang-Ch'ing tsou-i*, 33:26–27.

CHAPTER VII. ADMINISTRATION OF JUSTICE

1. Ku Yen-wu mentioned that the yamen of many magistrates displayed a sign reading "*Yüeh-sung* (to bypass the proper authorities and submit a complaint to the superior yamen) is punishable with fifty strokes." Quoting an edict by the Ming emperor T'ai-tsu (1368–1398), Ku held that this law meant that one should appeal to the *li-lao*, i.e., *li-chang* and the "elders" (*ch'i-lao*), before coming to the magistrate's court (*Jih-chih lu chi-shih*, 8:10; on the definition of *li-lao* see *Ming-lü chi-chieh*, 26:1). However, the Ming and Ch'ing law relating to the *li-lao* permits them merely to reconcile and settle disputes at the *shen-ming t'ing*, a pavilion in which were posted imperial edicts instructing the people to be good subjects, and the names of unfilial sons and evildoers (*Ming-lü chi-chieh*, 26:1; *Ch'ing lü-li*, 34:2a–b). The law does not specify that people must go to the *li-lao* before they appeal to the magistrates. The law of *yüeh-sung* in both the Ming and Ch'ing codes referred only to bypassing the government authorities having jurisdiction over the people (*pen-kuan kuan-ssu*). The original notes to this law in the Ch'ing code and the related statutes made it clear that the "lowest authorities" meant the magistrates and that anyone who bypassed them and submitted a complaint to a higher yamen was subject to the punishment of fifty strokes. Under the law of the Ming and Ch'ing, the *yüan*, *ssu, tao,* or *fu* was subject to indictment for receiving a complaint from a person who bypassed the proper tribunal (*Ming-lü chi-chieh*, 22:1; *Ch'ing lü-li*, 30:2a–b, 7b–9, 10b; Staunton, p. 359; Boulais, p. 630).

Moreover, it should be noted that the law concerning the role of *li-lao* had little actual significance. A Ming official mentions that most of the pavilions had already fallen into ruins in the fifteenth century, that the names of evildoers were no longer posted there, and that people went directly to the court of the magistrates instead of appealing first to the "elders" (quoted in *Jih-chih lu chi-shih*, 8:10a–b). Liu Ch'i mentions that *li-lao* were abolished in the Ch'ing after the introduction of the system of *kun-tan* ("rolling form," see below, Chap. VIII, sec. 1) and the regulation permitting taxpayers to seal the bag containing their tax money when delivering it to a clerk (*T'ang-i hsien-chih*, 2:10b; *Pao-chia shu*, 4:8b–9). Apparently Liu referred to the abolishing of *li-chang*.

2. *Ch'ing hui-tien*, 55:2b; 56:7; *P'ei-yüan-t'ang ou-ts'un kao*, 40:10; *Yung-li yung-yen*, p. 53b.

3. Two volumes, known as *hsün-huan pu*, were used alternatively to list the

civil cases referred to a magistrate. At the end of each month, copy A was sent to the prefect, or the subprefect of an independent subprefecture, or to the independent department magistrate, and the magistrate would then register cases in copy B. When copy A had been reviewed and sent back a month later, copy B was sent to the superior and copy A again came into use. The magistrate was also required to send monthly reports to all superior officials: prefect, intendant, provincial judge, governor, and governor-general. See *Ch'ing hui-tien*, 56:72; *Ch'ing lü-li*, 30:30b–32; *Liu-pu ch'u-fen tse-li*, 47:16a–b; *P'ei-yüan-t'ang ou-ts'un kao*, 10:28b ff; 11:7 ff; 40:11–12; *Mu-ling shu*, 23:29 ff.

4. A magistrate was subject to forfeiture of one year's nominal salary if any case was omitted from the court record, and to demotion of one grade if he failed to keep the brief of a case. If he purposely omitted any entries in the record or made a false report, the penalty was dismissal (*Liu-pu ch'u-fen tse-li*, 47:17).

5. *Ch'ing hui-tien*, 56:7; *Ch'ing lü-li*, 30:32a–b, 34a–b; *Ch'ing shih kao*, 155:2.

6. *Ch'ing hui-tien*, 55:2b; *Ch'ing hui-tien shih-li* (1818), 649:29a–b, 30b–31; *ibid.* (1899), *chüan* 843.

7. *Ch'ing hui-tien*, 55:2b–3b; *Ch'ing lü-li*, 37:44b; *Ch'ing shih kao*, 155:2, 6b; *Pan-an yao-lüeh*, p. 41b.

8. However, this procedure was not required in places far away from the provincial capital, where the provincial judge was stationed. Instead, cases were retried by an intendant and reported to the provincial judge, the governor, and the governor-general. But cases had to be retried by the provincial judge if the defendant retracted his testimony or if the offender sentenced to exile or banishment was involved in a homicide case (*Ch'ing lü-li*, 37:60 ff; *Liu-pu ch'u-fen tse-li*, 47:12 ff).

9. *Ch'ing lü-li*, 37:44b.

10. Only the chou and hsien which were at a great distance from the provincial capital were permitted not to deliver criminals to the provincial capital for retrial during the atumn assize. In such cases, criminals were retried by intendants who were responsible for reporting to the higher provincial authorities. But if a defendant retracted his testimony the case had to be referred to the provincial judge for retrial (*Ch'ing lü-li*, 37:31–32b, 44b–48b; *Ch'ing hui-tien*, 53:1–3, 57:13–15; *Ch'ing shih-kao*, 155:2–3).

11. When an appeal was made to the magistrate's superior officials, it could be referred back to the magistrate only if he had not yet passed sentence or if the case had not been submitted to the superior yamen for retrial. If the case had been closed by the magistrate, or if the magistrate was accused of having detained people unlawfully or of forcing a person to sign a confession, or if the clerks and runners were accused of abuse and corruption, the superior officials had to retry the case themselves or assign another official to retry it, depending upon the seriousness of the case. As a rule, however, the prefect or the magistrate of an independent chou had to retry the case himself. The governor-general and governor were obliged to retry the case personally if the

magistrate was accused of having tortured anyone to death, or if the emperor ordered the provincial authorities to hear a case which had been appealed to the capital. For details, see *Ch'ing hui-tien*, 55:3a–b; *Ch'ing hui-tien shih-li* (1818), 649:29–31; *ibid.* (1899), *chüan* 843; *Ch'ing lü-li*, 37:26–28b; *Ting-li hui-pien*, 11:127–130b; 16:46–48b; 38:63b–69b, 70b–71; 55:87b–90; 58:76–77; 61:71b–73b; *Liu-pu ch'u-fen tse-li*, 47:60a–b.

12. *Liu-pu ch'u-fen tse-li*, 48:18.

13. In the seventeenth and eighteenth centuries the days designated for this purpose were the 3rd, 6th, 9th, 13th, 16th, 19th, 23rd, 26th, and 29th of every month (*Fu-hui ch'üan-shu*, 11:5b; *T'ien-tai chih-lüeh*, 7:1b; *Ch'in-pan chou-hsien shih-i*, p. 9b). In the nineteenth century complaints were received only on the 3rd, 8th, 13th, 18th, 23rd and 28th days of each month (*Ho-pei ts'ai feng lu*, T'ang-yin hsien, 19, Lin-chang hsien, 25, Yen-chin hsien, 39; *Tseng Wen-cheng chi, tsa-chu*, 2:62; *Pu-ch'ien-chai man-ts'un*, 25:5).

14. During the farmers' busy season only criminal cases were heard. However, certain civil cases, such as disputes over the annulment of an engagement, or disputes over the use of irrigation facilities or boundaries of landed property which could interfere with farming, were handled without delay. Civil cases which did not involve persons engaged in farming were accepted as usual. See *Ch'ing shih lu*, Kao-tsung, 88:2a–b; *Ch'ing hui-tien*, 56:7a–b; *Ch'ing lü-li*, 30:30a–b, 33a–b; *P'ei-yüan-t'ang ou-ts'un kao*, 20:36 ff, 23:38 ff.

15. *Ch'in-pan chou-hsien shih-i*, p. 9; *Hsüeh-chih shuo-chui*, p. 2b; *Hsüeh-chih t'i-hsing lu*, A:13b.

16. *Yung-li yung-yen*, pp. 44–45b; *Ming-hsing kuan-chien lu*, pp. 32b–33; *P'ing-p'ing yen*, 2:42b. For rescripts written by a magistrate, Tai Chao-chia (*chin-shih* 1706), see his *T'ien-tai chih-lüeh*, *chüan* 8.

17. *Hsüeh-chih i-te pien*, p. 29.

18. *Ibid.*; *Tseng Wen-cheng chi, tsa-chu*, 2:62b; *P'ing-p'ing yen*, 2:42b; see above, Chap. VI, sec. 2.

19. *P'ing-p'ing yen*, 2:42b.

20. *Ch'ing hui-tien*, 55:2b; 56:5a–b; *Ch'ing lü-li*, 35:83b.

21. *P'ei-yüan-t'ang ou-ts'un kao*, 11:8, 44:38a–b; *Liu-pu ch'u-fen tse-li*, 47:16a–b. A law was finally formulated in 1810 which provided the following punishments: for procrastination of less than one month, forfeiture of three months' nominal salary; more than one month, one year's salary; more than half a year, two years' salary; more than one year, demotion of one grade and retention in the original post (*Liu-pu ch'u-fen tse-li*, 47:16b–17).

22. *Ch'ing shih kao*, 155:4b; *Yung-li yung-yen*, pp. 52a–b; *P'ing-p'ing yen*, 2:41.

23. *Yung-li yung-yen*, pp. 6a–b.

24. *Li-pu tse-li*, 40:5; *Liu-pu ch'u-fen tse-li*, 43:2.

25. *Ch'ing lü-li*, 37:77; Staunton, p. 452; Boulais, pp. 722–723.

26. The magistrate of a neighboring hsien who refused to conduct an inquest without giving any reason was to be demoted three grades and transferred to

another post (*Li-pu tse-li*, 40:5b; *Liu-pu ch'u-fen tse-li*, 43:2; *Ch'ing lü-li*, 37:82b; *Ch'ing hui-tien*, 55:7a–b).

27. A jail warden was authorized to conduct an inquest on behalf of the absent magistrate only in such places as Kweichow and Szechwan, where there was no assistant magistrate, or where the latter was not stationed in the same hsien seat as the magistrate and the neighboring magistrate was at a great distance. A subdistrict magistrate was allowed to conduct an inquest if the location was so far distant that the jail warden could not return from the trip within one day. A subdistrict magistrate was also allowed to conduct an inquest on behalf of an absent magistrate in Kweichow if a homicide occurred in the summer and the neighboring hsien was far away (*Ch'ing hui-tien*, 53:7a–b; *Li-pu tse-li*, 40:4a–b; *Liu-pu ch'u-fen tse-li*, 43:1a–b; *Ch'ing lü-li*, 37:82b–83, 84–85b, 88b–89; *Ting-li hui-pien*, 7:103–104b).

28. *Mu-hsüeh chü-yao*, p. 13; *Ming-hsing kuan-chien lu*, p. 6b; *Hsüeh-chih t'i-hsing lu*, A:18a–b.

29. *Ch'in-pan chou-hsien shih-i*, p. 20; *Yung-li yung-yen*, p. 36; *Mu-hsüeh chü-yao*, p. 14; *Ching-shih wen hsü-pien*, 22:8b.

30. *Ch'ing hui-tien*, 55:6a–b; *Li-pu tse-li*, 40:4b; *Ch'ing lü-li*, 37:81b.

31. See above, Chap. IV, n. 92.

32. *Yung-li yung-yen*, pp. 16, 32, 37; *P'ing-p'ing yen*, 3:58a–b.

33. *P'ing-p'ing yen*, 4:4b.

34. See above, Chap. IV, secs. 1, 4.

35. Wan Wei-han, a private secretary, reported that most of the coroners were not equipped to make an examination (*Mu-hsüeh chü-yao*, p. 13b; see above, Chap. IV, n. 81).

36. *Li-pu tse-li*, 40:6a–b; *Liu-pu ch'u-fen tse-li*, 43:2b.

37. The penalty for incorrectly reporting inquest findings was 60 strokes for a magistrate and 70 strokes for the jail warden. The penalty was the same for failure to ascertain the cause of death. For the same violation the clerk and the coroner were to receive 80 strokes. If an incorrectly conducted inquest had caused an increase or decrease in the punishment inflicted upon a person accused of homicide, the magistrate and the coroner were to be punished according to the law relating to the pronouncing through error of a sentence inadequate to the crime (*shih-ch'u*) or excessive for the crime (*shih-ju*) (see below, Chap. VII, sec. 5) (*Ch'ing lü-li*, 37:77a–b; Staunton, p. 452; Boulais, pp. 722–723).

38. *Ch'ing lü-li*, 37:79b–80; *Ch'ing hui-tien*, 55:6a–b; *Ch'ing shih kao*, 155:6. For the inquest form see *Hsi-yüan lu chi-cheng*, 1:12–13; *Fu-hui ch'üan-shu*, 15:9–11.

39. *Ch'ing hui-tien*, 55:6a–b; *Ch'in-pan chou-hsien shih-i*, p. 21a–b; *Hsi-yüan lu chi-cheng*, 21:1b–2; *Fu-hui ch'üan-shu*, 14:4b, 6; 15:6 ff, 17–19; *Hsüeh-chih i-shuo*, B:8b; *P'ing-p'ing yen*, 3:60a–b; *Ts'ung-cheng hsü-yü lu*, 1:3, 2:13; *Hsüeh-chih i-te pien*, p. 1; *Hsüeh-chih t'i-hsing lu*, A:18a–b; *Ming-hsing huan-chien lu*, pp. 6b, 11a–b; *Mu-ling shu*, 19:2a–b, 5, 7, 8a–b, 19a–b; *Tze-chih hsin-shu*, 2:32a–b; *Mu-hsüeh chü-yao*, p. 14; *Huan-yu sui-pi*, 1:12b.

40. *Ch'in-pan chou-hsien shih-i*, pp. 20b, 43b; *Mu-hsüeh chü-yao*, p. 14.

41. *Fu-hui ch'üan-shu*, 14:17b.

42. *Ch'in-pan chou-hsien shih-i*, pp. 20b, 43; *Meng-hen lu-yü*, p. 5b; *P'ing-p'ing yen*, 1:4b.

43. *Ch'ing shih kao*, 155:6. It was generally believed that a magistrate should always have a copy of *Hsi-yüan lu* at an inquest. In case the family members of the dead raised objections to the report on the inquest, the magistrate could show them the book and explain the procedure to them (*Hsüeh-chih i-shuo*, B:9; *Meng-hen lu-yü*, p. 10; *Hsüeh-chih t'i-hsing lu*, A:18; *Huan-yu sui-pi*, 1:13b–14).

44. See *Liu-pu ch'u-fen tse-li*, 43:7–8b.

45. Violation of this regulation meant forfeiture of one year's nominal salary (*Ch'ing lü-li*, 37:80b–81; *Liu-pu ch'u-fen tse-li*, 43:3).

46. *Hsi-yüan lu chi-cheng*, chüan 4.

47. *Ch'ing hui-tien*, 56:5 ff; *Liu-pu ch'u-fen tse-li*, 43:14–15b.

48. The total time limit included the time allowed for the magistrate as well as for his superiors. Thus a six-month limit included three months for the chou or hsien magistrate to complete the trial and deliver the criminals to the prefect or the independent department magistrate, one month for the latter to deliver the criminals to the provincial judge, one month for the provincial judge to deliver them to the governor-general and governor, and one month for the governor-general and governor to report to the Board of Punishment. In a four-month time limit, two months were allowed the magistrate, and twenty days for each of the ensuing officials. In a two-month time limit, one month was given to the magistrate and ten days to each of the ensuing officials (*Ch'ing hui-tien*, 56:5a–b; *Liu-pu ch'u-fen tse-li*, 47:1–2b; *Ch'ing lü-li*, 35:83, 94b).

49. Punishment was imposed on magistrates whenever they exceeded the first deadline (two or three months). Three-months' nominal salary was to be forfeited for a delay of less than one month, and one year's salary for a delay of more than one month (*Ch'ing hui-tien*, 56:5a–b; *Liu-pu ch'u-fen tse-li*, 47:1a–b; *Ch'ing lü-li*, 35:84, 94b–95).

50. *Liu-pu ch'u-fen tse-li*, 41:5.

51. *Ch'ing hui-tien*, 51:10b–11; *Li-pu tse-li*, 38:19a–b; *Liu-pu ch'u-fen tse-li*, 41:12.

52. For a one-day delay, demotion of one grade and transfer to another post; two-day delay, demotion of three grades and transfer; three-day delay, dismissal (*Liu-pu ch'u-fen tse-li*, 41:12a–b).

53. The magistrate of the neighboring hsien was subject to demotion of one grade if he declined to make the trip (*Li-pu tse-li*, 38:19b–20; *Liu-pu ch'u-fen tse-li*, 41:12b).

54. See *Liu-pu ch'u-fen tse-li*, 41:17a–b, 18b–19.

55. *Li-pu tse-li*, 38:11b; *Liu-pu ch'u-fen tse-li*, 42:41a–b.

56. The magistrate was given a promotion of one grade if he was able to apprehend all robbers involved in a case; three recordings of merit if he

apprehended more than half of the robbers and their leader; and two recordings of merit for apprehending half of the robbers without the leader (*Li-pu tse-li*, 38:11b; *Liu-pu ch'u-fen tse-li*, 42:41a–b).

57. *Liu-pu ch'u-fen tse-li*, 42:30b–31.

58. *Li-pu tse-li*, 38:3a–b; *Liu-pu ch'u-fen tse-li*, 4:20–21. A magistrate could be exempted from the first impeachment if he was able to apprehend within the given deadline half of the robbers, their leader, and anyone who harbored them. If he had arrested more than half of the robbers but was unable to catch their leader, he was subject to the following punishment: (1) Within the period of the first deadline, forfeiture of one year's nominal salary; forfeiture of two years' salary at the end of another year if he was still unable to catch the leader; demotion of one grade and retention in the same post at the end of the third year. (2) Within the period of the second deadline, forfeiture of two-years' nominal salary; demotion of one grade and retention in the same post at the end of another year. (3) Within the period of the third deadline, demotion of one grade and retention in the same post. (4) Within the period of the fourth deadline, the first impeachment (demotion of one grade) was to be canceled—on condition that he had committed no other faults—three years after the apprehension of more than half of the robbers. In all cases, the magistrate could be exempted from punishment, regardless of the deadline, if the leader of the robbers had died (*Liu-pu ch'u-fen tse-li*, 41:23, 24a–b).

59. *Li-pu tse-li*, 38:9b–10; *Liu-pu ch'u-fen tse-li*, 41:30.

60. *Liu-pu ch'u-fen tse-li*, 42:26; *Ch'ing shih-lu*, Mu-tsung, 40:18.

61. *Liu-pu ch'u-fen tsu-li*, 42:26a–b.

62. As the requests made by the various governors-general and governors varied in different cases, regulations were formulated in 1849 in an attempt at standardization. It was ruled that a magistrate was to be demoted one grade prior to the deadline if the highest provincial authority so requested. When a more severe punishment was requested, the magistrate could be demoted two or three grades instead of one or two grades. For details see *Liu-pu ch'u-fen tse-li*, 41:25 ff.

63. The four-month deadline included two months for the magistrate, and twenty days for each of the following three groups of officials: (1) prefect or independent department magistrate, (2) provincial judge, and (3) governor-general and governor (*Ch'ing hui-tien*, 56:5a–b; *Liu-pu ch'u-fen tse-li*, 47:1–2; *Ch'ing lü-li*, 35:83).

64. As in a case of homicide, there was a punishment for exceeding the first deadline (four months). Three-months' nominal salary was to be forfeited for a delay of less than one month, and one year's salary for a delay of more than one month (*Liu-pu ch'u-fen tse-li*, 47:1b).

65. When a magistrate had accumulated four demerits (*chi-kuo*), he was subject to forfeiture of six months' nominal salary. When he had accumulated four merits (*chi-kung*) he won one recording of merit (*chi-lu*) (*Liu-pu ch'u-fen tse-li*, 42:50a–b).

66. See above, Chap. IV, sec. 5.

67. A policeman who failed to apprehend a thief at the end of one month was subject to ten strokes; twenty strokes at the end of two months; and thirty strokes at the end of three months. In a case of robbery, the punishment was twenty strokes for one month; thirty for two months; and forty for three months. See *Ch'ing hui-tien*, 55:12; *Ch'ing lü-li*, 35:82; Staunton, pp. 429–430; Boulais, p. 708; cf. *Hsüeh-chih i-te pien*, p. 40b.

68. *Ch'ing hui-tien*, 55:12b; *Ts'ung-cheng hsü-yü lu*, 3:10b–11b; *Hsüeh-chih i-te pien*, p. 39b.

69. See above, Chap. IV, sec. 4.

70. *Hsüeh-chih t'i-hsing lu*, A:5.

71. *Ching-shih wen-pien*, 21:15b; see above, Chap. VI, sec. 2.

72. *P'ing-p'ing yen*, 1:14b; see above, Chap. VI, sec. 2.

73. Bamboo tallies (*ch'ien*) were used during a trial when the magistrate wanted to anounce corporal punishment (*Fu-hui ch'üan-shu*, 11:30b–31; Justus Doolittle, *Social Life of the Chinese: with some Account of Their Religious, Governmental, Educational, and Business Customs and Opinions*, 2 vols., New York, 1865, I, 304; Williams, I, 504). They were also used to authorize a runner to make an immediate arrest (see Chap. IV, n. 123).

74. *Fu-hui ch'üan-shu*, 2:9b–10.

75. According to Wang Hui-tsu, who encouraged people to go to hearings, there were usually three to four hundred people, including out-of-town traders, who came to watch the trials (*Meng-hen lu yü*, B:40b–41b; see also *Huan-yu chi-lüeh*, A:10).

76. *Ch'ing lü-li*, 36:48; Staunton, pp. 441–442; Boulais, p. 716.

77. There were two kinds of flogging: 10–50 strokes with a light bamboo stick (*ch'ih*) and 60–100 strokes with a heavy bamboo stick (*chang*), in both cases on the thighs and buttocks (*Ch'ing lü-li*, 2:34a–b; Staunton, p. xxiv; Boulais, pp. 2–3).

78. Face-slapping was ordinarily administered with an open hand and varied from five to ten blows. Sometimes a leather slapstick was used instead of the hand, and forty to eighty blows might be administered (*Hsüeh-chih i-shuo*, A:16b).

79. Squeezing the fingers with a wooden instrument known as *tsan* was reserved for women only (Boulais, p. 6).

80. *Chia-kun*, an instrument made of two pieces of wood, was used to squeeze the ankles (Boulais, p. 6).

81. *Ch'ing hui-tien*, 57:6a–b; *Ch'ing lü-li*, 4:6b; *Liu-pu ch'u-fen tse-li*, 50:1.

82. An official who made unlawful instruments of torture was to be dismissed and punished with 100 strokes, and a superior who failed to impeach such an official was subject to demotion. See *Ch'ing hui-tien*, 57:6a–b; *Ch'ing lü-li*, 36:14a–b; *Li-pu tse-li*, 50:2 ff; *Liu-pu ch'u-fen tse-li*, 50:1 ff.

83. *Ch'ing hui-tien*, 57:6a–b; *Ch'ing lü-li*, 36:10–11b; *Li-pu tse-li*, 43:3; *Liu-pu ch'u-fen tse-li*, 50:3.

84. *Liu-pu ch'u-fen tse-li*, 50:2a–b; *Ch'ing shih kao*, 155:6; *Hsüeh-chih i-shuo*, A:16b.

85. *Hsüeh-chih i-shuo*, A:15–16.

86. *Li-pu tse-li*, 42:33a–b; *Liu-pu ch'u-fen tse-li*, 48:30; *Ch'ing lü-li*, 37:124b.

87. If any change in the document caused a change in the punishment, the official was subject to dismissal. If the change had no effect on the punishment, the official was subject to forfeiture of nominal salary or demotion, depending on the seriousness of the case (*Ch'ing lü-li*, 37:18; *Liu-pu ch'u-fen tse-li*, 48:30a–b; cf. 48:14a–b, on punishment for failure to include the essential part of the deposition).

The magistrate was held responsible if he permitted the clerks to take the statement of deposition to their office and a change was thereby made in the document. The clerks were punishable in accordance with the law relating to the willful pronouncing of a sentence inadequate to or excessive for the crime (*ku-ch'u* or *ku-ju*), whereas the magistrate was punishable in accordance with the law relating to the pronouncing through error of a sentence inadequate to or excessive for the crime (*shih-ch'u* or *shih-ju*) (*Ch'ing lü-li*, 37:124–125; *Li-pu tse-li*, 42:35b; *Liu-pu ch'u-fen tse-li*, 48:30).

88. When a magistrate went over the statement of deposition, the customary practice was to mark a dot with a red brush at the beginning of the statement, and a check at the end, and then write down the date (*Fu-hui ch'üan-shu*, 12:10b; *Hsüeh-chih i-shuo*, A:21b; *P'ing-p'ing yen*, 4:27b; *Mu-ling shu*, 18:15. See above, Chap. V, sec. 2, for the service rendered by a court attendant).

89. *Ch'ing lü-li*, 37:101–102b; Staunton, pp. 455–456.

90. The statement signed by a plaintiff was called *tsun-i;* and a similar statement signed by a defendant was called *kan-chieh* (*Ko-hang shih-chien*, quoted in *Chung-ho*, 2.10:81).

91. An official who failed to secure such a statement from the convicted was to be punished with forty strokes where the sentence was penal servitude or banishment; in a case of capital punishment, sixty strokes (*Ch'ing lü-li*, 37:107a–b; Staunton, pp. 456–457; Boulais, pp. 723–724).

92. The statement of decision was used in cases under the jurisdiction of a magistrate, i.e., cases that would be judged by a magistrate without being referred to a superior yamen. For the style of this type of statement see *Fu-hui ch'üan-shu*, 12:10b, 23–26; *T'ien-tai chih-lüeh*, chüan 3; *Fu-weng chi, hsing-ming*, 4:15 ff; 5:27 ff.

93. *P'ing-p'ing yen*, 4:28b.

94. See above, Chap. VI, sec. 2.

95. See above, Chap. VI, sec. 2.

96. Imperial preface to *Ta-Ch'ing lü chi-chieh; Ch'in-pan chou-hsien shih-i*, pp. 36–37; *Hsüeh-chih shuo-chui*, p. 7b; *T'u-min lu*, 4:14; *Ming-hsing kuan-chien lu*, pp. 5b–6; *P'ing-p'ing yen*, 1:14b. When Wang Hui-tsu was asked for advice by his son, who became a *chin-shih* and was appointed a magistrate, he suggested that his son read the Penal Code and *Hsi-yüan lu* (*Meng-hen lu-yü*, p. 5b).

97. *Shu liao wen-ta*, p. 3a–b.

98. *Ming-hsing kuan-chien lu*, p. 6.

99. The Penal Code (*Ta-Ch'ing lü-li*) includes two parts: the law (*lü*) and the statutes (*li*). The former, promulgated in 1727, consists of 436 articles and was considered the fundamental law and could not be revised (*Ch'ing shih-kao*, 153:3). The statutes, known as the supplementary law, were added to and revised from time to time. The statutes embodied only 321 articles during the early K'ang-hsi period. In 1725 these were increased to 815, and in 1801 to 1573. In the T'ung-chih period there were as many as 1892 articles. See *Ch'ing lü-li, chüan-shou*, "Pu-pan fan-li," p. 30; *Ch'ing shih kao*, 153:3b–4.

100. *Shu liao wen ta*, p. 4.

101. It was commonly recommended that a magistrate be familiar with the general law (*ming-li*), the laws on indictments and information (*su-sung*), and the laws on judgment and imprisonment (*tuan-yü*). He should also have some knowledge of the laws governing the following: land and tenancy, marriage, debt, robbery and theft, homicide, quarrels and fights, forgeries and fraud, incest and adultery (*Hsüeh-chih shuo-chiu*, p. 7b; *Shu liao wen-ta*, pp. 4a–b; *Mu-ling shu*, 2:13a–b).

102. *Ming hsing kuan-chien lu*, p. 6b.

103. *Meng-hen lu-yü*, A:56a–57; *Shu liao wen-ta*, p. 2; *Mu-ling shu*, 17:3.

104. The punishment ranged from forfeiture of six months' nominal salary to dismissal, varying according to the seriousness of the case: six months' nominal salary in a case involving the penalty of beating or penal servitude; one year's salary in a case involving banishment or exile; demotion of two grades and transfer to another post in a case involving a sentence of strangling or beheading; demotion of two grades and transfer to another post in a case involving a sentence of death by dismemberment; and dismissal in a case of rebellion. The superior officials who were responsible for retrial, as well as the provincial judge, the governor, and the governor-general, were also subject to punishment accordingly (*Li-pu tse-li*, 42:16b–17; *Liu-pu ch'u-fen tse-li*, 48:12a–b).

105. The penalties were as follows: forfeiture of one year's nominal salary for sentencing an innocent person to beating or penal servitude; demotion of one grade and retention in the same post for sentencing to banishment or exile an innocent person or a person deserving beating or penal servitude; demotion of one grade and transfer to another post for sentencing to dismemberment a person deserving strangling or beheading, or for sentencing to immediate execution a man deserving detention for execution; demotion of three grades and transfer to another post for sentencing to strangling or beheading an innocent person or a person deserving banishment or exile; demotion of four grades for sentencing to dismemberment an innocent person or a person deserving banishment or exile. If a death sentence had been carried out, dismissal was the punishment (*Li-pu tse-li*, 42:12a–b; *Liu-pu ch'u-fen tse-li*, 48:9–10). A magistrate was also subject to dismissal if he made a decision carelessly and sentenced a person without justice and evidence (*Ch'ing lü-li*, 37:18).

106. The penalties were as follows: forfeiture of six months' nominal salary for acquitting a person deserving beating or penal servitude; one year's salary

for sentencing to beating or penal servitude, or pronouncing not guilty, a person deserving banishment or exile; the same punishment for sentencing to detention for execution a person deserving immediate execution; demotion of one grade and transfer to another post for sentencing to strangling or beheading a person deserving dismemberment, or for sentencing to banishment or exile a person deserving strangling or beheading, or pronouncing not guilty a person deserving strangling or beheading; demotion of two grades and transfer to another post for sentencing to banishment or exile a person deserving dismemberment, or for pronouncing such a person not guilty (*Li-pu tse-li*, 42:13a–b; *Liu-pu ch'u-fen tse-li*, 48:11a–b).

107. For details see *Li-pu tse-li*, 42:12–13b; *Liu-pu ch'u-fen tse-li*, 48:9–11b, 16a–b, 18a–b.

108. Under the 1740 statute, a magistrate who recommended a wrong sentence could be exempted from impeachment if he corrected the sentence after his superior officials had rejected his sentence and ordered him to retry the case. But the magistrate was to be punished according to the law if he insisted upon his original sentence but was subsequently corrected by a commissioner who retried the case, or if the magistrate's sentence was found incorrect after the case had been reported to the Board of Punishment and closed (*Ch'ing hui-tien shih-li*, 1818, 99:12b–13; *ibid.*, 1899, *chüan* 123; *Li-pu tse-li*, 42:14b–15). It was ruled in 1780 that if the sentence recommended by a magistrate was wrong and was corrected by his superior officials, or if it was rejected by his superiors and subsequently corrected by the magistrate, he was to be punished in the same manner as if a wrong sentence had been rejected by the board and subsequently corrected. Since the regulation concerning the rejection of a sentence by the board was different under the 1773 and 1804 statutes, the magistrate's punishment also differed. Under the 1773 statute, the magistrate was to be demoted or his punishment was to be subject to the consideration of the emperor. Under the 1804 statute the magistrate's punishment was to be one degree less than that stipulated in the law concerning *shih-ch'u* or *shih-ju* (see note 109). But the punishment could not be reduced if the magistrate insisted upon his original recommended sentence after it had been rejected by the superior officials or by a commissioner who retried the case (*Ch'ing hui-tien shih-li*, 1818, 99:23a–b; 649:23a–b; *ibid.*, 1899, *chüan* 123, *chüan* 843; *Liu-pu ch'u-fen tse-li*, 48:16a–b).

109. Under the 1725 statute, a magistrate who tried the case, as well as his superior officials who reviewed and retried it, could be exempted from punishment if the sentence approved by the governor-general and governor was rejected by the Board of Punishment and subsequently, after a retrial, the provincial authorities corrected the sentence; but the governor-general and governor and their subordinate officials who tried the case were subject to punishment if the governor-general and governor insisted upon the original sentence and it was rejected by the board three times (*Ch'ing hui-tien shih-li*, 1818, 99:9a–b; 649:18a–b; *ibid.*, 1899, *chüan* 123; *chüan* 843; *Li-pu tse-li*, 42:14b). In an edict issued in 1773, the emperor held that it was all right to

exempt the governors-general, governors, provincial judges, and intendants from punishment if they corrected a sentence after it had been rejected by the board, but that the magistrate who conducted the trial and the prefect who reviewed the case should be demoted or their punishment be considered by the emperor, depending upon the seriousness of the case. A new statute was formulated in 1804 to the effect that the governors-general, governors, provincial judges, and intendants were to be exempted from punishment under the condition outlined above, and that the magistrates and the prefects who were responsible for a wrong sentence could have their punishment reduced by one degree from the punishment as stipulated in the law concerning *shih-ch'u* or *shih-ju* (*Ch'ing hui-tien shih-li*, 1818, 99:21b–22b; 25b–26; 649:23a–b; *ibid.*, 1899, *chüan* 123, *chüan* 843; *Liu-pu ch'u-fen tse-li*, 48:18a–b).

Under the 1725 statute, the responsible officials were subject to impeachment if they wrongfully sentenced a man deserving the death penalty to exile or banishment, or vice versa. But in a case involving a sentence less severe than exile or banishment, the board would correct the sentence without ordering the provincial authorities to retry the case, and would exempt the responsible officials from impeachment. Under the 1804 statute, however, a magistrate could not have his punishment reduced when the board corrected a wrong sentence without ordering a retrial by the provincial authorities (*Ch'ing hui-tien shih-li*, 1818, 99:9b, 26b; 649:19; *ibid.*, 1899, *chüan* 123, *chüan* 852; *Liu-pu ch'u-fen tse-li*, 48:18b).

110. Although punishment for making a wrong decision, whether *shih-ch'u* or *shih-ju,* was provided in both the Punitive Regulations of the Board of Civil Office (*Li-pu ch'u-fen tse-li*) and the Penal Code (*Ta-Ch'ing lü-li*), ordinary cases of making a wrong decision, as pointed out by the Board of Punishment, were referred to the Board of Civil Office. Only when serious cases were referred to the Board of Punishment by an imperial edict would the officials involved in an impeachment be punished with the corporal punishment stipulated in the Penal Code (*Ting-li hui-pien*, 80:26a–b).

111. In order to figure out this difference, penal servitude was converted into beating, and banishment into penal servitude, in accordance with the following scale. Each half-year of penal servitude was computed as equivalent to 20 strokes, and each 500 li of the distance of banishment as equivalent to a half-year of penal servitude. In addition, 100 strokes were added to every 20 strokes for the magistrate if he had increased a sentence from beating to penal servitude, and 200 strokes were added to every half-year's penal servitude if the prisoner's penalty had been increased from beating or penal servitude to banishment. No additional strokes were given if the increased or decreased sentence had been in the same category. For details, see *Ch'ing lü-li*, 37:2–13b; Staunton, pp. 447–449; Boulais, pp. 717–718.

112. *Ch'ing lü-li*, 37:2a–b, 18.

113. *Ibid.*, 37:4b. A censor mentioned in his memorial in 1833 that as the clerks were never allowed to interfere with the administration, no punishment could be imposed on them when a wrong decision was made by the officials. He

therefore suggested formulating a law to deal with the situation. But the Board of Punishment held that there was no reason why clerks could not be punished, although they were not allowed to interfere with the administration. No special law was therefore necessary (*Ting-li hui-pien*, 80:26a–b). Their arguments seem to imply that, although the law put the principal responsibility on the clerks, the practicality of this law is doubtful.

114. The chief officers (*shou-ling kuan*)—*ching-li* (commissaries of records), *chih-shih* (archivists), *chao-mo* (commissaries of the seal), and *chien-chiao* (prefectural police inspectors)—in a prefecture yamen, and the jail wardens in a chou or hsien yamen (*Ch'ing hui-tien*, 5:13; see above, Chap. I, sec. 3) were incorrectly rendered as "the executive or deputy officer" by Staunton (p. 448).

115. The term "subordinate official" (*tso-erh*), which was rendered by Staunton as "the assessor or assessors of the court" (p. 448) actually refers to the subprefect or assistant magistrate (*Ch'ing hui-tien*, 5:1; see above, Chap. I, sec. 3).

116. The reduction was rather complicated. In a case of aggravation, the clerk's penalty was first reduced by three degrees from the pronounced sentence, and then was finally determined by the difference between the reduction and the sentence which should have been applied to the case. For example, if a man was sentenced through error to 100 strokes whereas he deserved only 30 strokes, the penalty for the clerk, three degrees reduced from the sentence, should be 70 strokes. The difference between 70 and 30, i.e., 40 strokes, would then be the punishment.

In a case of mitigation, the clerk's penalty was first reduced by five degrees from the sentence which should have been applied to the case, and then was finally determined by the difference between the reduction and the pronounced sentence. For example, if a man was sentenced through error to 30 strokes whereas he deserved 100 strokes, the penalty for the clerk, five degrees reduced from the sentence which should have been applied to the case, should be 50 strokes. The difference between 50 and 30, i.e., 20 strokes, would be the punishment for the clerk. For details see *Ch'ing lü-li*, 37:2b, 5, 13b–17; Staunton, p. 448; Boulais, p. 717.

117. *Ch'ing lü-li*, 37:2; Staunton, p. 448; Boulais, p. 717.

CHAPTER VIII. TAXATION

1. *Ch'ing hui-tien*, 18:2a–b.

2. The commissioners (*wei-yüan*) of the provincial likin bureaus, who were appointed by governor-general and governor, were recruited mainly from the intendants, prefects, and magistrates, including both the active and the expectant officials. The *wei-yüan* in turn appointed the commissioners of the numerous branch bureaus and stations (*Ch'ing hsü t'ung-k'ao*, 49:8043, 8045; *Huang-ch'ao cheng-tien lei-tsuan*, 98:1b, 2b, 4a–b, 8, 10, 14; 99:3; 100:5, 10b; *Sheng-shih wei-yen pu-pien*, 5:12; *Ching-shih wen san-pien*, 36:3b, 4b). The principle of "employing both officials and gentry members" (*kuan-shen ping-yung*) was often emphasized by the provincial authorities, and the likin bureau commis-

sioners were instructed to manage together with the local gentry (*Ch'ing hsü t'ung-k'ao*, 49:8042, 8045; *Huang-ch'ao cheng-tien lei-tsuan*, 98:2b, 4a–b, 8a–b, 10a–b; 100:3b–4). Thus many posts in the likin bureaus and stations were occupied by gentry members (*Ch'ing hsü t'ung-k'ao*, 49:8042–43; *Huang-ch'ao cheng-tien lei-tsuan*, 98:8, 12; 99:1, 2b, 3; 100:2, 3b–4; *Lo Wen-chung kung tsou-kao*, 8:48a–b; *Hu Wen-chung kung i-chi*, 24:6). On likin, consult Lo Yü-tung, *Chung-kuo li-chin shih.*

3. Upon the request of a censor, Ting Shao-chou, the 1862 edict ordered that the likin administration be transferred from the commissioners to the local officials, magistrates, or prefect and intendants, depending upon the local situation and the burden of the magistrates. A similar edict was issued in the next year (*Ch'ing shih-lu*, Mu-tsung, 45:23; *Ch'ing hsü t'ung-k'ao*, 49:8042–43; *Ch'ing shih kao*, 132:14b–15). The governor of Hupeh, Yen Shu-sen, memorialized that it was inadvisable to transfer the duty to the overburdened local officials and that the tax collection would fall into the hands of the clerks if such a transfer took place. His request to keep the commissioners in his province was granted (*Ch'ing hsü t'ung-k'ao*, 49:8042). Similar requests also came from the governor of Hunan, Mao Hung-pin, and the governor-general of Szechwan, Lo Ping-chang (*Ch'ing hsü t'ung-k'ao*, 49:8043; *Ching-shih wen hsü-pien*, 25:5–7b; *Huang-ch'ao cheng-tien lei-tsuan*, 98:8–9; 100:3–5).

4. For instance, likin in Honan was under the management of local officials (*Huang-ch'ao cheng-tien lei-tsuan*, 100:2). Kiangsi is reported to have replaced commissioners with local officials (*ibid.*, 100:11a–b). It should be pointed out that the imperial edict of 1862 and the one that succeeded it were ignored by most of the provincial authorities. Li Huang-chang mentioned the employment of commissioners in Kiangsu in his memorial dated 1865. In a memorial presented in 1867, an official in the central government, Wang Jui, stated that the likin bureaus and stations in the various provinces were under the management of commissioners (*Ch'ing hsü t'ung-k'ao*, 49:8043–45). In fact, as is indicated in an imperial edict of 1884 and four memorials presented by certain officials in 1895, 1900, and 1910, the appointment of commissioners continued to be the common pattern in likin administration in the empire (*Ch'ing hsü t'ung-k'ao*, 50:8047, 8051–53, 8055).

5. *Hu-pu tse-li*, 9:17, 18. A a rule, two copies were distributed to each hsien or chou. One was kept by the magistrate, and the other in the office of the director of studies (*Ch'ing shih kao*, 128:19b).

6. As the registration and assessment of the *ting* and their landed property (*pien-shen*) ceased to be taken after 1772 (see below, Chap. IX, sec. 1), no record of increase in *ting* appears in the Complete Books of Taxes and Labor Services after that date. See *Chi-fu fu-i ch'üan-shu, passim; Honan fu-i ch'üan-shu, passim; Chiang-hsi fu-i ch'üan-shu, fan-li,* p. 18b; *Hunan fu-i ch'üan-shu, passim; T'ai-ts'ang-chou fu-i ch'üan shu, passim.*

7. See *Chi-fu fu-i ch'üan-shu; Honan fu-i ch'üan-shu; Chiang-hsi fu-i ch'üan-shu; Hunan fu-i ch'üan-shu; T'ai-ts'ang chou fu-i ch'üan-shu.* For a brief description see *Ch'ing hui-tien* (1690), 24:1–2b; *ibid.* (1732), 31:1b–2; *ibid.* (1764), 10:17.

8. See *Fu-hui ch'üan-shu*, 6:1b; *Hsing-ch'ien pi-lan*, 5:11; *Ch'ien-ku pei-yao*, 1:1b, 2:1a–b; *Ch'ien-ku shih-ch'eng*, p. 4.

9. *Hu-pu tse-li*, 9:18.

10. For instance, according to the preface to *Honan fu-i ch'üan-shu*, the book had been revised in 1837, and not again until 1883.

11. *Ch'ien-ku pei-yao*, 1:1b; *Hsing-ch'ien pi-lan*, 5:11.

12. This was the record which listed all the funds delivered by a provincial government to the Board of Revenue (*Ch'ing hui-tien* [1690], 24:4; *ibid.* [1732], 31:4; *Ch'ing shih kao*, 128:1b; *Shih-ch'ü yü-chi*, 3:18). According to the last source, the preparation of this sort of record was suspended in 1688, and the list of funds was incorporated into the *tsou-hsiao ts'e* (see n. 13).

13. This was the annual report presented to the Board of Revenue by the provincial government for inspection and approval. It gave the amounts of land-and-labor-service tax collected and uncollected, and the amounts delivered to the superior yamen or kept by the local government. See *Ch'ing hui-tien* (1690), 24:3; *ibid.* (1764), 10:14a–b; *ibid.* (1899), 19:13a–b; *Ch'ing shih kao*, 128:1b; *Shih-ch'ü yü-chi*, 3:18; *Hsing-ch'ien pi-lan*, 6:8a–b.

14. According to Wang Yu-huai, there were the *K'uan-mu ts'e* (bill of items) and the account book in Kiangsu and Anhui, and the *Yin-mi k'uan-mu* (items of silver and rice) and *K'o-tse yu-tan* (list of tax items) in Chekiang (*Ch'ien-ku pei-yao*, 11:1b).

15. *Fu-hui ch'üan-shu*, 5:6; *Ch'ien-ku pei-yao*, 11:1b; *Ch'ien-ku shih-ch'eng*, pp. 4–5.

16. See above, Chap. VI, sec. 2.

17. *Fu-hui ch'üan-shu*, 3:17; *Liu-pu ch'eng-yü chu-chieh*, pp. 33–34.

18. For the rates in different provinces, see *Hu-pu tse-li*, 5:9–23b; for the rates in different localities in each province, see the Complete Book of Taxes and Labor Services of each province.

19. *Ch'ing hui-tien* (1764), 9:4b, reads: "The *ting* [male adults] pay money by heads in lieu of labor service. . . [This] is called *yao-yin* [labor service money]." See also *Ch'ing hui-tien* (1818), 11:15b; *ibid.* (1899), 18:1b–2; *Ch'ing t'ung-k'ao*, 19:5023; *Shih-ch'ü yü-chi*, 3:11, 12b.

20. *Ch'ing t'ung-k'ao*, 19:5023. For the rates in different provinces, see *Hu-pu tse-li*, 6:1–7; for the rates in various localities in each province see the Complete Book of Taxes and Labor Services of each province.

21. It is mentioned in *Ch'ing hui-tien* (1690), 23:1; *ibid.* (1732), 30:1; *ibid.* (1818), 11:15; *Ch'ing t'ung-k'ao*, 19:5023; *Shih-ch'ü yü-chi*, 3:10b–11, that the collection of labor-service tax either varied according to the three grades and nine divisions or was evenly distributed among the taxpayers; but no details as to the different practices in different regions are given in these sources. According to *Fu-hui ch'üan-shu*, 9:2b, the three grades and nine divisions were in practice in the north, whereas the adults in the south were classified as urban or rural population (*shih-min* and *hsiang-min*).

Our conclusion on regional differences is based upon the following *Fu-i ch'üan-shu* and local gazetteers: (1) Regions where labor-service tax was divided into grades and divisions: *Chi-fu fu-i ch'üan-shu, passim; Honan fu-i ch'üan-shu, passim; Shansi t'ung-chih,* 58:9; *Yang-ch'ü hsien-chih,* 4:5a–b; *Shensi t'ung-chih, chüan* 24, 25; *San-yüan hsien-chih,* 3:99b; *Hsien-yang hsien-chih,* 3:2; *Kansu t'ung-chih, chüan* 13; *Kung-ch'ang fu-chih,* 12:2 ff; *Ching-chou chih,* A:24a–b; *Ning-yüan hsien-chih,* 3:1b. (2) *Shantung t'ung-chih,* 12:2b, states that in some chou and hsien the rates for *ting* tax were classified into grades and divisions, and that in other chou and hsien such classification was absent. For instance, Chü-chou and Lai-yang used the classification (*Chü-chou chih,* 3:2a–b; *Lai-yang hsien-chih,* 3:7–8b); Kao-mi, Ting-t'ao, and Shou-chang did not (*Kao-mi hsien-chih,* 3:6a–b; *Ting-t'ao hsien-chih,* 3:1b; *Shou-chang hsien-chih,* 5:1b). (3) Regions where labor-service tax was not divided into grades and divisions: *Chiang-nan t'ung-chih* (1736), 74:8 ff; 75:1 ff; *Anhui t'ung-chih,* 74:5b ff; *T'ai-ts'ang chou fu-i ch'üan-shu, passim; Chiang-hsi fu-i ch'üan-shu, passim; Che-chiang t'ung-chih,* 71:9 ff; 72:2b ff; 73:2b ff; *P'u-t'ien hsien-chih,* 5:24b; *Tang-yang hsien-chih,* 4:3b; *Hunan fu-i ch'üan-shu, passim; Hunan t'ung-chih* (1757), 23:9b ff; *P'an-yü hsien-chih,* 9:1b; *P'ing-lo hsien-chih,* 3:1; *Hua-yang hsien-chih,* 8:2.

22. *Ch'ing hui-tien* (1690), 23:1; 16b–17b; *ibid.* (1732), 30:24a–b, 27a–b; *ibid.* (1764), 9:4b–5; *ibid.* (1818), 11:3a–b, 15; *ibid.* (1899), 18:1a–b; *Ch'ing lü-li,* 8:6b; *Ch'ing t'ung-k'ao,* 19:5024–26; *Shih-ch'ü yü-chi,* 3:14b. See also below, Chap. IX, sec. 1, and Ho Ping-ti, *Studies in the Population of China, 1368–1953* (Cambridge, Mass., 1959), chap. 2.

23. *Ch'ing hui-tien* (1764), 9:4b–5; *ibid.* (1818), 11:15a–b; *ibid.* (1899), 18:1b; *Ch'ing hui-tien shih-li* (1818), 133:11b ff; *Ch'ing t'ung-k'ao,* 19:5023. The practice of incorporating labor-service tax into land tax (*ting sui ti p'ai*) was already existent in Kwangtung in 1716 and in part of Szechwan in the latter years of K'ang-hsi (the exact year is unknown). It was extended to other provinces in the period between 1723 and 1729 (Chihli in 1723; Fukien in 1724; Shantung in 1725; Honan, Chekiang, Shensi, Kansu, Szechwan, and Yünnan in 1726; Kiangsu and Kiangsi in 1727; Hunan and Kwangsi in 1728; Hupeh in 1729). The practice did not reach Kweichow until 1777. See *Ch'ing hui-tien tse-li,* 33:10b ff; *Ch'ing hui-tien shih-li* (1818), 133:11b ff; *Ch'ing t'ung-k'ao,* 19:5023, 5026; *Shih-ch'ü yü-chi,* 3:22 ff; *Huang-Ch'ing tsou-i,* 56:19–23.

The merging of land tax and labor-service tax in Shansi underwent a long process, being effected in several chou and hsien at a time. According to Wang Ch'ing-yün, it began in 1736, and continued throughout the Ch'ien-lung, Chia-ch'ing, and Tao-kuang periods, until 1837. But owing to complications in Shansi, the combination did not take place in all chou and hsien. Instead, three different practices existed in this province: (1) separate collection of labor-service tax and land tax (e.g., Yang-ch'ü); (2) incorporation of a part of the labor-service tax into land tax (e.g., Chiao-ch'eng); (3) incorporation of all labor-service taxes into land tax (e.g., T'ai-yüan). See *Ch'ing hui-tien tse-li,* 33:14b ff; *Ch'ing hui-tien shih-li* (1818), 133:15b ff; *Ch'ing t'ung-k'ao,* 19:5029. For a highly detailed study of this subject see *Shih-ch'ü yü-chi,* 3:28–36b, for which the author, Wang Ch'ing-yün, had consulted the Complete Book of Taxes and Labor Services for Shansi and other official documents in addition to the *Hui-tien shih-li* and *Ch'ing t'ung-k'ao*.

24. Customarily the magistrate, after deducting from the *hao-hsien* for his own supplementary salary and that of other officials serving in the hsien or chou, and also for wages for his runners, delivered the remainder to the provincial treasurer. See Chap. II, n. 63, for magistrates' office expenses paid from *hao-hsien*.

25. In Kwangtung, the collection began in the seventh month, and in Yünnan and Kweichow in the ninth month.

26. A few exceptions may be cited: In Kiangsu, Shensi, and Szechwan, half of the land-and-labor-service tax was to be collected at the end of the seventh month; in Kwangtung, at the end of the eighth month; in Yünnan and Kweichow, at the end of the year.

The regulation governing the collection of half of the land-and-labor-service tax was not very strict. It permitted tax amounting to less than one tael of silver to be handed in through the eighth month (*Liu-pu ch'u-fen tse-li*, 25:1). Hsieh Ming-huang, a private secretary of taxation in the eighteenth century, pointed out that the regulation governing the collection of half of the tax in the fourth month pertained mainly to large taxpayers, and that small taxpayers were allowed to pay their taxes within the year or even just prior to the submission of the provincial annual expenditure report (*tsou-hsiao*) in the following spring (*Ch'ien-ku shih-ch'eng*, p. 19b).

27. In Fukien, however, the collection was resumed in the seventh month. In Shantung, Honan, and in some places in Anhui (Lu-chou, Feng-yang, Ying-chou, and Ssu-chou), tax might be collected in the six and seventh months (*Ch'ing hui-tien*, 18:11a-b).

28. *Ch'ing hui-tien*, 18:11a-b; *Hu-pu tse-li*, 9:5b-6; *Liu-pu ch'u-fen tse-li*, 25:1. In Kwangtung, the collection ended in the first month of the next year; in Yünnan and Kweichow, it ended in the second month of the next year.

29. If the original deficiency was less than ten per cent, the magistrate was demoted one grade at the end of the extension, but was kept in the same post and given a second extension of one year to collect the tax. He was actually demoted and transferred to another post at the end of the second extension if he had still failed to collect. If the original deficiency was ten per cent, the magistrate was demoted three grades and transferred to another post at the expiration of the one-year extension. If the original deficiency was twenty or thirty per cent, he was demoted four or five grades respectively and transferred to another post at the end of the extension period. If the original deficiency was more than forty per cent, he was dismissed at the end of the extension period (*Li-pu tse-li*, 23:1, 2a-b; *Liu-pu ch'u-fen tse-li*, 25:7, 8a-b).

30. For details see *Li-pu tse-li*, 23:1-3b; *Liu-pu ch'u-fen tse-li*, 25:7-9.

31. A much lower standard prevailed in the Ming. Officials who were able to collect seventy or eighty per cent of the tax quota were considered to have

done fairly well. According to Mu T'ien-yen, who served as the provincial treasurer of Kiangsu (1670–1675), an earlier Ch'ing regulation in the reign of Shun-chih was also more lenient. Officials at that time could avoid impeachment if the deficiency was less than ten per cent (*Tzu-chih hsin-shu*, 1:38; cf. Jen Yüan-hsiang's statement in *Ching-shih wen-pien*, 28:2b).

32. Mu T'ien-yen, in *Tzu-chih hsin-shu*, 1:38b, 39b.

33. Han Shih-ch'i, governor of Kiangsu 1662–1669, in *ibid.*, 1:7.

34. *Ibid.*, 1:7, 36a–b.

35. Under a regulation of 1665, a magistrate who collected land tax and labor-service tax in full quota was rewarded with one to three recordings of merit, depending upon the total amount of tax collected (*Ch'ing hui-tien shih-li* [1818], 85:3b; *Li-pu tse-li*, 23:18). A more generous reward, including advancement of grade, was prescribed in 1799, and revised in 1816 as follows.

Amount of tax collected (*in taels*)	Reward
300–less than 10,000	1 recording of merit
10,000–less than 20,000	2 recordings of merit
20,000–less than 30,000	3 recordings of merit
30,000–less than 50,000	Advancement of 1 grade
50,000–less than 80,000	Advancement of 2 grades
80,000 and above	Immediate promotion before completion of current term

See *Ch'ing hui-tien shih-li* (1818), 85:3b; *ibid.* (1899), *chüan* 107. For the revised regulation of 1849 concerning an additional reward for collecting a full quota of tax for more than two years, see *Liu-pu ch'u-fen tse-li*, 25:4–6b. Rewards were also given to the superior officials, from independent department magistrates to governors-general, if the land-and-labor-service tax in the area under their jurisdiction was collected in full quota (*Ch'ing hui-tien shih-li* [1818], 85:3b–4, 13a–b; *ibid.* [1899], *chüan* 107; *Li-pu tse-li*, 23:18a–b; *Liu-pu ch'u-fen tse-li*, 25:5a–b).

36. *Tzu-chih hsin-shu*, 1:39a–b; *Che-sheng ts'ang-k'u ch'ing-ch'a chieh-yao*, p. 22.

37. *Ping-t'a meng-hen lu*, B:33; *Tzu-chih hsin-shu*, 1:6; *Liu-pu ch'u-fen tse-li*, 25:51a–b.

38. *Mu-ling shu*, 11:39; *Tzu-chih hsin-shu*, 13:11.

39. *Fu-hui ch'üan-shu*, 6:9–11; *Fu-weng chi*, ch'ien-ku, 1:17b.

40. The tax notice was to be issued before the collection, and a sample was sent to the Board of Revenue within a specified time (*Ch'ing hui-tien* [1690], 24:5–6b; *ibid.* [1732], 31:5–7; *Li-pu tse-li*, 23:25b–26; *Ch'ing shih kao*, 128:1b).

41. *Ch'ing hui-tien* (1690), 24:5, 6; *ibid.* (1732), 31:5, 6a–b; *Shih-ch'ü yü-chi*, 3:18b; *Ch'ing shih kao*, 128:1b.

42. *Ch'ing hui-tien* (1732), 31:7b–8; *Shih-ch'ü yü-chi*, 3:18b.

43. *Hsing-ch'ien pi-lan*, 5:22; *Sung-chün chün-i ch'eng-shu*, ts'e 1:44b–45; 5:159b, 164b. However, the number of deadlines, as well as the percentage to be collected each month, might be adjusted according to the climate of a particular area (*Fu-hui ch'üan-shu*, 7:5b). Taking the practice of Huang

Liu-hung as an example, the tax, which was divided into ten equal parts, was to be paid within nine main deadlines and sixteen minor deadlines (one minor deadline for the fourth and fifth months and two for the other months), beginning with the second month and ending in the tenth month.

Deadlines	Percentage due
1 (2nd month)	20
2 (3rd month)	10
3 (4th month)	10
4 (5th month)	5
5 (6th month)	5
6 (7th month)	15
7 (8th month)	15
8 (9th month)	10
9 (10th month)	10

For details see *Fu-hui ch'üan-shu*, 7:1b–2, 4a–b. In a different system, there were three minor deadlines in each month (*Sung-chün chün-i ch'eng-shu, ts'e* 1:44b; 2:50a–b; 5:164b; *Hsing-ch'ien pi-lan*, 5:4).

44. *Fu-hui ch'üan-shu*, 7:3b–6b.

45. *Tzu-chih hsin-shu*, 12:20b.

46. *Hu-pu tse-li*, 12:45b; *P'ei-yüan-t'ang ou-ts'un kao*, 18:34–35; *Mu-ling shu*, 11:39b.

47. *Fu-hui ch'üan-shu*, 6:4b.

48. This procedure was known as *tzu-feng t'ou-kuei* (sealed by taxpayer himself and inserted into the silver chest). See *Ch'ing hui-tien* (1732), 31:21a–b, 27b–28; *ibid.* (1899), 18:1b; *Hu-pu tse-li*, 9:6b; *Fu-hui ch'üan-shu*, 6:4a–b; *Sung-chün chün-i ch'eng-shu, ts'e* 5:159b; *Fu-weng yü-chi*, p. 22.

49. The land-and-labor-service tax receipt, *ch'uan-p'iao*, or *chieh-p'iao*, was in two, three, or four parts. The two-part receipt (one part was given to the taxpayer) was first introduced in 1653, but was abolished in 1689. It was replaced by a three-part form consisting of the stub kept by the government (*p'iao-ken*), the receipt given to the taxpayer (*na-hu chih-chao*), and the deadline-hearing certificate (*pi-chao* or *pi-hsien ch'a-chieh*), which was given to the runner or tax agent. The four-part receipt, introduced in 1725, included a certificate sent to the prefectural yamen. This form was abolished in 1730, and the three-part form was again used. However, according to *Hsing-ch'ien pi-lan*, a four-part form, which included a canceling certificate (*hsiao-chao*, a form canceling the record of an overdue tax), was still in use after 1730. See *Ch'ing hui-tien* (1690), 24:3b; *ibid.* (1732), 31:19–21, 22b–23; *Ch'ing hui-tien tse-li*, 36:25b–26b, 27b–28; *Ch'ing hui-tien shih-li* (1818), 143:22b–23, 24a–b; *Hu-pu tse-li*, 9:7; *Ch'ing t'ung-k'ao*, 2:4866; *Shih-ch'ü yü-chi*, 3:18b–19; *Hsing-ch'ien pi-lan*, 5:25a–b; *Fu-hui ch'üan-shu*, 6:7b–8; *Ch'ing shih kao*, 128:3. For a description of the form see *Fu-hui ch'üan-shu*, 7:7b–8; *Sung-chün chün-i ch'eng-shu, ts'e* 2:50a–b.

50. H. B. Morse, comp., "Currency and Measures in China," *Journal of the China Branch of the Royal Asiatic Society*, new series, 24:58 ff. (1889–90).

51. *Ch'ing hui-tien*, 18:11b; *Hu-pu tse-li*, 9:8b; *Fu-hui ch'üan-shu*, 6:19b. Wang Yu-huai reported that the clerks in charge of silver chests often cooperated with the authorized silversmith and would not accept any silver without the seal of the silversmith (*Hsing-ch'ien pi-lan*, 5:21).

52. *Ch'in-pan chou-hsien shih-i*, pp. 12b, 46; *Fu-hui ch'üan-shu*, 6:19b; *Hsing-ch'ien pi-lan*, 5:21.

53. *Fu-hui ch'üan-shu*, 6:20.

54. *Ch'ing hui-tien*, 18:11b; *Hu-pu tse-li*, 9:7b; *Ch'ing shih kao*, 128:7.

55. According to *Ch'ing shih kao*, 128:9b–10, this practice became prevalent after the Ch'ien-lung and Chia-ch'ing periods. See also *P'ei-yüan-t'ang ou-ts'un kao*, 21:18.

56. According to Wang Hui-tsu, 180–190 coins were demanded from taxpayers in lieu of one *ch'ien* of silver in 1799 in Hsiao-shan, Chekiang, whereas the market rate was only 108.1. Wang states that the magistrate was ordered by an edict to reduce the "conversion rate" to the market rate; instead, the magistrate set the rate at 136 coins. Many taxpayers were willing to pay this, but several months later the rate was again raised, this time to 150–160 coins (*Meng-hen lu-yü*, pp. 34b–35). It was reported to the emperor that 3100–3200 coins had been collected in lieu of one *liang* of silver in Shantung during the Chia-ch'ing period (1796–1820) and that the rate was increased to 4000 in 1828 (e.g., 4200 in Ning-hai and 4260 in Chu-ch'eng), whereas the market rate at that time was only 2600. In 1879, 2000 to 2200 coins were collected in lieu of one *liang* of silver in Hsin-cheng and other places in Honan where the market rate was 1400 (*Ch'ing hsü t'ung-k'ao*, 2:7511–2). For additional information on the "conversion rate" in other provinces, see *Mu-ling shu*, 3:12b; 8:21; *Ch'ing lü-li*, 11:44b; *Hsien-chih-t'ang kao*, 5:33b; Morse, *Trade and Administration*, pp. 88–89.

57. *Mu-ling shu*, 3:12b.

58. *Ming-lü chi-chieh*, 4:20; *Ming shih*, 78:7b; *Ch'ing hui-tien* (1764), 9:4b; *Ch'ing hui-tien shih-li* (1818), 133:10b; *Ch'ing lü-li*, 8:47–48; *Ch'ing t'ung-k'ao*, 19:5024, 21:5045; *Ch'ing shih kao*, 128:11; *Fu-hui ch'üan-shu*, 6:2; *Mu-ling shu*, 11:19a–b, 20; *Ching-shih wen-pien*, 29:1; *Chiang-nan t'ung-chih*, 76:14; *Lou-hsien chih*, 7:2b. On the *li-chia* system in Ming times see Liang Fang-chung, *Single-whip Method*, pp. 5, 56–57, and *Ming-tai liang-chang chih-tu*, pp. 86 ff. On the *li-chia's* role in tax collection in the Ch'ing see Hsiao, *Rural China*, pp. 95 ff.

It may be noted that the details relating to *li-chia* units which were prescribed by the government were by no means uniformly followed in all places. In fact, the number of households in a *chia* as well as the number of *chia* in a *li* might deviate from the official system. In a detailed study based upon the local gazetteers, Hsiao found that whereas the *li-chia* system in the Northern provinces conformed to the official pattern more consistently, wide divergences appeared in the South, where a *li* was generally designated as *t'u* (Appendix I, *Rural China*, pp. 521 ff. See also my note on the usage of *t'u* in Chiang-nan and Chekiang, Chap. I, n. 10).

59. *Fu-hui ch'üan-shu*, 6:2, 11.

60. See above, n. 49.

61. For details see *Fu-hui ch'üan-shu*, 6:14b; 7:2b, 4–8b; *Sung-chün chün-i ch'eng-shu, ts'e* 2:51; *Lou-hsien chih*, 7:2b.

62. *Fu-hui ch'üan-shu*, 6:12b, 14b–15.

63. *Ibid.*, 6:18b–19; *Mu-ling shu*, 11:13; *Tzu-chih hsin-shu*, 1:2; *Chiang-nan t'ung-chih*, 68:6b; 76:14.

64. *Fu-hui ch'üan-shu*, 6:15.

65. *Ibid.* However, according to Chia Han-fu (1606–1677), governor of Shensi, since it was beneficial to both the magistrate and the runners, some officials still assigned *hsien-nien* privately, despite the edict which ordered their abolition (*Tzu-chih hsin-shu*, 13:2 ff). A similar observation was made by Li Wei, governor-general of Chekiang (*Ch'in pan chou-hsien shih-i*, p. 54). The following case illustrates the reluctance of magistrates to abolish the system which had been in practice since the Ming dynasty. In 1684 an order was issued by the governor-general of Chiang-nan and Kiangsi, Yü Ch'eng-lung (1617–1684), abolishing the system of *hsien-nien*. Yet two years later, it was discovered that *hsien-nien* were still employed in Kao-ch'un hsien, and the provincial treasurer was instructed by the governor, T'ang Pin, to enforce the edict by engraving the order of prohibition on stone tablets placed in Kao-ch'un and other chou and hsien. However, the system was still maintained in two hsien—Wu-hsi and Chin-kuei. The local gentry made an appeal in 1837 requesting its abolition, but the request was rejected by the two magistrates. The gentry then appealed to the governor, who ordered the provincial treasurer to investigate. In the end the two magistrates won and were permitted by their superior to continue to employ *hsien-nien* regardless of the edicts and the complaints of the local gentry (see *Chiang-nan t'ung-chih*, 76:14a–b; *Hsi-Chin chih-wai*, 5:1–6).

66. *Fu-hui ch'üan-shu*, 6:13–14; *Hsing-ch'ien pi-lan*, 5:5–6.

67. *Fu-hui ch'üan-shu*, 6:12b–14.

68. *Ibid.*, 6:13b–14b.

69. *Ibid.*, 6:11b–12, 15a–b, 18b; *Hsüeh-chih i-shuo*, B:7; *Hsing-ch'ien pi-lan*, 5:16; *Mu-ling shu*, 11:20; *Ching-shih wen-pien*, 29:12b.

70. *Ch'ing-hui-tien* (1732), 31:21a–b; *ibid.* (1764), 10:16a–b; *Hu-pu tse-li*, 9:6a–b; *Shih-ch'ü yü-chi*, 8:19; *Fu-hui ch'üan-shu*, 6:14a–b; *Fu-weng chi, ch'ien-ku*, 1:8, 9–10b, 12a–b; *Hsing-ch'ien pi-lan*, 5:21; *Mu-ling shu*, 11:16a–b, 18, 23b–24; *Tzu-chih hsin-shu*, 1:8b–9; *Shih-hsüeh ta-sheng*, 10:1 ff, 12 ff, 26 ff; *Ch'ien-ku pei-yao*, 1:7; *Ch'ing shih kao*, 128:3.

71. *Hsüeh-chih t'i-hsing lu*, B:19.

72. *Ch'in-pan chou-hsien shih-i*, p. 12a–b; *Mu-ling shu*, 11:15b, 17b–18, 33; *Tzu-chih hsin-shu*, 10:12; *Hsing-ch'ien pi-lan*, 5:21; *Mu-hsüeh chü-yao*, p. 20.

73. *Hsing-ch'ien pi-lan*, 5:6. Wang Hui-tsu reported that a runner was stationed in each of the thirty-six *li* in Ning-yüan hsien, Hunan (*Hsüeh-chih i-shuo*, B:7). Similar information was offered by another magistrate in Hunan,

Yüan Shou-ting, who then decided to stop assigning such runners (*T'u-min lu*, 3:28).

74. *Ch'in-pan chou-hsien shih-i*, p. 12; *Hsing-ch'ien pi-lan*, 5:21b; *Ch'ien-ku shih-ch'eng*, p. 15b; *Mu-ling shu*, 11:17a–b.

75. *Mu-hsüeh chü-yao*, p. 2b. According to Huang K'o-jun (*chin-shih* 1739), Ting-chou was the only place in Chihli where this system had been in practice continuously (*Mu-ling shu*, 11:33b).

76. *Hu-pu tse-li*, 9:7b.

77. For the form of the deadline-hearing record, see *Fu-hui chüan-shu*, 7:3b–5.

78. See above, Chap. VI, sec. 2.

79. See above, Chap. VI, sec. 2.

80. *Hsing-chien pi-lan*, 5:25b; *Hsüeh-chih t'i-hsing lu*, B:19; *Mu-ling shu*, 11:36. According to *Ch'ien-ku shih-ch'eng*, pp. 20b–21b, at the beginning of tax collection a notice of payment due was issued to the taxpayers. No action was taken until the second half of the third month, when about half of the largest taxpayers (*ta-hu*) were called for a hearing; ten days later, about half of the medium large taxpayers (*chung-ta hu*) were called. All the largest taxpayers were again called in the first ten days of the ninth month, and then all the medium large taxpayers who had been called in the spring and the middle taxpayers who had not yet been called were summoned. In the first ten days of the tenth month, all the small taxpayers were called. At that time, all taxpayers, whether large or small, who had failed to pay their overdue taxes, were summoned to appear for flogging.

81. *Fu-hui ch'üan-shu*, 6:13b, 17; 7:8a–b, 9b; *Mu-hsüeh chü-yao*, p. 20b.

82. *Hsing-ch'ien pi-lan*, 5:6a–b.

83. *Fu-hui ch'üan-shu*, 6:12b, 14b; 7:9b; *Mu-hsüeh chü-yao*, p. 20b.

84. *Fu-hui ch'üan-shu*, 7:8b, 9b, 12; *Fu-weng chi, ch'ien-ku*, 1:10b, 12b; *Ch'ien-ku pei-yao*, 1:6b; *Hsing-ch'ien pi-lan*, 5:23; *Mu-hsüeh chü-yao*, p. 20b.

85. *Hsiao-ts'ang shan-fang wen-chi*, 18:9b–10.

86. *P'ei-yüan-t'ang ou-ts'un kao*, 46:39b–40.

87. *Ch'in-pan chou-hsien shih-i*, pp. 13, 44a–b; *P'ei-yüan-t'ang ou-ts'un kao*, 46:39b; *Mu-ling shu*, 11:14; *Tzu-chih hsin-shu*, 1:3.

88. *Ch'in-pan chou-hsien shih-i*, pp. 10b–11; *Mu-ling shu*, 11:12b; *Tzu-chih hsin-shu*, 1:1.

89. *Hsüeh-chih i-shuo*, B:7b. Wang Feng-sheng said he knew that the poor people should be pitied, but since the government regulation required them to pay tax on time, there was nothing he could do (*Hsüeh-chih t'i-hsing lu*, B:19b).

90. *P'ing-p'ing yen*, 4:61.

91. *Hsüeh-chih hsü-shuo*, p. 12.

92. *Fu-hui ch'üan-shu*, 7:10a–b; *T'ien-tai chih-lüeh*, 5:22b; *Tzu-chih hsin-shu*, 1:3b.

93. See above, Chap. I, sec. 4.

94. *Ch'ing shih-lu; Kao-tsung*, 46:6a–b; *Hu-pu tse-li*, 9:17.

95. *Hu-pu tse-li*, 9:17.

96. *Ibid.*, 9:5b–6, 14. Delay incurred punishment ranging from forfeiture of nominal salary to demotion of three grades and transfer to another post (*Liu-pu ch'u-fen tse-li*, 23:3).

97. See above, Chap. V, sec. 2.

98. The magistrate who made the delivery was responsible for sixty per cent of the lost funds, and the magistrate of the locality within which the accident took place was responsible for the remaining forty per cent. If the local magistrate had not provided an escort, as he should have, he was liable for one half of the loss. The magistrate who made the delivery was held solely responsible if he had failed to request an escort from the local magistrate or had allowed his runners to take a short cut (*Hu-pu tse-li*, 9:16a–b).

99. Millet and black beans were collected in Shantung and Honan in addition to rice. Glutinous rice (*pai-liang*) was also collected in addition to the regular nonglutinous rice in some places in Kiangsu and Chekiang (*Hu-pu tse-li*, 19:10b–11; *Shih-ch'ü yü-chi*, 4:3a–b).

100. Sea transport was used only in 1826. In 1848 it was again used for grain tribute in the areas of Su-chou, Sung-chiang, Ch'ang-chou, Chen-chiang, and T'ai-ts'ang. From that year on it was in use periodically until the end of the dynasty. For details see *Ch'ing hui-tien shih-li*, *chüan* 210–213; *Ch'ing shih kao*, 129:19 ff; H. C. Hinton, *The Grain Tribute System of China (1845–1911)* (Harvard University, East Asian Research Center, 1956), pp. 23–27, 76 ff.

101. *Hu-pu tse-li*, 19:11.

102. See *ibid.*, 19:11–13b.

103. *Ibid.*, 19:14–15b; *Shih-ch'ü yü-chi*, 4:3b, 11a–b.

104. *Hu-pu tse-li*, 19:3b, 17–18b; *Shih-ch'ü yü-chi*, 4:3b–4.

105. *Hu-pu tse-li*, 19:19–22b.

106. For details see *Hu-pu ts'ao-yün ch'üan-shu*, 9:13 ff; *Hu-pu tse-li*, 19:9, 23b–25; *Shih-ch'ü yü-chi*, 4:4b–5; *Hsing-ch'ien pi-lan*, 6:10b–12.

107. *Hsien-chih-t'ang kao*, 5:37b.

108. *Ch'ing shih-lu*, Hsüan-tsung, 111:16b; *T'ao Yün-t'ing hsien-sheng tsou-su*, 17:8a–b; 19:21b; *Hsien-chih-t'ang kao*, 9:23, 26.

109. Thus the amount of extra surcharge collected by local officials varied not only among provinces but also among localities within the same province (*Hsien-chih-t'ang kao*, 5:31a–b).

110. *Shih-ch'ü yü-chi*, 4:5b.

111. *Mu-ling shu*, 11:46.

112. The law permitted taxpayers to use a wooden bar to strike at the upper edge of the grain container so that a fair measure could be made. If a grain measurer denied them this right, and, instead, shook the grain into as small a compass as possible or piled the grain into a heap in order to collect more grain, he was to be punished with 60 to 100 strokes. If a grain measurer applied the excess to his own advantage, he was to be punished in accordance with the law concerning embezzlement of government property. The magistrate who

connived at this practice was to be punished in the same way as the grain measurer (*Ch'ing lü-li*, 11:42a–b; *Liu-pu ch'u-fen tse-li*, 46:5b–6; Staunton, pp. 126–127; Boulais, p. 314).

113. *Ch'ing lü-li*, 46:5b–6; *Ch'ing shih kao*, 128:8. According to Wang Hui-tsu, in the early years of Ch'ien-lung, magistrates who collected grain that was "one or one-half finger higher than evenly full" were impeached; but after 1764 the grain was collected on a twenty to thirty per cent discount basis (*Ping-t'a meng-hen lu*, A:33).

114. *P'ing-ta meng-hen lu*, A:34; *Shih-ch'ü yü-chi*, 4:5a–b; *Hsien chih-t'ang kao*, 5:36a–b; *Mu-ling shu*, 11:47b.

115. *Ch'ing shih kao*, 128:8.

116. *Hsien-chih-t'ang kao*, 5:36a–b.

117. *Hu-pu tse-li*, 19:3b; 24:1.

118. *Ch'ing shih kao*, 129:3.

119. See *Hsien-chih-t'ang kao*, 10:2b, on the selling of collected grain to rice shops.

120. *Mu-ling shu*, 11:47, 50. According to Tseng Kuo-fan (1811–1872), in most cases grain tribute was collected in cash. Eevn when it was collected in kind, the part covering the cost of collection (i.e., the extra surcharges) was always collected in cash (*Tseng Wen-cheng chi, tsou-kao*, 1:36b).

121. *Ch'ing shih kao*, 128:10.

122. *Ch'ing t'ung-k'ao*, 2:7512.

123. *Ch'ing shih kao*, 128:9b–10; *Hu Wen-chung chi*, 26:4.

124. *Hsien-chih-t'ang kao*, 5:33. This, however, was the highest rate. Some taxpayers paid only 2 to 2.5 piculs for 1 picul of grain (*ibid.*, 5:31b; 10:1; for different rates imposed on taxpayers with different statutes see below, Chap. X, sec. 7).

125. *Liu-pu ch'u-fen tse-li*, 25:1; *Ch'ing lü-li*, 11:8a–b; *P'ei-yüan-t'ang ou-ts'un kao*, 46:33b; Staunton, pp. 125–126.

126. *Li-pu tse-li*, 23:4 ff; *Liu-pu ch'u-fen tse-li*, 25:16a–b.

127. *Hu-pu ts'ao-yün ch'üan-shu*, 9:3; *Ch'ien-ku shih-ch'eng*, pp. 19b–20, 22a–b; *Fu-hui ch'üan-shu*, 8:3; *Mu-ling shu*, 11:51a–b. According to Chen Hung-mou, the selection of delinquent taxpayers for flogging took place at the end of the tenth month (*P'ei-yüan-t'ang ou-ts'un kao*, 46:33b–34).

128. *Fu-hui ch'üan-shu*, 8:1b–2; *Mu-ling shu*, 11:45b.

129. *P'ei-yüan-t'ang ou-ts'un kao*, 25:45.

130. *Li-pu tse-li*, 16:8; *Liu-pu ch'u-fen tse-li*, 25:55; *Hu-pu tse-li*, 19:1a–b; *Fu-hui ch'üan-shu*, 8:3; *Hsing-ch'ien pi-lan*, 6:14.

131. *Hu-pu tse-li*, 19:1b–2. The magistrate was punishable by dismissal if the collected grain was spoiled by moisture or mildew (*Liu-pu ch'u-fen tse-li*, 18:6).

132. *Fu-hui ch'üan-shu*, 8:4b.

133. *Hu-pu tse-li*, 19:1; *Hu-pu ts'ao-yün ch'üan-shu*, 9:2, 5b, 6b–7; *P'ei-yüan-t'ang ou-ts'un kao*, 18:19b; 25:43.

134. *Hu-pu tse-li*, 24:2a–b; *Ch'ing lü-li*, 11:42a–b; Staunton, pp. 126–127; *P'ei-yüan-t'ang ou-ts'un k̩ao*, 25:43b.

135. See the experience related by Wang Chih, in *Mu-ling shu*, 11:40a–b.

136. *Hu-pu tse-li*, 19:1b, 24:1b; *Hu-pu ts'ao-yün ch'üan-shu*, 9:5; *Fu-hui ch'üan-shu*, 8:4b.

137. *Ch'in-pan chou-hsien shih-i*, p. 47a–b.

138. Chen Hung-mou instructed the magistrates to supervise the collection at the granary located in the district seat as often as possible and to bring their documents to the rural granaries so that they could attend to official business there (*P'ei-yüan-t'ang ou-ts'un k̩ao*, 25:45b).

139. *Ch'in-pan chou-hsien shih-i*, p. 47; *P'ei-yüan-t'ang ou-ts'un k̩ao*, 25:45a–b; *Hu-pu ts'ao-yün ch'üan-shu*, 9:5.

140. See above, Chap. V. sec. 5.

141. *Mu-ling shu*, 11:4b.

142. *Hu-pu ts'ao-yün ch'üan-shu*, 9:1; *Ch'ing shih k̩ao*, 129:4; *Shih-ch'ü yü-chi*, 4:5; *Fu-hui ch'üan-shu*, 8:1, 3b–4.

143. *Hu-pu tse-li*, 20:8; *Hu-pu ts'ao-yün ch'üan-shu*, 12:1. An exception occurred in Honan, where the magistrates were required to transport the grain tribute to Yüeh-chou within the eleventh month. Delay was punishable (*Hu-pu tse-li*, 20:9).

144. Delay beyond the twelfth month was punishable by forfeiture of six months' nominal salary, delay beyond the first month of the next year by forfeiture of one year's salary, delay beyond the second month by demotion of two grades and retention in the same post (*Li-pu tse-li*, 16:6a–b; *Liu-pu ch'u-fen tse-li*, 18:4; *Hu-pu ts'ao-yün ch'üan-shu*, 12:1).

145. *Hu-pu tse-li*, 19:35; *Hu-pu ts'ao-yün ch'üan-shu*, 12:9b–10b; *Ch'ing hui-tien shih-li, chüan* 205.

146. See *Hu-pu ts'ao-yün ch'üan-shu*, 12:5a–b.

147. *Ch'ing shih k̩ao*, 129:11a–b; *Fu-hui ch'üan-shu*, 8:4a–b; *Hsing-ch'ien pi-lan*, 6:15a–b.

148. *Hsing-ch'ien pi-lan*, 6:14b; *Mu-ling shu*, 4:12b.

149. *Fu-hui ch'üan-shu*, 8:3b–5; *Hsing-ch'ien pi-lan*, 6:13a, 14b; *Ch'ing hui-tien shih-li, chüan* 205; *Hu-pu ts'ao-yün ch'üan-shu*, 12:1b–2.

150. *Li-pu tse-li*, 16:15b–16, 19a–b; *Liu-pu ch'u-fen tse-li*, 18:11b–12, 30–31, 35b–36. The magistrate along the canal was required to enter the dates of arrival and departure of the junks on the sailing-schedule form (*hsien-tan*) issued by the governor (*Ch'ing hui-tien shih-li, chüan* 205).

151. *Li-pu tse-li*, 16:21a–b; *Liu-pu ch'u-fen tse-li*, 18:8a–b.

152. *Li-pu tse-li*, 16:15; *Liu-pu ch'u-fen tse-li*, 18:42a–b, 46.

153. *Ch'ing hui-tien*, 18:2; *Shih-ch'ü yü-chi*, 6:8b; *Fu-hui ch'üan-shu*, 3:17.

154. *Ch'ing hui-tien shih-li, chüan* 245, 247; *Ch'ing t'ung-k̩ao*, 31:5136–37; *Shih-ch'ü yü-chi*, 6:9; *Fu-hui ch'üan-shu*, 8:66–67.

155. Brokers' licenses bearing the seal of the provincial treasurer were issued by the magistrate and a fee was paid for the issuance and annual renewal of

the license. A magistrate was forbidden to issue a license bearing his own seal (*Ch'ing hui-tien shih-li, chüan* 245, 247; *Hu-pu tse-li*, 42:25 ff; *Li-pu tse-li*, 21:6b–7, 10a–b; *Liu-pu ch'u-fen tse-li*, 23:25–26; *Ch'ing t'ung-k'ao*, 31:5136–38; *Shih-ch'ü yü-chi*, 6:8b). However, according to *Ch'ien-ku pi-tu*, private licenses were in fact issued by magistrates. Many business transactions, such as the sale of land and houses, rice, used clothing, cattle, and donkeys, depended upon brokers for price negotiations. There were no brokers for food-shops, wineshops, carriage renters, grain-millers, vendors of vegetables, fruit, and other daily commodities. See *Li-pu tse-li*, 20:4a–b; *Fu-hui ch'üan-shu*, 8:6b–7; *Shih-ch'ü yü-chi*, 6:8b; *Tzu-chih hsin-shu*, 19:59; 20:60b–61.

156. *Ch'ing hui-tien shih-li, chüan* 245; *Hu-pu tse-li*, 42:24; *Fu-hui ch'üan-shu*, 8:6; *Su-fan k'uan-mu yüan-liu*.

157. *Ch'ing hui-tien shih-li, chüan* 245; *Hu-pu tse-li*, 41:8 ff; *Fu-hui ch'üan-shu*, 8:7; *Su-fan k'uan-mu yüan-liu*.

158. *Fu-hui ch'üan-shu*, 8:7b–8; *Sung-chün chün-i ch'eng-shu*, ts'e 2:62–63; cf. *Ming shih*, 81:9a–b.

159. *Ch'ing hui-tien shih-li, chüan* 245, 247; *Li-pu tse-li*, 17:13; *Su-fan k'uan-mu yüan-liu*.

160. *Ch'ing hui-tien*, 18:2; *Hu-pu tse-li*, 42:21 ff; *Ch'ing t'ung-k'ao*, 31:5136; *Fu-hui ch'üan-shu*, 8:8; *Shih-ch'ü yü-chi*, 6:9b; *Ch'ien-ku pei-yao*, 2:17b; *Su-fan k'uan-mu yüan-liu*.

161. See *Hu-pu tse-li*, 41:8 ff; *Ch'ing t'ung-k'ao*, 31:5135–41; *Shih-ch'ü yü-chi*, 6:8b–10; *Su-fan k'uan-mu yüan-liu*. Customs duties, under superintendents of customs houses, were not included in the miscellaneous taxes (*Ch'ing hui-tien*, 18:2a–b).

162. *Ch'ing hui-tien*, 18:2a–b.

163. In some provinces there was no quota for any of the miscellaneous taxes (e.g., see *Chi-fu fu-i ch'üan-shu*, Shun-t'ien fu, Pao-ting hsien, p. 41). In other provinces some items had a quota and some did not. For example, in Honan there were quotas for old taxes (i.e., taxes which had been in existence for a long time), newly added taxes, and brokerage taxes, but none for pawnshop taxes, "nonquota newly added taxes" (*huo-shui*), and taxes on title deeds (*Honan fu-i ch'üan-shu*, K'ai-feng fu, Hsiang-fu hsien, p. 84a–b; K'ai-feng fu, Ch'en-liu hsien, p. 34b). In Kiangsi there were quotas for the pawnshop tax, brokerage tax, and cattle tax, but none for the tax on title deeds (*Chiang-hsi fu-i ch'üan-shu*, Nan-ch'ang fu, Feng-ch'eng hsien, p. 44; Chiu-chiang fu, Jui-ch'ang hsien, p. 19). In Hunan there were quotas for the brokerage tax and pawnshop tax, but none for the tax on title deeds, or the tax on cattle and donkeys (*Hunan fu-i ch'üan-shu*, Ch'ang-sha fu, Hsiang-t'an hsien, pp. 43b–44; Pao-ch'ing fu, Wu-kang chou, pp. 39b–40; Heng-chou fu, Heng-yang hsien, p. 55b). No miscellaneous tax was listed in the *T'ai-ts'ang-chou fu-i ch'üan-shu*, Kiangsu.

164. *Liu-pu ch'u-fen tse-li*, 26:3b; *Hu-pu tse-li*, 41:8 ff; *Fu-hui ch'üan-shu*, 8:15a–b; *Hsing-ch'ien pi-lan*, 6:1.

165. Failure to collect "miscellaneous taxes" led to impeachment, and delay

in delivery was punishable by forfeiture of one year's nominal salary (*Ch'ing hui-tien*, 15:12b–13; *Li-pu tse-li*, 23:20b; *Liu-pu ch'u-fen tse-li*, 26:3b).

166. The proceeds varied from place to place. From a rough examination of the Complete Book of Taxes and Labor Services and local gazetteers of several provinces, I gain the impression that in a number of chou and hsien the total proceeds from the miscellaneous taxes were as little as several dozen taels; in most of the localities the range was several hundred to less than 2000 taels; and cases with proceeds above 3000 taels were rather rare. As a rule, the whole list of miscellaneous taxes appears on a single Chinese page in the Complete Book of Taxes and Labor Services.

167. *Fu-hui ch'üan-shu*, 8:8, 15–16.

168. This point was mentioned in an imperial edict of 1729 (*Ch'ing hui-tien shih-li, chüan* 247).

169. *Ch'ing hui-tien*, 6:14b.

170. *Hu-pu tse-li*, 29:42; *Fu-weng chi, ch'ien-ku*, 2:1, 11.

171. *Hu-pu tse-li*, 28:21b–22.

172. E.g., a lump sum for selling salt in a hsien (*pao-k'o*) was imposed in Hsüan-hua, Huai-lai, Hsi-ning, Pao-an chou, and Yen-ch'ing chou in Chihli, where people were allowed to buy salt imported from Mongolia. The same tax was imposed in two island hsien: Ting-hai in Chekiang, and Ch'ung-ming in Kiangsu. A tax on native salt (*t'u-yen shui*) was collected in Kao-lan, Chin-hsien, Ti-tao chou, Wei-hsien, and Ho chou in Kansu, where people were also permitted to buy native salt (*Hu-pu tse-li*, 28:21a–b, 24; *T'ai-ts'ang-chou fu-i ch'üan-shu*, Ch'ung-ming hsien, p. 21b).

173. *Li-pu tse-li*, 19:1, 2; *Liu-pu ch'u fen tse-li*, 21:1b, 4a–b, 11. There was a special regulation involving a slightly more severe punishment in Kwangtung and Kwangsi (*Li-pu tse-li*, 19:4a–b; *Liu-pu ch'u-fen tse-li*, 21:7a–b).

174. This was a reform introduced by T'ao Chu and others in the Huai River area. For details, see *Huai-nan yen-fa chih-lüeh;* Liu Chün, "Tao-kuang ch'ao Liang-Huai fei-yin kai-p'iao shih-mo," *Chung-kuo chin-tai ching-chi-shih yen-chiu chi-k'an*, 1.2:124–188 (May 1933); Saeki Tomi, "Shindai Dōkōchō ni okeru Wainan ensei no kaikaku," *Tōhōgaku ronshū*, 3:87–120 (Sept. 1955); *idem, Shindai ensei no kenkyū*, pp. 335–360.

175. *Ch'ing shih-kao*, 130:10.

176. *Hu-pu tse-li*, 31:3; *Ch'ing lü-li*, 13:18; *Ch'ing shih kao*, 130:6.

177. *Li-pu tse-li*, 19:1a–b; *Liu-pu ch'u-fen tse-li*, 21:12b.

178. *Li-pu tse-li*, 19:9a–b; *Liu-pu ch'u-fen tse-li*, 21:15a–b.

179. *Fu-hui ch'üan-shu*, 8:8b; *Mu-ling shu*, 22:33, 34b.

180. *Li-pu tse-li*, 19:7b; *Liu-pu ch'u-fen tse-li*, 21:13.

181. *Fu-hui ch'üan-shu*, 8:8b; *Sheng-shih wei-yen pu-pien*, 5:20; *Mu-ling shu*, 22:33.

182. The punishment was demotion of three grades and transfer to another post. If a magistrate reported the unlawful activities but failed to apprehend the lawbreakers, he was demoted three grades but kept in the same post and given another year to make the arrest. He was demoted and transferred if he

had still failed to make the arrest at the end of a year (*Li-pu tse-li*, 19:9b–10; *Liu-pu ch'u-fen tse-li*, 21:27–28).

183. The punishment varied according to the number of persons involved in the smuggling. A regulation of 1676 decreed that if a large group was involved (the law defined a "large group" as more than ten persons or a group carrying weapons) the magistrate was to be "dismissed" but kept in the same post for a year to apprehend the smugglers. His dismissal was canceled if he succeeded in arresting more than half of the smugglers. It was ruled in 1705 that if the smugglers were fewer than ten persons, the magistrate and the jail warden were to be demoted two grades for failing to detect the unlawful activities once, four grades for failing twice. They were given another year to make the arrest. If they had still not succeeded at the end of the year, they were punished with forfeiture of one year's nominal salary; their demotion was canceled if they succeeded. Dismissal was the punishment for failure to detect smuggling three times. The punishment prescribed in a revised regulation of 1873 was less severe: in a case of small-group smuggling, the magistrate and the jail warden forfeited two years' nominal salary and were given another year to apprehend the smugglers. If they failed, they were demoted one grade and kept in the same post. In large-group smuggling, the magistrate and the jail warden were demoted one grade, but they were kept in the same post and given another year to apprehend the smugglers. If they failed, they were demoted and transferred. See *Li-pu tse-li*, 19:11a–b, 12b; *Liu-pu ch'u-fen tse-li*, 21:37; *Ch'ing hui-tien shih-li* (1818), 83:13b, 15; *ibid.* (1899), *chüan* 105. For the punishment in cases where the smugglers resisted arrest and caused injury to the patrolmen, see *Li-pu tse-li*, 19:3, 13a–b; *Liu-pu ch'u-fen tse-li*, 21:39b.

184. One to three "recordings of merit" were given to a magistrate who succeeded in arresting one to three groups of small-group smugglers, respectively, within a year. An advancement of one grade was awarded a magistrate who made four arrests, and an additional advancement of one grade for every additional arrest.

A magistrate who succeeded in arresting one or two large groups of smugglers was given an advancement of one or two grades, respectively. He was rewarded with immediate promotion if he made three arrests (*Liu-pu ch'u-fen tse-li*, 21:36a–b).

185. The sale of salt was in the hands of government officials in a number of chou and hsien under the jurisdiction of Fu-chou, Hsing-hua, Chang-chou, and Ch'üan-chou in Fukien. (Such an arrangement was designated as *kuan-pang* or *hsien ao*.) The magistrates were obliged to receive salt certificates and report monthly to their superior yamen the quantity of salt sold and the amount derived from such transactions. This system came to an end, however, when a new system of issuing salt tickets (*p'iao-yen*) to merchants was introduced in 1865 (*Hu-pu tse-li*, 30:29–30; *Liu-pu ch'u-fen tse-li*, 21:8–9. For a brief history of the salt administration in Fukien see *Ch'ing shih kao*, 130:5, 18b). The transport and sale of salt was handled by officials also in a number of places in Shantung (e.g., Lin-ch'ü), Honan (e.g., Shang-ch'iu), Chihli (hsien under

the jurisdiction of the Yung-p'ing prefect), Shansi, and Shensi (*Hu-pu tse-li,* 30:22a–b, 24a–b, 27, 38b).

186. Tea certificates were issued by the magistrates of the following localities: Ch'ien-shan and sixteen other hsien in Anhui; Shan-hua and sixteen other hsien in Hunan. In Hupeh, certificates were issued by the magistrate of Chien-shih to tea merchants. In Hsien-ning and six other chou and hsien, tea planters also received certificates to sell tea (*Hu-pu tse-li,* 32:4–5).

187. For instance, certificates in Kiangsi to export tea to other provinces were examined at the customs station, whereas certificates issued to tea peddlers in nearby places were examined by magistrates. Certificates were also examined by magistrates in Anhui, Hupeh, Hunan, Szechwan, and Kweichow (*Hu-pu tse-li,* 32:20b–22; *Ch'ing hui-tien,* 21:3).

188. *Shih-ch'ü yü-chi,* 5:64b.

189. *Ch'ing shih kao,* 131:8. The tea tax was collected by magistrates in certain places in Shantung, Shansi, and Hunan. See *Hu-pu tse-li,* 32:11b–12; *Ch'ing hui-tien,* 21:3; *Hunan fu-i ch'üan-shu,* Ch'ang-sha fu, Hsiang-t'an hsien, p. 43b; Pao-ch'ing-fu, Shao-yang hsien, p. 25b; Ch'ang-te-fu, T'ao-yüan-hsien, p. 29b.

190. *Liu-pu ch'u-fen tse-li,* 23:19. See above, Chap. VIII, sec. 4.

CHAPTER IX. GENERAL ADMINISTRATION

1. *Ch'ing hui-tien* (1690), 24:3; *ibid.* (1732), 31:3b.

2. *Ibid.* (1690), 24:2b–4; *Ch'ing hui-tien tse-li,* 33:3a–b; *Ch'ing hui-tien shih-li* (1818), 133:1a–b; *Ch'ing t'ung-k'ao,* 19:5024; *Fu-hui ch'üan-shu,* 9:1; *Shih-ch'ü yü-chi,* 3:18. For a discussion of the meaning of *ting,* which has been misunderstood by modern students of demography in dealing with the population data of the Ch'ing, see Ho, *Studies on the Population of China,* chap. 2. See also Hsiao, *Rural China,* pp. 86 ff.

3. See above, Chap. VIII, sec. 1.

4. *Ch'ing hui-tien* (1690), 23:16b–17; *ibid.* (1732), 30:24a–b; 25b; *Ch'ing hui-tien tse-li,* 33:4a–b; *Ch'ing hui-tien shih-li* (1818), 133:2a–b; *Ch'ing t'ung-k'ao,* 19:5024; *Fu-hui ch'üan-shu,* 9:14b; *Shih-ch'ü yü-chi,* 3:10b.

5. See above, Chap. VIII, sec. 1.

6. *Fu-hui ch'üan-shu,* 9:2–3, 7 ff.

7. *Ch'ing hui-tien* (1732), 30:27b–28; *Ch'ing hui-tien tse-li,* 33:4a–b; *Ch'ing hui-tien shih-li* (1818), 133:2a–b.

8. *Ch'ing hui-tien tse-li,* 33:5; *Ch'ing hui-tien shih-li* (1818), 133:2b–3.

9. *Ch'ing hui-tien shih-li* (1818), 133:3a–b; *Ch'ing t'ung-k'ao,* 25:5073; *Shih-ch'ü yü-chi,* 3:11b, 14b–15. Thus no *ting* figure was given in the Complete Books of Taxes and Labor Services after 1772 (see Chap. VIII, note 6). *Hu-pu tse-li,* 3:2, explains that the number of *ting* listed is that of the year when the registration discontinued. As Wang Ch'ing-yün (1798–1862) pointed out, the record of *ting* for the various provinces kept by the Board of Revenue in his day was based on the quota of 1711. This was the tax quota, not the actual number of the increased population (*Shih-ch'ü yü-chi,* 3:16).

10. *Ch'ing hui-tien* (1764), 9:5; *ibid.* (1818), 11:5; *ibid.* (1899), 17:5; *Ch'ing t'ung-k'ao*, 19:5024, 5029; 22:5051; *Hu-pu tse-li*, 3:6; *Ch'ing lü-li*, 20:17; *Fu-hui ch'üan-shu*, 21:4; *Yung-li yung-yen*, p. 92; *P'ing-hu hsien pao-chia shih-i*, p. 5.

The *pao-cheng* or *pao-chang* should not be confused with the constable, *ti-pao*, who was also called *pao-chang* in some places (*Ts'ung-cheng hsü-yü lu*, 2:34b; *Hsing-ch'ien pi-lan*, 4:15. It was for this reason that Wang Feng-sheng, a magistrate, changed the name of *pao-chang* to *pao-ch'i* in order to avoid confusion—*P'ing-hu hsien pao-chia shih-i*, pp. 9b–10). The *ti-pao* was a government agent in charge of reporting homicide and robbery cases and other lawsuits to the magistrate (see above, Chap I, sec. 1. This was not the responsibility of the *p'ai-t'ou*, *chia-chang*, and *pao-chang* (*Ch'ing t'ung-k'ao*, 24:5062; *P'ing-hu hsien pao-chia shih-i*, pp. 9b–10).

11. For the form of the door placard see *Fu-hui ch'üan-shu*, 21:9b; *Yung-li yung-yen*, pp. 97 ff; *P'ing-hu hsien pao-chia shih-i*, pp. 15–18. Both *Ch'ing hui-tien*, 17:5, and *Hu-pu tse-li*, 3:6, mention that the door placards listed only the names of the adult males. This, however, was not universally true. In some cases the names of women were not listed (*Mu-ling shu*, 2:24a–b, 27, 32b; *Tzu-chih hsin-shu*, 13:24); in others, the names of the resident's wife, concubines, mother, aunts, sisters-in-law, daughters, and female slaves were all listed (*Yu Ch'ing-tuan kung cheng-shu*, 5:85b; 7:38b; *Fu-hui ch'üan-shu*, 21:9b; *P'ing-hu hsien pao-chia shih-i*, pp. 15–18; *Pao-chia shu*, 2A:4).

12. *Ch'ing hui-tien*, 17:5; *Hu-pu tse-li*, 3:6; *Yung-li yung-yen*, pp. 94b–95; *P'ing-hu hsien pao-chia shih-i*, pp. 15b, 18; *Mu-ling shu*, 2:36b.

13. *Hu-pu tse-li*, 3:5; *P'ing-hu hsien pao-chia shih-i*, pp. 5b–6b, 19a–b, 26a–b, 29a–b; *Pao-chia shu*, 2A:4a–b; 2B:28–29, 34a–b.

14. A certain magistrate insisted on including these groups in the *pao-chia* organization (*Yung-li yung-yen*, p. 94b). But another magistrate preferred not to include them on the ground that reputable people were not willing to be associated with them in the same organization. Instead he put their names in a separate record and entrusted their supervision to the *ti-pao* (*P'ing-hu hsien pao-chia shih-i*, pp. 7a–b, 15).

15. This point was explicitly indicated in one of the sixteen Sacred Edicts (see below, n. 161) and other statements concerning the meaning of *pao-chia*. See *Chi'n-pan chou-hsien shih-i*, pp. 18b–19; *Ch'ing t'ung-k'ao*, 24:5062; *Fu-hui ch'üan-shu*, 21:1; 23:11; *Hsiao-ts'ang shan-fang wen-chi*, 15:7b; *Tseng Wen-cheng chi, p'i-tu*, 1:1, 33; *P'ing-p'ing yen*, 4:45; *Tzu-chih hsin-shu*, 13:15, 22; *Ching-shih wen-pien*, 74:3; *Pao-chia shu*, A:9a–b, 3:12b, 22b, 27, 32b, 38b, 41. This is why *pao-chia* was customarily under the Office of Punishment (*Pao-chia shu*, 2A:9a–b).

16. *Pao-chia shu*, 3:7b–8; 12b; 22b.

17. *Ibid.*, 2A:6a–b; 2B:24; 3:7b; *Tseng Wen-cheng chi, tsou-kao*, 1:47; *ibid.*, p'i-tu, 1:33.

18. *Ch'ing hui-tien*, 17:5; *Ch'in-pan chou-hsien shih-i*, p. 18b; *Fu-hui ch'üan-shu*, 21a–b; *P'ing-hu hsien pao-chia shih-i*, pp. 1, 9b, 11, 18, 19, 21, 22, 26b–27.

19. *Fu-hui ch'üan-shu*, 23:1a–b.

20. A *p'ai-t'ou* who withheld information concerning anyone guilty of robbery or of harboring a robber was punishable with eighty strokes. The *chia-chang* and *pao-chang* were punishable with seventy and sixty strokes, respectively, if they failed to report a crime after they had been informed of it by the *p'ai-t'ou*. All three were punishable if they failed to detect robbers in areas under their jurisdiction: forty strokes for the *p'ai-t'ou*, thirty for the *chia-chang*, and twenty for the *pao-chang* (*Ch'ing lü-li*, 25:100a–b).

21. *Yu Ch'ing-tuan cheng-shu*, 5:89; 7:44a–b; *Fu-hui ch'üan-shu*, 21:7b, 10, 11, 18 ff; *Ch'in-pan chou-hsien shih-i*, p. 18b; *Yung-li yung-yen*, p. 89b; *Pao-chia shu*, 2:36b.

22. On the difference between *pao-chia* and *t'üan-lien*, see *Tseng Wen-cheng chi, p'i-tu*, 1:7, 8b, 16b, 17b, 18–19b, 55b; *Yung-li yung-yen*, pp. 46b ff, 89b; *Pao-chia shu*, 2B:25b.

23. *Pao-chia shu*, 2B:25b–26, 30a–b, 35b–36b.

24. *Mu-ling shu*, 2:53.

25. Cf. K. C. Hsiao, "Rural Control in Nineteenth Century China," *Far Eastern Quarterly*, 12.2:134–135 (1953); Hsiao, *Rural China*, pp. 45–46.

26. For instance, Wen Chün-t'ien holds that *pao-chia* was very successful in the Ch'ing. His conclusion, however, is based largely upon the regulations and on discussions of the system rather than on their actual application (*Chung-kuo pao-chia chih-tu*, pp. 272 ff).

27. Mary Wright holds that by the nineteenth century the *pao-chia* system "had declined into an ineffective instrument of local control, and its revival became one of the chief aims of the Restoration" (*The Last Stand of Chinese Conservatism*, p. 136). However, on a basis of the edicts issued by the K'ang-hsi, Yung-cheng, Ch'ien-lung, and Chia-ch'ing emperors, and the statements made by various officials mentioned below, I am inclined to believe that the system had been mainly ineffective from the beginning of the dynasty. K. C. Hsiao makes a similar appraisal of the *pao-chia*, concluding: "With the problem of personnel unsolved and with the difficulties confronting registration and reporting unremoved, the *pao-chia* system could not have operated with the efficiency which the founding emperors of Ch'ing expected . . . the same circumstances that rendered the *pao-chia* indispensable to the imperial rulers also limited its actual usefulness to them. This is a conclusion that applies not only to the *pao-chia* but also to other instruments of rural control, as subsequent discussions will show" (*Rural China*, pp. 82–83).

It seems to me that the intention of Tseng Kuo-fan and some of his contemporaries was to enforce more thoroughly the system which had been only ineffectively enforced previously, rather than to revive a system once effective but now declining. The *pao-chia* served a particular purpose in Tseng Kuo-fan's time, in that it made it difficult for the rebels to hide among the local residents. This explains why the *pao-chia* became comparatively effective during this period. However, as Feng Kuei-fen pointed out, the *t'uan-lien* was more effective than the *pao-chia* during the Taiping Rebellion (*Chiao-pin-lu k'ang-i*, A:13).

28. *Ch'ing t'ung-k'ao*, 22:5051, 23:5055.

29. See the edicts issued by the Ch'ien-lung emperor in 1757, and by the Chia-ch'ing emperor in 1799 and 1810, complaining that the local officials regarded *pao-chia* administration as a mere formality (*Ch'ing t'ung-k'ao*, 24:5061–62; *Ch'ing hsü t'ung-k'ao*, 25:7757–58).

30. *Yung-li yung-yen*, p. 88; *P'ing-hu hsien pao-chia shih-i*.

31. *Fu-hui ch'üan-shu*, 21:1; *Chu-p'i yü-chih*, T'ien Wen-ching's memorials, 5:106b. Wang Hui-tsu's personal experience was most interesting. He had intended to put *pao-chia* into practice while he was serving as a private secretary, but he was unable to persuade the magistrates to adopt his plan. He did not have a chance to adopt it until he himself became a magistrate (*Hsüeh-chih i-shuo*, B:5b). For additional remarks by other officials on the ineffectiveness of the *pao-chia* system, see Chou Liang-kung (*Tzu-chih hsin-shu*, 13:15b); Li Shih-chen (1619–1695) (*ibid.*, 13:23); Chang Po-hsing (1652–1725) (*Pao-chia shu*, 3:22b); Yeh P'ei-sun (1731–1784) (*ibid.*, 2A:1b); Yang Hsi-fu (1701–1768) (*Ching-shih wen-pien*, 74:12a–b); Hsü Wen-pi (*chü-jen* 1741) (*ibid.*, 74:11b); Hu Tse-huang (*chin-shih* 1742) (*ibid.*, 74:13).

32. *P'ing-hu hsien pao-chia shih-i*, p. 1; *Pao-chia shu*, 2B:2b.

33. *Chiao-pin-lu k'ang-i*, A:13.

34. *Pao-chia shu*, 2A:1b; 2B:2b.

35. *Hsüeh-chih i-shuo*, B:5b–6; *P'ing-hu hsien pao-chia shih-i*, p. 1; *Pao-chia shu*, 2A:1b; 2B:3b; 3:25a–b; *Tzu-chih hsin-shu*, 13:23; *Hsien-chih-t'ang kao*, 11:16.

36. *Pao-chia shu*, 2:23.

37. *Hsüeh-chih i-shuo*, B:5b–6; *Ping-t'a meng-hen lu*, B:13b; *Yung-li yung-yen*, p. 95b; *Pao-chia shu*, 3:25. The case of Tsung P'ei, magistrate of Hua-jung, Hunan (1811–1814), was exceptional. As his son recalled, he spent two years in checking the households door-to-door against the *pao-chia* records and door placards (*Kung-ch'ih-chai wen-ch'ao*, 4:1; *Hunan T'ung-chih*, 1882–85, 107:11b, also mentions that he diligently put into practice the *pao-chia* administration).

38. *Pao-chia shu*, 2B:23; *Tzu-chih hsin-shu*, 13:23.

39. *Ching-shih wen-pien*, 74:12a–b; *P'ing-hu hsien pao-chia shih-i*, p. 1.

40. *Tzu-chih hsin-shu*, 13:6; *Pao-chia shu*, 2A:2.

41. *Hsiao-ts'ang shan-fang wen-chi*, 15:6b–7.

42. *Pao-chia shu*, 2B:25a–b.

43. There were magistrates who voluntarily contributed money to provide meals for those who were assigned to register the households, for stationery, and for door placards (*Hsüeh-chih i-shuo*, B:5b–6; *Yung-li yung-yen*, pp. 88b, 95b–96; *P'ing-hu hsien pao-chia shih-i*, pp. 4b–5, 13b–14; *Pao-chia shu*, 2B:5b–6). Some instances indicate that magistrates were ordered by their superiors to pay the expenses out of their own pockets (*Pao-chia shu*, 2B:23, 27b). It was also mentioned in an edict that stationery expenses should be met by local officials (*Ch'ing lü-li*, 20:19b).

44. *Pao-chia shu*, 2B:23b–24. In one case each household was asked to pay 1000 coins for a door placard (*P'ing-p'ing yen*, 4:46b–47).

45. The fees included: fees for stationery, fees for making *pao-chia* records,

money for wine and meals and for shoes, fees for hiring horses, and fees for submitting the bonded statement, for getting the wooden tablet on which the names of the ten households of a *chia* appeared, and for checking and revising the *pao-chia* records. The clerks and runners demanded these fees from the *pao-chang*, and the latter collected them from the local residents (*Yung-li yung-yen*, p. 88a–b; *Pao-chia shu*, 2A:2; 2B:23a–b; *Tzu-chih hsin-shu*, 13:19b–20).

46. *Fu-hui ch'üan-shu*, 23:1; *Pao-chia shu*, 3:12b; *Tzu-chih hsin-shu*, 13:20.

47. *Yung-li yung-yen*, p. 88.

48. A member of the gentry was punishable with 80 to 100 strokes if he evaded inclusion in the *pao-chia* organization. The magistrate who permitted such evasion was also punishable (*Ch'ing lü-li*, 8:44a–b; *Hu-pu tse-li*, 3:6b–7; *Liu-pu ch'u-fen tse-li*, 20:1).

49. *Yü Ch'ing-tuan cheng-shu*, 5:88b; 7:42b–43b; *Fu-hui ch'üan-shu*, 21:8b; *Kung-ch'ih-chai wen-ch'ao*, 4:4; *Tzu-chih hsin-shu*, 13:23b–24.

50. See below, Chap. X. sec. 6. For a discussion of the government policy to exclude the gentry from *pao-chia* leadership, and attempts by some local officials to secure gentry cooperation in *pao-chia* administration, see Hsiao, *Rural China*, pp. 68–72.

51. *P'ing-p'ing yen*, 4:44.

52. *Ch'ing hui-tien*, 51:1–4; *Fu-hui ch'üan-shu*, 28:1; *Mu-ling shu*, 23:23b; *Ching-shih wen-pien*, 20:16.

53. *Ch'ing hui-tien*, 51:2; *Fu-hui ch'üan-shu*, 30:7; *Shih-hsüeh ta-sheng*, 11:30b.

54. *Ch'ing hui-tien*, 51:4.

55. *Ibid.*, 51:1; *Fu-hui ch'üan-shu*, 28:1a–b; 7:20b; *Mu-ling shu*, 23:6b–7; *Hsing-ch'ien pi-lan*, 6:21.

56. A magistrate or post station master was subject to dismissal for failure to buy horses in accordance with the quota, for neglect to feed the horses properly, and for other forms of mismanagement of the post stations (*Li-pu tse-li*, 32:9b–10; *Liu-pu ch'u-fen tse-li*, 35:1). Thus when a new magistrate took over the post much attention was given to examining the horses. Horses not in good health were often not accepted, and the outgoing magistrate was asked to replace them with good ones (*Ch'ien-ku pei-yao*, 3:2a–b, 3; *Hsing-ch'ien pi-lan*, 6:22; *Ch'ien-ku pi-tu*).

57. *K'an-ho* was a certificate issued to an official; *huo-p'ai*, to a messenger (*Ch'ing hui-tien*, 51:6 ff; *Fu-hui ch'üan-shu*, 28:1b, 10b–11b; *Hsing-ch'ien pi-lan*, 6:22b–25b; *Mu-ling shu*, 22:26b, 29–30b).

58. A delay was punishable by forfeiture of salary or demotion of one grade, depending upon the urgency of the dispatch (*Liu-pu ch'u-fen tse-li*, 35:25–26).

59. *Fu-hui ch'üan-shu*, 28:7b.

60. *Ibid.*, 28:9b–10; see above, Chap. V, sec. 2.

61. *Liu-pu ch'u-fen tse-li*, 35:10a–b; *Fu-hui ch'üan-shu*, 28:2b–4b, 16b–18; *Mu-ling shu*, 23:24–25; *Ching-shih wen-pien*, 20:16a–b; *Shih-hsüeh ta-sheng*, 4:7.

62. *Mu-ling shu*, 23:6b–7.

63. The magistrate could report directly to the Board of War any official who demanded more horses (*Liu-pu ch'u-fen tse-li*, 35:11–12b, 17b–18; *Hsing-ch'ien pi-lan*, 6:23b–24b).

64. *Ch'ing shih-lu*, Shih-tsung, 12:7a–b; *ibid.*, Jen-tsung, 170:19a–b; *Mu-ling shu*, 23:7.

65. *Liu-pu ch'u-fen tse-li*, 35:10a–b; *Fu-hui ch'üan-shu*, 28:2a–b, 4b ff; *Ching-shih wen-pien*, 20:16b.

66. *Liu-pu ch'u-fen tse-li*, 35:18.

67. *Tzu-chih hsin-shu*, 11:27b; *Mu-ling shu*, 8:43b. See *Liu-pu ch'u-fen tse-li*, 35:18, for a regulation concerning the punishment for demanding that the people pay such expenses.

68. *Mu-ling shu*, 8:43b; *Tzu-chih hsin-shu*, 11:28; *Hsing-ch'ien pi-lan*, 6:21, 26.

69. See above, Chap. VIII, sec. 1.

70. *Mu-ling shu*, 8:43b; *Tzu-chih hsin-shu*, 11:27b–28.

71. *Ch'ing hui-tien*, 51:3b.

72. *Fu-hui ch'üan-shu*, 29:18b–19; *Mu-ling shu*, 22:28a–b; *Ch'i-pu-fu-chai ch'üan-chi, cheng-shu*, 7:19a–b.

73. *Fu-hui ch'üan-shu*, 29:18b. An edict of 1728 mentioned that in many places the horses actually kept in a post station were far below the official quota and that the money secured from the government for the purchase of horses was not used to replace the dead ones. When there was a need for horses, they were demanded from the local people (*Ch'ing shih-lu*, Shih-tsung, 12:7b–8).

74. *Tzu-chih hsin-shu*, 11:28; *Mu-ling shu*, 8:43b.

75. *Ch'ing hui-tien shih-li*, chüan 927, 928; *Ch'ing lü-li*, 39:3b–4; *Fu-hui ch'üan-shu*, 31:2.

76. Thus the magistrate was authorized to determine whether dredging and repairing of a dam was necessary (*Ch'ing hui-tien shih-li*, chüan 927). As a rule, no punishment was imposed on a magistrate for failure to dredge a river, excepting in Shantung, where the magistrate who failed to perform this duty regularly was punishable by forfeiture of one year's nominal salary. Failure to repair the private dams was also punishable—for dams along the Chang River and Wei River in Honan and Shantung, by demotion of one grade; for dams in other places, by forfeiture of one year's salary (*Liu-pu ch'u-fen tse-li*, 51:6, 7, 8a–b).

77. *Ch'ing hui-tien shih-li*, chüan 925; *Chu-p'i yü-chih*, Li Wei's memorials, 2:71a–b.

78. *Ch'ing hui-tien shih-li*, chüan 925, 927; *Mu-ling shu*, 9:28b.

79. *Ch'ing shih-lu*, Kao-tsung, 12:22; 14:2a–b; *Ch'ing hui-tien shih-li*, chüan 927, 929; *Fu-weng chi, ch'ien ku*, 2:14; *Hsüeh-chih ou-ts'un*, 3:1b; *Mu-ling shu*, 9:28b; 22:22b–23; *Lou-hsien chih*, 5:19b–20b.

80. *Ping-t'a meng-hen lu*, B:52–54, 55b–56.

81. The punishment was forfeiture of one year's nominal salary when

important bridges on a main road collapsed (*Li-pu tse-li*, 47:2; *Liu-pu ch'u-fen tse-li*, 52:16). Another law stipulated that a magistrate was punishable by thirty strokes if he failed to repair a main road or bridge and thereby impeded communications (*Ch'ing lü-li*, 39:25).

82. The punishment was forfeiture of six months' nominal salary if the damage to the city wall was minor; forfeiture of six months' nominal salary or demotion of one grade if the wall had collapsed (*Li-pu tse-li*, 47:3a–b; *Liu-pu ch'u-fen tse-li*, 52:10). Failure to repair government buildings was punishable by forty strokes (*Ch'ing lü-li*, 38:33).

83. *Ch'ing t'ung-k'ao*, 24:5061.

84. *Li-pu tse-li*, 47:3a–b; *Liu-pu ch'u-fen tse-li*, 52:3; *Mu-ling shu*, 22:10.

85. *Li-pu tse-li*, 47:3a–b: *Liu-pu ch'u-fen tse-li*, 52:10.

86. *Mu-ling shu*, 22:10. There was a law which permitted a magistrate to impose a fine on people involved in ordinary lawsuits, in order to provide funds for the repair of roads, bridges, and temples. But such cases had to be reported to the superior yamen and permission had to be obtained from the emperor. Violation of this regulation was punishable with demotion of one to three grades (*Liu-pu ch'u-fen tse-li*, 48:25a–b).

87. *Ping-t'a meng-hen lu*, B:17.

88. *Ibid.*, B:12b; *Liu-pu ch'u-fen tse-li*, 52:15.

89. *Ping-t'a meng-hen lu*, B:29.

90. *Ch'ing shih-lu*, Shih-tsung, 55:40a–b.

91. For instance, there was a regulation requiring an official who had borrowed money from the government for the purpose of repairing the yamen building to guarantee it for a period of ten years. Within this period small repairs were to be done by his successor. But the original official was obliged to pay back the borrowed money if extensive repair became necessary (*Liu-pu ch'u-fen tse-li*, 52:15).

92. *Ts'ung-cheng hsü-yü lu*, 1:71a–b.

93. The normal proportion was seventy per cent to be kept, thirty per cent to be sold. But there were places where the portion of grain for sale was forty, fifty, or seventy per cent. There were also places where no definite portion was prescribed. These ratios, however, could be adjusted in accordance with the needs of the locality. Thus more could be sold when there was a famine, and no grain, or only ten to twenty per cent, was offered for sale when there had been a good harvest (*Ch'ing hui-tien*, 18:18; *Hu-pu tse-li*, 16:14, 15b).

94. The normal rate was five *fen* per picul less than the market price during a good harvest, and one *ch'ien* less during a poor harvest (*Ch'ing hui-tien*, 18:18; *Hu-pu tse-li*, 6:19a–b; *Ch'ing shih kao*, 128:19).

95. *Hu-pu tse-li*, 17:22b–23.

96. *Ibid.*, 17:24.

97. *Ibid.*, 16:16a–b.

98. *Ibid.*, 17:24.

99. *Ibid.*, 16:16a–b, 37–38; 17:20b; *Li-pu tse-li*, 25:9a–b; *Liu-pu ch'u-fen tse-li*, 27:33a–b.

100. *Hu-pu tse-li*, 16:5a–b.

101. *Ibid.*, 16:16.

102. *Fu-hui ch'üan-shu*, 27:7a–b; *P'ei-yüan-t'ang ou-ts'un kao*, 17:47; 38:18; *Mu-ling shu*, 12:1.

103. *Ch'ing shih-lu*, Jen-tsung, 58:19a–b; *Ch'in-pan chou-hsien shih-i*, 13b–14; *Fu-hui ch'üan-shu*, 27:8; *Hsing-ch'ien pi-lan*, 6:18b.

104. *Li-pu tse-li*, 25:12; *Liu-pu ch'u-fen tse-li*, 27:35a–b.

105. *Fu-hui ch'üan-shu*, 27:8; *Mu-ling shu*, 12:15b.

106. *Li-pu tse-li*, 25:12; *Liu-pu ch'u-fen tse-li*, 27:35a–b.

107. *Ch'ing shih-lu*, Kao-tsung, 50:6b–7b; 58:19a–b. Under the law a magistrate was punishable with demotion of three grades if he bought grain from the people at a price lower than the market price (*Li-pu tse-li*, 25:9b–10; *Liu-pu ch'u-fen tse-li*, 27:37–38).

108. *Hu-pu tse-li*, 17:20b–22; *Liu-pu ch'u-fen tse-li*, 27:37–38.

109. *Ch'in-pan chou-hsien shih-i*, p. 50b; *Ch'ing shih kao*, 128:18a–b, 20; *Hsing-ch'ien pi-lan*, 6:18a–b.

110. *Fu-hui ch'üan-shu*, 27:6b–8.

111. Both *she-ts'ang* and *i-ts'ang* stored grain contributed by the local people. The difference between them, as is pointed out in an edict of 1679, was that *she-ts'ang* were established in rural districts, *i-ts'ang* in towns (*Ch'ing t'ung-k'ao*, 22:5051). However this was not always the case (e.g., in Chihli). It may be noted that *i-ts'ang* were not found in some areas, such as Honan and Shensi (*Ch'ing shih-lu*, Kao-tsung, 283:14 ff; 287:9). A different distinction was made by Chu Yün-chin who said that *i-ts'ang* were under the management of both the government and people, whereas *she-ts'ang* were managed exclusively by the local people (*Yü-sheng shih-hsiao lu*, A:23). It seems that since the usage probably varied in different areas, there was no standard definition of the terms. Therefore the Ch'ien-lung emperor said in an edict that "they were merely different names for the same thing" (*Ch'ing shih-lu*, Kao-tsung, 287:9).

112. As a rule, ten-per-cent interest was charged for borrowing grain from the *she-ts'ang*, but the interest was waived during a bad harvest. Similar interest rates were charged in an *i-ts'ang*, but there were places where no interest was charged at all. For details see *Hu-pu tse-li*, 17:27b, 31b–32; *Ch'ien-ku pei-yao*. 2:39b; *Ch'ing shih kao*, 128:21a–b.

113. *Hu-pu tse-li*, 17:26a–b.

114. *Fu-hui ch'üan-shu*, 27:8b.

115. *Ch'ing hui-tien*, 19:17b; *Hu-pu tse-li*, 17:28a–b; *Liu-pu ch'u-fen tse-li*, 27:45a–b; *P'ei-yüan-t'ang ou-ts'un kao*, 22:9a–b.

116. *Hu-pu tse-li*, 17:26–28.

117. *Fu-hui ch'üan-shu*, 27:7b–9b; *P'ei-yüan-t'ang ou-ts'un kao*, 38:19b–20, 23a–b; *Ch'ien-ku pei-yao*, 6:20a–b; *Mu-ling shu*, 12:40b–41.

118. *Mu-hsüeh chü-yao*, 28a–b; *Ch'ien-ku pei-yao*, 2:38.

119. *Ch'ing shih kao*, 128:21.

120. *Ping-t'a meng-hen lu*, B:7.

121. *Hsüeh-chih t'i-hsing lu*, B:20b.

122. A picture of the decay of the public and community granary system in the nineteenth century, based upon information found in the various local gazetteers, is presented in Hsiao, *Rural China*, pp. 153 ff. Hsiao feels that the unsatisfactory conditions in the local granaries can be attributed not only to the difficulties connected with their operation and supervision, but also to the material destitution of the peasantry (pp. 159 ff).

123. The investigation was made either by the magistrate in person (*Ch'ien-ku pi-tu*) or by the educational officials and subordinate officials, who were assigned to cover specific areas. The report, including a chart, was prepared after the investigations had been made (*Ch'ien-ku shih-ch'eng*).

124. *Li-pu tse-li*, 22:1a–b; *Liu-pu ch'u-fen tse-li*, 24:1a–b.

125. A magistrate who failed to report a calamity was punishable by dismissal and permanently barred from reappointment. He was also punishable by dismissal if he had over- or under-reported the degree of calamity. If the over- or under-statement had not been made with intent and concerned holdings of no more than twenty *mou*, the punishment was demotion of three grades and retention in the same post (*Liu-pu ch'u-fen tse-li*, 24:2a–b; *Hu pu tse-li*, 84:10–11). In addition, the magistrate was also subject to corporal punishment under the penal code: 100 strokes if he had not conducted the investigation carefully, deceiving his superiors and causing harm to the people stricken by the calamity. He was punishable according to the law governing bribery if his false report had caused a taxpayer to pay land-and-labor-service tax from which he was exempt, or the reverse (*Ch'ing lü-li*, 9:7–8).

For the procedure in investigating a calamity, see *Ch'ien-ku pei-yao*, 8:10–12b; 9:2–4b; 10:1–2b; *Ch'ien-ku shih-ch'eng*.

126. The percentage of reduction varied from 10 to 30 per cent in the Shun-chih and K'ang-hsi periods; it was raised to 10 to 70 per cent in the Yung-cheng period (*Shih-ch'ü yü-chi*, 1:22b ff).

127. *Hu-pu tse-li*, 84:6b–7b.

128. *Ch'ien-ku shih-ch'eng*.

129. *Hu-pu tse-li*, 84:6b; *Liu-pu ch'u-fen tse-li*, 24:5a–b; 33:3a–b; *Ch'ien-ku shih-ch'eng*.

130. As a rule, one month's emergency relief was given to the people stricken by calamity. Two-months' additional relief was given only to widowers, widows, and others living alone. Regular relief thereafter was given in proportion to the seriousness of the calamity, to those who qualified as "extremely poor" or "less poor" (See *Hu-pu tse-li*, 84:12–13; *Mu-ling shu*, 13:21; *Ch'ien-ku pei-yao*, 7:27b ff; *Shih-ch'ü yü-chi*, 1:3b–5).

131. *Hu-pu tse-li*, 84:11b–12, 15a–b; *Liu-pu ch'u-fen tse-li*, 24:4; *Mu-ling shu*, 13:29b; *Ch'ien-ku pei-yao*, 8:7a–b, 22 ff, 45b–46b; 9:5–8; 10:7–9b, 17–19.

132. *Hu-pu tse-li*, 84:23 ff.

133. It may be noted that the government regulations prohibited local officials from leaving the investigation to the clerks and runners. It could be

conducted only by the magistrate, his subordinate officials, or the commissioners assigned by the superior yamen (*Hu-pu tse-li*, 84:15b; *Liu-pu ch'u-fen tse-li*, 24:4).

134. *P'ing-p'ing yen*, 4:48b; *Mu-ling shu*, 14:46–47; *Huang-cheng pei-lan*, A:14.

135. *Huang-cheng pei-lan*, A:16–17b, 23a–b.

136. *Ibid.*, A:27b–28; *Ch'ien-ku pei-yao*, 8:28b–29; 9:11–12, 26; 10:12a–b, 20–22b; *Mu-ling shu*, 13:43a–b.

137. *Hu-pu tse-li*, 84:13a–b.

138. *Ch'in-pan chou-hsien shih-i*, p. 52; *Ch'ien-ku pei-yao*, 10:28 ff; *Mu-ling shu*, 14:67b–71b; *Shih-ch'ü yü-chi*, 1:4.

139. *Huang-cheng pei-lan*, A:30–31; *Mu-ling shu*, 14:28b, 35–39b, 66.

140. *Huang-cheng pei-lan*, A:10 ff.

141. *Fu-hui ch'üan-shu*, 27:19. In one case, a magistrate contributed 1000 taels of silver for flood relief and set up a relief board, headed by members of the gentry, which raised 20,000 taels (*Hsüeh-chih t'i-hsing lu*, B:12–13). In another instance, a magistrate donated 300 taels and about 68,000 silver dollars were contributed by the gentry and merchants (*Mu-ling shu*, 14:37b, 52). For additional instances, see *Hsien-chih-t'ang kao*, 1:19; *Huang-cheng pei-lan*, B:9; *Mu-ling shu*, 13:6b; 14:28b–29b.

142. *Yung-li yung-yen*, 84:86b; *Mu-ling shu*, 14:31b–33b, 35, 36–38b, 48a–b, 54b.

143. *Hu-pu tse-li*, 84:28–29b; *Li-pu tse-li*, 22:3–4b; *Liu-pu ch'u-fen tse-li*, 24:10–14. For this reason, technical instructions on the wiping out of locusts were issued to the magistrates by the provincial authorities (*Ch'ien-ku pei-yao*, 9:27 ff).

144. A magistrate was punishable with sixty strokes if he failed to take care of the people who were entitled to care in the poorhouse (*Ch'ing lü-li*, 8:57a–b). For the quotas of persons to be kept in the poorhouse in different provinces, see *Hu-pu tse-li*, 90:1b ff, 17 ff.

145. *Mu-ling shu*, 15:18.

146. *Hu-pu tse-li*, 90:1. Two examples may be cited. The official quota in Liang-shan, Szechwan, was only five persons. Three additional persons were cared for through contributions made by the local magistrate. When another magistrate, Liu Heng, took over the post, he made more contributions and nineteen more persons were taken into the poorhouse. Further contributions from the gentry and well-to-do commoners built a 128-room poorhouse where 104 persons were housed (*Yung-li yung-yen*, pp. 77–78, 82–83b).

In Ta-ch'eng, Chihli, the magistrate and gentry deposited the money they themselves had donated in a pawnshop and used the interest to finance the establishment of six poorhouses, maintaining more than 200 persons (*Mu-ling shu*, 15:17).

147. *Hu-pu tse-li*, 90:8–12b.

148. E.g., chou and hsien in Chekiang (*ibid.*, 90:9b).

149. *Fu-hui ch'üan-shu*, 31:16b–19b; *Wu-ch'eng hsien-chih*, 7:13, 14.

150. *Hu-pu tse-li,* 90:8; *Ch'ien-ku pei-yao,* 2:19.

151. *Hu-pu tse-li,* 90:8; *Ch'ien-ku pei-yao,* 2:18b–19; *Mu-ling shu,* 15:26b.

152. The charity schools were to be set up in cities and countryside, whereas the community schools were to be in the rural districts. See *Li³-pu tse-li,* 82:4b–5; *Ch'ing hui-tien shih-li, chüan* 396; *Hsüeh-cheng ch'üan-shu,* 64:1, 2, 3, 6; *Mu-ling shu,* 16:29b, 30b, 32, 33b.

153. *Li³-pu tse-li,* 82:4b–5; *Hsüeh-cheng ch'üan-shu,* 64:6b.

154. *Fu-hui ch'üan-shu,* 25:12b–13. Instances of magistrates and gentry members contributing money to establish community schools or charity schools are mentioned in many local gazetteers. But most of the magistrates were unenthusiastic and unwilling to donate money for the schools. The lack of funds made it very difficult to maintain the schools, and many schools established by previous magistrates were soon out of existence (see Hsiao, *Rural China,* pp. 250–252).

155. *Fu-hui ch'üan-shu,* 2:16b; 24:21; *T'ien-tai chih-lüeh,* 4:2b ff; *Hsüeh-chih ou-ts'un,* 4:1b.

156. *Ping-t'a meng-hen lu,* B:15.

157. *Ch'ing hui-tien,* 32:3a–b; *Li³-pu tse-li,* 60:1; *Fu-hui ch'üan-shu,* 24:20b–21b.

158. *Hsüeh-chih ou-ts'un,* 4:13. It was ruled in *Li³-pu tse-li,* 60:4, that a prefect or magistrate who could not read the examination papers should invite a competent person to do it on his behalf.

159. The following were not eligible to take the examination: family members of prostitutes, entertainers, government runners, and slaves. For details, see *Hsüeh-cheng ch'üan-shu,* 43:1 ff.

160. *Liu-pu ch'u-fen tse-li,* 30:34.

161. The six Sacred Edicts which were first issued by the Ming emperor, Tai-tsu, and taken over by the Ch'ing dynasty and again promulgated officially in 1662 were: (1) Be filial and obedient to your parents; (2) Respect your elders and superiors; (3) Maintain harmonious relationships with your neighbors; (4) Instruct your sons and grandsons; (5) Be engaged in your work with content; (6) Do not commit wrongful deeds. These edicts were expanded to sixteen by the K'ang-hsi emperor in 1670 as follows: (1) Pay regard to filial and fraternal duties in order to emphasize the proper relationships; (2) Be kind to your kin in order to maintain harmony; (3) Let harmony prevail among neighbors in order to prevent disputes and litigations; (4) Give importance to farming and the culture of mulberry trees in order to produce adequate supplies of food and clothing; (5) Be frugal in order to prevent waste; (6) Give importance to education in order to improve the behavior of scholars; (7) Discard unorthodox doctrines in order to exalt orthodox learning; (8) Explain the laws in order to warn the ignorant and obstinate; (9) Illustrate the principles of politeness and deference in order to improve customs; (10) Attend to the essential employments in order to make firm the will of the people; (11) Instruct the youth in order to prevent them from doing evil; (12) Suppress all false accusations in order to protect the innocent; (13) Warn those who hide

deserters to avoid involvement; (14) Complete the payment of taxes in order to prevent frequent urging; (15) Unite the *pao* and *chia* in order to eliminate robbery and theft; (16) Dissolve feuds in observance of the value of lives (*Ch'ing hui-tien shih-li, chüan* 397; cf. William Milne's translation in *The Sacred Edict*, London, 1817; G. T. Staunton's translation in *Miscellaneous Notices Relating to China*, London, 1822, pp. 1–56; James Legge's translation in "Imperial Confucianism," *The China Review*, VI, 1877–78, pp. 147–158, 223–235, 299–310, 364–374).

162. *Ch'ing hui-tien shih-li, chüan* 397, 398; *Ch'ing hui-tien,* 30:12b–13; *Ch'in-pan chou-hsien shih-i,* p. 8b; *Wu-hsüeh lu ch'u-pien,* 23:5b; *Hsi Chin shih-hsiao lu,* 1:13a–b.

163. *Ch'ing hui-tien shih-li, chüan* 398; *Ch'in-pan chou-hsien shih-i,* p. 33b; *Fu-hui ch'üan-shu,* 31:11–13b, 19b–20; *Hsüeh-chih hsü-shuo,* p. 16; *P'ei-yüan-t'ang ou-ts'un kao,* 19:21 ff; *Hsüeh-chih t'i-hsing lu,* B:13b–14b, 18; *P'ing-p'ing yen,* 4:50b ff; *Tzu-chih hsin-shu,* 14:21b–23b, 29b–30, 34a–b; *Mu-ling shu,* 16:2, 4b, 7b, 9b–10, 17b, 20b–22b.

164. *P'ei-yüan-t'ang ou-ts'un kao,* 19:21 ff; *Mu-ling shu,* 16:9b–10.

165. *Ch'ing hui-tien,* 30:13; *Li³-pu tse-li,* 49:1. For a discussion of the social status of the guests invited to the local banquet, see Hsiao, *Rural China,* pp. 210 ff.

166. *Ch'ing hui-tien,* 30:13–15b, 36:10; *Ch'ing hui-tien shih-li, chüan* 444; *Li³-pu tse-li,* 48:1; *Fu-hui ch'üan-shu,* 24:27–28; *P'ing-p'ing yen,* 4:38b–39, 42; *Mu-ling shu,* 16:14b–15b; *Tzu-chih hsin shu,* 3:20b–22. Under the law the magistrate and the educational official were punishable by demotion of one grade if their recommendation did not accord with the facts (*Liu-pu ch'u-fen tse-li,* 30:38).

167. *Ping-t'a meng-hen lu,* B:13b–14; *Ching-te-t'ang chi,* 4:13; *Mu-ling shu,* 16:9b–10.

168. *Ch'ing shih-lu,* Jen-tsung, 279:25b. See also *Ch'ing hui-tien shih-li, chüan* 397; *Hsüeh-cheng ch'üan-shu,* 9:21; *Fu-hui ch'üan-shu,* 24:2b; *Hsüeh-chih i-te pien,* p. 34.

169. *Ch'ing hui-tien shih-li, chüan* 398, 399; *Pao-chia shu,* 2:44b; *Mu-ling shu,* 16:33b; *Ching-shih wen-pien,* 23:5b; *Hsüeh-chih i-te pien,* p. 34. Huang Ang (first half of eighteenth century) reported that upon the order of the provincial official, a *sheng-yüan* had been nominated as chief lecturer and two elders as assistant lecturers in each of the rural districts of Wu-hsi and Chin-kuei, Kiangsu, The elders read one of the Sacred Edicts, and the *sheng-yüan* explained it. As the provincial official did not supervise the lecture system, it was discontinued after three or four lectures had been held (*Hsi Chin shih-hsiao lu,* 1:13a–b).

170. *Ping-t'a meng-hen lu,* B:13b–14; *Hsüeh-chih t'i-hsing lu,* B:6b–7.

171. Hsiao (*Rural China,* p. 197) reaches the following conclusion in his appraisal of the lecture system: "Whatever may have been the intrinsic merits of the *hsiang-yüeh,* the majority of Chinese officials and quite a few of the emperors expressed disappointment in its performance. If we have to choose

between this view and the view of the apparently optimistic minority, it seems safer to subscribe to the former. . . Moreover, even if we take the favorable reports at their face value, it is doubtful that we can regard the operation of the *hsiang-yüeh* as a success." Hsiao believes that in addition to the difficulty of securing suitable persons to serve in the *hsiang-yüeh* in towns and villages, the unsatisfactory conditions under which the Chinese peasantry lived was a fundamental obstacle to successful ideological control (pp. 197–199).

172. *Ch'ing shih-lu*, Jen-tsung, 279:25b; *Ch'ing hui-tien shih-li, chüan* 398; *Fu-hui ch'üan-shu*, 24:23b; *P'ei-yüan-t'ang ou-ts'un kao*, 13:20; *Mu-ling shu*, 16:5b.

173. *Hsüeh-chih hsü-shuo*, p. 16; *Ping-t'a meng-hen lu*, B:12b.

174. *Hu-pu tse-li*, 93:22.

175. *Fu-hui ch'üan-shu*, 2:5.

176. *Ibid.*, 2:4b–5b, 7; *San-yü-t'ang wen-chi*, 12:1b–2; *T'ien-tai chih-lüeh*, 10:15b–16; *Yung-li yung-yen*, 3a–b; *Mu-ling shu*, 2:11; *Huan-hsiang yao-tse*, 2:5b–6.

177. *Fu-hui ch'üan-shu*, 2:5b–6, 7; *Huan-hsiang yao-tse*, 2:6.

178. *Fu-hui ch'üan-shu*, 2:16b.

179. *Ch'ing hui-tien*, 36:1, 4; *Li³-pu tse-li*, 134:1–2b, 6b; 135:4–5b; *Mu-ling shu*, 22:35b.

180. *Ch'ing hui-tien*, 36:14; *Li³-pu tse-li*, 135:6b–7.

181. This sacrifice was offered three times a year (*Li³-pu tse-li*, 134:4a–b).

182. *Li-pu tse-li*, 29:6b–7; *Liu-pu ch'u-fen tse-li*, 32:7; *Ch'ing lü-li*, 16:8; *Mu-ling shu*, 22:38a–b.

183. *Ch'ing hui-tien*, 47:42; *Li³-pu tse-li*, 134:4; *Fu-hui ch'üan-shu*, 24:11b–14; *Fu-weng chi, hsing-ming*, 9:1–6b; *Hsüeh-chih i-shuo*, B:1; *Meng-hen lu-yü*, 77a–b; *Mu-ling shu*, 22:35b, 37 ff.

184. *Ch'ien-ku pei-yao*, 9:55; *Mu-ling shu*, 22:46; *Tzu-chih hsin-shu*, 8:34b–35b.

185. *Hsüeh-chih i-shuo*, B:3; *Mu-ling shu*, 22:37a–b, 39b; *Tzu-chih hsin-shu*, 14:16b–17.

186. *Fu-hui ch'üan-shu*, 24:13b; *Mu-ling shu*, 22:37.

187. *Mu-ling shu*, 22:37b.

188. The local official was punishable with eighty strokes for offering a sacrifice to a god not listed in the Book of Sacrifices (*Ch'ing lü-li*, 16:8).

189. *Hsüeh-chih i-shuo*, B:3a–b; cf. remarks of Wang Chih in *Mu-ling shu*, 22:36b.

190. *Fu-hui ch'üan-shu*, 24:10b–11b; *Hsüeh-chih i-shuo*, B:1.

191. For example, the city god of Lou-hsien in Kiangsu was a former magistrate, Li Fu-hsing, who had died there in 1669. The gentry and the people, remembering his diligence and good administration, pronounced him the city god by presenting a request to the Supreme God through the petition of Chang T'ien-shih, the head priest of the Taoist sect (*Sung-chün chün-i ch'eng-shu, ts'e* 10:363–364b).

192. *T'ien-tai chih-lüeh*, 10:15b–16, 17b–18; *Tzu-chih hsin-shu*, 8:41b–42.

193. *Hsüeh-chih i-shuo*, B:1; *Meng-hen lu-yü*, 77a–b.

194. For the details of this case, see *Hsüeh-chih i-shuo*, B:1b–2b.

195. *Lu-chou kung-an*, A:17–19b; *Fu-hui ch'üan-shu*, 14:25b–26, 28a–b; see remarks on this point by Wang Hui-tsu in *Hsüeh-chih i-shuo*, B:2b.

196. *Fu-hui ch'üan-shu*, 24:15; *Mu-ling shu*, 22:39.

197. It corresponded to the system of the "Stems and Branches" (*kan-chih*) which makes the cycle.

198. *Ch'ing hui-tien*, 30:12b; *Fu-hui ch'üan-shu*, 24:16a–b.

199. *Ch'in-pan chou-hsien shih-i*, pp. 33–34.

200. *Mu-ling shu, chüan* 9, *passim*.

201. *Ping-t'a meng-hen lu*, B:60b; *Hsing-mu yao-lüeh*, p. 14.

202. *Fu-hui ch'üan-shu*, 23:16–17; *Fu-weng chi, hsing-ming*, pp. 28–29; *Mu-ling shu*, 22:31b; *Hsing-ch'ien pi-lan*, 7:21 ff; *Ch'ien-ku pei-yao*, 7:13.

203. The punishment varied from forfeiture of nominal salary to demotion of one grade, depending upon the number of rooms destroyed by fire. The magistrate was also subject to forfeiture of salary and demotion if the fire destroyed the treasury, jail, or the official documents (*Li-pu tse-li*, 22:8–9; *Liu-pu ch'u-fen tse-li*, 24:15–17b).

204. See above, Chap. II, sec. 1.

205. *Li-pu tse-li*, 20:2b ff; *Liu-pu ch'u-fen tse-li*, 22:3–6b, 8a–b.

206. *Li-pu tse-li*, 38:34b–36; *Liu-pu ch'u-fen tse-li*, 42:5, 25.

207. *Liu-pu ch'u-fen tse-li*, 45:43.

208. *Li-pu tse-li*, 45:4–14; *Liu-pu ch'u-fen tse-li*, 45:9b–10.

209. *Li-pu tse-li*, 45:2 ff; *Liu-pu ch'u-fen tse-li*, 45:38 ff.

210. *Li-pu tse-li*, 31:3a–b; *Liu-pu ch'u-fen tse-li*, 34:3a–b.

211. *Li-pu tse-li*, 39:19–20, 43:49 ff; *Chang wen-hsiang chi*, 111:1 ff.

212. *Liu-pu ch'u-fen tse-li*, 45:89b; *Ching-shih wen-pien*, 23:5b.

213. *Ch'ing hui-tien shih-li, chüan* 927.

214. *Hsüeh-chih hsü-shuo*, p. 16; *Mu-ling shu*, 16:5a–b.

CHAPTER X. THE GENTRY AND LOCAL ADMINISTRATION

1. By "elite" we mean the minority who were considered superior and had the most power in society. No value judgment is involved. Consult Vilfredo Pareto, *Mind and Society*, trans. A. Bonjiono and A. Livingston, 4 vols. (New York, 1935), I, 169; III, 1423; H. D. Lasswell, *Politics: Who Gets What, When, How* (New York, 1936), chap. 1; H. D. Lasswell and A. Kaplan, *Power and Society* (New Haven, 1950), p. 201.

2. The term "formal," as Lasswell and Kaplan suggest (p. 130), conveys "the idea of legitimacy and the idea of a symbolic status." Informal power, on the other hand, lacks authority and legality. Thus any person or group participating in the governing process but not recognized as a responsible part of the government represents informal power.

3. See Ch'üan Han-sheng, *Chung-kuo hang-hui chih-tu shih;* H. B. Morse, *The Guilds of China* (London, 1909).

4. For a study of the social life and mobility of salt merchants, particularly

their association with men of letters, see P. T. Ho, "The Salt Merchants of Yang-chou: a study of Commercial Capitalism in Eighteenth-Century China," *Harvard Journal of Asiatic Studies*, 17.1 and 2:130–168 (June 1954).

5. *Tung-hua hsü-lu*, 190:6b; 200:12b, 17b, 20; 201:4, 17; 202:4, 11; *Chang Wen-hsiang chi, tsou-i*, 57:1–3; *Yü-chai ts'un-kao*, 19:6b; 17:39; *Ch'ing shih kao*, 149:11.

6. The domination of gentry over merchants is clearly seen in the fact that although the latter also took part in railway construction plans in the last decade of the nineteenth century and the first decade of the present century, it was always the gentry who negotiated with the officials. For instance, in 1898 the gentry members and merchants of Hupeh, Hunan, and Kwangtung signed a joint petition to the government requesting that the Hankow-Canton railway run through Hunan and be built by the local people, but it was the gentry members, Hsiung Hsi-ling and others, who went to see Governor-general Chang Chih-tung (*Chang Wen-hsiang chi, tsou-i*, 57:1–3). Further, the managers of the local railway companies in the various provinces were selected from the gentry members (see below, note 100).

7. *Chin-shen* means, literally, the insertion of an official's tablet (*hu*), held during a court audience, into the belt worn by him. See *Chuang-tzu chi-chieh*, 8:28; *Shih-chi*, 28:3; *Han-shu*, 25A:4b.

8. After I had sent my manuscript to press, I read with great interest R. M. Marsh's *The Mandarin; the Circulation of Elite in China* (Glencoe, Ill., 1961). Marsh substitutes "local elite" for "gentry" for the reason that the latter term does not apply to the Chinese *shen-shih*. I agree with him on this point, although I still follow the popular usage and translate *shen-shih* as "gentry" in my book.

However, while both of us identify *shen-shih* as the local elite, we do not agree on the membership of the group. Marsh (p. 38) sees the officials in the imperial bureaucracy as persons performing the highly valued roles, whereas the group performing the roles of medium value, that is, degree-holders not in office, the "local literati," he classifies as the "local elite." Thus persons with bureaucratic status, called by him the "elite of the realm," are excluded from the local elite (pp. 35, 51). Presumably Marsh believes that officials holding a position in the bureaucracy could not perform leadership roles on the local (hsien) level, and that therefore these roles were left to the degree-holders not in office, who complemented the local bureaucracy. However, as we shall see, the *shen-shih* or local elite included the retired officials and officials on leave at home, who not only took an active part in local leadership on the hsien, prefectural, and provincial levels, but above all, were more influential and powerful than the degree-holders not in office. To exclude officials from the definition is to leave the core of the local elite out of the picture. Marsh is also confused over the meaning of the terms *shen-shih, shen-chin,* and *hsiang-shen,* which he associates with degree-holders below officialdom (p. 55). In fact, while *shih* and *chin* refer to degree-holders, and to *sheng-yüan* in particular, *shen* refers to officials.

Marsh includes another group in the local elite—the large landowners and wealthy merchants who did not hold degrees but assumed these medium-valued roles "because their income provided both the necessary leisure and the excess capital" (p. 38). As will become clear later in this chapter, merchants and landlords, regardless of their economic status, did not have the status of *shen-shih*. Marsh claims that "any given landowner or wealthy merchant could hold disparate positions, however high he might be in the system of economic stratification . . . his social status or prestige would be evaluated as low until he became involved in the above local leadership functions, at which time his social status would correlate more highly with his economic status" (p. 38). It is true, as Marsh says, that wealthy merchants and large landowners did contribute to certain aspects of leadership, such as raising funds for financing and operating irrigation projects, granaries, and public works, for maintaining temples, and for philanthropies. But they did not direct irrigation projects and public works; moreover, contrary to Marsh's contention, they did not lecture in academies; they did not perform "ideological functions in ceremonies"; they seldom arbitrated disputes; above all, they were not in a position to act as intermediaries between the government and the people. Thus they did not perform the important leadership roles generally associated with the *shen-shih*, because they did not possess the status and privileges of the *shen-shih*, nor had they a position in the power structure. A distinction must be made between financial contribution and actual local leadership in order to ascertain who were the local elite in a community.

9. For instance, Wolfram Eberhard defines gentry as "owners of substantial estates, who also held official positions, and later were also literati." (*A History of China*, trans. E. E. Dickes, Berkeley and Los Angeles, 1950, p. 72. In his *Conquerors and Rulers, Social Forces in Medieval China*, Leiden, 1952, p. 16, Eberhard defines gentry as a clan "comprising landowners, scholars, and politicians in one and the same class.") Certainly all three of these groups were power groups in China, but to lump them together in one definition confuses the issue and leaves unanswered the crucial question of the criterion or criteria for gentry membership.

Eberhard singles out the proprietary aspect in his recently revised edition of *A History of China* (Berkeley, 1960), p. 72, where he defines the gentry in Han times, the era seen by him as the beginning of the development of the "gentry state," as families which "owned substantial estates." They included old nobility, nonnoble officials, wealthy merchants, and nonnoble farmers. While one branch of the family lived in the country and collected rents from tenants, another branch, consisting of literati, was in the capital or in a provincial administrative center in official positions (pp. 72–73).

The validity of such a definition is subject to dispute, for officials were not always recruited from the landlord families. Persons without such a background did become officials and in later dynasties, after the examination system had been introduced, became degree holders. On the other hand, many landlords failed to become officials or degree holders.

The important point, as we shall see, is that the status and power of the Chinese gentry was politically based, that is, only when one attained the status of an official or a degree holder could he enjoy the privileges and power of the gentry and participate in the exercise of its functions in society. Since Eberhard fails to see this important feature of the Chinese gentry, his use of the term "gentry" becomes ambiguous and confusing. On p. 78 he says that the official class was "recruited from the gentry." Yet in other places he seems to indicate that it was association with political power that admitted a person to the gentry class. On p. 197 he divides the gentry of the Five Dynasties into two parts: the "big gentry," which directed policy in the capital, and the "small gentry," which operated mainly in the provincial cities, directing local affairs and bound by ties of loyalty to "big gentry" families. On p. 216, discussing the gentry in the Sung, he states that "all burghers were admitted to the examinations, and, thus, there was a certain social mobility allowed within the leading class of the society, and a new 'small gentry' developed by this system." For the Ming, on pp. 252–253 he mentions the existence of the old gentry who had been rich landowners, and the new "small gentry." Those of the latter who wanted "to play a political part in the central government or to gain a position there" got into close touch with "one of the families of the gentry," or approached the emperor or the eunuchs in the court. And finally, on p. 272, he mentions that literati and scholars streamed into Peking when the Ch'ing government was looking for Chinese scholars for its administrative posts. If the rise of these gentry was connected with political power and the examination system, then the membership and power of the Chinese gentry were not economically determined. Much of the confusion could have been avoided if Eberhard had used the term "landlord" instead of "gentry," and if he had made a distinction between those landlords who held official positions or degrees and those who did not.

10. Fei Hsiao-tung, "Peasantry and Gentry: An Interpretation of Chinese Social Structure and Its Changes," *The American Journal of Sociology*, 2.1:11 (July 1946).

11. On the purchase of official ranks see Hsü Ta-ling, *Ch'ing-tai chüan-na chih-tu*.

12. That the wealthy merchants were not considered members of the *shen-shih* is clearly indicated in a Tientsin *pao-chia* record made in 1842 in which the number of households in the city and the surrounding rural districts was given under various categories. The salt merchants were listed separately from the *shen-chin*, which always appears at the top of the list (*Chin-men pao-chia t'u-shuo, passim*).

Although there is no entry for landlords, it goes without saying that *shen-chin* by definition did not include landlords without the status of *shen* or *chin*. Obviously they would be listed instead under the category of *yen-hu*, a term ordinarily used for population in general, including commoner households (*min-hu*), soldiers, artisans, salt makers, fishermen, and minority groups (*Ch'ing hui-tien*, 17:1a–b). Since shopkeepers, peddlers, hired laborers, boatmen, fishermen, soldiers, physicians, Buddhist monks, Taoist priests, and some other groups are listed separately in this *pao-chia* record, the term *yen-hu* apparently refers to households other than those in the various occupations just mentioned—that is, to farmers, including both landowners and peasants.

13. T'ao Chu (1779–1839) mentioned that among the scholar-gentry who handled tax payment for others there were *sheng-yüan* and *chien-sheng* who owned no land (*Tao Yün-t'ing tsou-su,* 17:9b).

14. *Ch'ing hui-tien,* 18:2; *Hu-pu tse-li,* 84:13; *Hsüeh-cheng ch'üan-shu,* 32:1b–2b, 3b; *Ch'ien-ku pei-yao,* 7:21; 8:26a–b, 45b–46. Since the poor and degenerate *sheng-yüan* were ridiculed in novels it is reasonable to raise the question: did a *sheng-yüan* lose his status as a member of the gentry because of poverty? The answer is no. In a discussion of how to "treat the *shen-shih*," Huang Liu-hung suggested that a magistrate should donate stipends to the poor *sheng-yüan* who could not maintain themselves so that they could continue their studies (*Fu-hui ch'üan-shu,* 4:9a–b). Wang Feng-sheng made similar suggestions (*Hsüeh-chih t'i-hsing lu,* A:11a–b). These suggestions reflect the attitude of the local officials who not only showed respect to learned but poor men, but also made an effort to assist the poor scholars financially.

15. "Status group" designates a group of people having similar social honor. This notion, which is based on Max Weber, is helpful in distinguishing "status situation" from "class situation" (i.e., the ownership or lack of property), and in discussing the relationship between those two types of order (*From Max Weber: Essays in Sociology,* trans. H. H. Gerth and C. W. Mills, New York, 1946, pp. 181–187, 405).

16. For details about these examinations, see *Ch'ing hui-tien,* 32:2b–4; *Li[3]-pu tse-li,* 60:1 ff; Shang Yen-liu, *Ch'ing-tai k'o-chü k'ao-shih shu-lu,* pp. 1–17; Miyazaki Ichisada, *Kakyo;* Étienne Zi, *Pratique des examens litteraires en Chine,* Variétés Sinologiques (Shanghai, 1894); Chang, *Chinese Gentry,* pp. 10–11.

17. For example, a well-known commoner-scholar, Shih Ching, taught in Chiang-yin, Kiangsu. His scholarly reputation even reached the ears of the Ch'ien-lung emperor, who ordered the governor-general and governor to make a report on him. He was visited by the provincial director of studies. Yet he remained a commoner (*pu-i*) (*Ch'ing shih-lu,* Kao-tsung, 293:4b–5b).

18. A directive issued by Governor Ch'eng Han-chang (d. 1832) to the magistrates in Kwangtung instructed them to report the names of *shen-shih* in the following order: active officials, officials staying at home, degree-holders (*k'o-chia*), officials who purchased their rank (*Mu-ling shu,* 2:44). Customarily the gentry having bureaucratic status (*shen*) were classified into two categories: (1) active officials, and (2) officials who had held posts previously (*Fu-hui ch'üan-shu,* 2:13; 14:21b; *P'ei-yüan-t'ang ou-ts'un kao,* 17:6b; 34:24b; 37:10b; *Mu-ling shu,* 2:2b, 32b, 39). Or, following the practice of Huang Liu-hung, they were divided into the following three categories: (1) officials who held office either in the capital or away from their own native provinces; (2) officials on leave at home; (3) retired or dismissed officials staying at home

(*Fu-hui ch'üan-shu*, 4:9). Huang's classification is more satisfactory because it is more inclusive.

19. There were several types of *kung-sheng*: (1) *en-kung*, Senior Licentiates by imperial favor; (2) *pa-kung*, Senior Licentiates by selection—government school students who had passed a special examination held for this purpose at regular intervals (at first, once every six years; after 1742, once every twelve years); (3) *yu-kung*, Senior Licentiates by recommendation—government school students who were recommended by educational officials for their good conduct and accomplishments, and who had passed a special examination held once every three years for this purpose; (4) *sui-kung*, Senior Licentiates by seniority—selected from the stipendiaries who had seniority; (5) *fu-kung*, *fu-pang*, or *fu-pang chü-jen*, supplementary *chü-jen*—Senior Licentiates who had passed the provincial examination and whose names were on the supplementary list of successful candidates, the *fu-pang*; (6) *lin-kung*, stipendiaries who purchased the title of *kung-sheng*; (7) *tseng-kung*, "additional" government school students who purchased the title of *kung-sheng*; (8) *fu-kung*, "supplementary" government school students who purchased the title of *kung-sheng*; (9) commoner–*chien-sheng* who purchased the title of *kung-sheng*. The first five were *cheng-kung* (regular *kung-sheng*); the rest were irregulars, known as *li-kung* (Senior Licentiates by purchase). For details see *Ch'ing hui-tien*, 32:12b–15b; 33:2b; 76:4b–5; *Ch'ing shih kao*, 113:1b ff; Shang Yen-liu, pp. 26–32; Chang, *Chinese Gentry*, pp. 19–20, 27–29.

20. *Chien-sheng* comprised the following categories: (1) *en-chien*, Imperial Academy students by imperial favor; (2) *yu-chien*, Imperial Academy students by recommendation—"supplementary" government school students recommended to the Imperial Academy for their good conduct and accomplishments; (3) *yin-chien*, or *yin-sheng*, Honorary Licentiates, who were admitted to the Imperial Academy by virtue of their fathers' or grandfathers' bureaucratic status (*en-yin*) or by virtue of their fathers' or grandfathers' having died in the service of the government (*nan-yin*); (4) *lin-chien*, stipendiaries who purchased the title of *chien-sheng*; (5) *tseng-chien*, "additional" government school students who purchased the title of *chien-sheng*; (6) *fu-chien*, "supplementary" government school students who purchased the title of *chien-sheng*; (7) *chün-hsiu chien-sheng*, commoners who purchased the title of *chien-sheng*. The last four were also called irregular *chien-sheng*, or *li-chien* (Imperial Academy students by purchase). For details see *Ch'ing hui-tien*, 76:5; *Ch'ing shih kao*, 113:1b ff; Shang Yen-liu, pp. 23–26. Chang, *Chinese Gentry*, pp. 13–14, 19.

21. Only holders of the first degree were admitted to the prefectural, chou, and hsien schools. The civil *sheng-yüan* were classified into three grades: (1) *fu-sheng*, "supplementary" government school students—newly admitted students; (2) *tseng-sheng*, "additional" government school students—advanced from *fu-sheng* who received the second grade in the "annual" examination given by the provincial director of studies (*sui-shih*); (3) *lin-sheng*, stipendiaries—advanced from those in the above two groups of students who received the first grade in the same examination. But as there was a quota for *lin-sheng*

in each government school, the actual advancement to stipendiary depended upon whether there was a vacancy. For details see *Ch'ing hui-tien*, 31:7 ff; *Ch'ing shih kao*, 113:10b; *Kai-yü ts'ung-k'ao*, 28:2; Shang Yen-liu, pp. 18–22; Chang, *Chinese Gentry*, pp. 17–18.

22. P. T. Ho, in his "Aspects of Social Mobility in China, 1368–1911," *Comparative Studies in Society and History*, 1.4:330–359 (June 1959), rejects the term "gentry," and uses instead "ruling class." He classifies officials, *chin-shih*, *chü-jen*, and *kung-sheng* as ruling class; includes *chien-sheng* in the Ming ruling class, but excludes them in the Ch'ing ruling class; and excludes *sheng-yüan* from the ruling class in both dynasties (pp. 340–342). Ho's study is primarily concerned with the persons "entering into the ruling class," thus he uses qualification for official appointment as his criterion. But it is not clear whether he sees "ruling class" and *shen-shih* as identical. The latter term is never mentioned in his article.

In my opinion, we may or may not include *chien-sheng* and *sheng-yüan* in the ruling class, depending upon our definition of the ruling class. But according to the usage of the term *shen-shih* or *shen-chin* in the Ming and Ch'ing, *chien-sheng* and *sheng-yüan* must be included in the group, whether we classify them as ruling class or not. Few students of Chinese history would disagree that the term *shen* refers only to the officials, active or retired. And few would disagree that the term *shen-chin* definitely includes the *shen* and the *chin*, that is the *sheng-yüan*. The ambiguity seems to lie in the actual application of the term *shen-shih*, although literally it is synonymous with *shen-chin*. Did the term actually include *shen-yüan*? My answer is yes. Since this book is concerned only with the *shen-shih* in the Ch'ing, I will examine only the usage of the term in this period to illustrate my point. In *Fu-hui ch'üan-shu*, 4:9a–b, under the heading "treatment of the *shen-shih*," Huang Liu-hung gave advice on how to treat both the *hsiang-shen* (natives who were or had been officials) and the *shih* of the schools (students of government schools). Similarly Wang Feng-sheng, in his *Hsüeh-chih t'i-hsing lu*, A:11a–b, mentioned the *shih* under the heading *shen-shih*. He also used the term *shen-chin*. One other concrete example, which includes a list of the *shen-shih* in a certain locality, is even more conclusive. In a petition submitted by a group of "*shen-shih*" in Tientsin to the governor-general of Chihli in 1896, requesting the imperial government to bestow posthumous honor upon a deceased *shen*, the list of petitioners included the names of three ordinary *sheng-yüan* (two *lin-sheng* and one *fu-sheng*), besides a number of officials and several *chü-jen* (*Ching-shu-chai i-kao*, 1:1).

23. For the meaning of the term *shen* see above, notes 7 and 18.

24. *Chin*, which means the collar on a robe, refers to *sheng-yüan*, who wore a blue robe with a black collar and border, and to *chien-sheng*, who wore a black robe with a blue collar and border (*Ch'ing lü-li*, 4:29b; *Hsüeh-cheng ch'üan-shu*, 31:6b). The term is used interchangeably with *shih*.

25. This sort of demarcation is consistent with legal and conventional usage. *Ch'ing hui-tien* (1690), 24:19a–b; *ibid.* (1732), 31:30b–31; *Ch'ing hui-tien*

tse-li, 36:38b; *Ch'ing hui-tien shih-li* (1818), 144:15b; and *Ch'ing lü-li,* 11:14, refer to *shen-shih* in the following order: civil and military *hsiang-shen* (i.e., natives who were or had been officials), *chin-shih, chü-jen, kung-sheng, chien-sheng,* and *sheng-yüan.* The names of *hsiang-shen* or *hsiang-huan* (used interchangeably with *hsiang-shen,* meaning officials living in their home towns) in a locality were also listed separately from the names of degree-holders and holders of academic titles (*chin-shih, chü-jen, kung-sheng, chien-sheng,* and *sheng-yüan*) in the following official records: *Hsü-chih ts'e* ("must know" book, prepared by yamen clerks for the magistrate—see Chap. III, note 4); *Hsien-kang ts'e* (Essentials to government), a record prepared by magistrates for their superior provincial officials, containing general information on the locality, such as physical details of the territory, number of villages, population, information relating to taxes, granaries, and post stations, and the names of local officials and gentry members (for the form of this record see *Fu-hui ch'üan-shu,* 4:20b ff; *P'ei-yüan-t'ang ou-ts'un kao,* 37:8 ff; 41:30 ff); *Ch'ao-chin ts'e* (a court-audience record submitted by local officials to the central government; for its form see *Fu-hui ch'üan-shu,* 24:5 ff); and *pao-chia* records. (See *Fu-hui ch'üan-shu,* 2:13; 4:21a–b; 21:16; 24:5b–6; *P'ei-yüan-t'ang ou-ts'un-kao,* 36:16b; 37:10b; 41:33a–b. Among the above documents, only *Hsien-kang ts'e,* mentioned in *P'ei-yüan-tang ou-ts'un kao,* has an entry for *chin-shih.* The omission in other sources is due to the fact that as a rule *chin-shih* became officials.) When Chen Hung-mou instructed the magistrates under him to prepare a *Hsien-kang ts'e,* he made it clear that *chin-shih, chü-jen, kung-sheng,* and *chien-sheng* should be listed as *shen* if they had already entered officialdom (*P'ei-yüan-t'ang ou-ts'un kao,* 36:16b; 37; 10b; 41:33b). This clearly indicates the basic difference between the two groups, as well as the criterion for *shen.* In an effort to urge the *shen-shih* of Soochow to pay grain tribute at an adjusted rate, Feng Kuei-fen, himself a *shen,* wrote two essays addressed separately to the *shen* and *chin.* The latter includes not only *sheng-yüan,* but also *chü-jen, kung-cheng,* and *chien-sheng* (*Hsien-chih-t'ang kao,* 9:23–26).

26. I shall use the term "gentry" in this study to translate *shen-shih* or *shen-chin;* but whenever a distinction between *shen* and *shih* is necessary, I shall follow the traditional usage explained in note 25, and translate *shen* as "official-gentry," and *shih* or *chin* as "scholar-gentry."

Although both Chang Chung-li and I have the same definition for gentry, there is a difference between my terms "official-gentry" and "scholar-gentry" and his terms "upper gentry" and "lower gentry." An explanation is necessary in order to avoid confusion. My terms are derived from the traditional usage distinguishing officials from degree-holders not yet entered into officialdom. Chang in *Chinese Gentry,* pp. 6–9, classifies officials, *chin-shih, chü-jen,* and regular *kung-sheng* into "upper-gentry," and irregular *kung-sheng* (i.e., those who obtained the title of *kung-sheng* by purchase), *chien-sheng,* and *sheng-yüan* into "lower-gentry." As he does not take into account the traditional distinction between the *shen* and *shih* or *chin,* and arbitrarily lumps *shen* and part of the *shih* together under "upper-gentry," it is sometimes difficult for the reader to tell which of the terms in the Chinese sources he is referring to. Chang tries to justify his classification by pointing out, among other things, the difference in the ceremonies observed by the two groups. However, the merit of using this criterion is questionable. The regulations concerning marriage ceremonies are listed in *Ta-ch'ing t'ung-li* under three categories: *p'in-kuan* (ranking officials), *shu-shih* (mass of scholars), and *shu-jen* (commoners). Officials of the eighth rank and below were classified together with *sheng-yüan* and *chien-sheng* in the second category instead of the first. If this classification is followed, not all officials can be classified as "upper gentry" in the way that Chang proposes. (Cf. P. T. Ho's criticism on Chang's demarcation between "upper" and "lower" gentry, "Aspects of Social Mobility in China, 1368–1911," pp. 341–342)

27. On the concept of the intermediate class, see Lasswell and Kaplan, p. 206. The famous classical dichotomy of "the ruler" and "the ruled" was seen by Mencius as two groups in the Chinese political and social order (*Meng-tzu chu-su*, 5 B:1b–2; James Legge, *The Work of Mencius*, The Chinese Classics, 5 vols. in 8 vols., Hong Kong and London, 1861–1872, II, 125–126). For a systematic analysis of the ruling class see Gaetano Mosca, *The Ruling Class*, trans. H. D. Kahu (New York, 1939), p. 50; cf. Pareto, *Mind and Society*, III, 1427.

28. Under the "law of avoidance," an official could not hold office in his native province, or in a neighboring province within a distance of 500 li (*Li-pu tse-li*, 1:4a–b; *Liu-pu ch'u-fen tse-li*, 3:30b).

29. *T'u-min lu*, 3:18.

30. *Hsüeh-cheng ch'üan-shu*, 31:7.

31. Thus the official-gentry referred to themselves as *chih yü-ti* (humble younger brother under your jurisdiction) on their visiting cards and letters addressed to the magistrate; the *chü-jen* called themselves *chih chiao-ti* (instructed younger brother under your jurisdiction); the regular *kung-sheng* called themselves *chih wan-sheng* (junior under your jurisdiction). The *chien-sheng* and *sheng-yüan* could only refer to themselves as *chien-sheng*, *lin-sheng*, *fu-sheng*, or *tseng-sheng*. When addressing an official-gentry member, magistrates referred to themselves as *yü-ti* (your humble younger brother) (*Huan-hsiang yao-tse*, 3:19b, 57a–b). In a petition presented to their provincial authorities a group of *sheng-yüan* signed their names together with the commoners, referring to themselves as the *shih min* (scholars and commoners). At the same time, in a letter addressed to the provincial treasurer, the official-gentry called themselves *chih-ti* (younger brothers under your jurisdiction); the reply addressed them as *lao hsien-sheng* (old gentlemen); and the provincial treasurer called himself *ti* (younger brother) (*Sung-chün chün-i ch'eng-shu, ts'e* 8:300 ff; *ts'e* 9:317a–b). This instance indicates an interesting point: not only did the official-gentry have a status superior to that of the students, as is evident in the way they referred to themselves, but, more

important, they could approach the higher officials, whereas the scholar-gentry could not.

32. Take the ceremony of lectures (*hsiang-yüeh*) as an example: The official-gentry stood together with *chü-jen* and *kung-sheng*, bowing once to the magistrate. The students stood together, facing the north, bowing three times. When the magistrate was leaving, the official-gentry, *chü-jen*, and *kung-sheng* would see him off at the gate; the students bade him farewell by seeing him to the road and bowing (*Fu-hui ch'üan-shu*, 25:28b, 36).

33. Chang Chung-li states that "in contrast to the commoners, the gentry had free access to the officials" (*Chinese Gentry*, p. 33). This is an over-simplification which fails to show that not all members of the gentry had free access to the local officials. Whereas the official-gentry were encouraged to give advice to the officials, the *sheng-yüan* were not allowed to make any suggestions regarding the welfare of the local people, violation of this rule being punishable by dismissal. They were also not allowed to visit the yamen, to interfere with the lawsuits of others, or to appear in court as witnesses (these prohibitions were engraved on the "horizontal tablet" [*wo-pei*] erected in all government schools—see *Li³-pu tse-li*, 57:1a–b; *Hsüeh-cheng ch'üan-shu*, 4:1b–2). In order to keep track of their activities the magistrate was required to keep a "door record" (*men-pu*), noting the names of *sheng-yüan* who did visit the yamen, reasons for the visit, and whether they were involved in any lawsuit. These records had to be submitted to the provincial director of studies so that he would be informed of the activities of the *sheng-yüan*. (This regulation, first introduced in 1651, was originally applicable only to the *sheng-yüan*; *kung-sheng* and *chien-sheng* were not included until 1727. But the 1651 regulation was abolished in 1755 because the keeping of records was not strictly observed. Four years later the "door record" was resumed, but this time it listed only the names of *sheng-yüan* and *chien-sheng* who were involved in lawsuits—*Hsüeh-cheng ch'üan-shu*, 31:1, 2b, 4a–b, 7b, 9a–b; *Fu-hui ch'üan-shu*, 3:23b–24.)

34. *Sheng-yüan* were under the supervision of the educational officials of the locality; those who purchased the title of *kung-sheng* or *chien-sheng* were under the supervision of the magistrates (*Hsüeh-cheng ch'üan-shu*, 31:2b, 7b, 8a–b; 33:3; *Li³-pu tse-li*, 59:1).

It is clearly declared in *Li³-pu tse-li*, 59:3, that those who purchased the titles of *kung-sheng* or *chien-sheng* were subject to chastisement and dismissal, depending upon their offense, and that all regulations governing the *sheng-yüan* were equally applicable to them.

35. *Hsüeh-cheng ch'üan-shu*, 33:1 ff.

36. *Hsien-chih-t'ang kao*, 9:25. Fang Ta-chih also mentioned that many magistrates had a tendency to treat the *sheng-yüan* in a harsh and humiliating manner (*P'ing-p'ing yen*, 2:30b–31).

37. The hat buttons, belts, and robes worn by officials differed according to their ranks. *Chü-jen*, *kung-sheng*, and *chien-sheng* wore the same belt as

the eighth-rank official. *Sheng-yüan* wore the same belt as the ninth-rank official. But hat buttons and the design of garments worn by *chü-jen, kung-sheng, chien-sheng,* and *sheng-yüan* were different from those of the officials (*Ch'ing lü-li,* 17:27–29b).

38. *Li³-pu tse-li,* 58:2b; 98:1b, 3b. Customarily money for tablets and flagpoles were granted to *en-kung* and *sui-kung* (see note 19) only. No money was provided for other types of *kung-sheng,* but they were free to display a tablet and flagpole at their own expense. However, a ruling was made in 1867 that a distinction should be made between the regular and irregular *kung-sheng.* Under this regulation, *pa-kung, yu-kung,* and *fu-kung* could continue displaying tablets and flagpoles, but the irregular *kung-sheng* (*sheng-yüan* and commoners who purchased the title of *kung-sheng*) could no longer acquire them, although those who had already set up a tablet and flagpole were permitted to keep them (*Ch'ing hui-tien shih-li, chüan* 385). This regulation seems to imply that the status of regular *kung-sheng* was superior to that of the irregular ones.

39. Ch'ü, *Law and Society,* pp. 161 ff.

40. *Ch'ing lü-li,* 4:25, 34; Staunton, pp. 7, 9; Boulais, pp. 32–33, 37–38; Ch'ü, *Law and Society,* pp. 178–180. It may be noted that this law and the following laws concerning pecuniary redemption and disputes with commoners mention only the officials. But it is understood that these laws are applicable also to the official-gentry, for the latter were by definition the natives of a local community having the status of an official.

41. *Ch'ing lü-li,* 4:71.

42. *Ch'ing hui-tien,* 32:11b; *Li-pu tse-li,* 28:10b–11; 30:29–30; *Li³-pu tse-li,* 59:3.

43. At first punishment for the magistrate was forfeiture of nine months' salary; after 1800 it was changed to demotion of two grades (*Hsüeh-cheng ch'üan-shu,* 31:2, 3b, 8b, 10b; *Li³-pu tse-li,* 57:7; *Li-pu tse-li,* 28:18; *Liu-pu ch'u-fen tse-li,* 30:31).

44. A *sheng-yüan* could be deprived of his degree by the provincial director of studies; to deprive *kung-sheng* and *chien-sheng* of their titles, the authorization of the governor-general and/or governor was required (*Hsüeh-cheng ch'üan-shu,* 31:2, 3, 4b, 7b–8; 32:1; *Li³-pu tse-li,* 57:8; 59:3a–b; *Ch'ing lü-li,* 4:35b; *Pan-an yao-lüeh,* p. 46; *Hsing-mu yao-lüeh,* p. 8).

Chin-shih and *chü-jen* could be deprived of their titles only when this was recommended by the governor-general and governor and approved by the emperor (*Li³-pu tse-li,* 59:5b; *Hsüeh-cheng ch'üan-shu,* 49:12a–b). Thus they had more protection than the holders of the lower degree.

45. *Ch'ing lü-li,* 4:7a–b; *Pan-an yao-lüeh,* p. 46b.

46. *Ch'ing lü-li,* 30:99; *Hsüeh-cheng ch'üan-shu,* 4:2; Staunton, p. 377; *Kung-ch'ih-chai wen-ch'ao,* 2:57a–b. However, Hsü Keng-pi, a magistrate, ruled that although all gentry members were given the privilege of sending their family members or servants to lay a complaint (*pao-kao*), a *sheng-yüan* was obliged to appear in court. A subordinate official (one of the miscel-

laneous officials and chief officers), a *chü-jen*, a regular *kung-sheng*, or *chien-sheng* was required to appear in person during the first trial or when a complaint was submitted for the first time. The official-gentry members with the rank of magistrate or above (among the military officials, first captain [*tu-ssu*], second captain [*shou-pei*], and above) and mothers or wives of officials holding an honorary title (*ming-fu*) were not required to appear in person to make a statement, unless they were involved in a case in which either a plaintiff or a defendant was punishable with more than 100 strokes (*Pu-ch'ien-chai man-ts'un*, 2:6–7). This regulation reflects the fact that *sheng-yüan* and low-ranking official-gentry members were not received by the local officials with the same respect as gentry members with higher status.

47. The punishment varied according to the rank of the assaulted official (*Ch'ing lü-li*, 27:31b–32; Staunton, pp. 331–332). It is clearly mentioned in the Penal Code that a retired official was to be accorded the same treatment as an active official (*Ch'ing lü-li*, 4A:71a–b; 27:34b; Ch'ü, *Law and Society*, p. 183).

48. A magistrate, Yüan Shou-ting, observed that rich commoners were bullied by powerful persons and milked for money by the clerks when they were involved in dealings with a yamen, and that therefore few of them were able to protect themselves (*T'u-min lu*, 3:14).

49. Fei, "Peasantry and Gentry," p. 8.

50. *T'ing-lin wen-chi*, 1:17b–18.

51. Many disputes were settled in this way out of court. Sometimes cases were dropped from the court through the intervention of the gentry. Thus the people could avoid the expense and trouble inevitable in litigation. Probably such mediation was more satisfactory to the people, for the gentry were likely to be familiar with local customs and to have a knowledge of the background of the dispute. A certain magistrate who preferred to settle disputes in this way ordered some cases to be settled by the gentry out of court (*Hsüeh-chih ou-ts'un*, 6:4b, 5b, 6b, 10b, 15, 24a–b).

52. For a discussion of the gentry's leadership in rural communities, see Hsiao, *Rural China*, pp. 316 ff.

53. I agree with James G. March, "An Introduction to the Theory and Measurement of Influence," in Heinz Eulau, *et al.*, eds., *Political Behavior* (Glencoe, Ill., 1956), p. 387, who sees influence as the inducement of change.

54. The overbearing manner of *sheng-yüan* in village communities seems to have been quite common (*T'ing-lin wen-chi*, 1:19; *Ching-shih wen hsü-pien*, 21:11b). A magistrate once mentioned that they often behaved like members of the official-gentry in a small district (*Tzu-chih hsin-shu*, 3:7b).

55. For instance, when several official-gentry members planned to request the government to use foreign troops to defend Shanghai (see note 56), they went to see Yin Chao-yung, chief supervisor of imperial instruction (*chan-shih*), for they realized that the plan could not be realized without his participation. When the petition was submitted to the governor, signed by more than ten members of the official-gentry, the governor asked why the

names of two prominent gentry members, Feng Kuei-fen, junior secretary of the Supervisorate of Imperial Instruction (*yu chung-yün*), and P'an Tsun-ch'i, compiler of the second class (*pien-hsiu*) of the Hanlin Academy, were not included (*Hsien-chih-t'ang kao*, 4:20a–b). In another instance, when the gentry and merchants of Kiangsi requested the right to build the provincial railway in 1904, they mentioned in their petition that since such a big enterprise could be operated only under the leadership of a "big official-gentry member" (*chü-shen*), they nominated Li Yu-fen, a former provincial treasurer of Kiangsu, as president of the railway company (*Tung-hua hsü-lu*, 190:6b–7).

56. One or two examples will illustrate how the influential affected the decision-making of high provincial authorities. In 1860, after Soochow had been seized by the Taiping forces, three official-gentry members of Kiangsu (Ku Wen-pin, Feng Kuei-fen, and P'an Tseng-wei) planned to ask Tseng Kuo-fan to send troops to reinforce Shanghai. They got the approval of the governor of Kiangsu and the high commissioner of local militia, and a gentry member was sent to see Tseng, with letters from these two officials; one of the letters was drafted by Feng and included the signatures of five gentry members. Tseng agreed to send Li Hung-chang (1823–1901) to Shanghai with his troops (*Hsien-chih-t'ang kao*, 4:15b–18; *Tseng Wen-cheng chi, tsou-kao*, 18:41).

In 1861 the same three gentry members suggested using foreign troops to defend Shanghai and to recover other cities in Kiangsu. They communicated their plan to a former prefect and, through him, to the governor. The governor said: "It is all right if the idea comes from the gentry; it is not mine." The gentry members then submitted to the governor a plea signed by more than ten persons. The governor memorialized the throne and authorized the establishment of a Joint Defense Bureau (Hui-fang Chü) in Shanghai.

At the same time, one of the group, P'an Tseng-wei (department director of the Board of Punishment [*lang-chung*] and the son of P'an Shih-en, Grand Councilor of State), went to Peking to see Prince Kung, requesting that the central government consider the plan. The emperor ordered the Tsungli Yamen to discuss the matter with the British and French ministers. The emperor also asked the opinion of Tseng Kuo-fan, the governor-general of Liang-Chiang. Tseng did not favor the plan on the ground that it was a shame to require the assistance of foreign troops. But the emperor told him that permission should be granted (*Ch'ing shih-lu*, Mu-tsung, 15:56a–b; 18:14b–15; 20:21b–22; 21:10b–11b; 24:21–22b; *Tseng Wen-cheng chi, tsou-kao*, 18:43–45b; *Hsien-chih-t'ang kao*, 4:19–20b; *Shang-hai hsien-chih*, 11:38b–39).

57. The following instance is an illustration. A member of the official-gentry, Yin chao-yung (*q.v.*, note 55), who was observing mourning for a parent in Shanghai, presented a memorial to the capital in 1862 reporting on the things he had witnessed there. He complained about the corruption of the commissioners in charge of likin, the unlawful activities of a number

of high local officials, and the lack of discipline among the troops. The emperor then sent a copy of this memorial to Tseng Kuo-fan and to Li Hung-chang, the governor-general and governor, ordering them to investigate matters and punish one or two principal offenders (*Ch'ing shih-lu*, Mu-tsung, 28:58b–59b).

58. *Ch'ing shih-lu*, Shih-tsu, 106:12–13b; *ibid.*, Hsüan-tsung, 241:23b–24; Shang Yen-liu, p. 85. It may be noted that the "teacher-student" relation was not limited strictly to those whose connection was derived from the civil service examination system. It was also the practice for an inferior official to acknowledge his superior official, particularly one who had recommended him for promotion, as a teacher. The government complained about this practice and attempted to prohibit it (*Huang-Ch'ing tsou-i*, 10:1b–2; *Ch'ing shih-lu*, Hsüan-tsung, 241:23b–24; 318:12a–b).

59. *T'ing-lin wen-chi*, 1:20a–b.

60. *Hsüeh-cheng ch'üan-shu*, 7:10b–12, 15–16.

61. *Ibid.*, 7:15b–16.

62. *T'ing-lin wen-chi*, 1:19a–b. Chao Shen-chiao, a governor, declared that he found out from the documents of old cases in Hunan that many civil and military *sheng-yüan* "control the yamen, intimidate the officials, monopolize the transaction of land tax on behalf of others, [or] foment litigation, and their various forms of bad behavior are difficult to enumerate" (*Chao Kung-i sheng-kao*, 6:43b). Huang Ang, himself a *sheng-yüan*, reported in his *Hsi Chin shih-hsiao lu*, 1:13b–14, that among the *sheng-yüan* and *chien-sheng* of Wu-hsi and Chin-kuei, Kiangsu, who "visited the magistrate's court, controlled the yamen, and regarded the village people as fish and flesh," there were thirteen notorious persons in the Shun-chih and early K'ang-hsi periods and seven in the middle K'ang-hsi period.

63. *Feng* refers to the conferring of an honorary title on a living person, whereas *tseng* refers to a title conferred posthumously. The number of generations to which these honors were granted depended upon the rank of the official: first-rank official—great-grandparents, grandparents, and parents; second- to third-rank official—grandparents and parents; fourth- to seventh-rank official—parents. An honorary title was granted only to the wife of a seventh- to ninth-rank official, but the official could request the transfer (*i-feng* or *i-tseng*) of his and his wife's titles to his parents (*Ch'ing hui-tien*, 12:7b–9b). It may be mentioned that the gentry's family members who acquired honorary titles through the system of bestowal and secured *yin* privileges were usually listed in the local gazetteers under the heading of *feng-tseng* or *yin-hsi* (i.e., *yin* privileges and hereditary ranks), e.g., see *Cheng-ting hsien-chih, chüan* 25, 26, or *feng yin* (i.e., *feng-tseng* and *yin*), e.g., see *Luan-ch'eng hsien-chih, chüan* 10; *Hua-yang hsien-chih, chüan* 28. Thus their names appeared together with the names of the gentry members, who were listed under the heading of *hsüan-chü* (i.e., selection by examination or by purchase of an academic title).

64. *Ch'ing lü-li*, 4:71, 72.

65. There were eight groups of people whose punishment had to be deliber-

ated. One of them, *kuei,* included those who held a hereditary rank of nobility, officials with duties (*chih-shih kuan*) of the third rank and above, and officials without duties (*san-kuan*) of the second rank and above (*Ch'ing lü-li,* 4A:23–24b; Staunton, pp. 5–6; Boulais, p. 33).

66. *Ch'ing lü-li,* 4A:31a–b; Staunton, p. 8.

67. The names of fathers of gentry members who possessed an honorary title (*feng-chün*) were not included in the list of gentry appearing in *Hsien-kang ts'e* (see above, note 25). Their names appeared only in the *Hsü-chih ts'e* prepared by the Office of Rites, where they were listed as fathers of the official-gentry (*Fu-hui ch'üan-shu,* 2:13).

68. There was one case where the brother of an official-gentry member instigated an accusation against the magistrate. When the governor-general started an investigation the accuser would not appear in court until the emperor ordered his brother to deliver him to the yamen (*Ch'ing shih-lu,* Mu-tsung, 27:27a–b, 29:29a–b). In another instance, a man whose two sons were *sheng-yüan* relied upon their position in refusing to pay land tax and beating the tax-collecting runners (*Shih-hsüeh ta-sheng,* 8:105a–b).

69. As an illustration, Li Wei, the governor-general of Chekiang, once reported to the emperor that two of his first cousins, who were at home in their native province, behaved without regard for law and order. To get them under his control, the governor-general requested the local authorities in his native province to take them into custody and escort them to his yamen, where they were "confined" (*Chu-p'i yü-chih,* Li Wei's memorials, 3:57b–58).

70. *Ch'ing lü-li,* 4A:31; Staunton, p. 8.

71. *Ch'ing lü-li,* 4A:37a–b; *Li-pu tse-li,* 13:11a–b; *Liu-pu ch'u-fen tse-li,* 15:30.

72. *Shuang-chieh-t'ang yung-hsün,* 4:8a–b.

73. *Ch'in-pan chou-hsien shih-i,* p. 30.

74. For example, see *Yen-t'ang chien-wen tsa-chi,* p. 39.

75. For example, see *Tzu-chih hsin-shu,* 19:44.

76. *Ch'ing lü-li,* 4A:31b; Staunton, p. 8.

77. Readers will recall from the chapters on clerks and runners that wealthy commoners who were targets of extortion were unable to protect themselves. The only effective means of protection was to become a member of the gentry. Thus, as Ku Yen-wu pointed out, the aim in becoming a *sheng-yüan* in many cases was to protect one's family from injustice (*T'ing-lin wen-chi,* 1:17b–18). Fei Hsiao-t'ung correctly observed: "If they are not in alliance with the power hierarchy, their position as landowners is threatened" ("Peasantry and Gentry," p. 8).

78. *Ching-shih wen hsü-pien,* 82:45.

79. *Ch'in-pan chou-hsien shih-i,* p. 29b; *Fu-hui ch'üan-shu,* 1:5a–b; *Hsüeh-chih i-shuo,* A:11a–b; *Hsüeh-chih shuo-chui,* p. 3a–b; *Hsüeh-chih t'i-hsing lu,* A:11; *P'ing-p'ing yen,* 2:20, 29b–30; *Hsiao-ts'ang shan-fang wen-chi,* 18:10; *Mu-ling shu,* 7:3b, 4b.

80. *Hsüeh-chih shuo-chui,* p. 3; *Mu-ling shu,* 7:4b.

81. *Sung-chün chün-i ch'eng-shu, ts'e* 1:25b; *ts'e* 3:116a–b; *ts'e* 4:118–129b; *ts'e* 6:206b; *ts'e* 7:230 ff.

82. *Mu-ling shu*, 11:20b ff.

83. For instance, in 1853 the prefect of Soochow consulted with the gentry in determining a new tax rate for grain tribute (*Hsien-chih-t'ang kao*, 5:43b–44; 45b–46).

84. It is generally held that the people were closer to the gentry, the scholar-gentry in particular, and had more confidence in them than in the local officials (*Hsüeh-chih i-shuo*, A:11; *Hsüeh-chih t'i-hsing lu*, A:11; *Tung-ming wen-chi*, 3:19). As Kuo Sung-tao explained, while the officials enforced the law, the gentry reached the people through their feelings. What could not be prohibited by law could be prevented by an appeal to feelings. Hence only when there was a close connection between the local officials and the gentry could there be an effective response to the call of the officials (*Kuo shih-lang tsou-su*, 1:24b).

85. *Ch'in-pan chou-hsien shih-i*, p. 29b; *Mu-ling shu*, 7:3b.

86. Fei, "Peasantry and Gentry," p. 8; Chang, *Chinese Gentry*, p. 70.

87. On the concept of community sentiment in contrast to class sentiment, see R. M. MacIver, *Society* (New York, 1937), pp. 31, 173–174.

88. Fei, "Peasantry and Gentry," p. 10.

89. *Mu-ling shu*, 11:22–26.

90. *Shao-hsing hsien-chih tzu-liao, ts'e* 10:36b–37.

91. For example, the governor of Chekiang in 1792 ordered the prefect and the magistrate of Hsiao-shan to confer with the gentry to estimate the cost of repairing a dike. One of the gentry, Wang Hui-tsu, felt that the cost estimated by the officials was too high and should be reduced. The magistrate did not agree with him. Wang then wrote to the governor, who approved his suggestion and ordered the subprefect to re-estimate the cost with the gentry. (*Ping-t'a meng-hen lu*, B:52–53b).

92. The contribution of the gentry to public works and public welfare is mentioned in every local gazetteer. For a careful study based upon such data, see Chang, *Chinese Gentry*, pp. 56–63.

93. The situation was summed up by a chou magistrate, Yeh Chen, as follows: "A hsien cannot plan any construction without the honest gentry. For instance, in repairing city walls, school buildings and temples, in establishing a foundling home, and in road repair, the gentry are depended upon to lead, encourage, and manage from beginning to end" (*Mu-ling shu*, 7:4b).

94. There was a case where repairs on the dike of Ch'ien-t'ang River were financed by the gentry of Hsiao-shan, Shan-yin, and K'uai-chi, who contributed 40,000 taels of silver, and by salt merchants in Shao-hsing, who contributed 10,000 taels. Several conferences were held between the local authorities and the gentry, eleven of whom were appointed as directors of the bureau in charge of the project and its funds. It is interesting to note that the governor insisted that one of the gentry, Wang Hui-tsu, who had declined to participate because of illness, should join the bureau. The prefect and the magistrate were instructed

by the governor to call on Wang for consultation (*Ping-t'a meng-hen lu,* B:51–54b, 55b–56; *Ch'ing shih kao,* 484:16). In another instance, a charity bureau was under the direction of six gentry members in raising a fund to build a 128-*chien* poorhouse where 104 persons were to be housed (*Yung-li yung-yen,* p. 82b). In most cases poorhouses and foundling homes were managed by gentry members (*Mu-ling shu,* 15:17, 23).

95. *Ping-t'a meng-hen lu,* B:17; *Mu-ling shu,* 7:4b; 22:21b–23. According to the estimate of Ting Jih-ch'ang, governor of Kiangsu, seventy to eighty per cent of the funds might be used for charity when an organization was managed by the gentry, who feared public opinion. But if it was managed by clerks and runners, then they would embezzle thirty to forty per cent, with the person in charge of the magistrate's accounting embezzling twenty to thirty per cent, and the magistrate's personal servants twenty to thirty per cent, leaving only ten to twenty per cent for alms. Thus Governor Ting instructed his subordinates that the poorhouses and foundling homes should be managed by honest gentry members, and that clerks and runners should not be allowed to interfere (*Fu Wu kung-tu,* 18:2b–3).

96. According to Chou Jen-fu, a magistrate in Chekiang, the relief funds available to a district normally amounted to not more than several thousand taels. When it was distributed to the villages, each village could have only several dozen taels. Because of limited funds it was necessary to depend upon the gentry and wealthy families to contribute toward famine relief (*Mu-ling shu,* 14:38b, 43b). A similar point of view was expressed by another official, Ho Shih-ch'i, who mentioned that since government famine relief was limited, voluntary contributions were necessary to fill the gap (*Mu-ling shu,* 14:66).

97. *Hsien-chih-t'ang kao,* 1:19; *Hsüeh-chih t'i-hsing lu,* B:12–13; *Mu-ling shu,* 14:31b ff.

98. The gentry members who were asked to handle relief funds were authorized to interview the famine-stricken people, classifying them into groups according to degree of poverty. This record was the basis for determining who should receive relief (*Yung-li yung-yen,* pp. 84b–85; *Huang-cheng pei-lan,* A:10–20b, 26–28; B:8; *Hsüeh-chih t'i-hsing lu,* B:12–13; *Ch'ien-ku pei-yao,* 10:15a–b). Most officials found it more efficient to entrust this task to the gentry than to leave it to clerks and runners (*Mu-ling shu,* 14:30).

99. The director of a community granary (*she-ts'ang*), however, could be any wealthy man in the community, not necessarily a gentry member (see *Hu-pu tse-li,* 17:26b; *Mu-ling shu,* 12:32b; cf. Chang, *Chinese Gentry,* p. 62). The regulation with regard to community granaries in Hunan was that either a gentry member or a commoner-elder could be appointed as director (*Mu-ling shu,* 12:29a–b). Li Hu, governor of Kwangtung, preferred to select a director from wealthy *sheng-yüan* or *chien-sheng* who did not intend to take the next examination. If such a person could not be found, then the director was to be selected from the honest rural residents (*Mu-ling shu,* 12:40a–b).

100. *Tung-hua hsü-lu,* 190:6b–7; 194:11a–b; 200:12b–13, 17b; 201:4, 17a–b; 202:4, 11; 218:9b; *Ch'ing shih kao,* 149:10a–b. The gentry played a similar part

in internal navigation. For instance, in 1897 the gentry of Hunan and Hupeh requested permission to run steam boats between Ch'angsha and Hankow to transport mineral products and passengers. The governor-general authorized them to establish companies in both provinces, each directed by a gentry member (*Chang Wen-hsiang chi, kung-tu*, 118:2–6b, 8b–9b).

101. An imperial edict of 1724 mentioned that since the gentry had read the books of the sages they should express their gratitude by contributing voluntarily to the cost of repairs to Confucian temples and school buildings in their native communities (*Ch'ing shih-lu*, Shih-tsung, 23:24a–b). See also *Ping-t'a meng-hen lu*, B:12a–b, p. 24; *T'u-min-lu*, 3:29b; *Ch'i-pu-fu-chai ch'üan-chi, cheng-shu*, 3:10b–12; *Mu-ling shu*, 22:11a–b, 14b ff.

102. The provincial academies were established and maintained on government funds. An academy located in a prefecture, chou, or hsien was established either with government funds or with contributions from the local gentry (*Ch'ing hui-tien*, 33:29). For instance, P'eng Yü-lin (1816–1890), a gentry member in Heng-yang, Hunan, contributed 12,000 taels of silver for the establishment of Ch'uan-shan Academy (*Hsü pei-chuan chi*, 14:19b).

103. It may be noted that academies might be headed by either a local gentry member or a scholar from a different province. See cases of Chiang Shih-ch'üan, Yao Nai (1732–1815), Yü Yüeh (1821–1907), and Chu I-hsin (1846–1894) in *Pei chuan chi*, 49:23; 141:12b; *Hsü pei-chuan chi*, 19:17; 75:18. A government regulation also provided that either a native of a province or a person from a neighboring province could be appointed as the head of an academy (*Ch'ing hui-tien*, 33:29; *Li³-pu tse-li*, 82:2).

104. *Ch'ing shih-lu*, Hsüan-tsung, 325:13b; *Ch'in-pan chou-hsien shih-i*, p. 8b. *Hsi Chin shih-hsiao lu*, 1:13a–b. For an instance where a magistrate ordered the villages and towns to nominate gentry members as heads of lecture units (*Yüeh-cheng*), see *Chi-hsi hsien-chih*, 3:35.

105. See above, Chap. IX, sec. 2.

106. *P'ing-p'ing yen*, 4:44.

107. *P'ing-hu hsien pao-chia shih-i*, pp. 9, 10, 19–20b. Wang Feng-sheng mentioned that all the *pao-chia* heads (*hsiang-ch'i*) were members of the gentry. Only in one or two isolated villages were such posts held by commoners engaged in farming (*ibid.*, 25a–b). For further instances in which the local officials sought the gentry's assistance in *pao-chia* administration, see Hsiao, *Rural China*, pp. 70–72.

108. See Chang, *Chinese Gentry*, pp. 66–68; Hsiao, *Rural China*, pp. 294 ff.

109. Although the government was interested in promoting the *pao-chia* system in time of peace, it was not very enthusiastic about *t'uan-lien*, or local militia, and was cautious about allowing the people to keep weapons. This attitude was expressed clearly in Magistrate Liu Heng's report to his superior. He stated that since he had already ordered the local residents to organize *t'uan-lien*, it was difficult to stop them. Liu also explained that while he permitted the people to have wooden sticks and bamboo spears, which were examined and bore an official stamp, they were not authorized to keep any

other kind of weapon for their own use. Thus he told his superior to feel no concern on this subject (*Yung-li yung-yen,* 89b).

110. A number of cities (e.g., Chia-ting and Ch'ang-shu) were defended under the leadership of the gentry. In one instance the gentry captured and killed a local official newly appointed by the Manchu conquerors, closed the city, and organized a defense. For details, see *Ming-chi nan-lüeh,* 9:40–41b, 43–44b, 48a–b; *Chia-ting t'u ch'eng chi; Chia-ting-hsien i-yu chi-shih; Hai-chiao i-pien; Lu-chiao chi-wen,* A:23.

111. *Ch'ang Chao ho chih kao,* 27:48b–49; *Hai-yü tse-luan chih,* 5:347 ff; *Chi Wu-hsi hsien-ch'eng shih-shou k'o-fu pen-mo,* p. 246; *Ch'ing shih kao,* 411:1b ff; 427:11b.

112. Lü Hsien-chi, vice-minister of works, was given the title *t'uan-lien ta-ch'en* (high commissioner of local militia) to command the local militia in Anhui, with Li Hung-chang, compiler of the second class of the Hanlin Academy, as his assistant (*Ch'ing shih kao,* 405, 1a–b; 417:1; *Li Wen-chung kung ch'üan-chi,* pp. 12a–b, 67b).

113. *Chang Wen-hsiang chi, kung-tu,* 90:4a–b.

114. *Hai-yü tse-luan chih,* 5:348; *Ken-shen Chiang-yin tung-nan Ch'ang-shu hsi-pei-hsiang jih-chi,* pp. 426–427; *Chi Wu-hsi hsien-ch'eng shih-shou k'o-fu pen-mo,* 5:251–252.

115. See above, Chap. VIII.

116. In Chin-t'an a defense-supply bureau (*Ch'ou-fang Chü*) was established by the gentry to solicit and collect contributions in order to provide rations, supplies, and weapons for local defense. The bureau financed both the local corps and regular troops, which were unable to get rations from the government at that time (*Chin-t'an chien-wen chi,* 5:193, 208–214; *Chin-t'an hsien-chih,* 16:3, 4b, 7). In Liu-ho a defense and supply bureau (*T'uan-fang Ch'ou-hsiang Chü*) was established and managed by the gentry, and later a likin bureau was established to collect likin to finance the defense (*Liu-ho hsien-chih,* 4:12b, 8:1b, 4, 6b, 8b; *Liu-ho chi-shih,* 5:154–155, 160). For other examples see *Hai-yü tse-luan chih,* 5:347; *Meng-nan shu-ch'ao,* 5:53–55; *Feng-ming shih-lu,* 5:5, 8.

117. For instance, in Liu-ho, the eastern and southern sections of the city were defended by government troops, while the western and northern sections were defended by the local corps, under the command of a military *chü-jen* and a military *sheng-yüan,* respectively. In addition, some gentry members were assigned to watch and interrogate at the city gates. The chief inspector was Hsü Tzu (1810–1862), corrector (*chien-t'ao*) of the Hanlin Academy (see *Liu-ho chi-shih,* pp. 153–163; *Liu-ho hsien-chih,* 5:3b–4; *Pei-chuan chi pu,* 24:14). At Chin-t'an, while regular troops guarded the city, the local corps reinforced them by guarding the city gates, water gate, and cannons. A patrol bureau (*Hsün-fang Chü*) and a number of branch bureaus were established; each bureau was headed by a member of the gentry (*Chin-t'an hsien-chih,* 16:2a–b, 4b, 5b, 6b, 13–14b, 18b, 20b–21).

118. For instance, the defense of Liu-ho was under the command of the magistrate, Wen Shao-yüan (d. 1858), with the assistance of the gentry (*Liu-ho*

chi-shih, 5:153 ff; *Liu-ho hsien-chih*, 8:1 ff). The strategic areas in Ch'ien-shan were defended by the local militia led by the gentry, under the command of a magistrate (*Hu Wen-chung kung i-chi*, 39:19b–21b). The importance of unification of command was emphasized by Wei Yüan (1794–1856) in his essay "Ch'eng shou p'ien" (City defense), in which he advised that the local official should remain at the center of the city to give orders while the outlying area was guarded by his subordinates and the gentry. Wei added that the latter groups should not be allowed to change this arrangement and command without the local official's approval (*Mu-ling shu*, 21:40b–41).

119. *Hai-yü tse-luan chih*, 5:347 ff.

120. Following the Ming regulation, the Ch'ing government authorized the exemption in 1648 as follows: Officials in the capital were exempted from six to thirty piculs of grain, varying according to their ranks. The officials outside the capital were given an exemption of half this amount. For the retired officials with honor, the exemption was seven tenths of the exemption given to active officials; for those who were living at home without a post, one half of the amount for active officials. There was no exemption for officials dismissed for bribery. The *chü-jen, kung-sheng, chien-sheng,* and *sheng-yüan* were exempted from two piculs of grain (*Ch'ing shih-lu,* Shih-tsu, 37:21a–b; *Ch'ing hui-tien* (1690), 24:18a–b; *ibid.* (1732), 31:29a–b).

It was decreed in 1657 that only an actual official or degree-holder was exempted from labor service (*Ch'ing hui-tien* [1690], 24:18b; *ibid.* [1732], 31:29b–30b). The 1648 regulation concerning the amount of exemption in land tax and labor service was thus annulled.

121. This is the well-known *tsou-hsiao an* (taxation case reported to the Board of Revenue). The number 13,517 is taken from *Ch'ing shih-lu,* and is based on a report by the governor, Chu Kuo-chih, in 1661. *Yen-t'ang chien-wen tsa-chi* reports only 3700 tax delinquents. After their names had been reported to the court, the government issued an edict ordering the following punishments: all the active officials were demoted two grades; the official-gentry staying at home, including the famous scholar Wu Wei-yeh, were arrested and sent to the capital (but were released by the K'ang-hsi emperor in 1662 before they had reached the capital); punishment for the dismissed official-gentry was left to the governor; the scholar-gentry were deprived of their degrees. (*Ch'ing shih-lu,* Shih-tsu, 3:3; cf. *Yen-t'ang chien-wen tsa-chi,* pp. 34a–b, 35b–36. For more information on this case, see Meng Sen, *Hsin-shih ts'ung-k'an,* Series I, pp. 1–15. Meng's study, which is based mainly upon memoirs and epitaphs, is invaluable because *Ch'ing shih-lu* had not been published by that time and the case was not mentioned in *Tung-hua lu* and in official documents.) It was also disclosed in Chekiang that a large number of gentry members did not pay land tax to the government. Imperial commissioners were sent to the province in 1660 to investigate, and the names of delinquent taxpayers in Wu-ch'eng and Kuei-an were reported to the board in the following year. But they succeeded in avoiding punishment by paying up within half a month and by getting the cooperation of the governor, who

reported to the emperor that the delay in payment was largely due to the inefficiency of local officials (*Wu-ch'eng hsien-chih*, 34:28b–30). In short, as indicated in an edict of 1648, the gentry members' refusal to pay tax and the tolerance of the local officials were largely responsible for the government's failure to collect land tax in accordance with the quota for each province (*Ch'ing shih-lu*, Shih-tsu, 2:3b–4).

122. Meng, *Hsin-shih ts'ung-k'an*, Series I, pp. 1b–2, 3, 8.

123. *Ch'ing hui-tien* (1690), 24:20; *ibid.* (1732), 31:31b.

124. For details, see *Ch'ing hui-tien* (1690), 24:19a–b; *ibid.* (1732), 31:30b–31; *Ch'ing lü-li*, 11:11a–b, 14a–b, 44b–45; *Hsüeh-cheng ch'üan-shu*, 7:1b–2, 5, 6b–7b, 13b–15; *Li-pu tse-li*, 28:13a–b; *Liu-pu ch'u-fen tse-li*, 15:30b–31; *Hu-pu tse-li*, 9:9.

125. See above, Chap. VIII, sec. 1.

126. *Hsien-chih-t'ang kao*, 10:1, 5a–b.

127. The classification of taxpayers into *kuan-hu, ju-hu*, and *min-hu* in the tax records was authorized by the government in 1654 (*Ch'ing hui-tien* [1690], 24:18b; *ibid.* [1732], 31:30a–b). Although a 1724 edict ordered the abolition of these distinctions (*Ch'ing shih-lu*, Shih-tsung, 16:21b–22; *Ch'ing hui-tien* [1732], 31:33), the practice remained prevalent throughout the dynasty. It was even recognized by local officials in spite of the formal prohibition (*Ch'ing hiu-tien shih-li*, chüan 172; *Hu-pu tse-li*, 19:3b–4; *Ch'ing t'ung-k'ao*, 2:7513; 3:4871; *Chiang-nan t'ung-chih*, 76:11; *Fu-hui ch'üan-shu*, 6:5b–6; *Hsien-chih-t'ang kao*, 9:19a–b; *Tso Wen-hsiang chi, tsou-kao*, 8:69; *Fu Wu kung-tu*, 22:1–2b; *Ching-shih wen-pien*, 33:13; *Shih-hsüeh ta-sheng*, 5:21a–b; 10:23a–b).

128. See Chap. II, sec. 3, Chap. VIII, secs. 1, 2.

129. *Hsien-chih-t'ang kao*, 9:19, 23.

130. Feng Kuei-fen mentioned that the amount of the grain tribute payment in Kiangsu depended upon whether the taxpayer's status was superior or inferior and whether he was strong or weak. "Not only is [the rate] not uniform between the gentry and the commoners, but it is not uniform among the gentry, and it is also not uniform among the commoners" (*Hsien-chih-t'ang kao*, 10:1; see also 5:31b).

131. This point was made in an 1846 imperial edict (*Ch'ing hsü t'ung-k'ao*, 2:7513), and in the statements of Feng Kuei-fan (*Hsien-chih-t'ang kao*, 9:23–24) and Ting Jih-ch'ang (*Fu Wu kung-tu*, 22:2b).

132. *Tso Wen-hsiang chi, tsou-kao*, 8:69. For more details on tax rates in these districts, see *Shao-hsing hsien-chih tzu-liao*, ts'e 10:27b–29b; *Hsiao-shan hsien-chih kao*, 4:24b. According to *Hsiao-shan hsien-chih kao*, 4:27b, the market rate in the area as of 1877 was 1700:1 to 1800:1. This means that a commoner-taxpayer had to pay about 1000 to 2200 more coins per tael.

A similar report concerning different tax rates in K'uai-chi was given in a diary in the year 1859 by one of its natives, Li Tz'u-ming (1830–1894). According to him, the large households in K'uai-chi and Shan-yin paid only 1.25 to 1.3 taels for 1 tael of land-and-labor-service tax, whereas the medium rate was 1.4 taels, and the small households paid as much as 1.5 or 1.6 taels for 1 tael of tax. His own family paid 1.38 taels. Li also mentioned that only his and other big households paid in rice for grain tribute, and as a rule, for every *hu* (half picul) of grain, they paid 6 or 7 *sheng* in excess of the legal tax. The commoners always paid in copper coins instead of rice (*Yüeh-man-t'ang jih-chi pu, ts'e* 8, *chi-chi* 83a–b).

133. *Hsien-chih-t'ang kao,* 5:31b; 10:1.

134. *Fu Wu kung-tu,* 22:2a–b. In another instance, Ting gave the rate of grain tribute in T'ung-chou, Kiangsu, as follows: 6000 to 8000 up to 12,000 or 18,000 coins for 1 picul of grain for commoner-taxpayers; 2800 coins for gentry-taxpayers (*Fu Wu kung-tu,* 20:3b).

135. See above, note 127.

136. For example: In 1724 a magistrate in Honan ignored the customary difference between the gentry households and commoner households and ordered the local residents to share the burden of dike repairs according to the amount of land owned. Several dozen scholar-gentry got together and protested to the magistrate against his failure to discriminate between gentry households and commoner households in tax collection and labor service. They prevented him from passing through the city gate. They boycotted the current examination. And more than 100 gentry members, including holders of *chü-jen* and *chin-shih* degrees, accused the magistrate before the governor (*Chu-p'i yü-chih,* T'ien Wen-ching's memorials, 1:34b–35b). The only person I know to have held a different view was Feng Kuei-fen, who recommended to the provincial authorities of Kiangsu in 1853 that both the gentry and commoners pay grain tribute at the rate of 4052 coins per picul of grain—a rate requiring the gentry to pay more than usual and reducing the payment of the commoner-taxpayers almost by half. Feng wrote essays appealing to the conscience of the official-gentry and scholar-gentry in an effort to secure their cooperation (*Hsien-chih-t'ang kao,* 9:23 ff). There is no evidence that any of the gentry took his appeal to heart. When Governor Ting Jih-ch'ang ordered the magistrates in northern Kiangsu in 1868 to collect grain tribute from gentry and commoner taxpayers according to the new equal rate, he commented: "It would be unfair to continue the customary practice under which the gentry households . . . pay only 2000 or 3000 coins [for one picul of grain]. If all taxes are collected at the new [equal] rate, there will be many complications. If the local officials do not handle the matter properly, trouble may occur" (*Fu Wu kung-tu,* 22:3).

137. According to the law, a person guilty of transmitting tax for others was subject to the punishment of sixty strokes (*Ch'ing lü-li,* 11:49; Staunton, p. 128; Boulais, p. 315). Under an edict of 1658, a gentry member who acted as transmitter of tax payments for others and did not hand in the tax to the government was punishable with dismissal, forty strokes, and wearing of the cangue for three months (*Ch'ing hui-tien* [1690], 24:19b). It was ruled in 1727 that a *kung-sheng, chien-sheng,* or *sheng-yüan* was to be sent to Heilung-kiang to render service for this offense; if the amount embezzled was over eighty taels, he was to be sentenced to "detention for strangling" (*Ch'ing*

hui-tien [1732], 31:33a–b; cf. *Ch'ing hui-tien tse-li*, 36:43). This regulation was revised in 1736 to the effect that such a person guilty of embezzlement was to be punished in accordance with the law governing the stealing of government property (*Ta-Ch'ing lü-li an-yü*, 40:26). A similar regulation appears in the *Hu-pu tse-li*, 9:9b. It was also ruled that such a person was punishable for transmitting tax for others, even if he handed it over to the government: eighty strokes if the tax payment entrusted to him was more than eighty taels; sixty strokes if the payment was less than eighty taels (*Li³-pu tse-li*, 37:6b–7).

138. *Ch'ing hui-tien* (1732), 31:32; *Ch'ing hui-tien tse-li*, 36:41. Li Huan (1827–1891), provincial treasurer of Kiangsi, reported that the gentry members who acted as transmitters of grain tribute for others often collected cash in lieu of grain from taxpayers (apparently at a rate higher than the market rate), and handed in grain to the government. Or they collected cash from taxpayers at a very high rate and handed in the tax at a very low rate (*Pao-wei-chai lei-kao*, 11:2b).

139. *Fu-hui ch'üan-shu*, 9:3a–b.

140. *Ch'ing shih-lu*, Jen-tsung, 144:21.

141. *Ch'ing hui-tien* (1732), 31:32b.

142. *Ch'ing shih-lu*, Shih-tsu, 3:16b; *ibid.*, Hsüan-tsung, 111:12b; *Ch'ing hui-tien* (1732), 31:33; *Ch'ing hui-tien shih-li, chüan* 177; *Ch'ing t'ung-k'ao*, 2:4866, 7513; 3:4871; *Ch'in-pan chou-hsien shih-i*, p. 29b; *Fu-hui ch'üan-shu*, 4:2–4b, 5:26–28; *T'ao Yün-t'ing tsou-su*, 17:9 ff; *Li Wen-kung kung i-chi, tsou-i*, 9:37 ff; *Fu Wu kung-tu*, 22:3; *Hsien-chih-t'ang kao*, 5:36b; *Hsüeh-chih ou-ts'un*, 3:11b, 13b; *Mu-ling shu*, 11:51.

143. In Wu-chiang, Kiangsu, it was disclosed in 1805 that there was a deficit in government funds under the care of a magistrate from whom 315 *chien-sheng* and *sheng-yüan* had collected customary grain tribute fees (*Ch'ing shih-lu*, Jen-tsung, 144:21b–24). Governor T'ao Chu of Kiangsu reported that in some places the scholar-gentry who derived an income from such fees numbered 300 to 400, and that the fees amounted to 20,000 to 30,000 taels (*Ch'ing shih-lu*, Hsüan-tsung, 111:17b; *T'ao Yün-t'ing tsou-su*, 17:9–11b; 19:22b–23; see also *Hsüeh-cheng ch'üan-shu*, 31:12; *Fu Wu kung-tu*, 23:2).

A censor reported in 1827 that in addition to the grain tribute fees, a new fee called *mang-kuei* (land tax fee) was introduced by the *sheng-yüan* and *chien-sheng* in Kiangsu in his day. Such a fee, varying from twenty dollars to one or two hundred per person, was obtained from the magistrate when land tax was collected. Some *chü-jen, kung-sheng,* and even younger brothers or nephews of deceased gentry members also were accorded this privilege in certain districts (*Ch'ing shih-lu*, Hsüan-tsung, 120:25–26).

144. The exemptions, based on a Ming regulation of 1648, were as follows: The officials in the capital were entitled to an exemption of six to thirty units of *ting* tax, varying according to their rank. The officials outside the capital were given an exemption of half this amount. For the retired officials with honor, the exemption was seven-tenths the exemption given to active officials;

for those who were living at home without a post, one-half the amount for active officials. There was no exemption for officials dismissed for bribery. The *chü-jen, kung-sheng, chien-sheng,* and *sheng-yüan* were exempted from two units of *ting* tax (*Ch'ing shih-lu,* Shih-tsu, 37:21a–b; *Ch'ing hui-tien* [1690], 24:18a–b; *ibid.* [1732], 31:29a–b; *Ch'ing t'ung-k'ao,* 25:5072; *Ch'ing shih kao,* 128:14b).

145. *Ch'ing hui-tien* (1690), 24:18b; *ibid.* (1732), 31:29b–30b. The local officials were authorized to impeach any official who allowed his family members to use his name in order to avoid the labor-service tax. A *chien-sheng* or *sheng-yüan* guilty of this same action was similarly impeachable and could be deprived of his degree or academic title. Both officials and students were further punishable with 100 strokes (*Ch'ing lü-li,* 8:43b–44; *Hu-pu tse-li,* 8:37b).

146. *Ch'ing t'ung-k'ao,* 21:5045, 5073; *Ch'ing lü-li,* 8:44a–b; *Li-pu tse-li,* 38:17b–18; *Hsüeh-cheng ch'üan-shu,* 32:2; *Shih-ch'ü yü-chi,* 1:26–27; *Chu-p'i yü-chih,* T'ien Wen-ching's memorials, 5:53b; *T'ing-lin wen-chi,* 1:19b; *Tzu-chih hsin-shu,* 6:17b–18; *Mu-ling shu,* 9:42b–43; 11:56b; 20:43; *Ching-shih wen-pien,* 30:11, 13b; 33:5b–9; *Shih-hsüeh ta-sheng,* 10:35 ff; *Sung-chün chün-i ch'eng-shu, ts'e* 4:126b.

According to a censor and a magistrate, the gentry members in Chihli contributed money for only one kind of labor service, namely, labor service required in connection with the emperor's hunting trips and visits to mausoleums, including necessary repairs to bridges and roads (*huang-ch'ai,* "imperial labor service," or *ta-ch'ai,* "big labor service"). In the southern part of the province the gentry members either contributed thirty per cent of the cost of labor service while the people were responsible for the rest, or the gentry made no contribution at all. But in all places in Chihli, the burden of the "miscellaneous labor service" was borne by the commoners alone (*Ch'ing shih-lu,* Hsüan-tsung, 8:3–4b; *Mu-ling shu,* 1:56b; *Ching-shih wen-pien,* 33:8, 11; *Ch'ing shih kao,* 128:13b). Another magistrate reported that the gentry in Kiangsu contributed only to the cost of labor service involved in repairing dikes (*t'ang-kung*) and that all other "miscellaneous labor service" was the burden of the commoners (*Sung-chün chün-i ch'eng-shu, ts'e* 1:40).

147. For instance, when carriages were needed by the chou or hsien government to transport rice or coal, or to transport criminals, the villagers were asked to provide them or pay for the hiring of them (*Mu-ling shu,* 11:53b, 56a–b; *Shen-chou feng-t'u chi,* 3B:24b–25). Labor service in connection with such public works as repair of roads and dikes might also be rendered in money (*Sung-chün chün-i ch'eng-shu, ts'e* 1:40). As a rule the labor service, or the money paid in lieu of labor service, was imposed on the entire village or *t'u,* where the inhabitants shared the burden assigned to the unit. The customary practice was to apportion the labor service or money among the people according to the number of male adults or households, or the number of *mou* of land; in the matter of providing transportation facilities, it was apportioned according to the number of horses, oxen, or donkeys owned by a household (*Ch'ing hsü*

t'ung-k'ao, 27:7790–91; *Chien-shih* quoted in *Ch'ing lü-li*, 8:42; *Fu-hui ch'üan-shu*, 3:9; *Sung-chün chün-i ch'eng-shu*, ts'e 1:40–41; 4:144b–145; *Chao kung-i sheng-kao*, 5:2b; *Mu-ling shu*, 11:55b–56; *Shen-chou feng-t'u chi*, 3B:23b ff).

148. *T'ing-lin wen-chi*, 1:19b; *Chu-p'i yü-chih*, T'ien Wen-ching's memorials, 55:33a–b; *Chao Kung-i sheng-kao*, 5:2b; *Chiang-nan t'ung-chih*, 76:11; *Sung chün chün-i ch'eng-shu*, ts'e 1:44b; 3:103; *Ching-shih wen-pien*, 33:11; *Mu-ling shu*, 11:55a–b.

149. *T'ing-lin wen-chi*, 1:19b–20.

150. *Hu-pu tse-li*, 8:37b; *Chiang-nan t'ung-chih*, 76:11b; *Sung-chün chün-i ch'eng-shu*, ts'e 3:104b–105b; *Tzu-chih hsin-shu*, 6:17b–18; *Ching-shih wen-pien*, 30:13b; 33:5b, 8b, 10b; *Shih-hsüeh ta-sheng*, 5:34b; *Mu-ling shu*, 11:55.

151. *Ch'ing hui-tien* (1732), 31:33; *Ch'ing hui-tien tse-li*, 36:41; *Ch'ing hui-tien shih-li*, chüan 172; *Ch'ing t'ung-k'ao*, 2:4866; *Chiang-nan t'ung-chih*, 68:4b; 76:13b; *Sung-chün chün-i ch'eng-shu*, ts'e 1:44a–b; *Fu-hui ch'üan-shu*, 9:3b–4; *Ching-shih wen-pien*, 29:17; 33:4, 12b.

152. *Fu-hui ch'üan-shu*, 9:3b. *Yung-ch'ing hsien-chih*, 10:53b, lists 340 *kung-ting* in the district. Even the magistrate was often unable to control the situation. A magistrate complained that if a local official attempted to prevent the gentry members from "protecting" others, resentment and opposition would come from the gentry (*Fu-hui ch'üan-shu*, 9:4a–b, 14).

153. *Ching-shih wen-pien*, 33:8b.

154. *Ibid.*, 33:5b, 8b, 9, 10b; *Mu-ling shu*, 11:55.

155. *Fu-hui ch'üan-shu*, 23:18b. For specific examples of attempts made to obstruct the construction of water works by gentry members, see *T'ai-chou chih*, 4:16b–17; 32:30b–32.

156. *Ch'ing shih-lu*, Kao-tsung, 289:19a–b; 295:10b–11; 296:69; 298:16b–17b; *Ch'ing hui-tien shih-li*, chüan 928.

157. *Fu-hui ch'üan-shu*, 4:12b; *Hsi Chin shih-hsiao lu*, 1:15; *Shih-hsüeh ta-sheng*, 4:43a–b; *T'ao Yün-t'ing tsou-su*, 19:4; *Fu Wu kung-tu*, 36:5; *Ching-shih wen hsü-pien*, 21:15b.

158. *Ch'ing shih-lu*, Kao-tsung, 297:14. See also *Fu-weng chi*, hsing-ming, 1:16b; *Fu Wu kung-tu*, 35:9b; *Ching-shih wen hsü-pien*, 21:15b.

159. *Ch'ing hui-tien shih-li*, chüan 400; *Ch'in-pan chou-hsien shih-i*, p. 29b; *Chao Kung-i sheng-kao*, 6:43b; *Fu-hui ch'üan-shu*, 11:10b; *Hsüeh-chih i-shuo*, B:4b; *Hsi-chiang cheng-yao*, 36:2b–3; *Hsi Chin shih-hsiao lu*, 1:14; *Pao-chia shu*, 3:28. In one instance a *chien-sheng* opened an inn where he and several other *chien-sheng* and *sheng-yüan* under his direction wrote complaints for others. It was reported that the group handled all lawsuits for the people in the hsien (*T'ao Yün-t'ing tsou-su*, 19:3–8; for additional examples see *Fu Wu kung-tu*, 28:2; 36:5, 7).

160. *Li³-pu tse-li*, 57:1a–b; *Hsüeh-cheng ch'üan-shu*, 4:2; 7:4b–5.

161. There was a ruling that a *sheng-yüan* or a *chien-sheng* guilty of writing complaints or of being a pettifogger should receive a punishment one degree more severe than an ordinary offender. It was also ruled in 1727 that a *sheng-yüan* who made complaints on behalf of his relatives or appeared in court as

a witness should be deprived of his degree (*Hsüeh-cheng ch'üan-shu*, 7:4b–5, 7b–8, 13b).

162. *Ch'ing shih-lu*, Kao-tsung, 296:6a–b. "Previously" obviously refers to the Ming and early Ch'ing before the Yung-cheng period. The Ming gentry were notorious for their oppressiveness and unlawful activities (see Chao I's (1727–1814) essay, "Ming hsiang-kuan nüeh-min chih hai [On the Ming official-gentry's tyranny over the people], in *Nien-erh-shih cha-chi*, 34:13). In general the gentry in the Ch'ing seem to have been less tyrannical than those in the Ming, especially during the Yung-cheng period, when a stern policy was adopted by the emperor. Huang Ang (first half of the eighteenth century), who wrote about the gentry of Wu-hsi and Chin-kuei, Kiangsu, said that the members of the official-gentry living in these localities behaved much better than had those in the Ming. According to him, many members of the official-gentry in the K'ang-hsi period took concern in the lawsuits of others, negotiated with the officials on their behalf, and received money from them, but no such thing occurred in the Yung-cheng period. Although the gentry members had recently begun to have some contact with the local officials (i.e., early in the Ch'ien-lung period), they did not have a "bad reputation in the local communities, and were causing no mischief" (*Hsi Chin shih-hsiao lu*, 1:14b–15; see also, *ibid.*, 10:10b). Both the 1747 edict quoted above and Huang's statement indicate that although an effort had been made in the Yung-cheng period to control the gentry, the policy was effective only for a short time.

163. *Fu Wu kung-tu*, 7:7.

164. *Tzu-chih hsin-shu*, 20:47–50b; *Li-pu tse-li*, 28:16.

165. There was a special law dealing with the beating of tenants by the gentry (*Li-pu tse-li*, 17:13b; *Liu-pu ch'u-fen tse-li*, 15:31).

166. E.g., see *Fu-weng yü-chi*, p. 18a–b; *Tso Wen-hsiang chi, tsou-kao*, 5:18–19.

167. *Hsüeh-cheng ch'üan-shu*, 7:8. In another instance, a *chü-jen* unlawfully set up a station to collect likin (*Ch'ing shih-lu*, Mu-tsung, 45:23).

168. *Ching-shih wen hsü-pien*, 21:11b–12.

169. The commissioners in charge of local militia were thus accused by court officials, and as a result of these complaints, the emperor dismissed several commissioners of local militia in 1861 (*Ch'ing shih-lu*, Mu-tsung, 8:28a–b; 44:46–47). *T'ao Yün-t'ing tsou-su*, 4:11b, reports that a commissioner in charge of local militia in T'ung-chou killed other gentry members and merchants arbitrarily and seized the property of the commoners.

170. In one instance a gentry member in charge of local militia in Kweichow, Chao Kuo-chu, was accused of excessive killing. His cruelty led to the revolt of several tens of thousands of people, who killed a commissioner of likin and announced that they would attack the provincial capital and kill Chao (*Ch'ing shih-lu*, Mu-tsung, 17:49b–51; 24:12). In another instance, in Fukien in 1856, two villagers in Ou-ning, on orders given by the local security bureau (organized by the gentry), set fire to some grain stored in the village, to prevent it from falling into the hands of the approaching Taiping army.

The fire destroyed the house of a *chien-sheng*, who tied up the two villagers and took them to the local security bureau. The director of the bureau took the prisoners to the submagistrate with the suggestion that they be reported to the magistrate as bandits, to be executed on the spot. Permission for the execution was granted. The brother of one of the prisoners appealed to the governor-general, Tso Tsung-t'ang, who discovered that the charge against the two villagers was false. The submagistrate and the director of the local security bureau were thereupon sentenced to banishment and military service, respectively. The *chien-sheng* was deprived of his title (*Tso Wen-hsiang chi, tsou-kao*, 19:68–70b; 20:45–49).

171. *Ch'ing lü-li*, 4A:37b; 6:38b, 39; 33:41a–b; *Li-pu tse-li*, 28:16–17b; 42:32b; *Liu-pu ch'u-fen tse-li*, 30b; *Hsüeh-cheng ch'üan-shu*, 7:2, 8a–b.

172. K. C. Hsiao, who feels that "sometimes the rural gentry proved itself more of a disturbing than a tranquilizing element," concludes: "While not all gentry were selfish or oppressive, the stabilizing influences of 'upright gentry' were bound to be neutralized by the deeds of 'bad gentry'" (*Rural China*, pp. 317, 320).

173. E.g., on one occasion a magistrate was accused by the gentry of violating a certain regulation concerning grain purchase. One of the gentry members, Wang Hui-tsu, refused to join in the accusation, and was criticized by the rest of the group (*Meng-hen lu-yü*, p. 66).

174. *Hsüeh-chih i-te pien*, p. 30b. For a similar point of view held by a magistrate, Yao Ying (1785–1852), see *Tung-ming wen-chi*, 3:19.

175. The edict reads: "An official guilty of a deficit does not necessarily love the people. As the people may be rich or poor, it is not conceivable that the whole hsien should be willing to make up the deficit for the official. . . Perhaps [deficiencies have thus been made up] because the bad gentry frequently visit the yamen and are engaged in corruption together [with the magistrate]. When the magistrate has been impeached, he hopes that he can be appointed again. Therefore, the gentry present a petition [requesting permission to make up the deficit]. When it reaches the hands of the newly appointed magistrate, runners are sent to collect money from village to village. In name it is voluntary contribution; in actuality, it is involuntary assignment." For this reason, the emperor ordered that if the gentry were willing to help the magistrate to make up the deficit, they could do so, but if the petition was falsely presented in the name of the whole hsien, the person who led the petition would be severely punished (*Ch'ing shih-lu*, Shih-tsung, 19:11a–b; see also *Li-pu tse-li*, 23:7a–b; *Liu-pu ch'u-fen tse-li*, 27:13a–b).

176. *T'u-min lu*, 3:18; *Mu-ling shu*, 15:11.

177. *Ch'ing shih-lu*, Jen-tsung, 144:22b–23; *ibid.*, Mu-tsung, 36:8; *Hsien-chih-t'ang kao*, 9:25. Precautionary measures were accordingly taken by the Ch'ing government in an attempt to prevent gentry members and local officials from close association. It was ruled in 1679 that a newly appointed official was punishable with dismissal if he visited any official in the capital who was a

gentry member of the province where his own yamen was located, or if he sent his family members or yamen personnel to maintain contact with an official in the capital after he had arrived at his post. The regulation also prevented an official in the capital from visiting a man who was a newly appointed local official in his native province and from presenting a gift to him. Both the gentry who presented such a gift and the one who received it were subject to dismissal.

Under a similar regulation of 1729, a local official was prevented from receiving gifts from an offiical in the capital who was a gentry member of the province where his yamen was located, and they were prohibited from establishing a personal connection by acknowledging each other as "teacher" and "student." The same rule was applicable between a local official and a gentry member on leave at home. The local official was punishable with dismissal for violating this regulation, while the gentry member was punishable with dismissal, or loss of rank, title, or degree, depending upon his status. The regulation mentioned that the gentry members and the local official could see each other only when they discussed official business or when they attended the semimonthly lectures. See *Ch'ing hui-tien tse-li,* 14:23b–24; *Ch'ing hui-tien shih-li* (1818), 75:1b–2b, 3b–4b.

178. *Fu Wu kung-tu,* 23:1; *Sheng-shih wei-yen,* 2:29. There were instances where the servants of gentry members became clerks and runners in the local yamen. A regulation was issued in 1730 to prevent such a practice (*Ch'ing hui-tien shih-li, chüan* 98; *Ch'ing t'ung k'ao,* 23:5056).

179. *Hsüeh-chih t'i-hsing lu,* A:11b.

180. *Tseng Wen-cheng chi, tsa-chu,* 2:55. Liu Jung (1816–1873), a member of the official-gentry who himself had previously organized and commanded the local militia in his native place, Hsiang-hsiang, Hunan, related in a letter after he returned home from a post in another province, that the gentry in charge of local militia in Hsiang-hsiang accepted lawsuits from the local people and seized authority. As the magistrate listened only to them, "matters depend on the bureau, not on the hsien [government]; authority rests with the official-gentry, not with the officials" (*Ching-shih wen hsü-pien,* 21:7b–8).

181. In his essay discussing the bad effects of the local militia, Hsüeh Fu-ch'eng reports that Tu Ch'iao, an official-gentry member in charge of militia in Shantung, interfered with the local officials' exercise of their authority. In another instance, an official-gentry member in charge of local militia in Chekiang was impeached by the governor and dismissed. The relation between his successor, Wang Lü-ch'ien (another official-gentry member), and the governor was even worse. Hsüeh described the situation thus: "Above, the official and the gentry member opposed each other; below, the soldiers and the militia brawled." Before the fall of Hang-chou and the death of the governor, the latter presented a memorial to impeach Wang, who was then reprimanded by the emperor (*Yung-an ch'üan-chi, Hai-wai wen-pien,* 4:11a–b). The *Ch'ing shih kao,* 412:1b, also records the discord between the governor of Hunan and

Tseng Kuo-fan, then the gentry member in charge of local militia, who organized the Trial Bureau (*Fa-shen Chü*) to try and execute suspects without referring to the local authorities.

182. *Fu-hui ch'üan-shu*, 4:9b; *Tzu-chih hsin-shu*, 10:18b; *Pu-ch'ien-chai man-ts'un*, 5:120; *Hsüeh-chih ou-ts'un*, 3:13. A chou magistrate, Kao T'ing-yao (fl. 1786–1830), remarked that there were many large and old families in Liu-an chou, Anhui, and that the gentry members often capitalized on the errors of the magistrates and toyed with them. Many magistrates were thus ruined (*Huan-yu chi-lüeh*, A:21b).

183. For example, see *Ch'ing shih-lu*, Kao-tsung, 92:6a–b; *Fu-hui ch'üan-shu*, 4:3–4; *Ping-t'a meng-hen lu*, B:38b–40b; *Meng-hen lu-yü*, p. 66; *Hsüeh-cheng ch'üan-shu*, 7:15b–16; *Tzu-chih hsin-shu*, 20:20 ff. Various sources mention certain *chien-sheng* and *sheng-yüan* who were engaged in handling grain-tribute payments for others and who demanded customary fees from magistrates by intimidation. These scholar-gentry frequently made trouble for granaries during the period of collection by accusing the magistrates and clerks of irregularities (*Ch'ing shih-lu*, Jen-tsung, 144:22b–23; *ibid.*, Hsüan-tsung, 111:17a–b; *T'ao Yün-t'ing tsou-su*, 17:9b; *Ch'ing t'ung-k'ao*, 2:7513; *Hsüeh-cheng ch'üan-shu*, 31:11b; *Hsüeh-chih ou-ts'un*, 3:13a–b). Governor T'ao Chu reported that accusations in connection with grain tribute in Kiangsu numbered about two to three hundred per year (*T'ao Yün-t'ing tsou-su*, 17:11b).

CONCLUSION

1. *Jih-chih lu*, 9:15b–16a; 17a–b.

2. Ku Yen-wu observed that so many laws were formulated to keep officials from corruption and restrain their activities, that "the virtuous and intelligent officials are unable to proceed an inch outside the law. They merely carefully follow the law in the hope that they can avoid faults" (*Jih-chih lu*, 9:15b; see also *Ku chung sui-pi*, p. 53).

3. This negative aspect of bureaucracy, which has been overlooked by Max Weber and others whose almost exclusive concern has been its positive aspect, is seen by R. K. Merton as "the dysfunction of bureaucracy." Merton points out that this occurs when conformity to rules, originally conceived as a means, becomes an end in itself. "These very devices which increase the probability of conformance also lead to an over-concern with strict adherence to regulations which induce timidity, conservatism and technicism" (*Social Theory and Social Structure*, Glencoe, Ill., 1949, p. 156).

4. Chou Kao, an official, said: "Punishments are so numerous that there is almost a punishment for everything. As [the officials] are afraid of punishments, they cannot but attempt to avoid them skillfully" (*Mu-ling shu*, 23:17b–18a). Commenting on the insecurity of the officials, Wang Hui-tsu compared them with a glass screen which could be broken by a touch with the hand (*Hsüeh-chih i-shuo*, B:20b).

The Tao-kuang emperor, who was aware of this situation, mentioned in an edict of 1820 that as a result of the punishment provided for the numerous administrative regulations, "the good officials may lose their posts, whereas the bad ones are skillful in evading [the punishment]." The emperor also said that as the administrative regulations were numerous, the magistrates spent all their time in observing the formalities, and were unable to take care of such fundamental administrative matters as education and the nurturing of the people. For this reason the emperor had ordered the Board of Civil Office and the Board of War to reduce and revise the administrative regulations. Yet, as he noted in his edict, his order had not actually been carried out by the boards (*Ch'ing shih-lu*, Hsüan-tsung, 7:24b–25b).

5. An official in the eighteenth century observed that the administration was in the hands of these three groups and that the officials merely bore an empty title (*Hsüeh-chih hsü-shuo*, p. 13).

6. Gerth and Mills, *From Max Weber: Essays in Sociology*, pp. 215–216; Merton, *Social Theory and Social Structure*, pp. 157–159.

7. See C. K. Yang, "Some Characteristics of Chinese Bureaucratic Behavior," in D. S. Nivison and A. F. Wright, eds., *Confucianism in Action* (Stanford, 1959), pp. 156–163.

8. Morton Grodzins, "Public Administration and the Science of Human Relations," in Heinz Eulau, *et al.*, eds., *Political Behavior* (Glencoe, Ill., 1956), pp. 340–341, 344.

9. Recent studies on bureaucracy in both industrial and nonindustrial societies have questioned the advisability of maintaining a rigid distinction between "formal" and "informal" administrative behavior. Formal structure may provide conditions for the development of certain informal behavior patterns. It is convincingly suggested by S. H. Udy, Jr., that more fruitful results may be obtained through investigation of the interrelation between various bureaucratic and rational variables than by merely following the "formal" and "informal" ideal-type dichotomy. His empirical analysis indicates that the informal organization, thought of in terms of deviation from patterns described by a Weberian ideal-type construct, is an artifact which disappears when ideal-types are abandoned in favor of a system of variables ("Bureaucracy and Rationality in Weber's Oragnization Theory: An Empirical Study," *American Sociological Review*, 24.6:791–795, Dec. 1959).

10. On this concept see R. K. Merton, "Social Conformity, Deviation and Opportunity Structures: A Comment on the Contribution of Dubin and Gloward," *American Sociological Review*, 24.2:187 (April 1959).

11. Ch'ien Tuan-sheng, *Government and Politics of China* (Cambridge, Mass., 1950), p. 45.

12. Commenting on the contradictory views as to whether there was autonomy in Chinese villages, a modern political scientist, K. C. Hsiao, maintains that the view that autonomy was absent "comes nearer to the actual conditions of village life." His conclusion is based upon the fact (1) that the government exercised control in rural villages through the medium of agents who were directly responsible to the magistrates, and (2) that the village affairs were directed by the rural gentry "who often had interests distinguishable from

those of the nongentry elements." Thus, "even where government control was absent, the village as an organized community was not a democracy under the self-government of all the inhabitants" (*Rural China,* p. 264). Hsiao's argument that the interests of the gentry and of the villagers at large differed, a point which I have repeatedly stressed, is valid, and crucial to an understanding of whether gentry leadership meant self-government.

A similar conclusion was also reached by another student of Chinese government, T. S. Ch'ien, on the ground that the gentry were neither elected nor formally appointed, and that they had to defer to the wishes of the officials, having "no domain of their own, protected by constitutional or customary rights" (*Government and Politics of China,* p. 45).

13. Lasswell and Kaplan, p. 75.

INDEX

BIBLIOGRAPHY

GLOSSARY

BIBLIOGRAPHY

WORKS IN CHINESE AND JAPANESE

Abe Takeo 安部健夫. "Kōsen teikai no kenkyū" 耗羡提解の
研究; Tōyōshi kenkyū 東洋史研究, 16.4:108-251
(Mar. 1958).

Anhui t'ung-chih 安徽通志. 1877.

Chang Chien 張謇. Chang Chi-tzu chih lu 張季子九錄 Shanghai, 1931.

Chang Chien-ying 張鑒瀛. Huan-hsiang yao-tse 宦鄉要則. 1882.

Chang Chih-tung 張之洞. Chang Wen-hsiang kung ch'üan-chi 張文襄公
全集. Wen-hua-chai 文華齋 ed., 1928.

Chang Ch'un-ming 張純明 "Ch'ing-tai ti mu-chih" 清代的幕職;
Ling-nan hsüeh-pao 嶺南學報 9.2:33-37 (1950).

Chang Chung-ju 章中如. Ch'ing-tai k'ao-shih chih-tu 清代考試制度
Shanghai, 1931.

Chang Hsüeh-ch'eng 章學誠. Chang-shih i-shu 章氏遺書. Liu-shih
Chia-yeh-t'ang 劉氏嘉業堂 ed.

Chang Meng-yüan 張夢元. Ching-shu-chai i-kao 敬恕齋遺稿 1897.

Chang Wo-kuan 張我觀. Fu-weng chi 覆甕集 and Fu-weng yü-chi 覆甕
餘集. 1626.

Chang T'ing-hsiang 張廷驤. "Chui-yen shih tse" 贅言十則; in Hsing-mu
yao-lüeh.

Ch'ang-Chao ho-chih kao 常昭合志稿. 1904.

Ch'ang-sui lun 長隨論. MS, quoted in Ts'ai Shen-chih, "Ch'ing-tai
chou-hsien ku-shih."

Ch'ang-t'ing hsien-chih 長汀縣志. 1879.

i

Chao Erh-hsün 趙爾巽 et al. Ch'ing shih kao 清史稿. 1927.

Chao I 趙翼. Kai-yü ts'ung-k'ao 陔餘叢考. Ssu-pu pei-yao 四部
備要 ed.

-------Nien-erh-shih cha-chi 廿二史劄記. Ssu-pu pei-yao ed.

Chao Shen-ch'iao 趙申喬. Chao Kung-i kung sheng-kao 趙恭毅公
賸稿. Preface dated 1738.

Che-chiang t'ung-chih 浙江通志. 1736, reprint 1899.

Ch'en   陳. Shu-ch'i kao pu   書啟稿簿. MS in the Chinese-
Japanese Library, Harvard University.

Ch'en Chung-i 陳忠倚, comp. Huang-ch'ao ching-shih wen san-pien
皇朝經世文三編. 1901.

Ch'en Hung-mou 陳宏謀. P'ei-yüan-t'ang ou-ts'un kao 培遠堂偶
存稿.

-------Tsai-kuan fa-chieh lu 在官法戒錄; in Wu-chung i-kuei 五
種遺規. 1868.

------- Ts'ung-cheng i-kuei 從政遺規; in Wu-chung i-kuei.

Ch'en K'un 陳坤, comp. Ts'ung-cheng hsü-yü lu 從政緒餘錄;
in Ju-pu-chi-chai hui-ch'ao 如不及齋彙鈔. 1872.

Cheng Kuan-ying 鄭觀應. Sheng-shih wei-yen 盛世危言 and
pu-pien 補編.

Cheng-ting hsien-chih 正定縣志. 1875.

Cheng-yü tsa-chi 政餘雜記. MS, quoted in Ts'ai Shen-chih, "Ch'ing-
tai chou-hsien ku-shih."

Ch'eng-kung hsien-chih 呈貢縣志. 1885.

Chi-fu t'iao-pien fu-i ch'üan-shu 畿輔條鞭賦役全書. 1883.

Chi-fu t'ung-chih 畿輔通志. 1682.

Chi Liu-ch'i 計六奇. Ming-chi nan-lüeh 明季南略.

Chia-ting hsien chi-yu chi-shih 嘉定縣己酉紀事; in T'ung shih 痛史.

ii

Chia-ting hsien-chih 嘉定縣志 . 1673.

Chia-ting t'u-ch'eng chi 嘉定屠城記 ; in T'ung shih.

Chiang-hsi fu-i ching-chih ch'üan-shu 江西賦役經制全書 .

Chiang-nan t'ung-chih 江南通志 . 1736.

Chiang Shih-ch'üan 蔣士銓 . Chung-ya-t'ang wen-chi 忠雅堂文
    集 ; in Chiang-shih ssu-chung 蔣氏四種 .

Chiang-su ch'ing-sung chang-ch'eng 江蘇清訟章程 . Chiang-su
    shu-chü 江蘇書局 .

Chiang-su sheng li 江蘇省例 . Chiang-su shu-chü.

Ch'iang ju-hsün 強汝詢 . Chin-t'an chien-wen chi 金壇見聞記 ;
    in T'ai-p'ing t'ien-kuo 太平天國 , 5:193-214. Shanghai, 1953.

Chiao-tai k'uan-mu pei-k'ao 交代欵目備考 . MS in the Chinese-
    Japanese Library, Harvard University.

Ch'ien I-chi 錢儀吉 , comp. Pei-chuan chi 碑傳集 . 1893.

Ch'ien-liang ping kao 錢糧稟稿 . MS, 1875, in the Chinese-Japanese
    Library, Harvard University.

Chih Che ch'eng-kuei 治浙成規 .

Ch'ih Chuang 遲莊 . "Ch'ing-tai chih mu-pin yü men-ting" 清代之幕
    賓與門丁 ; Tu-lu, 5.2:15-16 (July 1952).

Chin-men pao-chia t'u-shuo 津門保甲圖說 . 1846.

Chin Po-fu hsien-sheng ch'eng-p'i ti-kao 金博夫先生呈批底稿 .
    MS in the Chinese-Japanese Library, Harvard University.

Chin-shen ch'üan-shu 搢紳全書 .

Chin-t'an hsien-chih 金壇縣志 . 1885.

Ching-chou chih 涇州志 . 1754.

Ching-yen hsien-chih 井研縣志 . 1900.

Ch'ing-ch'ao hsü wen-hsien t'ung-k'ao 清朝續文獻通考 . Shih-t'ung
    十通 ed.; Shanghai, 1936.

Ch'ing-ch'ao t'ung-chih 清朝通志 . Shih-t'ung ed.

Ch'ing-ch'ao t'ung-tien 清朝通典 . Shih-t'ung ed.

Ch'ing-ch'ao wen-hsien t'ung-k'ao 清朝文獻通考 . Shih-t'ung ed.

Ch'ing-ho chiao-tai po-ts'e kao 清和交代駁冊稿 . MS, 1907,
     in the Chinese-Japanese Library, Harvard University.

Ch'ing hsü t'ung-k'ao, see Ch'ing-ch'ao hsü wen-hsien t'ung-k'ao.

Ch'ing hui-tien, see Ta-Ch'ing hui-tien.

Ch'ing hui-tien shih-li, see Ta-Ch'ing hui-tien shih-li.

Ch'ing lü-li, see Ta-Ch'ing lü-li hui-chi pien-lan.

Ch'ing-shih 清史 . 8 vols.; Taipei, 1961.

Ch'ing shih kao 清史稿 . 1927- 1928.

Ch'ing-shih lieh-chuan 清史列傳 . Shanghai, 1928.

Ch'ing shih-lu, see Ta-Ch'ing li-ch'ao shih-lu.

Ch'ing t'ung-k'ao , see Ch'ing-ch'ao wen-hsien t'ung-k'ao.

Chou Ch'ang-sen 周長森 . Liu-ho chi-shih 六和紀事; in T'ai-p'ing
     t'ien-kuo, 5:153-163.

Chou Chia-mei 周家楣 . Ch'i-pu-fu-chai ch'üan-chi 期不負齋全
     集 . 1895.

Chou Pang-fu 周邦福 . Meng-nan shu-ch'ao 蒙難述鈔 ; in T'ang-p'ing
     t'ien-kuo, 5:45-78.

Chu Ch'un 朱椿 . "Kuan-chien" 管見 ; in Tso li yao yen.

Chu-p'i yü-chih 硃批御旨 . Ch'ien-lung emperor's preface dated 1738.

Chu Shou-p'eng 朱壽朋 , comp. Tung-hua hsü-lu 東華續錄 . 1909.

Chu Yün-chin 朱雲錦 . Yü-sheng shih-hsiao lu 豫乘識小錄 . 1873.

Ch'u-chou chih 滁州志 . 1897.

Chung Hsiang 鍾祥 . Kung tu che-yao 公牘摘要 ; in Ts'ung-cheng hsü-
     yü lu.

Ch'ung-lun 崇綸 . Ta-Ch'ing lü-li an-yü 大清律例案語. 1894.

iv

Chü-chou chih 莒州志 . 1796.

Ch'ü T'ung-tsu 瞿同祖. Chung-kuo fa-lü yü chung-kuo she-hui 中國 法律與中國社會 . Shanghai, 1947.

Ch'üan Han-sheng 全漢昇 . Chung-kuo hang-hui chih-tu shih 中國 行會制度史. Shanghai, 1934.

Ch'üan Tseng-hu 全增祐. "Ch'ing-tai mu-liao chih-tu lun" 清代幕 僚制度論 ; Ssu-hsiang yü shih-tai 思想與時代, 31:29-35 (Feb. 1944); 32:35-43 (Mar. 1944).

Fan Tseng-hsiang 樊增祥 Fan-shan p'an-tu 樊山判牘, cheng-pien 正編 and hsü-pien 續編. Shanghai, 1933.

Fang Chün-i 方濬頤. Huai-nan yen-fa chi-lüeh 淮南鹽法紀畧. 1873.

Fang Ta-chih 方大湜 . P'ing-p'ing yen 平平言 . 1887.

Feng Kuei-fen 馮桂芬. Chiao-pin-lu k'ang-i 校邠廬抗議 1884.

-------Hsien-chih-t'ang kao 顯志堂稿. 1876.

Feng Meng-lung 馮夢龍 . Ku-chin t'an-kai 古今譚概. Wen-hsüeh ku-chi k'an-hsing she 文學古籍刊行社 ed.

Fu-i k'uan-mu pu 阜邑欵目簿 (Fu-i e-cheng ti-ts'ao feng-kung teng-k'uan ch'ien-liang ping k'ou-lien k'uan-mu pu 阜邑額徵地漕俸 工等欵錢糧並扣廉欵目簿). MS, 1907, in the Chinese-Japanese Library, Harvard University.

Fu-ning chiao-tai teng-fu ts'e 阜寧交代登復冊. MS, 1906, in the Chinese-Japanese Library, Harvard University.

Fu Tseng-hsiang 傅增湘 Ch'ing-tai tien-shih k'ao-lüeh 清代殿試 考略 . Tientsin, 1933.

Fu-weng yü-chi, see Fu-weng chi.

Hai-chou chiao-tai po-ts'e 海州交代駁冊．MS, 1907, in the
　　　Chinese-Japanese Library, Harvard University.

Ho Ch'ang-ling 賀長齡, comp. Huang (Ch'ing)-ch'ao ching-shih wen-
　　　pien 皇(清)朝經世文編．1887.

-------Nai-an kung-tu ts'un-kao 耐庵公牘存稿．1882.

-------Nai-an tsou-i ts'un-kao 耐庵奏議存稿．1882.

Ho Keng-sheng 何耿繩．Hsüeh-chih i-te pien 學治一得編；in
　　　Hsiao-yüan ts'ung-shu.

Honan fu-i ch'üan-shu 河南賦役全書．1883.

Hosoi Shōji 細井昌治．"Shinsho no shori--shakaishiteki ichikōsatsu"
　　　清初の胥吏--社會史的一考察；Shakai keizai shigaku
　　　社會經濟史學, 14.6:1-23 (Sept. 1944).

Hou Fang-yü 侯方域．Chuang-hui-t'ang chi 壯悔堂集．

Hsi-chiang cheng yao 西江政要．Chiang-hsi an-t'sa ssu 江西按察
　　　司 yamen.

Hsi Yü-fu 席裕福, comp. Huang (Ch'ing)-ch'ao cheng-tien lei-tsuan
　　　皇(清)朝政典類纂．Shanghai, 1903.

Hsiang Ta 向達 et al.,comps. T'ai-p'ing t'ien-kuo 太平天國．
　　　8 vols.; Shanghai, 1953.

Hsiang-t'an hsien-chih 湘潭縣志．1756.

Hsiang-yin hsien t'u-chi 湘陰縣備記．1880.

Hsieh Chao-chih 謝肇淛．Wu tsa-tsu 五雜俎．Wu hang pao shu t'ang
　　　吳航寶樹堂, Ming ed.

Hsieh Ming-huang 謝鳴篁．Ch'ien-ku shih-ch'eng 錢穀視成．
　　　Preface dated 1788; copied by Chan Yün-hsiu 湛允修, 1907.
　　　MS in the Chinese-Japanese Library, Harvard University.

Hsien-ning hsien-chih 咸寧縣志．1668.

Hsien-yang hsien-chih 咸陽縣志．1751.

Hsin-hui hsien-chih 新會縣志 . 1840.

Hsin T'ang shu 新唐書 . Ssu-pu pei-yao ed.

Hsing-an hsien ti-ting k'uan-mu 興安縣地丁欵目 . MS, 1841-1853,
    in the Chinese-Japanese Library, Harvard University.

Hsing-fa chih-nan 刑法指南 . MS in the Chinese-Japanese Library,
    Harvard University.

Hsing-hua hsien chiao-tai ts'e 興化縣交代冊 . MS, 1910, in the
    Chinese-Japanese Library, Harvard University.

Hsing-mu yao-lüeh 刑幕要略 ; in Ju-mu hsü-chih wu chung 入幕須
    知五種 , ed. Chang Han-po 張翰伯 . 1884.

Hsü Keng-pi 徐賡陛 . Pu-ch'ien-chai man-ts'un 不懍齋漫存 .
    1882.

Hsü K'o 徐珂 . Ch'ing-pai lei-ch'ao 清稗類鈔. Shanghai, 1928.

Hsü Ta-ling 許大齡 . Ch'ing-tai chüan-na chih-tu 清代捐納制度.
    Peking, 1950.

Hsü Tung 徐棟, comp. Mu-ling shu 牧令書 . 1848.

Hsü Wen-pi 徐文弼 . Li-chih hsien-ching 吏治縣鏡 . Hung-tao-
    t'ang 宏道堂 ed.

Hsüeh-cheng ch'üan-shu 學政全書 . 1812.

Hsüeh Fu-ch'eng 薛福成 . Yung-an ch'üan-chi 庸庵全集 . 1897.

Hsüeh Yün-sheng 薛允升 . Tu-li ts'un-i 讀例存疑. 1905.

Hu Ch'ien-fu 胡潛甫 . Feng-ming shih-lu 鳳鳴實錄 ; in T'ai-p'ing
    t'ien-kuo, 5:5-22.

Hu Lin-i 胡林翼 . Hu Wen-chung kung i-chi 胡文忠公遺集 .
    Ch'ung-wen shu-chü 崇文書局 ed., 1875.

Hu-pu ts'ao-yün ch'üan-shu 戶部漕運全書 . 1844.

Hu-pu tse-li 戶部則例. 1874.

Hu Yen-yü 胡衍虞 . Chü-kuan kua-kuo lu 居官寡過錄 . 1775.

Hua-yang hsien-chih 華陽縣志 . 1816.

Huai-chi hsien-chih 懷集縣志 . 1916.

Huang Ang 黃卬 . Hsi Chin shih-hsiao lu 錫金識小錄 . 1896.

Huang-Ch'ing tsou-i 皇清奏議 . Peking.

Huang En-t'ung 黃恩彤 , comp. Yüeh-tung sheng-li hsin-tsuan 粵東省例新纂 .

Hunan fu-i ch'üan-shu 湖南賦役全書.

Hunan t'ung-chih 湖南通志. 1757; 1882-1885.

Hung Liang-chi 洪亮吉 . Chüan-shih-ko wen 卷施閣文 , chia-chi 甲集 ; in Hung Pei-chiang ch'üan-chi 洪北江全集 . 1877.

Iwami Hiroshi 岩見宏 . "Yōsei jidai ni okeru kōhi no ikkōsatsu" 雍正時代における公費の一考察 ; in Tōyōshi kenkyū , 15.4:65-99 (Mar. 1957).

Ju-kao chiao-tai ts'e 如皋交代冊 . MS, 1907, in the Chinese-Japanese Library, Harvard University.

Jun-fu 潤甫 , comp. Huang (Ch'ing)-ch'ao ching-shih wen t'ung-pien 皇(清)朝經世文統編 . Shanghai, 1901.

Kan-yü hsien chiao-tai teng-fu ts'e 贛榆縣交代登復冊 . MS, 1906, in the Chinese-Japanese Library, Harvard University.

Kang-i 剛毅, comp. Chin-cheng chi-yao 晉政輯要 . 1887.

-------Mu-ling hsü chih 牧令須知 . 1889.

-------Shen-k'an i-shih 審看擬式 . 1887.

K'ang-chi lu 康濟錄 . 1869.

Kano Naoki 狩野直喜 . "Shinchō chihō seido" 清朝地方制度 ; Dokusho san'yo 讀書纂餘 , pp. 133-176. Tokyo, 1947.

Kansu t'ung-chih 甘肅通志 . 1736.

Kao-mi hsien-chih 高密縣志 . 1754.

Kao T'ing-yao 高廷瑤 . Huan-yu chi-lüeh 宦游紀畧 . 1908.

Kitamura Hirotada 北村敬直 . "Shindai ni okeru sozei kaikaku
   (chitei heichō)" 清代における租税改革 (地丁併徵) ;
   Shakai keizai shigaku, 15.3-4:1-38 (Oct. 1949).

Ko hang shih chien 各行事件 . MS, quoted in Ts'ai Shen-chih,
   "Ch'ing-tai chou-hsien ku-shih. "

Ko Shih-chün 葛士濬 , comp. Huang (Ch'ing)-ch'ao ching-shih wen
   hsü-pien 皇 (清) 朝經世文續編 . Shanghai, 1888. To be
   differentiated from Huang (Ch'ing)-ch'ao ching-shih wen hsü-pien
   (A), comp. Sheng K'ang.

K'o-ch'ang t'iao-li 科場條例. 1790.

Kobayakawa Kingo 小早川欣吾 . "Shinjidai ni okeru chihōjichi
   dantai no hai no keishiki ni tsuite, tokuni hokō seido o chūshin
   toshite" 清時代に於ける地方自治團體の牌の形式につ
   いて ― 特に保甲制度を中心として ; Tōa jimbun gakuhō
   東亞人文學報 , 1.2:370-422 (Sept. 1941).

-------"Shinjidai ni okeru hokōsatsu no keishiki to sono hensei ni tsuite"
   清時代に於ける保甲冊の形式と其の編制につ
   いて ; Tōa jimbun gakuhō, 3.1:73-143 (Mar. 1943).

Ku Yen-wu 顧炎武 . Jih-chih lu chi-shih 日知錄集釋 . Ssu-pu
   pei-yao ed.

-------Ku chung sui-pi 菰中隨筆 ; in T'ing-lin hsien-sheng i-shu hui-
   chi 亭林先生遺書彙輯. 1885.

-------T'ing-lin wen-chi 亭林文集 ; in T'ing-lin hsien-sheng i-shu
   hui-chi. 1855.

Ku Ju-chüeh 顧汝鈺 , ed. Hai-yü tse luan chih 海虞賊亂志 ;
   in T'ai-p'ing t'ien-kuo, 5:347-396.

K'uai-chi hsien-chih 會稽縣志 . 1673, reprint 1936.

K'uai Te-mo 蒯德模. Wu-chung p'an-tu 吳中判牘 ; in Hsiao-yüan
　　ts'ung-shu 嘯園叢書 .

K'uan-mu yüan-liu 欵目源流 . MS in the Chinese-Japanese Library,
　　Harvard University.

K'uang Chung 況鍾. K'uang tai-shou chih Su chi 況太守治蘇集 .
　　1764.

Kung-ch'ang fu-chih 鞏昌府志 . 1687.

Kung-men yao-lüeh 公門要略. MS, quoted in Ts'ai Shen-chih,
　　"Ch'ing-tai chou-hsien ku-shih."

Kuo Sung-tao 郭嵩燾 . Kuo shih-lang tsou-su 郭侍郎奏疏. 1892.

-------Yang-chih shu-wu ch'üan-chi 養知書屋全集 . 1892.

Lai-yang hsien-chih 萊陽縣志 . 1673.

Lan Ting-yüan 藍鼎元 . Lu-chou kung-an 鹿洲公案 ; in Lu-chou
　　ch'üan-chi 鹿洲全集 .

Li Chen 李珍, comp. Ting-li ch'üan-pien 定例全編. 1715.

Li Hsing-yüan 李星沅. Li Wen-kung kung i-chi 李文恭公遺集 .
　　T'ung-chih ed.

Li Huan 李桓, comp. Kuo-ch'ao ch'i-hsien lei-cheng 國朝耆獻類
　　徵. Hsiang-yin Li-shih 湘陰李氏 ed.

------- Pao-wei-chai lei-kao 寶韋齋類稿 . 1880.

Li Hung-chang 李鴻章 . Li Wen-chung kung ch'üan-chi 李文忠公全
　　集. Shanghai, 1921.

Li Kung 李塨. Yüeh shih hsi shih 閱史郗視 ; in Chi-fu ts'ung-shu 畿
　　輔叢書 .

Li Po-yüan 李伯元 (Li Pao-chia 李寶嘉). Huo ti-yü 活地獄 .
　　Shanghai, 1956.

-------Kuan ch'ang hsien hsing chi 官場現形記 . Shanghai, 1927.

Li-pu ch'üan-hsüan tse-li 吏部銓選則例.

Li-pu tse-li 吏部則例. Ch'ien-lung ed.; 1843 ed. Citations herein
    are from the Ch'ien-lung ed.

Li[3]-pu tse-li 禮部則例. Memorial dated 1844. Note that tone number
    is used here to distinguish this book from Li-pu tse-li 吏部則例,
    in which no tone number is indicated.

Li Tz'u-ming 李慈銘. Yüeh-man-t'ang jih-chi 越縵堂日記.
    Peking, 1922.

-------Yüeh-man-t'ang jih-chi pu 越縵堂日記補. Shanghai, 1936.

Li-yang hsien-chih 溧陽縣志. 1813.

Li Yü 李漁, comp. Tzu-chih hsin-shu 資治新書, erh-chi 二集.
    Preface dated 1667.

Li Yüan-tu 李元度. Kuo-ch'ao hsien-cheng shih-lüeh 國朝先正事
    略. Ssu-pu pei-yao ed.

Liang Chang-chü 梁章鉅. Ch'eng-wei lu 稱謂錄 1884.

Liang Fang-chung 梁方仲. "I-t'iao-pien fa" 一條鞭法; Chung-kuo
    chin-tai ching-chi-shih yen-chiu chi-k'an 中國近代經濟史
    研究集刊, 4.1:1-65 (May 1936).

-------"Ming-tai liang-chang chih-tu" 明代糧長制度; Chung-kuo
    she-hui ching-chi shih chi-k'an 中國社會經濟史集刊,
    7.2:107-133 (Dec. 1944).

-------Ming-tai liang-chang chih-tu 明代糧長制度. Shanghai, 1957.

-------"Shih i-t'iao-pien fa" 釋一條鞭法; Chung-kuo she-hui ching-
    chi shih chi-k'an, 7.1:105-119 (June 1944).

Liang-shan hsien-chih 梁山縣志. 1894.

Ling-shou hsien-chih 靈壽縣志. 1685.

Liu Chün 劉雋. "Hsien-feng i-hou Liang Huai chih p'iao-fa" 咸豐以後
    兩淮之票法; Chung-kuo she-hui ching-chi shih chi-k'an,
    2.1:142-165 (Nov. 1933).

-------"Tao-kuang ch'ao Liang-Huai fei yin kai p'iao shih-mo 道光朝 兩淮廢引改票始末 ; Chung-kuo chin-tai ching-chi-shih yen-chiu chi-k'an, 1.2:124-188 (May 1933).

Liu Heng 劉衡. Shu liao wen-ta 蜀僚問答.

-------Yung-li yung-yen 庸吏庸言 and Yung-li yü-t'an 庸吏餘談. 1827.

Liu-ho hsien-chih 六合縣志. 1883.

Liu Ju-yü 劉如玉. Tzu-chih kuan-shu ou-ts'un 自治官書偶存. 1898.

Liu-pu ch'eng-yü chu-chieh 六部成語註解. Kyoto, 1940.

Liu-pu ch'u-fen tse-li 六部處分則例 (also known as Li-pu ch'u-fen tse-li 吏部處分則例). 1887.

Liu Yu-jung 劉有容. Ch'ien-ku pi-tu 錢穀必讀. Preface dated 1795; MS in the Chinese-Japanese Library, Harvard University.

Lo Cheng-chün 羅正鈞. Tso Wen-hsiang kung nien p'u 左文襄公年譜. 1897.

Lo Ping-chang 駱秉章. Lo Wen-chung kung tsou-kao 駱文忠公奏稿. 1891.

Lo Yü-tung 羅玉東. Chung-kuo li-chin shih 中國釐金史. 2 vols.; Shanghai, 1936.

Lou-hsien chih 婁縣志. 1788.

Lu I-t'ung 魯一同. T'ung-fu lei-kao 通甫類稿. 1859.

Lu Lung-ch'i 陸隴其. San-yü-t'ang wen-chi 三魚堂文集 and wai-chi 外集. 1701.

Lu Wei-ch'i 陸維祺. Hsüeh-chih ou-ts'un 學治偶存. 1893.

Lu Yao 陸燿, comp. Ch'ieh-wen-chai wen-ch'ao 切問齋文鈔. Preface dated 1775.

Lung Ch'i-jui 龍啟瑞. Ching-te-t'ang wen-chi 經德堂文集; in Yüeh-hsi wu-chia wen-ch'ao 粵西五家文鈔.

Lü Chih-t'ien 呂芝田 . Lü-fa hsü-chih 律法須知. Canton.

Lüan-ch'eng hsien-chih 欒城縣志. 1873.

Mai Chung-hua 麥仲華 , comp.　Ching-shih wen hsin-pien 經世文
　　　新編. 1898.

Man-yu yeh-shih 漫遊野史. Hai-chiao i-pien 海角遺編 ; in
　　　Yü-yang shuo-yüan 虞陽說苑.

Matsumoto Yoshimi 松本善海 . "Mindai ni okeru risei no sōritsu"
　　　明代に於ける里制の創立 ; Tōhō gakuhō, Tokyo
　　　東方學報, 12.1:109-122 (May 1941).

------- "Shindai ni okeru sōkōseido no sōritsu" 清代における總甲
　　　制度の創立 ; Tōhō gakuhō, Tokyo, 13.1:109-142 (May
　　　1942).

Mei-ts'un yeh-shih 梅村野史 .Lu-ch'iao chi-wen 鹿樵紀聞; in
　　　T'ung shih.

Men-wu che-yao 門務摘要. MS, quoted in Ts'ai Shen-chih, "Ch'ing-
　　　tai chou-hsien ku-shih."

Meng-hen lu-yü 夢痕錄餘, see Ping-t'a meng-hen lu.

Meng Sen 孟森 . Hsin-shih ts'ung-k'an 心史叢刊 , Series 1.
　　　Shanghai, 1936.

Miao Ch'üan-sun 繆荃孫, comp.　Hsü pei-chuan chi 續碑傳集 .
　　　1893.

Min Erh-ch'ang 閔爾昌 , comp.　Pei-chuan chi pu 碑傳集補 .
　　　Peking, 1931.

Ming-lü chi-chieh fu li 明律集解附例 . 1908.

Ming-shih 明史 . Ssu-pu pei-yao ed.

Miyazaki Ichisada 宮琦市定 . Kakyo 科舉 Osaka, 1946.

-------"Shindai no shori to bakuyu, toku ni Yōsei chō o chūshin toshite"
清代の胥吏と幕友 ― 特に雍正朝を中心として,
Tōyōshi kenkyū, 16.4:1-28 (Mar. 1958).

Motomura Shōichi 本村正一. "Shindai shakai ni okeru shinshi no sonzai"
清代社會に於ける紳士の存在 ; Shien 史淵, 24:61-78
(Nov. 1940).

Mu-han 穆翰. Ming-hsing kuan-chien lu 明刑管見錄 (preface
dated 1845); in Hsiao-yüan ts'ung-shu.

Mu-yün-sou 沐雲叟. Hsi Chin chih wai 錫金志外 ; in Pi-chi hsiao-
shuo ta-kuan 筆記小說大觀.

Nan-feng hsien-chih 南豐縣志. 1871.

Negishi Tadashi 根岸佶. Chūgoku shakai ni okeru shidōsō, kirō shinshi
no kenkyū 中國社會に於ける指導層 ― 耆老紳士の
研究. Tokyo, 1947.

Nei-huang hsien-chih 內黃縣志. 1739.

Ning-yüan hsien-chih 寧遠縣志. 1709.

O-sheng ting-ts'ao chih-chang 鄂省丁漕指掌. Hu-pei nieh-shu 湖
北臬署, 1875.

P'an-yü hsien-chih 番禺縣志. 1871.

Pao-an chou chiao che kao 保安州交摺稿. MS, 1864, in the
Chinese-Japanese Library, Harvard University.

Pao-shan hsien chiao-tai po-ts'e 寶山縣交代駁冊. MS, 1902,
in the Chinese-Japanese Library, Harvard University.

P'eng-shui hsien-chih 彭水縣志. 1875.

P'eng Yüan-tuan 彭元端, comp. Fu-hui ch'üan-shu 孚惠全書.
1931 reprint.

P'ien-t'u lun ko ssu shih 偏途論各司事 . MS in the Chinese-Japanese Library, Harvard University.

P'ing-hu hsien-chih 平湖縣志. 1790.

P'ing-lo hsien-chih 平樂縣志. 1884.

P'u-t'ai hsien-chih 蒲台縣志. 1763.

P'u-t'ien hsien-chih 莆田縣志. 1758, reprint 1879.

Saeki Tomi 佐伯富. "Min Shin jidai no minsō ni tsuite" 明清時代の民牡について ; Tōyōshi kenkyū, 15.4:33-64 (Mar. 1957).

-------"Shindai Dōkōchō ni okeru Wainan ensei no kaikaku" 清代道光朝における淮南鹽政の改革 ; Tōhōgaku ronshū 東方學論集, 3:87-120 (Sept. 1955).

-------Shindai ensei no kenkyū 清代鹽税の研究. Kyoto, 1956.

Sakai Tadao 酒井忠夫 . "Kyōshin ni tsuite" 鄉紳について; Shichō 史潮 , 47:1-18 (Dec. 1952).

San-yüan hsien-chih 三原縣志 . 1783.

Sano Manabu 佐野學. Shinchō shakai shi 清朝社會史. 3 parts, 8 vols.; Tokyo, 1947-1948.

Shan-yang chiao-tai po-ts'e 山陽交代駁冊. MS, 1907, in the Chinese-Japanese Library, Harvard University.

Shan-yin hsien-chih 山陰縣志. 1803.

Shan-yin hsien-chih kao 山陰縣志稿. 1935.

Shang-hai hsien-chih 上海縣志. 1871.

Shang-hai yen-chiu tzu-liao 上海研究資料 . Shanghai, 1936.

Shang Yen-liu 商衍鎏. Ch'ing-tai k'o-chü k'ao-shih shu-lu 清代科舉考試述錄. Peking, 1958.

Shansi t'ung-chih 山西通志 1892.

Shantung t'ung-chih 山東通志 . 1736, reprint 1837.

Shao-hsing fu-chih 紹興府志 . Ch'ien-lung ed.

Shao-hsing hsien-chih tzu-liao 紹興縣志資料 . Series 1, 1937.

Shen-chou feng-t'u chi 深州風土記. 1900.

Shen Pao-chen 沈寶楨. Shen Wen-su kung cheng-shu 沈文肅公 政書. 1880.

Shen-tse hsien-chih 深澤縣志 . 1735-1744.

Shen Yen-ch'ing 沈衍慶. Huai-ch'ing cheng-chi 槐卿政績. 1905.

Sheng Hsüan-huai 盛宣懷. Yü-chai ts'un-kao 愚齋存稿 .

Sheng K'ang 盛康 , comp. Huang (Ch'ing)-ch'ao ching-shih wen hsü-pien (A) 皇 (清) 朝經世文續編 . Shanghai, 1897.

Shensi t'ung-chih 陝西通志. 1735.

Shih Chien-lieh 施建烈 . Chi Wu-hsi hsien-ch'eng shih-shou k'o-fu pen-mo 紀無錫縣城失守克復本末 ; in T'ai-p'ing t'ien-kuo, 5:245-268.

Shih hsiang pi lu 石香秘錄 ; in Pu-chu hsi-yüan lu chi-cheng. 1873.

Shih-hsüeh ta-sheng 仕學大乘 . K'ang-hsi ed.

Shimizu Morimitsu 清水盛光 . Chūgoku kyōson shakai ron 中國鄉 村社會論 . Tokyo, 1951.

-------Chūgoku no kyōson tōchi to sonraku 中國の鄉村統治と村落. Tokyo, 1949.

Shou-chang hsien-chih 壽張縣志 . 1717.

Shou-yang hsien-chih 壽陽縣志 . 1771.

Shun-t'ien fu Pa-chou fu-i ts'e 順天府霸州賦役冊 .

Sogabe Shizuo 曾我部靜雄 . "Chūgoku no gyōsei kukaku toshite no zu no kigen" 中國の行政區劃としての圖の起源; Tōyōshi kenkyū, 17.1:97-104 (June 1958).

-------"Min Taiso rokuyu no denshō ni tsuite" 明太祖六諭の傳承 について; Tōyōshi kenkyū, 12.4:27-36 (June 1953).

Su-chou fu-chih 蘇州府志. 1796.

Su-fan cheng-yao 蘇藩政要. MS in the Chinese-Japanese Libra[ry,]
    Harvard University.

Su-fan k'uan-mu yüan-liu 蘇藩欵目源流. MS in the Chinese-
    Japanese Library, Harvard University.

Sun Chia-kan 孫嘉淦. Sun Wen-ting kung tsou-su 孫文定公奏疏.

Sun Lun 孫綸, comp. Ting-li ch'eng-an ho-chien 定例成案合鐫.
    Preface dated 1707.

Sung-chün chün-i ch'eng-shu 松郡均役成書 (also known as Sung-chün
    Lou-hsien chün-i yao-lüeh 松郡婁縣均役要略). 1671-1788.

Sung shih 宋史. Ssu-pu pei-yao ed.

Ta-Ch'ing hui-tien 大清會典. 1690; 1732; 1764; 1818; 1899.
    Unless otherwise specified, citations herein are always from the
    1899 edition.

Ta-Ch'ing hui-tien shih-li 大清會典事例. 1818; 1899. Unless
    otherwise specified, citations herein are always from the
    1899 edition.

Ta-Ch'ing hui-tien tse-li 大清會典則例. 1764.

Ta-Ch'ing li-ch'ao shih-lu 大清歷朝實錄. Tokyo, 1937.

Ta-Ch'ing shih-ch'ao sheng-hsün 大清十朝聖訓.

Tai Chao-ch'en 戴肇辰, comp. Hsüeh-shih lu 學仕錄. 1867.

Tai Chao-chia 戴兆佳. T'ien-t'ai chih-lüeh 天台治略. Preface
    dated 1721, reprint 1897.

T'ai-chou chih 泰州志. 1827.

T'ai-ts'ang chou fu-i ch'üan-shu 太倉州賦役全書.

Tang-yang hsien-chih 當陽縣志. 1866.

T'ang-i hsien-chih 堂邑縣志. 1711, reprint 1892.

T'ao Chu 陶澍．T'ao Yün-t'ing hsien-sheng tsou-su 陶雲汀先生奏
　　疏　．

T'ao-yüan hsien chiao-tai po-ts'e 桃源縣交代駁冊　．MS, 1907, in
　　the Chinese-Japanese Library, Harvard University.

Te-yang hsien-chih 德陽縣志．1874.

Teng Ch'eng-hsiu 鄧承修．Yü-ping-ko tsou-i 語冰閣奏議．

T'ien Wen-ching 田文鏡 and Li Wei 李衛．Ch'in-pan chou-hsien
　　shih-i 欽頒州縣事宜　；in Huan-hai chih-nan wu chung 宦海
　　指南五種．1886.

Ting Jih-ch'ang 丁日昌．Fu Wu kung-tu 撫吳公牘．1877.

Ting-li hui-pien 定例彙編．Chiang-hsi an-ch'a-ssu yamen.

Ting-li hui-pien (A) 定例彙編．Chiang-hsi pu-cheng-ssu 江西布政
　　司　yamen.

Ting-t'ao hsien-chih 定陶縣志．1753, reprint 1876.

Tsai ch'eng hsiang ko-chia fu-shu e-ts'e pu 在城鄉各甲副書額冊
　　簿．MS in the Chinese-Japanese Library, Harvard University

Ts'ai-heng-tzu 采衡子．Ch'ung-ming man-lu 蟲鳴漫錄；in Pi-chi
　　hsiao-shuo ta-kuan 筆記小說大觀．

Ts'ai Shen-chih 蔡申之．"Ch'ing-tai chou-hsien ku-shih" 清代州
　　縣故事；Chung-ho 中和, 2.9:49-67 (Sept. 1941); 2.10:72-95
　　(Oct. 1941); 2.11:89-101 (Nov. 1941); 2.12:100-108 (Dec. 1941).

Tseng Kuo-fan 曾國藩．Tseng Wen-cheng kung ch'üan-chi 曾文正公
　　全集．1876.

Tso Tsung-t'ang 左宗棠．Tso Wen-hsiang kung ch'üan-chi 左文襄
　　公全集．1888.

Tsung Chi-ch'en 宗稷辰．Kung-ch'ih-chai wen-ch'ao 躬耻齋文鈔．
　　1851.

Tu Yu 杜佑．T'ung tien 通典．Shih-t'ung ed.

Tung-a hsien-chih 東阿縣志．1829.

Tung-p'ing chou chih 東平州志. 1878.

Tzu-t'ung hsien-chih 梓潼縣志. 1858.

Tz'u-chou chih 磁州志. 1703.

Wada Sei 和田清, ed. Shina chihō jichi hattatsu shi 支那地方自治發達史. Tokyo, 1939.

Wan Wei-han 萬維翰. Mu-hsüeh chü-yao 幕學舉要 (preface dated 1770); in Ju-mu hsü-chih wu chung.

Wang An-shih 王安石. Lin-ch'uan hsien-sheng wen-chi 臨川先生文集. Ssu-pu ts'ung-k'an 四部叢刊 ed.

Wang Ch'ing-yün 王慶雲. Shih-ch'ü yü-chi 石渠餘紀 (also known as Hsi-ch'ao chi-cheng 熙朝紀政). 1890.

Wang Feng-sheng 王鳳生. Che-sheng ts'ang-k'u ch'ing-ch'a chieh-yao 浙省倉庫清查節要; in Yüeh-chung ts'ung-cheng lu 越中從政錄. Preface dated 1824.

-------Ho-pei ts'ai-feng lu 河北采風錄 1826.

-------Hsüeh-chih t'i-hsing lu 學治體行錄; in Yüeh-chung ts'ung-cheng lu.

-------Huang-cheng pei-lan 荒政備覽; in Yüeh-chung ts'ung-cheng lu.

-------P'ing-hu hsien pao-chia shih-i 平湖縣保甲事宜; in Yüeh-chung ts'ung-cheng lu.

-------Sung-chou ts'ung-cheng lu 宋州從政錄. 1826.

Wang Hsi-hsün 汪喜荀. Ts'ung-cheng lu 從政錄; in Chiang-tu Wang-shih ts'ung-shu 江都汪氏叢書. Preface dated 1841.

Wang Hsien-ch'ien 王先謙. Chuang-tzu chi chieh 莊子集解.

-------, comp. Tung-hua lu 東華錄 and Tung-hua hsü-lu 東華續錄. 1911.

Wang Hsien-i 王賢儀. Chia yen sui chi 家言隨記. 1866.
    Chüan 1 includes "Shen Han lun" 申韓論, "Tso-chih yao-yen

xix

che-yao" 佐治藥言摘要　　, and "Yüeh-li ou-t'an" 閱歷偶談　.

Wang Hui-tsu 汪輝祖. Hsüeh-chih i-shuo 學治臆說, Hsüeh-chih hsü-shuo 學治續說, and Hsüeh-chih shuo-chui 學治說贅；in Wang Lung-chuang hsien-sheng i-shu 汪龍莊先生遺書　. 1882–1886.

-------Ping-t'a meng-hen lu 病榻夢痕錄　and Meng-hen lu yü 夢痕錄餘；in Wang Lung-chuang hsien-sheng i-shu.

-------Shuang-chieh-t'ang yung-hsün 雙節堂庸訓　；in Wang Lung-chuang hsien-sheng i-shu.

-------Tso-chih yao-yen 佐治藥言　and Hsü tso-chih yao-yen 續佐治藥言　；in Wang Lung-chuang hsien-sheng i-shu.

Wang K'an 王侃. Chiang-chou pi-t'an 江州筆談；in Pa-shan ch'i-chung 巴山七種. 1865.

-------Fang yen 放言；in Pa-shan ch'i-chung.

Wang Yen-hsi 王延熙　and Wang Shu-min 王樹敏. Huang (Ch'ing)-ch'ao Tao Hsien T'ung Kuang tsou-i 皇(清)朝道咸同光奏議. 1902.

Wang Yu-huai 王又槐. Ch'ien-ku pei-yao 錢穀備要. Preface dated 1793.

-------Hsing-ch'ien pi-lan 刑錢必覽. Preface dated 1793.

-------Pan-an yao-lüeh 辦案要略；in Ju-mo hsü-chih wu chung.

-------et al. Pu-chu hsi-yüan lu chi-cheng 補註洗寃錄集證. 1843; 1873.

Wen Chün-t'ien 聞鈞天. Chung-kuo pao-chia chih-tu 中國保甲制度. Shanghai, 1935.

Weng Tsu-lieh 翁祖烈. Huan-yu sui-pi 宦遊隨筆. 1880.

Wu-ch'eng hsien-chih 烏程縣志. 1881.

Wu-chiang hsien-chih 烏江縣志. 1747.

Wu Jung-kuang 吳榮光 . Wu-hsüeh lu, ch'u-pien 吾學錄初編. 1870.

Wu-ling hsien-chih 武陵縣志 . 1867.

Wu T'an 吳壇 . Ta-Ch'ing lü-li t'ung-k'ao 大清律例通考 . 1886.

Wu Wen-jung 吳文榕 . Wu Wen-chieh kung i-chu 吳文節公遺著 .
    1857.

Yamada Hideji 山田秀二 . "Min-Shin jidai no sonraku jichi ni
    tsuite" 明清時代の村落自治について ; Rekishigaku
    kenkyū 歷史學研究 2.3:214-230 (July 1934); 2.5:15-22
    (Sept. 1934); 2.6:2-30 (Oct. 1934).

Yang-ch'ü hsien-chih 陽曲縣志 . 1682.

Yang-i chiao-tai po-ts'e 揚邑交代駮册 . MS, 1910, in the
    Chinese-Japanese Library, Harvard University.

Yao Hsi-kuang 姚錫光. Li-Wan ts'un-tu 吏皖存牘 . 1908.

Yao Te-yü 姚德豫. Hsi-yüan lu chieh 洗寃錄解 ; in Pu-chu hsi-
    yüan lu chi cheng, 1865 ed.

Yao Ying 姚瑩 . Tung-ming wen-chi 東溟文集 ; in Chung-fu-t'ang
    ch'üan-chi 中復堂全集 . 1867.

Yeh Chen 葉鎮 . Tso li yao yen 作吏要言 ; in Pu-chu hsi-yüan lu chi
    cheng, 1843 ed.

Yen-t'ang chien-wen tsa-chi 研堂見聞雜記 ; in T'ung-shih.

Yung-cheng shang-yü 雍正上諭 . 1741.

Yung-ch'ing hsien-chih 永清縣志. 1779.

Yü-che hui-ts'un 諭摺彙存 . 1893-1907.

Yü Ch'eng-lung 于成龍 . Yu Ch'ing-tuan kung cheng-shu 于清端公
    政書 . 1683.

Yüan Mei 袁枚 . Hsiao-ts'ang shan-fang wen-chi 小倉山房文集 .
    Sui-yüan sa-chung 隨園卅種 ed.

Yüan Shou-ting 袁守定 . T'u-min lu 畜民錄 . 1839.

WORKS IN WESTERN LANGUAGES

Alabaster, Ernest. Notes and Commentaries on Chinese Law and Cognate Topics, with Special Relation to Ruling Cases, Together with a Brief Excursus on the Law of Property. London, 1899.

-------"Notes on Chinese Law and Practice Preceding Revision, " Journal of the North China Branch of the Royal Asiatic Society, 37:83-149 (1906).

Beal, E. G. Jr. The Origin of Likin (1853-1864). Cambridge, Mass., 1958.

Boulais, Gui, trans. Manuel du code chinois (Variétés sinologiques). Shanghai, 1923.

Brenan, Byron. "The Office of District Magistrate in China, " Journal of the China Branch of the Royal Asiatic Society, new series, 32:36-65 (1897-1898). Also published as a pamphlet, Shanghai, 1899.

Brunnert, H. S. and V. V. Hagelstrom. Present Day Political Organization of China. Shanghai, 1912.

Chang Chung-li. The Chinese Gentry; Studies on Their Role in Nineteenth Century Chinese Society. Seattle, 1955.

Ch'ien Tuan-sheng. The Government and Politics of China. Cambridge, Mass., 1950.

Ch'ü T'ung-tsu. "Chinese Class Structure and its Ideology, " in J. K. Fairbank, ed., Chinese Thought and Institutions, pp. 235-250. Chicago, 1957.

-------Law and Society in Traditional China (Le Monde d'outre-mer-- passé et présent). Paris and The Hague, 1961.

Doolittle, Justus. Social Life of the Chinese, with Some Account of their Religious, Governmental, Educational, and Business Customs and Opinions. 2 vols.; New York, 1865.

Eberhard, Wolfram. A History of China, trans. E. W. Dickes. Berkeley, 1950; 2nd and rev. ed., Berkeley, 1960.

Fairbank, J. K. and S. Y. Teng. Ch'ing Administration: Three Studies. Cambridge, Mass., 1960.

Fei Hsiao-t'ung. China's Gentry: Essays in Rural-Urban Relations; with Six Life-Histories of Chinese Gentry Collected by Yung-teh Chow. Chicago, 1953.

-------"Peasantry and Gentry: An Interpretation of Chinese Social Structure and its Changes," American Journal of Sociology, 52.1:1-17 (July 1946).

Gulik, R. H. van, trans. T'ang-Yin-Pi-shih, Parallel Cases from under the Pear Tree (Sinica Leidensia). Leiden, 1956.

Hinton, H. C. The Grain Tribute System of China (1845-1911). Cambridge, Mass., 1956.

Ho Ping-ti. "Aspects of Social Mobility in China, 1368-1911," Comparative Studies in Society and History, 1.4:330-359 (June 1959).

-------"The Salt Merchants of Yang-chou: A Study of Commercial Capitalism in Eighteenth-Century China," Harvard Journal of Asiatic Studies, 17.1 and 2:130-168 (June 1954).

-------Studies in the Population of China, 1368-1953. Cambridge, Mass., 1959.

Hsiao Kung-chuan. Rural China: Imperial Control in the Nineteenth Century. Seattle, 1960.

-------"Rural Control in Nineteenth Century China," Far Eastern Quarterly, 12.2:173-181 (Feb. 1953).

Hsieh Pao-chao. The Government of China, 1644-1911. Baltimore, 1925.

Jamieson, George, et al. "Tenure of Land in China and the Condition of the Rural Population," Journal of the China Branch of the Royal Asiatic Society, new series, 23:59-174 (1888).

Legge, James. "Imperial Confucianism," The China Review, 6:147-158, 223-235, 299-310, 364-374 (1877-1878).

Liang Fang-chung. The Single-whip Method of Taxation in China, trans. Wang Yü-chuan. Cambridge, Mass., 1956.

Liu Wang Hui-chen. The Traditional Chinese Clan Rules (Monographs of the Association for Asian Studies). New York, 1959.

Macgowan, D. J. "China Guilds or Chambers of Commerce and Trade Unions," Journal of the China Branch of the Royal Asiatic Society, new series, 21.3-4:133-192 (1886).

Marsh, Robert M. The Mandarins; The Circulation of Elites in China, 1600-1900. Glencoe, Ill., 1961.

Mayers, W. F. The Chinese Government, A Manual of Chinese Titles, Categorically Arranged and Explained, with an Appendix. 3rd and rev. ed.; Shanghai, 1897.

Meadows, T. T. Desultory Notes on the Government and People of China and on the Chinese Language, Illustrated with a Sketch of the Province of Kwangtung. London, 1847.

Milne, William, trans. The Sacred Edict, containing Sixteen Maxims of the Emperor Kang-He, Amplified by His Son, the Emperor Yoong-Ching; together with A Paraphrase on the Whole, by A Mandarin. London, 1817.

Morse, H. B., comp. "Currency and Measures in China," Journal of the China Branch of the Royal Asiatic Society, new series, 24:48-135 (1889-1890).

-------The Guilds of China, with an Account of the Guild Merchant or Co-hong of Canton. London, 1909.

-------The Trade and Administration of the Chinese Empire. Shanghai, 1908.

Staunton, G. T. Miscellaneous Notices Relating to China, and Our Commercial Intercourse with that Country, including a Few Translations from the Chinese Language. London, 1822.

-------, trans. Ta Tsing Leu Lee; being the Fundamental Laws and a Selection from the Supplementary Statutes of the Penal Code of China. London, 1810.

Sun Zen E-tu, trans. Ch'ing Administrative Terms (Harvard East Asian Studies). Cambridge, Mass., 1961.

Weber, Max. The Religion of China: Confucianism and Taoism, trans. H. H. Gerth. Glencoe, Ill., 1951.

Williams, S. W.   The Middle Kingdom; A Survey of the Geography, Government, Literature, Social Life, Arts, and History of the Chinese Empire and its Inhabitants.   2 vols.; New York, 1883.

Yang Ch'ing-k'un.   "Some Characteristics of Chinese Bureaucratic Behavior," in D. S. Nivison and A. F. Wright, eds., Confucianism in Action, pp. 134-164.   Stanford, 1959.

Yang Hsien-yi and G. Yang, trans.   The Scholars.   Peking, 1957.

Zi, Étienne.   Pratique des examens litteraires en Chine   (Variétés sinologiques).   Shanghai, 1894.

an-chien 案件

an-tsung 案總

An-yang 安陽

ao-yu 廒友

cha 札

ch'a-i 茶儀

ch'a-kuan 牖官

ch'a-kuo ch'ien 茶果錢

Ch'a-ling 茶陵

ch'a-shui 茶稅

ch'a-yin 茶引

ch'ai-ch'ien 差錢

ch'ai-tsung 差總

ch'ai-wu 差務

ch'ai-yao 差徭

chan chien-hou 斬監候

chan-shih 詹事

chang 杖

Chang Ch'ien 張謇

chang-ch'ien 杖錢

Chang Chih-tung 張之洞

Chang-chou 漳州

chang-fang 賬房

Chang-ho 漳河

Chang Hsüeh-ch'eng 章學誠

Chang Ju-hsin 張汝炘

Chang Liang-chi 張亮基

Chang P'eng-chan 張鵬展

Chang Po-hsing 張伯行

Chang-te 彰德

Chang T'ien-shih 張天師

Chang T'ing-hsiang 張廷驤

Chang Wo-kuan 張我觀

Ch'ang-an 長安

Ch'ang-chai 長寨

Ch'ang-chou 長洲

Ch'ang-hsing 長興

Ch'ang-hua 昌化

Ch'ang-lu 長蘆

ch'ang-p'ing ts'ang 常平倉

Ch'ang-sha 長沙

Ch'ang-shu 常熟

ch'ang-ssu 常祀

ch'ang-sui 長隨

ch'ang-tan 長單

xxvii

Ch'ang-te 常德

Ch'ang-t'ing 長汀

chao 照

chao chieh 招解

chao chieh fei 招解費

chao-chuang 招狀

chao-fang 招房

Chao I 趙翼

Chao Kuo-chu 趙國澍

chao-mo 照磨

Chao Shen-ch'iao 趙申喬

chao-shih 名試

chao-shu 招書

Chao-ssu t'ai-t'ai 趙四太太

Chao-ssu t'ai-yeh 趙四太爺

Chao-wen 昭文

Ch'ao-chin ts'e 朝覲冊

ch'ao-k'ao 朝考

chen-chang 鎮長

Chen-chiang 鎮江

Chen-hsiung 鎮雄

Chen-yüan 鎮遠

Ch'en Hung-mou 陳宏謀

Ch'en-liu 陳留

Ch'en Pi-ning 陳必寧

cheng 政

Cheng-chou 鄭州

cheng-ch'u 正出

cheng-hsiang ch'ien-liang 正項錢
糧

cheng-ju 正入

Cheng Kuan-ying 鄭觀應

cheng-kung 正貢

cheng-pi 徵比

cheng-shu 政書

cheng-t'ang 正堂

cheng-t'u 正途

cheng-tui 正兌

cheng-yin kuan 正印官

ch'eng 誠

ch'eng fa fang 承發房

Ch'eng Han-chang 程含章

ch'eng-hsüan pu-cheng shih 承宣布
政使

Ch'eng-huang 城隍

Ch'eng-kung 呈貢

"Ch'eng shou p'ien" 城守篇

ch'eng-tz'u 呈詞

Ch'eng Yung-yen 程永言

chi-chi 己集

chi-kung 記功

chi-kung pu 記功簿

chi-kuo 記過

chi-lu 記錄

Chi-pu chang-ch'eng 緝捕章程

chi-shih 記室

ch'i-lao 耆老

ch'i-ting 旗丁

ch'i-wei 契尾

ch'i-yün 起運

chia 甲

chia-chang 甲長

chia-chi 甲集

chia-chi 加級

Chia-ch'ing 嘉慶

Chia Han-fu 賈漢復

Chia-hsing 嘉興

chia-jen 家人

chia-kun 夾棍

Chia-shan 嘉善

chia-shou 甲首

Chia-ting 嘉定

Chiang-hsia 江夏

Chiang-ling 江陵

Chiang-nan 江南

Chiang-ning 江寧

Chiang-pei 江北

Chiang Shih-ch'üan 蔣士銓

Chiang-yin 江陰

Chiao-ch'eng 交城

chiao chien-hou 絞監候

chiao-chih 教職

Chiao-chou 膠州

chiao-fu 轎夫

chiao-hsi 教習

chiao hu 較斛

chiao-p'an ts'e 交盤冊

chiao-tai ts'e 交代冊

chiao-ti 教弟

chiao-yü 教諭

chieh-an fei 結案費

chieh-ch'ai 解差

chieh fei 解費

Chieh-hsiao tz'u 節孝祠

chieh-p'iao 截票

chieh-so ch'ien 解鎖錢

Chien-ch'ang 建昌

chien-chiao 檢校

chien-ch'üeh 簡缺

chien-fang 柬房

chien-hsüan 揀選

chien-hsü 奸胥

chien-k'uai 健快

chien-kuan yen-wu 兼管鹽務

Chien-li 監利

chien-min 賤民

chien-p'u 簡譜

chien-sheng 監生

Chien-shih 建始

chien-shih 箋釋

chien-t'ao 檢討

ch'ien 虔

ch'ien 錢

ch'ien 籤

Ch'ien Ch'en-ch'ün 錢陳羣

ch'ien-ku 錢穀

ch'ien-liang 錢糧

ch'ien-liang ching-ch'eng 錢糧經承

ch'ien-liang men-ting 錢糧門丁

ch'ien-liang ts'e 錢糧冊

ch'ien-liang tsung 錢糧總

Ch'ien-lung 乾隆

Ch'ien-shan 潛山

Ch'ien-t'ang 錢塘

ch'ien-ts'ao 錢漕

ch'ien-ts'ao men-ting 錢漕門丁

ch'ien-ya 簽押

ch'ien-ya fang 簽押房

chih chiao-ti 治教弟

chih-chou 知州

chih-chün 制軍

chih-fu 知府

chih-hsien 知縣

chih-kuan chih kuan 治官之官

chih-kung yin 紙工銀

chih-li chou 直隸州

chih-li chou chih-chou 直隸州知州

chih-li t'ing 直隸廳

chih-li t'ing t'ung-chih 直隸廳同知

chih-li t'ing t'ung-p'an 直隸廳通判

chih-pi fei 紙筆費

chih-shih 知事

chih-shih chih kuan 治事之官

chih-shih fu 執事夫

chih-shih kuan 職事官

chih-t'ang 值堂

chih-ti 治弟

chih-t'ieh ch'uan-hua 執帖傳話

chih wan-sheng 治晚生

chih yü-ti 治愚弟

chih-yüan 職員

ch'ih 笞

chin 衿

chin ao ch'ien 進廒錢

Chin-hsien 金縣

Chin-kuei 金匱

chin-shen 搢(縉)紳

chin-shih 進士

Chin-t'an 金壇

chin-ts'ang ch'ien 進倉錢

chin-tsu 禁卒

ch'in-min chih kuan 親民之官

ching 敬

ching-ch'eng 經承

<u>Ching-chih ch'üan-shu</u> 經制全書

xxx

Ching-chou 涇州   Chu I-hsin 朱一新

ching-li 經歷   Chu Kuo-chih 朱國治

Ching-pao 京報   chu-mo 硃墨

ching-piao 旌表   chu-pu 主簿

Ching-yang 涇陽   chu-shih 主事

Ch'ing-chou 青州   Chu Yün-chin 朱雲錦

Ch'ing-ho 清河   Ch'u-chou 滁州

Ch'ing-li ssu 清吏司 ch'u-chieh ch'ien 出結錢

Ch'ing-p'u 青浦   ch'u-p'iao fei 出票費

Ch'ing-yüan 清苑   ch'u-pien 初編

Chiu-chiang 九江   ch'uan-ch'eng fei 傳呈費

chiu-kuan 舊管   ch'uan-p'iao 串票

ch'iu-shen 秋審   Ch'uan-shan shu-yüan 船山書院

Ch'iu Shu-t'ang 邱樹堂 ch'uan-sheng ch'ien 串繩錢

Cho-chou 涿州   chuang-pang 狀榜

cho-i 卓異   chuang-t'ou 莊頭

ch'o-ch'ien 戳錢   ch'ui ku shou 吹鼓手

chou 州   chung-ch'üeh 中缺

chou erh-shou 州貳守 chung-hu 中戶

Chou Jen-fu 周壬福 Chung-i tz'u 忠義祠

Chou Kao 周鎬   Chung-mou 中牟

Chou Liang-kung 周亮工 chung-ta hu 中大戶

chou-p'an 州判   Chung-wei 中衛

chou-t'ung 州同   ch'ung 衝

ch'ou-ch'üeh 醜缺 Ch'ung-ming 崇明

Ch'ou-fang Chü 籌防局 Chü-chou 莒州

Chu-ch'eng 諸城   chü-hsiang shih-ta-fu 居鄉士大夫

chü-jen 樂人

Chü-jung 句容

chü-shen 巨紳

ch'ü 區

chüan 卷

chüan-shou 卷首

Ch'üan-chou 泉州

ch'üeh 缺

ch'üeh-ti 缺底

chün-hsiu chien-sheng 俊秀監生

chün-yao 均徭

e-tseng pang-i 額增幫役

En-an 恩安

en-chien 恩監

en-kung 恩貢

En-lo 恩樂

en-yin 恩廕

erh-chia 二甲

erh-yin 貳尹

fa-fang 發房

fa-hsing 發行

fa-shen 發審

Fa-shen Chü 發審局

fan 繁

fan-ch'üeh 繁缺

fan-li 凡例

fan-shih yin 飯食銀

fan-yin 飯銀

fang 房

fang 坊

fang-kao 放告

fang-po 方伯

fang-shih 房師

Fang Ta-chih 方大湜

fei 飛

fen 分

fen-chou 分州

fen-fang 分防

fen-hsien 分縣

fen-hsün tao 分巡道

fen-shou tao 分守道

fen-ssu 分司

feng 封

feng 俸

Feng Chen-tung 馮宸東

Feng-ch'eng 豐城

feng-ch'ien 風籤

feng-chün 封君

Feng-huang t'ing 鳳凰廳

Feng Kuei-fen 馮桂芬

feng-man chi-sheng 俸滿即陞

Feng-t'ien 奉天

feng-tseng 封贈

feng-tseng kuan 封贈官

Feng-yang 鳳陽

feng yin 封麾

feng-yin 封印

fu 府

fu 撫

fu-chien 附監

Fu-chou 福州

fu-feng 腹俸

fu-hsin 腹心

Fu-i ch'üan-shu 賦役全書

fu-jen 夫人

fu-kung 副貢

fu-kung 附貢

fu-mu kuan 父母官

Fu-ning 阜寧

fu-pang 副榜

fu-pang chü-jen 副榜舉人

fu-sheng 附生

fu-shih 府試

Fu-shun 富順

fu-t'an 府攤

fu-tsao 浮躁

fu tsung-ho 副總河

Fu Wei-lin 傅維鱗

hai 亥

Hai-ning 海寧

Hai-wai wen-pien 海外文編

Han Chen 韓振

Han Shih-ch'i 韓世琦

hang-hu 行戶

hao-chien 號件

hao-hsien 耗羨

hao-mi 耗米

Heng-chou 衡州

Heng-yang 衡陽

Ho-chou 河州

ho-hsi fei 和息費

Ho Keng-sheng 何耿繩

ho-po-so kuan 河泊所官

Ho Shih-ch'i 何士祁

ho-tao 河道

ho-tao shui-li tsung-tu 河道水利總督

Ho-tung 河東

Hou Fang-yü 侯方域

Hou-kuan 侯官

Hou T'ung 侯桐

Hsi-lung 西隆

Hsi-ning 西寧

Hsi-yüan lu 洗寃錄

hsiang 詳

hsiang 廂

hsiang 鄉

hsiang-chang 鄉長

hsiang-ch'i 鄉耆

Hsiang-fu 祥符

Hsiang-hsiang 湘鄉

Hsiang-hsien tz'u 鄉賢祠

hsiang-huan 鄉官

hsiang-min 鄉民

Hsiang-shan 香山

hsiang-shen 鄉紳

hsiang-shen t'i-mien 鄉紳體面

Hsiang-t'an 湘潭

hsiang-wen 詳文

hsiang-yin 鄉飲

hsiang-yüeh 鄉約

hsiao-chao 銷照

hsiao ch'üeh 小缺

hsiao-hu 小戶

hsiao-lien fang-cheng 孝廉方正

Hsiao-shan 蕭山

Hsiao-ti tz'u 孝弟祠

Hsieh Chao-chih 謝肇淛

Hsieh Chen-ting 謝振定

hsieh-ch'ien 鞋錢

Hsieh Chin-luan 謝金鑾

Hsieh Ming-huang 謝鳴篁

hsieh-tzu 楔子

hsieh-wa ch'ien 鞋襪錢

hsien 限

hsien 縣

hsien ao 縣澳

hsien-ch'eng 縣丞

Hsien-feng 咸豐

Hsien-kang ts'e 憲綱

hsien-nien 現年

Hsien-ning 咸寧

Hsien-nung 先農

hsien-shih 縣試

hsien-tan 限單

Hsien-te 憲德

hsien-ts'ao 閒曹

Hsien-yang 咸陽

Hsin-cheng 新鄭

Hsin-chien 新建

Hsin-hui 新會

hsin-kung yin 辛工銀

hsin-shou 新收

hsing 行

Hsing-hua 興化

hsing-ming 刑名

Hsiu-shui 秀水

hsiu-ts'ai 秀才

Hsiung Hsi-ling 熊希齡

hsiung-ti 兄弟

hsü 戌

Hsü-chih ts'e 須知冊

hsü-k'an 敘勘

Hsü Keng-pi 徐賡陛

Hsü Tzu 徐鼐

Hsü Wen-pi 徐文弼

Hsü-yung t'ing 敘永廳

Hsüan-ch'eng 宣城　　　Huang Ang 黃印

hsüan-chü 選舉　　　huang-ch'ai 皇差

Hsüan-hua 宣化　　　Huang K'o-jun 黃可潤

Hsüan-tsung 宣宗　　　Huang Liu-hung 黃六鴻

hsüeh-cheng 學正　　　Huang-ts'e 黃册

Hsüeh Fu-ch'eng 薛福成　　　hui-chao 迴照

hsün 汎　　　Hui-fang Chü 會防局

hsün-chien 巡檢　　　hui-pi 迴避

Hsün-fang Chü 巡防局　　　hung-hei pi 紅黑筆

hsün-fu 巡撫　　　Hung Liang-chi 洪亮吉

hsün-huan pu 循環簿　　　huo 獲

hsün-tao 訓導　　　huo-ch'ien 火籤

hsün-tsai 巡宰　　　huo-fu 伙夫

hu 笏　　　huo-hao 火耗

hu 斛　　　huo-p'ai 火牌

hu 護　　　huo-shui 活稅

Hu-chou 湖州

Hu Lin-i 胡林翼　　　i-chan 驛站

hu-ming 戶名　　　I Chao-hsiung 宜兆熊

hu-shu 戶書　　　I-cheng 宜徵

Hu Tse-huang 胡澤璜　　　i-ch'eng 驛丞

hu-ts'e 戶册　　　i-chih yu-tan 易知由單

hua-hu 花戶　　　i-ch'uan tao 驛傳道

Hua-jung 筆容　　　I-fang 翼房

Hua-yang 華陽　　　i-feng 毗封

Huai-chi 懷集　　　i-hsü 議敍

Huai-lai 懷來　　　i-hsüeh 義學

i-hu 役戶

i-kao 遺稿
i-men 儀門
i-shu 驛書
i-ts'ai hsing-ch'iu 以財行求
i-ts'ang 義倉
i-tseng 貤贈
i-t'u 異途
i-yen tao 驛鹽道
Ili 伊犂

Jao-chou 饒州
Jen-ho 仁和
Jen-tsung 仁宗
jen-yin pi-tao ch'ien 人銀必到籤
Jen Yüan-hsiang 任原祥
ju-hsüeh men-tou 儒學門斗
ju-hu 儒戶
ju-jen 孺人
Ju-kao 如皋
Ju-lin wai-shih 儒林外史
Jui-ch'ang 瑞昌
Jui-chou 瑞州
Jung-hsien 融縣
jung-kuan 冗官

kai-tui 改兌
k'ai-ch'u 開除
K'ai-feng 開封
k'ai-tan fei 開單費

k'ai-yin 開印
kan-chieh 甘結
kan-chih 干支
Kan-en 感恩
kan-hsiu 乾修
k'an-ho 勘合
k'an ts'ang 看倉
k'an-yin 看印
k'an-yü 看語
K'ang-hsi 康熙
Kao-an 高安
kao-an 稿案
kao-an ch'ien-ya 稿案簽押
kao-an men-ting 稿案門丁
kao-ch'i 告期
Kao-ch'un 高淳
Kao-lan 皋蘭
Kao-mi 高密
Kao P'an-lung 高攀龍
kao-shih 告示
Kao-t'ang 高唐
Kao T'ing-yao 高廷瑤
Kao-tsung 高宗
k'ao-ch'eng 考成
k'ao chih 考職
k'ao san kuan 考散館
k'ao-yü 考語
ken-pan 跟班

keng-fu 更夫

k'o-chia 科甲

K'o Sung 柯聳

k'o-tse yu-tan 科則由單

kou-she jen-fan 勾攝人犯

kou-she kung-shih 勾攝公事

K'ou Yung-hsiu 冠永修

ku-ch'u 故出

ku-i ch'ien 雇役錢

ku-ju 故入

Ku Wen-pin 顧文彬

Ku Yen-wu 顧炎武

k'u 庫

k'u 酷

k'u-fang 庫房

k'u-li 庫吏

k'u-p'ing 庫平

k'u-shu 庫書

k'u-ting 庫丁

k'u-tzu 庫子

kua-hao 掛號

kua-hao fei 掛號費

kua-ming shu-li 掛名書吏

kua-ming ya-i 掛名衙役

k'uai 快

K'uai-chi 會稽

k'uai-chi ts'e 會計冊

k'uai-pan 快班

k'uai-shou 快手

kuan-chia 官價

kuan-chien 管監

kuan-chien p'eng-yu 管監朋友

kuan-ch'u 管厨

kuan-hao 管號

kuan-ho chou-p'an 管河州判

kuan-ho chou-t'ung 管河州同

kuan-ho chu-pu 管河主簿

kuan-ho hsien-ch'eng 管河縣丞

kuan-ho shui-li chou-p'an 管河水利
州判

kuan-hu 官户

kuan-li 官吏

kuan-liang chu-pu 管糧主簿

kuan-pan 官辦

kuan-pang 官幫

kuan-shen ping-yung 官紳並用

kuan-tai 冠帶

Kuan-ti 關帝

kuan yin-chiang 官銀匠

k'uan-mu ts'e 欵目冊

Kuang-ch'ang 廣昌

Kuang-chi 廣濟

K'uang Chung 況鍾

kuei 貴

Kuei-an 歸安

kuei-nung mien-pi p'iao 歸農免比
票

kuei-shu 櫃書
kun-tan 滾單
Kung-ch'ang 鞏昌
kung-chuang 供狀
kung-sheng 貢生
kung-shih 供事
kung-shih 工食
kung-ting 供丁
kung-tsui 公罪
kung-tu 公牘
kuo-ko 過割
Kuo-shih Kuan 國史館
Kuo Sung-tao 郭嵩燾

Lai-yang 萊陽
lang-chung 郎中
lao-fu-tzu 老夫子
lao hsien-sheng 老先生
lao-hu pan 老虎班
lao-i 牢役
lao-tung 老東
lei-ch'ien 雷籤
li 吏
li 里
li 例
li 屬
li-ch'ai 里差
li-chang 里長

Li-ch'eng 歷城
li-chia 里甲
li-chien 例監
li-ch'un 立春
li-chüeh 立決
Li Fu-hsing 李復興
Li Hu 李湖
Li Huan 李桓
Li Hung-chang 李鴻章
Li Kung 李塨
li-kung 例貢
li-lao 里老
li-mu 吏目
li-nien k'uei-k'ung 歷年虧空
Li-po 荔波
Li Po-yüan 李伯元
Li Shih-chen 李士禎
li-shu 吏書
li-shu 里書
li-ts'ui 里催
Li Tz'u-ming 李慈銘
Li Wei 李衛
Li-yang 溧陽
Li Yu-fen 李有棻
li-yüan 吏員
liang 兩
Liang-Che 兩浙

xxxviii

Liang-Chiang tsung-tu 兩江總督

liang-ch'u tao 糧儲道

Liang-hsiang 良鄉

Liang-Huai 兩淮

liang-p'iao 糧票

liang pu chou-p'an 糧捕州判

liang pu chou-t'ung 糧捕州同

liang pu shui-li hsien-ch'eng 糧捕
水利縣丞

Liang-shan 梁山

liang-t'ing 糧廳

liang-wu shui-li chou-p'an 糧務水
利州判

liang-wu shui-li chu-pu 糧務水
利主簿

liang-wu shui-li hsien-ch'eng 糧務
水利縣丞

lieh-shen 劣紳

lien-pu 廉捕

likin 釐金

Lin-chang 臨漳

lin-chien 廩監

Lin-ch'ü 臨朐

Lin-kuei 臨桂

lin-kung 廩貢

lin-sheng 廩生

lin-tsun 懍遵

ling-chuang 領狀

Ling-hu 菱湖

Ling-shou 靈壽

Ling-shui 陵水

liu 流

Liu-an 六安

liu-ch'ai 流差

Liu Ch'i 劉淇

Liu Chien-shao 劉建韶

liu-fa 六法

Liu Heng 劉衡

Liu-ho 六合

Liu Ju-chi 劉汝驥

Liu Jung 劉蓉

liu-shui shou-pu 流水收簿

liu-yang chü 留養局

Lo Ping-chang 駱秉章

lo-ti shui 落地稅

Lou-hsien 婁縣

lou-kuei 陋規

Lu-chou 廬州

Lu-i 鹿邑

Lu I-t'ung 魯一同

Lu Lung-ch'i 陸隴其

Lu Wei-ch'i 陸維祺

Luan-ch'eng 欒城

Lung-kuan chen 龍關鎮

lü 律

Lü Hsien-chi 呂賢基

ma-fu 馬夫

ma-k'uai 馬快

ma-p'ai 馬牌

Ma-p'ing 馬平

mai-mien 買免

mai-p'i fei 買批費

mang-kuei 忙規

Mang-shen 芒神

Mao Hung-pin 毛鴻賓

mao-pu 卯簿

mei-ch'üeh 美缺

men-chün 門軍

men-pao 門包

men-pu 門簿

men-shang 門上

men-sheng 門生

men-t'an shui 門攤稅

Men-t'ou kou 門頭溝

men-tzu 門子

Meng Sen 孟森

Miao-chiang ch'üeh 苗疆缺

Mien-yang 沔陽

min-chuang 民壯

Min-hou 閩侯

Min-hsien 閩縣

min-hu 民戶

ming-an chien-yen fei 命案檢驗費

Ming-chiang 明江

ming-fa 明法

ming-fu 命婦

"Ming hsiang-kuan nüeh-min chih hai" 明鄉官虐民之害

Ming-huan tz'u 名宦祠

ming-li 名例

ming-lo fu 鳴鑼夫

Ming-lun-t'ang 明倫堂

mou 畝

mu-fu 幕府

Mu-han 穆翰

mu-liao 幕僚

mu-pin 幕賓

Mu T'ien-yen 慕天顏

Mu-tsung 穆宗

Mu-tu chen 木瀆鎮

mu-yu 幕友

na-hu chih-chao 納戶執照

Na-yen-ch'eng 那彥成

nan 難

Nan-ch'ang 南昌

Nan-feng 南豐

Nan-hai 南海

Nan-k'ang 南康

nan-yin 難廕

nan yin-sheng 難廕生

nei-chai nei-hsiao 內摘內銷

Nei-huang 内黃

nei-ko chung-shu 内閣中書

Nei-wu Fu 内務府

nien 年

nien-lao 年老

nien-po 年伯

Ning-erh 寧洱

Ning-hai 寧海

Ning-ming 寧明

Ning-yüan 寧遠

No-min 諾敏

nung-mang 農忙

Ou-ning 甌寧

Pa-chou 巴州

Pa-chou 霸州

pa-fa 八法

Pa-hsien 巴縣

pa-i 八議

pa-ku 八股

pa-kung 拔貢

Pa-ling 巴陵

pai-i 白役

pai-liang 白糧

pai-pu 白捕

Pai-se 百色

p'ai 牌

p'ai-chang 牌長

p'ai-nien 排年

p'ai-t'ou 牌頭

pan 班

pan-ch'ai 伴差

pan-ch'ai 辦差

pan-fang 班房

p'an 判

p'an-ch'a 盤查

p'an-fa 判發

P'an Shao-ts'an 潘杓燦

P'an Shih-en 潘世恩

P'an Tseng-wei 鄱曾瑋

P'an Tsun-ch'i 潘遵祁

P'an-yü 番禺

p'an-yü 判語

pang 梆

pang-i 幫役

P'ang Chung-lu 龐鍾璐

pao 保

Pao-an 保安

pao-chang 保長

pao-cheng 保正

pao-ch'i 保耆

pao-chia 保甲

Pao-ch'ing 寶慶

pao-chü 保舉

pao-hsieh 保歇

pao-kao 抱告

pao-k'o 包課

pao-lan 包攬

pao-lan ch'ien-liang 包攬錢糧

Pao-shan 寶山

Pao-ting 保定

P'ei-chou 邳州

pen-kuan kuan-ssu 本管官司

P'eng-shui 彭水

P'eng Yü-lin 彭玉麟

pi-chao 比照

pi-chi 筆記

pi-fei 比費

pi-hsien ch'a-chieh 比限查截

pi-pu 比簿

pi-tan 比單

pi-tse 比責

pi-wan ch'ien 必完籤

p'i 批

p'i 疲

p'i-hui 批迴

p'i-juan wu-wei 罷軟無為

p'i-tu 批牘

piao-p'an 標判

p'iao 票

p'iao-fa 票法

p'iao kao 票稿

p'iao-ken 票根

p'iao-yen 票鹽

pien-feng 邊俸

pien-hsiu 編修

pien-shen 編審

p'ien-t'i 駢體

Pin-chou 濱州

pin-shih 賓師

p'in-kuan 品官

ping 稟

ping-t'ieh 稟帖

P'ing-hu 平湖

P'ing-lo 平樂

p'ing-ti 平糴

P'ing-wu 平武

P'ing-yüan 平遠

po-an 駁案

P'o-yang 鄱陽

pu-chin 不謹

pu-ho tse-ch'ü 不合則去

pu-i 布衣

pu-i 捕役

pu-k'uai 捕快

pu-k'uai 步快

pu-kuan 捕官

pu-lin 補廩

pu-lun feng-man chi-sheng 不論俸滿即陞

pu-pan 捕班

"Pu-pan fan-li" 部頒凡例

pu-pan t'ou-i 捕班頭役

pu-su ch'ien 不宿籤

pu-t'ing 捕廳

pu wang-fa tsang 不枉法贓

p'u 鋪

p'u-chi t'ang 普濟堂

p'u-pan fei 鋪班費

p'u-ping 鋪兵

P'u-t'ai 蒲台

p'u-t'ang fei 鋪堂費

P'u-t'ien 莆田

san-chia 三甲

san-chou 散州

san-i 散役

san-kuan 散官

san pan 三班

san shan fu 傘扇夫

san-t'ing 散廳

san-yin 三尹

San-yüan 三原

shan 扇

Shan-hua 善化

shan-shu 扇書

Shan-yang 山陽

Shan-yin 山陰

Shang-ch'iu 商邱

Shang-yüan 上元

Shao-hsing 絽興

Shao-hsing shih-yeh 絽興師爺

shao-wei 少尉

Shao-yang 邵陽

shao-yin 少尹

she-chang 社長

She-chi 社稷

she-hsüeh 社學

she-ts'ang 社倉

shen 紳

shen 慎

shen-chia ch'ing-pai 身家清白

shen-chin 紳衿

Shen Chin-men 沈金門

Shen Chin-ssu 沈近思

Shen-chou 深州

shen-ch'uan 審轉

shen-hu 紳戶

shen-ming t'ing 申明亭

Shen Pao-chen 沈葆楨

shen shang 紳商

shen-shih 紳士

Shen-tse 深澤

shen-wen 申文

shen-yü 審語

sheng 升

sheng-shih tzu-sheng jen-ting 盛世滋生人丁

Sheng Ta 盛大

sheng-yüan 生員

shih 示

shih 士

shih-cheng ts'e 實徵冊

Shih-ch'ien 石阡

Shih Ching 是鏡

shih-ch'u 失出

shih-ju 失入

Shih Lin 石麟

shih-ling lei 時令類

Shih-lu Kuan 實錄館

shih min 士民

shih-min 市民

shih-t'ieh 實貼

shih-tsai 實在

Shih-tsu 世祖

Shih-tsung 世宗

shih-yeh 師爺

shou 守

Shou-chang 壽張

shou-ling kuan 首領官

shou-pei 守備

Shou-yang 壽陽

shu-ch'ang kuan 庶常館

shu chi shih 庶吉士

shu-ch'i 書啟

shu-chou 屬州

Shu-i t'iao-kuei 書役條規

shu-jen 庶人

Shu-kuei 署規

shu-li 書吏

shu-p'iao 書票

shu-ping 書稟

shu-shih 庶士

shu-t'ing 屬廳

shu-yüan 書院

shuang yüeh 雙月

shui-ch'i men-ting 稅契門丁

shui-k'o-ssu ta-shih 稅課司大使

shui-li chou-p'an 水利州判

shui-li hsien-ch'eng 水利縣丞

shui-t'u o-tu 水土惡毒

shui-wu 稅務

shun-ch'ai 順差

Shun-chih 順治

Shun-te 順德

Shun-t'ien 順天

ssu 巳

ssu 司

Ssu-chou 泗州

ssu-chu ts'e 四柱冊

ssu-hun 司閽

ssu-lu t'ing 四路廳　　　　tai-shu 代書

ssu-t'an 司攤　　　　　　T'ai-an 泰安

ssu-ts'ang 司倉　　　　　T'ai-p'ing 太平

ssu-tsui 私罪　　　　　　T'ai-ts'ang 太倉

su 速　　　　　　　　　T'ai-tsu 太祖

Su-chou 蘇州　　　　　　T'ai-yüan 太原

su-fang 疏防　　　　　　t'an 貪

su-sung 訴訟　　　　　　T'an Ch'eng-tsu 譚承祖

sui-kung 歲貢　　　　　　t'an-chüan 攤捐

sui-shih 歲試　　　　　　Tang-yang 當陽

Sung-chiang 松江　　　　t'ang-ch'ien 堂籤

sung-ch'ien 送籤　　　　t'ang-kung 塘工

sung-kao 送稿　　　　　　T'ang Pin 湯斌

sung-kao chih-pi fei 送稿紙筆費　T'ang-yin 湯陰

　　　　　　　　　　　tao 道

ta-a-ko 大阿哥　　　　　tao-an fei 到案費

ta-ch'ai 大差　　　　　　tao-jen li 到任禮

Ta-ch'eng 大城　　　　　Tao-kuang 道光

ta-chi 大計　　　　　　　tao-tan 到單

ta-ch'üeh 大缺　　　　　tao-t'an 道攤

Ta-hsing 大興　　　　　　T'ao Chu 陶澍

ta-hu 大戶　　　　　　　T'ao-yüan 桃源

Ta-li Ssu 大理寺　　　　Te-chou 德州

Ta-t'ang 大塘　　　　　　Teng Ch'eng-hsiu 鄧承修

ta-t'iao 大挑　　　　　　Teng-ching kuan 鄧井關

t'a-k'an fei 踏勘費　　　teng-fu 燈夫

tai-an fei 帶案費　　　　t'eng-lu 謄錄

Tai Chao-chia 戴兆佳　　ti 弟

Ti-ch'ao 邸鈔
ti-ch'ien 地錢
ti-fang 地方
ti-fang kuan 地方官
ti-pao 地保
Ti-tao 狄道
ti-ting yin 地丁銀
t'i-hsing an-ch'a shih 提刑按察使
t'ieh-hsieh 貼寫
tien 點
tien-li 典吏
tien-shih 典史
T'ien Wen-ching 田文鏡
ting 丁
Ting-chou 定州
Ting-fan 定番
Ting-hai 定海
Ting-hsing 定興
Ting Jih-ch'ang 丁日昌
Ting Shao-chou 丁紹周
ting sui ti p'ai 丁隨地派
Ting-t'ao 定陶
ting-t'u lao-hu ch'uan 頂圖老虎船
ting yin 丁銀
t'ing 廳
tou 斗

tou-chi 斗級
t'ou-i 頭役
tsa-chih 雜職
tsa-chu 雜著
tsa-ch'u 雜出
tsa-fan ch'ai-yao 雜泛差徭
tsa-ju 雜入
tsa-shui 雜稅
tsa-shui men-ting 雜稅門丁
ts'ai 才
ts'ai-li pu-chi 才力不及
tsan 欑
tsang-fan 贓犯
ts'ang-fang 倉房
ts'ang-fu 倉夫
ts'ang ta-shih 倉大使
Ts'ang-wu 蒼梧
tsao 皂
tsao-k'o 竈課
tsao-li 皂隸
tsao-li ch'iang-shou 皂隸搶手
tsao-pan 皂班
ts'ao-fei 漕費
ts'ao-kuei 漕規
ts'ao-kung 草供
ts'ao-shu 漕書
ts'ao-tsung 漕總

ts'ao-yün tsung-tu 漕運總督

Tse-ch'eng chou-hsien t'iao-yüeh 責成州縣條約

ts'e 冊

ts'e-chieh 冊結

ts'e-shu 冊書

tseng 贈

tseng-chien 增監

tseng-kung 增貢

Tseng Kuo-fan 曾國藩

tseng-sheng 增生

tso-ch'ai 坐差

tso-erh 佐貳

tso-fu chia-jen 坐府家人

tso-sheng chia-jen 坐省家人

tso-shih 座師

tso-t'ang 左堂

tso-t'ang li 坐堂禮

tso-tsa 佐雜

Tso Tsung-t'ang 左宗棠

tsou-hsiao 奏銷

tsou-hsiao an 奏銷案

tsou-hsiao ts'e 奏銷冊

tsou-i 奏議

tsou-kao 奏稿

tsuan-tien 攢典

tsui-yao ch'üeh 最要缺

ts'ui-ch'ai 催差

ts'ui-liang k'uai-shou 催糧快手

ts'ui-t'ou 催頭

tsun 遵

tsun-i 遵依

ts'un-chang 村長

ts'un-liu 存留

Tsung Chi-ch'en 宗稷辰

tsung-fang 總房

tsung-ho 總河

Tsung P'ei 宗霈

tsung-shu 總書

tsung-tu 總督

tsung-tu Chiang-nan ho-tao 總督江南河道

tsung-tu Honan Shantung ho-tao 總督河南山東河道

Tu-ch'a Yüan 都察院

Tu Ch'iao 杜喬

tu-fan 蠹犯

tu-i 蠹役

Tu Kuei-ch'ih 杜貴墀

tu-liang tao 督糧道

tu-pu t'ing 督捕廳

tu-ssu 都司

t'u 徒

t'u 圖

t'u-ch'ai 圖差

t'u-ssu 土司

T'u-ti 土地

t'u-yen shui 土鹽稅

t'u yen-yin 土鹽引

tuan-yü 斷獄

T'uan-fang Ch'ou-hsiang Chü 團防
　　籌餉局

t'uan-lien 團練

t'uan-lien ta-ch'en 團練大臣

t'ui-kuan 推官

t'ui-shou 推收

Tung-kuan 東莞

Tung-p'ing 東平

tung-weng 東翁

t'ung-chih 同知

T'ung-chou 通州

t'ung-kuan 通關

t'ung-nien 同年

t'ung-p'an 通判

t'ung-sheng 童生

t'ung-shih 童試

tzu 字

tzu-feng t'ou-kuei 自封投櫃

tzu-li tz'u-sung 自理詞訟

Tzu-liu ching 自流井

Tz'u-hsi 慈谿

wai-pien 外編

wan-pang 晚梆

Wan-p'ing 宛平

wan-sheng 晚生

wan-t'ang 晚堂

Wan Wei-han 萬維翰

Wang An-shih 王安石

Wang Chih 王植

Wang Ch'ing-yün 王慶雲

Wang Chung-lin 王鍾霖

wang-fa shou-ts'ai 枉法受財

wang-fa tsang 枉法贓

Wang Feng-sheng 王鳳生

Wang Hsien-i 王賢儀

Wang Hui-tsu 汪輝祖

Wang Jui 王瑞

Wang K'an 王侃

Wang Lan-kuang 王蘭廣

Wang Lü-ch'ien 王履謙

Wang Tsung-lu 王宗魯

Wang Yu-huai 王又槐

wei 為

Wei-ho 衛河

Wei-hsien 渭縣

Wei Yüan 魏源

wei-yüan 委員

Wen-ch'ang 文昌

Wen-shang 汶上

Wen Shao-yüan 溫紹原
Weng Tsu-lieh 翁祖列
wo-pei 卧碑
Wu 吳
Wu-ch'eng 烏程
Wu-chiang 吳江
Wu-ch'ing 武清
Wu-hsi 吳錫
Wu-hsien 吳縣
Wu-kang 武岡
Wu-ling 武陵
wu-lu jen 無祿人
Wu Shou-ch'un 吳壽椿
wu-tso 仵作
wu-wei 無違
Wu Wei-yeh 吳偉業
Wu Wen-jung 吳文鎔
Wu Ying-fen 吳應棻

Ya-chou 崖州
ya-hang 牙行
ya-hu 牙户
ya-i 衙役
ya-pu tsung t'ou-i 押捕總頭役
yang-chi yüan 養濟院
Yang-chou 揚州
Yang-ch'ü 陽曲
Yang Hsi-fu 楊錫綬
Yang Hsiang-chi 楊象濟

Yang-lien yin 養廉銀
Yang Tsung-jen 楊宗仁
yao-ch'üeh 要缺
yao-li yin 徭里銀
Yao Nai 姚鼐
yao-yin 徭銀
Yao Ying 姚瑩
Yeh Chen 葉鎮
Yeh P'ei-sun 葉佩蓀
yen ch'a tao 鹽茶道
yen-chang ch'üeh 煙瘴缺
Yen-chin 延津
Yen-ch'ing 延慶
yen-fa tao 鹽法道
yen-hai ch'üeh 沿海缺
yen-ho ch'üeh 沿河缺
yen-hu 煙户
yen shu-sen 嚴樹森
yen-yün shih 鹽運使
yin 寅
yin 蔭
Yin Chao-yung 殷兆鏞
yin-chien 引見
yin-chien 蔭監
yin-hsi 蔭襲
yin-k'o 引課
Yin-mi k'uan-mu 銀米欵目
yin-sheng 蔭生

Ying-chou 潁州

Ying-ho 英和

ying-pu 應捕

yu 酉

yu-chi 有疾

yu-chien 優監

yu chung-yün 右中允

yu-kung 優貢

yu-lu jen 有祿人

Yu Po-ch'uan 游百川

yu-tan 由單

yu-t'ang 右堂

yu-yang 右仰

yung-che 永折

Yung-cheng 雍正

Yung-ch'ing 永清

Yung-feng 永豐

Yung-p'ing 永平

yung pu hsü-yung 永不敍用

Yung-shan 永善

Yung-ting 永定

yung-yin 用印

yü 諭

Yü Ch'eng-lung 于成龍

Yü-chou 禹州

yü-p'ing 餘平

yü-ti 愚弟

Yü-tieh Kuan 玉牒館

Yü Yüeh 俞樾

yüan 院

Yüan-ho 元和

Yüan Mei 袁枚

yüan-shih 院試

Yüan Shou-ting 袁守定

Yüeh 越

yüeh 閱

yüeh-cheng 約正

Yüeh-chou 岳州

yüeh-fu 約副

yüeh-sung 越訴

Yün-lung 雲龍

yün-pan 雲板